Applied Computational Economics and Finance

Applied Computational Economics and Finance

Mario J. Miranda and Paul L. Fackler

The MIT Press
Cambridge, Massachusetts
London, England

This book was set in 11/13 Times Roman by ICC and was printed and bound in the United States of America.

Library of Congress Cataloging-in-Publication Data

Miranda, Mario J.
    Applied computaional economics and finance / Mario J. Miranda and Paul L. Fackler.
      p.   c.m.
    Includes bibliographical references and index.
    ISBN 0-262-13420-9
    1. Economics—Data processing. 2. Economics, Mathematical. 3. Finance—Data processing.
  I. Fackler, Paul L. II. Title.

HB 143.5 .M567 2002
330′.01′51—dc21   2002026492

This book is dedicated to the memories of our fathers:
Mario S. Miranda
M.D.
1923–1995
and
Walter D. Fackler
Economist and Teacher
1921–1993

Contents

Many interesting economic models cannot be solved analytically using the standard mathematical techniques of algebra and calculus. Models that cannot be solved in this way are often applied economic models that attempt to capture the complexities inherent in real-world economic behavior. For example, to be useful in applied economic analysis, the conventional Marshallian partial static equilibrium model of supply and demand must often be generalized to allow for multiple goods, interregional trade, intertemporal storage, and government interventions such as tariffs, taxes, and trade quotas. In such models, the structural economic constraints are of central interest to the economist, making it undesirable, if not impossible, to "assume an internal solution" to render the model analytically tractable.

Another class of interesting models that typically cannot be solved analytically consists of stochastic dynamic models of rational, forward-looking economic behavior. Dynamic economic models typically give rise to functional equations in which the unknown is not simply a vector in Euclidean space, but rather an entire function defined on a continuum of points. For example, the Bellman and Euler equations that describe dynamic optima are functional equations, as often are the conditions that characterize rational expectations and arbitrage pricing market equilibria. Except in a very limited number of special cases, the functional equation lacks a known closed-form solution, even though the solution can be shown theoretically to exist and to be unique.

Models that lack closed-form analytical solution are not unique to economics. Analytically insoluble models are common in biological, physical, and engineering sciences. Since the introduction of the digital computer, scientists in these fields have turned increasingly to computer methods to solve their models. In many cases where analytical approaches fail, numerical methods are used successfully to compute highly accurate approximate solutions. In recent years, the scope of numerical applications in the biological, physical, and engineering sciences has grown dramatically. In most of these disciplines, computational model building and analysis is now recognized as a legitimate subdiscipline of specialization. Numerical analysis courses have also become standard in many graduate and undergraduate curricula in these fields.

Economists, however, have not embraced numerical methods as eagerly as other scientists. Many economists have shunned numerical methods out of a belief that numerical solutions are less elegant or less general than closed-form solutions. The former belief is a subjective, aesthetic judgment that is outside of scientific discourse and beyond the scope of this book. The generality of the results obtained from numerical economic models, however, is another matter. Of course, given an economic model, it is always preferable to derive a closed-form solution—provided such a solution exists. However, when essential features of an economic system being studied cannot be faithfully captured in an algebraically soluble model, a choice must be made. Either essential features of the system must be ignored in order to obtain an algebraically tractable model, or numerical techniques must be applied. Too often economists chose algebraic tractability over economic realism.

Numerical economic models are often criticized by economists on the grounds that they rest on specific assumptions regarding functional forms and parameter values. Such criticism, however, is unwarranted when strong empirical support exists for the specific functional form and parameter values used to specify a model. Moreover, even when there is some uncertainty about functional forms and parameters, the model may be solved under a variety of assumptions in order to assess the robustness of its implications. Although some doubt will persist as to the implications of the model outside the range of functional forms and parameter values examined, this uncertainty must be weighed against the lack of relevance of an alternative model that is explicitly soluble but ignores essential features of the economic system of interest. We believe that it is better to derive economic insights from a realistic numerical model of an economic system than to derive irrelevant results, however general, from an unrealistic but explicitly soluble model.

Despite resistance by some, an increasing number of economists are becoming aware of the potential benefits of numerical economic model building and analysis. This trend is evidenced by the recent introduction of journals and an economic society devoted to the subdiscipline of computational economics. The growing popularity of computational economics, however, has been impeded by the absence of adequate textbooks and computer software. The methods of numerical analysis and much of the available computer software have been largely developed for noneconomic disciplines, most notably the physical, mathematical, and computer sciences. The scholarly literature can also pose substantial barriers for economists, both because of its mathematical prerequisites and because its examples are unfamiliar to economists. Many available software packages, moreover, are designed to solve problems that are specific to the physical sciences.

This book addresses the difficulties typically encountered by economists attempting to learn and apply numerical methods in several ways. First, the book emphasizes practical numerical methods, not mathematical proofs, and focuses on techniques that will be directly useful to economic analysts, not those that would be useful exclusively to physical scientists. Second, the examples used in the book are drawn from a wide range of subspecialties of economics and finance, with particular emphasis on problems in financial, agricultural, and resource economics as well as macroeconomics. And third, we supply with the textbook an extensive library of computer utilities and demonstration programs to provide interested economic researchers with a starting point for their own computer models.

We make no attempt to be encyclopedic in our coverage of numerical methods or potential economic applications. We have instead chosen to develop only a relatively small number of techniques that can be applied easily to a wide variety of economic problems. In some instances, we have deviated from the standard treatments of numerical methods in existing textbooks in order to present a simple, consistent framework that may be readily learned and applied by economists. In many cases we have elected not to cover certain numerical techniques when we considered them to be of limited benefit to economists, relative to their complexity. Throughout the book, we try to explain our choices and to give references to more advanced numerical textbooks where appropriate.

The book is divided into two major sections. In the first six chapters we develop basic numerical methods, including linear and nonlinear equation methods, complementarity methods, finite-dimensional optimization, numerical integration and differentiation, and function approximation. In these chapters we develop appreciation for basic numerical techniques by illustrating their application to equilibrium and optimization models familiar to most economists. The last five chapters are devoted to methods for solving dynamic stochastic models in economics and finance, including dynamic programming, rational expectations, and arbitrage pricing models in discrete and continuous time.

The book is aimed at graduate students, advanced undergraduate students, and practicing economists. We have attempted to write a book that can be used both as a classroom text and for self-study. We have also attempted to make the various sections reasonably self-contained. For example, the sections on discrete time continuous state models are largely independent from those on discrete time discrete state models. Although this approach results in some duplication of material, we felt that it would increase the usefulness of the text by allowing readers to skip sections.

Although we have attempted to keep the mathematical prerequisites for this book to a minimum, some mathematical training and insight are necessary to work with computational economic models and numerical techniques. We assume that the reader is familiar with ideas and methods of linear algebra and calculus. Appendix A provides an overview of the basic mathematics used throughout the book.

One barrier to the use of numerical methods by economists is lack of access to functioning computer code. This presents an apparent dilemma to us as book authors, given the variety of computer languages available. On the one hand, it is useful to have working examples of code in the book and to make the code available to readers for immediate use. On the other hand, using a specific language in the text could obscure the essence of the numerical routines for those unfamiliar with the chosen language. We believe, however, that the latter concern can be substantially mitigated by conforming to the syntax of a vector-processing language. Vector-processing languages are designed to facilitate numerical analysis, and their syntax is often simple enough that the language is transparent and easily learned and implemented.

Because of its facility of use and its wide availability on university campus computing systems, we have chosen to illustrate algorithms in the book using MATLAB® and have provided a toolbox of utilities, the CompEcon Toolbox, to assist interested readers in developing their own computational economic applications. The CompEcon Toolbox can be obtained via the Internet at the web site http://mitpress.mit.edu/CompEcon. All the figures and tables in this book were generated by MATLAB files provided with the toolbox. For those not familiar with the MATLAB programming language, a primer is provided in Appendix B. (MATLAB is a registered trademark of The MathWorks, Inc.)

The text contains many code fragments, which, in some cases, have been abridged or otherwise simplified for expositional clarity. This simplification generally consists of eliminating the explicit setting of optional parameters and not displaying code that actually generates tabular or graphical output. The demonstration files provided in the CompEcon Toolbox contain fully functioning versions. In many cases the toolbox versions of functions described in the text have optional parameters that can be altered by the user.

Our ultimate goal in writing this book is to motivate a broad range of economists to use numerical methods in their work by demonstrating the essential principles underlying computational economic models across subdisciplines. It is our hope that this book will make accessible a range of computational tools that will enable economists to analyze economic and financial models that they have been unable to solve within the confines of traditional mathematical economic analysis.

Any book of this scope involves the efforts of many people besides the authors. We would like to thank our graduate students at Ohio State University and North Carolina State University for helping us write a more user-friendly book. We are grateful for reviews and suggestions by Kenneth Judd of Stanford University, Larry Karp of the University of California at Berkeley, Sergio Lence of the University of Iowa, Bob King of the University of Minnesota, and Dmitry Vedenov of the University of Georgia, as well as to the many users of early versions of the CompEcon Toolbox.

We also thank Jane MacDonald and Elizabeth Murry at MIT Press, Peggy Gordon at P. M. Gordon Associates, and Kathy Ewing at Interactive Composition Corporation for their efforts (and their patience) in the often frustrating effort to turn a draft into a finished product. Last but not least we thank our families for their indulgence. In particular, we thank our wives, Barbara Lucey and Marilyn Hartman, for their support of this project.

1 Introduction

1.1 Some Apparently Simple Questions

Consider the constant elasticity demand function

$$q = p^{-0.2}$$

This is a function because, for each price p, there is a unique quantity demanded q. Given a handheld calculator, any economist could easily compute the quantity demanded at any given price.

An economist would also have little difficulty computing the price that clears the market of a given quantity. Flipping the demand expression about the equality sign and raising each side to the power of -5, the economist would derive a closed-form expression for the inverse demand function

$$p = q^{-5}$$

Again, using a calculator any economist could easily compute the price that will exactly clear the market of any given quantity.

Suppose now that the economist is presented with a slightly different demand function

$$q = 0.5\, p^{-0.2} + 0.5\, p^{-0.5}$$

This function contains two terms, a domestic demand term and an export demand term. Using standard calculus, the economist could easily verify that the demand function is continuous, differentiable, and strictly decreasing. The economist once again could easily compute the quantity demanded at any price using a calculator and could easily and accurately draw a graph of the demand function.

However, suppose that the economist is asked to find the price that clears the market of, say, a quantity of 2 units. The question is well posed. Formal arguments based on the Intermediate Value and Implicit Function Theorems would establish that the inverse demand function is well defined, continuous, and strictly decreasing. A unique market clearing price clearly exists.

But what is the inverse demand function? And what price clears the market of the given quantity? After considerable effort, even the best trained economist will not find an explicit answer using algebra and calculus. No closed-form expression for the inverse demand function exists. The economist cannot answer the apparently simple question of what the market clearing price will be.

Consider now a simple model of an agricultural commodity market. In this market, acreage supply decisions are made before the per-acre yield and harvest price are known.

Planting decisions are based on the price expected at harvest:

$a = 0.5 + 0.5Ep$

After the acreage is planted, a random yield $\tilde{y}$ is realized, giving rise to a quantity

$q = a\tilde{y}$

that is entirely sold at a market clearing price

$p = 3 - 2q$

Assume the random yield $\tilde{y}$ is exogenous and distributed normally with mean 1 and variance 0.1.

Most economists would have little difficulty deriving the rational expectations equilibrium of this market model. Substituting the first expression into the second, and then the second into the third, the economist would write

$p = 3 - 2(0.5 + 0.5Ep)\tilde{y}$

Taking expectations on both sides

$Ep = 3 - 2(0.5 + 0.5Ep)$

she would solve for the equilibrium expected price $Ep = 1$. She would conclude that the equilibrium acreage is $a = 1$ and the equilibrium price distribution has a variance of 0.4.

Suppose now that the economist is asked to assess the implications of a proposed government price support program. Under this program, the government guarantees each producer a minimum price, say 1. If the market price falls below this level, the government simply pays the producer the difference per unit produced. The producer thus receives an effective price of $\max(p, 1)$ where p is the prevailing market price. The government program transforms the acreage supply relation to

$a = 0.5 + 0.5E \max(p, 1)$

Before proceeding with a formal mathematical analysis, the economist exercises a little economic intuition. The government support, she reasons, will stimulate acreage supply, raising acreage planted. Increased acreage will shift the equilibrium price distribution to the left, reducing the expected market price below 1. Price would still occasionally rise above 1, however, implying that the expected effective producer price will exceed 1. The difference between the expected effective producer price and the expected market price represents a positive expected government subsidy.

The economist now attempts to formally solve for the rational expectations equilibrium of the revised market model. She performs the same substitutions as before and writes

$$p = 3 - 2[0.5 + 0.5E \max(p, 1)]\tilde{y}$$

As before, she takes expectations on both sides

$$Ep = 3 - 2[0.5 + 0.5E \max(p, 1)]$$

In order to solve the expression for the expected price, the economist uses a fairly common and apparently innocuous trick: she interchanges the max and E operators, replacing $E \max(p, 1)$ with $\max(Ep, 1)$. The resulting expression is easily solved for $Ep = 1$. This solution, however, asserts that the expected market price and acreage planted remain unchanged by the introduction of the government price support policy. This assertion is inconsistent with the economist's intuition.

The economist quickly realizes her error. The expectation operator cannot be interchanged with the maximization operator because the latter is a nonlinear function. But if this operation is not valid, then what mathematical operations would allow the economist to solve for the equilibrium expected price and acreage?

Again, after considerable effort, our economist is unable to find an answer using algebra and calculus. No apparent closed-form solution exists for the model. The economist cannot answer the apparently simple question of how the equilibrium acreage and expected market price will change with the introduction of the government price support program.

1.2 An Alternative Analytic Framework

The two problems discussed in the preceding section illustrate how even simple economic models cannot always be solved using standard mathematical techniques. These problems, however, can easily be solved to a high degree of accuracy using numerical methods.

Consider the inverse demand problem. An economist who knows some elementary numerical methods and who can write basic MATLAB code would have little difficulty solving the problem. The economist would simply write the following elementary MATLAB program:

```
p = 0.25;
for i=1:100
  deltap = (.5*p^-.2+.5*p^-.5-2)/(.1*p^-1.2 + .25*p^-1.5);
  p = p + deltap;
  if abs(deltap) < 1.e-8, break, end
end
disp(p);
```

He would then execute the program on a computer and, in an instant, compute the solution: the market clearing price is 0.154. The economist has used Newton's rootfinding method, which is discussed in section 3.3.

Consider now the rational expectations commodity market model with government intervention. The source of difficulty in solving this problem is the need to evaluate the truncated expectation of a continuous distribution. An economist who knows some numerical analysis and who knows how to write basic MATLAB code, however, would have little difficulty computing the rational expectation equilibrium of this model. The economist would approximate the original normal yield distribution with a discrete distribution that has identical lower moments, say, one that assumes values $y_1, y_2, \ldots, y_n$ with probabilities $w_1, w_2, \ldots, w_n$. After constructing the discrete distribution approximant, which would require only a single call to the CompEcon library routine qnwnorm, the economist would code and execute the following elementary MATLAB program:

```
[y,w] = qnwnorm(10,1,0.1);
a = 1;
for it=1:100
  aold = a;
  p = 3 - 2*a*y;
  f = w'*max(p,1);
  a = 0.5 + 0.5*f;
  if abs(a-aold)<1.e-8, break, end
end
disp(a);disp(w'*p);disp(f)
```

In an instant, the program would compute and display the rational expectations equilibrium acreage, 1.10; the expected market price, 0.81; and the expected effective producer price, 1.19. The economist has combined fixed-point function iteration methods and Gaussian quadrature techniques to solve the problem. Function iteration and Gaussian quadrature are discussed in sections 3.2 and 5.2, respectively.

Exercises

1.1. Plot the function $f(x) = 1 - e^{2x}$ on the interval $[-1, 1]$ using a grid of evenly spaced points 0.01 units apart.

1.2. Consider the matrices

$$A = \begin{bmatrix} 0 & -1 & 2 \\ -2 & -1 & 4 \\ 2 & 7 & -3 \end{bmatrix}$$

and

$$B = \begin{bmatrix} -7 & 1 & 1 \\ 7 & -3 & -2 \\ 3 & 5 & 0 \end{bmatrix}$$

and the vector

$$y = \begin{bmatrix} 3 \\ -1 \\ 2 \end{bmatrix}$$

a. Formulate the *standard* matrix product $C = A * B$, and solve the linear equation $Cx = y$. What are the values of C and x?

b. Formulate the *element-by-element* matrix product $C = A * B$, and solve the linear equation $Cx = y$. What are the values of C and x?

1.3. Using the MATLAB standard normal pseudo–random number generator `randn`, simulate a hypothetical time series $\{y_t\}$ governed by the structural relationship

$$y_t = 5 + 0.05t + \epsilon_t$$

for years $t = 1960, 1961, \dots, 2001$, assuming that the ϵ_t are independently and identically distributed with mean 0 and standard deviation 0.2. Using only MATLAB elementary matrix operations, regress the simulated observations of y_t on a constant and time, then plot the actual values of y and estimated trend line against time.

1.4. Consider the rational expectations commodity market model discussed on page 1, except now assume that the yield has a simple two-point distribution in which yields of 0.7 and 1.3 are equally probable.

a. Compute the expectation and variance of price without government support payments.

b. Compute the expectation and variance of the effective producer price assuming a support price of 1.

c. What is the expected government subsidy per planted acre?

2 Linear Equations and Computer Basics

The *linear equation* is the most elementary problem that arises in computational economic analysis. In a linear equation, an $n \times n$ matrix A and an n-vector b are given, and one must compute the n-vector x that satisfies

$$Ax = b$$

Linear equations arise, directly or indirectly, in most computational economic applications. For example, a linear equation may be solved when computing the steady-state distribution of a discrete-state stochastic economic process or when computing the equilibrium prices and quantities of a multicommodity market model with linear demand and supply functions. Linear equations also arise as elementary tasks in solution procedures designed to solve more complicated nonlinear economic models. For example, a nonlinear partial equilibrium market model may be solved using Newton's method, which involves solving a sequence of linear equations. And the Euler functional equation of a rational expectations model may be solved using a collocation method, which yields a nonlinear equation that in turn is solved as a sequence of linear equations.

Various practical issues arise when solving a linear equation numerically. Digital computers are capable of representing arbitrary real numbers with only limited precision. Numerical arithmetic operations, such as computer addition and multiplication, produce rounding errors that may, or may not, be negligible. Unless the rounding errors are controlled in some way, the errors can accumulate, rendering a computed solution that may be far from correct. Speed and storage requirements are also important considerations in the design of a linear equation solution algorithm. In some applications, such as the stochastic simulation of a rational expectations model, linear equations may have to be solved millions of times. And in other applications, such as computing option prices using finite difference methods, linear equations with a very large number of variables and equations may be encountered.

Over the years, numerical analysts have studied linear equations extensively and have developed algorithms for solving them quickly, accurately, and with a minimum of computer storage. In most applied work, one can typically rely on Gaussian elimination, which may be implemented in various different forms depending on the structure of the linear equation. Iterative methods offer an alternative to Gaussian elimination and are especially efficient if the A matrix is large and consists mostly of zero entries.

2.1 L-U Factorization

Some linear equations $Ax = b$ are relatively easy to solve. For example, if A is a lower triangular matrix,

$$A = \begin{bmatrix} a_{11} & 0 & 0 & \ldots & 0 \\ a_{21} & a_{22} & 0 & \ldots & 0 \\ a_{31} & a_{32} & a_{33} & \ldots & 0 \\ & & & & \\ a_{n1} & a_{n2} & a_{n3} & \ldots & a_{nn} \end{bmatrix}$$

then the elements of x can be computed recursively using *forward substitution:*

$$x_1 = b_1/a_{11}$$
$$x_2 = (b_2 - a_{21}x_1)/a_{22}$$
$$x_3 = (b_3 - a_{31}x_1 - a_{32}x_2)/a_{33}$$
$$\vdots$$
$$x_n = (b_n - a_{n1}x_1 - a_{n2}x_2 - \ldots - a_{nn-1}x_{n-1})/a_{nn}$$

The algorithm can be written more compactly using summation notation as

$$x_i = \left(b_i - \sum_{j=1}^{i-1} a_{ij}x_j \right) /a_{ii}, \qquad \forall i$$

In the vector processing language MATLAB, this computation may be implemented as follows:

```
for i=1:length(b)
  x(i)=(b(i)-A(i,1:i-1)*x(1:i-1))/A(i,i);
end
```

If A is an upper triangular matrix, then the elements of x can be computed recursively using *backward substitution.*

Most linear equations encountered in practice, however, do not have a triangular A matrix. In such cases, the linear equation is often best solved using the *L-U factorization algorithm.* The L-U algorithm is designed to decompose the A matrix into the product of lower and upper triangular matrices, allowing the linear equation to be solved using a combination of backward and forward substitution. The L-U algorithm involves two phases. In the *factorization* phase, Gaussian elimination is used to factor the matrix A into the product

$$A = LU$$

of a row-permuted lower triangular matrix L and an upper triangular matrix U. A row-permuted lower triangular matrix is simply a lower triangular matrix that has had its rows rearranged. Any nonsingular square matrix can be decomposed in this way.

In the *solution* phase of the L-U algorithm, the factored linear equation

$$Ax = (LU)x = L(Ux) = b$$

is solved by first solving

$$Ly = b$$

for y using forward substitution, accounting for row permutations, and then solving

$$Ux = y$$

for x using backward substitution.

Consider, for example, the linear equation $Ax = b$ where

$$A = \begin{bmatrix} -3 & 2 & 3 \\ -3 & 2 & 1 \\ 3 & 0 & 0 \end{bmatrix} \quad \text{and} \quad b = \begin{bmatrix} 10 \\ 8 \\ -3 \end{bmatrix}$$

The matrix A can be decomposed into the product $A = LU$ where

$$L = \begin{bmatrix} 1 & 0 & 0 \\ 1 & 0 & 1 \\ -1 & 1 & 0 \end{bmatrix} \quad \text{and} \quad U = \begin{bmatrix} -3 & 2 & 3 \\ 0 & 2 & 3 \\ 0 & 0 & -2 \end{bmatrix}$$

The matrix L is row-permuted lower triangular; by interchanging the second and third rows, a lower diagonal matrix results. The matrix U is upper triangular. Solving $Ly = b$ for y using forward substitution involves first solving for y_1, then for y_3, and finally for y_2. Given the solution $y = [10\ 7\ -2]^\top$, the linear equation $Ux = y$ can then be solved using backward substitution, yielding the solution of the original linear equation, $x = [-1\ 2\ 1]^\top$.

The L-U factorization algorithm is faster than other linear equation solution methods that are typically presented in elementary linear algebra courses. For large n, it takes approximately $n^3/3 + n^2$ long operations (multiplications and divisions) to solve an $n \times n$ linear equation using L-U factorization. Explicitly computing the inverse of A and then computing $A^{-1}b$ requires approximately $n^3 + n^2$ long operations. Solving the linear equation using Cramer's rule requires approximately $(n + 1)!$ long operations. To solve a 10×10 linear equation, for example, L-U factorization requires exactly 430 long operations, whereas matrix inversion and multiplication requires exactly 1,100 long operations, and Cramer's rule requires nearly 40 million long operations.

Linear equations arise so frequently in numerical analysis that most numerical subroutine packages and software programs include an intrinsic routine for solving a linear equation using L-U factorization. In MATLAB, the solution to the linear equation $Ax = b$ is returned by the statement $x = A \setminus b$. The "\", or "backslash," operator is designed to solve the linear equation using L-U factorization, unless a special structure for A is detected, in which case MATLAB may implicitly use another, more efficient method. In particular, if MATLAB detects that A is triangular or permuted triangular, it will dispense with L-U factorization and solve the linear equation directly using forward or backward substitution. MATLAB also uses special algorithms when the A matrix is positive definite (see section 2.5).

Although L-U factorization is the best general method for solving a linear equation, situations can arise in which alternative methods may be preferable. For example, in many computational economic applications, one must solve a series of linear equations, all having the same A matrix, but different b vectors, $b_1, b_2, \ldots, b_m$. In this situation, it is often computationally more efficient to directly compute and store the inverse of A first and then compute the solutions $x = A^{-1}b_j$ by performing only direct matrix-vector multiplications. Whether explicitly computing the inverse is faster than L-U factorization depends on the size of the linear equation system n and the number of times, m, an equation system is to be solved. Computing $x = A \setminus b_j$ a total of m times involves $mn^3/3 + mn^2$ long operations. Computing A^{-1} once and then computing $A^{-1}b_j$ a total of m times requires $n^3 + mn^2$ long operations. Thus explicit computation of the inverse should be faster than L-U factorization whenever the number of equations to be solved m is greater than three or four. The actual break-even point will vary across numerical analysis packages, depending on the computational idiosyncrasies and overhead costs of the L-U factorization and inverse routines implemented in the package.

2.2   Gaussian Elimination

The L-U factors of a matrix A are computed using *Gaussian elimination*. Gaussian elimination is based on two elementary row operations: subtracting a constant multiple of one row of a linear equation from another row, and interchanging two rows of a linear equation. Either operation may be performed on a linear equation without altering its solution.

The Gaussian elimination algorithm begins with matrices L and U initialized as $L = I$ and $U = A$, where I is the identity matrix. The algorithm then uses elementary row operations to transform U into an upper triangular matrix, while preserving the permuted lower diagonality of L and the factorization $A = LU$.

Consider the matrix

$$A = \begin{bmatrix} 2 & 0 & -1 & 2 \\ 4 & 2 & -1 & 4 \\ 2 & -2 & -2 & 3 \\ -2 & 2 & 7 & -3 \end{bmatrix}$$

The first stage of Gaussian elimination is designed to nullify the subdiagonal entries of the first column of the U matrix. The U matrix is updated by subtracting 2 times the first row from the second, subtracting 1 times the first row from the third, and subtracting -1 times the first row from the fourth. The L matrix, which initially equals the identity, is updated by storing the multipliers 2, 1, and -1 as the subdiagonal entries of its first column. These operations yield updated L and U matrices:

$$L = \begin{bmatrix} 1 & 0 & 0 & 0 \\ 2 & 1 & 0 & 0 \\ 1 & 0 & 1 & 0 \\ -1 & 0 & 0 & 1 \end{bmatrix}, \quad U = \begin{bmatrix} 2 & 0 & -1 & 2 \\ 0 & 2 & 1 & 0 \\ 0 & -2 & -1 & 1 \\ 0 & 2 & 6 & -1 \end{bmatrix}$$

After the first stage of Gaussian elimination, $A = LU$, and L is lower triangular, but U is not yet upper triangular.

The second stage of Gaussian elimination is designed to nullify the subdiagonal entries of the second column of the U matrix. The U matrix is updated by subtracting -1 times the second row from the third and subtracting 1 times the second row from the fourth. The L matrix is updated by storing the multipliers -1 and 1 as the subdiagonal elements of its second column. These operations yield updated L and U matrices:

$$L = \begin{bmatrix} 1 & 0 & 0 & 0 \\ 2 & 1 & 0 & 0 \\ 1 & -1 & 1 & 0 \\ -1 & 1 & 0 & 1 \end{bmatrix}, \quad U = \begin{bmatrix} 2 & 0 & -1 & 2 \\ 0 & 2 & 1 & 0 \\ 0 & 0 & 0 & 1 \\ 0 & 0 & 5 & -1 \end{bmatrix}$$

After the second stage of Gaussian elimination, $A = LU$, and L is lower triangular, but U still is not upper triangular.

In the third stage of Gaussian elimination, one encounters an apparent problem. The third diagonal element of the matrix U is zero, making it impossible to nullify the subdiagonal entry as before. This difficulty is easily remedied, however, by interchanging the third and fourth rows of U. The L matrix is updated by interchanging the previously computed multipliers residing in the third and fourth columns. These operations yield updated L and U matrices:

$$L = \begin{bmatrix} 1 & 0 & 0 & 0 \\ 2 & 1 & 0 & 0 \\ 1 & -1 & 0 & 1 \\ -1 & 1 & 1 & 0 \end{bmatrix}, \quad U = \begin{bmatrix} 2 & 0 & -1 & 2 \\ 0 & 2 & 1 & 0 \\ 0 & 0 & 5 & -1 \\ 0 & 0 & 0 & 1 \end{bmatrix}$$

The Gaussian elimination algorithm terminates with a permuted lower triangular matrix L and an upper triangular matrix U whose product is the matrix A. In theory, Gaussian elimination will compute the L-U factors of any matrix A, provided A is invertible. If A is not invertible, Gaussian elimination will detect this fact by encountering a zero diagonal element in the U matrix that cannot be replaced with a nonzero element below it.

2.3 Rounding Error

In practice, Gaussian elimination performed on a computer can sometimes render inaccurate solutions as a result of rounding errors. The effects of rounding errors, however, can often be controlled by *pivoting*.

Consider the linear equation

$$\begin{bmatrix} -M^{-1} & 1 \\ 1 & 1 \end{bmatrix} \begin{bmatrix} x_1 \\ x_2 \end{bmatrix} = \begin{bmatrix} 1 \\ 2 \end{bmatrix}$$

where M is a large positive number.

To solve this equation using Gaussian elimination, a single row operation is required: subtracting $-M$ times the first row from the second row. In principle, this operation yields the L-U factorization

$$\begin{bmatrix} -M^{-1} & 1 \\ 1 & 1 \end{bmatrix} = \begin{bmatrix} 1 & 0 \\ -M & 1 \end{bmatrix} \begin{bmatrix} -M^{-1} & 1 \\ 0 & M+1 \end{bmatrix}$$

In theory, applying forward and backward substitution yields the solution $x_1 = M/(M+1)$ and $x_2 = (M+2)/(M+1)$, which are both very nearly one.

In practice, however, Gaussian elimination may yield a very different result. In performing Gaussian elimination, one encounters an operation that cannot be carried out precisely on a computer and that should be avoided in computational work: adding or subtracting values of vastly different magnitudes. On a computer, it is not meaningful to add or subtract two values whose magnitudes differ by more than the number of significant digits that the computer can represent. If one attempts such an operation, the smaller value is effectively treated as zero. For example, the sum of 0.1 and 0.0001 may be 0.1001, but on a hypothetical machine with three-digit precision the result of the sum is rounded to 0.1 before it is stored.

In the present linear equation, adding 1 or 2 to a sufficiently large M on a computer simply returns the value M. Thus, in the first step of the backward substitution, x_2 is computed, not as $(M+2)/(M+1)$, but rather as M/M, which is exactly one. Then, in the second step of backward substitution, $x_1 = -M(1 - x_2)$ is computed to be zero. Rounding error thus produces a computed solution for x_1 that has a relative error of 100 percent.

Fortunately, there is a partial remedy for the effects of rounding error in Gaussian elimination. Rounding error arises in this example because the diagonal element $-M^{-1}$ is very small. Interchanging the two rows at the outset of Gaussian elimination does not alter the theoretical solution to the linear equation, but allows one to perform Gaussian elimination with a diagonal element of larger magnitude.

Consider the equivalent linear equation system after the rows have been interchanged:

$$\begin{bmatrix} 1 & 1 \\ -M^{-1} & 1 \end{bmatrix} \begin{bmatrix} x_1 \\ x_2 \end{bmatrix} = \begin{bmatrix} 2 \\ 1 \end{bmatrix}$$

After interchanging the rows, the new A matrix may be factored as

$$\begin{bmatrix} 1 & 1 \\ -M^{-1} & 1 \end{bmatrix} = \begin{bmatrix} 1 & 0 \\ -M^{-1} & 1 \end{bmatrix} \begin{bmatrix} 1 & 1 \\ 0 & M^{-1}+1 \end{bmatrix}$$

Backward and forward substitution yield the theoretical results $x_1 = 1 - M^{-1}$ and $x_2 = M^{-1} + 1 + M^{-1}(1 - M^{-1})$. In evaluating these expressions on the computer, one again encounters rounding error. Here, x_2 is numerically computed to be exactly one as before. However, x_1 is also computed to be exactly one. The computed solution, though not exactly correct, is correct to the precision available on the computer, and it is certainly more accurate than the one obtained without interchanging the rows.

Interchanging rows during Gaussian elimination in order to make the magnitude of diagonal element as large as possible is called *pivoting*. Pivoting substantially enhances the reliability and accuracy of a Gaussian elimination routine. For this reason, all good Gaussian elimination routines designed to perform L-U factorization, including the ones implemented in MATLAB, employ some form of pivoting.

2.4   Ill Conditioning

Pivoting cannot cure all the problems caused by rounding error. Some linear equations are inherently difficult to solve accurately on a computer, despite pivoting. This difficulty occurs when the A matrix is structured in such a way that a small perturbation δb in the data vector b induces a large change δx in the solution vector x. In such cases the linear equation or, more generally, the A matrix is said to be *ill conditioned*.

One measure of ill conditioning in a linear equation $Ax = b$ is the "elasticity" of the solution vector x with respect to the data vector b

$$\epsilon = \sup_{||\delta b|| > 0} \frac{||\delta x||/||x||}{||\delta b||/||b||}$$

The elasticity gives the maximum percentage change in the size of the solution vector x induced by a 1 percent change in the size of the data vector b. If the elasticity is large, then small errors in the computer representation of the data vector b can produce large errors in the computed solution vector x. Equivalently, the computed solution x will have far fewer significant digits than the data vector b.

The elasticity of the solution is expensive to compute and thus is virtually never computed in practice. In practice, the elasticity is estimated using the *condition number* of the matrix A, which for invertible A is defined by

$$\kappa \equiv ||A|| \cdot ||A^{-1}||$$

The condition number of A is the least upper bound of the elasticity. The bound is tight in that for some data vector b, the condition number equals the elasticity. The condition number is always greater than or equal to one. Numerical analysts often use the rough rule of thumb that for each power of 10 in the condition number, one significant digit is lost in the computed solution vector x. Thus, if A has a condition number of 1,000, the computed solution vector x will have about three fewer significant digits than the data vector b.

Consider the linear equation $Ax = b$ where $A_{ij} = i^{n-j}$ and $b_i = (i^n - 1)/(i - 1)$. In theory, the solution x to this linear equation is a vector containing all ones for any n. In practice, however, if one solves the linear equation numerically using MATLAB's "\" operator, one can get quite different results. Following is a table that gives the supremum norm approximation error in the computed value of x and the condition number of the A matrix for different n:

n	Approximation Error	Condition Number
5	2.5e-013	2.6e+004
10	5.2e-007	2.1e+012
15	1.1e+002	2.6e+021
20	9.6e+010	1.8e+031
25	8.2e+019	4.2e+040

In this example the computed answers are accurate to seven decimals up to $n = 10$. The accuracy, however, deteriorates rapidly after that point. In this example the matrix A is a member of a class of notoriously ill-conditioned matrices called the Vandermonde matrices, which we will encounter again in Chapter 6.

Ill conditioning ultimately can be ascribed to the limited precision of computer arithmetic. The effects of ill conditioning can often be mitigated by performing computer arithmetic using the highest precision available on the computer. The best way to handle ill conditioning, however, is to avoid it altogether. Avoiding it is often possible when the linear equation problem is an elementary task in a more complicated solution procedure, such as solving a nonlinear equation or approximating a function with a polynomial. In such cases one can sometimes reformulate the problem or alter the solution strategy to avoid the ill-conditioned linear equation. We will see several examples of this avoidance strategy later in the book.

2.5   Special Linear Equations

Gaussian elimination can be accelerated for matrices possessing certain special structures. Two such classes arising frequently in computational economic analysis are symmetric positive definite matrices and sparse matrices.

Linear equations $Ax = b$ in which A is a symmetric positive definite arise frequently in least-squares curve fitting and optimization applications. A special form of Gaussian elimination, the Cholesky factorization algorithm, may be applied to such linear equations. Cholesky factorization requires only half as many operations as general Gaussian elimination and has the added advantage that it is less vulnerable to rounding error and does not require pivoting.

The essential idea underlying Cholesky factorization is that any symmetric positive definite matrix A can be uniquely expressed as the product

$$A = U^\top U$$

of an upper triangular matrix U and its transpose. The matrix U is called the Cholesky factor or square root of A. Given the Cholesky factor of A, the linear equation

$$Ax = U^\top U x = U^\top (Ux) = b$$

may be solved efficiently by using forward substitution to solve

$$U^\top y = b$$

and then using backward substitution to solve

$$Ux = y.$$

The MATLAB "\" operator will automatically employ Cholesky factorization, rather than L-U factorization, to solve the linear equation if it detects that A is symmetric positive definite.

Another situation that often arises in computational practice involves linear equations $Ax = b$ in which the A matrix is sparse, that is, A consists largely of zero entries. For example, in solving differential equations, one often encounters tridiagonal matrices, which are zero except on or near the diagonal. When the A matrix is sparse, the conventional Gaussian elimination algorithm consists largely of meaningless, but costly, operations involving either multiplication or addition with zero. The execution speed of the Gaussian elimination algorithm in these instances can often be dramatically increased by avoiding these useless operations.

MATLAB has special routines for efficiently storing sparse matrices and operating with them. In particular, the MATLAB command `S=sparse(A)` creates a version S of the matrix A stored in a sparse matrix format, in which only the nonzero elements of A and their indices are explicitly stored. Sparse matrix storage requires only a fraction of the space required to store A in standard form if A is sparse. Also, the operator "\" is designed to recognize whether a sparse matrix is involved in the operation and adapts the Gaussian elimination algorithm to exploit this property. In particular, both `x=S\b` and `x=A\b` will compute the answer to $Ax = b$. However, the former expression will be executed substantially faster by avoiding operations with zeros when A is sparse.

2.6   Iterative Methods

Algorithms based on Gaussian elimination are called *exact* or, more properly, *direct methods* because they would generate exact solutions for the linear equation $Ax = b$ after a finite number of operations, if not for rounding error. Such methods are ideal for moderately sized linear equations but may be impractical for large ones. Other methods, called *iterative methods,* can often be used to solve large linear equations more efficiently if the A matrix is sparse, that is, if A is composed mostly of zero entries. Iterative methods are designed to generate a sequence of increasingly accurate approximations to the solution of a linear equation, but they generally do not yield an exact solution after a prescribed number of steps, even in theory.

The most widely used iterative methods for solving a linear equation $Ax = b$ are developed by choosing an easily invertible matrix Q and writing the linear equation in the equivalent form

$$Qx = b + (Q - A)x$$

or

$$x = Q^{-1}b + (I - Q^{-1}A)x$$

This form of the linear equation suggests the iteration rule

$$x^{(k+1)} \leftarrow Q^{-1}b + (I - Q^{-1}A)x^{(k)}$$

which, if convergent, must converge to a solution of the linear equation.

Ideally, the so-called *splitting matrix* Q will satisfy two criteria. First, $Q^{-1}b$ and $Q^{-1}A$ should be relatively easy to compute. This criterion is met if Q is either diagonal or triangular. Second, the iterates should converge quickly to the true solution of the linear equation. If

$$||I - Q^{-1}A|| < 1$$

in any matrix norm, then the iteration rule is a contraction mapping and is guaranteed to converge to the solution of the linear equation from any initial value. The smaller the value of the matrix norm $||I - Q^{-1}A||$, the faster the guaranteed rate of convergence of the iterates when measured in the associated vector norm.

The two most popular iterative methods are the Gauss-Jacobi and Gauss-Seidel methods. The Gauss-Jacobi method sets Q equal to the diagonal matrix formed from the diagonal entries of A. The Gauss-Seidel method sets Q equal to the upper triangular matrix formed from the upper triangular elements of A. Using the row-sum matrix norm to test the convergence criterion, both methods are guaranteed to converge from any starting value if A is diagonally dominant, that is, if

$$|A_{ii}| > \sum_{\substack{i=1 \\ i \neq j}}^{n} |A_{ij}| \quad \forall i$$

Diagonally dominant matrices arise naturally in many computational economic applications, including the solution of differential equations and the approximation of functions using cubic splines, both of which will be discussed in later sections. The following MATLAB script solves the linear equation $Ax = b$ using Gauss-Jacobi iteration:

```
d = diag(A);
for it=1:maxit
   dx = (b-A*x)./d;
   x  = x+dx;
   if norm(dx)<tol, break, end
end
```

Here, the user specifies the data A and b and an initial guess x for the solution of the linear equation, typically the zero vector or b. Iteration continues until the norm of the change dx in the iterate falls below the specified convergence tolerance tol or until a specified maximum number of allowable iterations maxit are performed.

The following MATLAB script solves the same linear equation using Gauss-Seidel iteration:

```
Q = tril(A);
for it=1:maxit
  dx = Q\(b-A*x);
  x  = x+lambda*dx;
  if norm(dx)<tol, break, end
end
```

Here, we have incorporated a so-called *overrelaxation parameter,* λ. Instead of using $x + dx$, we use $x + \lambda dx$ to compute the next iterate. It is often true, though not universally so, that a value of λ between 1 and 2 will accelerate convergence of the Gauss-Seidel algorithm.

The CompEcon Toolbox includes functions gjacobi and gseidel that solve linear equations using Gauss-Jacobi and Gauss-Seidel iteration, respectively. The following script solves a linear equation using Gauss-Seidel iteration with default value of 1 for the overrelaxation parameter:

```
A = [3 1 ; 2 5];
b = [7 ; 9];
x = gseidel(A,b)
```

Execution of this script produces the result x=[2;1]. When A=[3 2; 4 1], however, the algorithm diverges. The subroutines are extensible in that they allow the user to override the default values of the convergence parameters and, in the case of gseidel, the default value of the overrelaxation parameter.

A general rule of thumb is that if A is large and sparse, then the linear equation is a good candidate for iterative methods, provided that sparse matrix storage functions are used to reduce storage requirements and computational effort. Iterative methods, however, have some drawbacks. First, iterative methods, in contrast to direct methods, can fail to converge. Furthermore, it is often difficult or computationally costly to check whether a specific problem falls into a class of problems known to be convergent. It is therefore always a good idea to monitor whether the iterations seem to be diverging and try something else if they are. Second, satisfaction of the termination criteria does not necessarily guarantee a similar level of accuracy in the solution, measured as the deviation of the approximate solution from the true (but unknown) solution.

Exercises

2.1. Solve $Ax = b$ for

$$A = \begin{bmatrix} 54 & 14 & -11 & 2 \\ 14 & 50 & -4 & 29 \\ -11 & -4 & 55 & 22 \\ 2 & 29 & 22 & 95 \end{bmatrix}, \quad b = \begin{bmatrix} 1 \\ 1 \\ 1 \\ 1 \end{bmatrix}$$

by

a. L-U decomposition.

b. Gauss-Jacobi iteration.

c. Gauss-Seidel iteration.

How many Gauss-Jacobi and Gauss-Seidel iterations are required to get answers that agree with the L-U decomposition solution to four significant digits?

2.2. Use the MATLAB function `randn` to generate a random 100-by-100 matrix A and a random 100-vector b. Then use the MATLAB functions `tic` and `toc` to compute the time needed to solve the linear equation $Ax = b$ 1, 10, and 50 times for each of the following algorithms:

a. $x = A \backslash b$.

b. $x = U \backslash (L \backslash b)$, computing the L-U factors of A only once using the MATLAB function `lu`.

c. $x = A^{-1}b$, computing A^{-1} only once using the MATLAB function `inv`.

2.3. Prove theoretically that Gauss-Jacobi iteration applied to the linear equation $Ax = b$ must converge if A is diagonally dominant. You will need to use the Contraction Mapping Theorem (Appendix A, p. 461) and the result that $||My|| \le ||M|| \, ||y||$ for any square matrix M and conformable vector y.

2.4. It is well known that a quadratic equation

$$ax^2 + bx + c = 0$$

has two roots given by

$$\frac{-b \pm \sqrt{b^2 - 4ac}}{2a}$$

There are, however, other mathematically correct ways of expressing the quadratic equation.

For example, the quadratic equation could be written as

$$\frac{-2c}{b \pm \sqrt{b^2 - 4ac}}$$

or, indeed, as either

$$\frac{b}{2a}\left(-1 \pm \sqrt{1 - 4ac/b^2}\right)$$

or

$$\frac{-2c}{b\left(1 \pm \sqrt{1 - 4ac/b^2}\right)}$$

(You can derive these by noting that $4ac = (b + \sqrt{b^2 - 4ac})(b - \sqrt{b^2 - 4ac})$.) Discuss the relative merits of these alternative ways of computing the roots. Under what circumstances will each produce inaccurate results. Based on these considerations, write a MATLAB function that accepts a, b, and c and returns the two roots.

Appendix 2A: Computer Arithmetic

Some knowledge of how computers perform numerical computations and how programming languages work is useful in applied numerical work, especially if one is to write efficient programs and avoid errors. It often comes as an unpleasant surprise to learn that exact arithmetic and computer arithmetic do not always give the same answers, even in programs without programming errors. For example, consider the following two statements

```
x = (1e-20 + 1) - 1
```

and

```
x = 1e-20 + (1 - 1)
```

Here, 1e-20 is computer shorthand for 10^{-20}. Mathematically the two statements are equivalent because addition and subtraction are associative. A computer, however, would evaluate these statements differently. The first statement would, incorrectly, likely result in $x = 0$, whereas the second would result, correctly, in $x = 10^{-20}$. The reason has to do with how computers represent numbers. Typically, computer languages such as Fortran and C allow several ways of representing a number. MATLAB makes things simple by only having one representation for a number. MATLAB uses what is often called a double precision floating point number. The exact details of the representation depend on the hardware, but it will suffice for our purposes to suppose that floating point numbers are stored in the form $m2^e$, where m and e are integers with $-2^b \le m < 2^b$ and $-2^d \le e < 2^d$. For example, the number -3210.48 cannot be represented precisely as an ordinary double precision number but is approximately equal to $-7059920181484585 \times 2^{-41}$. The value of the approximation, to 32 decimal digits, is equal to $-3210.48000000000181898940354586$, implying that the error in representing -3210.48 is approximately 2^{-42}.

Consider now what happens when arithmetic operations are performed. If $m_1 2^{e_1}$ is multiplied by $m_2 2^{e_2}$, the exact result is $m_1 m_2 2^{e_1 + e_2}$. If $m_1 m_2$ is outside the range $[-2^b, 2^b)$, it will need to be divided by powers of 2 until it is within this range, and the exponent will need to be adjusted accordingly. In the process of dividing $m_1 m_2$, any remainders will be lost. Therefore, it is possible to perform the operation $(x*y)/y$ and have the result not equal x; instead it may be off by 1 in its least significant digit. Furthermore, if $e_1 + e_2$ (plus any adjustment arising from the division) is greater than 2^d or less than -2^d, the result cannot be represented. This is a situation known as *overflow*. In MATLAB, overflow produces a result that is set to `inf` or `-inf`. Further operations may produce sensible results, but, more often than not, the end result of overflow is useless.

Addition is also problematic. Suppose $e_1 > e_2$; then

$$m_1 2^{e_1} + m_2 2^{e_2} = \left(m_1 + \frac{m_2}{2^{e_1 - e_2}} \right) 2^{e_1}$$

The computer, however, will truncate $m_2 / 2^{e_1 - e_2}$, so the result will not be exact. It is therefore possible to perform $x+y$, for $y \ne 0$ and have the result equal x; this will occur if $m_2 < 2^{e_1 - e_2}$. Although odd, the result is nonetheless accurate to its least significant digit.

Of all the operations on floating point numbers, the most troublesome is subtraction, particularly when a large number is subtracted from another large number. Consider, for example, what happens when one performs `1000000.2-1000000.1`. The result, of course, should equal 0.1 but instead equals (on a Pentium processor) 0.09999999997672. The reason for this strange behavior is that the two numbers being operated on cannot be represented exactly. On a Pentium processor, the floating point numbers used are actually

$8589935450993459 \times 2^{-33} = 1000000.09999999999767169356346130$

and

$8589936309986918 \times 2^{-33} = 1000000.19999999999534338712692261.$

The result obtained from subtracting the first from the second is therefore

$$(8589936309986918 - 8589935450993459)2^{-33} = 0.09999999997672$$

as we found previously. The error is approximately -2.3283×10^{-11}, which is roughly the same order of magnitude as 2^{-34}.

Although one's first impression may be to minimize the importance of finite precision arithmetic, serious problems can arise if one is not careful. Furthermore, these problems may result in strange behavior that is hard to track down or erroneous results that may, or may not, be detected.

Consider, for example, the computation of the function

$$\phi^-(y, z) = y + z - \sqrt{y^2 + z^2}$$

This function is used in solving complementarity problems and is discussed in section 3.8. Most of the time it can be computed as written, and no problems will arise. When one of the values gets large relative to the other, however, the obvious way of coding can fail as a result of overflow or, worse, can produce an incorrect answer.

Suppose that $|y| > |z|$. One problem that can arise is that y is so big that y^2 overflows. The largest real number representable on a machine can be found with the MATLAB command `realmax` (it is approximately $2^{1024} \approx 10^{308}$ for most double precision environments). Although this kind of overflow may not happen often, it could have unfortunate consequences and cause problems that are hard to detect.

Even when y is not so big, several problems can arise if it is big relative to z. The first of these is easily dealt with. Suppose we evaluate

$$y + z - \sqrt{y^2 + z^2}$$

when $|y|$ is large enough so that $y + z$ is evaluated as y. This evaluation implies that $\sqrt{y^2 + z^2}$ will be evaluated as $|y|$. When $y < 0$, the expression is evaluated as $2y$, which is correct to the most significant digit. When $y > 0$, however, we get 0, which may be very far from correct. If the expression is evaluated in the order

$$y - \sqrt{y^2 + z^2} + z$$

the result will be z, which is much closer to the correct answer.

An even better approach is to use

$$\phi^-(y, z) = y\left(1 - \text{sign}(y)\sqrt{1 + \epsilon^2} + \epsilon\right)$$

where $\epsilon = z/y$. Although this is algebraically equivalent, it has very different properties. First notice that the chance of overflow is greatly reduced because $1 \le 1 + \epsilon^2 \le 2$, and so the expression within the parentheses is bounded on $[\epsilon, 4]$. If $1 + \epsilon^2$ is evaluated as 1 (i.e., if ϵ is less than the square root of machine precision), this expression yields $2y$ if $y < 0$ and $y\epsilon = z$ if $y > 0$.

This approach is better, but one further problem arises when $y > 0$ with $|y| \gg |z|$. In this case there is a cancellation due to the expression of the form

$$z = 1 - \sqrt{1 + \epsilon^2}$$

The obvious way of computing this term will result in loss of precision as ϵ gets small. Another expression for z is

$$z = -\frac{\left(1 - \sqrt{1 + \epsilon^2}\right)^2 + \epsilon^2}{2\sqrt{1 + \epsilon^2}}$$

Although this is more complicated, it is accurate regardless of the size of ϵ. As ϵ gets small, this expression will be approximately $\epsilon^2/2$. Thus, if ϵ is about the size of the square root of machine precision (2^{-26} on most double precision implementations), z would be computed to machine precision with the second expression, but would be computed to be 0 using the first; that is, no significant digits would be correct.

Putting all this together, a good approach to computing $\phi^-(y, z)$ when $|y| \geq |z|$ uses

$$\phi^-(y, z) = \begin{cases} y\left(1 + \sqrt{1 + \epsilon^2} + \epsilon\right) & \text{if } y < 0 \\ y\left(\epsilon - \frac{\left(1 - \sqrt{1 + \epsilon^2}\right)^2 + \epsilon^2}{2\sqrt{1 + \epsilon^2}}\right) & \text{if } y > 0 \end{cases}$$

where $\epsilon = z/y$ (reverse z and y if $|y| < |z|$).

MATLAB has a number of special numerical representations relevant to this discussion. We have already mentioned `inf` and `-inf`. These arise not only from overflow but from division by 0. The number `realmax` is the largest floating point number that can be represented; `realmin` is the smallest positive (normalized) number representable.[1] In addition, `eps` represents the machine precision, defined as the first number greater than 0 that can be represented as a floating point number. Another way to state this definition is: For any $0 \leq \epsilon \leq$ `eps`/2, $1 + \epsilon$ will be evaluated as 1 (i.e., `eps` is equal to 2^{1-b}).[2] All three of these special values are hardware specific. In addition, floating point numbers may get set to `NaN`, which stands for "not a number." This result typically follows from a mathematically undefined operation, such as `inf-inf` and `0/0`. This result, however,

---

1. A denormalized number is one that is nonzero but has an exponent equal to its smallest possible value.

2. The expression $2^0 + 2^{-b} = (2^b + 1)2^{-b}$ cannot be represented and must be truncated to $(2^{b-1})2^{1-b} = 1$. However, $2^0 + 2^{1-b} = (2^{b-1} + 1)2^{1-b}$ can be represented.

does not follow from `inf/0`, `0/inf`, or `inf*inf` (these result in `inf`, `0`, and `inf`). Any arithmetic operation involving a `NaN` results in a `NaN`.

Round-off error is only one of the pitfalls in evaluating mathematical expressions. In numerical computations, error is also introduced by the computer's inherent inability to evaluate certain mathematical expressions exactly. For all its power, a computer can only perform a limited set of operations in evaluating expressions. Essentially this list includes the four arithmetic operations of addition, subtraction, multiplication, and division, as well as logical operations of comparison. Other common functions, such as exponential, logarithmic, and trigonometric functions, cannot be evaluated directly using computer arithmetic. They can only be evaluated approximately using algorithms based on the four basic arithmetic operations.

For the common functions very efficient algorithms typically exist, and these are sometimes "hardwired" into the computer's processor or coprocessor. An important area of numerical analysis involves determining efficient approximations that can be computed using basic arithmetic operations. For example, the exponential function has the series representation

$$\exp(x) = \sum_{i=0}^{\infty} x^n/n!$$

Obviously one cannot compute the infinite sum, but one could compute a finite number of these terms, with the hope that one will obtain sufficient accuracy for the purpose at hand. The result, however, will always be inexact.[3]

For nonstandard problems, we must often rely on our own abilities as numerical analysts (or know when to seek help). Being aware of some of the pitfalls should help us avoid them.

Appendix 2B: Data Storage

MATLAB's basic data type is the matrix, with a scalar just a 1×1 matrix and an n-vector an $n \times 1$ or $1 \times n$ matrix. MATLAB keeps track of matrix size by storing row and column information about the matrix along with the values of the matrix itself. This is a significant advantage over writing in low-level languages like Fortran or C because it relieves one of the necessity of keeping track of array size and memory allocation.

---

3. Incidentally, the Taylor series representation of the exponential function does not result in an efficient computational algorithm.

One can represent an $m \times n$ matrix of numbers in a computer in a number of ways. The most simple way is to store all the elements sequentially in memory, starting with the one indexed (1,1) and working down successive columns or across successive rows until the (m, n)th element is stored. Different languages make different choices about how to store a matrix. Fortran stores matrices in column order, whereas C stores in row order. MATLAB, although written in C, stores them in column order, thereby conforming with the Fortran standard.

Many matrices encountered in practice are sparse, meaning that they consist mostly of zero entries. Clearly, it is a waste of memory to store all the zeros, and it is time-consuming to process the zeros in arithmetic matrix operations. MATLAB supports a sparse matrix data type, which efficiently keeps track of only the nonzero elements of the original matrix and their locations. In this storage scheme, the nonzero entries and the row indices are stored in two vectors of the same size. A separate vector is used to keep track of where the first element in each column is located. If one wants to access element (i, j), MATLAB checks the jth element of the column indicator vector to find where the jth column starts and then searches the row indicator vector for the ith element (if one is not found, then the element must be zero).

Although sparse matrix representations are useful, they come at a cost. To access element (i, j) of a full matrix, one simply goes to storage location $(j - 1)m + i$. Accessing an element in a sparse matrix involves a search over row indices and hence can take longer. This additional overhead can add up significantly and actually slow down a computational procedure.

A further consideration in using sparse matrices concerns memory allocation. If a procedure repeatedly alters the contents of a sparse matrix, the memory needed to store the matrix may change, even if its dimension does not. As a result, more memory may be needed each time the number of nonzero elements increases. This memory allocation both is time-consuming and may eventually exhaust computer memory.

The decision whether to use a sparse or full matrix representation depends on a balance between a number of factors. Clearly for very sparse matrices (less than 10% nonzero) one is better off using sparse matrices, and for anything over 67% nonzeros one is better off with full matrices (which actually require less storage space at that point). In between, some experimentation may be required to determine which is better for a given application.

Fortunately, for many applications users don't even need to be aware of whether matrices are stored in sparse or full form. MATLAB is designed so most functions work with any mix of sparse or full representations. Furthermore, sparsity propagates in a reasonably intelligent fashion. For example, a sparse times a full matrix or a sparse plus a full matrix results in a full matrix, but if a sparse and a full matrix are multiplied element by element (using the ". *" operator), a sparse matrix results.

Bibliographic Notes

Good introductory discussions of computer basics are contained in Gill, Murray, and Wright (1981), Press et al. (1992), and Kennedy and Gentle (1980). These references also all contain discussions of computational aspects of linear algebra and matrix factorizations. A standard in-depth treatment of computational linear algebra is Golub and van Loan (1989). Most textbooks on linear algebra also include discussions of Gaussian elimination and other factorizations; see, for example, Leon (1980).

We have discussed only the two matrix factorizations that are most important for the remainder of this text. A number of other factorizations exist and have uses in computational economic analysis, making them worth mentioning briefly (see references cited previously for more details).

The first is the eigenvalue/eigenvector factorization. Given an $n \times n$ matrix A, this factorization finds $n \times n$ matrices Z and D, with D diagonal, that satisfy $AZ = ZD$. The columns of Z and the diagonal elements of D form eigenvector, eigenvalue pairs. If Z is nonsingular, the result is a factorization of the form $A = ZDZ^{-1}$. It is possible, however, that Z is singular (even if A is not); such matrices are called defective. The eigenvalue/eigenvector factorization is unique (up to rearrangement and possible linear combinations of columns of Z associated with repeated eigenvalues). In general, both Z and D may be complex valued, even if A is real valued. Complex eigenvalues arise in economic models that display cyclic behavior. In the special case that A is real valued and symmetric, the eigenvector matrix is not only guaranteed to be nonsingular but is orthonormal (i.e., $Z^{\top}Z = I$), so $A = ZDZ^{\top}$ and Z and D are real valued.

Another factorization is the QR decomposition, which finds a representation $A = QR$, where Q is orthonormal and R is triangular. This factorization is not unique; there are a number of algorithms that produce different values of Q and R, including Householder and Givens transformations. The matrix A need not be square to apply the QR decomposition.

Finally, we mention the singular-value decomposition (SVD), which finds U, D, and V, with U and V orthonormal and D diagonal, that satisfies $A = UDV^{\top}$. The diagonal elements of D are known as the *singular values* of A and are nonnegative and generally ordered highest to lowest. In the case of a square, symmetric A, this is identical to the eigenvalue/eigenvector decomposition. The SVD can be used with nonsquare matrices.

The SVD is the method of choice for determining matrix condition and rank. The condition number is the ratio of the highest to the lowest singular value; the rank is the number of nonzero singular values. In practice, one would treat a singular value D_{jj} as zero if $D_{jj} < \max_i(D_{ii})\epsilon$, for some specified value of ϵ (MATLAB sets ϵ equal to the value of the machine precision `eps` times the maximum of the number of rows and columns of A).

We have only touched on iterative methods. These are mainly useful when solving large sparse systems that cannot be stored directly. See Golub and Ortega (1992), Section 9.3, for further details and references.

Numerous software libraries that perform basic linear algebra computations are available, including LINPACK, LAPACK, IMSL, and NAG.

3 Nonlinear Equations and Complementarity Problems

One of the most basic numerical problems encountered in computational economics is to find the solution of a system of nonlinear equations. Nonlinear equations generally arise in one of two forms. In the nonlinear *rootfinding problem,* a function f from $\mathbb{R}^n$ to $\mathbb{R}^n$ is given, and one must compute an n-vector x, called a *root* of f, that satisfies

$$f(x) = 0$$

In the nonlinear *fixed-point problem,* a function g from $\mathbb{R}^n$ to $\mathbb{R}^n$ is given, and one must compute an n-vector x, called a *fixed-point* of g, that satisfies

$$x = g(x)$$

The two forms are equivalent. The rootfinding problem may be recast as a fixed-point problem by letting $g(x) = x - f(x)$; conversely, the fixed-point problem may be recast as a rootfinding problem by letting $f(x) = x - g(x)$.

In the related *complementarity problem,* two n-vectors a and b, with $a < b$, and a function f from $\mathbb{R}^n$ to $\mathbb{R}^n$ are given, and one must compute an n-vector $x \in [a, b]$, that satisfies

$$x_i > a_i \implies f_i(x) \geq 0 \quad \forall i = 1, \dots, n$$

$$x_i < b_i \implies f_i(x) \leq 0 \quad \forall i = 1, \dots, n$$

The rootfinding problem is a special case of the complementarity problem in which $a_i = -\infty$ and $b_i = +\infty$ for all i. However, the complementarity problem is not simply to find a root that lies within specified bounds. An element $f_i(x)$ may be nonzero at a solution of the complementarity problem, provided that x_i equals one of the bounds a_i or b_i.

Nonlinear equations and complementarity problems arise directly in many economic applications. For example, the typical economic equilibrium model characterizes market prices and quantities with an equal number of supply, demand, and market clearing equations. If one or more of the equations is nonlinear, a nonlinear rootfinding problem arises. If the model is generalized to include constraints on prices and quantities arising from price supports, quotas, nonnegativity conditions, or limited production capacities, a nonlinear complementarity problem arises.

One also encounters nonlinear rootfinding and complementarity problems indirectly when maximizing or minimizing a real-valued function. An unconstrained optimum may be characterized by the condition that the first derivative of the function is zero—a rootfinding problem. A constrained optimum may be characterized by the Karush-Kuhn-Tucker conditions—a complementarity problem. Nonlinear equations and complementarity problems also arise as elementary tasks in solution procedures designed to solve more complicated functional equations. For example, the Euler functional equation of a dynamic optimization problem might be solved using a collocation method, which gives rise to a nonlinear equation or complementarity problem, depending on whether the actions are unconstrained or constrained, respectively.

Various practical difficulties arise with nonlinear equations and complementarity problems. In many applications, it is not possible to solve the nonlinear problem analytically. In these instances, the solution is often computed numerically using an iterative method that reduces the nonlinear problem to a sequence of linear problems. Such methods can be very sensitive to initial conditions and inherit many of the potential problems of linear equation methods, most notably rounding error and ill conditioning. Nonlinear problems also present the added difficulty that they may have more than one solution.

Over the years, numerical analysts have studied nonlinear equations and complementarity problems extensively and have devised a variety of algorithms for solving them quickly and accurately. In many applications, one may use simple derivative-free methods, such as function iteration, which is applicable to fixed-point problems, or the bisection method, which is applicable to univariate rootfinding problems. In many applications, however, one must rely on more sophisticated Newton and quasi-Newton methods, which use derivatives or derivative estimates to help locate the root or fixed point of a function. These methods can be extended to complementarity problems using semismooth approximation methods.

3.1   Bisection Method

The *bisection method* is perhaps the simplest and most robust method for computing the root of a continuous real-valued function defined on a bounded interval of the real line. The bisection method is based on the Intermediate Value Theorem, which asserts that if a continuous real-valued function defined on an interval assumes two distinct values, then it must assume all values in between. In particular, if f is continuous, and $f(a)$ and $f(b)$ have different signs, then f must have at least one root x in $[a, b]$.

The bisection method is an iterative procedure. Each iteration begins with an interval known to contain or to bracket a root of f, because the function has different signs at the interval endpoints. The interval is bisected into two subintervals of equal length. One of the two subintervals must have endpoints of different signs and thus must contain a root of f. This subinterval is taken as the new interval with which to begin the subsequent iteration. In this manner, a sequence of intervals is generated, each half the width of the preceding one, and each known to contain a root of f. The process continues until the width of the bracketing interval containing a root shrinks below an acceptable convergence tolerance.

The bisection method's greatest strength is its robustness. In contrast to other rootfinding methods, the bisection method is guaranteed to compute a root to a prescribed tolerance in a known number of iterations, provided valid data are entered. Specifically, the method computes a root to a precision ϵ in no more than $\log((b - a)/\epsilon)/\log(2)$ iterations. The bisection method, however, is applicable only to one-dimensional rootfinding problems and typically requires more iterations than other rootfinding methods to compute a root to a given precision, largely because it ignores information about the function's curvature. Given its relative strengths and weaknesses, the bisection method is often used in conjunction with other rootfinding methods. In this context, the bisection method is first used to obtain a crude approximation for the root. This approximation then becomes the starting point for a more precise rootfinding method that is used to compute a sharper, final approximation to the root.

The following MATLAB script computes the root of a user-supplied univariate function f using the bisection method. The user specifies two points at which f has different signs, a and b, and a convergence tolerance tol. The script makes use of the intrinsic MATLAB function sign, which returns -1, 0, or 1 if its argument is negative, zero, or positive, respectively:

```
s = sign(f(a));
x = (a+b)/2;
d = (b-a)/2;
while d>tol;
   d = d/2;
   if s == sign(f(x))
      x = x+d;
   else
      x = x-d;
   end
end
```

In this implementation of the bisection algorithm, d begins each iteration equal to the distance from the current root estimate x to the boundaries of the bracketing interval. The value of d is cut in half, and the iterate is updated by increasing or decreasing its value by this amount, depending on the sign of $f(x)$. If $f(x)$ and $f(a)$ have the same sign, then the current x implicitly becomes the new left endpoint of the bracketing interval, and x is moved d units toward b. Otherwise, the current x implicitly becomes the new right endpoint of the bracketing interval, and x is moved d units toward a.

The CompEcon Toolbox includes a routine bisect that computes the root of a univariate function using bisection. Suppose that one wished to compute the cube root of 2, or, equivalently, the root of the function $f(x) = x^3 - 2$. To apply bisect, one first codes a stand-alone MATLAB function f that returns the value of the function at an arbitrary point:

```
function y = f(x)
y = x^3-2;
```

One then passes the function name, along with two bracketing points, to bisect:

```
x = bisect('f',1,2)
```

Execution of the preceding script computes the root 1.2599 to a default tolerance of 1.5×10^{-8} starting with the bracketing interval $[1, 2]$.

3.2 Function Iteration

Function iteration is a relatively simple technique that may be used to compute a fixed point $x = g(x)$ of a function from $\mathbb{R}^n$ to $\mathbb{R}^n$. The technique is also applicable to a rootfinding problem $f(x) = 0$ by recasting it as the equivalent fixed-point problem $x = x - f(x)$.

Function iteration begins with the analyst supplying a guess $x^{(0)}$ for the fixed point of g. Subsequent iterates are generated using the simple iteration rule

$$x^{(k+1)} \leftarrow g\left(x^{(k)}\right)$$

Since g is continuous, if the iterates converge, they converge to a fixed point of g.

In theory, function iteration is guaranteed to converge to a fixed point of g if g is differentiable and if the initial value of x supplied by the analyst is "sufficiently" close to a fixed point x^* of g at which $\|g'(x^*)\| < 1$. Function iteration, however, often converges even when the sufficiency conditions are not met. Given that the method is relatively easy to implement, it is often worth trying before attempting to use more robust, but ultimately more complex, methods, such as the Newton and quasi-Newton methods, which are discussed in the following sections.

Computation of the fixed point of a univariate function $g(x)$ using function iteration is graphically illustrated in Figure 3.1. In this example, g possesses a unique fixed point x^*, which is graphically characterized by the intersection of g and the 45-degree line. The algorithm begins with the analyst supplying a guess $x^{(0)}$ for the fixed point of g. The next iterate $x^{(1)}$ is obtained by projecting upward to the g function and then rightward to the 45-degree line. Subsequent iterates are obtained by repeating the projection sequence, tracing out a step function. The process continues until the iterates converge.

The CompEcon Toolbox includes a routine fixpoint that computes a fixed point of a multivariate function using function iteration. Suppose that one wished to compute a fixed point of the function $g(x) = x^{0.5}$. To apply fixpoint, one first codes a stand-alone

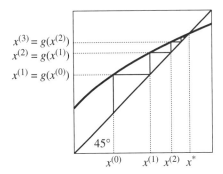

Figure 3.1
Function Iteration

MATLAB function g that returns the value of the function at an arbitrary point:

```
function y = g(x)
y = x^0.5;
```

One then passes the function name, along with an initial guess for the fixed point, to `fixpoint`:

```
x = fixpoint('g',0.4)
```

Execution of the preceding script computes the fixed point 1 to a default tolerance of 1.5×10^{-8} starting from the initial guess $x = 0.4$.

3.3 Newton's Method

In practice, most nonlinear problems are solved using *Newton's method* or one of its variants. Newton's method is based on the principle of *successive linearization*. Successive linearization calls for a hard nonlinear problem to be replaced with a sequence of simpler linear problems whose solutions converge to the solution of the nonlinear problem. Newton's method is typically formulated as a rootfinding technique, but may be used to solve a fixed-point problem $x = g(x)$ by recasting it as the rootfinding problem $f(x) = x - g(x) = 0$.

The univariate Newton method is graphically illustrated in Figure 3.2. The algorithm begins with the analyst supplying a guess $x^{(0)}$ for the root of f. The function f is then approximated by its first-order Taylor series expansion about $x^{(0)}$, which is graphically represented by the line tangent to f at $x^{(0)}$. The root $x^{(1)}$ of the tangent line is then accepted as an improved estimate for the root of f. The step is repeated, with the root $x^{(2)}$ of the line

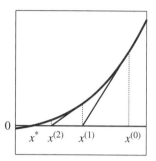

Figure 3.2
Univariate Newton Method

tangent to f at $x^{(1)}$ taken as an improved estimate for the root of f, and so on. The process continues until the roots of the tangent lines converge.

More generally, the multivariate Newton method begins with the analyst supplying a guess $x^{(0)}$ for the root of f. Given $x^{(k)}$, the subsequent iterate $x^{(k+1)}$ is computed by solving the linear rootfinding problem obtained by replacing f with its first-order Taylor approximation about $x^{(k)}$:

$$f(x) \approx f\left(x^{(k)}\right) + f'\left(x^{(k)}\right)\left(x - x^{(k)}\right) = 0$$

This approach yields the iteration rule

$$x^{(k+1)} \leftarrow x^{(k)} - \left[f'\left(x^{(k)}\right)\right]^{-1} f\left(x^{(k)}\right)$$

The following MATLAB script computes the root of a function f using Newton's method. It assumes that the user has provided an initial guess x for the root, a convergence tolerance tol, and an upper limit maxit on the number of iterations. It calls a user-supplied routine f that computes the value fval and Jacobian fjac of the function at an arbitrary point x. To conserve on storage, only the most recent iterate is stored:

```
for it=1:maxit
  [fval,fjac] = f(x);
  x = x - fjac\fval;
  if norm(fval) < tol, break, end
end
```

In theory, Newton's method converges if f is continuously differentiable and if the initial value of x supplied by the analyst is "sufficiently" close to a root of f at which f' is invertible. There is, however, no generally practical formula for determining what sufficiently close is. Typically, an analyst makes a reasonable guess for the root f and counts his blessings if the iterates converge. If the iterates do not converge, then the analyst must look more closely at the properties of f to find a better starting value or change to another rootfinding method. Newton's method can be robust to the starting value if f is well behaved. Newton's method can be very sensitive to starting value, however, if the function behaves erratically. Finally, in practice it is not sufficient for f' to be merely invertible at the root. If f' is invertible but ill conditioned, then rounding errors in the vicinity of the root can make it difficult to compute a precise approximation to the root using Newton's method.

The CompEcon Toolbox includes a routine newton that computes the root of a function using the Newton method. The user inputs the name of the function file that computes f, a starting vector, and any additional parameters to be passed to f (the first input to f must be x). The function has default values for the convergence tolerance and the maximum number of steps to attempt. The subroutine newton, however, is extensible in that it allows the user to override the default tolerance and limit on the number of iterations.

To illustrate the use of the routine newton, consider a simple Cournot duopoly model, in which the inverse demand for a good is

$$P(q) = q^{-1/\eta}$$

and the two firms producing the good face cost functions

$$C_i(q_i) = \tfrac{1}{2}c_i q_i^2, \quad \text{for } i = 1, 2$$

The profit for firm i is

$$\pi_i(q_1, q_2) = P(q_1 + q_2)q_i - C_i(q_i)$$

If firm i takes the other firm's output as given, it will choose its output level so as to solve

$$\partial \pi_i / \partial q_i = P(q_1 + q_2) + P'(q_1 + q_2)q_i - C_i'(q_i) = 0$$

Thus the market equilibrium outputs, q_1 and q_2, are the roots of the two nonlinear equations

$$f_i(q) = (q_1 + q_2)^{-1/\eta} - (1/\eta)(q_1 + q_2)^{-1/\eta-1}q_i - c_i q_i = 0, \quad \text{for } i = 1, 2$$

Suppose one wished to use the CompEcon routine newton to compute for the market equilibrium quantities, assuming $\eta = 1.6$, $c_1 = 0.6$, and $c_2 = 0.8$. The first step would be to write a MATLAB function that gives the value and Jacobian of f at an arbitrary vector of quantities q:

```
function [fval,fjac] = cournot(q)
c = [0.6; 0.8]; eta = 1.6; e = -1/eta;
fval = sum(q)^e + e*sum(q)^(e-1)*q - diag(c)*q;
fjac = e*sum(q)^(e-1)*ones(2,2) + e*sum(q)^(e-1)*eye(2) ...
       + (e-1)*e*sum(q)^(e-2)*q*[1 1] - diag(c);
```

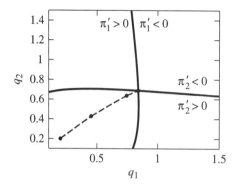

Figure 3.3
Solving a Cournot Model Using the Newton Method

Making an initial guess of, say $q_1 = q_2 = 0.2$, a call to newton

```
q = newton('cournot',[0.2;0.2]);
```

will compute the equilibrium quantities $q_1 = 0.8396$ and $q_2 = 0.6888$ to the default tolerance
of 1.5×10^{-8}.

The path taken by newton to the Cournot equilibrium solution from an initial guess of
$(0.2, 0.2)$ is illustrated by the dashed line in Figure 3.3. Here, the Cournot market equilibrium
is the intersection of the zero contours of f_1 and f_2, which may be interpreted as the reaction
functions for the two firms. In this case Newton's method works very well, needing only a
few steps to effectively land on the root.

3.4 Quasi-Newton Methods

Quasi-Newton methods offer an alternative to Newton's method for solving rootfinding
problems. Quasi-Newton methods are based on the same successive linearization principle
as Newton's method, except that they replace the Jacobian f' with an approximation that
is easier to compute. Quasi-Newton methods are easier to implement and are less likely
to fail because of programming errors than Newton's method because the analyst need not
explicitly code the derivative expressions. Quasi-Newton methods, however, often converge
more slowly than Newton's method and additionally require an initial approximation of the
function's Jacobian.

The *secant method* is the most widely used univariate quasi-Newton method. The secant
method is identical to the univariate Newton method, except that it replaces the derivative of

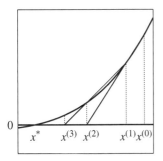

Figure 3.4
Secant Method

f with an approximation constructed from the function values at the two previous iterates:

$$f'\left(x^{(k)}\right) \approx \frac{f\left(x^{(k)}\right) - f\left(x^{(k-1)}\right)}{x^{(k)} - x^{(k-1)}}$$

This approach yields the iteration rule

$$x^{(k+1)} \leftarrow x^{(k)} - \frac{x^{(k)} - x^{(k-1)}}{f\left(x^{(k)}\right) - f\left(x^{(k-1)}\right)} f\left(x^{(k)}\right)$$

Unlike the Newton method, the secant method requires two starting values rather than one.

The secant method is graphically illustrated in Figure 3.4. The algorithm begins with the analyst supplying two distinct guesses $x^{(0)}$ and $x^{(1)}$ for the root of f. The function f is approximated using the secant line passing through $(x^{(0)}, f(x^{(0)}))$ and $(x^{(1)}, f(x^{(1)}))$, whose root $x^{(2)}$ is accepted as an improved estimate for the root of f. The step is repeated, with the root $x^{(3)}$ of the secant line passing through $(x^{(1)}, f(x^{(1)}))$ and $(x^{(2)}, f(x^{(2)}))$ taken as an improved estimate for the root of f, and so on. The process continues until the roots of the secant lines converge.

Broyden's method is the most popular multivariate generalization of the univariate secant method. Broyden's method generates a sequence of vectors $x^{(k)}$ and matrices $A^{(k)}$ that approximate the root of f and the Jacobian f' at the root, respectively. Broyden's method begins with the analyst supplying a guess $x^{(0)}$ for the root of the function and a guess $A^{(0)}$ for the Jacobian of the function at the root. Often, $A^{(0)}$ is set equal to the numerical Jacobian of f at $x^{(0)}$.[1] Alternatively, some analysts use a rescaled identity matrix for $A^{(0)}$, though this approach typically will require more iterations to obtain a solution than if a numerical

---

1. Numerical differentiation is discussed in section 5.6.

Jacobian is computed at the outset. Given $x^{(k)}$ and $A^{(k)}$, one updates the root approximation by solving the linear rootfinding problem obtained by replacing f with its first-order Taylor approximation about $x^{(k)}$:

$$f(x) \approx f\left(x^{(k)}\right) + A^{(k)}\left(x - x^{(k)}\right) = 0$$

This step yields the root approximation iteration rule

$$x^{(k+1)} \leftarrow x^{(k)} - \left(A^{(k)}\right)^{-1} f\left(x^{(k)}\right)$$

Broyden's method then updates the Jacobian approximant $A^{(k)}$ by making the smallest possible change, measured in the Frobenius matrix norm, that is consistent with the *secant condition,* a condition that any reasonable Jacobian estimate should satisfy:

$$f\left(x^{(k+1)}\right) - f\left(x^{(k)}\right) = A^{(k+1)}\left(x^{(k+1)} - x^{(k)}\right)$$

This condition yields the iteration rule

$$A^{(k+1)} \leftarrow A^{(k)} + \left[f\left(x^{(k+1)}\right) - f\left(x^{(k)}\right) - A^{(k)}d^{(k)}\right]\frac{d^{(k)\top}}{d^{(k)\top}d^{(k)}}$$

where $d^{(k)} = x^{(k+1)} - x^{(k)}$.

In practice, Broyden's method may be accelerated by avoiding the linear solve. This acceleration may be achieved by retaining and updating the Broyden estimate of the inverse of the Jacobian, rather than that of the Jacobian itself. Broyden's method with inverse update generates a sequence of vectors $x^{(k)}$ and matrices $B^{(k)}$ that approximate the root of f and the inverse Jacobian f'^{-1} at the root, respectively. It uses the iteration rule

$$x^{(k+1)} \leftarrow x^{(k)} - B^{(k)} f\left(x^{(k)}\right)$$

and inverse update rule[2]

$$B^{(k+1)} \leftarrow B^{(k)} + \left[\left(d^{(k)} - u^{(k)}\right)d^{(k)\top}B^{(k)}\right] / \left(d^{(k)\top}u^{(k)}\right)$$

where $u^{(k)} = B^{(k)}[f(x^{(k+1)}) - f(x^{(k)})]$. Most implementations of Broyden's methods employ the inverse update rule because of its speed advantage over Broyden's method with Jacobian update.

In theory, Broyden's method converges if f is continuously differentiable, if $x^{(0)}$ is "sufficiently" close to a root of f at which f' is invertible, and if $A^{(0)}$ and $B^{(0)}$ are

---

2. This is a straightforward application of the Sherman-Morrison formula:

$$(A + uv^\top)^{-1} = A^{-1} + \frac{1}{1 + u^\top A^{-1}v}A^{-1}uv^\top A^{-1}$$

"sufficiently" close to the Jacobian or inverse Jacobian of f at that root. There is, however, no generally practical formula for determining what sufficiently close is. Like Newton's method, the robustness of Broyden's method depends on the regularity of f and its derivatives. Broyden's method may also have difficulty computing a precise root estimate if f' is ill conditioned near the root. It is also important to note that the sequence approximants $A^{(k)}$ and $B^{(k)}$ need not, and typically do not, converge to the Jacobian and inverse Jacobian of f at the root, respectively, even if the $x^{(k)}$ converge to a root of f.

The following MATLAB script computes the root of a user-supplied multivariate function f using Broyden's method with inverse update. The script assumes that the user has written a MATLAB routine f that evaluates the function at an arbitrary point and that the user has specified a starting point x, a convergence tolerance tol, and a limit on the number of iterations maxit. The script also computes an initial guess for the inverse Jacobian by inverting the finite difference derivative computed using the CompEcon toolbox function fdjac, which is discussed in section 5.6.

```
fjacinv = inv(fdjac(f,x));
fval = f(x);
for it=1:maxit
  fnorm = norm(fval);
  if fnorm<tol; break; end
  d = -(fjacinv*fval);
  x = x+d;
  fold = fval;
  fval = f(x);
  u = fjacinv*(fval-fold);
  fjacinv = fjacinv + ((d-u)*(d'*fjacinv))/(d'*u);
end
```

The CompEcon Toolbox includes a routine broyden that computes the root of a function using Broyden's method with inverse update. To illustrate the use of this function, consider the simple Cournot duopoly model, introduced in the preceding subsection. The function cournot discussed on page 35 could be passed to broyden, with an initial guess of, say $q_1 = q_2 = 0.2$:

```
q = broyden('cournot',[0.2;0.2]);
```

yielding the equilibrium quantities $q_1 = 0.8396$ and $q_2 = 0.6888$ to the default tolerance of 1.5×10^{-8}. Note that the function cournot need not return the Jacobian of f because the Broyden method does not require it. The subroutine broyden is extensible in that it allows

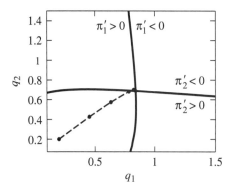

Figure 3.5
Solving a Cournot Model Using Broyden's Method

the user to enter an initial estimate of the Jacobian estimate, if available, and allows the user
to override the default tolerance and limit on the number of iterations. The subroutine also
allows the user to pass additional arguments for the function f, if necessary.

The path taken by `broyden` to the Cournot equilibrium solution from an initial guess
of $(0.2, 0.2)$ is illustrated by the dashed line in Figure 3.5. In this case Broyden's method
works well and is not altogether very different from Newton's method. However, a close
comparison of Figures 3.3 and 3.5 demonstrates that Broyden's method takes more iterations
and follows a somewhat more circuitous route than Newton's method.

3.5   Problems with Newton Methods

Several difficulties commonly arise in the application of Newton and quasi-Newton methods when solving multivariate nonlinear equations. The most common cause of failure of
Newton-type methods is coding error committed by the analyst. The next most common
cause of failure is the specification of a starting point that is not sufficiently close to a
root. And yet another common cause of failure is an ill-conditioned Jacobian at the root.
These problems can often be mitigated by appropriate action, though they cannot always
be eliminated altogether.

The first cause of failure, coding error, may seem obvious and not specific to rootfinding
problems. It must be emphasized, however, that with Newton's method, the likelihood of
committing an error in coding the analytic Jacobian of the function is often high. A careful
analyst can avoid Jacobian coding errors in two ways. First, the analyst could use Broyden's
method instead of Newton's method to solve the rootfinding problem. Broyden's method is

derivative-free and does not require the explicit coding of the function's analytic Jacobian. Second, the analyst can perform a simple but highly effective check of his code by comparing the values computed by his analytic derivatives to those computed using finite difference methods. Such a check will almost always detect an error in either the code that returns the function's value or the code that returns its Jacobian.

A comparison of analytic and finite difference derivatives can easily be performed using the checkjac routine provided with the CompEcon Toolbox. This function computes the analytic and finite difference derivatives of a function at a specified evaluation point and returns the index and magnitude of the largest deviation. The function may be called as follows:

```
[error,i,j] = checkjac(f,x)
```

Here, we assume that the user has coded a MATLAB function f that returns the function value and analytic derivatives at a specified evaluation point x. Execution returns error, the highest absolute difference between an analytic and finite difference cross-partial derivative of f, and its index i and j. A large deviation indicates that either the ijth partial derivative or the ith function value may be incorrectly coded.

The second problem, a poor starting value, can be partially addressed by "backstepping." If taking a full Newton (or quasi-Newton) step dx does not offer an improvement over the current iterate x, then one "backsteps" toward the current iterate x by repeatedly cutting dx in half until $x + dx$ does offer an improvement. Whether a step dx offers an improvement is measured by the Euclidean norm $\|f(x)\| = \frac{1}{2}f(x)^{\top}f(x)$. Clearly, $\|f(x)\|$ is precisely zero at a root of f and is positive elsewhere. Thus one may view an iterate as yielding an improvement over the previous iterate if it reduces the function norm, that is, if $\|f(x)\| > \|f(x+dx)\|$. Backstepping prevents Newton and quasi-Newton methods from taking a large step in the wrong direction, substantially improving their robustness.

A simple backstepping algorithm will not necessarily prevent Newton-type methods from getting stuck at a local minimum of $\|f(x)\|$. If $\|f(x)\|$ must decrease with each step, it may be difficult to find a step length that moves away from the current value of x. Most good root-finding algorithms employ some mechanism for getting unstuck. We use a very simple one in which the backsteps continue until either $\|f(x)\| > \|f(x+dx)\|$ or $\|f(x+dx/2)\| > \|f(x+dx)\|$.

The following MATLAB script computes the root of a function using a safeguarded Newton's method. It assumes that the user has specified a maximum number maxit of Newton iterations, a maximum number maxsteps of backstep iterations, and a convergence tolerance `tol`, along with the name of the function `f` and an initial value `x`:

```
for it=1:maxit
  [fval,fjac] = f(x);
  fnorm = norm(fval);
  if fnorm<tol, return, end
  d = -(fjac\fval);
  fnormold = inf;
  for backstep=1:maxsteps
    fvalnew = f(x+d);
    fnormnew = norm(fvalnew);
    if fnormnew<fnorm, break, end
    if fnormold<fnormnew, d=2*d; break, end
    fnormold = fnormnew;
    d = d/2;
  end
  x = x+d;
end
```

Safeguarded backstepping may also be implemented with Broyden's method; the `newton` and `broyden` routines supplied with the CompEcon Toolbox both employ safeguarded backstepping.

The third problem, an ill-conditioned Jacobian at the root, occurs less often, but should not be ignored. An ill-conditioned Jacobian can result in an inaccurately computed Newton step dx, creating severe difficulties for the convergence of Newton and Newton-type methods. In some cases, ill conditioning is a structural feature of the underlying model and cannot be eliminated. However, in many cases, ill conditioning is inadvertently and unnecessarily introduced by the analyst. A common source of avoidable ill conditioning arises when the natural units of measurements for model variables yield values that vary vastly in order of magnitude. When such variability occurs, the analyst should consider rescaling the variables so that their values have comparable orders of magnitude, preferably close to unity. Rescaling will generally lead to faster execution time and more accurate results.

3.6   Choosing a Solution Method

Numerical analysts have special terms that they use to classify the rates at which iterative routines converge. Specifically, a sequence of iterates $x^{(k)}$ is said to converge to x^* at a rate of order p if there is constant $C > 0$ such that

$$\|x^{(k+1)} - x^*\| \leq C \|x^{(k)} - x^*\|^p$$

for sufficiently large k. In particular, the rate of convergence is said to be *linear* if $C < 1$ and $p = 1$, *superlinear* if $1 < p < 2$, and *quadratic* if $p = 2$.

The rates of convergence of the nonlinear equation solution methods discussed earlier are well known. The bisection method converges at a linear rate with $C = 1/2$. The function iteration method converges at a linear rate with C equal to $\|f'(x^*)\|$. The secant and Broyden methods converge at a superlinear rate, with $p \approx 1.62$. And Newton's method converges at a quadratic rate. The rates of convergence are asymptotically valid, provided that the algorithms are given "good" initial data.

Consider a simple example. The function $g(x) = \sqrt{x}$ has a fixed point $x^* = 1$. Function iteration may be used to compute the fixed point. One can also compute the fixed point by applying Newton's method or the secant method to the equivalent rootfinding problem $f(x) = x - \sqrt{x} = 0$. Table 3.1 gives the approximation error $|x^{(k)} - x^*|$ produced by the three methods starting from $x^{(0)} = 0.5$ and using a finite difference derivative for the first secant method iteration. The convergence patterns illustrated in the table are typical for the various iterative nonlinear equation solution algorithms used in practice. Newton's method converges in fewer iterations than the quasi-Newton method, which in turn converges in fewer iterations than function iteration. Both the Newton and quasi-Newton methods converge to machine precision very quickly, in this case five or six iterations. As the iterates approach the solution, the number of significant digits in the Newton and quasi-Newton approximants begins to double with each iteration.

Table 3.1
Convergence Rates for Nonlinear Equation Methods

k	Function Iteration	Broyden's Method	Newton's Method
1	2.9e-001	-2.1e-001	-2.1e-001
2	1.6e-001	3.6e-002	-8.1e-003
3	8.3e-002	1.7e-003	-1.6e-005
4	4.2e-002	-1.5e-005	-6.7e-011
5	2.1e-002	6.3e-009	0.0e+000
6	1.1e-002	2.4e-014	0.0e+000
7	5.4e-003	0.0e+000	0.0e+000
8	2.7e-003	0.0e+000	0.0e+000
9	1.4e-003	0.0e+000	0.0e+000
10	6.8e-004	0.0e+000	0.0e+000
15	2.1e-005	0.0e+000	0.0e+000
20	6.6e-007	0.0e+000	0.0e+000
25	2.1e-008	0.0e+000	0.0e+000

However, the rate of convergence, measured in number of iterations, is only one determinant of the computational efficiency of a solution algorithm. Algorithms differ in the number of arithmetic operations, and thus in the computational effort required per iteration. For multivariate problems, function iteration requires only a function evaluation; Broyden's method with inverse update requires a function evaluation and a matrix-vector multiplication; and Newton's method requires a function evaluation, a derivative evaluation, and the solution of a linear equation. In practice, function iteration tends to require more overall computational effort to achieve a given accuracy than the other two methods. However, whether Newton's method or Broyden's method requires more overall computational effort to achieve convergence in a given application depends largely on the dimension of x and complexity of the derivative. Broyden's method will tend to be computationally more efficient than Newton's method if the derivative is costly to evaluate.

An important factor that must be considered when choosing a nonlinear equation solution method is developmental effort. Developmental effort is the effort exerted by the analyst to produce a viable, convergent computer code—this includes the effort to write the code, the effort to debug and verify the code, and the effort to find suitable starting values. Function iteration and quasi-Newton methods involve the least developmental effort because they do not require the analyst to correctly code the derivative expressions. Newton's method typically requires more developmental effort because it additionally requires the analyst to correctly code derivative expressions. The developmental cost of Newton's method can be quite high if the derivative matrix involves many complex or irregular expressions.

Experienced analysts use certain rules of thumb when selecting a nonlinear equation solution method. If the nonlinear equation is of small dimension, say univariate or bivariate, *or* if the function derivatives follow a simple pattern and are relatively easy to code, then development costs will vary little among the different methods, and computational efficiency should be the main concern, particularly if the equation is to be solved many times. In this instance, Newton's method is usually the best first choice.

If the nonlinear equation involves many complex or irregular function derivatives, or if the derivatives are expensive to compute, then Newton's method is less attractive. In such instances, quasi-Newton and function iteration methods may make better choices, particularly if the nonlinear equation is to be solved very few times. If the nonlinear equation is to be solved many times, however, the faster convergence rate of Newton's method may make the development costs worth incurring.

3.7 Complementarity Problems

Many economic models naturally take the form of a complementarity problem rather than a rootfinding or fixed-point problem. In the complementarity problem, two n-vectors a and

b, with $a < b$, and a function f from $\mathbb{R}^n$ to $\mathbb{R}^n$ are given, and one must find an n-vector $x \in [a, b]$, that satisfies

$$x_i > a_i \Rightarrow f_i(x) \geq 0 \quad \forall i = 1, \ldots, n$$

$$x_i < b_i \Rightarrow f_i(x) \leq 0 \quad \forall i = 1, \ldots, n$$

The complementarity conditions require that $f_i(x) = 0$ whenever $a_i < x_i < b_i$. The complementarity problem thus includes the rootfinding problem as a special case in which $a_i = -\infty$ and $b_i = +\infty$ for all i. The complementarity problem, however, is not to find a root that lies within specified bounds. An element $f_i(x)$ may be nonzero at a solution of a complementarity problem, though only if x_i equals one of its bounds. For the sake of brevity, we denote the complementarity problem CP(f, a, b).

Complementarity problems arise naturally in economic equilibrium models. In this context, x is an n-vector that represents the levels of certain economic activities. For each $i = 1, 2, \ldots, n$, a_i denotes a lower bound on activity i, b_i denotes an upper bound on activity i, and $f_i(x)$ denotes the marginal arbitrage profit associated with activity i. Disequilibrium arbitrage profit opportunities exist if either $x_i < b_i$ and $f_i(x) > 0$, in which case an incentive exists to increase x_i, or $x_i > a_i$ and $f_i(x) < 0$, in which case an incentive exists to decrease x_i. An arbitrage-free economic equilibrium obtains if and only if x solves the complementarity problem CP(f, a, b).

Complementarity problems also arise naturally in economic optimization models. Consider maximizing a function $F : \mathbb{R}^n \mapsto \mathbb{R}$ subject to the simple bound constraint $x \in [a, b]$. The Karush-Kuhn-Tucker theorem asserts that x solves the bounded maximization problem only if it solves the complementarity problem CP(f, a, b) where $f_i(x) = \partial F / \partial x_i$. Conversely, if F is strictly concave at x and x solves the complementarity problem CP(f, a, b), then x solves the bounded maximization problem (see section 4.6).

As a simple example of a complementarity problem, consider the well-known Marshallian competitive price equilibrium model. In this model, competitive equilibrium obtains if and only if excess demand $E(p)$, the difference between quantity demanded and quantity supplied at price p, is zero. Suppose, however, that the government imposes a price ceiling $\bar{p}$ that it enforces through fiat or direct market intervention. It is then possible for excess demand to exist at equilibrium, but only if the price ceiling is binding. In the presence of a price ceiling, the equilibrium market price is the solution to the complementarity problem CP($E, 0, \bar{p}$).

A more interesting example of a complementarity problem is the single commodity competitive spatial price equilibrium model. Suppose that there are n distinct regions and that excess demand for the commodity in region i is a function $E_i(p_i)$ of the price p_i in the region. In the absence of trade among regions, equilibrium is characterized by the condition that $E_i(p_i) = 0$ in each region i, a rootfinding problem. Suppose, however, that trade can take place among regions, and that the cost of transporting one unit of the good from region i to region j is a constant c_{ij}. Denote by x_{ij} the amount of the good that is shipped from region i to region j, and suppose that this quantity cannot exceed a given shipping capacity b_{ij}.

In this market, $p_j - p_i - c_{ij}$ is the unit arbitrage profit available from shipping one unit of the commodity from region i to region j. When the arbitrage profit is positive, an incentive exists to increase shipments; when the arbitrage profit is negative, an incentive exists to decrease shipments. Equilibrium obtains only if all spatial arbitrage profit opportunities have been eliminated. This condition requires that, for all pairs of regions i and j, $0 \leq x_{ij} \leq b_{ij}$ and

$$x_{ij} > 0 \quad \Rightarrow \quad p_j - p_i - c_{ij} \geq 0$$

$$x_{ij} < b_{ij} \quad \Rightarrow \quad p_j - p_i - c_{ij} \leq 0$$

To formulate the spatial price equilibrium model as a complementarity problem, note that market clearing requires that net imports equal excess demand in each region i:

$$\sum_k [x_{ki} - x_{ik}] = E_i(p_i)$$

This expression implies that

$$p_i = E_i^{-1}\left(\sum_k [x_{ki} - x_{ik}]\right)$$

If

$$f_{ij}(x) = E_j^{-1}\left(\sum_k [x_{kj} - x_{jk}]\right) - E_i^{-1}\left(\sum_k [x_{ki} - x_{ik}]\right) - c_{ij}$$

then x is a spatial equilibrium trade flow if and only if x solves the complementarity problem CP$(f, 0, b)$, where x, f, and b are vectorized and written as $n^2 \times 1$ vectors.

In order to understand the mathematical structure of the complementarity problem, it is instructive to consider the simplest case: the univariate linear complementarity problem. Figures 3.6a–3.6c illustrate the three possible subcases when f is negatively sloped. In all three subcases, a unique equilibrium solution exists. In Figure 3.6a, $f(a) < 0$, and the unique equilibrium solution is $x^* = a$; in Figure 3.6b, $f(b) > 0$, and the unique equilibrium solution is $x^* = b$; and in Figure 3.6c, $f(a) > 0 > f(b)$, and the unique equilibrium solution lies between a and b. In all three subcases, the equilibrium is stable in that the economic incentive at nearby disequilibrium points is to return to the equilibrium.

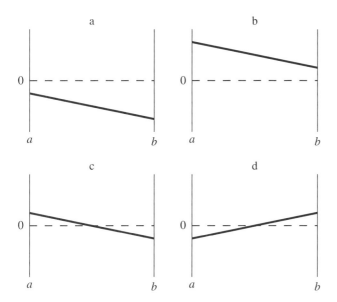

Figure 3.6
The Univariate Linear Complementarity Problem

Figure 3.6d illustrates the difficulties that can arise when f is positively sloped. Here, multiple equilibrium solutions arise, one in the interior of the interval and one at each endpoint. The interior equilibrium, moreover, is unstable in that the economic incentive at nearby disequilibrium points is to move away from the interior equilibrium toward one of the corner equilibria.

More generally, multivariate complementarity problems are guaranteed to possess a unique solution if f is strictly negative monotone, that is, if $(x - y)^\top (f(x) - f(y)) < 0$ whenever $x, y \in [a, b]$ and $x \neq y$. This condition will be true for most well-posed economic equilibrium models. It will also be true when the complementarity problem derives from a bound-constrained maximization problem in which the objective function is strictly concave.

3.8 Complementarity Methods

Although the complementarity problem appears quite different from the ordinary rootfinding problem, it actually can be reformulated as one. In particular, x solves the complementarity problem CP(f, a, b) if and only if it solves the rootfinding problem

$$\hat{f}(x) = \min(\max(f(x), a - x), b - x) = 0$$

where min and max are applied row-wise. A formal proof of the equivalence between the complementarity problem CP(f, a, b) and its "minmax" rootfinding formulation $\hat{f}(x) = 0$ is straightforward, but it requires a somewhat tedious enumeration of several possible cases, which we leave as an exercise for the reader. The equivalence, however, can easily be demonstrated graphically for the univariate complementarity problem.

Figure 3.7 illustrates a minmax rootfinding formulation of the same four univariate complementarity problems examined in Figure 3.6. In all four plots, the curves $y = a - x$ and $y = b - x$ are drawn with narrow dashed lines, the curve $y = f(x)$ is drawn with a narrow solid line, and the curve $y = \hat{f}(x)$ is drawn with a thick solid line; clearly, in all four figures, $\hat{f}$ lies between the lines $y = x - a$ and $y = x - b$ and coincides with f inside the lines. In Figure 3.7a, $f(a) < 0$, and the unique solution to the complementarity problem is $x^* = a$, which coincides with the unique root of $\hat{f}$; in Figure 3.7b, $f(b) > 0$, and the unique solution to the complementarity problem is $x^* = b$, which coincides with the unique root of $\hat{f}$; in Figure 3.7c, $f(a) > 0 > f(b)$, and the unique solution to the complementarity problem

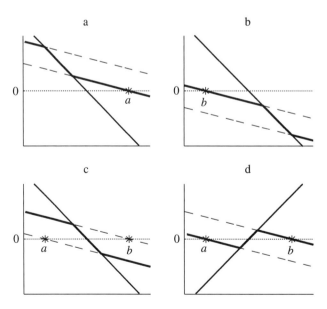

Figure 3.7
Minmax Rootfinding Formulation

lies between a and b and coincides with the unique root of $\hat{f}$ (and f). In Figure 3.7d, f is upwardly sloped and possesses multiple roots, all of which, again, coincide with roots of $\hat{f}$.

The reformulation of the complementarity problem as a rootfinding problem suggests that it may be solved using standard rootfinding algorithms, such as Newton's method. To implement Newton's method for the minmax rootfinding formulation requires computation of the Jacobian $\hat{J}$ of $\hat{f}$. The ith row of $\hat{J}$ may be derived directly from the Jacobian J of f:

$$\hat{J}_i(x) = \begin{cases} J_i(x), & \text{for } a_i - x_i < f_i(x) < b_i - x_i \\ -I_i, & \text{otherwise} \end{cases}$$

Here, I_i is the ith row of the identity matrix.

The following MATLAB script computes the solution of the complementarity problem $CP(f, a, b)$ by applying Newton's method to the equivalent minmax rootfinding formulation. The script assumes that the user has provided the lower and upper bounds a and b, a guess x for the solution of the complementarity problem, a convergence tolerance tol, and an upper limit maxit on the number of iterations. It calls a user-supplied routine f that computes the value fval and Jacobian fjac of the function at an arbitrary point x:

```
for it=1:maxit
  [fval,fjac] = f(x);
  fhatval = min(max(fval,a-x),b-x);
  fhatjac = -eye(length(x));
  i = find(fval>a-x & fval<b-x);
  fhatjac(i,:) = fjac(i,:);
  x = x - fhatjac\fhatval;
  if norm(fhatval)<tol, break, end
end
```

Using Newton's method to find a root of $\hat{f}$ will often work well. However, in many cases, the nondifferentiable kinks in $\hat{f}$ create difficulties for Newton's method, undermining its ability to converge rapidly and possibly even causing it to cycle. One way to deal with the kinks is to replace $\hat{f}$ with a function that has the same roots but is smoother and therefore less prone to numerical difficulties. One function that has proven very effective for solving the complementarity problem in practical applications is Fischer's[3] function

$$\tilde{f}(x) = \phi^- \big(\phi^+ \big(f(x), a - x \big), b - x \big),$$

3. One could also use $\tilde{f}(x) = \phi^+ (\phi^- (f(x), b - x), a - x)$.

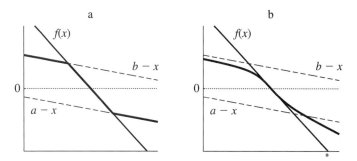

Figure 3.8
Minmax (a) and Semismooth (b) Formulations of a Representative Complementarity Problem

where

$$\phi_i^{\pm}(u, v) = u_i + v_i \pm \sqrt{u_i^2 + v_i^2}$$

In Figures 3.8a and 3.8b, the functions $\hat{f}$ and $\tilde{f}$, respectively, are drawn as thick solid lines for a representative complementarity problem. Clearly, $\hat{f}$ and $\tilde{f}$ can differ substantially. What is important for solving the complementarity problem, however, is that $\hat{f}$ and $\tilde{f}$ possess the same signs and roots and that $\tilde{f}$ is smoother than $\hat{f}$.

The CompEcon Toolbox includes a routine `ncpsolve` that solves the complementarity problem by applying Newton's method with safeguarded backstepping to either the minmax or semismooth rootfinding formulations. To apply this function, one defines a MATLAB function `f` that returns the function value and Jacobian at an arbitrary point, and specifies the lower and upper bounds, `a` and `b`, and, optionally, a starting value `x`. To solve the complementarity problem using the semismooth formulation, one writes the MATLAB script `x=ncpsolve('f',a,b,x)`; to solve the complementarity problem using the minmax formulation, one must change the default option using the MATLAB script `optset('ncpsolve','type','minmax')` before executing the `x=ncpsolve('f',a,b,x)` script.

In practice, Newton's method applied to either the minmax rootfinding formulation $\hat{f}(x) = 0$ or the semismooth rootfinding formulation $\tilde{f}(x) = 0$ will often successfully solve the complementarity problem CP(f, a, b). The semismooth formulation is generally more robust than the minmax formulation because it avoids the problematic kinks found in $\hat{f}$. However, the semismooth formulation also requires more arithmetic operations per iteration.

As an example of a complementarity problem for which the semismooth formulation is successful, but for which the minmax formulation is not, consider the surprisingly difficult complementarity problem CP(f, 0, $+\infty$) where

$$f(x) = 1.01 - (x-1)^2$$

The function f has a root at $x = 1 - \sqrt{1.01}$, but this is not a solution to the complementarity problem because it is negative. Also, 0 is not a solution because $f(0) = 0.01$ is positive. The complementarity problem has a unique solution $x = 1 + \sqrt{1.01} \approx 2.005$.

Figure 3.9a displays $\hat{f}$ (dashed) and $\tilde{f}$ (solid) for the complementarity problem, and Figure 3.9b magnifies the plot near the origin, making it clear why the problem is hard. Newton's method starting at any value slightly less than 1 will tend to move toward 0. In order to avoid convergence to this false root, Newton's method must take a sufficiently large step to exit the region of attraction. This result will not occur with $\hat{f}$ because 0 poses an upper bound on the positive Newton step. With $\tilde{f}$, however, the function is smooth at its local minimum near the origin, meaning that the Newton step can be very large.

To solve the complementarity problem using the semismooth formulation, one codes the function

```
function [fval,fjac] = f(x)
fval = 1.01-(1-x).^2;
fjac = 2*(1-x);
```

and then executes the MATLAB script

```
x = ncpsolve('f',0,inf,0);
```

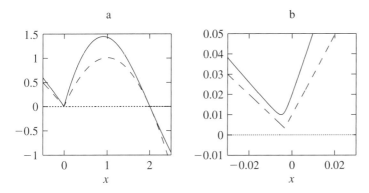

Figure 3.9
A Difficult Newton Complementarity Problem (a) and the Problem Magnified (b)

(this uses $x = 0$ as a starting value). To solve the complementarity problem using the minmax formulation, one executes the MATLAB script

```
optset('ncpsolve','type','minmax')
x = ncpsolve('f',0,inf,0);
```

In this example, the semismooth formulation will successfully compute the solution of the complementarity problem, but the minmax formulation will not.

   Algorithms for solving complementarity problems are still an active area of research, especially for cases that are not well behaved. Algorithms will no doubt continue to improve, and existing methods vary considerably in terms of robustness and speed. Our suggestion, however, is first to use a well-implemented general-purpose rootfinding algorithm in conjunction with a semismooth formulation. This approach has the virtue of simplicity and requires only a standard rootfinding utility.

Exercises

3.1. If $x = \sqrt{c}$, then $x^2 - c = 0$.

a. Use this root condition to construct a Newton method for determining the square root that uses only simple algebraic operations (addition, subtraction, multiplication, and division).

b. Given an arbitrary value of $c > 0$, how would you find a starting value to begin Newton's method?

c. Write a MATLAB procedure `function x=newtroot(c)` that implements the method. The procedure should be self-contained (i.e., it should not call a generic rootfinding algorithm).

3.2. If $x = \sqrt{1 + c^2} - 1$, then $(x + 1)^2 - (1 + c^2) = 0$.

a. Use this root condition to construct a Newton method for determining x that uses only simple algebraic operations (addition, subtraction, multiplication, and division).

b. Given an arbitrary value of $c > 0$, how would you find a starting value to begin Newton's method?

c. Write a MATLAB procedure `function x=newtroot(c)` that implements the method. The procedure should be self-contained (i.e., it should not call a generic rootfinding algorithm).

Note that the computation of $\sqrt{1 + c^2} - 1$ can fail as a result of overflow or underflow. In particular, when c is large, squaring it can exceed the largest representable number on the computer, whereas when c is small, the addition $1 + c^2$ will be truncated to 1. Be sure to deal with the overflow and underflow problem in your implementation.

3.3. The Black-Scholes option pricing formula expresses the value of an option as a function of the current value S of the underlying asset, the option's strike price K, the time to maturity τ, the current risk-free interest rate r, a dividend rate δ, and the volatility of the price of the underlying asset σ. The formula for a call option is[4]

$$V(S, K, \tau, r, \delta, \sigma) = e^{-\delta\tau} S\Phi(d) - e^{-r\tau} K\Phi\left(d - \sigma\sqrt{\tau}\right)$$

where

$$d = \frac{\ln(e^{-\delta\tau} S) - \ln(e^{-r\tau} K)}{\sigma\sqrt{\tau}} + \tfrac{1}{2}\sigma\sqrt{\tau}$$

and Φ is the standard normal cumulative distribution function (CDF):

$$\Phi(x) = \frac{1}{\sqrt{2\pi}} \int_{-\infty}^{x} e^{-\frac{1}{2}z^2} dz$$

a. Write a MATLAB procedure that takes the six inputs and returns the Black-Scholes option value: `V=BSVal(S,K,tau,r,delta,sigma)`. Use CompEcon Toolbox function `cdfn` to compute the standard normal CDF.

b. All of the inputs to the Black-Scholes formula are readily observable except σ. Market participants often want to determine the value of σ implied by the market price of an option. Write a program that computes the so-called implied volatility. The function should have the following calling syntax: `sigma=ImpVol(S,K,tau,r,delta,V)`. The algorithm should use Newton's method to solve (for σ) the rootfinding problem $V - \texttt{BSVal}(S, K, \tau, r, \delta, \sigma)$. To do so you will need to use the derivative of the Black-Scholes formula with respect to σ, which can be shown to equal

$$\frac{\partial V}{\partial\sigma} - Se^{-\delta\tau}\sqrt{\tau/(2\pi)}e^{-0.5d^2}$$

The program should be stand-alone, meaning that it should not call any rootfinding solver such as `newton` or `broyden` or a numerical derivative algorithm. It may, however, call `BSVal` from part a.

---

4. This is known as the extended Black-Scholes formula because it includes the parameter δ not found in the original formula. The inclusion of δ generalizes the formula. For options on stocks δ represents a continuous percentage dividend flow, for options on currencies it is set to the interest rate in the foreign country, and for options on futures it is set to r.

3.4. It was claimed (page 38) that the Broyden method chooses the approximate Jacobian to minimize a matrix norm subject to a constraint. Specifically

$$A^* \leftarrow A + (g - Ad)\frac{d^\top}{d^\top d}$$

with $g = f(x^{(k+1)}) - f(x^{(k)})$ and $d = x^{(k+1)} - x^{(k)}$, solves the problem

$$\min_{A^*} \sum_i \sum_j \left(A_{ij}^* - A_{ij}\right)^2$$

subject to

$$g = A^*d.$$

Provide a proof of this claim.

3.5. Consider the function $f : \mathbb{R}^2 \mapsto \mathbb{R}^2$ defined by

$$f_1(x) = 200x_1(x_2 - x_1^2) - x_1 + 1$$
$$f_2(x) = 100(x_1^2 - x_2)$$

Write a MATLAB function that takes a column 2-vector x as input and returns `fval`, a column 2-vector that contains the value of f at x, and `fjac`, a 2-by-2 matrix that contains the Jacobian of f at x.

a. Compute numerically the root of f using Newton's method.

b. Compute numerically the root of f using Broyden's method.

3.6. A common problem in computation is finding the inverse of a cumulative distribution function (CDF). A CDF is a function, F, that is nondecreasing over some domain $[a, b]$ and for which $F(a) = 0$ and $F(b) = 1$. Write a function that uses Newton's method to solve inverse CDF problems. The function should take the following form:

```
x=icdf(p,F,x0,varargin)
```

where p is a probability value (a real number on [0,1]), F is the name of a MATLAB function file, and x0 is a starting value for the Newton iterations. The function file should have the form:

```
[F,f]=cdf(x,additional parameters)
```

For example, the normal CDF with mean μ and standard deviation σ would be written

```
function [F,f]=cdfnormal(x,mu,sigma)
z=(x-mu)./sigma;
F=cdfn(z);
f=exp(-0.5*z.^2)./(sqrt(2*pi)*sigma);
```

You can test your code with the statement:

```
x-icdf(cdfnormal(x,0,1),'cdfnormal',0,0,1)
```

which should return a number close to 0.

3.7. Consider a simple endowment economy with three agents and two goods. Agent i is initially endowed with e_{ij} units of good j and maximizes utility

$$U_i(x) = \sum_{j=1}^{2} a_{ij}(v_{ij} + 1)^{-1} x_{ij}^{v_{ij}+1}$$

subject to the budget constraint

$$\sum_{j=1}^{2} p_j x_{ij} = \sum_{j=1}^{2} p_j e_{ij}$$

Here, x_{ij} is the amount of good j consumed by agent i, p_j is the market price of good j, and $a_{ij} > 0$ and $v_{ij} < 0$ are preference parameters.

A competitive general equilibrium for the endowment economy is a pair of relative prices, p_1 and p_2, normalized to sum to one, such that all the goods markets clear if each agent maximizes utility subject to his budget constraints.

Compute the competitive general equilibrium for the following parameters:

(i, j)	a_{ij}	v_{ij}	e_{ij}
$(1, 1)$	2.0	-2.0	2.0
$(1, 2)$	1.5	-0.5	3.0
$(2, 1)$	1.5	-1.5	1.0
$(2, 2)$	2.0	-0.5	2.0
$(3, 1)$	1.5	-0.5	4.0
$(3, 2)$	2.0	-1.5	0.0

3.8. Consider the market for potatoes, which are storable intraseasonally, but not inter-seasonally. In this market, the harvest is entirely consumed over two marketing periods, $i = 1, 2$. Denoting initial supply by s and consumption in period i by c_i, material balance requires that

$$s = c_1 + c_2$$

Competition among storers possessing perfect foresight eliminates interperiod arbitrage opportunities; thus,

$$p_1 + \kappa = \delta p_2$$

where p_i is equilibrium price in period i, $\kappa = 0.2$ is per-period unit cost of storage, and $\delta = 0.95$ is per-period discount factor. Demand, assumed the same across periods, is given by

$$p_i = c_i^{-5}$$

Compute the equilibrium period 1 and period 2 prices for $s = 1$, $s = 2$, and $s = 3$.

3.9. Provide a formal proof that the complementarity problem $CP(f, a, b)$ is equivalent to the rootfinding problem $\hat{f}(x) = \min(\max(f(x), a - x), b - x) = 0$ in that both have the same solutions.

3.10. Commodity X is produced and consumed in three countries. Let quantity q be measured in units and price p be measured in dollars per unit. Demand and supply in the three countries are given by the following table:

	Demand	Supply
Country 1	$p = 42 - 2q$	$p = 9 + 1q$
Country 2	$p = 54 - 3q$	$p = 3 + 2q$
Country 3	$p = 51 - 1q$	$p = 18 + 1q$

The unit costs of transportation are as follows:

	To Country 1	To Country 2	To Country 3
From Country 1	0	3	9
From Country 2	3	0	3
From Country 3	6	3	0

a. Formulate and solve the linear equation that characterizes competitive equilibrium, assuming that intercountry trade is not permitted.

b. Formulate and solve the linear complementarity problem that characterizes competitive spatial equilibrium, assuming that intercountry trade is permitted.

c. Using standard measures of surplus, which of the six consumer and producer groups in the three countries gain, and which ones lose, from the introduction of trade?

Bibliographic Notes

Rootfinding problems have been studied for centuries (Newton's method bears its name for a reason). They are discussed in most standard references on numerical analysis. In-depth treatments can be found in Dennis and Schnabel (1983) and in Ortega and Rheinboldt (1970). Press et al. (1992) provides a discussion, with computer code, of both Newton's and Broyden's methods and of backstepping.

Standard references on complementarity problems include Balinski and Cottle (1978); Cottle, Giannessi, and Lions (1980); Cottle, Pang, and Stone (1992); and Ferris, Mesnier, and More (1996). Ferris and Pang (1997) provides an overview of applications of complementarity problems.

We have broken with standard expositions of complementarity problems; the complementarity problem is generally stated to be

$$f(x) \geq 0, \quad x \geq 0, \quad \text{and} \quad x^\top f(x) = 0$$

This approach imposes only a one-sided bound on x at 0. Doubly bounded problems are often called mixed complementarity problems (MCPs). If standard software for MCPs is used, the sign of f should be reversed.

A number of approaches exist for solving complementarity problems other than reformulation as a rootfinding problem. A well-studied and robust algorithm based on successive linearization is incorporated in the PATH algorithm described by Ferris, Mesnier, and More (1996) and Ferris and Munson (1999). The linear complementarity problem (LCP) has received considerable attention and forms the underpinning for methods based on successive linearization. Lemke's method is perhaps the most widely used and robust LCP solver. It is described in the standard works already cited. Recent work on LCPs includes Kremers and Talman (1994).

We have not discussed homotopy methods for solving nonlinear equations, but these may be desirable to explore, especially if good initial values are hard to guess. Judd (1998, chap. 5) contains a good introduction, with economic applications and references for further study.

4 Finite-Dimensional Optimization

In this chapter we examine methods for optimizing a function with respect to a finite number of variables. In the finite-dimensional optimization problem, one is given a real-valued function f defined on $X \subseteq \mathbb{R}^n$ and asked to find an $x^* \in X$ such that $f(x^*) \geq f(x)$ for all $x \in X$. We denote this problem

$$\max_{x \in X} f(x)$$

and call f the objective function, X the feasible set, and x^*, if it exists, a maximum.[1]

Finite-dimensional optimization problems are ubiquitous in economics. For example, the standard neoclassical models of firm and individual decision making involve the maximization of profit and utility functions, respectively. Competitive static price equilibrium models can often be equivalently characterized as optimization problems in which a hypothetical social planner maximizes total surplus. Finite-dimensional optimization problems arise in econometrics, as in the minimization of the sum of squares or the maximization of a likelihood function. And one also encounters finite-dimensional optimization problems embedded within the Bellman equation that characterizes the solution to continuous-space dynamic optimization models.

There is a close relationship between the finite-dimensional optimization problems discussed in this chapter and the rootfinding and complementarity problems discussed in the previous chapter. The first-order necessary conditions of an unconstrained problem pose a rootfinding problem; the Karush-Kuhn-Tucker first-order necessary conditions of a constrained optimization problem pose a complementarity problem. The rootfinding and complementarity problems associated with optimization problems are special in that they possess a natural merit function, the objective function itself, which may be used to determine whether iterations are converging on a solution.

Over the years, numerical analysts have studied finite-dimensional optimization problems extensively and have devised a variety of algorithms for solving them quickly and accurately. We begin our discussion with derivative-free methods, which are useful if the objective function is rough or if its derivatives are expensive to compute. We then turn to Newton-type methods for unconstrained optimization, which employ derivatives or derivative estimates to locate an optimum. Univariate unconstrained optimization methods are of particular interest because many multivariate optimization algorithms use the strategy of first determining a linear direction to move in, and then finding the optimal point in that direction. We conclude with a discussion of how to solve constrained optimization problems.

---

1. We focus our discussion on maximization. To solve a minimization problem, one simply maximizes the negative of the objective function.

Before proceeding, we review some facts about finite-dimensional optimization and define some terms. By the Wierstrass Theorem, if f is continuous and X is nonempty, closed, and bounded, then f has a maximum on X. A point $x^* \in X$ is a local maximum of f if there is an ϵ-neighborhood N of x^* such that $f(x^*) \geq f(x)$ for all $x \in N \cap X$. The point x^* is a strict local maximum if, additionally, $f(x^*) > f(x)$ for all $x \neq x^*$ in $N \cap X$. If x^* is a local maximum of f that resides in the interior of X and f is twice differentiable there, then $f'(x^*) = 0$ and $f''(x^*)$ is negative semidefinite. Conversely, if $f'(x^*) = 0$ and $f''(x)$ is negative semidefinite in an ϵ-neighborhood of x^* contained in X, then x^* is a local maximum; if, additionally, $f''(x^*)$ is negative definite, then x^* is a strict local maximum. By the Local-Global Theorem, if f is concave, X is convex, and x^* is a local maximum of f, then x^* is a global maximum of f on X.[2]

4.1 Derivative-Free Methods

As was the case with univariate rootfinding, optimization algorithms exist that will place progressively smaller brackets around a local maximum of a univariate function. Such methods are relatively slow, but they do not require the evaluation of function derivatives and are guaranteed to find a local optimum to a prescribed tolerance in a known number of steps.

The most widely used derivative-free method is the *golden search method*. Suppose we wish to find a local maximum of a continuous univariate function $f(x)$ on the interval $[a, b]$. Pick any two numbers in the interior of the interval, say x_1 and x_2 with $x_1 < x_2$. Evaluate the function and replace the original interval with $[a, x_2]$ if $f(x_1) < f(x_2)$ or with $[x_1, b]$ if $f(x_2) \geq f(x_1)$. A local maximum must be contained in the new interval because the endpoints of the new interval have smaller function values than a point on the interval's interior (or the local maximum is at one of the original endpoints). We can repeat this procedure, producing a sequence of progressively smaller intervals that are guaranteed to contain a local maximum, until the length of the interval is shorter than some desired tolerance level.

A key issue is how to pick the interior evaluation points. Two simple criteria lead to the most widely used strategy. First, the length of the new interval should be independent of whether the upper or lower bound is replaced. Second, on successive iterations, one should be able to reuse an interior point from the previous iteration so that only one new function evaluation is performed per iteration. These conditions are uniquely satisfied by selecting

---

2. These results also hold for minimization, provided one changes concavity of f to convexity and negative (semi) definiteness of f'' to positive (semi) definiteness.

$x_i = a + \alpha_i(b - a)$, where

$$\alpha_1 = \frac{3 - \sqrt{5}}{2} \quad \text{and} \quad \alpha_2 = \frac{\sqrt{5} - 1}{2}$$

The value α_2 is known as the golden ratio, a number dear to the hearts of Greek philosophers and Renaissance artists.

The following MATLAB script computes a local maximum of a univariate function f on an interval $[a, b]$ using the golden search method. The script assumes that the user has written a MATLAB routine f that evaluates the function at an arbitrary point. The script also assumes that the user has specified interval endpoints a and b and a convergence tolerance tol:

```
alpha1 = (3-sqrt(5))/2;
alpha2 = (sqrt(5)-1)/2;
x1 = a+alpha1*(b-a);  f1 = f(x1);
x2 = a+alpha2*(b-a);  f2 = f(x2);
d  = alpha1*alpha2*(b-a);
while d>tol
   d = d*alpha2;
   if f2<f1
      x2 = x1;  x1 = x1-d;
      f2 = f1;  f1 = f(x1);
   else
      x1 = x2;  x2 = x2+d;
      f1 = f2;  f2 = f(x2);
   end
end
if f2>f1
   x = x2;
else
   x = x1;
end
```

The CompEcon Toolbox includes a routine golden that computes a local maximum of a univariate function using golden search. Suppose that one wished to compute a local maximum of the function $f(x) = x \cos(x^2)$ on the interval $[0, 3]$. To apply golden, one first codes a stand-alone MATLAB function that returns the value of the objective function

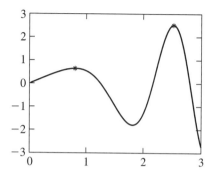

Figure 4.1
Maximization of $x \cos(x^2)$ Using Golden Search

at an arbitrary point:

```
function y = f(x);
y = x*cos(x^2);
```

One then passes the function name, along with the lower and upper bounds for the search interval, to `golden`:

```
x = golden('f',0,3)
```

Execution of this script yields the result $x = 0.8083$. As can be seen in Figure 4.1, this point is a local maximum but not a global maximum in [0, 3]. The golden search method is guaranteed to find the global maximum when the function is concave. However, as the present example makes clear, this guarantee does not hold when the optimand is not concave.

A derivative-free optimization method for multivariate functions is the Nelder-Mead algorithm. The algorithm begins by evaluating the objective function at $n + 1$ points. These $n + 1$ points form a so-called *simplex* in the n-dimensional decision space. This algorithm is most easily visualized when x is two-dimensional, in which case a simplex is a triangle.

At each iteration, the algorithm determines the point on the simplex with the lowest function value and alters that point by reflecting it through the opposite face of the simplex. This step is illustrated in Figure 4.2a (reflection), where the original simplex is lightly shaded and the heavily shaded simplex is the simplex arising from reflecting point A. If the reflection succeeds in finding a new point that is higher than all the others on the simplex, the algorithm checks to see if it is better to expand the simplex further in this direction, as shown in Figure 4.2b (expansion). However, if the reflection strategy fails to produce a point that is at least as good as the second-worst point, the algorithm contracts the simplex by halving

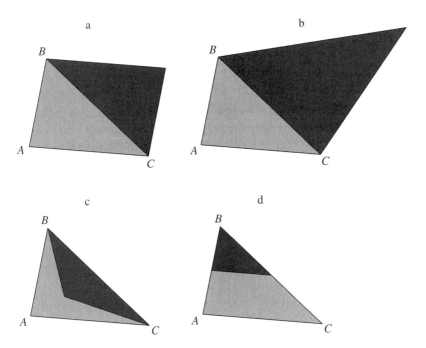

Figure 4.2
Simplex Transformations in the Nelder-Mead Algorithm: (a) Reflection, (b) Expansion, (c) Contraction, (d) Shrinkage

the distance between the original point and its opposite face, as in Figure 4.2c (contraction). Finally, if this new point is not better than the second-worst point, the algorithm shrinks the entire simplex toward the best point, point B in Figure 4.2d (shrinkage).

One thing that may not be clear from the description of the algorithm is how to compute a reflection. For a point x_i, the reflection is equal to $x_i + 2d_i$ where $x_i + d_i$ is the point in the center of the opposite face of the simplex from x_i. That central point can be found by averaging the n other point of the simplex. Denoting the reflection by r_i, therefore,

$$r_i = x_i + 2\left(\frac{1}{n}\sum_{j\neq i} x_j - x_i\right) = \frac{2}{n}\sum_{j=1}^{n} x_j - \left(1 + \frac{2}{n}\right) x_i$$

An expansion can then be computed as

$$1.5r_i - 0.5x_i$$

and a contraction as

$$0.25r_i + 0.75x_i$$

The Nelder-Mead algorithm is simple but slow and unreliable. However, if a problem involves only a single optimization or costly function and derivative evaluations, the Nelder-Mead algorithm is worth trying. In many problems an optimization problem that is embedded in a larger problem must be solved repeatedly, with the function parameters perturbed slightly with each iteration. For such problems, which are common in dynamic models, one generally will want to use a method that moves more quickly and reliably to the optimum, given a good starting point.

The CompEcon Toolbox includes a routine `neldmead` that computes the maximum of a multivariate function using the Nelder-Mead method. Suppose that one wished to maximize the "banana" function $f(x) = -100(x_2 - x_1^2)^2 - (1 - x_1)^2$ (so-called because its contours resemble bananas). To apply `neldmead`, one first codes a stand-alone MATLAB function that returns the value of the objective function at an arbitrary point:

```
function y = f(x);
y = -100*(x(2)-x(1)^2)^2-(1-x(1))^2;
```

One then passes the function name, along with a starting value, to `neldmead`:

```
x = neldmead('f',[1;0]);
```

Execution of this script yields the result $x = (1, 1)$, which indeed is the global maximum of the function. The contours of the banana function and the path followed by the first 55 Nelder-Mead iterates are illustrated in Figure 4.3.

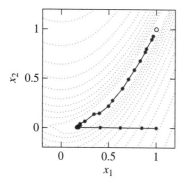

Figure 4.3
Nelder-Mead Maximization of Banana Function

4.2   Newton-Raphson Method

The Newton-Raphson method for maximizing an objective function uses successive quadratic approximations to the objective in the hope that the maxima of the approximants will converge to the maximum of the objective. The Newton-Raphson method is intimately related to the Newton method for solving rootfinding problems. Indeed, the Newton-Raphson method is identical to applying Newton's method to compute the root of the gradient of the objective function.

The Newton-Raphson method begins with the analyst supplying a guess $x^{(0)}$ for the maximum of f. Given $x^{(k)}$, the subsequent iterate $x^{(k+1)}$ is computed by maximizing the second-order Taylor approximation to f about $x^{(k)}$:

$$f(x) \approx f\left(x^{(k)}\right) + f'\left(x^{(k)}\right)\left(x - x^{(k)}\right) + \tfrac{1}{2}\left(x - x^{(k)}\right)^{\top} f''\left(x^{(k)}\right)\left(x - x^{(k)}\right)$$

Solving the first-order condition

$$f'\left(x^{(k)}\right) + f''\left(x^{(k)}\right)\left(x - x^{(k)}\right) = 0$$

yields the iteration rule

$$x^{(k+1)} \leftarrow x^{(k)} - \left[f''\left(x^{(k)}\right)\right]^{-1} f'\left(x^{(k)}\right)$$

In theory, the Newton-Raphson method converges if f is twice continuously differentiable and if the initial value of x supplied by the analyst is "sufficiently" close to a local maximum of f at which the Hessian f'' is negative definite. There is, however, no generally practical formula for determining what sufficiently close is. Typically, an analyst makes a reasonable guess for the maximum of f and counts his blessings if the iterates converge. The Newton-Raphson method can be robust to the starting value if f is well behaved, for example, if f is globally concave. The Newton-Raphson method, however, can be very sensitive to starting value if the function is not globally concave. Also, in practice, the Hessian f'' must be well conditioned at the optimum; otherwise, rounding errors in the vicinity of the optimum can make it difficult to compute a precise approximate solution.

The Newton-Raphson algorithm has numerous drawbacks. First, the algorithm requires computation of both the first and second derivatives of the objective function. Second, the Newton-Raphson algorithm offers no guarantee that the objective function value may be increased in the direction of the Newton step. Such a guarantee is available only if the Hessian $f''(x^{(k)})$ is negative definite; otherwise, one may actually move toward a saddle point of f (if the Hessian is indefinite) or even a minimum (if the Hessian is positive definite). For this reason, the Newton-Raphson method is rarely used in practice, and then only if the objective function is globally concave.

4.3   Quasi-Newton Methods

Quasi-Newton methods employ a strategy similar to the Newton-Raphson method, but they replace the Hessian of the objective function (or its inverse) with a negative definite approximation, guaranteeing that the function value can be increased in the direction of the Newton step. The most efficient quasi-Newton algorithms employ an approximation to the inverse Hessian, rather than the Hessian itself, in order to avoid performing a linear solve, and employ updating rules that do not require second-derivative information to ease the burden of implementation and the cost of computation.

In analogy with the Newton-Raphson method, quasi-Newton methods use a search direction of the form

$$d^{(k)} = -B^{(k)} f'\left(x^{(k)}\right)$$

where $B^{(k)}$ is an approximation to the inverse Hessian of f at the kth iterate $x^{(k)}$. The vector $d^{(k)}$ is called the Newton or quasi-Newton step.

The more robust quasi-Newton methods do not necessarily take the full Newton step, but rather shorten it or lengthen it in order to obtain improvement in the objective function. This adjustment is accomplished by performing a line search in which one seeks a step length $s > 0$ that maximizes or nearly maximizes $f(x^{(k)} + sd^{(k)})$. Given the computed step length $s^{(k)}$, one updates the iterate as follows:

$$x^{(k+1)} = x^{(k)} + s^{(k)}d^{(k)}$$

Line search methods are discussed in the following section.

Quasi-Newton methods differ in how the inverse Hessian approximation B^k is constructed and updated. The simplest quasi-Newton method sets $B^k = -I$, where I is the identity matrix. This approach leads to a Newton step that is identical to the gradient of the objective function at the current iterate:

$$d^{(k)} = f'\left(x^{(k)}\right)$$

The choice of gradient as a step direction is intuitively appealing because the gradient always points in the direction which, to a first order, promises the greatest increase in f. For this reason, this quasi-Newton method is called the *method of steepest ascent*. The steepest ascent method is simple to implement, but it is numerically less efficient in practice than competing quasi-Newton methods that incorporate information regarding the curvature of the objective function.

The most widely used quasi-Newton methods that employ curvature information produce a sequence of inverse Hessian estimates that satisfy two conditions. First, given that, for the

Newton step,

$$d^{(k)} \approx f''^{-1}\left(x^{(k)}\right)\left[f'\left(x^{(k)} + d^{(k)}\right) - f'\left(x^{(k)}\right)\right]$$

the inverse Hessian estimate B^k is required to satisfy the so-called *quasi-Newton* condition:

$$d^{(k)} = B^{(k+1)}\left[f'\left(x^{(k)} + d^{(k)}\right) - f'\left(x^{(k)}\right)\right]$$

Second, the inverse Hessian estimate $B^{(k)}$ is required to be both symmetric and negative definite, as must be true of the inverse Hessian at a local maximum. The negative definiteness of the Hessian estimate assures that the objective function value can be increased in the direction of the Newton step.

Two methods that satisfy the quasi-Newton and negative definiteness conditions are the Davidson-Fletcher-Powell (DFP) and Broyden-Fletcher-Goldfarb-Shano (BFGS) updating methods. The DFP method uses the updating scheme

$$B \leftarrow B + \frac{dd^\top}{d^\top u} - \frac{Buu^\top B}{u^\top Bu}$$

where

$$d = x^{(k+1)} - x^{(k)}$$

and

$$u = f'\left(x^{(k+1)}\right) - f'\left(x^{(k)}\right)$$

The BFGS method uses the update scheme

$$B \leftarrow B + \frac{1}{d^\top u}\left(wd^\top + dw^\top - \frac{w^\top u}{d^\top u}dd^\top\right)$$

where $w = d - Bu$.

The BFGS algorithm is generally considered superior to DFP, although there are problems for which DFP outperforms BFGS. Except for the updating formulas, the two methods are identical, so it is easy to implement both and give users the choice.[3]

The following MATLAB script computes the maximum of a user-supplied multivariate function f using the quasi-Newton method. The script assumes that the user has written a MATLAB routine f that evaluates the function at an arbitrary point and that the user has

---

3. Modern implementations of quasi-Newton methods store and update the Cholesky factors of the inverse Hessian approximation. This approach is numerically more stable and computationally efficient, but it is also somewhat more complicated and requires routines to update Cholesky factors.

specified a starting point x, an initial guess for the inverse Hessian B, a convergence tolerance tol, and a limit on the number of iterations maxit. The script uses an auxiliary algorithm optstep to determine the step length (discussed in the next section). The algorithm also offers the user a choice on how to select the search direction, searchmeth (1, steepest ascent; 2, DFP; 3, BFGS).

```
k = size(x,1);
[fx0,g0] = f(x);
if all(abs(g0)<eps), return; end
for it=1:maxit
  d = -B*g0;
  [s,fx] = optstep(stepmeth,f,x,fx0,g0,d,maxstep);
  if fx<=fx0
    warning('Iterations stuck in qnewton'), return;
  end
  d = s*d;
  x = x+d;
  [fx,g] = f(x);
  if all(abs(d)/(abs(x)+eps0)<tol))|all(abs(g)<eps);return;end
  u = g-g0; ud = u'*d;
  if searchmeth==1 | abs(ud)<eps
    B = -eye(k)./max(abs(fx),1);
  elseif searchmeth==2;
    v = B*u;
    B = B + d*d'./ud - v*v'./(u'*v);
  elseif SearchMeth==3;
    w = d-B*u; wd = w*d';
    B = B + ((wd + wd') - ((u'*w)*(d*d'))./ud)./ud;
  end
  fx0 = fx; g0 = g;
end
```

Quasi-Newton methods are susceptible to certain problems. Notice that in both update formulas there is a division by $d^\top u$. If this value becomes very small in absolute value, numerical instabilities will result. It is best to monitor this value and skip updating $B^{(k)}$ if it becomes too small. A useful rule for what is too small is

$$|d^\top u| < \epsilon \, ||d|| \, ||u||$$

where ϵ is the precision of the computer. An alternative to skipping the update, used in the CompEcon Toolbox, is to reset the inverse Hessian approximant to a scaled negative identity matrix.

The CompEcon Toolbox includes a routine `qnewton` that computes the maximum of a multivariate function using the quasi-Newton method. Suppose that one wished to maximize the "banana" function $f(x) = -100(x_2 - x_1^2)^2 - (1 - x_1)^2$. To apply `qnewton`, one first codes a stand-alone MATLAB function that returns the value of the objective function and its gradient at an arbitrary point:

```
function [y,dy] = f(x);
y = -100*(x(2)-x(1)^2)^2-(1-x(1))^2;
dy = [2*(1-x(1))+400*(x(2)-x(1)^2)*x(1); -200*(x(2)-x^2)];
```

One then passes the function name, along with a starting value, to `qnewton`:

```
x = qnewton('f',[1;0]);
```

Execution of this script yields the global maximum $x = (1, 1)$ in 18 iterations starting from the initial point [1, 0] using the default BFGS Hessian update. To maximize the function using the steepest ascent method, one may override the default update method as follows:

```
optset('qnewton','searchmeth',1); x = qnewton(f,[1;0]);
```

Execution of this script fails to find the optimum after 250 iterations, the default maximum allowable. The paths followed by the quasi-Newton method iterates in these two examples are illustrated in Figures 4.4 and 4.5.

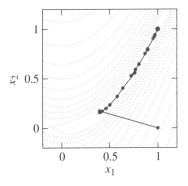

Figure 4.4
BFGS Quasi-Newton Maximization of Banana Function

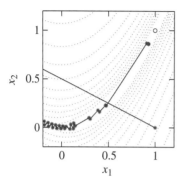

Figure 4.5
Steepest Ascent Maximization of Banana Function

4.4 Line Search Methods

Just as was the case with rootfinding problems, it is not always best to take a full Newton
step. In fact, it may be better to either stop short or move past the Newton step. If we view
the Newton step as defining a *search direction,* performing a one-dimensional search in that
direction will generally produce improved results. In practice, it is not necessary to perform
a thorough search for the best point in the Newton direction. Typically, it is sufficient to
assure that successive quasi-Newton iterations are raising the value of the objective. A
number of different *line search* methods are used in practice, including the golden search
method. The golden search algorithm is very reliable but computationally inefficient. Two
alternative schemes are typically used in practice to perform line searches. The first, known
as the Armijo search, is similar to the backstepping algorithm used in rootfinding and
complementarity problems. The idea is to find the minimum power j such that

$$\frac{f(x+sd) - f(x)}{s} \geq \mu f'(x)^\top d$$

where $s = \rho^j$ for $0 < \rho < 1$, and $0 < \mu < 0.5$. Note that the left-hand side is the slope of
the line from the current iteration point to the candidate for the next iteration and the right-
hand side is the directional derivative at x in the search direction d, that is, the instantaneous
slope at the current iteration point. The Armijo approach is to backtrack from a step size of
1 until the slope on the left-hand side is a given fraction μ of the slope on the right-hand
side.

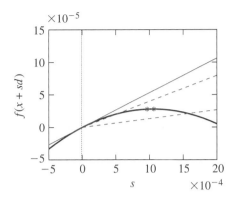

Figure 4.6
Step Length Determination

Another widely used approach, known as Goldstein search, is to find any value of s that satisfies

$$\mu_0 f'(x)^\top d \leq \frac{f(x+sd) - f(x)}{s} \leq \mu_1 f'(x)^\top d$$

for some values of $0 < \mu_0 \leq 0.5 \leq \mu_1 < 1$. Unlike the Armijo search, which is both a method for selecting candidate values of the step size s and a stopping rule, the Goldstein criterion is simply a stopping rule that can be used with a variety of search approaches.

Figure 4.6 illustrates the typical situation at a given iteration. The figure plots the objective function, expressed as deviations from $f(x)$, that is, $f(x+sd) - f(x)$, against the step size s in the Newton direction d. The objective function is highlighted, and the line tangent to it at the origin has slope equal to the directional derivative $f'(x)^\top d$. The values μ_0 and μ_1 define a cone within which the function value must lie to be considered an acceptable step. In Figure 4.6 the cone is bounded by dashed lines with $\mu_0 = 0.25$ and $\mu_1 = 0.75$. These values are for illustrative purposes and define a far narrower cone than is desirable; typical values are on the order of 0.0001 and 0.9999.

A simple strategy for locating an acceptable point is to first find a point in or below the cone using step doubling (doubling the value of s at each iteration). If a point below the cone is found first, we have a bracket within which points in the cone must lie, and we can backstep until a point inside the cone is obtained. We call this the bhhhstep approach.

Another approach, stepbt, checks to see if $s = 1$ is in the cone and, if so, maximizes a quadratic approximation to the objective function in the Newton direction constructed from knowledge of $f(x)$, $f'(x)d$, and $f(x + d)$. If the computed step s is acceptable, it is taken. Otherwise, the algorithm iterates until an acceptable step is found using a cubic approximation to the objective function in the Newton direction constructed from knowledge of $f(x)$, $f'(x)d$, $f(x + s^{(j-1)}d)$, and $f(x + s^{(j)}d)$. The stepbt approach is fast and generally gives good results. It is recommended as the default line search procedure for general maximization algorithms.

In Figure 4.6 we have included stars representing the step lengths determined by stepbhhh, stepbt, and our implementation of the golden search step length maximizer, stepgold. The stepbhhh method yielded $s = 0.00977$, whereas both the stepbt and stepgold methods yielded $s = 0.00105$. The stepgold method first brackets a maximum in the direction d and then uses the golden search approach to narrow the bracket. This method differs from the other two in that it terminates when the size of the bracket is less than a specified tolerance (here set at 0.0004).

In this example, the three methods took 11, 4, and 20 iterations to find an acceptable step length, respectively. Notice that stepbt found the maximum in far fewer steps than did stepgold. This result will generally occur when the function is reasonably smooth and hence well approximated by a cubic function. It is difficult to make generalizations about the performance of the step line search algorithm, however. In this example, the step size was very small, so both stepbhhh and stepgold took many iterations to get the order of magnitude correct. In many cases, if the initial distance is well chosen, the step size will typically be close to unity in magnitude, especially as the maximizer approaches the optimal point. When this statement is true, the advantage of stepbt is less important. Having said all that, we recommend stepbt as a default. We have also implemented our algorithm optstep to use stepgold if the other methods fail.

4.5 Special Cases

Two special cases arise often enough in economic practice (especially in econometrics) to warrant additional discussion. Nonlinear least squares and the maximum likelihood problems have objective functions with special structures that give rise to their own special quasi-Newton methods. The special methods differ from other Newton and quasi-Newton methods only in the choice of the matrix used to approximate the Hessian. Because these problems generally arise in the context of statistical applications, we alter our notation to conform with the conventions for those applications. The optimization takes place with respect to a k-dimensional parameter vector θ, and n will refer to the number of observations.

The nonlinear least squares problem takes the form

$$\min_{\theta} \tfrac{1}{2} f(\theta)^\top f(\theta)$$

where $f : \mathbb{R}^k \to \mathbb{R}^n$ (the $\frac{1}{2}$ is for notational convenience). The gradient of this objective function is

$$\sum_{i=1}^{n} f_i'(\theta)^\top f_i(\theta) = f'(\theta)^\top f(\theta)$$

The Hessian of the objective function is

$$f'(\theta)^\top f'(\theta) + \sum_{i=1}^{n} f_i(\theta) \frac{\partial^2 f_i(\theta)}{\partial\theta\, \partial\theta^\top}$$

If we ignore the second term in the Hessian, we are assured of having a positive definite matrix with which to determine the search direction:

$$d = -[f'(\theta)^\top f'(\theta)]^{-1} f'(\theta)^\top f(\theta)$$

All other aspects of the problem are identical to the quasi-Newton methods already discussed, except for the adjustment to minimization. It is also worth pointing out that, in typical applications, $f(\theta)$ is composed of error terms each having expectation 0. Assuming that the usual central limit assumptions apply to the error term, the inverse of the approximate Hessian

$$[f'(\theta)^\top f'(\theta)]^{-1}$$

can be used as a covariance estimator for θ.

Maximum likelihood problems are specified by a choice of a distribution function for the data, y, that depends on a parameter vector, θ. The log-likelihood function is the sum of the logs of the likelihoods of each of the data points:

$$l(\theta; y) = \sum_{i=1}^{n} \ln f(y_i; \theta)$$

The score function is defined as the matrix of derivatives of the log-likelihood function evaluated at each observation:

$$s_i(\theta; y) = \frac{\partial l(\theta; y_i)}{\partial\theta}$$

Viewed as a matrix, the score function is $n \times k$.

A well-known result in statistical theory is that the expectation of the inner product of the score function is equal to the negative of the expectation of the second derivative of the likelihood function, which is known as the information matrix. Either the information matrix or the sample average of the inner product of the score function provides a positive definite matrix that can be used to determine a search direction. In the latter case, the search direction is defined by

$$d = -[s(\theta; y)^{\top} s(\theta, y)]^{-1} s(\theta, y)^{\top} \underline{1}_n$$

where $\underline{1}_n$ is an n-vector of ones. This approach is known as the *modified method of scoring*.[4] As in the case of the nonlinear least squares, a covariance estimator for θ is immediately available using

$$[s(\theta; y)^{\top} s(\theta, y)]^{-1}$$

4.6   Constrained Optimization

The simplest constrained optimization problem involves the maximization of an objective function subject to simple bounds on the choice variable:

$$\max_{a \leq x \leq b} f(x)$$

According to the Karush-Kuhn-Tucker theorem, if f is differentiable on $[a, b]$, then x^* is a constrained maximum for f only if it solves the complementarity problem CP(f', a, b):[5]

$$a_i \leq x_i \leq b_i$$

$$x_i > a_i \Rightarrow f_i'(x) \geq 0$$

$$x_i < b_i \Rightarrow f_i'(x) \leq 0$$

Conversely, if f is concave and differentiable on $[a, b]$ and x^* solves the complementarity problem CP($f'(x)$, a, b), then x^* is a constrained maximum of f; if additionally f is strictly concave on $[a, b]$, then the maximum is unique.

Two bounded maximization problems are displayed in Figure 4.7. In this figure, the bounds are displayed with dashed lines and the objective function with a solid line. In Figure 4.7a the objective function is concave and achieves its unique global maximum on the interior of the feasible region. At the maximum, the derivative of f must be zero, for otherwise one could improve the objective by moving either up or down, depending on

---

4. If the information matrix is known in closed form, it could be used rather than $s^{\top}s$, and the method would be known as the *method of scoring*.

5. Complementarity problems are discussed in section 3.7.

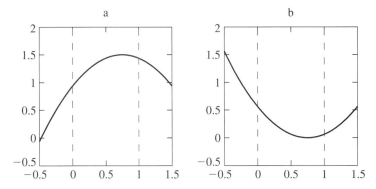

Figure 4.7
One-Dimensional Maximization Problems: (a) $f(x) = 1.5 - (x - 3/4)^2$, $x^* = 3/4$; (b) $f(x) = -2 + (x - 3/4)^2$, $x^* = 0$ and 1

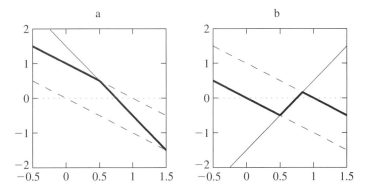

Figure 4.8
Complementarity Conditions for Maximization Problems: (a) $f'(x) = -2(x - 3/4)$; (b) $f'(x) = 2(x - 3/4)$

whether the derivative is positive or negative. In Figure 4.7b we display a more complicated case. Here, the objective function is convex. It achieves a global maximum at the lower bound and a local, nonglobal maximum at the upper bound. It also achieves a global minimum in the interior of the interval.

In Figure 4.8 we illustrate the complementarity problem presented by the Karush-Kuhn-Tucker conditions associated with the bounded optimization problems in Figure 4.7. The complementarity problems are represented in their equivalent rootfinding formulation $\min(\max(f'(x), a - x), b - x) = 0$. In Figure 4.8a we see that the Karush-Kuhn-Tucker conditions possess a unique solution at the unique global maximum of f. In Figure 4.8b there are three solutions to the Karush-Kuhn-Tucker conditions, corresponding to the two local maxima and the one local minimum of f on $[a, b]$. These figures illustrate that one may reliably solve a bounded maximization problem using standard complementarity methods only if the objective function is concave. Otherwise, the complementary algorithm could lead to local, nonglobal maxima or even minima.

The sensitivity of the optimal value of the objective function f^* to changes in the bounds of the bounded optimization problem is relatively easy to characterize. According to the envelope theorem,

$$\frac{df^*}{da} = \min\left(0, \, f'(x^*)\right)$$

$$\frac{df^*}{db} = \max\left(0, \, f'(x^*)\right)$$

More generally, if f, a, and b all depend on some parameter p, then

$$\frac{df^*}{dp} = \frac{\partial f}{\partial p} + \min\left(0, \frac{\partial f}{\partial x}\right)\frac{da}{dp} + \max\left(0, \frac{\partial f}{\partial x}\right)\frac{db}{dp}$$

where the derivatives of f, a, and b are evaluated at (x^*, p).

The most general constrained finite-dimensional optimization problem that we consider is

$$\max_{a \leq x \leq b} f(x), \quad \text{s.t. } R(x) \genfrac{}{}{0pt}{}{\leq}{\genfrac{}{}{0pt}{}{=}{\geq}} r$$

where $R : [a, b] \rightarrow \mathbb{R}^m$.

According to the Karush-Kuhn-Tucker Theorem, a regular point x maximizes f subject to the general constraints only if there is a vector $\lambda \in \mathbb{R}^m$ such that (x, λ) solves the complementarity problem

$$CP\left(\begin{bmatrix} f'(x)^\top - R'(x)^\top \lambda^\top \\ R(x) - r \end{bmatrix}, \begin{bmatrix} a \\ p \end{bmatrix}, \begin{bmatrix} b \\ q \end{bmatrix}\right)$$

where the values of p and q depend on the type of constraint:

	$\leq$	$=$	$\geq$
p_i	0	$-\infty$	$-\infty$
q_i	∞	∞	0

A point x is regular if the gradients of all constraint functions R_i that satisfy $R_i(x) = r_i$ are linearly independent.[6] Conversely, if f is concave, R is convex, and (x, λ) satisfies the Karush-Kuhn-Tucker conditions, then x solves the general constrained optimization problem.

In the Karush-Kuhn-Tucker conditions, the λ_i are called Lagrangian multipliers or shadow prices. The significance of the shadow prices is given by the Envelope Theorem, which asserts that under mild regularity conditions,

$$\frac{\partial f^*}{\partial r} = \lambda$$

that is, λ_i is the rate at which the optimal value of the objective will change with changes in the constraint constant r_i. The sensitivity of the optimal value of the objective function f^* to changes in the bounds on the choice variable is given by

$$\frac{df^*}{da} = \min\left(0, f'(x) - R'(x)\lambda^\top\right)$$

$$\frac{df^*}{db} = \max\left(0, f'(x) - R'(x)\lambda^\top\right)$$

The Karush-Kuhn-Tucker complementarity conditions typically have a natural arbitrage interpretation. Consider the problem of maximizing profits from certain economic activities when the activities employ fixed factors or resources that are available in limited supply. Specifically, suppose $x_1, x_2, \ldots, x_n$ are the levels of n economic activities, which must be nonnegative, and the objective is to maximize profit $f(x)$ generated by those activities. Also suppose that these activities employ m resources and that the usage of the ith resource $R_i(x)$ cannot exceed a given availability r_i. Then λ_i^* represents the opportunity cost or shadow price of the ith resource, and

$$MP_j = \frac{\partial f}{\partial x_j} - \sum_i \lambda_i^* \frac{\partial R_i}{\partial x_j}$$

represents the economic marginal profit of the jth activity, accounting for the opportunity cost of the resources employed in the activity. The Karush-Kuhn-Tucker conditions may

6. The regularity conditions may be omitted either if the constraint function R is linear, or if f is concave, R is convex, and the feasible set has nonempty interior.

thus be interpreted as follows:

$x_j \geq 0$	Activity levels are nonnegative.
$MP_j \leq 0$	Otherwise, raise profit by raising x_j.
$x_j > 0 \Rightarrow MP_j \geq 0$	Otherwise, raise profit by lowering x_j.
$\lambda_i^* \geq 0$	Shadow price of resource is nonnegative.
$R_i(x) \leq r_i$	Resource use cannot exceed availability.
$\lambda_i > 0 \Rightarrow R_i(x) = r_i$	Valuable resources should not be wasted.

There are many approaches to solving general optimization problems that would take us beyond what we can hope to accomplish in this book. Solving general optimization problems is difficult, and the best advice we can give here is that you should obtain a good package and use it. However, if your problem is reasonably well behaved in the sense that the Karush-Kuhn-Tucker conditions are both necessary and sufficient, then the problem is simply to solve the Karush-Kuhn-Tucker conditions. To do so, one writes the Karush-Kuhn-Tucker conditions as a complementarity problem and solves the problem using the methods of the previous chapter.

Exercises

4.1. Suppose that the probability density function of a nonnegative random variable y is

$\exp(-y_i/\mu_i)/\mu_i$

where $\mu_i = X_i\beta$ for some observable data X_i (X_i is $1 \times k$ and β is $k \times 1$).

a. Show that the first-order conditions for the maximum likelihood estimator of β can be written as

$$\sum \frac{X_i^\top X_i}{(X_i\beta)^2}\beta = \sum \frac{X_i^\top y_i}{(X_i\beta)^2}$$

b. Use this result to design a recursive algorithm to estimate β.

c. Write a MATLAB function of the form `[beta,sigma]=example(y,X)` that computes the maximum likelihood estimator of β and its asymptotic covariance matrix Σ. The function should be a stand-alone procedure (i.e., do not call any optimization or rootfinding solvers) that implements the recursive algorithm.

d. Show that the recursive algorithm can be interpreted as a quasi-Newton method. Explain fully.

4.2. The two-parameter gamma probability distribution function has density

$$f(x; \theta) = \frac{\theta_2^{\theta_1} x^{\theta_1 - 1} e^{-\theta_2 x}}{\Gamma(\theta_1)}$$

a. Derive the first-order conditions associated with maximizing the log-likelihood associated with this distribution. Note that the first and second derivatives of the log of the Γ function are the psi and trigamma functions. The CompEcon Toolbox contains procedures to evaluate these special functions.

b. Solve the first-order condition for θ_2 in terms of θ_1. Use this to derive an optimality condition for θ_1 alone.

c. Write a MATLAB function that is passed a vector of observations (of positive numbers) and returns the maximum likelihood estimates of θ and their covariance matrix. Implement the function to use Newton's method without calling any general optimization or rootfinding solvers. Notice that the maximum likelihood estimator of θ depends on the data only through $Y_1 = \frac{1}{n} \sum_{i=1}^{n} x_i$, the arithmetic mean, and $Y_2 = \exp(\frac{1}{n} \sum_{i=1}^{n} \ln(x_i))$, the geometric mean ($Y_1$ and Y_2 are known as sufficient statistics for θ). Your code should exploit this fact by only computing these sufficient statistics once.

d. Plot θ_1 as a function of Y_1/Y_2 over the range $[1.1, 3]$.

4.3. The Cox-Ingersoll-Ross (CIR) bond-pricing model uses the function

$$Z(r, \tau; \kappa, \alpha, \sigma) = A(\tau) \exp\left(- B(\tau) r \right)$$

with

$$A(\tau) = \left[\frac{2\gamma e^{(\gamma + \kappa)\tau/2}}{(\gamma + \kappa)(e^{\gamma\tau} - 1) + 2\gamma} \right]^{2\kappa\alpha/\sigma^2}$$

and

$$B(\tau) = \frac{2(e^{\gamma\tau} - 1)}{(\gamma + \kappa)(e^{\gamma\tau} - 1) + 2\gamma}$$

where $\gamma = \sqrt{\kappa^2 + 2\sigma^2}$. Here r is the current instantaneous rate of interest, τ is the time to maturity of the bond, and κ, α, and σ are model parameters. The percent rate of return on a bond is given by

$$r(\tau) = -100 \ln \left(Z(r, \tau) \right)/\tau$$

In the following table, rates of return on Treasury bonds for nine values of τ are given for five days:

Date	τ								
	.25	.5	1	2	3	5	7	10	30
01/07	4.44	4.49	4.51	4.63	4.63	4.62	4.82	4.77	5.23
01/13	4.45	4.48	4.49	4.61	4.61	4.60	4.84	4.74	5.16
01/20	4.37	4.49	4.53	4.66	4.66	4.65	4.86	4.76	5.18
01/27	4.47	4.47	4.51	4.57	4.57	4.57	4.74	4.68	5.14
02/03	4.48	4.55	4.59	4.72	4.73	4.74	4.91	4.83	5.25

a. For each date, find the values of r, κ, α, and σ that minimize the squared differences between the model and the actual rates of return. This is one way that model parameters can be "calibrated" to the data and ensures that model parameters yield a term structure that is close to the observed term structure.

b. In this model the values of the parameters are fixed, but the value of r varies over time. In fact, part a showed that the three parameter values vary from week to week. As an alternative, find the values of the parameters and the five values of r that minimize the squared deviations between the model and actual values. Compare these to the parameter values obtained by calibrating to each date separately.

4.4. An important theorem in finance demonstrates that the value of a European put option is equal to the expected return on the option, with the expectation taken with respect to the so-called risk-neutral probability measure[7]

$$V(k) = \int_0^\infty (k-p)^+ f(p)\,dp = \int_0^k (k-p) f(p)\,dp$$

where $f(p)$ is the probability distribution of the price of the underlying asset at the option's maturity, k is the option's strike price, and $(x)^+ = \max(0, x)$.

This relationship has been used to compute estimates of $f(p)$ based on observed asset prices. Two approaches have been taken. The first is to choose a parametric form for f and find the parameters that best fit the observed option price. To illustrate, define the discrepancy between observed and model values as

$$e(k) = V_k - \int_0^k (k-p) f(p;\theta)\,dp$$

7. This is strictly true only if the interest rate is 0 or, equivalently, if the option values are interest rate adjusted appropriately. Also, the price of the underlying asset should not be correlated with the interest rate.

and then fit θ by, for example, minimizing the sum of squared errors:

$$\min_{\theta} \sum_{j} e(k_j)^2$$

The other approach is to discretize the price p_i and its probability distribution f_i. Values of the f_i can be computed that correctly reproduce observed option value and that satisfy some auxiliary condition. That condition could be a smoothness condition, such as minimizing the sum of the $f_{i+1} - 2f_i + f_{i-1}$; if the p_i are evenly spaced, this quantity is proportional to an approximation to the second derivative of $f(p)$.

An alternative is to compute the maximum entropy values of the f_i:

$$\max_{\{f_i\}} \sum_{i} f_i \ln(f_i)$$

subject to the constraints that the f_i are nonnegative and sum to 1. It is easy to show that the f_i satisfy

$$f_i = \frac{\exp\left(\sum_j \lambda_j (k_j - p_i)^+\right)}{\sum_i \exp\left(\sum_j \lambda_j (k_j - p_i)^+\right)}$$

where λ_j is the Lagrange multiplier on the constraint that the jth option is correctly priced. The problem is thus converted to the rootfinding problem of solving for the Lagrange multipliers:

$$V_j - \sum_{i} f_i (k_j - p_i)^+ = 0$$

where the f_i are as given previously.

Write a program that takes as input a vector of price nodes p and associated vectors of strike prices k, along with observed put option values v, and returns a vector of maximum entropy probabilities f associated with p:

```
f = riskneutral(p,k,v)
```

The function can pass an auxiliary function to a root-finding algorithm such as `newton` or `broyden`.

The procedure just described has the peculiar property that (if put options alone are used) the upper tail probabilities are all equal above the highest value of the k_j. To correct for this, one can add in the constraint that the expected price at the option's expiration date is the current value of the asset, as would be true in a 0-interest-rate situation. Thus it is necessary to modify the original program to accept the current value of the price of the underlying asset:

```
f = RiskNeutral(p,k,v,p0)
```

To test your program, use the script file riskneutd.m.

4.5. A consumer's preferences over the commodities x_1, x_2, and x_3 are characterized by the Stone-Geary utility function

$$U(x) = \sum_{i=1}^{3} \beta_i \ln(x_i - \gamma_i)$$

where $\beta_i > 0$ and $x_i > \gamma_i \geq 0$. The consumer wants to maximize his utility subject to the budget constraint

$$\sum_{i=1}^{3} p_i x_i \leq I$$

where $p_i > 0$ denotes the price of x_i, I denotes income, and $I - \sum_{i=1}^{3} p_i \gamma_i > 0$.

a. Write the Karush-Kuhn-Tucker necessary conditions for the problem.

b. Verify that the Karush-Kuhn-Tucker conditions are sufficient for optimality.

c. Derive analytically the associated demand functions.

d. Derive analytically the shadow price, and interpret its meaning.

e. Prove that the consumer will utilize his entire income.

4.6. Suppose that the returns on a set of n assets has mean μ ($n \times 1$) and variance Σ ($n \times n$). A portfolio of assets can be characterized by a set of share weights, ω, an $n \times 1$ vector of nonnegative values summing to 1. The mean return on the portfolio is $\mu^\top \omega$, and its variance is $\omega^\top \Sigma \omega$.

A portfolio is said to be on the mean-variance efficient frontier if its variance is as small as possible for a given mean return.

Write a program that calculates and plots a mean-variance efficient frontier. Write it so it returns two vectors that provide points on the frontier:

```
[mustar,Sigmastar]=mv(mu,Sigma,n)
```

Here n represents the desired number of points.

Run the program mvdemo.m to test your program.

Hint: Determine the mean return from the minimium variance portfolio, and determine the maximum mean return portfolio. These provide lower and upper bounds for mustar. Then solve the optimization problem for the remaining $n - 2$ values of mustar.

4.7. Consider the nonlinear programming problem

$$\min_{x_1,\ldots,x_4} \quad x_1^{0.25} x_3^{0.50} x_4^{0.25}$$

s.t. $x_1 + x_2 + x_3 + x_4 \geq 4$

$x_1, x_2, x_3, x_4 \geq 0$

a. What can you say about the optimality of the point $(1, 0, 2, 1)$?

b. Does this problem possess all the correct curvature properties for the Karush-Kuhn-Tucker conditions to be sufficient for optimality throughout the feasible region? Why or why not?

c. How do you know that the problem possesses an optimal feasible solution?

4.8. Consider the nonlinear programming problem

$$\min_{x_1,x_2} \quad 2x_1^2 - 12x_1 + 3x_2^2 - 18x_2 + 45$$

s.t. $3x_1 + x_2 \leq 12$

$x_1 + x_2 \leq 6$

$x_1, x_2 \geq 0$

The optimal solution to this problem is $x_1^* = 3$ and $x_2^* = 3$.

a. Verify that the Karush-Kuhn-Tucker conditions are satisfied by this solution.

b. Determine the optimal values for the shadow prices λ_1 and λ_2 associated with the structural constraints, and interpret λ_1^* and λ_2^*.

c. If the second constraint were changed to $x_1 + x_2 \leq 5$, what would be the effect on the optimal values of $x_1, x_2, \lambda_1,$ and λ_2?

Bibliographic Notes

A number of very useful references exist on computational aspects of optimization. Perhaps the most generally useful for practitioners are Gill, Murray, and Wright (1981) and Fletcher (2000). Ferris and Sinapiromsaran (2000) discuss solving nonlinear optimization problems by formulating them as complementarity problems.

5 Numerical Integration and Differentiation

In many computational economic applications, one must compute the definite integral of a real-valued function f with respect to a "weight" function w over an interval I of $\mathbb{R}^n$:

$$\int_I f(x)w(x)\,dx$$

The weight function may be the identity, $w \equiv 1$, in which case the integral represents the area under the function f. In other applications, w may be the probability density function of a continuous random variable $\tilde{X}$ with support I, in which case the integral represents the expectation of $f(\tilde{X})$.

In this chapter, we discuss three classes of numerical integration or *numerical quadrature* methods. All methods approximate a definite integral with a weighted sum of function values:

$$\int_I f(x)w(x)\,dx \approx \sum_{i=0}^{n} w_i f(x_i)$$

The methods differ only in how the *quadrature weights* w_i and the *quadrature nodes* x_i are chosen. Newton-Cotes methods approximate the integrand f between nodes using low-order polynomials and sum the integrals of the polynomials to estimate the integral of f. Gaussian quadrature methods choose the nodes and weights to satisfy moment-matching conditions. Monte Carlo and quasi–Monte Carlo integration methods use equally weighted "random" or "equidistributed" nodes.

In this chapter, we also present an overview of how to compute *finite difference* approximations for the derivatives of a real-valued function. As we have seen in previous chapters, it is often desirable to compute derivatives numerically because analytic derivative expressions are difficult or impossible to derive, or expensive to evaluate. Finite difference methods can also be used to solve differential equations, which arise frequently in dynamic economic models, especially models formulated in continuous time. In this chapter, we introduce methods for solving differential equations and illustrate their application to *initial value problems*.

5.1 Newton-Cotes Methods

Univariate Newton-Cotes quadrature methods are designed to approximate the integral of a real-valued function f defined on a bounded interval $[a, b]$ of the real line. Two Newton-Cotes rules are widely used in practice: the *trapezoid rule* and *Simpson's rule*. Both rules are very easy to implement and are typically adequate for computing the area under a continuous function.

The trapezoid rule partitions the interval $[a, b]$ into subintervals of equal length, approximates f over each subinterval using linear interpolants, and then sums the areas under the linear segments. The trapezoid rule draws its name from the fact that the area under f is approximated by a series of trapezoids.

More formally, let $x_i = a + (i - 1)h$ for $i = 1, 2, \ldots, n$, where $h = (b - a)/(n - 1)$. The nodes x_i divide the interval $[a, b]$ into $n - 1$ subintervals of equal length h. Over the ith subinterval, $[x_i, x_{i+1}]$, the function f may be approximated by the line segment passing through the two graph points $(x_i, f(x_i))$ and $(x_{i+1}, f(x_{i+1}))$. The area under this line segment defines a trapezoid that provides an estimate of the area under f over this subinterval:

$$\int_{x_i}^{x_{i+1}} f(x)\, dx \approx \frac{h}{2}[f(x_i) + f(x_{i+1})]$$

Summing up the areas of the trapezoids across subintervals yields the trapezoid rule:

$$\int_a^b f(x)\, dx \approx \sum_{i=1}^n w_i\, f(x_i)$$

where $w_1 = w_n = h/2$ and $w_i = h$ otherwise.

The trapezoid rule is simple and robust. It is said to be first-order exact because, if not for rounding error, it will exactly compute the integral of any first-order polynomial, that is, a line. In general, if the integrand f is smooth, the trapezoid rule will yield an approximation error that is $O(h^2)$; that is, the error shrinks quadratically with the width of the subintervals.

Simpson's rule is based on piecewise quadratic, rather than piecewise linear, approximations to the integrand f. More formally, let $x_i = a + (i - 1)h$ for $i = 1, 2, \ldots, n$, where $h = (b - a)/(n - 1)$ and n is odd. The nodes x_i divide the interval $[a, b]$ into an even number $n - 1$ of subintervals of equal length h. Over the jth pair of subintervals, $[x_{2j-1}, x_{2j}]$ and $[x_{2j}, x_{2j+1}]$, the function f may be approximated by the unique quadratic function that passes through the three graph points $(x_{2j-1}, f(x_{2j-1}))$, $(x_{2j}, f(x_{2j}))$, and $(x_{2j+1}, f(x_{2j+1}))$. The area under this quadratic function provides an estimate of the area under f over the subinterval:

$$\int_{x_{2j-1}}^{x_{2j+1}} f(x)\, dx \approx \frac{h}{3}[f(x_{2j-1}) + 4f(x_{2j}) + f(x_{2j+1})]$$

Summing up the areas under the quadratic approximants across subintervals yields

Simpson's rule:

$$\int_a^b f(x)\, dx \approx \sum_{i=1}^n w_i f(x_i)$$

where $w_1 = w_n = h/3$ and, otherwise, $w_i = 4h/3$ if i is even and $w_i = 2h/3$ if i is odd.

Simpson's rule is as simple as the trapezoid rule, and thus it is not much harder to program. Even though Simpson's rule is based on locally quadratic approximation of the integrand, it is third-order exact. That is, it exactly computes the integral of any cubic polynomial. In general, if the integrand is smooth, Simpson's rule yields an approximation error that is $O(h^4)$ and thus falls at twice the geometric rate of the error associated with the trapezoid rule.

Simpson's rule is preferred to the trapezoid rule when the integrand f is smooth because it retains the algorithmic simplicity of the trapezoid rule while offering twice the degree of approximation. However, the trapezoid rule will often be more accurate than Simpson's rule if the integrand exhibits discontinuities in its first derivative, which can occur in economic applications exhibiting corner solutions.

Newton-Cotes rules based on fourth and higher order piecewise polynomial approximations exist, but they are more difficult to work with and thus are rarely used. Through the use of tensor product principles, univariate Newton-Cotes quadrature schemes can be generalized for higher dimensional integration. Suppose one wishes to integrate a real-valued function defined on a rectangle $\{(x_1, x_2) | a_1 \leq x_1 \leq b_1,\ a_2 \leq x_2 \leq b_2\}$ in $\mathbb{R}^2$. One way to proceed is to compute the Newton-Cotes nodes and weights $\{(x_{1i}, w_{1i}) | i = 1, 2, \ldots, n_1\}$ for the real interval $[a_1, b_1]$ and the Newton-Cotes nodes and weights $\{(x_{2j}, w_{2j}) | j = 1, 2, \ldots, n_2\}$ for the real interval $[a_2, b_2]$. The tensor product Newton-Cotes rule for the rectangle would comprise of the $n = n_1 n_2$ grid points of the form $\{(x_{1i}, x_{2j}) | i = 1, 2, \ldots, n_1;\ j = 1, 2, \ldots, n_2\}$ with associated weights $\{w_{ij} = w_{1i} w_{2j} | i = 1, 2, \ldots, n_1;\ j = 1, 2, \ldots, n_2\}$. This construction principle can be applied to higher dimensions using repeated tensor product operations.

In most computational economic applications it is not possible to determine a priori how many partition points are needed to compute an integral to a desired level of accuracy using a Newton-Cotes quadrature rule. One solution to this problem is to use an *adaptive quadrature* strategy whereby one increases the number of points at which the integrand is evaluated until the sequence of estimates of the integral converge. Efficient adaptive Newton-Cotes quadrature schemes are especially easy to implement. One simple but powerful scheme calls for the number of intervals to be doubled with each iteration. Because the new partition points include the partition points used in the previous iteration, the computational effort required to form the new integral estimate is cut in half. More sophisticated adaptive

Newton-Cotes quadrature techniques relax the requirement that the intervals be equally spaced and concentrate new evaluation points in those areas where the integrand appears to be most irregular.

5.2 Gaussian Quadrature

Gaussian quadrature rules are constructed with respect to specific weight functions. For a weight function w defined on an interval $I \subset \mathbb{R}$ of the real line, and for a given order of approximation n, the quadrature nodes $x_1, x_2, \ldots, x_n$ and quadrature weights $w_1, w_2, \ldots, w_n$ are chosen so as to satisfy the $2n$ "moment-matching" conditions:

$$\int_I x^k w(x) \, dx = \sum_{i=1}^{n} w_i x_i^k, \quad \text{for } k = 0, \ldots, 2n - 1$$

The integral approximation is then computed by forming the prescribed weighted sum of function values at the prescribed nodes:

$$\int_I f(x) w(x) \, dx \approx \sum_{i=1}^{n} w_i \, f(x_i)$$

By construction, an n-point Gaussian quadrature rule is order $2n - 1$ exact. That is, if not for rounding error, it will exactly compute the integral of any polynomial of order $2n - 1$ or less with respect to the weight function. Thus, if f can be closely approximated by a polynomial, Gaussian quadrature should provide an accurate approximation to the integral.

Gaussian quadrature over a bounded interval with respect to the identity weight function, $w(x) \equiv 1$, is called Gauss-Legendre quadrature. Gauss-Legendre quadrature is special interest because it is the Gaussian quadrature scheme appropriate for computing the area under a curve. Gauss-Legendre quadrature is consistent for Riemann-integrable functions. That is, if f is Riemann integrable, then the approximation afforded by Gauss-Legendre quadrature can be made arbitrarily precise by increasing the number of nodes n.

Table 5.1 compares the accuracy afforded by Gauss-Legendre quadrature and Newton-Cotes quadrature. The table demonstrates that Gauss-Legendre quadrature is the numerical integration method of choice when f possesses continuous derivatives, as in $f(x) = \exp(-x)$, but should be applied with great caution if the function has discontinuous derivatives, as in $f(x) = |x|^{0.5}$. If the function f possesses known kink points, it is often possible to break the integral into the sum of two or more integrals of smooth functions. If these or similar steps do not produce smooth integrands, then Newton-Cotes quadrature methods may be more efficient than Gaussian quadrature methods because they limit the error caused by the kinks and singularities to the interval in which they occur.

Table 5.1
Errors for Selected Quadrature Methods

Function	Degree (n)	Trapezoid Rule	Simpson Rule	Gauss-Legendre
$\exp(-x)$	10	1.36e+001	3.57e-001	8.10e-002
	20	3.98e+000	2.31e-002	2.04e-008
	30	1.86e+000	5.11e-003	1.24e-008
$|x|^{0.5}$	10	7.45e-001	7.40e-001	6.49e-001
	20	5.13e-001	4.75e-001	1.74e+001
	30	4.15e-001	3.77e-001	4.34e+003

When the weight function w is the probability density function of some continuous random variable $\tilde{X}$, Gaussian quadrature has a very straightforward interpretation. In this context, Gaussian quadrature essentially "discretizes" the continuous random variable $\tilde{X}$ by replacing it with a discrete random variable with mass points x_i and probabilities w_i that approximates $\tilde{X}$ in the sense that both random variables have the same moments of order less than $2n$:

$$\sum_{i=1}^{n} w_i x_i^k = E\tilde{X}^k \quad \text{for } k = 0, \ldots, 2n - 1$$

Given the mass points and probabilities of the discrete approximant, the expectation of any function of the continuous random variable $\tilde{X}$ may be approximated using the expectation of the function of the discrete approximant, which requires only the computation of a weighted sum:

$$Ef(\tilde{X}) = \int_I f(x)\, w(x)\, dx \approx \sum_{i=1}^{n} w_i f(x_i)$$

For example, the three-point approximation to the standard univariate normal distribution $\tilde{Z}$ is characterized by the condition that moments 0 through 5 match those of the standard normal: $E\tilde{Z}^0 = 1$, $E\tilde{Z}^1 = 0$, $E\tilde{Z}^2 = 1$, $E\tilde{Z}^3 = 0$, $E\tilde{Z}^4 = 3$, and $E\tilde{Z}^5 = 0$. One can easily verify that these conditions are satisfied by a discrete random variable with mass points $x_1 = -\sqrt{3}$, $x_2 = 0$, and $x_3 = \sqrt{3}$ and associated probabilities $w_1 = 1/6$, $w_2 = 2/3$, and $w_3 = 1/6$.

Computing the n-degree Gaussian nodes and weights is a nontrivial task that involves solving $2n$ nonlinear equations for $\{x_i\}$ and $\{w_i\}$. Efficient, specialized numerical routines for computing Gaussian quadrature nodes and weights are available for different weight functions, including virtually all the better known probability distributions such as the uniform, normal, gamma, exponential, Chi-square, and beta distributions.

As was the case with Newton-Cotes quadrature, tensor product principles may be used to generalize Gaussian quadrature rules to higher-dimensional integration. Suppose, for example, that $\tilde{X}$ is a d-dimensional normal random variable with mean vector μ and variance-covariance matrix Σ. Then $\tilde{X}$ is distributed as $\mu + \tilde{Z}R$ where R is the Cholesky square root of Σ (e.g., $\Sigma = R^\top R$) and $\tilde{Z}$ is a row d-vector of independent standard normal variates. If $\{z_i, w_i\}$ are the degree-n Gaussian nodes and weights for a standard normal variate, then an n^d degree approximation for $\tilde{X}$ may be constructed using tensor products. For example, in two dimensions the nodes and weights would take the form

$$x_{ij} = (\mu_1 + R_{11}z_i + R_{21}z_j, \ \mu_2 + R_{12}z_i + R_{22}z_j)$$

and

$$p_{ij} = p_i p_j$$

The Gaussian quadrature scheme for normal variates may also be used to develop a reasonable scheme for discretizing lognormal random variates. By definition, $\tilde{Y}$ is lognormally distributed with parameters μ and σ^2 if, and only if, it is distributed as $\exp(\mu + \sigma\tilde{Z})$ where $\tilde{Z}$ is standard normally distributed with mean 0 and variance 1. It follows that if $\{z_i, w_i\}$ are nodes and weights for a standard normal distribution, then $\{y_i, w_i\}$, where $y_i = \exp(\mu + \sigma z_i)$, provides a reasonable discrete approximant for a lognormal(μ, σ^2) distribution. Given this discrete approximant for the lognormal distribution, one can estimate the expectation of a function of $\tilde{Y}$ as follows: $Ef(\tilde{Y}) = \int f(y)\, w(y)\, dy \approx \sum_{i=1}^n w_i f(y_i)$. This integration rule for lognormal distributions will be exact if f is a polynomial of degree $2n - 1$ and less in $\log(y)$ (*not* in y).

5.3 Monte Carlo Integration

Monte Carlo integration methods are motivated by the Strong Law of Large Numbers. One version of the law states that if $x_1, x_2, \ldots$ are independent realizations of a random variable $\tilde{X}$ and f is a continuous function, then

$$\lim_{n\to\infty} \frac{1}{n} \sum_{i=1}^n f(x_i) = Ef(\tilde{X})$$

with probability one.

The Monte Carlo integration scheme is thus a simple one. To compute an approximation to the expectation of $f(\tilde{X})$, one draws a random sample $x_1, x_2, \ldots, x_n$ from the distribution of $\tilde{X}$ and sets

$$Ef(\tilde{X}) \approx \frac{1}{n} \sum_{i=1}^{n} f(x_i)$$

Most numerical software packages provide a routine that generates pseudorandom variables that are uniformly distributed on the interval [0, 1]. A uniform random number generator is useful for generating random samples from other distributions. Suppose $\tilde{X}$ has a cumulative distribution function

$$F(x) = \Pr(\tilde{X} \leq x)$$

whose inverse has a well-defined closed form. If $\tilde{U}$ is uniformly distributed on (0, 1), then $F^{-1}(\tilde{U})$ has the same distribution as $\tilde{X}$. Thus, to generate a random sample $x_1, x_2, \ldots, x_n$ from the $\tilde{X}$ distribution, one generates a random sample $u_1, u_2, \ldots, u_n$ from the uniform distribution and sets $x_i = F^{-1}(u_i)$.

Most numerical software packages also provide an intrinsic routine that generates pseudorandom standard normal variables. The routine may also be used to generate pseudorandom sequences of lognormal and multivariate normal variables. For example, to generate a pseudorandom sample $\{x_j\}$ of lognormal (μ, σ^2) variates, one generates a sequence $\{z_j\}$ of pseudorandom standard normal variates and sets $x_j = \exp(\mu + \sigma z_j)$. To generate a pseudorandom sample $\{(x_{1j}, x_{2j})\}$ of bivariate normal random vectors with mean μ and variance matrix Σ, one generates two sequences $\{z_{1j}\}$ and $\{z_{2j}\}$ of pseudorandom standard normal variates and sets

$$x_{ij} = \mu_i + R_{1i}z_{1j} + R_{2i}z_{2j}$$

for $i = 1, 2$, where R is the Cholesky square root of Σ.

A fundamental problem that arises with Monte Carlo integration is that it is almost impossible to generate a truly random sample of variates for any distribution. Most compilers and vector-processing packages provide intrinsic routines for computing so-called random numbers. These routines, however, employ iteration rules that generate a purely deterministic, not random, sequence of numbers. In particular, if the generator is repeatedly initiated at the same point, it will return the same sequence of "random" variates each time. About all that can be said of numerical random number generators is that good ones will generate sequences that appear to be random, in that they pass certain statistical tests for randomness. For this reason, numerical random number generators are more accurately said to generate sequences of "pseudorandom" rather than random numbers.

Monte Carlo integration is easy to implement and may be preferred over Gaussian quadrature if the routine for computing the Gaussian mass points and probabilities is not readily available or if the integration is over many dimensions. Monte Carlo integration, however, is subject to a sampling error that cannot be bounded with certainty. The approximation can be made more accurate, in a dubious statistical sense, by increasing the size of the random sample, but doing so can be expensive if evaluating f or generating the pseudorandom variate is costly. Approximations generated by Monte Carlo integration will vary from one integration to the next, unless initiated at the same point, making the use of Monte Carlo integration in conjunction within other iterative schemes, such as dynamic programming or maximum likelihood estimation, problematic. So-called quasi–Monte Carlo methods can circumvent some of the problems associated with Monte Carlo integration.

5.4   Quasi–Monte Carlo Integration

Although Monte Carlo integration methods originated using insights from probability theory, recent extensions have severed that connection and, in the process, demonstrated ways in which the methods can be improved. Quasi–Monte Carlo methods rely on sequences $\{x_i\}$ with the property that

$$\lim_{n \to \infty} \frac{b - a}{n} \sum_{i=1}^{\infty} f(x_i) = \int_a^b f(x)\,dx$$

without regard to whether the sequence passes standard tests of randomness. Any sequence that satisfies this condition for arbitrary (Riemann) integrable functions can be used to approximate an integral on $[a, b]$. Although the Law of Large Numbers assures us that this statement is true when the x_i are independent and identically distributed random variables, other sequences also satisfy this property. Indeed, it can be shown that sequences that are explicitly nonrandom, but instead attempt to fill in space in a regular manner, can often provide more accurate approximations to definite integrals.

There are numerous schemes for generating equidistributed sequences, including the Neiderreiter, Weyl, and Haber sequences. Let x_{ij} denote the jth coordinate of the ith vector in a sequence of equidistributed vectors on the d-dimensional unit hypercube. Then these three equidistributed sequences involve iterates of the form $x_{ij} = frac(2^{q_{ij}})$ where for the Neiderreiter

$$q_{ij} = ij/(d + 1)$$

for the Weyl

$$q_{ij} = ip_j$$

and for the Haber

$$q_{ij} = i(i+1)p_j/2$$

Here, p_j represents the jth positive prime number, and $frac(x)$ represents the fractional part of x, that is, x minus the greatest integer less than or equal to x. Through appropriate linear transformation, equidistributed sequences on the d-dimensional unit hypercube may be used to construct equidistributed sequences on any bounded interval of d-dimensional Euclidean space.

Two-dimensional examples of equidistributed sequences and a pseudorandom sequence are illustrated in Figure 5.1. Each of the plots shows 4,000 values. It is evident that the Neiderreiter and Weyl sequences are very regular, showing far less blank space than

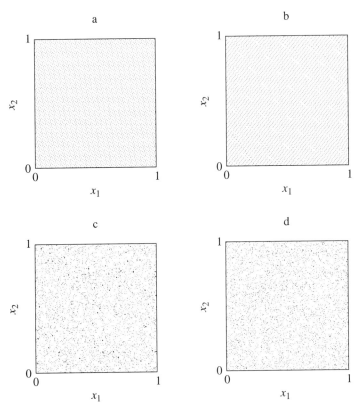

Figure 5.1
Alternative Two-Dimensional Equidistributed Sequences: (a) Neiderreiter; (b) Weyl; (c) Haber; (d) Pseudorandom

Table 5.2
Approximation Errors for Alternative Quasi–Monte Carlo Methods

n	Neiderreiter	Weyl	Haber	Random
1,000	0.00291	0.00210	0.05000	0.10786
10,000	0.00190	0.00030	0.01569	0.01118
100,000	0.00031	0.00009	0.00380	0.01224
1,000,000	0.00002	0.00001	0.00169	0.00197

the Haber sequence or the pseudorandom sequence. This figure demonstrates that it is possible to have sequences that are not only uniformly distributed in an ex ante or probabilistic sense but also in an ex post sense, thereby avoiding the clumpiness exhibited by truly random sequences.

To illustrate the quality of the approximations produced by equidistributed sequences, Table 5.2 displays the approximation error for the integral

$$\int_{-1}^{1}\int_{-1}^{1} \exp(-x_1)\cos\left(x_2^2\right) dx_1\, dx_2$$

which, to seven significant digits, equals 4.580997. It is clear that the methods require many evaluation points for even modest accuracy and that large increases in the number of points reduce the error very slowly. Regardless of the number of nodes, however, it is also clear that the Neiderreiter and Weyl equidistributed sequences consistently produce integral approximations that are two orders of magnitude more accurate than those produced by Monte Carlo simulation.

5.5   An Integration Tool Kit

The CompEcon Toolbox includes a series of routines that may be used to compute definite integrals of real-valued functions over bounded intervals of Euclidean space. These include qnwtrap and qnwsimp, which generate the nodes and weights associated with the trapezoid and Simpson rules, respectively; qnwlege, which generates the nodes and weights associated with Gauss-Legendre quadrature; and qnwequi, which generates the nodes and weights associated with equidistributed and uniform pseudorandom sequences.

The calling syntax for qnwtrap, qnwsimp, and qnwlege is the same and is illustrated here with qnwtrap:

```
[x,w] = qnwtrap(n,a,b);
```

The inputs, for one-dimensional integration, are the number nodes and weights n, the left endpoint a, and the right endpoint b. The outputs are the $n \times 1$ vectors of nodes x and weights w. The calling syntax for qnwequi takes the form

```
[x,w] = qnwequi(n,a,b,type);
```

The routine takes the additional input type, which refers to the type of equidistributed sequence: 'N' indicates Neiderrieter (the default), 'W' indicates Weyl, 'H' indicates Haber, and 'R' indicates pseudorandom uniformly distributed variates.

For example, to compute the definite integral of $\exp(x)$ on $[-1, 2]$ using a 10-point trapezoid rule, one would write:

```
[x,w] = qnwtrap(10,-1,2);
integral = w'*exp(x);
```

To compute the definite integral using a 100-point Neiderrieter rule, one would instead generate the nodes and weights as follows:

```
[x,w] = qnwequi(100,-1,2,'N');
```

Each of these routines also may be used to compute definite integrals of real-valued multivariate functions over bounded intervals in higher dimensional spaces. The routines generate nodes and weights for higher dimensional quadrature by forming the tensor products of univariate nodes and weights. For example, suppose one wished to compute the integral of $\exp(x_1 + x_2)$ over the rectangle $[1, 2] \times [0, 5]$ in $\mathbb{R}^2$. One could call qnwtrap to construct a grid of, say, 300 quadrature nodes produced by taking the cross product of 10 nodes in the x_1 direction and 20 nodes in the x_2 direction:

```
[x,w] = qnwtrap([10 20],[1 0],[2 5]);
integral = w'*exp(x(:,1)+x(:,2));
```

A similar calling syntax is used for qnwsimp and qnwlege.

The calling syntax for qnwequi when performing multidimensional integration requires n to be an integer indicating the total number of integration nodes. Thus, to compute the definite integral using a 10,000-point Neiderrieter rule, one would generate the nodes and weights as follows:

```
[x,w] = qnwequi(10000,[1 0],[2 5],'N');
```

In addition to the general integration routines, the CompEcon Toolbox also includes several functions for computing Gaussian nodes and weights associated with common probability distribution functions. The routine qnwnorm generates the Gaussian quadrature nodes and weights for normal random variables. For univariate normal distributions, the calling syntax takes the form

```
[x,w] = qnwnorm(n,mu,var);
```

where x are the nodes, w are the probability weights, n is the number of nodes and weights, mu is the mean of the distribution, and var is the variance of the distribution. If mu and var are omitted, the mean and variance are assumed to be 0 and 1, respectively. For example, suppose one wanted to compute the expectation of $\exp(\tilde{X})$ where $\tilde{X}$ is normally distributed with mean 2 and variance 4. An approximate expectation could be computed using the following MATLAB code:

```
[x,w] = qnwnorm(3,2,4);
expectation = w'*exp(x);
```

The routine qnwnorm also generates nodes and weights for multivariate normal random variables. For example, suppose one wished to compute the expectation of $\exp(\tilde{X}_1 + \tilde{X}_2)$ where $\tilde{X}_1$ and $\tilde{X}_2$ are jointly normal with $E\tilde{X}_1 = 3$, $E\tilde{X}_2 = 4$, $\text{Var}\,\tilde{X}_1 = 2$, $\text{Var}\,\tilde{X}_2 = 4$, and $\text{Cov}(\tilde{X}_1, \tilde{X}_2) = -1$. One could then invoke qnwnorm to construct a grid of 150 Gaussian quadrature nodes as the cross product of 10 nodes in the x_1 direction and 15 nodes in the x_2 direction, and then form the weighted sum of the assigned weights and function values at the nodes:

```
[x,w] = qnwnorm([10 15],[3 4],[2 -1; -1 4]);
expectation = w'*exp(x(:,1)+x(:,2));
```

Other quadrature routines included in the CompEcon Toolbox generate quadrature nodes and weights for computing the expectations of functions of lognormal, beta, and gamma random variates. For univariate lognormal distributions, the calling syntax takes the form

```
[x,w] = qnwlogn(n,mu,var);
```

where mu and var are the mean and variance of the log of x. For the beta distribution, the calling syntax is

```
[x,w] = qnwbeta(n,a,b);
```

where a and b are the shape parameters of the beta distribution. For the gamma distribution, the calling syntax is

```
[x,w] = qnwgamma(n,a);
```

where a is the shape parameter of the (one-dimensional) gamma distribution. For both the beta and gamma distributions the parameters may be passed as vectors, yielding nodes and weights for multivariate independent random variables.

MATLAB also offers two intrinsic random number generators. The routine `rand` generates a random sample from the Uniform(0,1) distribution stored in either vector or matrix format. Similarly, the routine `randn` generates a random sample from the standard normal distribution stored in either vector or matrix format. In particular, a call of the form `x=rand(m,n)` or `x=randn(m,n)` generates a random sample of mn realizations and stores it in an $m \times n$ matrix.

The MATLAB standard normal random number generator is useful for generating random samples from related distributions. For example, to generate a random sample of n lognormal variables, one may use the script

```
x = exp(mu+sigma*randn(n));
```

where `mu` and `sigma` are the mean and standard deviation parameters of the distribution. To generate a random sample of n d-dimensional normal variates one may use the script

```
x = randn(n,d)*chol(Sigma)+mu(ones(n,1),:);
```

where `Sigma` is the $d \times d$ variance-covariance matrix and `mu` is the $d \times 1$ mean vector.

5.6 Numerical Differentiation

The most natural way to approximate a derivative is to replace it with a finite difference. The definition of a derivative,

$$f'(x) = \lim_{h \to 0} \frac{f(x+h) - f(x)}{h}$$

suggests a way to compute this approximation. One can simply take h to be a small number, knowing that, for h small enough, the error of the approximation will also be small. We will return to the question of how small h should be, but first we address the issue of how large an error is produced using this finite difference approach. An error bound for the approximation can be obtained using a Taylor expansion. We know, for example, that

$$f(x+h) = f(x) + f'(x)h + O(h^2)$$

where $O(h^2)$ means that other terms in the expression are expressible in terms of second or higher powers of h. If we rearrange this expression we see that

$$f'(x) = [f(x+h) - f(x)]/h + O(h)$$

(since $O(h^2)/h = O(h)$), so the approximation to the derivative $f'(x)$ has an $O(h)$ error.

It is possible, however, to compute a more accurate finite difference approximation to the derivative of f at x. Consider the two second-order Taylor expansions

$$f(x+h) = f(x) + f'(x)h + f''(x)\frac{h^2}{2} + O(h^3)$$

and

$$f(x-h) = f(x) - f'(x)h + f''(x)\frac{h^2}{2} + O(h^3)$$

If we subtract the second expression from the first, rearrange, and divide by $2h$, we get

$$f'(x) = \frac{f(x+h) - f(x-h)}{2h} + O(h^2) \tag{5.1}$$

This is called the centered finite difference approximation to the derivative of f at x. Its error is $O(h^2)$, or one order more accurate than the preceding one-sided finite difference approximation.

Other three-point approximations are also possible. To see how these can be constructed, consider evaluating the function at three points, x, $x + h$, and $x + \lambda h$, and approximating the derivative with a weighted sum of these values:

$$f'(x) \approx af(x) + bf(x+h) + cf(x+\lambda h)$$

To determine both the appropriate values of a, b, and c and to determine the size of the approximation error, expand the Taylor series for $f(x + h)$ and $f(x + \lambda h)$ around x, obtaining

$$af(x) + bf(x+h) + cf(x+\lambda h) = (a+b+c)f(x) + h(b+c\lambda)f'(x)$$
$$+ \frac{h^2}{2}(b+c\lambda^2)f''(x) + \frac{h^3}{6}\left[bf^{(3)}(z_1) + c\lambda^3 f^{(3)}(z_2)\right]$$

(for some $z_1 \in [x, x+h]$ and $z_2 \in [x, x+\lambda h]$). We obtain an approximation to $f'(x)$ by forcing the terms on $f(x)$ and $f''(x)$ equal to zero and the coefficient multiplying $f'(x)$ equal to 1:

$$a + b + c = 0$$
$$b + c\lambda = 1/h$$
$$b + c\lambda^2 = 0$$

These conditions uniquely determine a, b, and c, which are easily verified to equal

$$\begin{bmatrix} a \\ b \\ c \end{bmatrix} = \frac{1}{h\lambda(1-\lambda)} \begin{bmatrix} \lambda^2 - 1 \\ -\lambda^2 \\ 1 \end{bmatrix}$$

and results in

$$af(x) + bf(x+h) + cf(x+\lambda h) = f'(x) + O(h^2).$$

Thus, by using three points, we can ensure that the approximation converges at a quadratic rate in h.

Some important special cases arise when the evaluation points are evenly spaced. When $\lambda = -1$, x lies halfway between the other points, and we obtain as a special case the approximation in the centered finite difference approximation in equation (5.1). If $\lambda = 2$, we obtain a formula that is useful when a derivative is needed at a boundary of a domain. In this case

$$f'(x) = \frac{1}{2h}[-3f(x) + 4f(x+h) - f(x+2h)] + O(h^2)$$

(Use $h > 0$ for a lower bound and $h < 0$ for an upper bound.)

Finite difference approximations for higher order derivatives can be found using a similar approach. For example, an order $O(h^2)$ centered finite difference approximation to the second derivative may be constructed using the two third-order Taylor expansions

$$f(x+h) = f(x) + f'(x)h + f''(x)\frac{h^2}{2} + f'''(x)\frac{h^3}{6} + O(h^4)$$

and

$$f(x-h) = f(x) - f'(x)h + f''(x)\frac{h^2}{2} - f'''(x)\frac{h^3}{6} + O(h^4)$$

If we add the two expressions, rearrange, and divide by h^2, we get

$$f''(x) = \frac{f(x+h) - 2f(x) + f(x-h)}{h^2} + O(h^2)$$

To obtain general formulas for second derivatives with second-order accuracy, we will (in general) require a weighted sum composed of four points

$$f''(x) \approx af(x) + bf(x+h) + cf(x+\lambda h) + df(x+\psi h)$$

Expand the Taylor series to the third order, obtaining

$$af(x) + bf(x+h) + cf(x+\lambda h) + df(x+\psi h)$$

$$= (a+b+c+d)f(x) + h(b+c\lambda+d\psi)f'(x) + \frac{h^2}{2}(b+c\lambda^2+d\psi^2)f''(x)$$

$$+ \frac{h^3}{6}(b+c\lambda^3+d\psi^3)f'''(x) + \frac{h^4}{24}\left[bf^{(4)}(z_1)+c\lambda^4 f^{(4)}(z_2)+d\psi^4 f^{(4)}(z_3)\right]$$

We obtain an approximation to $f''(x)$ by forcing the terms on $f(x)$, $f'(x)$, and $f'''(x)$ equal to zero and the coefficient multiplying $f''(x)$ equal to 1:

$$a+b+c+d = 0$$

$$b+c\lambda+d\psi = 0$$

$$b+c\lambda^2+d\psi^2 = 2/h^2$$

$$b+c\lambda^3+d\psi^3 = 0$$

These conditions uniquely determine a, b, c, and d, which are easily verified to equal

$$
\begin{bmatrix} a \\ b \\ c \\ d \end{bmatrix} = \frac{2}{h^2}
\begin{bmatrix}
\dfrac{1+\lambda+\psi}{\lambda\psi} \\[2mm]
\dfrac{\lambda^2-\psi^2}{(\lambda-1)(\psi-1)(\psi-\lambda)} \\[2mm]
\dfrac{\psi^2-1}{\lambda(\lambda-1)(\psi-1)(\psi-\lambda)} \\[2mm]
\dfrac{1-\lambda^2}{\psi(\lambda-1)(\psi-1)(\psi-\lambda)}
\end{bmatrix}
$$

This step gives the approximation

$$af(x) + bf(x+h) + cf(x+\lambda h) + df(x+\psi h) = f''(x) + O(h^2)$$

Thus, by using four points, we can ensure that the approximation converges at a quadratic rate in h.

Some important special cases arise when the evaluation points are evenly spaced. When x lies halfway between $x+h$ and one of the other two points (i.e., when either $\lambda = -1$ or $\psi = -1$), we obtain the centered finite difference approximation given previously, which is second-order accurate even though only three approximation points are used. If $\lambda = 2$

and $\psi = 3$, we obtain a formula that is useful when a derivative is needed at a boundary of the domain. In this case,

$$f''(x) = \frac{1}{h^2}[2f(x) - 5f(x+h) + 4f(x+2h) - f(x+3h)] + O(h^2)$$

An important use of second derivatives is in computing Hessian matrices. Given some function $f : \mathbb{R}^n \mapsto \mathbb{R}$, the Hessian is the $n \times n$ matrix of second partial derivatives, the ijth element of which is $\partial^2 f(x)/\partial x_i \partial x_j$. We consider only centered, evenly spaced approximations, which can be obtained as a weighted sum of the function values evaluated at the point x and eight points surrounding it obtained by adding or subtracting $h_i u_i$ and/or $h_j u_j$, where the h terms are scalar step increments and the u terms are n-vectors of zeros but with the ith element equal to 1 (the ith column of I_n).

To facilitate notation, let subscripts indicate a partial derivative of f evaluated at x, for example, $f_i = \partial f(x)/\partial x_i$, $f_{iij} = \partial^3 f(x)/\partial x_i^2 \partial x_j$, and so on, and let superscripts on f denote the function evaluated at one of the nine points of interest, so $f^{++} = f(x + h_i u_i + h_j u_j)$, $f^{00} = f(x)$, $f^{0-} = f(x - h_j u_j)$, and so on (see Figure 5.2).

With this notation, we can write Taylor expansions up to the third order for each of the f^{ij}. For example,

$$f^{+0} = f^{00} + h_i f_i + \frac{h_i^2}{2} f_{ii} + \frac{h_i^3}{6} f_{iii} + O(h^4)$$

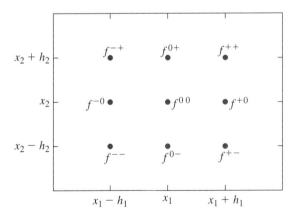

Figure 5.2
Evaluation Points for Finite Difference Hessians

and

$$f^{++} = f^{00} + h_i f_i + h_j f_j + \frac{h_i^2}{2} f_{ii} + h_i h_j f_{ij} \frac{h_j^2}{2} f_{jj}$$
$$+ \frac{h_i^3}{6} f_{iii} + \frac{h_i^2 h_j}{2} f_{iij} + \frac{h_i h_j^2}{2} f_{ijj} + \frac{h_j^3}{6} f_{jjj} + O(h^4)$$

With simple but tedious computations, it can be shown that the only $O(h^2)$ approximations to f_{ii} composed of these nine points are convex combinations of the usual centered approximation

$$f_{ii} \approx \frac{1}{h_i^2}(f^{+0} - 2f^{00} + f^{-0})$$

and an alternative

$$f_{ii} \approx \frac{1}{2h_i^2}(f^{++} - 2f^{0+} + f^{-+} + f^{-+} - 2f^{-0} + f^{--})$$

More importantly, for computing cross partials, the only $O(h^2)$ approximations to f_{ij} are convex combinations of

$$f_{ij} \approx \frac{1}{2h_i h_j}(f^{0+} + f^{-0} + f^{0-} + f^{+0} - f^{+-} - f^{-+} - 2f^{00})$$

or

$$f_{ij} \approx \frac{1}{2h_i h_j}(2f^{00} + f^{++} + f^{--} - f^{0+} - f^{-0} - f^{0-} - f^{+0})$$

The obvious combination of taking the mean of the two results in

$$f_{ij} \approx \frac{1}{4h_i h_j}(f^{++} + f^{--} - f^{-+} - f^{+-})$$

This approach requires less computation than the other two forms since only a single cross partial is evaluated. Using either of the other two schemes, however, along with the usual centered approximation for the diagonal terms of the Hessian, enables one to compute the entire Hessian with second-order accuracy in $1 + n + n^2$ function evaluations.

There are typically two situations in which numerical approximations of derivatives are needed. The first arises when one can compute the function at any value of x but it is difficult to derive a closed-form expression for the derivatives. In this case one is free to choose the evaluation points (x, $x + h$, $x + 2h$, etc.). The other situation is one

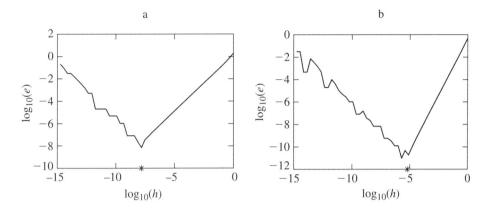

Figure 5.3
Errors in One-Sided (a) and Two-Sided (b) Numerical Derivatives

in which the value of f is known only at a fixed set of points x_1, x_2, and so on. When a function can be evaluated at any point, the choice of evaluation points must be considered. As with convergence criteria, there is no one rule that always works. On the one hand, if h is made too small, round-off error can make the results meaningless. On the other hand, too large an h provides a poor approximation, even if exact arithmetic is used.

This difficulty is illustrated in Figure 5.3a, which displays the errors in approximating the derivative of $\exp(x)$ at $x = 1$ as a function of h. The approximation improves as h is reduced to the point where it is approximately equal to $\sqrt{\epsilon}$ (the square root of the machine precision), shown as a star on the horizontal axis. Further reductions in h actually worsen the approximation because of the inaccuracies due to inexact computer arithmetic. This graph gives credence to the rule of thumb that, for one-sided approximations, h should be chosen to be of size $\sqrt{\epsilon}$ relative to $|x|$. When x is small, however, it is better not to let h get too small. We suggest the rule of thumb of setting

$$h = \max(|x|, 1)\sqrt{\epsilon}$$

Figure 5.3b shows an analogous plot for two-sided approximations. It is evident that the error is minimized at a much higher value of h, at approximately $\sqrt[3]{\epsilon}$. A good rule of thumb is to set

$$h = \max(|x|, 1)\sqrt[3]{\epsilon}$$

when using two-sided approximations.

There is a further, and more subtle, problem. If $x + h$ cannot be represented exactly but is instead equal to $x + h + e$, then we are actually using the approximation

$$\frac{f(x+h+e) - f(x+h)}{e}\frac{e}{h} + \frac{f(x+h) - f(x)}{h} \approx f'(x+h)\frac{e}{h} + f'(x)$$

$$\approx \left(1 + \frac{e}{h}\right) f'(x)$$

Even if the rounding error e is on the order of machine precision ϵ and h on the order of $\sqrt{\epsilon}$, we have introduced an error on the order of $\sqrt{\epsilon}$ into the calculation. It is easy to deal with this problem, however. Letting xh represent $x + h$, define h in the following way:

```
h=sqrt(eps)*max(abs(x),1); xh=x+h; h=xh-x;
```

for one-sided approximations and

```
h=eps.^(1/3)*max(abs(x),1); xh1=x+h; xh0=x-h; hh=xh1-xh0;
```

for two-sided approximations (hh represents $2h$).

The following function computes two-sided finite difference approximations for the Jacobian of an arbitrary function. For a real-valued function, $f : \mathbb{R}^n \mapsto \mathbb{R}^m$, the output is an $m \times n$ matrix:

```
function fjac = fdjac(f,x);
h = eps^(1/3)*max(abs(x),1);
xh1 = x+h; xh0 = x-h; hh = xh1-xh0;
for j = 1:length(x);
   xx = x;
   xx(j) = xh1(j); f1 = feval(f,xx);
   xx(j) = xh0(j); f0 = feval(f,xx);
   fjac(:,j) = (f1-f0)/hh(j);
end
```

For second derivatives, the choice of h encounters the same difficulties as with first derivatives, and similar reasoning leads to the rule of thumb that

$$h = \max(|x|, 1)\sqrt[4]{\epsilon}$$

A procedure for computing finite difference Hessians, fdhess, is provided in the CompEcon Toolbox. It is analogous to fdjac, with calling syntax

```
fhess = fdhess(f,x);
```

5.7   Initial Value Problems

Differential equations pose the problem of inferring a function given information about its derivatives and additional "boundary" conditions. Differential equations may be characterized as either ordinary differential equations (ODEs), whose solutions are functions of a single argument, or partial differential equations (PDEs), whose solutions are functions of multiple arguments. Both ODEs and PDEs may be solved numerically using finite difference methods.

From a numerical point of view, the distinction between ODEs and PDEs is less important than the distinction between initial value problems (IVPs), which can be solved in a recursive or evolutionary fashion, and boundary value problems (BVPs), which require the entire solution to be computed simultaneously because the solution at one point (in time and/or space) depends on the solution everywhere else. For ODEs, the solution of an IVP is known at some point and the solution near this point can then be (approximately) determined. This determination, in turn, allows the solution at still other points to be approximated and so forth. BVPs, however, require simultaneous solution of the differential equation and the boundary conditions. We take up the solution of IVPs in this section, but defer discussion of BVPs until the next chapter (section 6.9).

The most common initial value problem is to find a function $x : [0, T] \mapsto \mathbb{R}^d$ whose initial value $x(0)$ is known and which, over its domain, satisfies the differential equation

$$x'(t) = f\big(t, x(t)\big)$$

Here, x is a function of a scalar t (often referring to time in economic applications), and $f : [0, T] \times \mathbb{R}^d \mapsto \mathbb{R}^d$ is a given function. Many problems in economics are time-autonomous, in which case the differential equation takes the form

$$x'(t) = f\big(x(t)\big)$$

Although the differential equation contains no derivatives of order higher than one, the equation is more general than it might at first appear, because higher-order derivatives can always be eliminated by expanding the number of variables. For example, consider the second-order differential equation

$$y''(t) = f\big(t, y(t), y'(t)\big)$$

By defining z to be the first derivative of x, so that $z' = x''$, the differential equation may be written in first-order form in (y, z):

$$y' = z$$

$$z' = f(t, y, z)$$

Initial value problems can be solved using a recursive procedure. First, the direction of motion is calculated based on the current position of the system, and a small step is taken in that direction. This step is then repeated as many times as is desired. The inputs needed for these methods are the function defining the system f, an initial value x_0, the time step size h, and the number of steps to take n (or, equivalently, the stopping point T).

The most simple form of such a procedure is Euler's method. Define time nodes $t_i = ih$, $i = 0, \ldots, n$. The solution values x_i at the time nodes are defined iteratively using

$$x_{i+1} = x_i + hf(t_i, x_i)$$

with the procedure beginning at the prescribed $x_0 = x(0)$. This method is fine for rough approximations, especially if the time step is small enough. Higher-order approximations can yield better results, however.

Among the numerous refinements on the Euler method, the most commonly used are the Runge-Kutta methods. Runge-Kutta methods are a class of methods characterized by an order of approximation and by selection of certain key parameters. The derivation of these methods is fairly tedious for high-order methods but is easily demonstrated for a second-order model.

Runge-Kutta methods are based on Taylor approximations at a given starting point t.

$$x(t + h) = x + hf + \frac{h^2}{2}(f_t + f_x f) + O(h^3)$$

where $x = x(t)$, $f = f(t, x)$, and f_t and f_x are the partial derivatives of f evaluated at (t, x). This equation could be used directly, but doing so would require obtaining explicit expressions for the partial derivatives f_t and f_x. A method that relies only on function evaluations is obtained by noting that

$$f(t + \lambda h, x + \lambda hf) = f + \lambda h(f_t + f_x f) + O(h^2)$$

Substituting this into the previous expression yields

$$x(t + h) = x + h\left[\left(1 - \frac{1}{2\lambda}\right)f(t, x) + \frac{1}{2\lambda}f(t + \lambda h, x + \lambda hf)\right] + O(h^3) \qquad (5.2)$$

Two simple choices for λ are $\frac{1}{2}$ and 1, leading to the following second-order Runge-Kutta methods:

$$x(t + h) \approx x + hf\left(t + \frac{h}{2}, x + \frac{h}{2}f\right)$$

and

$$x(t + h) \approx x + \frac{h}{2}[f(t, x) + f(t + h, x + hf)]$$

It can be shown that an optimal choice, in the sense of minimizing the absolute value of the h^3 term in the truncation error, is to set $\lambda = 2/3$:

$$x(t + h) \approx x + \frac{h}{4}\left[f(t, x) + 3f\left(t + \frac{2h}{3}, x + \frac{2h}{3}f\right)\right]$$

(We leave this demonstration as an exercise.)

The most widely used Runge-Kutta method is the classical fourth-order method. A derivation of this approach is tedious, but the algorithm is straightforward:

$$x(t + h) = x + [F_1 + 2(F_2 + F_3) + F_4]/6$$

where

$$F_1 = hf(t, x)$$

$$F_2 = hf\left(t + \tfrac{1}{2}h, x + \tfrac{1}{2}F_1\right)$$

$$F_3 = hf\left(t + \tfrac{1}{2}h, x + \tfrac{1}{2}F_2\right)$$

$$F_4 = hf\left(t + h, x + F_3\right)$$

It can be shown that the truncation error in any order-k Runge-Kutta method is $O(h^{k+1})$, that second-order Runge-Kutta methods can be related to the trapezoid rule for numerical integration, and that the fourth-order Runge-Kutta methods can be related to Simpson's rule. (We leave this as an exercise.)

The CompEcon routine `rk4` implements the classical fourth-order Runge-Kutta approach to compute an approximate solution $x(T)$ to $x' = f(t, x)$, s.t. $x(T(1)) = x0$, where T is a vector of values. The calling syntax is

```
[T,x]=rk4(f,T,x0,[],additional parameters)
```

The inputs are the name of a problem file that returns the function f, the vector of time values T, and the initial conditions, x_0. The fourth input is an empty matrix to make the calling syntax for `rk4` compatible with the MATLAB's ODE solvers. The two outputs are the vector of time values (for compatibility with MATLAB's ODE solvers) and the solution values.

Unlike the suite of ODE solvers provided by MATLAB, rk4 is designed to be able to compute solutions for multiple initial values. If $x0$ is $d \times k$ and there are n time values in T, rk4 will return x as an $n \times d \times k$ array. Avoiding a loop over multiple starting points results in much faster execution when a large set of trajectories are computed. To take advantage of this feature, however, the function passed to rk4 that defines the differential equation must be able to return a $d \times k$ matrix when its second input argument is a $d \times k$ matrix (see the example that follows for an illustration of how this procedure is carried out).

There are numerous other approaches and refinements to solving initial value problems. Briefly, these include so-called multistep algorithms that utilize information from previous steps to determine the current step direction (Runge-Kutta methods are single-step methods). Also, any method can adapt the step size to the current behavior of the system by monitoring the truncation error, reducing (increasing) the step size if this error is unacceptably large (small). Adaptive schemes are important if one requires a given level of accuracy.[1]

As an example of an initial value problem, consider the following model of a commercial fishery:

$p = \alpha - \beta K y$ Inverse demand for fish

$\pi = py - cy^2/(2S) - f$ Profit function of representative fishing firm

$S' = (a - bS)S - Ky$ Fish population dynamics

$K' = \delta\pi$ Entry/exit from industry

where p is the price of fish, K is the size of the industry, y is the catch rate of the representative firm, π is the profit of the representative firm, and S is the fish population (α, β, c, f, a, b, and δ are parameters).

The behavior of this model can be analyzed by first determining the short-run (instantaneous) equilibrium given the current size of the fish stock and the size of the fishing industry. This equilibrium is determined by the demand for fish and a fishing firm profit function, which together determine the short-run equilibrium catch rate and firm profit level. The industry is competitive in the sense that catch rates are chosen by setting marginal cost equal to price:

$p = cy/S$

a relationship that can be interpreted as the short-run inverse supply function per unit of capital. The short-run (market-clearing) equilibrium is determined by equating demand and

---

1. The MATLAB functions ODE23 and ODE45 are implemented in this way, with ODE45 a fourth-order method.

supply:

$$\alpha - \beta K y = cy/S$$

yielding a short-run equilibrium catch rate:

$$y = \alpha S/(c + \beta S K)$$

price

$$p = \alpha c/(c + \beta S K)$$

and profit function

$$\pi = \frac{c\alpha^2 S}{2(c + \beta S K)^2} - f$$

All these relationships are functions of the industry size and the stock of fish. The model's dynamic behavior is governed by a growth rate for the fish stock and a rate of entry into the fishing industry. The former depends on the biological growth of the fish population and on the current catch rate, whereas the later depends on the current profitability of fishing. The capital stock adjustment process is myopic, as it depends only on current profitability and not on expected future profitability. The result is a two-dimensional IVP:

$$S' = (a - bS)S - \frac{\alpha S K}{c + \beta S K}$$

$$K' = \delta \left[\frac{c\alpha^2 S}{2(c + \beta S K)^2} - f \right]$$

which can be solved for any initial fish stock (S) and industry size (K).

To use the `rk4` solver, a function returning the time derivatives for the system must be supplied. (We normalize by setting $a = b = c = \alpha = 1$.)

```
function dx=fdif03(t,x,flag,beta,f,delta);
s=x(1,:);
k=x(2,:);
temp=1+beta*s.*k;
ds=(1-s).*s-s.*k./temp;
dk=delta*(s./(2*temp.^2)-f);
dx=[ds;dk];
```

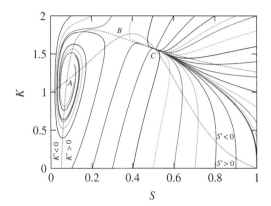

Figure 5.4
Phase Diagram for Commercial Fishery Example

As previously mentioned, the flag variable is not used but is supplied to make `rk4` compatible with the ODE solvers provided by MATLAB. The solver itself is called using

```
[t,x]=rk4('fdif03',t,x0,[],beta,f,delta);
```

where `x0` is a matrix of starting values.

A useful device for summarizing the behavior of a dynamic system is the phase diagram, which shows the movement of the system for selected starting values; these curves are known as the trajectories. A phase diagram for the fishing model is exhibited in Figure 5.4 for parameter values $\beta = 2.75$, $f = 0.06$, and $\delta = 20$. The zero-isoclines (the points in the state space for which one of the variables' time rate of change is zero) are shown as dashed lines. In the phase diagram in Figure 5.4, the dashed lines represent the zero-isoclines, and the solid lines the trajectories.

There are three long-run equilibria in this system; these are the points where the zero-isoclines cross. Two of the equilibria are locally stable (points A and C), and one is a saddle point (point B). The state space is divided into two regions of attraction, one in which the system moves toward point A and the other toward point C. The dividing line between these regions consists of points that move the system toward point B. Also note that point A exhibits cyclic convergence.

Exercises

5.1. Demand for a commodity is given by $q = 2p^{-0.5}$. The price of a good falls from 4 to 1. Compute the change in consumer surplus

a. analytically using Calculus.

b. numerically using an 11-node trapezoid rule.

c. numerically using an 11-node Simpson rule.

d. numerically using an 11-node Gauss-Legendre rule.

e. numerically using an 11-node equidistributed sequence rule.

5.2. Write a program that solves numerically the following expression for α:

$$\alpha \int_0^\infty \exp(\alpha\lambda - \lambda^2/2)\, d\lambda = 1$$

and demonstrate that the solution (to four significant digits) is $\alpha = 0.5061$.

5.3. Using Monte Carlo and Neiderreiter quasi–Monte Carlo integration, estimate the expectation of $f(\tilde{X}) = \tilde{X}^2$ where $\tilde{X}$ is exponentially distributed with cumulative distribution function (CDF) $F(x) = 1 - \exp(-x)$ for $x \geq 0$. Compute estimates using 1,000, 10,000, and 100,000 nodes and compare.

5.4. A government stabilizes the supply of a commodity at $S = 2$ but allows the price to be determined by the market. Domestic and export demand for the commodity are given by

$$D = \tilde{\theta}_1 P^{-1.0}$$

$$X = \tilde{\theta}_2 P^{-0.5}$$

where $\log\tilde{\theta}_1$ and $\log\tilde{\theta}_2$ are normally distributed with means 0, variances 0.02 and 0.01, respectively, and covariance 0.01.

a. Compute the expected price Ep and the ex ante variance of price $\text{Var}\, p$ using 100-node Gaussian discretization for the demand shocks.

b. Compute the expected price Ep and the ex ante variance of price $\text{Var}\, p$ using a 1,000-replication Monte Carlo integration scheme.

5.5. Consider a market for an agricultural commodity in which farmers receive a government payment $\bar{p} - p$ per unit of output whenever the market price p drops below an announced target price $\bar{p}$. In this market, producers base their acreage-planting decisions on their expectation of the effective producer price $f = \max(p, \bar{p})$; specifically, acreage planted a is given by

$$a = 1 + (Ef)^{0.5}$$

Production q is acreage planted a times a random yield $\tilde{y}$, unknown at planting time:

$$q = a\tilde{y}$$

and quantity demanded at harvest is given by

$$q = p^{-0.2} + p^{-0.5}$$

Conditional on information known at planting time, log y is normally distributed with mean 0 and variance 0.03. For $\bar{p} = 0$, $\bar{p} = 1$, and $\bar{p} = 2$, compute

a. the expected subsidy $E[q(f - p)]$.

b. the ex ante expected producer price Ef.

c. the ex ante variance of producer price Var f.

d. the ex ante expected producer revenue Efq.

e. the ex ante variance of producer revenue Var fq.

5.6. A standard biological model for predator-prey interactions, known as the Lokta-Volterra model, can be written

$$x' = \alpha x - xy$$

$$y' = xy - y$$

where x is the population of a prey species and y is the population of a predator species. To make sense, we restrict attention to x, $y > 0$ and $\alpha > 0$. (The model is scaled to eliminate excess parameters.) Although admittedly a simple model, it captures some of the essential features of the relationship. The prey population grows at rate α when there are no predators present. The greater the number of predators, the more slowly the prey population grows, and it declines when the predator population exceeds α. The predator population, however, declines if it grows too large unless prey is plentiful. Determine the equilibria (there are two) and draw the phase diagram. (Hint: This model exhibits cycles.)

5.7. A well-known model for pricing bonds and futures, the affine diffusion model, requires solving a system of quadratic Riccati differential equations of the form

$$\frac{dX}{dt} = A^\top X + \tfrac{1}{2}B^\top \mathrm{diag}(C^\top X)C^\top X - g$$

$$\frac{dx}{dt} = a^\top X + \tfrac{1}{2}b^\top \mathrm{diag}(C^\top X)C^\top X - g_0$$

where $X(t) : \mathbb{R}_+ \mapsto \mathbb{R}^n$ and $x(t) : \mathbb{R}_+ \mapsto \mathbb{R}$. The problem parameters a, b, and g are $n \times 1$; A, B, and C are $n \times n$; and g_0 is a scalar. In addition, the functions must satisfy boundary conditions of the form $X(0) = X_0$ and $x(0) = x_0$.

a. Write a program to solve this class of problems with the following input/output syntax:

```
[X,x]=affsolve(t,a,A,b,B,C,g,g0,X0,x0)
```

The solution should be computed at the time values specified by t. If there are m time values, the outputs should be $m \times n$ and $m \times 1$. The program may use $rk4$ or one of MATLAB's ODE solvers. You will need to write an auxiliary function to pass to the solver. Also note that $\text{diag}(z)z$ can be written in MATLAB as $z.*z$.

   Plot your solution functions over the interval $t \in [0, 30]$ for the following parameter values:

$$a = \begin{bmatrix} 0.0217 \\ 0.0124 \\ 0.00548 \end{bmatrix} \quad A = \begin{bmatrix} -17.4 & 17.4 & -9.309 \\ 0 & -0.226 & 0.879 \\ 0 & 0 & -0.362 \end{bmatrix}$$

$$b = \begin{bmatrix} 0 \\ .0002 \\ 0 \end{bmatrix} \quad B = \begin{bmatrix} 0 & 0 & 1 \\ 0 & 0 & 0 \\ 0 & 0 & .00782 \end{bmatrix}$$

$$g = \begin{bmatrix} 1 \\ 0 \\ 0 \end{bmatrix} \quad C = \begin{bmatrix} 1 & -3.42 & 4.27 \\ -.0943 & 1 & 0 \\ 0 & 0 & 1 \end{bmatrix}$$

with $g_0 = x_0 = 0$ and $X_0 = 0$.

b. When the eigenvalues of A are all negative (or have negative real parts when complex), X has a long-run stationary point $X(\infty)$. Write a fixed-point algorithm to compute the long-run stationary value of X, noting that it satisfies $dX/dt = 0$, testing it with the parameter values given. You should find that

$$X(\infty) = \begin{bmatrix} -0.0575 \\ -4.4248 \\ -8.2989 \end{bmatrix}$$

Also write a a stand-alone algorithm implementing Newton's method for this problem (it should not call other functions like $newton$ or $fjac$). To calculate the relevant Jacobian, it helps to note that

$$\frac{dAz}{dz} = A$$

and

$$\frac{d\,\text{diag}(z)z}{dz} = 2\,\text{diag}(z)$$

5.8. Show that the absolute value of the $O(h^3)$ truncation error in the second-order Runge-Kutta formula (5.2):

$$x(t+h) = x + h\left[\left(1 - \frac{1}{2\lambda}\right)f + \frac{1}{2\lambda}f(t + \lambda h, x + \lambda h f)\right] + O(h^3)$$

is minimized by setting $\lambda = 2/3$. (Hint: expand to the fourth order and minimize the $O(h^3)$ term.)

Bibliographic Notes

Treatments of numerical integration are contained in most general numerical analysis texts. Press et al. (1992) contains a excellent treatment of Gaussian quadrature techniques and provides fully functioning code for computing the Gaussian quadrature nodes and weights for several standard weight functions. Our discussion of quasi–Monte Carlo techniques largely follows that of Judd (1998).

A detailed treatment of the issues in computing finite-difference approximations to derivatives is contained in Gill, Murray, and Wright (1981, especially section 8.6).

The subject of solving initial value problems is one the most studied in numerical analysis. See discussions, for example, in Atkinson (1989), Press et al. (1992), and Golub and Ortega (1992). MATLAB has a whole suite of ODE solvers, of which ODE45 and ODE15s are good for most problems. ODE15s is useful for stiff problems and can also handle the slightly more general problem:

$$M(t)x'(t) = f(t, x(t))$$

which includes M, the so-called mass matrix. We will encounter (potentially) stiff problems with mass matrices in section 11.1.2. The commercial fishery example was developed by Smith (1969).

6 Function Approximation

Two types of function approximation problems arise often in computational economic applications. In the *interpolation* problem, one must approximate an analytically intractable real-valued function f with a computationally tractable function $\hat{f}$, given limited information about f. Interpolation methods were originally developed to approximate the value of mathematical and statistical functions from published tables of values. In most modern computational economic applications, however, the analyst is free to choose the data to obtain about the function to be approximated. Modern interpolation theory and practice are concerned with ways to optimally extract data from a function and with computationally efficient methods for constructing and working with its approximant.

In the *functional equation* problem, one must find a function f that satisfies

$$Tf = 0$$

where T is an operator that maps a vector space of functions into itself. In the equivalent *functional fixed-point* problem, one must find a function f such that

$$f = Tf$$

Functional equations are common in dynamic economic analysis. For example, the Bellman equation that characterizes the solution of an infinite horizon dynamic optimization model is a functional fixed-point equation. The Euler equation and the differential equations arising in asset pricing models are also functional equations.

Functional equations are difficult to solve because the unknown is not simply a vector in $\mathbb{R}^n$, but an entire function f whose domain contains an infinite number of points. Functional equations, moreover, typically impose an infinite number of conditions on the solution f. Except in very few special cases, functional equations lack explicit closed-form solutions and thus cannot be solved exactly. One must therefore settle for an approximate solution that satisfies the functional equation closely. In many cases, one can compute accurate approximate solutions to functional equations using techniques that are natural extensions of interpolation methods.

In this chapter we discuss methods for approximating functions and focus on the two most generally practical techniques: Chebychev polynomial and polynomial spline approximation. Univariate function interpolation methods are developed in detail and then generalized to multivariate function interpolation methods through the use of tensor product principles. In section 6.8 we introduce the collocation method, a natural generalization of interpolation methods that may be used to solve a variety of functional equations.

6.1 Interpolation Principles

Interpolation involves approximating an analytically intractable real-valued function f with a computationally tractable function $\hat{f}$. The first step in designing an interpolation scheme is choosing a family of functions from which the approximant $\hat{f}$ will be drawn. For practical reasons, we confine ourselves to approximants that can be written as a linear combination of a set of n known linearly independent *basis functions* $\phi_1, \phi_2, \ldots, \phi_n$,

$$\hat{f}(x) = \sum_{j=1}^{n} c_j \phi_j(x)$$

whose *basis coefficients* $c_1, c_2, \ldots, c_n$ are to be determined.[1] Polynomials of increasing order are often used as basis functions, although other types of basis functions, most notably spline functions, which are discussed later in this chapter, are also common. The number n of independent basis functions is called the *degree of interpolation*.

The second step in designing an interpolation scheme is to specify the properties of the original function f that one wishes the approximant $\hat{f}$ to replicate. Because there are n undetermined coefficients, n conditions are required to fix the approximant. The simplest and most common conditions imposed are that the approximant *interpolate* or match the value of the original function at selected *interpolation nodes* $x_1, x_2, \ldots, x_n$.

Given n interpolation nodes and n basis functions, computing the basis coefficients reduces to solving a linear equation. Specifically, one fixes the n undetermined coefficients $c_1, c_2, \ldots, c_n$ of the approximant $\hat{f}$ by solving the *interpolation conditions*

$$\sum_{j=1}^{n} c_j \phi_j(x_i) = f(x_i), \quad \forall i = 1, 2, \ldots, n$$

Using matrix notation, the interpolation conditions may be written as the matrix linear *interpolation equation* whose unknown is the vector of basis coefficients c:

$$\Phi c = y$$

Here, $y_i = f(x_i)$ is the function value at the ith interpolation node, and

$$\Phi_{ij} = \phi_j(x_i)$$

---

1. Approximations that are nonlinear in basis function are possible (e.g., rational approximations) but are more difficult to work with and hence are not often used in practical applications except in approximating special functions such as cumulative distribution functions.

the typical element of the *interpolation matrix* Φ, is the jth basis function evaluated at the ith interpolation node. In theory, an interpolation scheme is well defined if the interpolation nodes and basis functions are chosen such that the interpolation matrix is nonsingular.

Interpolation may be viewed as a special case of the curve fitting problem. The curve fitting problem arises when there are fewer basis functions than function evaluation nodes. In this case it will not generally be possible to satisfy the interpolation conditions exactly at every node. One can, however, construct a reasonable approximant by minimizing the sum of squared errors

$$e_i = f(x_i) - \sum_{j=1}^{n} c_j \phi_j(x_i)$$

This strategy leads to the well-known least-squares approximation

$$c = (\Phi'\Phi)^{-1}\Phi'y$$

which is equivalent to the interpolation equation when the number of basis functions and nodes are exactly the same and Φ is invertible.

Interpolation schemes are not limited to using only function value information. In some applications, one may wish to interpolate both function values and derivatives at specified points. Suppose, for example, that one wishes to construct an approximant $\hat{f}$ that replicates the function's values at nodes $x_1, x_2, \ldots, x_{n_1}$ and its first derivatives at nodes $x_1', x_2', \ldots, x_{n_2}'$. An approximant that satisfies these conditions may be constructed by selecting $n = n_1 + n_2$ basis functions and fixing the basis coefficients $c_1, c_2, \ldots, c_n$ of the approximant by solving the interpolation equation

$$\sum_{j=1}^{n} c_j \phi_j(x_i) = f(x_i), \quad \forall i = 1, \ldots, n_1$$

$$\sum_{j=1}^{n} c_j \phi_j'(x_i') = f'(x_i'), \quad \forall i = 1, \ldots, n_2$$

for the undetermined coefficients c_j. This principle applies to any combination of function values, derivatives, or even antiderivatives at selected points. All that is required is that the associated interpolation matrix be nonsingular.

In developing an interpolation scheme, the analyst should choose interpolation nodes and basis functions that satisfy certain criteria. First, the approximant should be capable of producing an accurate approximation of the original function f. In particular, the interpolation scheme should allow the analyst to achieve, at least in theory, an arbitrarily accurate approximation by increasing the number of basis functions and nodes. Second, it should be possible to compute the basis coefficients quickly and accurately. In particular, the interpolation equation should be well conditioned and easy to solve—diagonal, near diagonal, or orthogonal interpolation matrices are best. Third, the approximant should be easy to work with. In particular, the basis functions should be easy and relatively costless to evaluate, differentiate, and integrate.

Interpolation schemes may be classified as either *spectral* methods or *finite element* methods. A spectral method uses basis functions that are nonzero over the entire domain of the function being approximated, except possibly at a finite number of points. In contrast, a finite element method uses basis functions that are nonzero over subintervals of the approximation domain. Polynomial interpolation, which uses polynomials of increasing degree as basis functions, is the most common spectral method. Spline interpolation, which uses basis functions that are polynomials of low degree over subintervals of the approximation domain, is the most common finite element method. We examine both these methods in greater detail in the following sections.

6.2 Polynomial Interpolation

According to the Weierstrass Theorem, any continuous real-valued function f defined on a bounded interval $[a, b]$ of the real line can be approximated to any degree of accuracy using a polynomial. More specifically, for any $\epsilon > 0$, there exists a polynomial p such that

$$||f - p||_\infty \equiv \sup_{x \in [a,b]} |f(x) - p(x)| < \epsilon$$

The Weierstrass Theorem provides strong motivation for using polynomials to approximate continuous functions. The theorem, however, is not very useful. It does not give any guidance on how to find a good polynomial approximant or even tell us what order polynomial is required to achieve a required level of accuracy.

One apparently reasonable way to construct an nth-degree polynomial approximant for a function f on the interval $[a, b]$ is to form the unique $(n - 1)$th-order polynomial that interpolates f at the n evenly spaced interpolation nodes

$$x_i = a + \frac{i - 1}{n - 1}(b - a), \quad \forall i = 1, 2, \dots, n$$

In practice, however, polynomial interpolation at evenly spaced nodes often does not produce an accurate approximant. In fact, there are smooth functions for which polynomial approximants with evenly spaced nodes rapidly deteriorate, rather than improve, as the degree of approximation n rises. The classic example is Runge's function $f(x) = 1/(1 + 25x^2)$.

Table 6.1 gives the base 10 logarithm of the supremum norm approximation error associated with uniform node polynomial interpolation of Runge's function. As can be seen in the table, the approximation error rises rapidly, rather than falling, with the number of nodes.

Numerical analysis theory and empirical experience both suggest that polynomial approximants over a bounded interval $[a, b]$ should be constructed by interpolating the underlying function at the so-called *Chebychev nodes:*

$$x_i = \frac{a+b}{2} + \frac{b-a}{2} \cos\left(\frac{n-i+0.5}{n}\pi\right), \quad \forall i = 1, 2, \ldots, n$$

As illustrated in Figure 6.1 for $n = 9$, the Chebychev nodes are not evenly spaced. They are more closely spaced near the endpoints of the interpolation interval and less so near the center.

Chebychev-node polynomial interpolants possess some strong theoretical properties. According to Rivlin's Theorem, Chebychev-node polynomial interpolants are very nearly optimal polynomial approximants. Specifically, the approximation error associated with the

Table 6.1
Uniform Node Polynomial Interpolation Error
for Runge's Function on $[-5, 5]$

Nodes	$\log_{10} \|f - \hat{f}\|$
10	−0.06
20	1.44
30	4.06
40	6.72
50	9.39

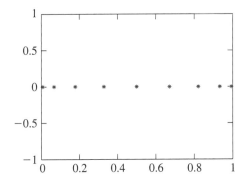

Figure 6.1
Chebychev Nodes on $[0, 1]$

nth-degree Chebychev-node polynomial interpolant cannot be larger than $2\pi \log(n) + 2$ times the lowest error attainable with any other polynomial approximant of the same order. For $n = 100$, this factor is approximately 30, which is very small when one considers that other polynomial interpolation schemes typically produce approximants with errors that are orders of magnitude, that is, powers of 10, larger than the optimum. In practice, the accuracy afforded by the Chebychev-node polynomial interpolant is often much better than indicated by Rivlin's bound, especially if the function being approximated is smooth.

Another theorem, Jackson's Theorem, provides a more useful result. Specifically, if f is continuously differentiable, then the approximation error afforded by the nth-degree Chebychev-node polynomial interpolant p_n can be bounded above:

$$||f - p_n|| \leq \frac{6}{n}||f'||(b - a)[\log(n)/\pi + 1]$$

This error bound can often be accurately estimated in practice, giving the analyst a good indication of the accuracy afforded by the Chebychev-node polynomial interpolant. More importantly, however, the error bound goes to zero as n rises. Thus, in contrast to polynomial interpolation with evenly spaced nodes, one can achieve any desired degree of accuracy by interpolating the function at a sufficiently large number of Chebychev nodes.

To illustrate the difference between Chebychev-node and evenly-spaced-node polynomial interpolations, consider approximating the function $f(x) = \exp(-x)$ on the interval $[-5, 5]$. The approximation error associated with ten-node polynomial interpolants is illustrated in Figure 6.2. The Chebychev-node polynomial interpolant exhibits errors that oscillate fairly evenly throughout the interval of approximation, a common feature of

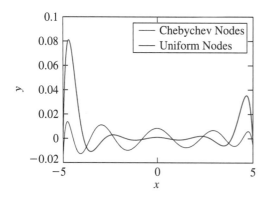

Figure 6.2
Approximation Error for $\exp(-x)$

Chebychev-node interpolants commonly referred to as the *equi-oscillation property*. The evenly-spaced-node polynomial interpolant, however, exhibits significant instability near the endpoints of the interval. The Chebychev-node polynomial interpolant avoids endpoint instabilities because the nodes are more heavily concentrated there.

The most intuitive basis for expressing polynomials, regardless of the interpolation nodes chosen, is the *monomial basis,* which consists of the simple power functions $1, x, x^2, x^3, \ldots$ pictured in Figure 6.3. The monomial basis produces an interpolation matrix Φ that is a so-called Vandermonde matrix:

$$\Phi = \begin{bmatrix} 1 & x_1 & \cdots & x_1^{n-2} & x_1^{n-1} \\ 1 & x_2 & \cdots & x_2^{n-2} & x_2^{n-1} \\ \vdots & \vdots & \ddots & \vdots & \vdots \\ 1 & x_n & \cdots & x_n^{n-2} & x_n^{n-1} \end{bmatrix}$$

Vandermonde matrices are notoriously ill conditioned, and increasingly so as the degree of approximation n is increased. Thus efforts to compute the basis coefficients of the monomial basis polynomials often fail because of rounding error, and attempts to compute increasingly

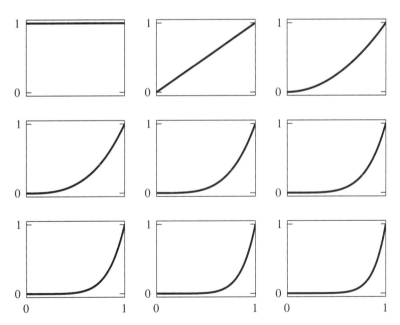

Figure 6.3
Monomial Basis Functions

more accurate approximations by raising the number of interpolation nodes are often futile.

Fortunately, alternatives to the standard monomial basis exist. In fact, any sequence of n polynomials having exact orders $0, 1, 2, \ldots, n - 1$ respectively can serve as a basis for all polynomials of order less than n. One such basis for the interval $[a, b]$ on the real line is the Chebychev polynomial basis. Defining $z = 2(x - a)/(b - a) - 1$, to normalize the domain to the interval $[-1, 1]$, the Chebychev polynomials are defined recursively as[2]

$$\phi_j(x) = T_{j-1}(z)$$

where

$$T_0(z) = 1$$
$$T_1(z) = z$$
$$T_2(z) = 2z^2 - 1$$
$$T_3(z) = 4z^3 - 3z$$
$$\vdots$$
$$T_j(z) = 2zT_{j-1}(z) - T_{j-2}(z)$$

The first nine Chebychev basis polynomials for the interval $x \in [0, 1]$ are displayed in Figure 6.4.

Chebychev polynomials are an excellent basis for constructing polynomials that interpolate function values at the Chebychev nodes. Chebychev basis polynomials in combination with Chebychev interpolation nodes yield an extremely well-conditioned interpolation equation that can be accurately and efficiently solved, even with high-degree approximants. The interpolation matrix Φ associated with the Chebychev interpolation has typical element

$$\Phi_{ij} = \cos((n - i + 0.5)(j - 1)\pi/n)$$

The Chebychev interpolation matrix is orthogonal

$$\Phi^\top \Phi = \text{diag}\{n, n/2, n/2, \ldots, n/2\}$$

and has a Euclidean norm condition number $\sqrt{2}$ regardless of the degree of interpolation, which is very near the absolute minimum of 1. This fact implies that the Chebychev basis coefficients can be computed quickly and accurately, regardless of the degree of interpolation.

---

2. The Chebychev polynomials also possess the alternate trigonometric definition $T_j(z) = \cos(\arccos(z)j)$.

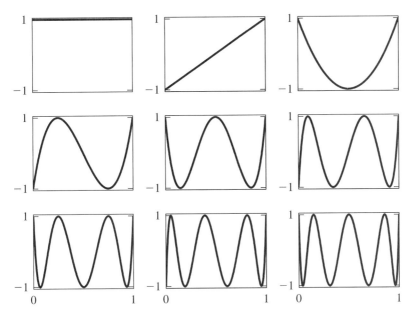

Figure 6.4
Chebychev Polynomial Basis Functions

6.3 Piecewise Polynomial Splines

Piecewise polynomial splines, or simply splines for short, constitute a rich, flexible class of functions that may be used instead of high-degree polynomials to approximate a real-valued function over a bounded interval. Generally, an order-k spline consists of a series of kth-order polynomial segments spliced together so as to preserve continuity of derivatives of order $k-1$ or less. The points at which the polynomial pieces are spliced together, $v_1 < v_2 < \cdots < v_p$, are called the *breakpoints* of the spline. By convention, the first and last breakpoints are the endpoints of the interval of approximation $[a, b]$.

A general order-k spline with p breakpoints may be characterized by $(p-1)(k+1)$ parameters, given that each of the $p-1$ polynomial segments is defined by its $k+1$ coefficients. By definition, however, a spline is required to be continuous and have continuous derivatives up to order $k-1$ at each of the $p-2$ interior breakpoints; these requirements impose $k(p-2)$ conditions. Thus an order-k spline with p breakpoints is actually characterized by $n = (k+1)(p-1) - k(p-2) = p+k-1$ free parameters. It should not be surprising that a general order-k spline with p breakpoints can be written as a linear combination of $n = p+k-1$ basis functions.

There are many ways to express basis functions for splines, but for applied numerical work the most useful way is to employ the so-called B-splines, or basic splines. B-splines for an order-k spline with breakpoint vector v can be computed using the recursive definition

$$B_j^{k,v}(x) = \frac{x - v_{j-k}}{v_j - v_{j-k}} B_{j-1}^{k-1,v}(x) + \frac{v_{j+1} - x}{v_{j+1} - v_{j+1-k}} B_j^{k-1,v}(x)$$

for $i = 1, \ldots, n$, with the recursion starting with

$$B_j^{0,v}(x) = \begin{cases} 1 & \text{if } v_j \le x < v_{j+1} \\ 0 & \text{otherwise} \end{cases}$$

This definition requires that we extend the breakpoint vector v for $j < 1$ and $j > p$

$$v_j = \begin{cases} a & \text{if } j \le 1 \\ b & \text{if } j \ge p \end{cases}$$

and at the endpoints set the terms

$$B_0^{k-1,v} = B_n^{k-1,v} = 0$$

Given a B-spline representation of a spline, the spline can easily be differentiated by computing simple differences, and it can be integrated by computing simple sums. Specifically,

$$\frac{dB_j^{k,v}(x)}{dx} = \frac{k}{v_j - v_{j-k}} B_{j-1}^{k-1,v}(x) - \frac{k}{v_{j+1} - v_{j+1-k}} B_j^{k-1,v}(x)$$

and

$$\int_a^x B_j^{k,v}(z)\, dz = \sum_{i=j}^n \frac{v_i - v_{i-k}}{k} B_{i+1}^{k+1,v}(x)$$

Although these formulas appear a bit complicated, their application in computer programs is relatively straightforward. First notice that the derivative of a B-spline of order k is a weighted sum of two order $k - 1$ B-splines. Thus the derivative of an order-k spline is an order $k - 1$ spline with the same breakpoints. Similarly, the integral of a B-spline can be represented as the sum of B-splines of order $k + 1$. Thus the antiderivative of an order-k spline is an order $k + 1$ spline with the same breakpoints. The family of splines, therefore, are closed under differentiation and integration.

Two classes of splines are often employed in practice. A first-order or *linear spline* is a series of line segments spliced together to form a continuous function. A third-order or *cubic spline* is a series of cubic polynomial segments spliced together to form a twice continuously differentiable function.

Linear splines are particularly easy to construct and evaluate in practice, a fact that explains their widespread popularity. Linear splines use line segments to connect points on the graph of the function to be approximated. A linear spline with n evenly spaced breakpoints on the interval $[a, b]$ may be written as a linear combination of the basis functions

$$\phi_j(x) = \begin{cases} 1 - \dfrac{|x - v_j|}{h} & \text{if } |x - v_j| \leq h \\ 0 & \text{otherwise} \end{cases}$$

Here, $h = (b - a)/(n - 1)$ is the distance between breakpoints, and $v_j = a + (j - 1)h$, $j = 1, 2, \ldots, n$, are the breakpoints. The linear spline basis functions are popularly called the "hat" functions, for reasons that are clear from Figure 6.5, which illustrates linear spline basis functions on the unit interval with evenly spaced breakpoints. Each basis function is zero everywhere, except over a narrow support of width $2h$. Each basis function also achieves a maximum of 1 at the midpoint of its support.

One can fix the coefficients of an n-degree linear spline approximant for a function f by interpolating its values at any n points of its domain, provided that the resulting interpolation matrix is nonsingular. However, if the interpolation nodes $x_1, x_2, \ldots, x_n$ are chosen to

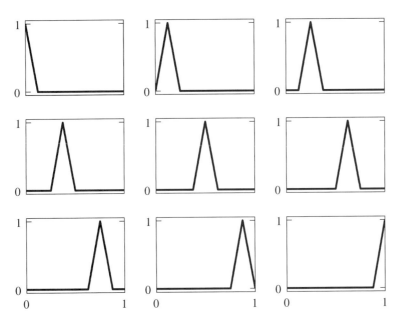

Figure 6.5
Linear Spline Basis Functions

coincide with the spline breakpoints $v_1, v_2, \ldots, v_n$, then computing the basis coefficients of the linear spline approximant becomes a trivial matter. In this case, $\phi_i(x_j)$ equals one if $i = j$, but it equals zero otherwise; that is, the interpolation matrix Φ is simply the identity matrix, and the interpolation equation reduces to the identity $c = y$, where y is the vector of function values at the interpolation nodes. The linear spline approximant of f when nodes and breakpoints coincide thus takes the form

$$\hat{f}(x) = \sum_{j=1}^{n} f(x_j)\phi_j(x)$$

When interpolation nodes and breakpoints coincide, no computations other than function evaluations are required to form the linear spline approximant. For this reason linear spline interpolation nodes in practice are always chosen to be the spline's breakpoints.

Evaluating a linear spline approximant and its derivative at an arbitrary point x is also straightforward. Since at most two basis functions are nonzero at any point, only two basis function evaluations are required. Specifically, if i is the greatest integer less than $1 + (x - a)/h$, then x lies in the interval $[v_i, v_{i+1}]$. Thus,

$$\hat{f}(x) = [(x - v_i)c_{i+1} + (v_{i+1} - x)c_i]/h$$

and

$$\hat{f}'(x) = (c_{i+1} - c_i)/h$$

Higher-order derivatives are zero, except at the breakpoints, where they are undefined.

Linear splines are attractive for their simplicity, but possess certain limitations that often make them a poor choice for computational economic applications. By construction, linear splines produce first derivatives that are discontinuous step functions and second derivatives that are zero almost everywhere. Linear spline approximants thus typically do a very poor job of approximating the first derivative of a nonlinear function and are incapable of approximating its second derivative. In some economic applications, however, the derivative represents a measure of marginality that is of as much interest to the analyst as the function itself. And the derivatives of the function approximant may be needed to compute its optimum using Newton-like methods.

Cubic splines offer an even better alternative to linear splines when a smooth approximant is required. Cubic splines retain much of the flexibility and simplicity of linear splines but possess continuous first and second derivatives, and thus they typically produce adequate approximations for both the function and its first and second derivatives.

The basis functions for an n-degree cubic spline with evenly spaced breakpoints on the interval $[a, b]$ are generated using the $n - 2$ breakpoints $v_j = a + h(j - 1)$, $j = 1, 2, \ldots,$

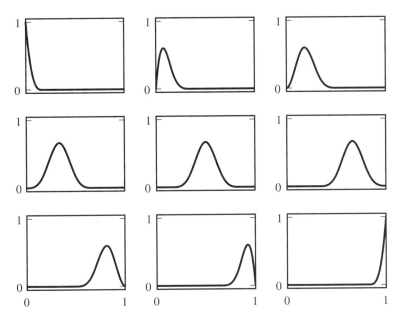

Figure 6.6
Cubic Spline Basis Functions

$n-2$, where $h = \frac{b-a}{n-3}$. Cubic spline basis functions generated with evenly spaced break-points are nonzero over a support of width $4h$. As such, at any point of $[a, b]$, at most four basis functions are nonzero. The basis functions for cubic splines of degree nine with equally spaced breakpoints on the unit interval are illustrated in Figure 6.6.

Although cubic spline breakpoints are often chosen to be evenly spaced, this need not be the case. Indeed, the ability to distribute breakpoints unevenly and to stack them on top of one another adds considerably to the flexibility of cubic splines, allowing them to accurately approximate a wide range of functions. In general, functions that exhibit wide variations in curvature are difficult to approximate numerically with polynomials of high degree. With splines, however, one can often finesse curvature difficulties by concentrating breakpoints in regions displaying the highest degree of curvature.

To illustrate the importance of breakpoint placement, consider the problem of form-ing a cubic spline approximant for Runge's function $f(x) = (1 + 25x^2)^{-1}$ on the interval $x \in [-5, 5]$. Figure 6.7 displays the errors associated with two cubic spline approxima-tions, one using 13 evenly spaced breakpoints, the other using 13 breakpoints (marked with "×"s) concentrated near zero, where Runge's function exhibits a high degree of curva-ture. As can be seen in the figure, the error associated with even breakpoints is orders of

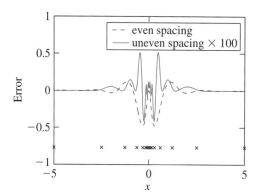

Figure 6.7
Approximation Errors for Runge's Function

magnitude greater than that obtained with unevenly spaced breakpoints. The figure clearly demonstrates the power of cubic spline approximations with good breakpoint placement.

The placement of the breakpoints can also be used to control the continuity of the spline approximant and its derivatives. By stacking breakpoints on top of one another, we can reduce the smoothness at the breakpoints. Normally, an order-k spline has continuous derivatives to order $k - 1$ at the breakpoints. By stacking q breakpoints, we can reduce this to $k - q$ continuous derivatives at this breakpoint. For example, a cubic spline with two equal breakpoints possesses a discontinuous second derivative at that point, and a cubic spline with three equal breakpoints possesses a discontinuous first derivative at that point; that is, it exhibits a kink there. Stacking breakpoints is a useful practice if the function is known a priori to exhibit a kink at a given point.

Regardless of the placement of breakpoints, splines have several important and useful properties. We have already commented on the limited support of the basis function. This limited support implies that spline interpolation matrices are sparse and for this reason can be stored and manipulated using sparse matrix methods. This property is extremely useful in high-dimensional problems for which a fully expanded interpolation matrix would strain any computer's memory. Another useful feature of splines is that their values are bounded, thereby reducing the likelihood that scaling effects will cause numerical difficulties. In general, the limited support and bounded values make spline interpolation matrices very well conditioned.

If the spline interpolation matrix must be reused, one must resist the temptation to form and store its inverse, particularly if the size of the matrix is large. Inversion destroys the sparsity structure. More specifically, the inverse of the interpolation matrix will be dense, even though the interpolation matrix is not. When n is large, solving the sparse $n \times n$ linear equation using sparse L-U factorization will generally be less costly than performing the matrix-vector multiplication required with the dense inverse interpolation matrix.

6.4   Piecewise Linear Basis Functions

Despite their simplicity, linear splines have many virtues. For problems in which the function being approximated is not smooth and may even exhibit discontinuities, linear splines can still provide reasonable approximations. Unfortunately, derivatives of linear splines are discontinuous, piecewise constant functions.

There is no reason, however, to limit ourselves to using the actual derivative of the approximating function if a more suitable alternative exists. If a function is approximated by a linear spline, a reasonable candidate for an approximation of its derivative is a linear spline constructed using finite-difference approximations (see section 5.6). Given a breakpoint sequence v for the function's approximant, a continuous approximant for the derivative can be constructed by defining a new breakpoint sequence with $n - 1$ values placed at the midpoints of the original sequence, $z_i = (v_i + v_{i+1})/2, i = 1, \ldots, n - 1$, and requiring the new function to equal the centered finite-difference derivative at the new breakpoints:

$$f'(z_i) \approx \frac{f(v_{i+1}) - f(v_i)}{v_{i+1} - v_i}$$

Values between and beyond the z_i sequence can be obtained by linear interpolation and extrapolation. We leave it as an exercise to show that this piecewise linear function, evaluated at the original breakpoints (the v_i), is equal to the centered finite difference approximations derived in the preceding chapter. Approximations to higher order derivatives can be obtained by repeated application of this idea.

For completeness, we define an approximate integral that is also a linear spline, with a breakpoint sequence $z_i = (v_i + v_{i+1})/2$ for $i = 2, \ldots, n$ and with additional breakpoints defined by extrapolating beyond the original sequence: $z_1 = (3v_1 - v_2)/2$ and $z_{n+1} = (3v_n - v_{n-1})/2$. The approximation to the integral

$$F(x) = \int_{v_1}^{x} f(x)\, dx$$

at the new breakpoints is

$$F(z_i) = F(z_{i-1}) + (z_i - z_{i-1}) f(v_{i-1})$$

where

$$F(z_1) = \tfrac{1}{2}(v_1 - v_2)f(v_1)$$

(This approach ensures the normalization that $F(v_1) = 0$.) [3] This definition produces an approximation to the integral at the original breakpoints that is equal to the approximation obtained by applying the trapezoid rule (see section 5.1):

$$\int_{v_i}^{v_{i+1}} f(x)\,dx \approx \tfrac{1}{2}(v_{i+1} - v_i)[f(v_{i+1}) + f(v_i)]$$

(We leave the verification of this assertion as exercise for the reader.)

It should be recognized that the "derivatives" and "integrals" associated with this family of approximating functions are approximations, unlike the case of the polynomial and spline functions already discussed. We will, however, refer to the derivative of $\phi(X)c$ as $\phi'(X)c$, although this usage is not technically correct. When we define the operations in this way, the family of piecewise linear functions obtained using these approximations is closed under the differentiation and integration operations, as are the other families of functions discussed. Unlike splines, however, for which differentiation and integration cause a decrease or increase in the order of the piecewise segments, leaving the breakpoint sequence unchanged, with the piecewise linear family differentiation and integration do not change the polynomial order of the pieces (they remain linear) but cause a decrease or increase in the number of breakpoints. The piecewise linear family makes computation using finite difference operators quite easy, without a need for special treatment to distinguish them from other families of basis functions (including finite-element families such as splines). We will return to this point in Chapter 11 when we discuss solving partial differential equations (PDEs).

6.5   Multidimensional Interpolation

The interpolation methods for univariate functions discussed in the preceding sections may be extended in a natural way to multivariate functions through the use of tensor products.

Consider the problem of interpolating a d-variate function f on a d-dimensional interval

$$I = \{(x_1, x_2, \ldots, x_d) \mid a_i \le x_i \le b_i, i = 1, 2, \ldots, d\}$$

---

3. It should be pointed out that the breakpoint sequence obtained by integrating and then differentiating will not produce the original breakpoint sequence unless the original breakpoints are evenly spaced. This fact leads to the unfortunate property that differentiating the integral will only produce the original function if the breakpoints are evenly spaced. It can also be shown that, although the first derivatives are $O(h^2)$, the second derivatives are only $O(h)$ when the breakpoints are not evenly spaced.

For $i = 1, 2, \ldots, d$, let $\{\phi_{ij} \mid j = 1, 2, \ldots, n_i\}$ be an n_i-degree univariate basis for real-valued functions defined on $[a_i, b_i]$, and let $\{x_{ij} \mid j = 1, 2, \ldots, n_i\}$ be a sequence of n_i interpolation nodes for the interval $[a_i, b_i]$. Then an $n = \Pi_{i=1}^{d} n_i$–degree function basis defined on I may be obtained by letting

$$\phi_{j_1 j_2 \ldots j_d}(x_1, x_2, \ldots, x_d) = \phi_{1 j_1}(x_1)\phi_{2 j_2}(x_2) \ldots \phi_{d j_d}(x_d)$$

for $i = 1, 2, \ldots, d$ and $j_i = 1, 2, \ldots, n_i$. Similarly, a grid of n interpolation nodes for I may be obtained by forming the Cartesian product of the univariate interpolation nodes:

$$\left\{ \left(x_{1 j_1}, x_{2 j_2}, \ldots, x_{d j_d} \right) \mid i = 1, 2, \ldots, d; \ j_i = 1, 2, \ldots, n_i \right\}$$

An approximant for f in the tensor product basis takes the form

$$\hat{f}(x_1, x_2, \ldots, x_d) = \sum_{j_1=1}^{n_1} \sum_{j_2=1}^{n_2} \cdots \sum_{j_d=1}^{n_d} c_{j_1 \ldots j_d} \phi_{j_1 j_2 \ldots j_d}(x_1, x_2, \ldots, x_d)$$

In tensor notation, the approximant can be written

$$\hat{f}(x_1, x_2, \ldots, x_d) = [\phi_d(x_d) \otimes \phi_{d-1}(x_{d-1}) \otimes \cdots \otimes \phi_1(x_1)]c$$

where c is an $n \times 1$ column vector and each ϕ_i is the $1 \times n_i$ row vector of basis functions over dimension i.[4] An even more compact notation is

$$\hat{f}(x) = \phi(x)c$$

where $\phi(x)$ is a function of d variables that produces an $1 \times n$ row vector.

The coefficients of the approximant are computed by solving the linear interpolation equation

$$\Phi c = y \tag{6.1}$$

where

$$\Phi = \Phi_d \otimes \Phi_{d-1} \otimes \cdots \otimes \Phi_1$$

the $n \times n$ interpolation matrix, is the tensor product of the univariate interpolation matrices, and y is the $n \times 1$ vector containing the values of f at the n interpolation nodes, properly

---

4. In principle the tensor product may be evaluated in any order, but using reverse order, as we do here, makes indexing easier in MATLAB.

stacked. Using a standard result from tensor algebra,

$$c = \left[\Phi_d^{-1} \otimes \Phi_{d-1}^{-1} \otimes \cdots \otimes \Phi_1^{-1}\right] y$$

Thus, to solve the multivariate interpolation equation, there is no need to invert the $n \times n$ multivariate interpolation matrix Φ. Instead, it suffices to invert the univariate interpolation matrices individually and multiply them together. This approach leads to substantial savings in storage and computational effort. For example, if the problem is three-dimensional and there are 10 evaluation points in each dimension, only three 10×10 matrices need to be inverted, rather than a single $1,000 \times 1,000$ matrix.

To illustrate tensor product constructions and operations, consider a two-dimensional basis built from univariate monomial bases with $n_1 = 3$ and $n_2 = 2$. (Of course, one should use Chebychev polynomials, but it makes the example harder to follow.) The elementary basis functions are

$$\phi_{11}(x_1) = 1$$

$$\phi_{21}(x_1) = x_1$$

$$\phi_{31}(x_1) = x_1^2$$

$$\phi_{12}(x_2) = 1$$

$$\phi_{22}(x_2) = x_2$$

The elementary basis vectors are

$$\phi_1(x_1) = \begin{bmatrix} 1 & x_1 & x_1^2 \end{bmatrix}$$

and

$$\phi_2(x_2) = \begin{bmatrix} 1 & x_2 \end{bmatrix}$$

Finally, the full basis function is

$$\phi(x) = \begin{bmatrix} 1 & x_2 \end{bmatrix} \otimes \begin{bmatrix} 1 & x_1 & x_1^2 \end{bmatrix} = \begin{bmatrix} 1 & x_1 & x_1^2 & x_2 & x_1 x_2 & x_1^2 x_2 \end{bmatrix}$$

which has $n = n_1 n_2 = 6$ columns.

Now suppose that we construct a grid of nodes from the univariate nodes $x_1 = \{0, 1, 2\}$ and $x_2 = \{0, 1\}$. Then

$$\Phi_1 = \begin{bmatrix} 1 & 0 & 0 \\ 1 & 1 & 1 \\ 1 & 2 & 4 \end{bmatrix}, \qquad \Phi_2 = \begin{bmatrix} 1 & 0 \\ 1 & 1 \end{bmatrix}$$

and

$$
\Phi = \Phi_2 \otimes \Phi_1 =
\begin{bmatrix}
1 & 0 & 0 & 0 & 0 & 0 \\
1 & 1 & 1 & 0 & 0 & 0 \\
1 & 2 & 4 & 0 & 0 & 0 \\
1 & 0 & 0 & 1 & 0 & 0 \\
1 & 1 & 1 & 1 & 1 & 1 \\
1 & 2 & 4 & 1 & 1 & 4
\end{bmatrix}
$$

The proper stacking of the grid nodes yields a 6×2 matrix X containing all possible combinations of the values of the univariate nodes, with the lowest dimension changing most rapidly:

$$
X =
\begin{bmatrix}
0 & 0 \\
1 & 0 \\
2 & 0 \\
0 & 1 \\
1 & 1 \\
2 & 1
\end{bmatrix}
$$

Interpolation using tensor product schemes tends to become computationally more challenging as the dimension rises. In one-dimensional interpolation, the number of nodes and the dimension of the interpolation matrix can generally be kept small with good results. For smooth functions, Chebychev polynomial approximants of order 10 or less can often provide extremely accurate approximations. If performing d-dimensional interpolation, one could approximate the function using the same number of points in each dimension, but this approach increases the number of nodes to 10^d and the size of the interpolation matrix to 10^{2d} elements. The tendency of computational effort to grow exponentially with the dimension of the function domain is known as the *curse of dimensionality*. To mitigate the effects of the curse requires that careful attention be paid to both storage and computational efficiency when designing and implementing numerical routines that perform approximation.

Typically, tensor product node-basis schemes inherit the favorable qualities of their univariate node-basis parents. For example, if a multivariate linear spline basis is used and the interpolation nodes are chosen to coincide with the breakpoints, then the interpolation matrix will be the identity matrix, just as in the univariate case. Also, if a multivariate Chebychev polynomial basis is used and the interpolation nodes are chosen to coincide with the Cartesian product of the Chebychev nodes in each dimension, then the interpolation matrix will be orthogonal.

6.6   Choosing an Approximation Method

The most significant difference between spline and polynomial interpolation methods is that spline basis functions have narrow supports, but polynomial basis functions have supports that coincide with the entire interpolation interval. This can lead to differences in the quality of approximation when the function being approximated is irregular or exhibits a high degree of curvature. Discontinuities in the first or second derivatives can create problems for all interpolation schemes. However, spline functions, because of their narrow support, can often contain the effects of such discontinuities. Polynomial approximants, in contrast, allow the ill effects of discontinuities to propagate over the entire interval of interpolation. Thus, when a function exhibits kinks, spline interpolation may be preferable to polynomial interpolation.

In order to illustrate the differences between spline and polynomial interpolation, we compare in Table 6.2 the approximation error for three different functions defined on $[-5, 5]$ and three different approximation schemes: linear spline interpolation, cubic spline interpolation, and Chebychev polynomial interpolation. The approximation errors are measured as the maximum absolute deviation between the function and the approximant on $[-5, 5]$. The degree-7 approximants, along with the actual functions, are displayed in Figures 6.8 through 6.10.

The three functions examined are ordered in increasing difficulty of approximation. The first function, $\exp(-x)$, is quite smooth and hence can be approximated well with either cubic splines or polynomials. The second function, $(1 + 25x^2)^{-1}$, also known as Runge's function, has continuous derivatives of all orders but has a high degree of curvature at the origin. The third function, $|x|^{0.5}$, is kinked at the origin; that is, its derivative is not continuous.

Table 6.2
Errors for Selected Interpolation Methods

Function	Degree	Linear Spline	Cubic Spline	Chebychev Polynomial
$\exp(-x)$	10	1.36e+001	3.57e-001	1.41e-002
	20	3.98e+000	2.31e-002	1.27e-010
	30	1.86e+000	5.11e-003	9.23e-014
$(1 + 25x^2)^{-1}$	10	8.85e-001	9.15e-001	9.25e-001
	20	6.34e-001	6.32e-001	7.48e-001
	30	4.26e-001	3.80e-001	5.52e-001
$|x|^{0.5}$	10	7.45e-001	7.40e-001	7.57e-001
	20	5.13e-001	4.75e-001	5.33e-001
	30	4.15e-001	3.77e-001	4.35e-001

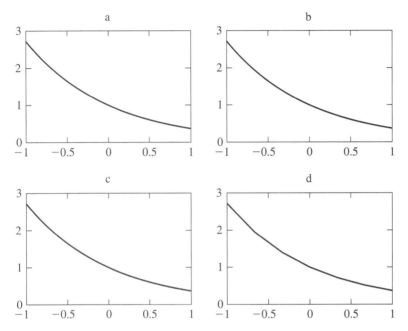

Figure 6.8
Approximation of $\exp(-x)$: (a) Function; (b) Chebychev Polynomial; (c) Cubic Spline; (d) Linear Spline

The results presented in Table 6.2 and in Figures 6.8–6.10 lend support to two rules of thumb: First, Chebychev-node polynomial interpolation dominates spline function interpolation whenever the function is smooth. Second, spline interpolation may perform better than polynomial interpolation if the underlying function exhibits a high degree of curvature or a derivative discontinuity. Of course, as with all rules of thumb, there are plenty of exceptions. However, these rules should guide initial selection of approximation schemes.

6.7   An Approximation Tool Kit

Implementing routines for multivariate function approximation involves a number of book-keeping details that are tedious at best. In this section we describe a set of numerical tools that take much of the pain out of this process. This tool kit contains several high-level functions that use a structured variable to store the essential information that defines the function space from which approximants are drawn. The tool kit also contains a set of middle-level

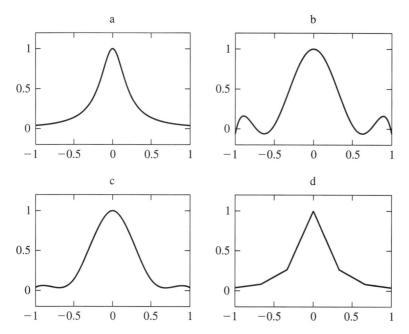

Figure 6.9
Approximation of $(1 + 25x^2)^{-1}$: (a) Function; (b) Chebychev Polynomial; (c) Cubic Spline; (d) Linear Spline

routines that define the basis functions and nodes and a set of low-level utilities to handle basic computations, including tensor product manipulations.

The most basic of the high-level routines is `fundefn`, which creates a structured variable that contains the essential information about the function space from which approximants will be drawn. There are several pieces of information that must be specified and stored in the structured variable in order to define the function space: the type of basis function (e.g., Chebychev polynomial, spline, etc.), the number of basis functions, and the endpoints of the interpolation interval. If the approximant is multidimensional, the number of basis functions and the interval endpoints must be supplied for each dimension.

The routine `fundefn` defines the approximation function space using the calling syntax

```
fspace = fundefn(bastype,n,a,b,order);
```

Here, on input, `bastype` is string referencing the basis function family, which can take the values `'cheb'` for Chebychev polynomial basis, `'spli'` for spline basis, or `'lin'` for a linear spline basis with finite difference derivatives; `n` is the vector containing the degree of approximation along each dimension; `a` is the vector of left endpoints of

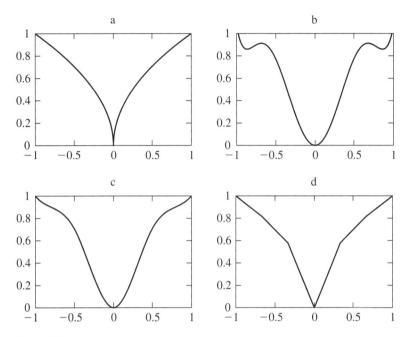

Figure 6.10
Approximation of $|x|^{0.5}$: (a) Function; (b) Chebychev Polynomial; (c) Cubic Spline; (d) Linear Spline

interpolation intervals in each dimension; b is the vector of right endpoints of interpolation intervals in each dimension; and `order` is an optional input that specifies the order of the interpolating spline. On output, `fspace` is a structured MATLAB variable containing numerous fields of information necessary for forming approximations in the chosen function space.

For example, suppose one wished to construct 10th-degree Chebychev approximants for univariate functions defined on the interval $[-1, 2]$. Then one would define the appropriate function space for approximation as follows:

```
fspace = fundefn('cheb',10,-1,2);
```

Suppose instead that one wished to construct cubic spline approximants for bivariate functions defined on the two-dimensional interval $\{(x_1, x_2) \mid -1 \leq x_1 \leq 2, 4 \leq x_2 \leq 9\}$ using 10 basis functions for the x_1 dimension and 15 basis functions for the x_2 dimension. Then one would issue the following command:

```
fspace = fundefn('spli',[10 15],[-1 2],[4 9]);
```

For spline interpolation, cubic spline interpolation is the default. However, other order splines may also be used for interpolation by specifying `order`. In particular, if one wished to construct a linear spline approximant instead of cubic spline approximant, one would issue the following command:

```
fspace = fundefn('spli',[10 15],[-1 2],[4 9],1);
```

Two routines are provided for function approximation and data fitting. The routine `funfitf` may be used to construct an approximant for a function using interpolation at standard nodes. The calling syntax for this routine is

```
c = funfitf(fspace,f,additional parameters);
```

Here, on input, `fspace` is the approximation function space defined using `fundef`, and `f` is the string name of the file that evaluates the function to be approximated at arbitrary points. Any additional parameters passed to `funfitf` are simply passed to the function `f`. On output, `c` is the vector of basis function coefficients for the unique member of the function space that interpolates the function f at the standard interpolation nodes associated with that space.[5]

A second routine, `funfitxy`, computes the basis coefficients of the approximant that interpolates the function values supplied at arbitrary points that may, or may not, coincide with the standard interpolation nodes. The calling syntax for this function approximation routine is

```
c = funfitxy(fspace,x,y);
```

Here, on input, `fspace` is an approximation function space defined using `fundef`, `x` is a matrix of points at which the function has been evaluated (each row represents one point in R^d), and `y` is a matrix of function values at those points. On output, `c` is the vector of basis function coefficients for the member of the function space that interpolates `f` at the interpolation nodes supplied in `x`. If there are more data points than coefficients, `funfitxy` returns the basis function coefficients of the least-squares fit.[6]

Once the approximant function space has been chosen and a specific approximant in that space has been constructed, then the routine `funeval` may be used to evaluate the approximant at one or more points. The calling syntax for this function approximation routine is

```
y = funeval(c,fspace,x);
```

5. Although we generally refer to `c` as a vector, it can also be an $n \times m$ matrix, making $\phi(x)c$ a mapping from $\mathbb{R}^d$ to $\mathbb{R}^m$.

6. The argument `x` may also be passed as a cell array containing the coordinates of a grid on which `y` is defined.

Here, on input, fspace is the approximation function space defined using fundefn, c is the vector of basis function coefficients that uniquely identifies the approximant within that function space, and x is the point at which the approximant is to be evaluated. On output, y is the value of the approximant at x. If one wishes to evaluate the approximant at m points, then one may pass all these points to funeval as an $m \times d$ array x, in which case y returns as an $m \times 1$ vector of function values.

The routine funeval may also be used to evaluate the derivatives or the approximant at one or more points. The calling syntax for evaluating derivatives is

```
d = funeval(c,fspace,x,order);
```

where, on input, order is a $1 \times d$ array specifying the order of integration in each dimension. On output, d is the derivative of the approximant at x. For example, to compute the first and second derivatives of a univariate approximant, one issues the commands:

```
f1 = funeval(c,fspace,x,1);
f2 = funeval(c,fspace,x,2);
```

To compute the partial derivatives of a bivariate approximant with respect to its first two arguments, one would issue the commands:

```
f1 = funeval(c,fspace,x,[1 0]);
f2 = funeval(c,fspace,x,[0 1]);
```

The single command

```
J = funeval(c,fspace,x,eye(d));
```

where eye(d) is the d-dimensional identity matrix, computes the Jacobian of multivariate function approximant. To compute the second partial derivatives and the cross partial of a bivariate function, one would issue the commands

```
f11 = funeval(c,fspace,x,[2 0]);
f12 = funeval(c,fspace,x,[1 1]);
f22 = funeval(c,fspace,x,[0 2]);
```

A simple example will help clarify how all of these routines may be used to construct and evaluate function approximants. Suppose we are interested (for whatever reason) in approximating the univariate function $f(x) = \exp(-\alpha x)$ on $[-1, 1]$. The first step is to create a file that computes the desired function:

```
function y = f(x,alpha)
y = exp(-alpha*x);
```

The file should be named f.m. The following script constructs the Chebychev approximant for $\alpha = 2$ and then plots the errors using a finer grid than used in interpolation:

```
alpha    = 2;
fspace = fundefn('cheb',10,-1,1);
c = funfitf(fspace,'f',alpha);
x = nodeunif(1001,-1,1);
y = funeval(c,fspace,x);
plot(x,y-f(x,alpha));
```

The steps used here are to first initialize the parameter α. Second, we use fundefn to define the function space fspace from which the approximant is to be drawn; in this case the function space is the linear subspace spanned by the first 10 Chebychev polynomials on $[-1, 1]$. Third, we use funfitf to compute the coefficient vector for the approximant that interpolates the function at the standard Chebychev nodes. Fourth, we generate a fine grid of 1,001 equally spaced values on the interpolation interval and plot the difference between the actual function values $f(x)$ and the approximated values $\hat{f}(x)$ at those values. The approximation error is plotted in Figure 6.11.

Two other routines are useful in applied computational economic analysis. For many problems it is necessary to work directly with the basis matrices. For this purpose funbas can be used. The command

```
B = funbas(fspace,x);
```

returns the matrix containing the values of the basis functions evaluated at the points x. The matrix containing the value of the basis functions associated with a derivative of given

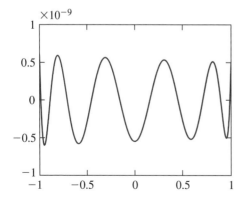

Figure 6.11
Approximation Error

order at x may be retrieved by issuing the command

```
B = funbas(fspace,x,order);
```

When a function is to be repeatedly evaluated at the same points but with different values of the coefficients, substantial time savings are achieved by avoiding repeated recalculation of the basis. The commands

```
B = funbas(fspace,x);
y = B*c;
```

have the same effect as

```
y = funeval(c,fspace,x);
```

Finally, the procedure `funnode` computes standard nodes for interpolation and function fitting. It returns a $1 \times d$ cell array (or an n-vector if $d = 1$) associated with a specified function space. Its syntax is

```
x = funnode(fspace);
```

The CompEcon Toolbox also contains a number of functions for "power users." These functions either automate certain procedures (for example `funjac` and `funhess`, which compute the Jacobians and Hessians of approximant) or give the user more control over how information is stored and manipulated (for example, `fundef` can define spline function spaces with unevenly spaced nodes). All these tools are are extensible, allowing nonstandard families of approximating functions to be defined. Complete documentation is available at the CompEcon Toolbox web site.

6.8   The Collocation Method

In this section we introduce the *collocation method,* a straightforward generalization of the function approximation methods covered earlier in this chapter that can be used to solve a wide variety of functional equations, including the functional equations that arise with dynamic economic models in discrete and continuous time. In order to introduce the collocation method as plainly as possible, we present it initially for a relatively simple functional equation problem, the univariate implicit function problem, which involves finding a function $f : [a, b] \mapsto \mathbb{R}$ that satisfies

$$g(x, f(x)) = 0 \quad \text{for } x \in [a, b]$$

where $g : \mathbb{R}^2 \mapsto \mathbb{R}$ is a known function.

The collocation method employs a conceptually straightforward strategy to solve functional equations. Specifically, the unknown function f is approximated using a linear combination of n known basis functions

$$\hat{f}(x) = \sum_{j=1}^{n} c_j \phi_j(x)$$

whose n coefficients $c_1, c_2, \ldots, c_n$ are fixed by requiring the approximant to satisfy the functional equation, not at all possible points of the domain, but rather at n prescribed points $x_1, x_2, \ldots, x_n$ in $[a, b]$ called the *collocation nodes*.

Solving the implicit function problem by collocation thus requires finding the n coefficients c_j that simultaneously satisfy the n nonlinear equations

$$g\left(x_i, \sum_{j=1}^{n} c_j \phi_j(x_i)\right) = 0 \quad \text{for } i = 1, 2, \ldots, n$$

The collocation method thus effectively replaces the hard infinite-dimensional functional equation problem with a simpler finite-dimensional rootfinding problem that can be solved with any standard rootfinding method, such as Newton's method or Broyden's method.

In general, the approximant constructed by means of collocation will not solve the functional equation exactly. That is, $g(x, \hat{f}(x))$ will not equal zero on $[a, b]$, except at the collocation nodes, where it is zero by definition. However, the approximant $\hat{f}$ is deemed acceptable if the *residual function* $r(x) = g(x, \hat{f}(x))$, though not identically zero, is very nearly zero over the domain $[a, b]$. As a practical matter, one assesses the accuracy of the approximant by inspecting the residual function and computing its maximum absolute value over the domain. If the maximum absolute residual is not below a prescribed tolerance, the process is repeated with more nodes and basis functions until the approximation error falls to acceptable levels.

To illustrate implementation of the collocation method for implicit function problems, consider the example of Cournot oligopoly. In the standard microeconomic model of the firm, the firm maximizes profit by equating marginal revenue to marginal cost (MC). An oligopolistic firm, recognizing that its actions affect price, takes the marginal revenue to be $p + q\frac{dp}{dq}$, where p is price, q is quantity produced, and $\frac{dp}{dq}$ is the marginal impact of output on market price. The Cournot assumption is that the firm acts as if any change in its output will be unmatched by its competitors. This implies that

$$\frac{dp}{dq} = \frac{1}{D'(p)}$$

where $D(p)$ is the market demand curve.

Suppose we wish to derive the effective supply function for the firm, which specifies the quantity $q = S(p)$ it will supply at any price. The firm's effective supply function is characterized by the functional equation

$$p + \frac{S(p)}{D'(p)} - MC(S(p)) = 0$$

for all positive prices p. In simple cases, this function can be found explicitly.[7] However, in more complicated cases, no explicit solution exists. Suppose, for example, that

$$D(p) = p^{-\eta}$$

and

$$MC(q) = \alpha \sqrt{q} + q^2$$

Then the functional equation to be solved for $S(p)$,

$$\left[p - \frac{S(p)p^{\eta+1}}{\eta} \right] - \left[\alpha \sqrt{S(p)} + S(p)^2 \right] = 0$$

has no known closed-form solution.

An approximate solution for $S(p)$, however, may be computed numerically in MATLAB using the collocation method. First, one enters the model parameters. Here, the demand elasticity and the marginal cost function parameter are entered:

```
alpha = 1.0;
eta   = 1.5;
```

Second, one specifies the approximation space. Here, a degree-25 Chebychev basis on the interval [0.1, 3.0] is selected; also, the associated collocation nodes p are computed:

```
n = 25; a = 0.1; b = 3.0;
fspace = fundefn('cheb',n,a,b);
p = funnode(fspace);
```

Third, one solves the collocation equation using Broyden's method:

```
c = zeros(n,1);
c = broyden('resid',c,p,fspace,alpha,eta);
```

---

7. For example, if $MC(q) = c$ and $D(p) = p^{-\eta}$, then $S(p) = \eta(p - c)p^{-\eta}$.

Here, the CompEcon routine `broyden` computes the coefficient vector c, starting from an initial guess of the zero vector. The routine takes as input the name of the MATLAB file `resid` that computes the residual at an arbitrary set of price nodes, as well as parameters that must be passed to the residual function. The function `resid`, which must be coded in a separate file, takes the form

```
function r = resid(c,p,fspace,alpha,eta);
q  = funeval(c,fspace,p);
r  = p+q.*[(-1./eta)*p.^(eta+1)] - alpha*sqrt(q) - q.^2;
```

In the first line, the function employs the CompEcon routine `funeval` to compute the quantities q supplied at the prices p, as implied by the current supply function approximant, which is characterized by the function space `fspace` and coefficient vector c. In the second line, the residual, which equals marginal revenue minus marginal cost, is computed.

Finally, in order to assess the quality of the approximation, one plots the residual function over the approximation domain. Here, the residual function is plotted by computing the residual at a refined grid of 501 equally spaced points:

```
pplot = nodeunif(501,a,b);
splot = funeval(c,fspace,pplot);
plot(splot,pplot);
```

The result, shown in Figure 6.12, makes clear that the Chebychev polynomial approximation obtained with 10 nodes provides a solution that is accurate to an order of 1×10^{-6}.

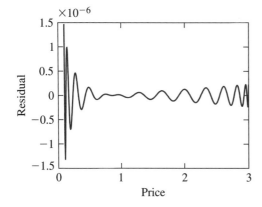

Figure 6.12
Residual Function for Cournot Problem

Once the collocation equation has been solved and an approximation for the firm's effective supply curve $S(p)$ has been computed, one may conduct additional economic analysis. For example, one may draw the industry supply curve $mS(p)$ under the assumption that the industry consists of m identical firms. The demand curve and industry supply curves for different values of m and for $\alpha = 1$ and $\eta = 1.5$ are illustrated in Figure 6.13. The equilibrium price, which is determined by the intersection of the industry supply and demand curves, is drawn as a function of the number of firms in Figure 6.14.

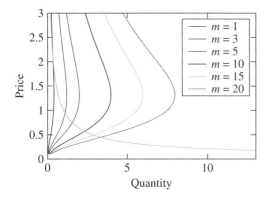

Figure 6.13
Industry Supply and Demand Functions

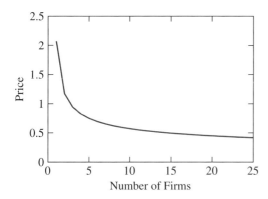

Figure 6.14
Cournot Equilibrium Price as Function of Industry Size

6.9   Boundary Value Problems

In the boundary value problem, or BVP for short, one seeks a solution function $x(t)$: $[0, T] \mapsto \mathbb{R}^d$ that satisfies the differential equation

$$r(t, x(t), x'(t)) = 0$$

where $r : [0, T] \times \mathbb{R}^{2d} \mapsto \mathbb{R}^d$, subject to d boundary conditions

$$b_i\left(t_i^b, x\left(t_i^b\right), x'\left(t_i^b\right)\right) = 0, \quad i = 1, 2, \dots, d$$

where $t_i^b \in [0, T]$ and $b_i : [0, T] \times \mathbb{R}^{2d} \mapsto \mathbb{R}$ for $i = 1, 2, \dots, d$. Boundary value problems arise often in economics and finance in deterministic optimal control problems. We consider such problems in more detail in Chapter 11, especially in sections 11.4 and 11.5.

Although there are many different strategies for solving BVPs, application of the collocation method is straightforward. The collocation method for BVPs calls for the unknown functions x_k, $i = 1, 2, \dots, d$, to be approximated using linear combinations of n known basis functions

$$\hat{x}_k(t) = \sum_{j=1}^{n} c_{jk}\phi_j(t)$$

whose coefficients $c_{11}, c_{12}, \dots, c_{nd}$ are to be determined. The nd basis function coefficients are fixed by requiring the approximants $\hat{x}_i$ to satisfy the differential equation at $n - 1$ prescribed nodes $t_1, t_2, \dots, t_{n-1}$ in $[0, T]$

$$r(t_i, \hat{x}(t_i), \hat{x}'(t_i)) = 0, \quad i = 1, 2, \dots, n - 1$$

subject to the boundary conditions

$$b_i\left(t_i^b, \hat{x}\left(t_i^b\right), \hat{x}'\left(t_i^b\right)\right) = 0, \quad i = 1, 2, \dots, d$$

The $(n - 1)d$ residual conditions and the d boundary conditions provide a total of nd nonlinear equations to be solved for the nd unknowns.

To illustrate implementation of the collocation method for boundary value problems, consider the example of a market for a periodically produced storable commodity. Assume that at time $t = 0$ there are s_0 units of of the commodity available for consumption. No more of the commodity will be produced until time $t = 1$, at which time all of the currently available good must be consumed. The change in the level of commodity stocks s is the negative of the rate of consumption, here assumed to be a constant elasticity function of the prevailing market price p:

$$s'(t) = -p^{-\eta}$$

To eliminate arbitrage opportunities and to induce storage, the price must rise at a rate that covers the interest rate r and the cost of physical storage k:

$$p'(t) = rp + k$$

Since no stocks are carried into the next production cycle, which begins at time $t = 1$, the terminal condition $s(1) = 0$ must be observed in addition to the initial condition $s(0) = s_0$. Defining $x = (p, s)$, the commodity market model poses a two-dimensional boundary value problem with vector differential equation

$$r(t, x, x') = x' - \left[rx_1 + c \quad -x_1^{-\eta} \right] = 0$$

and boundary conditions $x_2(0) - s_0 = 0$ and $x_2(1) = 0$.

An approximate solution for $x(t)$ may be computed numerically in MATLAB using the collocation method. First, one enters the model parameters. Here, the interest rate, cost of storage, demand elasticity, and initial stocks are entered:

```
r   = 0.1;
k   = 0.5;
eta = 5;
s0  = 1;
```

Second, one specifies the approximation space. Here, a degree-15 Chebychev polynomial basis on the interval $[0, 1]$ is selected for approximation, and the degree-14 Chebychev nodes `tnodes` are selected to impose the residual condition on the differential equation:

```
T = 1;
n = 15;
tnodes = chebnode(n-1,0,T);
fspace = fundefn('cheb',n,0,T);
```

Third, one solves the collocation equation using Broyden's method:

```
c = zeros(n,2); c(1,:) = 1;
c = broyden('resid',c(:),tnodes,T,n,fspace,r,k,eta,s0);
```

Here, the CompEcon routine `broyden` computes the coefficient vector c, starting from an initial guess in which the coefficient associated with the first Chebychev polynomial is one, but the remaining coefficients are zero. The routine takes as input the name of the MATLAB file `resid` that computes the differential equation and boundary condition residuals at an arbitrary set of time nodes, as well as parameters that must be passed to the residual function.

The function `resid`, which must be coded in a separate file, takes the form

```
function r = resid(c,tnodes,T,n,fspace,r,k,eta,s0);
c   = reshape(c,n,2);
x   = funeval(c,fspace,tnodes);
d   = funeval(c,fspace,tnodes,1);
r   = d - [r*x(:,1)+k  -x(:,1).^(-eta)];
x0  = funeval(c,fspace,0);
x1  = funeval(c,fspace,T);
r   = [r(:); x0(2)-s0 ; x1(2)0];
```

In the first line, the function employs the CompEcon routine `funeval` to compute the vectors x and d at the time nodes `tnodes`, as implied by the current approximants, which are characterized by the function space `fspace` and coefficient matrix c. These are used to compute the differential equation residual r, to which the boundary condition residuals are then appended. Note that the residuals are returned as a $2n \times 1$ vector.

Finally, in order to assess the quality of the approximation, we plot the differential equation residual over the approximation domain. Here, the residual function is plotted by computing the residual at a refined grid of 501 equally spaced points:

```
nplot = 501;
t = nodeunif(nplot,0,T);
c = reshape(c,n,2);
x = funeval(c,fspace,t);
d = funeval(c,fspace,t,1);
r = d - [r*x(:,1)+k  -x(:,1).^(-eta)];
```

The result, which is shown in Figure 6.15, makes clear that the Chebychev polynomial approximation obtained with 15 nodes generates residuals that are of order 10^{-9}. The solution functions are shown in Figure 6.16.

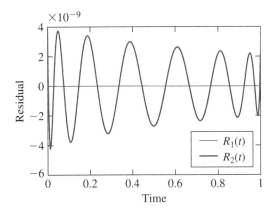

Figure 6.15
Residual Functions for Equilibrium Storage Problem

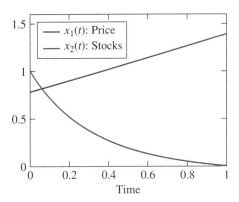

Figure 6.16
Solution Functions for Equilibrium Storage Problem

Exercises

6.1. Construct the 5- and 50-degree approximants for the function $f(x) = \exp(-x^2)$ on the interval $[-1, 1]$ using each of the interpolation schemes that follow. For each scheme and degree of approximation, plot the approximation error.

a. Uniform node, monomial basis polynomial approximant

b. Chebychev node, Chebychev basis polynomial approximant

c. Uniform node, linear spline approximant

d. Uniform node, cubic spline approximant

6.2. In the Cournot oligopoly model, each firm takes its competitors' output as fixed when determining its output level. An alternative assumption is that each firm takes its competitors' output *decision functions* as fixed when determining its output level. This can be expressed as the assumption that

$$\frac{dp}{dq_i} = \frac{1}{D'(p)} \sum_{j=1}^{n} \frac{dq_j}{dq_i} = \frac{1}{D'(p)} \left[1 + \sum_{j\neq i} \frac{dS_j(p)}{dp} \frac{dp}{dq_i} \right]$$

Solving this expression for dp/dq_i yields

$$\frac{dp}{dq_i} = \frac{1}{D'(p) - \sum_{j\neq i} S_j'(p)}$$

In an industry with m identical firms, each firm assumes the other firms will react in the same way it does, so this expression simplifies to

$$\frac{dp}{dq} = \frac{1}{D'(p) - (m-1)S'(p)}$$

This expression differs from the Cournot case in the extra term in the denominator (which only equals 0 in the monopoly situation of $m = 1$). Notice also that, unlike the Cournot case, the firm's "supply" function depends on the number of firms in the industry.

Solve this model using the collocation method, and produce plots similar to those found in section 6.8.

6.3. Consider the potato market model discussed in problem 3.8 (page 56). Assume that supply s at the beginning of the first marketing period is the product of the acreage planted a and a random yield y that is unknown at planting time. Also assume that acreage planted is a function $a = 0.5 + 0.5Ep_1$ of the period-1 price expected at planting time and that log yield is normally distributed with mean zero and standard deviation 0.1.

a. Construct a degree-20 Chebychev polynomial approximant on the interval $[1.5, 2.5]$ for the function $p_1 = f(s)$ that gives the period-1 price p_1 as a function the supply available at the beginning of period 1. You will need to use the routine that you wrote for problem 3.8.

b. Using the constructed approximant and an appropriate 5-point Gaussian quadrature scheme, solve the fixed-point problem

$$a = 0.5 + 0.5E_y f(ay)$$

for the rational expectations equilibrium acreage employing the univariate rootfinding problem of your choice. Caution: function iteration will fail. Why?

6.4. Using collocation with the basis functions of your choice, solve the following differential equation for $x \in [0, 1]$:

$$(1 + x^2)v(x) - v''(x) = x^2$$

with $v(0) = v(1) = 0$. Plot the residual function to ensure that the maximum value of the residual is less than 10^{-8}. What degree of approximation is needed to achieve this level of accuracy?

6.5. A simple model of lifetime savings/consumption choice considers an agent with a projected income flow by $y(t)$, who must choose a consumption rate $c(t)$ to maximize discounted lifetime utility:

$$\max_{c(t)} \int_0^T e^{-\rho t} U(c(t)) \, dt$$

subject to an intertemporal wealth constraint $dw/dt = rw(t) + y(t) - c(t)$, where r is the rate of return on investments (or the interest rate on borrowed funds, if $w < 0$). The solution to this optimal control problem can be expressed as the system of differential equations

$$c' = -\frac{U'(c)}{U''(c)}(r - \rho)$$

and

$$w' = rw + y - c$$

It is assumed that the agent begins with no wealth $[w(0) = 0]$ and leaves no bequests $[w(T) = 0]$.

a. Solve this boundary value problem assuming a utility function $U(c) = (c^{1-\lambda} - 1)/(1 - \lambda)$ and parameter values $T = 45$, $r = 0.1$, $\rho = 0.6$, $\lambda = 0.5$, and $y(t) = 1/(1 + e^{-\alpha t})$, with $\alpha = 0.15$. Plot the solution and residual functions.

b. In part a the agent works until time T and then dies. Suppose, instead, that the agent retires at time T and lives an additional $R = 15$ retirement years with no additional income ($y(t) = 0$ for $T < t \le T + R$). Resolve the problem with this assumption. What additional problem is encountered? How can the problem be addressed?

6.6. The complementary Normal cumulative distribution function is defined as

$$\Phi^c(x) = \frac{1}{\sqrt{2\pi}} \int_x^\infty e^{-z^2/2} dz$$

Define

$$u(x) = e^{x^2/2} \Phi^c(x)$$

a. Express u as a differential equation with boundary condition $u(\infty) = 0$.

b. Use the change of variable $t = x/(K + x)$ (for some constant K) to define a differential equation for the function $v(t) = u(x)$, for $v \in [0, 1]$.

c. Solve the transformed differential equation using Chebychev polynomial collocation.

d. Plot the residual function for different values of K between 0.1 and 20. Make a recommendation about the best choice of K.

6.7. Write a MATLAB routine that automates the approximation of function inverses. The function should have the following syntax:

```
function c = finverse(f,fspace,varargin)
```

You will also need to write an auxiliary function to compute the appropriate residuals used by the rootfinding algorithm.

Bibliographic Notes

Most general numerical analysis texts contain discussions of interpolation and function approximation using polynomials and splines. Introductory textbooks that provide clear discussions of one-dimensional function approximation include Cheney and Kincaid (1985) and Kincaid and Cheney (1991). Thorough but advanced theoretical treatments are found in Judd (1998) and Atkinson (1989). More practical discussions, including working computer code, may be found in de Boor (1978) and Press et al. (1992). The most complete reference on Chebychev approximation is Rivlin (1990). For a discussion focused on solving differential equations see Golub and Ortega (1992).

Collocation is just one example of a more general class of approximation methods known as weighted residual methods. Two weighted residual methods besides collocation are commonly used in physical science applications. The least-squares method calls for the coefficient vector c to be chosen so as to solve

$$\min_c \int_a^b r^2(x, \phi(x)c) \, dx$$

The Galerkin method (also called Bubnov–Galerkin method), calls for the coefficient vector

c to be chosen so that

$$\int_a^b r(x, \phi(x)c)\phi_i(x)\,dx = 0, \quad \text{for } i = 1, \ldots, n$$

When the integrals in these expressions can be solved explicitly, these methods seem to be somewhat more efficient than collocation. However, if r is nonlinear, as is typically the case in economic and financial applications, these methods will necessitate the use of quadrature techniques to compute the necessary integrals, eliminating any potential advantages these methods may have relative to collocation. For this reason, we have chosen to focus exclusively on collocation in this book as the preferred method for solving economic and financial models. A thorough treatment of weighted residual methods may be found in Fletcher (1984) and Judd (1998).

7 Discrete Time, Discrete State Dynamic Models

With this chapter, we begin our study of dynamic economic models. Dynamic economic models often present three complications rarely encountered together in dynamic physical science models. First, humans are cogent, future-looking beings capable of assessing how their actions will affect them in the future as well as in the present. Thus, most useful dynamic economic models are future looking. Second, many aspects of human behavior are unpredictable. Thus, most useful dynamic economic models are inherently stochastic. Third, the predictable component of human behavior is often complex. Thus, most useful dynamic economic models are inherently nonlinear.

The complications inherent in forward-looking, stochastic, nonlinear models make it impossible to obtain explicit analytic solutions to all but a small number of dynamic economic models. However, the proliferation of affordable personal computers, the phenomenal increase of computational speed, and the development of theoretical insights into the efficient use of computers over the last two decades now make it possible for economists to analyze dynamic models much more thoroughly using numerical methods.

The next three chapters are devoted to the numerical analysis of dynamic economic models in discrete time and are followed by two chapters on dynamic economic models in continuous time. In this chapter we study the simplest of these models: the discrete time, discrete state Markov decision model. Though the discrete Markov decision model is relatively simple, the methods used to solve and analyze the model lay the foundations for the methods developed in subsequent chapters to solve and analyze more complicated models with continuous states and time.

7.1 Discrete Dynamic Programming

The discrete time, discrete state Markov decision model has the following structure: in every period t, an agent observes the state of an economic system s_t, takes an action x_t, and earns a reward $f(s_t, x_t)$ that depends on both the state of the system and the action taken. The state space S, which enumerates all the states attainable by the system, and the action space X, which enumerates all actions that may be taken by the agent, are both finite. The state of the economic system is a controlled Markov process. That is, the probability distribution of the next period's state, conditional on all currently available information, depends only on the current state and the agent's action:[1]

$$\Pr(s_{t+1} = s' \mid s_t = s, x_t = x, \text{ other information at } t) = P(s' \mid s, x)$$

The agent seeks a sequence of policies $\{x_t^*\}$ that prescribe the action $x_t = x_t^*(s_t)$ that should

---

1. See section A.4 in Appendix A for a discussion of discrete Markov processes.

be taken in any given state and period so as to maximize the present value of current and expected future rewards over a time horizon T, discounted at a per-period factor δ.

A discrete Markov decision model may have an infinite horizon ($T = \infty$) or a finite horizon ($T < \infty$). A discrete Markov decision model may also be either deterministic or stochastic. It is deterministic if the next period's state is known with certainty once the current period's state and action are known. In this case, it is beneficial to dispense with the transition probabilities P as a description of how the state evolves and use instead a deterministic state transition function g that explicitly gives the state transitions:

$$s_{t+1} = g(s_t, x_t)$$

Discrete Markov decision models may be analyzed and understood using the dynamic programming methods developed by Richard Bellman (1957). Dynamic programming is based on the *principle of optimality*, which was articulated by Bellman as follows: "An optimal policy has the property that, whatever the initial state and decision are, the remaining decisions must constitute an optimal policy with regard to the state resulting from the first decision."

The principle of optimality formally may be expressed in the form of the *Bellman equation*. Denote by $V_t(s)$ the maximum attainable sum of current and expected future rewards, given that the system is in state s in period t. Then the principle of optimality implies that the *value functions* $V_t : S \mapsto \mathbb{R}$ must satisfy

$$V_t(s) = \max_{x \in X(s)} \left\{ f(s, x) + \delta \sum_{s' \in S} P(s' \mid s, x) V_{t+1}(s') \right\}, \quad s \in S, \ t = 1, 2, \ldots, T$$

The Bellman equation captures the essential problem faced by a dynamic, future-regarding optimizing agent: the need to optimally balance an immediate reward $f(s_t, x_t)$ against expected future rewards $\delta E_t V_{t+1}(s_{t+1})$.

In a finite horizon model, we adopt the convention that the optimizing agent faces decisions in periods 1 through $T < \infty$. The agent faces no decisions after the terminal decision period T, but may earn a final reward $V_{T+1}(s_{T+1})$ in the subsequent period that depends on the realization of the state in that period. The terminal value is typically fixed by some economically relevant terminal condition. In many applications, V_{T+1} is identically zero, indicating that no rewards are earned by the agent beyond the terminal decision period. In other applications, V_{T+1} may specify a salvage value earned by the agent after making his final decision in period T.

For the finite horizon discrete Markov decision model to be well posed, the terminal value V_{T+1} must be specified by the analyst. Given the terminal value function, the finite-horizon decision model in principle may be solved recursively by repeated application of the Bellman equation: having V_{T+1}, solve for $V_T(s)$ for all states s; having V_T, solve for $V_{T-1}(s)$ for all states s; having V_{T-1}, solve for $V_{T-2}(s)$ for all states s; and so on. The process continues until $V_1(s)$ is derived for all states s. Because only finitely many actions are possible, the optimization problem embedded in the Bellman equation can always be solved by performing finitely many arithmetic operations. Thus the value functions of a finite horizon discrete Markov decision model are always well defined, although in some cases more than one sequence of policies may yield the maximum expected stream of rewards.

If the decision problem has an infinite horizon, the value functions will not depend on time t. We may, therefore, discard the time subscripts and write the Bellman equation as a vector fixed-point equation whose single unknown is the common value function V:

$$V(s) = \max_{x \in X(s)} \left\{ f(s, x) + \delta \sum_{s' \in S} P(s' \mid s, x) V(s') \right\}, \quad s \in S$$

If the discount factor δ is less than one, the mapping underlying the Bellman fixed-point equation is a strong contraction on Euclidean space. The Contraction Mapping Theorem thus guarantees the existence and uniqueness of the infinite horizon value function.[2]

7.2 Economic Examples

A discrete Markov decision model is composed of several elements: the state space, the action space, the reward function, the state transition function or state transition probabilities, the discount factor δ, the time horizon T, and, if the model has finite horizon, the terminal value function V_{T+1}. This section provides six economic examples that illustrate how these elements are specified and how the Bellman equation is formulated.

7.2.1 Mine Management

A mine operator must decide how much ore to extract from a mine that will be shut down and abandoned after T years of operation. The price of extracted ore is p dollars per ton, and the total cost of extracting x tons of ore in any year, given that the mine contains s tons at the beginning of the year, is $c(s, x)$ dollars. The mine currently contains $\bar{s}$ tons of ore. Assuming the amount of ore extracted in any year must be an integer number of tons, what extraction schedule maximizes profits?

This is a finite horizon, deterministic model with time t measured in years. The state variable

$$s \in \{0, 1, 2, \dots, \bar{s}\}$$

is the amount of ore remaining in the mine at the beginning of the year, measured in tons.

---

2. Infinite horizon models with time-dependent rewards and transition probabilities are conceivable, but are generally difficult to solve. We have chosen not to explicitly consider them here.

The action variable

$$x \in \{0, 1, 2, \ldots, s\}$$

is the amount of ore extracted over the year, measured in tons. The state transition function is

$$g(s, x) = s - x$$

The reward function is

$$f(s, x) = p\, x - c(s, x)$$

The value of the mine, given that it contains s tons of ore at the beginning of year t, satisfies the Bellman equation

$$V_t(s) = \max_{x \in \{0,1,2,\ldots,s\}} \{p\, x - c(s, x) + \delta V_{t+1}(s - x)\}$$

subject to the terminal condition

$$V_{T+1}(s) = 0$$

7.2.2 Asset Replacement

At the beginning of each year, a manufacturer must decide whether to continue to operate an aging physical asset or replace it with a new one. An asset that is a years old yields a profit contribution $p(a)$ up to n years, at which point the asset becomes unsafe and must be replaced by law. The cost of a new asset is c. What replacement policy maximizes profits?

This is an infinite horizon, deterministic model with time t measured in years. The state variable

$$a \in \{1, 2, 3, \ldots, n\}$$

is the age of the asset in years. The action variable

$$x \in \{\text{keep}, \text{replace}\}$$

is the hold-replacement decision. The state transition function is

$$g(a, x) = \begin{cases} a + 1, & x = \text{keep} \\ 1, & x = \text{replace} \end{cases}$$

The reward function is

$$f(a, x) = \begin{cases} p(a), & x = \text{keep} \\ p(0) - c, & x = \text{replace} \end{cases}$$

The value of an asset of age a satisfies the Bellman equation

$$V(a) = \max\{p(a) + \delta V(a+1), \ p(0) - c + \delta V(1)\}$$

where we set $p(n) = -\infty$ to enforce replacement of an asset of age n. The Bellman equation asserts that if the manufacturer keeps an asset of age a, he earns $p(a)$ over the coming year and begins the subsequent year with an asset that is one year older and worth $V(a+1)$; if he replaces the asset, however, he starts the year with a new asset, earns $p(0) - c$ over the year, and begins the subsequent year with an asset that is one year old and worth $V(1)$. Actually, our language is a little loose here. The value $V(a)$ measures not only the current and future net earnings of an asset of age a, but also the net earnings of all future assets that replace it.

7.2.3 Asset Replacement with Maintenance

Consider the preceding example, but suppose that the productivity of the asset may be enhanced by performing annual service maintenance. Specifically, at the beginning of each year, a manufacturer must decide whether to replace the asset with a new one or, if he elects to keep the asset, whether to service it. An asset that is a years old and has been serviced s times yields a profit contribution $p(a, s)$ up to an age of n years, at which point the asset becomes unsafe and must be replaced by law. The cost of a new asset is c, and the cost of servicing an asset is k. What replacement-maintenance policy maximizes profits?

This is an infinite horizon, deterministic model with time t measured in years. The state variables

$$a \in \{1, 2, 3, \ldots, n\}$$

$$s \in \{0, 1, 2, \ldots, n-1\}$$

are the age of the asset in years and the number of servicings it has undergone, respectively. The action variable

$$x \in \{\text{no action, service, replace}\}$$

is the hold-replacement-maintenance decision. The state transition function is

$$g(a, s, x) = \begin{cases} (a+1, s), & x = \text{no action} \\ (1, 0), & x = \text{service} \\ (a+1, s+1), & x = \text{replace} \end{cases}$$

The reward function is

$$f(a, s, x) = \begin{cases} p(a, s), & x = \text{no action} \\ p(0, 0) - c, & x = \text{service} \\ p(a, s+1) - k, & x = \text{replace} \end{cases}$$

The value of asset of age a that has undergone s servicings satisfies the Bellman equation

$$V(a, s) = \max \{p(a, s) + \delta V(a + 1, s), \; p(a, s + 1) - k + \delta V(a + 1, s + 1),$$
$$p(0, 0) - c + \delta V(1, 0)\}$$

where we set $p(n, s) = -\infty$ for all s to enforce replacement of an asset of age n. The Bellman equation asserts that if the manufacturer replaces an asset of age a with servicings s, he earns $p(0, 0) - c$ over the coming year and begins the subsequent year with an asset worth $V(1, 0)$; if he services the asset, he earns $p(a, s + 1) - k$ over the coming year and begins the subsequent year with an asset worth $V(a + 1, s + 1)$. As with the previous example, the value $V(a, s)$ measures not only the current and future net earnings of the asset, but also the net earnings of all future assets that replace it.

7.2.4 Option Pricing

An American put option gives the holder the right, but not the obligation, to sell a specified quantity of a commodity at a specified strike price on or before a specified expiration date. In the Cox-Ross-Rubinstein binomial option-pricing model, the price of the commodity is assumed to follow a two-state discrete jump process. Specifically, if the price of the commodity is p at time t, then its price in time $t + \Delta t$ will be pu with probability q and p/u with probability $1 - q$ where

$$u = \exp(\sigma \sqrt{\Delta t})$$

$$q = \frac{1}{2} + \frac{\sqrt{\Delta t}}{2\sigma} \left(r - \frac{1}{2}\sigma^2 \right)$$

$$\delta = \exp(-r \Delta t)$$

Here, r is the annualized interest rate, continuously compounded, σ is the annualized volatility of the commodity price, and Δt is the length of time between decisions measured in years. Assuming the price of the commodity is p_0 at time $t = 0$, what is the value of an unexercised American put option with strike price K if it expires T years from today?

This is a finite horizon, stochastic model with time measured in periods of length $\Delta t = T/N$ years each. The state[3]

$$p \in \{p_0 u^i \mid i = -N, -N + 1, \ldots, N - 1, N\}$$

---

3. In this example, we alter our notation to conform with standard treatment of option valuation in the finance literature: t measures continuous time, T measures time to expiration (in years), i indexes periods, and N indicates the number of periods to expiration. For additional option pricing examples, see section 10.1.

is the commodity price. The action variable

$$x \in \{\text{hold, exercise}\}$$

is the exercise decision. The state transition probabilities are

$$P(p' \mid p, x) = \begin{cases} q, & p' = pu \\ 1 - q, & p' = p/u \\ 0, & \text{otherwise} \end{cases}$$

The reward function is

$$f(p, x) = \begin{cases} 0, & x = \text{hold} \\ K - p, & x = \text{exercise} \end{cases}$$

The value of the option at the beginning of period i, given that the underlying commodity price is p, satisfies the Bellman equation

$$V_i(p) = \max\{K - p, q\delta V_{i+1}(pu) + (1 - q)\delta V_{i+1}(p/u)\}$$

subject to the terminal condition

$$V_{N+1}(p) = 0$$

Here, $i = 0, 1, 2, \ldots, N$ indexes the decision points, which are associated with times $t = i \Delta t$. If the option is exercised, the owner receives $K - p$. If he holds the option, however, he earns no immediate reward but will have an option in hand the following period worth $V_{i+1}(pu)$ with probability q and $V_{i+1}(p/u)$ with probability $1 - q$. An option expires in the terminal decision period, making it valueless the following period.

7.2.5   Water Management

Water from a reservoir can be used for either irrigation or recreation. Irrigation during the spring benefits farmers but reduces the reservoir level during the summer, damaging the interests of recreational users. Specifically, if the reservoir contains s units of water at the beginning of the year and x units are released for irrigation, farmer and recreational user benefits during the year will be $F(x)$ and $U(s - x)$, respectively. Reservoir levels are replenished by random rainfall during the winter. Specifically, it rains k units with probability p_k, for $k = 0, 1, 2, \ldots, K$. The reservoir can hold only M units of water, and excess rainfall flows out without benefit to either farmer or recreational user. What irrigation policy maximizes the sum of farmer and recreational user benefits over an infinite time horizon?

This is an infinite horizon, stochastic model with time t measured in years. The state variable

$$s \in \{0, 1, 2, \ldots, M\}$$

is the reservoir level at beginning of the year, measured in units. The action variable

$$x \in \{0, 1, 2, \ldots, s\}$$

is the amount of water released for irrigation during the year, measured in units. The state transition probabilities are

$$P(s' \mid s, x) = \sum_{s'=\min(s-x+k,M)} p_k$$

The reward function is

$$f(s, x) = F(x) + U(s - x)$$

The value of the reservoir, given that it contains s units of water at the beginning of the year, satisfies the Bellman equation

$$V(s) = \max_{x=0,1,\ldots,s} \left\{ F(x) + U(s - x) + \delta \sum_k p_k V(\min(s - x + k, M)) \right\}$$

7.2.6 Bioeconomic Model

In order to survive, an animal must forage for food in one of m distinct areas. In area k, the animal survives predation with probability p_k, finds food with probability q_k, and, if it finds food, gains e_k energy units. The animal expends one energy unit every period and has a maximum energy carrying capacity $\bar{s}$. If the animal's energy stock drops to zero, it dies. What foraging pattern maximizes the animal's probability of surviving T periods to reproduce at the beginning of period $T + 1$?

This is a finite horizon, stochastic model with time t measured in foraging periods. The state variable

$$s \in \{0, 1, 2, \ldots, \bar{s}\}$$

is the stock of energy at the beginning of the period. The action variable

$$k \in \{1, 2, \ldots, m\}$$

is the choice of foraging area. The state transition probabilities are, for $s = 0$,

$$P(s' \mid s, k) = \begin{cases} 1, & s' = 0 \\ 0, & \text{otherwise} \end{cases}$$

and, for $s > 0$,

$$P(s' \mid s, k) = \begin{cases} p_k q_k, & s' = \min(\bar{s}, s - 1 + e_k) & \text{(survives, finds food)} \\ p_k(1 - q_k), & s' = s - 1 & \text{(survives, finds no food)} \\ (1 - p_k), & s' = 0 & \text{(does not survive)} \\ 0, & \text{otherwise} \end{cases}$$

Here, $s = 0$ represents death, an absorbing state that, once entered, is never exited. The reward function is

$$f(s, k) = 0$$

because the only reward is to procreate, which is realized only in period $T + 1$. The probability of surviving to procreate, given the animal has energy stock s in period t, satisfies the Bellman equation

$$V_t(s) = \max_{k \in \{1, 2, \dots, m\}} \{p_k q_k V_{t+1}(\min(\bar{s}, s - 1 + e_k)) + p_k(1 - q_k)V_{t+1}(s - 1)\}$$

for $s > 0$, with $V_t(0) = 0$, subject to the terminal condition

$$V_{T+1}(s) = \begin{cases} 0, & s = 0 \\ 1, & s > 0 \end{cases}$$

In this example, the value function represents an iterated probability, not a monetary value, and thus is not discounted.

7.3 Solution Algorithms

In this section we develop numerical solution algorithms for stochastic discrete time, discrete space Markov decision models. The algorithms apply to deterministic models as well, provided one views a deterministic model as a special case of the stochastic model for which the state transition probabilities are all zeros or ones.

To develop solution algorithms, we must introduce some vector notation and operations. Assume that the states $S = \{1, 2, \dots, n\}$ and actions $X = \{1, 2, \dots, m\}$ are indexed by the first n and m integers, respectively. Let $v \in \mathbb{R}^n$ denote an arbitrary value vector:

$$v_i \in \mathbb{R} = \text{value in state } i$$

and let $x \in X^n$ denote an arbitrary policy vector:

$$x_i \in X = \text{action in state } i$$

Also, for each policy $x \in X^n$, let $f(x) \in \mathbb{R}^n$ denote the n-vector of rewards earned in each state when one follows the prescribed policy:

$$f_i(x) = \text{Reward in state } i, \text{ given action } x_i \text{ taken}$$

For problems with constrained actions, we set $f_i(x) = -\infty$ if x_i is not an admissible action in state i. Finally, let $P(x) \in \mathbb{R}^{n \times n}$ denote the $n \times n$ state transition probabilities when one follows the prescribed policy:

$$P_{ij}(x) = \text{probability of jump from state } i \text{ to } j, \text{ given that action } x_i \text{ is taken}$$

Given this notation, the Bellman equation for the finite horizon model may be succinctly expressed as a recursive vector equation. Specifically, if $v_t \in \mathbb{R}^n$ denotes the value function in period t, then

$$v_t = \max_x \{f(x) + \delta P(x)v_{t+1}\}$$

where "max" is the vector operation of taking the maximum element of each row individually. Similarly, the Bellman equation for the infinite horizon model may be succinctly expressed as a vector fixed-point equation

$$v = \max_x \{f(x) + \delta P(x)v\}$$

We now consider three algorithms for solving the Bellman equation, one for finite horizon models and two for infinite horizon models.

7.3.1   Backward Recursion

Given the recursive nature of the finite horizon Bellman equation, one may compute the optimal value and policy functions v_t and x_t using backward recursion:

0. Initialization: Specify the rewards f, transition probabilities P, discount factor δ, terminal period T, and terminal value function v_{T+1}; set $t \leftarrow T$.

1. Recursion step: Given v_{t+1}, compute v_t and x_t:

$$v_t \leftarrow \max_x \{f(x) + \delta P(x)v_{t+1}\}$$

$$x_t \leftarrow \text{argmax}_x \{f(x) + \delta P(x)v_{t+1}\}$$

2. Termination check: If $t = 1$, stop; otherwise set $t \leftarrow (t-1)$ and return to step 1.

Each recursive step involves a finite number of algebraic operations, implying that the finite horizon value functions are well defined for every period. Note, however, that it may be possible to have more than one sequence of optimal policies if ties occur when performing the maximization embedded in the Bellman equation. Since the algorithm requires exactly T iterations, it terminates in finite time with the value functions precisely computed and at least one sequence of optimal policies obtained.

7.3.2   Function Iteration

Because the infinite horizon Bellman equation is a vector fixed-point equation, one may compute the optimal value and policy functions v and x using standard function iteration methods:

0. Initialization: Specify the rewards f, transition probabilities P, discount factor δ, convergence tolerance τ, and an initial guess for v.

1. Function iteration: Update the value function v:

$$v \leftarrow \max_x \{ f(x) + \delta P(x)v \}$$

2. Termination check: If $||\Delta v|| < \tau$, set

$$x \leftarrow \operatorname{argmax}_x \{ f(x) + \delta P(x)v \}$$

and stop; otherwise return to step 1.

Function iteration does not guarantee an exact solution in finitely many iterations. However, if the discount factor δ is less than one, the fixed-point mapping can be shown to be a strong contraction. Thus the infinite horizon value function exists and is unique, and theoretically may be computed to an arbitrary accuracy using function iteration. Moreover, an upper bound on the approximation error may be explicitly computed. Specifically, if the algorithm terminates at iteration k with iterate v_k, then

$$||v_k - v^*||_\infty \leq \frac{\delta}{1 - \delta} ||v_k - v_{k-1}||_\infty$$

where v^* is the true value function.

7.3.3   Policy Iteration

The Bellman fixed-point equation for an infinite horizon model may alternatively be recast as a rootfinding problem

$$v - \max_x \{ f(x) + \delta P(x)v \} = 0$$

and solved using Newton's method. By the Envelope Theorem, the derivative of the left-hand side with respect to v is $I - \delta P(x)$, where x is optimal for the embedded maximization problem. As such, the Newton iteration rule is

$$v \leftarrow v - [I - \delta P(x)]^{-1}[v - f(x) - \delta P(x)v]$$

where P and f are evaluated at the optimal x. After algebraic simplification, the iteration rule may be written

$$v \leftarrow [I - \delta P(x)]^{-1} f(x)$$

Newton's method applied to the Bellman equation of a discrete Markov decision model traditionally has been referred to as *policy iteration:*

0. Initialization: Specify the rewards f, transition probabilities P, discount factor δ, and an initial guess for v.

1. Policy iteration: Given the current value approximant v, update the policy x

$$x \leftarrow \operatorname*{argmax}_{x}\{f(x) + \delta P(x)v\}$$

and then update the value

$$v \leftarrow [I - \delta P(x)]^{-1} f(x)$$

2. Termination check: If $\Delta v = 0$, stop; otherwise return to step 1.

At each iteration, policy iteration either finds the optimal policy or offers a strict improvement in the value function in at least one state. Because the total number of states and actions is finite, the total number of admissible policies is also finite, guaranteeing that policy iteration will terminate after finitely many iterations with an exact optimal solution (at least as exact as floating point arithmetic allows). Policy iteration, however, requires the solution of a linear equation system at each iteration. If $P(x)$ is large and dense, the linear equation could be expensive to solve, making policy iteration slow and possibly infeasible because of memory limitations. In these instances, the function iteration algorithm may be the better choice.

7.3.4   Curse of Dimensionality

The backward recursion, function iteration, and policy iteration algorithms are structured as a series of three nested loops. The outer loop involves either a backward recursion, function iteration, or policy iteration; the middle loop involves visits to each state; and the inner loop involves visits to each action. The computational effort needed to solve a discrete Markov decision model is roughly proportional to the product of the number of times each loop must be executed. More precisely, if n is the number of states and m is the number of actions, then nm total actions need to be evaluated with each outer iteration.

The computational effort needed to solve a discrete Markov decision model is particularly sensitive to the dimensionality of the state and action variables. Suppose, for the sake of argument, that the state variable is k-dimensional and each dimension of the state variable has l different levels. Then the number of states will equal $n = l^k$, which implies that the computational effort required to solve the discrete Markov decision model will grow exponentially, not linearly, with the dimensionality of the state space. The same conclusion will be true regarding the dimensionality of the action space. The tendency for the solution time to grow exponentially with the dimensionality of the state or action space is called the *curse of dimensionality*. Historically, the curse of dimensionality has represented the most severe practical problem encountered in solving discrete Markov decision models.

7.4   Dynamic Simulation Analysis

The optimal value and policy functions provide some insight into the nature of the controlled dynamic economic process. The optimal value function describes the benefits of being in a given state, and the optimal policy prescribes the optimal action to be taken there. However, the optimal value and policy functions provide only a partial, essentially static, picture of the controlled process. Typically, one wishes to analyze the process further to learn about its dynamic behavior. Furthermore, one often wishes to know how the dynamic behavior is affected by changes in model parameters.

To analyze the dynamics of the controlled economic process, one will typically perform dynamic-path and steady-state analysis. Dynamic-path analysis examines how the controlled process evolves over time starting from some initial state. Specifically, dynamic-path analysis describes the path or expected path followed by the state or some other endogenous variable over time and how the path or expected path will vary with the model parameters.

Steady-state analysis examines the long-run tendencies of the controlled economic process over an infinite horizon, without regard to the path followed over time. Steady-state analysis of a deterministic model seeks to find the values to which the state or other endogenous variables will converge over time and to determine how the limiting values will vary with the model parameters. Steady-state analysis of a stochastic model requires derivation of the steady-state distribution of the state or other endogenous variable. In many cases, one is satisfied to find the steady-state means and variances of these variables and to determine how they vary with the model parameters.

The path followed by the controlled deterministic process of a finite horizon Markov decision model is easily computed. Given the state transition function g and the sequence of optimal policy functions x_t^*, the path taken by the process from an initial state through the terminal period can be computed iteratively as follows:

$$s_{t+1} = g\left(s_t, x_t^*(s_t)\right)$$

Given the state path, it is straightforward to derive the path of optimal actions through the relationship $x_t = x_t^*(s_t)$. Similarly, given the state and action paths, one is able to derive the path taken by any function of the state and action. The path followed by the controlled deterministic process of an infinite horizon Markov decision model is analyzed similarly. Given the state transition function g and optimal policy x^*, the path taken by the process from an initial state can be computed iteratively as follows:

$$s_{t+1} = g\left(s_t, x^*(s_t)\right)$$

The steady state of the controlled-state process can be computed by continuing to form iterates until they converge. Alternatively, the steady state can be found by testing which states s, if any, satisfy $s = g(s, x^*(s))$. The path and steady-state values of other endogenous variables, including the action variable, can then be computed from the path and steady state of the controlled-state process.

Analysis of stochastic problems is a bit more complicated because the controlled-state processes follow a random path, not a deterministic one. Consider a finite-horizon process model whose optimal policies x_t^* have been derived for each period t. Under the optimal policy, the controlled-state process will be a finite horizon Markov chain with nonstationary transition probability matrices P_t^* whose typical ijth element is the probability of jumping from state i in period t to state j in period $t+1$, given that the optimal policy $x_t^*(i)$ is followed in period t:

$$P_{tij}^* = \Pr\left(s_{t+1} = j | s_t = i, x_t = x_t^*(i)\right)$$

The controlled-state process of an infinite horizon stochastic model with optimal policy x^* will be a stationary Markov chain with transition probability matrix P^* whose typical ijth element is the probability of jumping from state i in one period t to state j in the following period, given that the optimal policy $x^*(i)$ is followed:

$$P_{ij}^* = \Pr\left(s_{t+1} = j | s_t = i, x_t = x^*(i)\right)$$

Given the transition probability matrix P^* of the controlled-state process, it is possible to simulate a representative state path, or, for that matter, many representative state paths, by performing Monte Carlo simulation. To perform Monte Carlo simulation, one picks an initial state, say s_0. Having the state $s_t = i$, one may simulate s_{t+1} by randomly picking a new state j with probability P_{ij}^*. The path taken by the controlled-state process of an infinite-horizon stochastic model may also be described probabilistically. To this end, let

Q_t denote the matrix whose typical ijth element is the probability that the process will be in state j in period t, given that it is in state i in period 0. Then the t-period transition probability matrices Q_t are simply the matrix powers of the transition probability matrix P^*:

$$Q_t = (P^*)^t$$

Given the t-period transition probability matrices Q_t, one can fully describe, in a probabilistic sense, the path taken by the controlled process from any initial state $s_0 = i$ by looking at the ith row of the matrices Q_t.

In most economic applications, the multiperiod transition matrices Q_t will converge to a matrix Q as t goes to infinity. In such cases, each entry of Q will indicate the relative frequency with which the controlled decision process will visit a given state in the long run, when starting from a given initial state. In the event that all the rows of Q are identical, the long-run probability of visiting a given state is independent of initial state, and the controlled state process is said to possess a steady-state distribution. The steady-state distribution is given by the probability vector π that is the common row of the matrix Q. Given the steady-state distribution of the controlled state process, it becomes possible to compute summary measures about the long-run behavior of the controlled process, such as its long-run mean or variance. Also, it is possible to derive the long-run probability distributions of the optimal action variable and other endogenous variables that are functions of the state and action. Examples of these analyses will be presented in the numerical examples in section 7.6.

7.5   A Discrete Dynamic Programming Tool Kit

In order to simplify the process of solving and analyzing discrete Markov decision models, the CompEcon Toolbox contains a series of MATLAB routines that perform many of the necessary operations.

The central routine is `ddpsolve`, which solves discrete Markov decision models using the dynamic programming algorithms discussed in the section 7.3. The routine, in its most general form, is executed as follows:

```
[v,x,pstar] = ddpsolve(model,vinit)
```

Here, on input, `model` is a structured variable that contains all relevant model information, and `vinit` is an optional initial guess for the value function of an infinite horizon model (default is the zero function). On output, `v` is the optimal value function, `x` is the optimal policy, and `pstar` is the transition probability matrix of the controlled state process. As defaults, the routine uses policy iteration if the horizon is infinite and backward recursion if the horizon is finite; however, if the horizon is infinite, function iteration may be used by executing the following command before calling ddpsolve:

```
optset('ddpsolve','algorithm','funcit');
```

The structured variable model contains the fields horizon, discount, reward, and, if needed, vterm. The field horizon contains the time horizon, a positive integer, which is specified only if the horizon is finite. The field discount contains the discount factor; it must be a positive scalar less than or equal to one if the horizon is finite and less than one if the horizon is infinite. The field reward contains the $n \times m$ matrix of rewards; its elements are real numbers, and its rows and columns are associated with states and actions, respectively. The field vterm contains an $n \times 1$ vector of terminal values that is specified only if the horizon is finite; its default value is the zero vector.

The structured variable model also contains a field transprob or transfunc, depending on whether the model is stochastic or deterministic, respectively. The field transprob, which must be specified for stochastic models, contains the $m \times n \times n$ three-dimensional array of state transition probabilities; the first dimension is associated with the action, the second dimension is associated with this period's state, and the third dimension is associated with next period's state. The field transfunc, which must be specified for deterministic models, contains the $n \times m$ matrix of deterministic state transitions; its rows are associated with this period's state, and its columns are associated with this period's action.

The CompEcon routine ddpsolve implements dynamic programming algorithms relying on two elementary routines. One elementary routine, valmax, takes a value function v, reward matrix f, transition probability array P, and discount factor delta and solves the optimization problem embedded in the Bellman equation, yielding an updated value function v and optimal policy x:

```
[v,x] = valmax(v,f,P,delta);
```

The second elementary routine, valpol, takes a policy x, reward matrix f, and transition probability array P and returns the state reward function fstar and state transition probability matrix pstar induced by the policy:

```
[pstar,fstar] = valpol(x,f,P);
```

Given the CompEcon Toolbox routines valmax and valpol, it is straightforward to implement the backward recursion, function iteration, and policy iteration algorithms. A MATLAB script that performs backward recursion for a finite horizon model is

```
for t=T:-1:1
  [v(:,t),x(:,t)] = valmax(v(:,t+1),f,P,delta);
end
```

A MATLAB script that performs function iteration for the infinite horizon model is

```
for it=1:maxit
  vold = v;
  [v,x] = valmax(v,f,P,delta);
  if norm(v-vold)<tol, return, end;
end
```

And a MATLAB script that performs policy iteration for the infinite horizon model is

```
for it=1:maxit
  vold = v;
  [v,x] = valmax(v,f,P,delta);
  [pstar,fstar] = valpol(x,f,P);
  v = (speye(n)-delta*pstar)\fstar;
  if norm(v-vold)<tol, return, end;
end
```

In these implementations, `maxit` and `tol` are the maximum iterations allowed and the convergence tolerance, respectively, which have specified default values that may be overridden with the routine `optset` as suggested by the following examples:

```
optset('ddpsolve','maxit',100);
optset('ddpsolve','tol',1E-8);
```

The CompEcon Toolbox also provides two utilities for performing dynamic analysis. The first routine, `ddpsimul` is employed as follows:

```
spath = ddpsimul(pstar,sinit,N);
```

On input, `pstar` is the transition probability matrix induced by the optimal policy, which is generated by the routine `ddpsolve`; `sinit` is a $k \times 1$ vector of initial state indices, each entry of which initiates a distinct replication of the controlled state process; and `N` is the number of periods over which the controlled state process will be simulated. On output, `spath` is a $k \times (N + 1)$ matrix containing the indices of k replications of the controlled state process, each $N + 1$ periods in duration. When the model is deterministic, the path is deterministic. When the model is stochastic, the path is generated by Monte Carlo methods.

The CompEcon Toolbox also provides a second utility for performing dynamic analysis called `markov`, which is employed as follows:

```
pi = markov(pstar);
```

On input, `pstar` is the transition probability matrix induced by the optimal policy, which is generated by the routine `ddpsolve`. On output, `pi` is a vector containing the steady-state distribution of the controlled state process, if it exists.

Finally, the CompEcon Toolbox also provides a utility `getindex` that facilitates working with state transition functions and transition probability matrices by computing the index associated with a given state. The routine is employed as follows:

```
i = getindex(s,S);
```

On input, `s` is an element of the state space, and `S` is the state space. The element `s` is $1 \times d$, and the state space `S` is $n \times d$, where n is the total number of states and d is the dimensionality of the state space. On output, `i` is an integer between 1 and n indicating the row index of the state element. The routine is useful because the state transitions are often easier to compute in terms of the elements of the state space, rather than their corresponding integer indices, although specifying the state transition and transition probability matrices requires knowledge of the indices.

Given the aforementioned discrete dynamic programming routines, the most significant practical difficulty typically encountered when solving discrete Markov decision models is correctly initializing the reward and state transition matrices. We demonstrate how to apply these routines in the following section.

7.6   Numerical Examples

7.6.1   Mine Management

Consider the mine-management model of section 7.2.1 assuming a market price $p = 1$, initial stock of ore $\bar{s} = 100$, cost of extraction $c(s, x) = x^2/(1 + s)$, and annual discount factor $\delta = 0.9$. One may solve the mine-management model using CompEcon library routines as follows:

First, one enters the model parameters. Here, the market price, initial stock of ore, and discount factor are specified, respectively:

```
price = 1;
sbar  = 100;
delta = 0.9;
```

Second, one specifies the state and action spaces:

```
S = (0:sbar)';
X = (0:sbar)';
```

```
n = length(S);
m = length(X);
```

Third, one constructs the reward matrix. Here, the reward is set to negative infinity if the extraction level exceeds the available stock in order to preclude the choice of an infeasible action:

```
f = zeros(n,m);
for i=1:n
for k=1:m
  if X(k)<=S(i)
    f(i,k) = price*X(k)-(X(k)^2)./(1+S(i));
  else
    f(i,k) = -inf;
  end
end
end
```

Fourth, one constructs the deterministic state transition rule g:

```
g = zeros(n,m);
for i=1:n
for k=1:m
  snext = S(i)-X(k);
  g(i,k) = getindex(snext,S);
end
end
```

Here, the routine getindex is used to find the index of the following period's state.

Fifth, one packs the model structure. Here, model is a structured variable whose fields contain the reward matrix, state transition function, and discount factor, respectively:

```
model.reward    = f;
model.transfunc = g;
model.discount  = delta;
```

Sixth, one solves the decision model. To solve the model using Newton's method, the default solution algorithm, one issues the command:

```
[v,x,pstar] = ddpsolve(model)
```

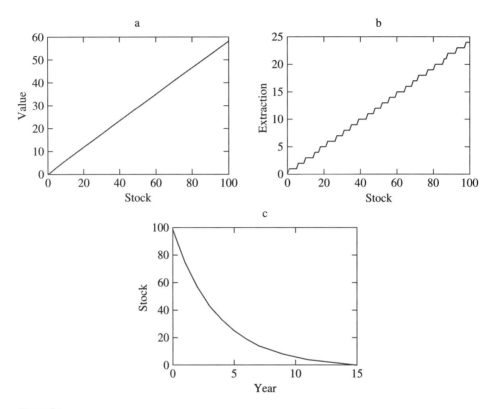

Figure 7.1
Solution to Mine-Management Model: (a) Optimal Value Function; (b) Optimal Extraction Policy; (c) Optimal State Path

To solve the model via function iteration, one issues the following command prior to calling `ddpsolve`:

```
optset('ddpsolve','algorithm','funcit');
```

In either case, `ddpsolve` returns the $n \times 1$ vector of values v, the $n \times 1$ vector of optimal actions x, and the $n \times n$ controlled state transition probability matrix `pstar`.

Finally, one performs postoptimality analysis. Figures 7.1a and 7.1b give the value function and the optimal extraction policy, respectively. The value of the firm is very nearly proportional to the stock level. Figure 7.1c gives the path followed by the stock level over time, beginning from a stock level of 100. The path was computed by performing a deterministic simulation of 15 years in duration using the CompEcon library routine

```
ddpsimul:
```

```
sinit = max(S); nyrs = 15;
spath = ddpsimul(pstar,sinit,nyrs);
```

As seen in this figure, the content of the mine is optimally exhausted in 15 years.

7.6.2   Asset Replacement

Consider the asset replacement model of section 7.2.2 assuming a profit contribution $p(a) = 50 - 2.5a - 2.5a^2$ that is a function of the asset age a in years. Further assume a maximum asset age of 5 years, asset replacement cost $c = 75$, and annual discount factor $\delta = 0.9$. One may solve the asset replacement model using CompEcon library routines as follows:

First, one enters the model parameters. Here, the maximum asset age, replacement cost, and discount factor are specified, respectively:

```
maxage  = 5;
repcost = 75;
delta   = 0.9;
```

Second, one specifies the state space:

```
S = (1:maxage)';
n = length(S);
```

Third, one constructs the reward matrix. Here, the columns of the reward matrix correspond to the two admissible decisions, keep and replace:

```
f = [50-2.5*S-2.5*S.^2 (50-repcost)*ones(n,1)];
```

Fourth, one constructs the deterministic state transition rule g:

```
g = zeros(n,2);
for i=1:n
  g(i,1) = min(i+1,n);
  g(i,2) = 1;
end
```

Fifth, one packs the model structure. Here, model is a structured variable whose fields contain the reward matrix, state transition function, and discount factor, respectively:

```
model.reward    = f;
model.transfunc = g;
model.discount  = delta;
```

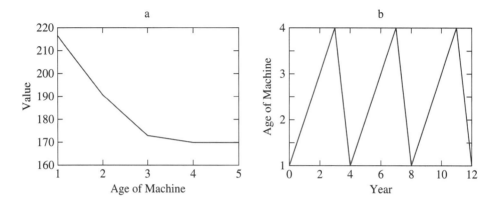

Figure 7.2
Solution to Asset Replacement Model: (a) Optimal Value Function; (b) Optimal State Path

Sixth, one solves the decision model:

```
[v,x,pstar] = ddpsolve(model);
```

Finally, one performs postoptimality analysis. Figure 7.2a gives the value of the firm at the beginning of the period as a function of the asset's age. Figure 7.2b gives the age of the asset along the optimal path. As can be seen in this figure, the asset is replaced every four years. The path was computed by performing a deterministic simulation of 12 years in duration using the CompEcon library routine ddpsimul:

```
sinit = 1; nyrs = 12;
spath = ddpsimul(pstar,sinit,nyrs);
```

7.6.3   Asset Replacement with Maintenance

Consider the asset replacement with maintenance model of section 7.2.3 assuming a profit contribution $p(a, s) = (1 - (a - s)/5)(50 - 2.5a - 2.5a^2)$ that is a function of the asset age a in years and annual servicings s. Further assume a maximum asset age of 5 years, asset replacement cost $c = 75$, cost of servicing $k = 10$, and annual discount factor $\delta = 0.9$. One may solve the asset replacement with maintenance model using CompEcon library routines as follows:

First, one enters the model parameters. Here, the maximum asset age, replacement cost, maintenance cost, and discount factor are specified, respectively:

```
maxage  = 5;
repcost = 75;
```

```
mancost = 10;
delta   = 0.9;
```

Second, one specifies the state space. Here, the set of possible asset ages and servicings are generated individually, and then a two-dimensional state grid is constructed by forming their Cartesian product using the CompEcon routine `gridmake`:

```
s1 = (1:maxage)';
s2 = (0:maxage-1)';
S  = gridmake(s1,s2);
n  = length(S);
```

Note that `s1` enumerates all possible ages, `s2` enumerates all possible servicings, and `S` enumerates all conceivable combinations of ages and servicings.

Third, one constructs the reward matrix. Here, the columns of the reward matrix, which correspond to the three admissible decisions (no action, service, replace), are computed individually and then combined:

```
q  = (50-2.5*S(:,1)-2.5*S(:,1).^2);
f1 = q.*min(1,1-(S(:,1)-S(:,2))/maxage);
f2 = q.*min(1,1-(S(:,1)-S(:,2)-1)/maxage) - mancost;
f3 = (50 - repcost)*ones(n,1);
f  = [f1 f2 f3];
```

Fourth, one constructs the deterministic state transition rule `g`:

```
g = zeros(n,3);
for i=1:n
  g(i,1) = getindex([S(i,1)+1 S(i,2)],S);
  g(i,2) = getindex([S(i,1)+1 S(i,2)+1],S);
  g(i,3) = getindex([1 0],S);
end
```

Here, the routine `getindex` is used to find the index of the following period's state.

Fifth, one packs the model structure. Here, `model` is a structured variable whose fields contain the reward matrix, state transition function, and discount factor, respectively:

```
model.reward    = f;
model.transfunc = g;
model.discount  = delta;
```

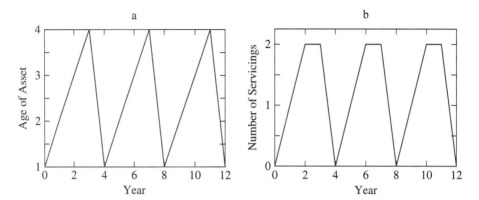

Figure 7.3
Solution to Asset Replacement with Maintenance Model: (a) Optimal State Path, Age of Asset; (b) Optimal State
Path, Number of Servicings

Sixth, one solves the decision model:

```
[v,x,pstar] = ddpsolve(model);
```

Finally, one performs postoptimality analysis. Figure 7.3a and 7.3b give the age of the
asset and the number of times it has been serviced, respectively, along the optimal path. As
can be seen in these figures, the asset is replaced every four years and is serviced twice,
at the beginning of the second and third years of operation. The paths were computed by
performing a deterministic simulation of 12 years in duration using the CompEcon library
routine ddpsimul:

```
sinit = 1; nyrs = 12;
spath = ddpsimul(pstar,sinit,nyrs);
```

7.6.4 Option Pricing

Consider the binomial option pricing model (section 7.2.4) assuming a current asset price
$p_0 = 2.00$, strike price $\bar{p} = 2.10$, annual interest rate $r = 0.05$, annual volatility $\sigma = 0.2$,
and time to expiration $T = 0.5$ years that is to be divided into $N = 100$ intervals. One may
solve the option pricing model using CompEcon library routines as follows:

First, one enters the model parameters. Here, the time to expiration in years, annual
volatility, annual interest rate, strike price, current asset price, and number of time intervals
are specified, respectively. In addition, the length of the time interval, discount factor,

up-jump factor, and up-jump probability are computed:

```
T       = 0.5;
sigma   = 0.2;
r       = 0.05;
strike  = 2.1;
p0      = 2;
N       = 100;
tau     = T/N;
delta   = exp(-r*tau);
u       = exp(sigma*sqrt(tau));
q       = 0.5+sqrt(tau)*(r-(sigma^2)/2)/(2*sigma);
```

Second, one specifies the state space:

```
price = p0*(u.^(-N:N))';
n = length(price);
```

Third, one constructs the reward matrix. Here, the columns of the reward matrix correspond to the two admissible decisions, hold and exercise:

```
f = [zeros(n,1) strike-price];
```

Fourth, one constructs the transition probability matrix P:

```
P = zeros(2,n,n);
for i=1:n
  P(1,i,min(i+1,n)) = q;
  P(1,i,max(i-1,1)) = 1-q;
end
```

Note how the transition probability matrix associated with the decision to exercise the option is identically the zero matrix, to ensure that the expected future value of an exercised option always is computed to zero.

Fifth, one packs the model structure. Here, model is a structured variable whose fields contain the reward matrix, transition probability matrix, and discount factor, respectively:

```
model.reward    = f;
model.transprob = P;
model.horizon   = N;
model.discount  = delta;
```

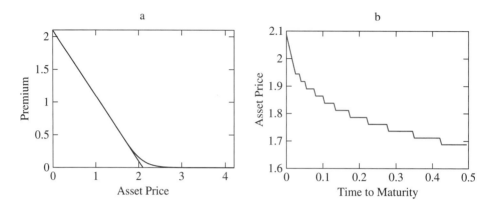

Figure 7.4
Solution to Option Pricing Model: (a) Put Option Value; (b) Put Option Optimal Exercise Boundary

Sixth, one solves the decision model. To solve the finite horizon model using backward recursion, one issues the command:

```
[v,x] = ddpsolve(model);
```

On exit, $v(:,1)$ is an $n \times 1$ vector that contains the value of the American option in the current period for different asset prices.

Finally, one performs postoptimality analysis. Figure 7.4a gives value of the American option in the current period as a function of the asset price. Figure 7.4b gives a crude approximation of the critical asset price below which it is optimal to exercise the option. As can be seen in the figure, the critical exercise price rises and converges to the strike price as time to expiration diminishes to zero.

7.6.5 Water Management

Consider the water management model of section 7.2.5 assuming a farmer benefit function $F(x) = \alpha_1 x^{\beta_1}$ and a recreational user benefit function $G(x) = \alpha_2(s-x)^{\beta_2}$, where $\alpha_1 = 14$, $\beta_1 = 0.8, \alpha_2 = 10$, and $\beta_2 = 0.4$. Further assume a reservoir capacity $M = 30$ and a discount factor $\delta = 0.9$, and assume that it rains 0, 1, 2, 3, and 4 units with probabilities 0.1, 0.2, 0.4, 0.2, and 0.1, respectively. One may solve the water management model using CompEcon library routines as follows:

First, one enters the model parameters. Here, the farmer and user benefit function parameters, reservoir capacity, rainfall probability distribution, and discount factor are specified, respectively:

```
alpha1 =  14;
beta1  = 0.8;
alpha2 =  10;
beta2  = 0.4;
maxcap =  30;
r = [0 1 2 3 4];
p = [0.1 0.2 0.4 0.2 0.1];
delta  = 0.9;
```

Second, one specifies the state and action spaces:

```
S = (0:maxcap)';
X = (0:maxcap)';
n = length(S);
m = length(X);
```

Third, one constructs the reward matrix. Here, the reward is set to negative infinity if the amount released for irrigation exceeds the reservoir level, in order to prohibit an infeasible action:

```
f = zeros(n,m);
for i=1:n
for k=1:m
  if k>i
    f(i,k) = -inf;
  else
    f(i,k) = alpha1*X(k).^beta1+alpha2*(S(i)-X(k)).^beta2;
  end
end
end
```

Fourth, one constructs the transition probability matrix P:

```
P = zeros(m,n,n);
for k=1:m
for i=1:n
for j=1:length(r)
  snext = min(S(i)-X(k)+r(j),maxcap);
```

```
  inext = getindex(snext,S);
  P(k,i,inext) = P(k,i,inext) + p(j);
end
end
end
```

Here, the routine `getindex` is used to find the index of the following period's state.

Fifth, one packs the model structure. Here, `model` is a structured variable whose fields contain the reward matrix, transition probability matrix, and discount factor, respectively:

```
model.reward     = f;
model.transprob  = P;
model.discount   = delta;
```

Sixth, one solves the decision model:

```
[v,x,pstar] = ddpsolve(model);
```

Finally, one performs postoptimality analysis. Figure 7.5a gives the optimal irrigation policy. As can be seen in this figure, no water is released for irrigation if the reservoir level is below 3 units, whereas 5 units of water are released if the reservoir level is above 25 units. Figure 7.5b gives the value of the reservoir content.

Figure 7.5c gives the expected reservoir level over time beginning with an empty reservoir. As can be seen in this figure, the expected reservoir level rises steadily, converging on its steady-state mean of 12.5 units. The expected reservoir level was computed by performing 10,000 stochastic simulations of 30 years in duration using the CompEcon library routine `ddpsimul`:

```
sinit = ones(10000,1); nyrs = 30;
spath = ddpsimul(pstar,sinit,nyrs);
```

Figure 7.5d gives the steady-state distribution of the reservoir level. As can be seen in this figure, the steady-state distribution is symmetric about a mean of 12.5 units. The steady-state distribution `pi` was computed using the CompEcon library routine `markov`:

```
pi = markov(pstar);
```

7.6.6   Bioeconomic Model

Consider the bioeconomic model of section 7.2.6 assuming a terminal decision period $T = 10$ and a maximum energy carrying capacity $\bar{s} = 8$. Further assume that there are three foraging areas whose energy offerings are 2, 4, and 5 units, respectively; whose predation survival probabilities are 1.0, 0.7, and 0.8, respectively; and whose foraging

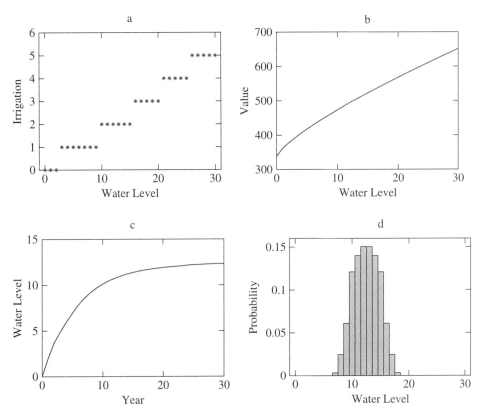

Figure 7.5
Solution to Water-Management Model: (a) Optimal Irrigation Policy; (b) Optimal Value Function; (c) Optimal State Path; (d) Steady-State Distribution

success probabilities are 0.5, 0.8, and 0.7, respectively. One may solve the bioeconomic model using CompEcon library routines as follows:

First, one enters the model parameters. Here, the time horizon, maximum energy-carrying capacity, area energy offerings, predation survival probabilities, and foraging success probabilities are specified, respectively:

```
T    = 10;
emax =  8;
e = [2 4 5];
p = [1.0 0.7 0.8];
q = [0.5 0.8 0.7];
```

Second, one specifies the state space:

```
S = 0:emax;
n = length(S);
```

Third, one constructs the reward matrix. Here, the reward matrix is identically zero, since the reward is earned only after the terminal decision period:

```
f = zeros(n,3);
```

Fourth, one constructs the transition probability matrix P:

```
P = zeros(m,n,n);
for k=1:m
  P(k,1,1) = 1;
  for i=2:n;
     snext = 0; j=getindex(snext,S);
     P(k,i,j) = P(k,i,j) + (1-p(k));
     snext = S(i)-1+e(k); j=getindex(snext,S);
     P(k,i,j) = P(k,i,j) + p(k)*q(k);
     snext = S(i)-1; j=getindex(snext,S);
     P(k,i,j) = P(k,i,j) + p(k)*(1-q(k));
  end
end
```

Here, the routine `getindex` is used to find the index of the following period's state.

Fifth, one specifies the terminal value function `vterm`. Upon reaching period $T + 1$, if the energy stock is positive, the animal procreates with probability 1; if the stock is zero, however, the animal procreates with probability 0:

```
vterm = ones(n,1);
vterm(1) = 0;
```

Sixth, one packs the model structure. Here, `model` is a structured variable whose fields contain the reward matrix, transition probability matrix, time horizon, discount factor, and terminal value function, respectively:

```
model.reward    = f;
model.transprob = P;
model.horizon   = T;
model.discount  = 1;
model.vterm     = vterm;
```

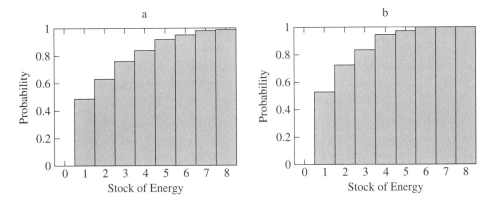

Figure 7.6
Solution to Bioeconomic Model: (a) Survival Probability, Period 0; (b) Survival Probability, Period 5

Seventh, one solves the decision model. To solve the finite horizon model using backward recursion, one issues the command:

```
[v,x] = ddpsolve(model);
```

On exit, v is an $n \times (T + 1)$ vector that contains the survival probabilities for different energy levels over time; x will be an $n \times T$ matrix containing the indices of the optimal foraging areas for different energy levels over time.

Finally, one performs postoptimality analysis. Figures 7.6a and 7.6b give the survival probabilities as functions of the energy level for periods 0 and 5, respectively. Clearly, survival probabilities increase with the energy level and as the procreation period approaches.

Exercises

7.1. Consider a timber stand that grows by one unit of biomass per year. Harvesting decisions are made at the beginning of each year. If the stand is harvested, new seedlings are replanted immediately (so the stand has biomass 1 at the beginning of the following year). The price of harvested timber is p dollars per unit of biomass, and the cost of harvesting and replanting is c. The firm discounts the future using an annual discount factor of δ.

a. Formulate the firm's dynamic optimization problem. Specifically, formulate the Bellman equation, clearly identifying the state and action variables, the state and action spaces, the reward function, and the state transition function.

b. For $\delta = 0.95$, $p = 1$, and $c = 5$, determine the optimal harvesting policy. What is the optimal policy if $p = 2$?

7.2. A firm operates in an uncertain profit environment. At the beginning of each period, the firm observes its potential short-run variable profit π, which may be negative, and decides whether to operate, making a short-run variable profit π, or to temporarily shut down, making a short-run variable profit of zero. Although the firm faces no fixed costs or shutdown costs, it incurs a start-up cost c if it reopens after a period of inactivity. The short-run variable profit π is an exogenous Markov process that assumes five values, p_1, p_2, p_3, p_4, and p_5, with transition probabilities $P_{ij} = \Pr(\pi_{t+1} = p_j | \pi_t = p_i)$.

a. Formulate the firm's dynamic optimization problem. Specifically, formulate the Bellman equation, clearly identifying the state and action variables, the state and action spaces, the reward function, and the transition probabilities.

b. In the standard static model of the firm, a firm will shut down if its short-run variable profit p_t is negative. Is this condition sufficient in the current model? If not, what is the sufficient condition?

7.3. Consider the preceding problem assuming a start-up cost $c = 0.8$, discount factor $\delta = 0.95$, and short-run variable profit that assumes five values, $p_1 = -1.0$, $p_2 = -0.2$, $p_3 = 0.4$, $p_4 = 1.2$, and $p_5 = 2.0$, with the following transition probabilities:

		To				
		p_1	p_2	p_3	p_4	p_5
	p_1	0.1	0.2	0.3	0.4	0.0
	p_2	0.1	0.3	0.2	0.2	0.2
From	p_3	0.1	0.5	0.2	0.1	0.1
	p_4	0.2	0.1	0.3	0.2	0.2
	p_5	0.3	0.2	0.2	0.1	0.2

a. What is the optimal operation policy? Specifically, under what short-run profits will a previously closed firm open, and under what short-run profits will a previously open firm close?

b. Graph the expected short-run profit less start-up costs over a 10-year horizon. Assume that the short-run profit for this year is -1 and the firm is currently closed.

c. In the long run, what percentage of the time will be firm be open? How does this result change if the start-up cost rises to 1.5?

7.4. Consider a competitive price-taking firm that wishes to maximize profits from harvesting a nonrenewable resource. In any year, the firm earns revenue px where p is the market price for the harvested resource and x is the amount harvested by the firm; the firm also incurs cost $0.2x^{1.5}$. The market price is an exogenous Markov process that assumes two values, $p = 1$ and $p = 2$, according to the transition probability matrix

$\Pr[p_{t+1} = 1 | p_t = 1] = 0.8$

$\Pr[p_{t+1} = 2 | p_t = 1] = 0.2$

$\Pr[p_{t+1} = 1 | p_t = 2] = 0.3$

$\Pr[p_{t+1} = 2 | p_t = 2] = 0.7$

Assume an annual discount factor $\delta = 0.95$.

a. Formulate the firm's dynamic optimization problem. Specifically, formulate the Bellman equation, clearly identifying the state and action variables, the state and action spaces, the reward function, and the transition probabilities.

b. Plot on the same graph the value of the firm as a function of the initial stock for $p = 1$ and $p = 2$, respectively, with the initial stock ranging from 0 to 100.

c. Plot on the same graph the optimal harvest as a function of the initial stock for $p = 1$ and $p = 2$, respectively, with the initial stock ranging from 0 to 100.

d. Assuming an initial stock of 100 units and a price of $p = 1$, graph expected stocks over a 20-year horizon.

7.5. At the beginning of every year, a firm must decide how much to produce over the coming year in order to meet the demand for its product. The demand over any year is known at the beginning of the year, but it varies annually, assuming serially independent values of 5,000, 6,000, 7,000, or 8,000 units with probabilities 0.1, 0.3, 0.4, and 0.2, respectively. The firm's cost of production in year t is $10q_t + (q_t - q_{t-1})^2$ thousand dollars, where q_t is thousands of units produced in year t. The product sells for \$20 per unit, and excess production can be either carried over to the following year at a cost of \$2 per unit or disposed of for free. The firm's production and storage capacities are 8,000 and 5,000 units per annum, respectively. The annual discount factor is 0.9. Assuming that the firm meets its annual demand exactly and that production and storage levels must be integer multiples of 1,000 units, answer the following questions:

a. Formulate the firm's dynamic optimization problem. Specifically, formulate the Bellman equation, clearly identifying the state and action variables, the state and action spaces, the reward function, and the transition probabilities.

b. What is the value of the firm, and what is its optimal production if its previous year's production was 5,000 units, its carry-in (inventories at the beginning of the period) is 2,000 units, and the demand for the coming year is 7,000 units?

c. Under the same initial conditions as in part b, plot expected production and stock levels over a 10-year horizon.

7.6. A dairy producer must decide whether to keep and lactate a cow or replace it with a new one. A cow yields $y_i = 8 + 2i - 0.25i^2$ tons of milk over its ith lactation up to ten lactations, after which she becomes barren and must be replaced. Assume that the net cost of replacing a cow is 500 dollars, the profit contribution of milk is 150 dollars per ton, and the per-lactation discount factor is $\delta = 0.9$.

a. Formulate the firm's dynamic optimization problem. Specifically, formulate the Bellman equation, clearly identifying the state and action variables, the state and action spaces, the reward function, and the transition probabilities.

b. What lactation-replacement policy maximizes profits? How is this policy affected if the profit contribution of milk rises to 200 dollars per ton?

c. What is the optimal policy if the cost of replacement c_t follows a three-state Markov chain with possible values $400, $500, and $600 and transition probabilities?

		c_{t+1}	
c_t	$400	$500	$600
$400	0.5	0.4	0.1
$500	0.2	0.6	0.2
$600	0.1	0.4	0.5

Bibliographic Notes

There are many books that provide good introductions to dynamic programming and provide examples of its application to discrete time, discrete space dynamic optimization models. Among the best are the classic texts Bellman (1957) and Bellman and Dreyfus (1962). Other, more recent introductions include Ross (1983), Bertsekas (1976), and Bertsekas and Shreve (1978).

Many of the models discussed in the chapter are generic versions of models appearing in the academic literature. We offer only a limited number of references. Discussion of dynamic resource economic models can be found in Clark (1976), Conrad and Clark (1987), Hotelling (1931), and Pindyck (1978, 1984). Numerous examples of agricultural and resource management problems can also be found in J.O.S. Kennedy (1986). The mine management model is discussed in Conrad and Clark (1987); the binomial option-pricing model is discussed in Ross (1983); the water management model is discussed in J.O.S. Kennedy (1986); and the bioeconomic model is discussed in Clark (1976).

8 Discrete Time, Continuous State Dynamic Models: Theory and Examples

We now turn our attention to discrete time dynamic economic models whose state variables may assume a continuum of values. Three classes of discrete time, continuous state dynamic economic models are examined. One class includes models of centralized decision making by individuals, firms, or institutions that may involve either discrete or continuous choices. Examples of continuous state dynamic decision models involving discrete choices include a financial investor deciding when to exercise a put option, a capitalist deciding whether to enter or exit an industry, and a producer deciding whether to keep or replace a physical asset. Examples of continuous state decision models admitting a continuum of choices include a central planner managing the harvest of a natural resource, an entrepreneur planning production and investment, and a consumer making consumption and savings decisions.

A second class of discrete time, continuous state dynamic models examined includes models of strategic gaming among a small number of individuals, firms, or institutions. Dynamic game models attempt to capture the behavior of a small group of dynamically optimizing agents when the policy pursued by one agent affects the welfare of another. Examples of such models include national grain marketing boards deciding how much grain to sell on world markets, producers of substitute goods deciding whether to expand factory capacity, and individuals deciding how much work effort to exert within an income risk-sharing arrangement.

A third class of discrete time, continuous state dynamic economic models examined includes partial and general equilibrium models of collective, decentralized economic behavior. Dynamic equilibrium models characterize the behavior of a market, economic sector, or entire economy through intertemporal arbitrage conditions that are enforced by the collective action of atomistic dynamically optimizing agents. Often the behavior of agents at a given date depends on their expectations of what will happen at a future date. If it is assumed that agents' expectations are consistent with the implications of the model, then the model is said to be a rational expectations model. Rational expectations models may be used to study asset returns in a pure exchange economy, futures prices in a primary commodity market, and producer responses to government price support programs.

Dynamic optimization and equilibrium models are closely related. The solutions to continuous state, continuous action dynamic optimization models may often be equivalently characterized by first-order intertemporal equilibrium conditions obtained by differentiating the Bellman equation. Conversely, many dynamic equilibrium problems can be "integrated" into equivalent optimization formulations. Whether cast in optimization or equilibrium form, most discrete time, continuous state dynamic economic models pose infinite-dimensional fixed-point problems that lack closed-form solution. This chapter introduces the theory of discrete time, continuous state dynamic economic models and provides illustrative examples. The subsequent chapter is devoted to numerical methods that may be used to solve and analyze such models.

8.1   Continuous State Dynamic Programming

The discrete time, continuous state Markov decision model has the following structure: in every period t, an agent observes the state of an economic system s_t, takes an action x_t, and earns a reward $f(s_t, x_t)$ that depends on both the state of the system and the action taken. The state of the economic system is a controlled Markov process. Specifically, the state of the economic system in period $t + 1$ will depend on the state and action in period t and an exogenous random shock ϵ_{t+1} that is unknown in period t:

$$s_{t+1} = g(s_t, x_t, \epsilon_{t+1})$$

The agent seeks a sequence of policies $\{x_t^*\}$ that prescribe the action $x_t = x_t^*(s_t)$ that should be taken in any given state and period so as to maximize the present value of current and expected future rewards over a time horizon T, discounted at a per-period factor δ.

A continuous state Markov decision model may have an infinite horizon ($T = \infty$) or a finite horizon ($T < \infty$). A continuous state Markov decision model may also be either deterministic or stochastic. If the model is stochastic, the exogenous random shocks ϵ_t are assumed to be independently and identically distributed over time, and independent of preceding states and actions.

The state space S, which enumerates all the states attainable by the system, includes continuous state variables whose ranges are intervals of the real line. The state space, however, may also include discrete state variables whose ranges are finite. If all states are continuous, the state space is said to be purely continuous; if some states are continuous and some are discrete, the state space is said to be mixed.

The action space X, which enumerates all actions that may be taken by the agent, may possess continuous action variables whose ranges are intervals of the real line or discrete action variables whose ranges are finite. We limit our discussion, however, to models whose actions are all of one form or the other. If all actions are continuous, the model is said to be a continuous choice model; if all actions are discrete, the model is said to be a discrete choice model. In some instances, the set of actions available to the agent may vary with the state of the economic process s. In such cases, the restricted action space is denoted $X(s)$.

Like the discrete Markov decision problem, the discrete time, continuous state Markov decision problem may be analyzed using dynamic programming methods based on Bellman's principle of optimality, which was articulated by Bellman (1957) as follows: "An optimal policy has the property that, whatever the initial state and decision are, the remaining decisions must constitute an optimal policy with regard to the state resulting from the first decision."

The principle of optimality formally may be expressed in the form of the *Bellman equation*. Denote by $V_t(s)$ the maximum attainable sum of current and expected future rewards, given that the economic process is in state s in period t. Then the principle of optimality implies that the *value functions* $V_t : S \mapsto \mathbb{R}$ must satisfy

$$V_t(s) = \max_{x \in X(s)} \{f(s, x) + \delta E_\epsilon V_{t+1}(g(s, x, \epsilon))\}, \quad s \in S, \quad t = 1, 2, \ldots, T$$

The Bellman equation captures the essential problem faced by a dynamic, future-regarding optimizing agent: the need to optimally balance an immediate reward $f(s_t, x_t)$ against expected future rewards $\delta E_t V_{t+1}(s_{t+1})$.

In a finite horizon model, we adopt the convention that the optimizing agent faces decisions in periods 1 through $T < \infty$. The agent faces no decisions after the terminal decision period T, but may earn a final reward $V_{T+1}(s_{T+1})$ in the subsequent period that depends on the realization of the state in that period. The terminal value is typically fixed by some economically relevant terminal condition. In many applications, V_{T+1} is identically zero, indicating that no rewards are earned by the agent beyond the terminal decision period. In other applications, V_{T+1} may specify a salvage value earned by the agent after making his final decision in period T.

If the decision problem has an infinite horizon, the value functions will not depend on time t. We may, therefore, discard the time subscripts and write the Bellman equation as a functional fixed-point equation whose single unknown is the common value function V:

$$V(s) = \max_{x \in X(s)} \{f(s, x) + \delta E_\epsilon V(g(s, x, \epsilon))\}, \quad s \in S$$

If the discount factor δ is less than one and the reward function f is bounded, the mapping underlying the Bellman equation is a strong contraction on the space of bounded continuous functions and, thus, by the Contraction Mapping Theorem, will possess a unique solution.

8.2 Euler Conditions

Markov decision models with purely continuous state and action spaces are special because their solutions can often be characterized by "first-order" equilibrium conditions. Characterizing the solution to a Markov decision problem in terms of its equilibrium conditions, the so-called Euler conditions, provides an intertemporal arbitrage interpretation that helps the analyst understand and explain the essential features of the controlled dynamic economic process. In this section we derive the Euler conditions for the infinite horizon model, leaving derivation of the Euler conditions for finite horizon models as an exercise. We assume that the reward functions f and the state transition functions g are twice continuously differentiable over S and X and that the per-period discount factor δ is less than one.

The equilibrium conditions of a purely continuous Markov decision problem involve not the value function but its derivative

$$\lambda(s) \equiv V'(s)$$

We call λ the shadow price function. It represents the marginal value of the state variable to the optimizer or, equivalently, the price that the optimizer imputes to the state variable.

The equilibrium conditions for discrete time, continuous state, continuous choice Markov decision problems are derived by applying the Karush-Kuhn-Tucker and Envelope Theorems to the optimization problem embedded in the Bellman equation. Assuming actions are unconstrained, the Karush-Kuhn-Tucker conditions for the embedded optimization problem imply that the optimal action x, given state s, satisfies the equimarginality condition

$$f_x(s, x) + \delta E_\epsilon \left[\lambda \big(g(s, x, \epsilon) \big) g_x(s, x, \epsilon) \right] = 0$$

The Envelope Theorem applied to the same problem implies

$$f_s(s, x) + \delta E_\epsilon \left[\lambda \big(g(s, x, \epsilon) \big) g_s(s, x, \epsilon) \right] = \lambda(s)$$

Here, f_x, f_s, g_x, and g_s denote partial derivatives whose dimensions are $1 \times d_x$, $1 \times d_s$, $d_s \times d_x$, and $d_s \times d_s$, respectively, where d_s and d_x are the dimensions of the state and action spaces, respectively.

In certain applications, the state transition depends only on the action taken by the agent, so that $g_s = 0$. In these instances, it is possible to substitute the expression derived using the Envelope Theorem into the expression derived using the Karush-Kuhn-Tucker condition. This procedure eliminates the shadow price function as an unknown and simplifies the Euler conditions into a single functional equation in a single unknown, the optimal policy x:

$$f_x\big(s, x(s)\big) + \delta E_\epsilon \left[f_s \big(g \big(s, x(s), \epsilon \big), x \big(g \big(s, x(s), \epsilon \big) \big) \big) g_x \big(s, x(s), \epsilon \big) \right] = 0$$

This equation, when it exists, is called the Euler equation.

The Euler conditions take a different form when actions are subject to constraints. Suppose, for example, that actions are subject to bounds of the form

$$a(s) \le x \le b(s)$$

where $a : S \mapsto X$ and $b : S \mapsto X$ are differentiable functions of the state s. In these instances, the Euler conditions take the form

$$f_x(s, x) + \delta E_\epsilon \left[\lambda \big(g(s, x, \epsilon) \big) g_x(s, x, \epsilon) \right] = \mu$$

$$f_s(s, x) + \delta E_\epsilon \left[\lambda \big(g(s, x, \epsilon) \big) g_s(s, x, \epsilon) \right] + \min(\mu, 0) a'(s) + \max(\mu, 0) b'(s) = \lambda(s)$$

where x and μ satisfy the complementarity condition

$$a(s) \le x \le b(s), \qquad x_i > a_i(s) \Rightarrow \mu_i \ge 0, \qquad x_i < b_i(s) \Rightarrow \mu_i \le 0$$

Here, μ is a $1 \times d_x$ vector whose ith element, μ_i, measures the current and expected future reward from a marginal increase in the ith action variable x_i. At the optimum, μ_i must be nonpositive if x_i is less than its upper bound, for otherwise rewards can be increased by raising x_i; similarly, μ_i must be nonnegative if x_i is greater than its lower bound, for otherwise rewards can be increased by lowering x_i. And if x_i is neither at its upper or lower bound, μ_i must be zero to preclude the possibility of increasing rewards as a result of marginal changes in x_i in either direction.

An analyst is often interested in the long-run tendencies of the controlled economic process. If the model is deterministic, it may possess a well-defined steady state to which the controlled economic process will converge over time. The steady state is characterized by the solution to a nonlinear equation. More specifically, the steady state of an unconstrained deterministic problem, if it exists, consists of a state s^*, an action x^*, and shadow price λ^* that satisfy the Euler and state stationarity conditions

$$f_x(s^*, x^*) + \delta\lambda^* g_x(s^*, x^*) = 0$$

$$\lambda^* = f_s(s^*, x^*) + \delta\lambda^* g_s(s^*, x^*)$$

$$s^* = g(s^*, x^*)$$

The steady-state conditions of a constrained deterministic dynamic optimization problem can be similarly stated, except that they take the form of a nonlinear complementarity problem, rather than a system of nonlinear equations. Whether the action is constrained or not, the steady-state conditions pose a finite-dimensional problem that can typically be solved numerically using standard nonlinear equation or complementarity methods. In simpler applications, the conditions can often be solved analytically, even if the Bellman and Euler equations do not possess closed-form solutions. In such situations, it is often further possible through implicit differentiation to derive explicit closed-form expressions for the derivatives of the steady-state state, action, and shadow price with respect to critical model parameters.

Knowledge of the steady state of a deterministic Markov decision problem is often useful in applied work. For most well-posed deterministic problems, the controlled economic process will converge to the steady state, regardless of initial condition. The steady state, therefore, unequivocally characterizes the long-run behavior of the controlled process. The analyst will often be satisfied to understand the dynamics of the controlled process around the steady state, given that this is the region where the process tends to reside. For stochastic models, however, the state and action generally will not converge to specific values, and the long-run behavior of the model can only be described probabilistically. Nonetheless, in these cases, it is often practically useful to derive the steady state of the deterministic "certainty-equivalent" problem obtained by fixing all exogenous random shocks at their respective means. Knowledge of the certainty-equivalent steady state can assist the analyst by providing a reasonable initial guess for the optimal policy, value, and shadow price functions in iterative numerical solution algorithms designed to solve the Bellman equation or Euler conditions. Also, one can often solve a hard stochastic dynamic model by first solving the certainty-equivalent model, and then solving a series of models obtained by gradually perturbing the variance of the shock from zero back to its true level, always using the solution of one model as the starting point for the algorithm used to solve the subsequent model.

8.3   Continuous State, Discrete Choice Models

8.3.1   Asset Replacement

At the beginning of each year, a manufacturer must decide whether to continue to operate an aging physical asset or replace it with a new one. An asset that is a years old produces $q(a)$ units of output up to $\bar{a}$ years, at which point the asset becomes unsafe and must be replaced by law. The cost of a new asset is c, and the profit contribution per unit of output p is an exogenous continuous-valued Markov process

$$p_{t+1} = h(p_t, \epsilon_{t+1})$$

What replacement policy maximizes profits?

This is an infinite horizon, stochastic model with time t measured in years. The state variables

$$p \in (0, \infty)$$

$$a \in \{1, 2, 3, \ldots, \bar{a}\}$$

are the current unit profit contribution of output, a continuous variable, and the age of the asset in years, a discrete variable. The action variable

$$x \in \{\text{keep, replace}\}$$

is the keep-replacement decision, a discrete variable. The state transition function is

$$g(p, a, x, \epsilon) = \begin{cases} (h(p, \epsilon), a + 1), & x = \text{keep} \\ (h(p, \epsilon), 1), & x = \text{replace} \end{cases}$$

The reward function is

$$f(p, a, x) = \begin{cases} pq(a), & x = \text{keep} \\ pq(0) - c, & x = \text{replace} \end{cases}$$

The value of an asset of age a, given that the unit profit contribution of output is p, satisfies the Bellman equation

$$V(p, a) = \max \left\{ pq(a) + \delta E_\epsilon V\left(h(p, \epsilon), a + 1\right), pq(0) - c + \delta E_\epsilon V\left(h(p, \epsilon), 1\right) \right\}$$

The Bellman equation asserts that if the manufacturer keeps an asset of age a, he earns $pq(a)$ over the coming year and begins the subsequent year with an asset that is one year older and worth $V(p', a + 1)$, where p' is the following year's unit profit contribution; if he replaces the asset, however, he starts the year with a new asset, earns $pq(0) - c$ over the coming year, and begins the subsequent year with an asset that is one year old and worth $V(p', 1)$.

8.3.2   Industry Entry and Exit

A firm operates in an uncertain profit environment. At the beginning of each period, the firm observes its potential short-run operating profit over the coming period π, which may be negative, and decides whether to operate, making a short-run profit π, or not operate, making a short-run profit 0. Although the firm faces no fixed costs, it incurs a shutdown cost K_0 when it closes and a start-up cost K_1 when it reopens. The short-run profit π is an exogenous continuous-valued Markov process

$$\pi_{t+1} = h(\pi_t, \epsilon_{t+1})$$

What is the optimal entry-exit policy? In particular, how low must the short-run profit be for an operating firm to close, and how high must the short-run profit be for nonoperating firm to reopen?

   This is an infinite horizon, stochastic model with time t measured in years. The state variables

$$\pi \in (-\infty, \infty)$$

$$d \in \{0, 1\}$$

are the current short-run profit, a continuous variable, and the operational status of the firm, a binary variable that equals 1 if the firm is operating and 0 if the firm is not operating. The action variable

$$x \in \{0, 1\}$$

is the operating decision for the coming year, a binary variable that equals 1 if the firm operates and 0 if does not operate. The state transition function is

$$g(\pi, d, x, \epsilon) = \left(h(\pi, \epsilon), x\right)$$

The reward function is

$$f(\pi, d, x) = \pi x - K_1(1 - d)x - K_2 d(1 - x)$$

The value of the firm, given that the current short-run profit is π and the firm's operational status is d, satisfies the Bellman equation

$$V(\pi, d) = \max_{x=0,1} \left\{ \pi x - K_1(1 - d)x - K_2 d(1 - x) + \delta E_\epsilon V \big(h(\pi, \epsilon), x \big) \right\}$$

8.3.3 American Option Pricing

An American put option gives the holder the right, but not the obligation, to sell a specified quantity of a commodity at a specified strike price K on or before a specified expiration period T. In the discrete time, continuous state Black-Scholes option pricing model, the price of the commodity follows an exogenous continuous-valued Markov process

$$p_{t+1} = h(p_t, \epsilon_{t+1})$$

What is the value of an American put option in period t if the commodity price is p? At what critical price is it optimal to exercise the put option, and how does this critical price vary over time?

This is a finite horizon, stochastic model with time t measured in periods. The state variables

$$p \in (0, \infty)$$

$$d \in \{0, 1\}$$

are the current commodity price, a continuous variable, and the exercise status of the option, a discrete variable that equals 1 if the option has been exercised previously and equals 0 otherwise. The action variable

$$x \in \{0, 1\}$$

is the exercise decision, a discrete variable that equals 1 if the option is exercised and equals 0 otherwise. The state transition function is

$$g(p, d, x, \epsilon) = \big(h(p, \epsilon), x \big)$$

The reward function is

$$f(p, d, x) = \begin{cases} K - p, & d = 0, x = 1 \\ 0, & \text{otherwise} \end{cases}$$

The value of an unexercised option in period t, given that the commodity price is p, satisfies the Bellman equation

$$V_t(p, 1) = \max \left\{ K - p, \delta E_\epsilon V_{t+1}\big(h(p, \epsilon), 1\big) \right\}$$

subject to the terminal condition $V_{T+1}(p, 1) = 0$. The value of a previously exercised option is zero, regardless of the price of the commodity; that is, $V_t(p, 0) = 0$ for all p and t.

8.4   Continuous State, Continuous Choice Models

8.4.1   Economic Growth

Consider an economy that produces and consumes a single composite good. Each year begins with a predetermined amount of the good s in stock, of which an amount x is invested and the remainder $s - x$ is consumed, yielding a social benefit $u(s - x)$. The amount of the good available at the beginning of each year is a controlled continuous-valued Markov process

$$s_{t+1} = \gamma x_t + \epsilon_{t+1} h(x_t)$$

where γ is the capital survival rate (1 minus the depreciation rate), h is the aggregate production function, and ϵ is a positive production shock with mean 1. What consumption-investment policy maximizes the sum of current and expected future social benefits?

This is an infinite horizon, stochastic model with time t measured in years. The state variable

$$s \in [0, \infty)$$

is the stock of good at the beginning of the year. The action variable

$$x \in [0, s]$$

is the amount of good invested. The state transition function is

$$g(s, x, \epsilon) = \gamma x + \epsilon h(x)$$

The reward function is

$$f(s, x) = u(s - x)$$

The sum of current and expected future social benefits, given a stock s, satisfies the Bellman equation

$$V(s) = \max_{0 \le x \le s} \left\{ u(s - x) + \delta E_\epsilon V\big(\gamma x + \epsilon h(x)\big) \right\}$$

Assuming $u'(0) = \infty$ and $h(0) = 0$, the constraints will never be binding at an optimum, and the shadow price of the composite good $\lambda(s)$ will satisfy the Euler equilibrium conditions

$$u'(s - x) - \delta E_\epsilon \left[\lambda \left(\gamma x + \epsilon h(x) \right) \left(\gamma + \epsilon h'(x) \right) \right] = 0$$

$$\lambda(s) = u'(s - x)$$

These conditions imply that along the optimal path

$$u'_t = \delta E_t [u'_{t+1} (\gamma + \epsilon_{t+1} h'_t)]$$

where u'_t is current marginal utility and $\epsilon_{t+1} h'_t$ is the following period's marginal product of capital. Thus the utility derived from consuming a unit of the good today must equal the discounted expected utility derived from investing it and consuming its yield tomorrow.

The certainty-equivalent steady state, which is obtained by fixing the production shock ϵ at its mean 1, are the stock level s^*, investment level x^*, and shadow price λ^* that solve the nonlinear equation system

$$u'(s^* - x^*) = \delta \lambda^* \left(\gamma + h'(x^*) \right)$$

$$\lambda^* = u'(s^* - x^*)$$

$$s^* = \gamma x^* + h(x^*)$$

The certainty-equivalent steady-state conditions imply the golden rule: $1 - \gamma + r = h'(x^*)$, where $\delta = 1/(1 + r)$. That is, the marginal product of capital must equal the capital depreciation rate plus the discount rate.

8.4.2   Renewable Resource Management

A social planner wishes to maximize social benefits derived from harvesting a publicly owned resource. Each year begins with a predetermined stock of the resource s, of which an amount x is harvested at a total cost $c(x)$ and sold at a market-clearing price $p(x)$. The remainder $s - x$ is retained for reproduction. The stock of resource available at the beginning of each period is a controlled deterministic process

$$s_{t+1} = h(s_t - x_t)$$

What harvest policy maximizes net social surplus over time? What are the steady-state resource stock and harvest, and how do they vary with the discount rate?

This is an infinite horizon, deterministic model with time t measured in years. The state variable

$$s \in [0, \infty)$$

is the stock of resource at beginning of the year. The action variable

$$x \in [0, s]$$

is the amount of resource harvested. The state transition function is

$$g(s, x) = h(s - x)$$

The reward function is

$$f(s, x) = \int_0^x p(\xi) \, d\xi - c(x)$$

The sum of current and future social benefits, given a stock s, satisfies the Bellman equation

$$V(s) = \max_{0 \le x \le s} \left\{ \int_0^x p(\xi) \, d\xi - c(x) + \delta V\big(h(s - x)\big) \right\}$$

Assuming $p(0) = \infty$ and $h(0) = 0$, the constraints will never be binding at an optimum, and the shadow price of the resource $\lambda(s)$ will satisfy the Euler equilibrium conditions

$$p(x) = c'(x) + \delta\lambda\big(h(s - x)\big)h'(s - x)$$
$$\lambda(s) = \delta\lambda\big(h(s - x)\big)h'(s - x)$$

These conditions imply that along the optimal path

$$p_t = c'_t + \lambda_t$$
$$\lambda_t = \delta\lambda_{t+1}h'_t$$

where p_t is the market price, c'_t is the marginal harvest cost, and h'_t is the marginal future yield of stock in year t. Thus the market price of the harvested resource must cover both the shadow price of the unharvested resource and the marginal cost of harvesting it. Moreover, the current value of one unit of the resource equals the discounted value of its yield in the subsequent period.

The steady-state resource stock s^*, harvest x^*, and shadow price λ^* solve the equation system

$$p(x^*) = c'(x^*) + \delta\lambda^*h'(s^* - x^*)$$
$$\lambda^* = \delta\lambda^*h'(s^* - x^*)$$
$$s^* = h(s^* - x^*)$$

These conditions imply $h'(s^* - x^*) = 1 + r$. That is, in steady state, the marginal rate of growth of resource stock equals the discount rate.

8.4.3   Nonrenewable Resource Management

A mine owner wishes to maximize profit obtained from extracting and selling ore. Each year begins with a predetermined stock of ore s, of which an amount x is extracted at a total cost $c(s, x)$ and sold at a market price $p(x)$, where $c_s \leq 0$, $c_x \geq 0$, $c_s(s, 0) = 0$, and $p' < 0$. Given that the current stock of ore is $\bar{s}$, what extraction policy maximizes profit over time?

This is an infinite horizon, deterministic model with time t measured in years. The state variable

$$s \in [0, \bar{s}]$$

is the stock of ore at beginning of the year. The action variable

$$x \in [0, s]$$

is the amount of ore extracted. The state transition function is

$$g(s, x) = s - x$$

The reward function is

$$f(s, x) = p(x)\, x - c(s, x)$$

The value of the mine, given that is contains an ore stock s, satisfies the Bellman equation

$$V(s) = \max_{0 \leq x \leq s} \left\{ p(x)\, x - c(s, x) + \delta V(s - x) \right\}$$

One cannot preclude a priori the possibility that at some stock level it will be optimal to abandon the mine. As a result, the Euler conditions take the form of a complementarity condition. More specifically, the shadow price of the resource $\lambda(s)$ is characterized by

$$p(x) + p'(x)\, x - c_x(s, x) - \delta\lambda(s - x) = \mu$$

$$\lambda(s) = c_s(s, x) + \delta\lambda(s - x) + \max(\mu, 0)$$

where the ore extracted x and the long-run marginal profit of extraction μ must satisfy the complementarity condition

$$0 \leq x \leq s, \qquad x > 0 \Rightarrow \mu \geq 0, \qquad x < s \Rightarrow \mu \leq 0$$

Thus, in any period, either ore is extracted until the long-run marginal profit is driven to zero, or the mine is abandoned because it is not possible to do so. Under the assumption

$p(0) > c_x(0, 0)$, the model admits only one steady state, which is characterized by the conditions $\lambda^* = x^* = 0$ and $c_s(s^*, 0) = 0$. That is, the mine will be abandoned when the ore stock reaches the critical level s^*. Until such time that the mine is abandoned,

$$p_t + p_t' x_t = c_{x_t} + \delta \lambda_{t+1}$$

$$\lambda_t = c_{s_t} + \delta \lambda_{t+1}$$

That is, the marginal revenue of extracted ore will equal the shadow price of unextracted ore plus the marginal cost of extraction. Also, the present-valued shadow price of unextracted ore will grow at the rate at which the cost of extraction rises as a result of the depletion of the ore stock.

8.4.4   Water Management

Water from a reservoir can be used for either irrigation or recreation. Irrigation during the spring benefits farmers, but reduces the reservoir level during the summer, damaging the interests of recreational users. Specifically, if the reservoir contains s units of water at the beginning of the year and x units are released for irrigation, farmer and recreational user benefits during the year will be $F(x)$ and $U(s - x)$, respectively. Reservoir levels are replenished by by i.i.d. random rainfalls ϵ during the winter. The reservoir can hold only M units of water, and excess rainfall flows out without benefit to either farmer or recreational user. What irrigation policy maximizes the sum of farmer and recreational user benefits over an infinite time horizon?

   This is an infinite horizon, stochastic model with time t measured in years. The state variable

$$s \in [0, M]$$

is the reservoir level at the beginning of the year. The action variable

$$x \in [0, s]$$

is the amount of water released for irrigation. The state transition function is

$$g(s, x, \epsilon) = \min(s - x + \epsilon, M)$$

The reward function is

$$f(s, x) = F(x) + U(s - x)$$

The social value of the reservoir, given that it contains s units of water at the beginning of the year, satisfies the Bellman equation

$$V(s) = \max_{0 \leq x \leq s} \left\{ F(x) + U(s - x) + \delta E_\epsilon V \left(\min(s - x + \epsilon, M) \right) \right\}$$

Assuming $F'(0)$, $U'(0)$, and M are sufficiently large, the constraints will not be binding at an optimal solution, and the shadow price of water $\lambda(s)$ will satisfy the Euler equilibrium conditions

$$F'(x) - U'(s - x) - \delta E_\epsilon \lambda(s - x + \epsilon) = 0$$

$$\lambda(s) = U'(s - x) + \delta E_\epsilon \lambda(s - x + \epsilon)$$

It follows that along the optimal path

$$F'_t = U'_t + \delta E_t \lambda_{t+1}$$

where F'_t and U'_t are the marginal farmer and recreational user benefits, respectively. Thus, on the margin, the benefit received by farmers this year from releasing one unit of water must equal the marginal benefit received by recreational users this year from retaining the unit of water plus the expected benefits of having that unit of water available for either irrigation or recreation the following year.

The certainty-equivalent steady-state reservoir level s^*, irrigation level x^*, and shadow price λ^* solve the equation system

$$x^* = \bar{\epsilon}$$

$$F'(x^*) = \lambda^*$$

$$U'(s^* - x^*) = (1 - \delta) F'(x^*)$$

where $\bar{\epsilon}$ is mean annual rainfall. These conditions imply that the certainty-equivalent steady-state irrigation level and shadow price of water are not affected by the discount rate. The certainty-equivalent steady-state reservoir level, however, is affected by the discount rate.

8.4.5 Monetary Policy

A monetary authority wishes to control the nominal interest rate x in order to minimize the variation of the inflation rate s_1 and the gross domestic product (GDP) gap s_2 around specified targets s_1^* and s_2^*, respectively. Specifically, the authority wishes to minimize expected discounted stream of weighted squared deviations

$$L(s) = \tfrac{1}{2}(s - s^*)^\top \Omega (s - s^*)$$

where s is a 2×1 vector containing the inflation rate and the GDP gap, s^* is a 2×1 vector of targets, and Ω is a 2×2 constant positive definite matrix of preference weights. The inflation rate and the GDP gap are a joint controlled exogenous linear Markov process

$$s_{t+1} = \alpha + \beta s_t + \gamma x_t + \epsilon_{t+1}$$

where α and γ are 2×1 constant vectors, β is a 2×2 constant matrix, and ϵ is a 2×1 random vector with mean zero. For institutional reasons, the nominal interest rate x cannot be negative. What monetary policy minimizes the sum of current and expected future losses?

This is an infinite horizon, stochastic model with time t measured in years. The state vector

$$s \in \mathbb{R}^2$$

contains the inflation rate and the GDP gap. The action variable

$$x \in [0, \infty)$$

is the nominal interest rate. The state transition function is

$$g(s, x, \epsilon) = \alpha + \beta s + \gamma x + \epsilon$$

In order to formulate this problem as a maximization problem, one posits a reward function that equals the negative of the loss function

$$f(s, x) = -L(s)$$

The sum of current and expected future rewards satisfies the Bellman equation

$$V(s) = \max_{0 \leq x} \left\{ -L(s) + \delta E_\epsilon V\big(g(s, x, \epsilon)\big) \right\}$$

Given the structure of the model, one cannot preclude the possibility that the nonnegativity constraint on the optimal nominal interest rate will be binding in certain states. Accordingly, the shadow-price function $\lambda(s)$ is characterized by the Euler conditions

$$\delta \gamma^\top E_\epsilon \lambda\big(g(s, x, \epsilon)\big) = \mu$$

$$\lambda(s) = -\Omega(s - s^*) + \delta \beta^\top E_\epsilon \lambda\big(g(s, x, \epsilon)\big)$$

where the nominal interest rate x and the long-run marginal reward μ from increasing the nominal interest rate must satisfy the complementarity condition

$$x \geq 0, \quad \mu \leq 0, \quad x > 0 \Rightarrow \mu = 0$$

It follows that along the optimal path

$$\delta \gamma^\top E_t \lambda_{t+1} = \mu_t$$

$$\lambda_t = -\Omega(s_t - s^*) + \delta \beta^\top E_t \lambda_{t+1}$$

$$x_t \geq 0, \qquad \mu_t \leq 0, \qquad x_t > 0 \Rightarrow \mu_t = 0$$

Thus, in any period, the nominal interest rate is reduced until either the long-run marginal reward or the nominal interest rate is driven to zero.

8.4.6 Production-Adjustment Model

A monopolist wishes to manage production so as to maximize long-run profit, given that production is subject to adjustment costs. In any given period, if the firm produces a quantity q, it incurs production costs $c(q)$ and adjustment costs $a(q - l)$, where l is the preceding period's (lagged) production. The firm faces a stochastic downward-sloping demand curve and can sell the quantity it produces at the price $dP(q)$, where d is a positive i.i.d. demand shock. What production policy maximizes the value of the firm?

This is an infinite horizon, stochastic model with time t measured in periods. The state variables

$$d \in (0, \infty)$$

$$l \in [0, \infty)$$

are the current period's demand shock and the previous period's (lagged) production, respectively. The action variable

$$q \in [0, \infty)$$

is the amount produced in the current period. The state transition function is

$$g(d, l, q, \epsilon) = (\epsilon, q)$$

where ϵ is the following period's demand shock. The reward function is

$$f(d, l, q) = dP(q)q - c(q) - a(q - l).$$

The value of the firm, given that the current demand shock is d and the lagged production is l, satisfies the Bellman equation

$$V(d, l) = \max_{0 \leq q}\{dP(q)q - c(q) - a(q - l) + \delta E_\epsilon V(\epsilon, q)\}$$

Assuming a positive optimal production level in all states, the shadow price of lagged production $\lambda(d, l)$ will satisfy the Euler equilibrium conditions

$$d(P(q) + P'(q)q) - c'(q) - a'(q - l) + \delta E_\epsilon \lambda(\epsilon, q) = 0$$

$$\lambda(d, l) = a'(q - l).$$

It follows that along the optimal path

$$d_t(P(q_t) + P'(q_t)q_t) = c'_t + (a'_t - \delta E_t a'_{t+1})$$

where c'_t and a'_t are the marginal production and adjustment costs in period t. Thus, marginal revenue equals marginal cost of production plus net (current less future) marginal adjustment cost.

The certainty-equivalent steady-state production q^* is obtained by assuming that d is fixed at its mean $\bar{d}$:

$$\bar{d}(P(q^*) + P'(q^*)q^*) = c'(q^*) + (1 - \delta)a'(0)$$

8.4.7   Production-Inventory Model

A competitive price-taking firm wishes to manage production and inventories so as to maximize long-run profit. The firm begins each period with a predetermined stock of inventory s and decides how much to produce q and how much to store x, buying or selling the resulting difference $s + q - x$ on the open market at the prevailing price p. The firm's production and storage costs are given by $c(q)$ and $k(x)$, respectively, and the market price is an exogenous Markov process

$$p_{t+1} = h(p_t, \epsilon_{t+1})$$

What production policy and inventory policy maximize the value of the firm?

This is an infinite horizon, stochastic model with time t measured in periods. The state variables

$$s \in [0, \infty)$$

$$p \in [0, \infty)$$

are beginning inventories and the current period's market price, respectively. The action variables

$$q \in [0, \infty)$$

$$x \in [0, \infty)$$

are the amount produced in the current period and the ending inventories, respectively. The state transition function is

$$g(s, p, q, x, \epsilon) = \big(x, h(p, \epsilon)\big)$$

The reward function is

$$f(s, p, q, x) = p(s + q - x) - c(q) - k(x)$$

The value of the firm, given that the beginning inventories are s and market price is p satisfies the Bellman equation

$$V(s, p) = \max_{0 \le q, 0 \le x} \big\{ p(s + q - x) - c(q) - k(x) + \delta E_\epsilon V\big(x, h(p, \epsilon)\big) \big\}$$

If production is subject to increasing marginal costs and $c'(0)$ is sufficiently small, then production will be positive in all states, and the shadow price of beginning inventories $\lambda(s, p)$ will satisfy the Euler equilibrium conditions

$$p = c'(q)$$

$$\delta E_\epsilon \lambda\big(x, h(p, \epsilon)\big) - p - k'(x) = \mu$$

$$\lambda(s, p) = p$$

$$x \ge 0, \qquad \mu \le 0, \qquad x > 0 \Rightarrow \mu = 0$$

It follows that along the optimal path,

$$p_t = c'_t$$

$$x_t \ge 0, \qquad \delta E_t p_{t+1} - p_t - k'_t \le 0, \qquad x > 0 \Rightarrow \delta E_t p_{t+1} - p_t - k'_t = 0$$

where p_t denotes the market price, c'_t denotes the marginal production cost, and k'_t denotes the marginal storage cost. Thus the firm's production and storage decisions are independent. Production is governed by the conventional short-run profit-maximizing condition that price equal the marginal cost of production. Storage, however, is entirely driven by intertemporal arbitrage profit opportunities. If the expected marginal profit from storing is negative, then no storage is undertaken. Otherwise, stocks are accumulated up to the point at which the marginal cost of storage equals the present value of the expected appreciation in the market price.

The certainty-equivalent steady state obtains when p is fixed at its long-run mean $\bar{p}$, in which case there is no appreciation in the value of commodity stocks, and optimal inventories will be zero. The certainty-equivalent steady-state production is implicitly defined by the short-run profit-maximization condition.

8.4.8 Livestock Feeding

A livestock producer feeds his stock up to period T and then sells it at the beginning of period $T + 1$ at a fixed price p per unit weight. Each period, the producer must determine how much grain x to feed his livestock, given that grain sells at a constant unit cost κ. The weight of the livestock is a controlled deterministic process

$$s_{t+1} = g(s_t, x_t)$$

What feeding policy maximizes profit, given that the livestock weighs $\bar{s}$ in period 0?

This is a finite horizon, deterministic model with time t measured in periods. The state variable

$$s \in [0, \infty)$$

is the weight of the livestock. The action variable

$$x \in [0, \infty)$$

is the amount of feed supplied to the livestock. The state transition function is $g(s, x)$. The reward function is

$$f(s, x) = -\kappa x$$

The value of livestock, given that it weighs s at the beginning of period t, satisfies the Bellman equation

$$V_t(s) = \max_{x \geq 0} \left\{ -\kappa x + \delta V_{t+1}\big(g(s, x)\big) \right\}$$

subject to the terminal condition

$$V_{T+1}(s) = ps$$

If the marginal weight gain g_x at zero feed is sufficiently large, the nonnegativity constraint of feed will never be binding. Under these conditions, the shadow price of livestock weight in period t, $\lambda_t(s)$, will satisfy the Euler equilibrium conditions

$$\delta \lambda_{t+1}\big(g(s, x)\big) g_x(s, x) = \kappa$$

$$\lambda_t(s) = \delta \lambda_{t+1}\big(g(s, x)\big) g_s(s, x)$$

subject to the terminal condition

$$\lambda_{T+1}(s) = p$$

It follows that along the optimal path

$$\delta \lambda_{t+1} g_{x,t} = \kappa$$

$$\lambda_t = \delta \lambda_{t+1} g_{s,t}$$

where $g_{x,t}$ and $g_{s,t}$ represent, respectively, the marginal weight gain from feed and the marginal decline in the livestock's ability to gain weight as it grows in size. Thus the cost of feed must equal the value of the marginal weight gain. Also, the present value of the shadow price grows at a rate that exactly counters the marginal decline in the livestock's ability to gain weight.

8.5 Dynamic Games

Dynamic game models attempt to capture strategic interactions among a small number of dynamically optimizing agents when the actions of one agent affect the welfare of the others. To simplify notation, we consider only infinite horizon games. The theory and methods developed, however, can be easily adapted to accommodate finite horizons.

The discrete time, continuous state Markov m-agent game has the following structure: In every period, each agent p observes the state of an economic system $s \in S$, takes an action $x_p \in X$, and earns a reward $f_p(s, x_p, x_{-p})$ that depends on the state of the system and both the action taken by the agent x_p and the actions taken by the $m - 1$ other agents x_{-p}. The state of the economic system is a jointly controlled Markov process. Specifically, the state of the economic system in period $t + 1$ will depend on the state in period t, the actions taken by all m agents in period t, and an exogenous random shock ϵ_{t+1} that is unknown in period t:

$$s_{t+1} = g(s_t, x_t, \epsilon_{t+1})$$

As with static games, the equilibrium solution to a Markov game depends on the information available to the agents and the strategies they are assumed to pursue. We will limit discussion to noncooperative Markov perfect equilibria, that is, equilibria that yield a Nash equilibrium in every proper subgame. Under the assumption that each agent can perfectly observe the state of the system and knows the policies followed by the other agents, a Markov perfect equilibrium is a set of m policies of state-contingent actions $x_p^* : S \mapsto X$, $p = 1, 2, \ldots, m$, such that policy x_p^* maximizes the present value of agent p's current and expected future rewards, discounted at a per-period factor δ, given that other agents pursue their policies $x^*_{-p}(\cdot)$. That is, for each agent p, $x^*_p(\cdot)$ solves

$$\max_{x_p(\cdot)} E_0 \sum_{t=0}^{\infty} \delta^t f_p\left(s_t, x_p(s_t), x^*_{-p}(s_t)\right)$$

The Markov perfect equilibrium for the m-agent game is characterized by a set of m simultaneous Bellman equations

$$V_p(s) = \max_{x \in X_p(s)} \left\{ f_i\left(s, x, x^*_{-p}(s)\right) + \delta E_\epsilon V_p\left(g\left(s, x, x^*_{-p}(s), \epsilon\right)\right) \right\}$$

whose unknowns are the value functions $V_p(\cdot)$ and optimal policies $x^*_p(\cdot)$, $p = 1, 2, \ldots, m$ of the different agents. Here, $V_p(s)$ denotes the maximum current and expected future rewards that can be earned by agent p, given that other agents pursue their equilibrium strategies.

8.5.1 Capital-Production Game

Consider two firms that produce the same perishable good. Firm p begins each period with a predetermined capital stock k_p and must decide how much to produce q_p. The firm's production cost $c_p(q_p, k_p)$ depends on both the quantity produced and the capital stock. Price for the good is determined by short-run market clearing conditions under Cournot competition. More specifically, the market clearing price $P(q_1, q_2)$ is a function of the output of both firms. Each firm must also decide how much to invest in capital. Specifically, if firm p invests x_p, it incurs a cost $h_p(x_p)$, and its capital stock at the beginning of the following period will be $(1 - \psi)k_p + x_p$ where ψ is the capital depreciation rate. What are the firm's optimal production and investment policies?

This is an infinite horizon, deterministic, two-agent dynamic game with time t measured in periods. The state variables

$k_1 \in [0, \infty)$

$k_2 \in [0, \infty)$

are firm 1's and firm 2's capital stocks, respectively. The action variables for firm p

$x_p \in [0, \infty)$

$q_p \in [0, \infty)$

are the amount invested and produced in the current period, respectively. The state transition function is

$$g(k_1, k_2, x_1, x_2, q_1, q_2) = \left((1 - \psi)k_1 + x_1, (1 - \psi)k_2 + x_2\right)$$

Firm p's reward function is

$$f_p(k_1, k_2, x_1, x_2, q_1, q_2) = P(q_1, q_2)q_p - c_p(q_p, k_p) - h_p(x_p)$$

The Markov perfect equilibrium for the capital-production game is captured by a pair of Bellman equations, one for each firm, which take the form

$$V_p(k_1, k_2) = \max_{q_p \geq 0, x_p \geq 0} \{ P(q_1, q_2)q_p - c_p(q_p, k_p) - h_p(x_p) + \delta E_\epsilon V_p(\hat{k}_1, \hat{k}_2) \}$$

where $\hat{k}_p = (1 - \psi)k_p + x_p$. Here, $V_p(k_1, k_2)$ denotes the maximum current and expected future income that can be earned by firm p, given capital stocks k_1 and k_2.

8.5.2   Income Redistribution Game

Consider two infinitely lived agents who must make consumption and investment decisions. Each period, agent p begins with a predetermined level of wealth s_p, of which an amount x_p is invested, and the remainder is consumed, yielding a utility $u_p(s_p - x_p)$. Agent p's wealth at the beginning of period $t + 1$ is determined entirely by his investment in period t and an income shock ϵ_{pt+1} that is unknown at the time the investment decision is made. More specifically, wealth is a controlled Markov process

$$s_{pt+1} = h_p(x_{pt}, \epsilon_{pt+1})$$

Suppose now that the two agents coinsure against exogenous income shocks by agreeing to share their wealth. Specifically, the agents agree that, at the beginning of any given period, the wealthier of the two agents will transfer a certain proportion ψ of the wealth differential to the poorer agent. Under this scheme, agent p's wealth in period $t + 1$, after the transfer, will equal

$$s_{pt+1} = (1 - \psi)h_p(x_{pt}, \epsilon_{pt+1}) + \psi h_q(x_{qt}, \epsilon_{qt+1})$$

where $q \neq p$. If wealth transfers are enforceable, but agents otherwise may consume and invest freely, how will the agents' investment policies be affected by the income redistribution agreement?

This is an infinite horizon, stochastic, two-agent dynamic game with time t measured in periods. The state variables

$$s_1 \in [0, \infty)$$

$$s_2 \in [0, \infty)$$

are agent 1's and agent 2's posttransfer wealths, respectively. The action variable for agent p

$$x_p \in [0, s_p]$$

is the amount invested in the current period. The state transition function is

$$g(s_1, s_2, x_1, x_2, \epsilon_1, \epsilon_2) = \left(s_1', s_2'\right)$$

where

$$s_p' = (1 - \psi)h_p(x_p, \epsilon_p) + \psi h_q(x_q, \epsilon_q)$$

Marketing board p's reward function is

$$f_p(s_1, s_2, x_1, x_2) = u_p(s_p - x_p)$$

The Markov perfect equilibrium of the income redistribution game is captured by a pair of Bellman equations, one for each agent, which take the form

$$V_p(s_1, s_2) = \max_{0 \leq x_p \leq s_p} \left\{ u_p(s_p - x_p) + \delta E_\epsilon V_p\left(s_1', s_2'\right) \right\}$$

Here, $V_p(s_1, s_2)$ denotes the maximum expected lifetime utility that can be obtained by agent p under the income redistribution arrangement, given posttransfer wealth levels s_1 and s_2.

8.5.3   Marketing Board Game

Suppose that two countries are the sole producers of a commodity and that, in each country, a government marketing board has the exclusive power to sell the commodity on the world market. The marketing boards compete with each other, attempting to maximize the present value of their own current and expected future income from commodity sales. More specifically, the marketing board in country p begins each period with a predetermined supply s_p of the commodity, of which it exports a quantity q_p and stores the remainder x_p at a total cost $c_p(x_p)$. The world market price $P(q_1 + q_2)$ will depend on the total amount exported by both marketing boards. The supplies available in the two countries at the beginning period $t + 1$ are given by

$$s_{it+1} = x_{it} + \epsilon_{it+1}$$

where new production in both countries, ϵ_{1t} and ϵ_{2t}, is exogenous and independently and identically distributed over time. What are the optimal export strategies for the two marketing boards?

This is an infinite horizon, stochastic, two-agent dynamic game with time t measured in years. The state variables

$$s_1 \in [0, \infty)$$

$$s_2 \in [0, \infty)$$

are the available supplies at the beginning of the year in country 1 and country 2, respectively. The action variable for marketing board p

$$x_p \in [0, s_p]$$

is the amount to store in the current year. The state transition function is

$$g(s_1, s_2, x_1, x_2, \epsilon_1, \epsilon_2) = (x_1 + \epsilon_1, x_2 + \epsilon_2)$$

Marketing board p's reward function is

$$f_p(s_1, s_2, x_1, x_2) = P(s_1 - x_1 + s_2 - x_2)(s_p - x_p) - c_p(x_p)$$

The Markov perfect equilibrium for the marketing board game is captured by a pair of Bellman equations, one for each marketing board, which take the form

$$V_p(s_1, s_2) = \max_{0 \le x_p \le s_p} \{P(s_1 - x_1 + s_2 - x_2)(s_p - x_p) - c_p(x_p) + \delta E_\epsilon V_p(x_1 + \epsilon_1, x_2 + \epsilon_2)\}$$

Here, $V_p(s_1, s_2)$ denotes the maximum current and expected future income that can be earned by marketing board p, given available supplies s_1 and s_2.

8.6   Rational Expectations Models

We now examine dynamic stochastic models of economic systems in which arbitrage-free equilibria are enforced through the collective, decentralized actions of atomistic dynamically optimizing agents. We assume that agents are rational in the sense that their expectations are consistent with the implications of the model as a whole.

We limit attention to dynamic models of the following general form: At the beginning of period t, an economic system emerges in a state s_t. Agents observe the state of the system and, by pursuing their individual objectives, produce a systematic response x_t governed by an equilibrium condition that depends on expectations of the following period's state and action:

$$f\left(s_t, x_t, E_t h(s_{t+1}, x_{t+1})\right) = 0$$

The economic system then evolves to a new state s_{t+1} that depends on the current state s_t, the response x_t, and an exogenous random shock ϵ_{t+1} that is realized only after the system responds at time t:

$$s_{t+1} = g(s_t, x_t, \epsilon_{t+1})$$

In many applications, the equilibrium condition $f = 0$ admits a natural arbitrage interpretation. In these instances, $f_i > 0$ indicates that activity i generates a profit on the margin, so that agents have an incentive to increase x_i; $f_i < 0$ indicates that activity i generates a loss on the margin, so that agents have an incentive to decrease x_i. An arbitrage-free equilibrium exists if and only if $f = 0$.

The state space $S \subseteq \mathbb{R}^{d_s}$, which contains the states attainable by the economic system, and the response space $X \subseteq \mathbb{R}^{d_x}$, which contains the admissible system responses, are both closed convex nonempty sets. The functions $f : \mathbb{R}^{d_s+d_x+d_h} \mapsto \mathbb{R}^{d_x}$, $g : \mathbb{R}^{d_s+d_x+d_\epsilon} \mapsto \mathbb{R}^{d_s}$, and $h : \mathbb{R}^{d_s+d_x} \mapsto \mathbb{R}^{d_h}$ are continuously differentiable. The exogenous random shocks ϵ_t are identically distributed over time, mutually independent, and independent of past states and responses. The stipulation that the response in any period depends only on the expectation of the subsequent period's state and response is more general than first appears. By introducing new accounting variables, responses can be made dependent on expectations of states and responses further in the future.

The primary task facing an economic analyst is to derive the rational expectations equilibrium system response $x = x(s)$ for each state s. The response function $x(\cdot)$ is characterized implicitly as the solution to a functional equation

$$f\big(s, x(s), E_\epsilon\big[h\big(g\big(s, x(s), \epsilon\big), x\big(g\big(s, x(s), \epsilon\big)\big)\big)\big]\big) = 0$$

The equilibrium condition takes a different form when the system response is constrained. Suppose, for example, that responses are subject to bounds of the form

$$a(s) \leq x \leq b(s)$$

where $a : S \mapsto X$ and $b : S \mapsto X$ are continuous functions of the state s. In these instances, the arbitrage condition takes the form

$$f\big(s_t, x_t, E_t h(s_{t+1}, x_{t+1})\big) = \mu_t$$

where x_t and μ_t satisfy the complementarity condition

$$a(s_t) \leq x \leq b(s_t), \qquad x_{ti} > a_i(s_t) \Rightarrow \mu_{ti} \geq 0, \qquad x_{ti} < b_i(s) \Rightarrow \mu_{ti} \leq 0$$

Here, μ_t is a d_x-vector whose ith element, μ_{ti}, measures the marginal benefit from activity i. In equilibrium, μ_{ti} must be nonpositive if x_{ti} is less than its upper bound, for otherwise agents can gain by increasing activity i; similarly, μ_{ti} must be nonnegative if x_{ti} is greater than its lower bound, for otherwise agents can gain by reducing activity i. And if x_{ti} is at neither its upper nor lower bound, μ_{ti} must be zero to ensure the absence of arbitrage opportunities from revising the level of activity i.

8.6.1 Asset Pricing Model

Consider a pure exchange economy in which a representative infinitely lived agent allocates wealth between immediate consumption and investment. Wealth is held in shares of claims s_t that trade at a price p_t and pay a dividend d_t per share. The representative agent's objective is to choose consumption levels c_t to maximize the sum of discounted expected utilities $u(c_t)$ over time subject to an intertemporal budget constraint, which stipulates that the value of net shares purchased in any period must equal the dividends paid at the beginning of the period less consumption in that period:

$$p_t(s_{t+1} - s_t) = d_t s_t - c_t$$

or, equivalently,

$$s_{t+1} = s_t + (d_t s_t - c_t)/p_t$$

Under mild regularity conditions, the agent's dynamic optimization problem has a unique solution that satisfies the first-order Euler equation

$$u'(c_t)p_t = \delta E_t[u'(c_{t+1})(p_{t+1} + d_{t+1})]$$

(see exercise 8.8). The Euler equation shows that, along an optimal consumption path, the marginal utility of consuming one unit of wealth today equals the marginal benefit of investing the unit of wealth and consuming it and its dividend tomorrow.

In a representative agent economy, all agents behave in an identical fashion, and hence no shares are bought or sold. If we normalize the total number of shares to equal one, then the consumption level will equal dividends paid, $c_t = d_t$. The model is closed by assuming that the dividends d_t follow an exogenous Markov process

$$d_{t+1} = g(d_t, \epsilon_{t+1})$$

The asset pricing model is an infinite horizon, stochastic model that may be formulated with one state variable, the dividend level d; one response variable, the asset price p; and one equilibrium condition,

$$u'(d_t)p_t - \delta E_t[u'(d_{t+1})(p_{t+1} + d_{t+1})] = 0$$

A solution to the rational expectations asset pricing model is a function $p(d)$ that gives the equilibrium asset price p in terms of the exogenous dividend level d. From the dynamic equilibrium conditions, the asset return function is characterized by the functional equation

$$u'(d)p(d) - \delta E_\epsilon\big[u'\big(g(d, \epsilon)\big)\big(p\big(g(d, \epsilon)\big) + g(d, \epsilon)\big)\big] = 0$$

In the notation of the general model, with state variable d and action variable p:

$$h(d, p) = u'(d)(p + d)$$

and

$$f(d, p, Eh) = u'(d)p - \delta Eh$$

8.6.2 Competitive Storage

Consider a market for a storable primary commodity. Each period t begins with a prede-termined supply of the commodity s_t, of which an amount q_t is sold to consumers at a market clearing price $p_t = P(q_t)$ and the remainder x_t is stored. Supply at the beginning of the following period is the sum of carry in and exogenous new production ϵ_{t+1}, which is uncertain in period t:

$$s_{t+1} = x_t + \epsilon_{t+1}$$

Competitive storers seeking to maximize expected profit guarantee that profit opportunities are fully exploited in equilibrium. In particular,

$$\delta E_t p_{t+1} - p_t - c = \mu_t$$

$$x_t \geq 0, \qquad \mu_t \leq 0, \qquad x_t > 0 \Rightarrow \mu_t = 0$$

where μ_t equals the expected profit from storing one unit of the commodity. Whenever expected profit is positive, storers increase stocks, raising the current market price and lowering the expected future price, until profit is eliminated. Conversely, whenever expected profit is negative, storers decrease stocks, lowering the current market price and raising the expected future price, until either expected losses are eliminated or stocks are depleted.

The commodity storage model is an infinite horizon, stochastic model. The model may be formulated with one state variable, the supply s available at the beginning of the period; one response variable, the storage level x; and one equilibrium condition,

$$\delta E_t P(s_{t+1} - x_{t+1}) - P(s_t - x_t) - c = \mu_t$$

$$x_t \geq 0, \qquad \mu_t \leq 0, \qquad x_t > 0 \Rightarrow \mu_t = 0$$

A solution to the commodity storage model formulated in this fashion is a function $x(\cdot)$ that gives the equilibrium storage in terms of the available supply. From the dynamic equilibrium conditions, the equilibrium storage function is characterized by the functional complementarity condition

$$\delta E_\epsilon P\big(x(s) + \epsilon - x\big(x(s) + \epsilon\big) - P(s - x(s))\big) - c = \mu(s)$$

$$x(s) \geq 0, \qquad \mu(s) \leq 0, \qquad x(s) > 0 \Rightarrow \mu(s) = 0$$

In the notation of the general model

$$h(s, x) = P(s - x)$$

$$g(s, x, \epsilon) = x + \epsilon$$

and

$$f(s, x, Eh) = \delta Eh - P(s - x) - c$$

The commodity storage model also admits an alternate formulation with the market price p as the sole response variable. In this formulation, the equilibrium condition takes the form

$$\delta E_t p_{t+1} - p_t - c = \mu_t$$

$$p_t \geq P(s_t), \qquad \mu_t \leq 0, \qquad p_t > P(s_t) \Rightarrow \mu_t = 0$$

A solution to the commodity storage model formulated in this fashion is a function $\lambda(\cdot)$ that gives the equilibrium market price in terms of the available supply. From the dynamic equilibrium conditions, the equilibrium price function is characterized by the functional complementarity condition

$$\delta E_y \big[\lambda\big(s - D\big(\lambda(s)\big) + \epsilon\big)\big] - \lambda(s) - c = \mu(s)$$

$$\lambda(s) \geq P(s), \qquad \mu(s) \leq 0, \qquad \lambda(s) > P(s) \Rightarrow \mu(s) = 0$$

where $D = P^{-1}$ is the demand function. In the notation of the general model,

$$h(s, p) = p$$

$$g(s, p, y) = s - D(p) + \epsilon$$

and

$$f(s, p, Eh) = \delta Eh - p - c$$

The two formulations are mathematically equivalent. The equilibrium price function may be derived from the equilibrium storage function through the relation

$$\lambda(s) = P\big(s - x(s)\big)$$

The equilibrium storage function may be derived from the equilibrium price function through the relation

$$x(s) = s - D\big(\lambda(s)\big)$$

8.6.3 Government Price Controls

Consider a market for an agricultural commodity in which the government is committed to maintaining a minimum price through the management of a public buffer stock. In particular, the government stands ready to purchase and store unlimited quantities of the commodity at a fixed price p^* in times of excess supply and to sell any quantities in its stockpile at the price p^* in times of short supplies. Assume that there is no private stock holding.

Each year t begins with a predetermined supply of the commodity s_t, of which an amount q_t is sold to consumers at a market-clearing price $p_t = P(q_t)$ and the remainder x_t is stored by the government. Supply at the beginning of the following year is the sum of government stocks and new production, which equals the acreage planted by producers a_t times an exogenous per-acre yield y_{t+1}, which is uncertain in year t:

$$s_{t+1} = x_t + a_t y_{t+1}$$

In making planting decisions, producers maximize expected profit by equating expected per-acre revenue to the marginal cost of production, which is a function of the acreage planted

$$\delta E_t p_{t+1} y_{t+1} = c(a_t)$$

This is an infinite horizon, stochastic model with two state variables, the supply s available at the beginning of the period and the current yield y; two response variables, the acreage planted a and government storage x; and two equilibrium conditions,

$$\delta E_t P(s_{t+1} - x_{t+1}) y_{t+1} - c(a_t) = 0$$

which asserts that the marginal expected profit from planting is zero, and

$$x_t \geq 0, \qquad p^* \leq P(s_t - x_t), \qquad x_t > 0 \Rightarrow p^* = P(s_t - x_t)$$

which asserts that the government will enforce the price floor. A solution to the government price control model is a pair of functions $x(\cdot)$ and $a(\cdot)$ that give government storage and acreage planting in terms of available supply. From the dynamic equilibrium conditions, the equilibrium government storage and acreage response functions are characterized by the simultaneous functional complementarity problem

$$\delta E_y P\big(x(s) + a(s)y - x\big(x(s) + a(s)y\big)\big)y - c\big(x(s)\big) = 0$$

and

$$x(s) \geq 0, \qquad p^* \leq P\big(s - x(s)\big), \qquad x(s) > 0 \Rightarrow p^* = P\big(s - x(s)\big)$$

In the notation of the general model, with state variable (s, y), response variable (x, a), and shock ϵ,

$$h(s, y, x, a) = P(s - x)y$$

$$g(s, y, x, a, \epsilon) = (x + a\epsilon, \epsilon)$$

and

$$f(s, y, x, a, Eh) = \big(p^* - P(s - x), \delta Eh - c(a)\big)$$

with $a \geq 0$ and $x \geq 0$. Here, y is used to denote current yield and ϵ is used to denote the following period's yield.

Exercises

8.1. An industrial firm's profit in period t

$$\pi(q_t) = \alpha_0 + \alpha_1 q_t - 0.5 q_t^2$$

is a function of its output q_t. The firm's production process generates an environmental pollutant. Specifically, if x_t is the level of pollutant in the environment in period t, then the level of the pollutant the following period will be

$$x_{t+1} = \beta x_t + q_t$$

where $0 < \beta < 1$.

A firm operating without regard to environmental consequences produces at its profit-maximizing level $q_t = \alpha_1$. Suppose that the social welfare, accounting for environmental damage, is measured by

$$\sum_{t=0}^{\infty} \delta^t \left[\pi(q_t) - cx_t\right]$$

where c is the unit social cost of suffering the pollutant and $\delta < 1$ is the social discount factor.

a. Formulate the social planner's dynamic optimization problem. Specifically, formulate the Bellman equation, clearly identifying the state and action variables, the state and action spaces, and the reward and transition functions.

b. Assuming an internal solution, derive the Euler conditions and interpret them. What does the shadow price function represent?

c. Solve for the steady-state socially optimal production level q^* and pollution level x^* in terms of the model parameters $(\alpha_0, \alpha_1, \delta, \beta, c)$.

d. Determine the per-unit tax on output τ that will induce the firm to produce at the steady-state socially optimal production level q^*.

8.2. Consider the problem of harvesting a renewable resource over an infinite time horizon. For year t, let s_t denote the resource stock at the beginning of the year, let x_t denote the amount of the resource harvested, let $p_t = p(x_t) = \alpha_0 - \alpha_1 x_t$ denote the market-clearing price, and let $c_t = c(s_t) = \beta_0 + \beta_1 s_t$ denote the unit cost of harvest. Assume an annual discount rate r and a stock growth dynamic $s_{t+1} = s_t + \gamma(\bar{s} - s_t) - x_t$ where $\bar{s}$ is the no-harvest steady-state stock level.

a. Formulate the social planner's problem of maximizing the discounted sum of net social surplus over time. Specifically, formulate the Bellman equation, clearly identifying the state and action variables, the state and action spaces, and the reward and transition functions.

b. Formulate the monopolist's problem of maximizing the discounted sum of profits over time. Specifically, formulate the Bellman equation, clearly identifying the state and action variables, the state and action spaces, and the reward and transition functions.

c. Solve for the steady-state harvest and stock levels, x^* and s^*, for both the social planner and the monopolist. Who maintains the larger resource stock in steady state?

d. How does the steady-state equilibrium stock level change if demand rises (i.e., if α_0 rises)? How does it change if the harvest cost rises (i.e., if β_0 rises)?

8.3. At time t, a firm earns net revenue

$$\pi_t = p y_t - r k_t - \tau_t k_t - c_t$$

where p is the market price, y_t is output, r is the capital rental rate, k_t is capital at the beginning of the period, c_t is the cost of adjusting capital, and τ_t is tax paid per unit of capital. The firm's production function, adjustment costs, and tax rate are given by

$$y_t = \alpha k_t$$

$$c_t = 0.5\beta(k_{t+1} - k_t)^2$$

$$\tau_t = \tau + 0.5\gamma k_t$$

Assume that the unit output price p and the unit capital rental rate r are both exogenously fixed and known; also assume that the parameters $\alpha > 0$, $\beta > 0$, $\gamma > 0$, and $\tau > 0$ are given.

a. Formulate the firm's problem of maximizing the discounted sum of profits over time. Specifically, formulate the Bellman equation, clearly identifying the state and action variables, the state and action spaces, and the reward and transition functions.

b. Assuming an internal solution, derive the Euler conditions and interpret them. What does the shadow price function represent?

c. What effect does an increase in the base tax rate τ have on output in the long run?

d. What effect does an increase in the discount factor δ have on output in the long run?

8.4. A firm wishes to minimize the cost of meeting a contractual obligation to deliver Q units of its product to a buyer T periods from now. The cost of producing q units in any period is $c(q)$, where $c' > 0$. The unit cost of storage is k dollars per period; due to spoilage, a proportion β of inventories held at the beginning of one period does not survive to the following period. Initially, the firm has no quantities in stock. Assume a per-period discount factor $\delta < 1$.

a. Formulate the firm's problem of minimizing the discounted sum of costs over time. Specifically, formulate the Bellman equation, clearly identifying the state and action variables, the state and action spaces, and the reward and transition functions.

b. Derive the Euler conditions and interpret them. What does the shadow-price function represent?

c. Assuming increasing marginal cost, $c'' > 0$, qualitatively describe the optimal production plan.

d. Assuming decreasing marginal cost, $c'' < 0$, qualitatively describe the optimal production plan.

8.5. A firm competes in a mature industry whose total profit is a fixed amount X every year. If the firm captures a fraction p_t of total industry sales in year t, it makes a profit $p_t X$. The fraction of sales captured by the firm in year t is a function $p_t = f(p_{t-1}, a_{t-1})$ of the fraction it captured the preceding year and its advertising expenditures the preceding year, a_{t-1}. Assume p_0 and a_0 are known.

a. Formulate the firm's problem of maximizing the discounted sum of profit over time. Specifically, formulate the Bellman equation, clearly identifying the state and action variables, the state and action spaces, and the reward and transition functions.

b. Derive the Euler conditions and interpret them. What does the shadow-price function represent?

c. What conditions characterize the steady-state optimal solution?

8.6. Show that the competitive storage model of section 8.6.2 can be recast as a dynamic optimization problem. In particular, formulate a dynamic optimization problem in which a hypothetical social planner maximizes the discounted expected sum of consumer surplus less storage costs. Derive the Euler conditions to show that, under a suitable interpretation, they are identical to the rational expectations equilibrium conditions of the storage model.

8.7. Consider the production-inventory model of section 8.4.7. Show that the value function is of the form $V(p, s) = ps + W(p)$ where W is the solution to a Bellman-like functional equation involving only one state variable p. Derive general conditions under which one can reduce the dimensionality of a Bellman equation.

8.8. Demonstrate that the representative agent's problem in section 8.6.1

$$\max E_0 \sum_{t=0}^{\infty} \delta^t u(c_t)$$

s.t. $0 \leq c_t \leq d_t s_t$

$$s_{t+1} = s_t + (d_t s_t - c_t)/p_t$$

leads to the Euler condition

$$\delta E_t[u'(c_{t+1})(p_{t+1} + d_{t+1})] = u'(c_t)p_t$$

Bibliographic Notes

Those interested in the theory underlying dynamic optimization models are referred to Stokey and Lucas (1989), which offers an extensive treatment at a high mathematical level. The classic articles discussing existence and uniqueness of solutions to discrete-time dynamic optimization models are Denardo (1967) and Blackwell (1962, 1965). Many of the models discussed in the chapter are generic versions of more complicated models appearing in the academic literature. Discussion of dynamic resource economic models can be found in Clark (1976), Conrad and Clark (1987), Hotelling (1931), and Pindyck (1978, 1984). Numerous examples of agricultural and resource management problems can also be found in J.O.S. Kennedy (1986).

Examples of discrete-time dynamic optimization models arising in finance can be found in Dixit and Pindyck (1994). Examples of models arising in macroeconomics, including the optimal growth problem, can be found in Sargent (1987) and Turnovsky (2000). The industry entry-exit model was derived from Dixit (1989). The optimal monetary policy model was derived from Kato and Nishiyama (2001).

Rational expectations abound in the academic literature. Numerous macroeconomic models are discussed in Judd (1998) and Sargent (1987). The asset pricing model is discussed in Lucas (1978), Lucas and Prescott (1971), and Miranda and Rui (1997). Rational expectations models of commodity markets similar to those presented in this chapter appear in Williams and Wright (1991), Wright and Williams (1982), Miranda and Helmberger (1988), Miranda (1989), Miranda and Glauber (1993), Miranda and Rui (1996), and Scheinkman and Schechtman (1983). The dynamic games appearing in this chapter were drawn from Vedenov and Miranda (2001) and Nguyen and Miranda (1997).

9 Discrete Time, Continuous State Dynamic Models: Methods

This chapter discusses numerical methods for solving discrete time, continuous state dynamic economic models. Such models give rise to functional equations whose unknowns are entire functions defined on a subset of Euclidean space. For example, the unknown of the Bellman equation

$$V(s) = \max_{x \in X(s)} \left\{ f(s, x) + \delta E_\epsilon V\big(g(s, x, \epsilon)\big) \right\}$$

is the value function $V(\cdot)$. And the unknown of a rational expectations equilibrium condition

$$f\Big(s, x(s), E_\epsilon h\big(g\big(s, x(s), \epsilon\big), x\big(g\big(s, x(s), \epsilon\big)\big)\big)\Big) = 0$$

is the response function $x(\cdot)$.

In most applications, these functional equations lack known closed-form solutions and can only be solved approximately using computational methods. Among the various computational methods available, linear-quadratic approximation has been especially popular among economists because of the relative ease with which it can be implemented. However, in many applications, linear-quadratic approximation provides unacceptably poor approximations that yield misleading results.

In recent years, economists have begun to experiment with numerical functional equation methods developed by physical scientists. Among the various methods available, the collocation method is the most useful for solving dynamic models in economics and finance. In most applications, the collocation method is flexible, accurate, and numerically efficient. It can also be developed directly from basic numerical integration, approximation, and rootfinding techniques.

Unfortunately, the widespread applicability of the collocation method to dynamic economic and financial models has been hampered by the absence of publicly available general-purpose computer code. We address this problem by providing, with the CompEcon Toolbox, a series of high-level computer routines that perform the essential computations for a broad class of dynamic economic and financial models. In this chapter the collocation method is developed in greater detail for single- and multiple-agent dynamic decision models and rational expectations models. Application of the method is illustrated with a variety of examples.

9.1 Linear-Quadratic Control

Before addressing solution methods for general continuous state Markov decision models, let us first examine a special case, the linear-quadratic control model, which historically has been used extensively by economists.

The linear-quadratic control model is an unconstrained Markov decision model with a quadratic reward function

$$f(s, x) = F_0 + F_s s + F_x x + 0.5 s^\top F_{ss} s + s^\top F_{sx} x + 0.5 x^\top F_{xx} x$$

and a linear state transition function

$$g(s, x, \epsilon) = G_0 + G_s s + G_x x + \epsilon$$

Here, s is an $d_s \times 1$ state vector, x is an $d_x \times 1$ action vector, and ϵ is an $d_s \times 1$ exogenous random shock vector. The parameters of the model are F_0, a constant; F_s, a $1 \times d_s$ vector; F_x, a $1 \times d_x$ vector; F_{ss}, a $d_s \times d_s$ matrix; F_{sx}, a $d_s \times d_x$ matrix; F_{xx}, a $d_x \times d_x$ matrix; G_0, a $d_s \times 1$ vector; G_s, a $d_s \times d_s$ matrix; and G_x, a $d_s \times d_x$ vector.

The linear-quadratic control model is of special importance because it is one of the few continuous state Markov decision models known to have a finite-dimensional solution. By a conceptually simple but algebraically burdensome induction proof omitted here, one can show that the optimal policy and shadow price functions of the infinite-horizon linear-quadratic control model are both linear in the state variable:

$$x(s) = \Gamma_0 + \Gamma_s s$$

$$\lambda(s) = \Lambda_0 + \Lambda_s s$$

Here, Γ_0 is a $d_x \times 1$ vector, Γ_s is a $d_x \times d_s$ matrix, Λ_0 is a $d_s \times 1$ vector, and Λ_s is a $d_s \times d_s$ matrix.

The parameters Λ_0 and Λ_s of the shadow price function are characterized by the nonlinear vector fixed-point *Riccati equations*

$$\Lambda_0 = -\left[\delta G_s^\top \Lambda_s G_x + F_{sx}\right]\left[\delta G_x^\top \Lambda_s G_x + F_{xx}\right]^{-1}\left[\delta G_x^\top [\Lambda_s G_0 + \Lambda_0] + F_x^\top\right]$$
$$+ \delta G_s^\top [\Lambda_s G_0 + \Lambda_0] + F_s^\top$$

$$\Lambda_s = -\left[\delta G_s^\top \Lambda_s G_x + F_{sx}\right]\left[\delta G_x^\top \Lambda_s G_x + F_{xx}\right]^{-1}\left[\delta G_x^\top \Lambda_s G_s + F_{sx}^\top\right]$$
$$+ \delta G_s^\top \Lambda_s G_s + F_{ss}$$

These finite-dimensional fixed-point equations can typically be solved in practice using function iteration. The recursive structure of these equations allows one to first solve for Λ_s by applying function iteration to the second equation, and then solve for Λ_0 by applying function iteration to the first equation. Once the parameters of the shadow price function have been computed, one can compute the parameters of the optimal policy using direct algebraic operations:

$$\Gamma_0 = -\left[\delta G_x{}^\top \Lambda_s G_x + F_{xx}\right]^{-1}\left[\delta G_x{}^\top [\Lambda_s G_0 + \Lambda_0] + F_x{}^\top\right]$$

$$\Gamma_s = -\left[\delta G_x{}^\top \Lambda_s G_x + F_{xx}\right]^{-1}\left[\delta G_x{}^\top \Lambda_s G_s + F_{sx}{}^\top\right]$$

The relative simplicity of the linear-quadratic control model derives from the fact that the optimal policy and shadow price functions are known to be linear functions whose parameters are characterized by a well-defined nonlinear vector fixed-point equation. Thus linear-quadratic models may be solved using standard nonlinear equation solution methods. This simplification, unfortunately, is not generally possible for other types of discrete time, continuous state Markov decision models.

A second simplifying feature of the linear-quadratic control model is that the shadow price and optimal policy functions depend only on the mean of the state shock, but not its variance or higher moments. This is known as the certainty-equivalence property of the linear-quadratic control model. It asserts that the optimal policy and shadow price functions of the stochastic model are the same as those of the deterministic model obtained by fixing the state shock ϵ at its mean. Certainty equivalence also is not a property of more general discrete time, continuous state Markov decision models.

Because linear-quadratic control models are relatively easy to solve, many analysts compute approximate solutions to more general Markov decision models using the method of linear-quadratic approximation. Linear-quadratic approximation calls for the state transition function g and objective function f of the general model to be replaced with linear and quadratic approximants and for all constraints on the action, if any, to be discarded. The resulting linear-quadratic control model is then solved using nonlinear equation methods, and the optimal policy is accepted as an approximate solution to the original general Markov decision model.

Typically, linear and quadratic approximants of g and f are constructed by forming the first- and second-order Taylor expansions around the certainty-equivalent steady state. If ϵ^* denotes the mean shock, the certainty-equivalent steady-state state s^*, optimal action x^*, and shadow price λ^* are characterized by the nonlinear equation system

$$f_x(s^*, x^*) + \delta\lambda^* g_x(s^*, x^*, \epsilon^*) = 0$$

$$\lambda^* = f_s(s^*, x^*) + \delta\lambda^* g_s(s^*, x^*, \epsilon^*)$$

$$s^* = g(s^*, x^*, \epsilon^*)$$

Here, f_x, f_s, g_x, and g_s denote partial derivatives whose dimensions are $1 \times d_x$, $1 \times d_s$, $d_s \times d_x$, and $d_s \times d_s$, respectively, where d_s and d_x are the dimensions of the state and action spaces, respectively; also, λ^* is expressed as a $1 \times d_s$ row vector. Typically, the nonlinear equation system may be solved using standard numerical nonlinear equation methods. In one-dimensional state and action models, the conditions can often be solved analytically.

Given the certainty-equivalent steady-state state, the state transition function g and reward function f are replaced, respectively, by their first- and second-order Taylor series approximants expanded around the steady state:

$$f(s, x) \approx f^* + f_s^*(s - s^*) + f_x^*(x - x^*) + 0.5(s - s^*)^\top f_{ss}^*(s - s^*)$$
$$+ (s - s^*)^\top f_{sx}^*(x - x^*) + 0.5(x - x^*)^\top f_{xx}^*(x - x^*)$$

$$g(s, x, \epsilon) \approx g^* + g_s^*(s - s^*) + g_x^*(x - x^*)$$

Here, f^*, g^*, f_s^*, f_x^*, g_s^*, g_x^*, f_{ss}^*, f_{sx}^*, and f_{xx}^* are the values and partial derivatives of f and g evaluated at the certainty-equivalent steady state. The orders of these vectors and matrices are as follows: f^* is a constant, f_s^* is $1 \times d_s$, f_x^* is $1 \times d_x$, f_{ss}^* is $d_s \times d_s$, f_{sx}^* is $d_s \times d_x$, f_{xx}^* is $d_x \times d_x$, g^* is $d_s \times 1$, g_s^* is $d_s \times d_s$, and g_x^* is $d_s \times d_x$.

The shadow price and optimal policy functions of the resulting linear-quadratic control model take the form

$$\lambda(s) = \lambda^* + \Lambda(s - s^*)$$

$$x(s) = x^* + \Gamma(s - s^*)$$

where the slope matrices Λ and Γ are characterized by the nonlinear vector fixed-point equations

$$\Lambda = -\left[\delta g_s^{*\top} \Lambda g_x^* + f_{sx}^*\right]\left[\delta g_x^{*\top} \Lambda g_x^* + f_{xx}^*\right]^{-1}\left[\delta g_x^{*\top} \Lambda g_s^* + f_{sx}^{*\top}\right] + \delta g_s^{*\top} \Lambda g_s^* + f_{ss}^*$$

$$\Gamma = -\left[\delta g_x^{*\top} \Lambda g_x^* + f_{xx}^*\right]^{-1}\left[\delta g_x^{*\top} \Lambda g_s^* + f_{sx}^{*\top}\right]$$

These fixed-point equations can usually be solved numerically using function iteration, typically with an initial guess $\Lambda = 0$, or, if the model is one-dimensional, analytically by applying the quadratic formula. In particular, if the model has one-dimensional state and action spaces, and if $f_{ss}^* f_{xx}^* = f_{sx}^{*2}$, a condition often encountered in economic problems, then the slope of the shadow-price function may be computed analytically as follows:

$$\Lambda = \left[f_{ss}^* g_x^{*2} - 2 f_{ss}^* f_{xx}^* g_s^* g_x^* + f_{xx}^* g_s^{*2} - f_{xx}^*/\delta\right]/g_x^{*2}$$

Linear-quadratic approximation works well in some instances, for example, if the state-transition rule is linear, if the constraints are nonbinding or nonexistent, and if the shocks have relatively small variation. However, in many economic applications, linear-quadratic approximation will render highly inaccurate approximate solutions. The basic problem with linear-quadratic approximation is that it relies on Taylor series approximations that are accurate only in the vicinity of the certainty-equivalent steady state. Linear-quadratic approximation will thus yield poor approximations if random shocks repeatedly throw the state variable far from the certainty-equivalent steady state and if the reward and state transition functions are not accurately approximated by second- and first-degree polynomials over their entire domains. Linear-quadratic approximation will yield especially poor approximations if the true controlled process is likely to encounter any constraints discarded in passing to a linear-quadratic approximation. For these reasons, we discourage the use of linear-quadratic approximation, except in those cases where the assumptions of the linear-quadratic model are known to hold globally, or very nearly so.

9.2 Bellman Equation Collocation Methods

In order to describe the collocation method for continuous state Markov decision models, we limit our discussion to infinite-horizon models with one-dimensional state and action spaces and univariate shocks. The presentation generalizes to models with higher dimensional states, actions, and shocks, but at the expense of cumbersome additional notation required to track the different dimensions.[1]

Consider, then, the Bellman equation for an infinite horizon, discrete time, continuous state dynamic decision problem

$$V(s) = \max_{x \in X(s)} \left\{ f(s, x) + \delta E_\epsilon V\big(g(s, x, \epsilon)\big) \right\}$$

Assume that the state space is a bounded interval S of the real line and the actions either are discrete or are continuous and subject to simple bounds $a(s) \le x \le b(s)$ that are continuous functions of the state.

To compute an approximate solution to the Bellman equation using collocation, one employs the following strategy: First, write the value function approximant as a linear combination of n known basis functions $\phi_1, \phi_2, \ldots, \phi_n$ on S whose coefficients $c_1, c_2, \ldots, c_n$ are to be determined:

$$V(s) \approx \sum_{j=1}^{n} c_j \phi_j(s)$$

Second, fix the basis function coefficients $c_1, c_2, \ldots, c_n$ by requiring the value function

---

1. The routines included in the CompEcon Toolbox admit multidimensional states, actions, and shocks.

approximant to satisfy the Bellman equation, not at all possible states, but rather at n collocation nodes $s_1, s_2, \ldots, s_n$.

The collocation strategy replaces the Bellman functional equation with a system of n nonlinear equations in n unknowns. Specifically, to compute the value function approximant, or more precisely, to compute the n coefficients $c_1, c_2, \ldots, c_n$ in its basis representation, one must solve the nonlinear equation system

$$\sum_{j=1}^{n} c_j \phi_j(s_i) = \max_{x \in X(s_i)} \left\{ f(s_i, x) + \delta E_\epsilon \sum_{j=1}^{n} c_j \phi_j \big(g(s_i, x, \epsilon) \big) \right\}$$

The nonlinear equation system may be compactly expressed in vector form as the *collocation equation*

$$\Phi c = v(c)$$

Here, Φ, the *collocation matrix*, is the $n \times n$ matrix whose typical ijth element is the jth basis function evaluated at the ith collocation node

$$\Phi_{ij} = \phi_j(s_i)$$

and v, the *collocation function*, is the function from $\mathbb{R}^n$ to $\mathbb{R}^n$ whose typical ith element is

$$v_i(c) = \max_{x \in X(s_i)} \left\{ f(s_i, x) + \delta E_\epsilon \sum_{j=1}^{n} c_j \phi_j \big(g(s_i, x, \epsilon) \big) \right\}$$

The collocation function evaluated at a particular vector of basis coefficients c yields a vector whose ith entry is the value obtained by solving the optimization problem embedded in the Bellman equation at the ith collocation node s_i, replacing the value function V with its approximant $\sum_j c_j \phi_j$.

In principle, the collocation equation may be solved using any nonlinear equation solution method. For example, one may write the collocation equation as a fixed-point problem $c = \Phi^{-1} v(c)$ and employ function iteration, which uses the iterative update rule

$$c \leftarrow \Phi^{-1} v(c)$$

Alternatively, one may write the collocation equation as a rootfinding problem $\Phi c - v(c) = 0$ and solve for c using Newton's method, which employs the iterative update rule

$$c \leftarrow c - [\Phi - v'(c)]^{-1}[\Phi c - v(c)]$$

Here, $v'(c)$ is the $n \times n$ Jacobian of the collocation function v at c. The typical element of

v' may be computed by applying the Envelope Theorem to the optimization problem in the definition of $v(c)$. Specifically,

$$v'_{ij}(c) = \frac{\partial v_i}{\partial c_j}(c) = \delta E_\epsilon \phi_j \big(g(s_i, x_i, \epsilon) \big)$$

where x_i is optimal for the maximization problem producing $v_i(c)$. As a variant to Newton's method one could also employ a quasi-Newton method to solve the collocation equation.[2]

If the model is stochastic, one must compute expectations in a numerically practical way. Regardless of the quadrature scheme selected, the continuous random variable ϵ in the state transition function is replaced with a discrete approximant, say, one that assumes values $\epsilon_1, \epsilon_2, \ldots, \epsilon_K$ with probabilities $w_1, w_2, \ldots, w_K$, respectively. In this instance, the collocation function v takes the form

$$v_i(c) = \max_{x \in X(s_i)} \left\{ f(s_i, x) + \delta \sum_{k=1}^{K} \sum_{j=1}^{n} w_k c_j \phi_j \big(g(s_i, x, \epsilon_k) \big) \right\}$$

and its Jacobian takes the form

$$v'_{ij}(c) = \delta \sum_{k=1}^{K} w_k \phi_j \big(g(s_i, x_i, \epsilon_k) \big)$$

When applying the collocation method, the analyst faces a number of practical decisions. First, the analyst must choose the basis functions and collocation nodes. Second, the analyst must choose an algorithm for solving the collocation equation. And third, the analyst must select a numerical quadrature technique for computing expectations. A careful analyst will often try a variety of basis-node combinations and may employ more than one solution algorithm in order to assure the robustness of the results.

In implementing a collocation strategy, many basis-node schemes are available to the analyst, including all the function approximation schemes discussed in Chapter 6. The best choice of basis-node scheme will typically depend on the curvature of the value function. If the basis functions and nodes are chosen wisely, it will be possible to reduce the approximation error by increasing the number of basis functions, collocation nodes, and quadrature points. The larger the number of basis functions and nodes, however, the more expensive the computation. For this reason, choosing good approximation and quadrature schemes is critical for achieving computational efficiency.

---

2. The Newton update rule is equivalent to $c \leftarrow [\Phi - v'(c)]^{-1} f$, where f is the $n \times 1$ vector of optimal rewards at the state nodes. This approach is analogous to the "policy iteration" method used in discrete state dynamic programming.

Collocation methods address many of the shortcomings of linear-quadratic approximation. Unlike linear-quadratic approximation, collocation methods employ global, rather than
local, function approximation schemes and are not limited to the first- and second-degree
approximations afforded by linear-quadratic approximation.

Collocation methods, however, are not without problems. First, polynomial and spline
approximants can behave strangely outside the range of approximation and should be ex-
trapolated with extreme caution. Even when state variable bounds are observed by the final
solution, states outside the bounds can easily be visited in the early stages of the solution
algorithm, leading to convergence problems. Also, polynomial and spline approximants can
behave strangely in the vicinity of nondifferentiabilities in the value function. In particular, the approximant can fail to preserve monotonicity near such points, undermining the
rootfinding algorithm used to compute the optimum action at each state node.

9.3   Implementation of the Collocation Method

Let us now consider the practical steps that must be taken to implement the collocation
method in a computer programming environment. In this section, we outline the key operations using the MATLAB vector-processing language, presuming access to the function
approximation and numerical quadrature routines contained in the CompEcon Toolbox.
The necessary steps can be implemented in virtually any other vector-processing or high-
level algebraic programming language, with a level of difficulty that will depend mainly on
the availability of general code that performs the required approximation and quadrature
operations.

Consider first a dynamic decision model with a discrete action space in which the possible
actions are identified with the first m positive integers. The initial steps in any implementation of the collocation method are to specify the basis functions that will be used to express
the value function approximant and to specify the collocation nodes at which the Bellman
equation will be required to hold exactly. These steps may be executed using the CompEcon
Toolbox routines fundefn, funnode, and funbas, which are discussed in Chapter 6:

```
fspace  = fundefn('cheb',n,smin,smax);
s       = funnode(fspace);
Phi     = funbas(fspace);
```

Here, it is presumed that the analyst has previously specified the lower and upper endpoints
of the state interval, smin and smax, and the number of basis functions and collocation
nodes n. After execution, fspace is a structured variable that contains the information
needed to define the approximation basis, s is the $n \times 1$ vector of standard collocation nodes

associated with the basis, and `Phi` is the $n \times n$ collocation matrix associated with the basis. In this specific example, a Chebychev polynomial approximation scheme is chosen.

Next, a numerical routine must be coded to evaluate the collocation function and its derivative at an arbitrary basis coefficient vector. A simple version of such a routine would have a calling sequence of the form

```
[v,x,vjac] = vmax(s,c)
```

Here, on input, `s` is an $n \times 1$ vector of collocation nodes, and `c` is an $n \times 1$ vector of basis coefficients. On output, `v` is an $n \times 1$ vector of optimal values at the collocation nodes, `x` is an $n \times 1$ vector of associated optimal actions at the nodes, and `vjac` is an $n \times n$ Jacobian of the collocation function at `c`.

Given the collocation nodes `s`, collocation matrix `Phi`, and collocation function routine `vmax`, and given an initial guess for the basis coefficient vector `c`, the collocation equation may be solved either by function iteration

```
for it=1:maxit
  cold = c;
  [v,x] = vmax(s,c);
  c = Phi\v;
  if norm(c-cold)<tol, break, end;
end
```

or by Newton iteration

```
for it=1:maxit
  cold = c;
  [v,x,vjac] = vmax(s,c);
  c = c - [Phi-vjac]\[Phi*c-v];
  if norm(c-cold)<tol, break, end;
end
```

Here, `tol` and `maxit` are iteration-control parameters set by the analyst, specifying the convergence tolerance and the maximum number of iterations. The MATLAB backslash operator is used to perform the linear solve.

The main challenge in implementing the collocation method for a general class of dynamic optimization problems is coding the routine `vmax` that solves the optimization problem embedded in the Bellman equation at the collocation nodes and returns the collocation function values and derivatives. A simple routine that performs the required optimizations for the discrete choice model is as follows:[3]

```
function [v,x,vjac] = vmax(s,c)
Ev = 0;
for i=1:m
  x = i*ones(n,1);
  f(:,i) = ffunc(s,x);
  for k=1:K
    g = gfunc(s,x,e(k));
    Ev(:,i) = Ev(:,i) + w(k)*funeval(c,fspace,g);
  end
end
[v,x] = max(f+delta*Ev,[],2);
vjac = 0;
for k=1:K
  g = gfunc(s,x,e(k));
  vjac = vjac + delta*w(k)*funbas(fspace,g);
end
```

This routine assumes that the analyst has coded separate ancillary routines ffunc and gfunc that return the rewards and state transitions specific to the dynamic decision model being solved. The routine ffunc accepts $n \times 1$ vectors of state nodes s and actions x and returns an $n \times 1$ vector f of associated reward function values. The routine gfunc accepts $n \times 1$ vectors of state nodes s and actions x and a particular value of the shock e and returns an $n \times 1$ vector g of associated state transitions.

The routine vmax begins with the execution of a series of loops, one for each possible action. The loops produce $n \times m$ matrices f and Ev containing, respectively, the current reward and value expected next period associated with the n state nodes (rows) and the m possible actions (columns). The value expected next period is computed by looping over all K possible realizations of the discrete shock and forming the probability weighted sum of values next period (here, e(k) and w(k) are the kth shock and its probability). For each realization of the shock, the state next period g is computed and passed to the routine funeval, which returns next period's value using the value function approximant associated with the coefficient vector c.

3. For clarity, the code omits several bookkeeping operations and programming tricks that accelerate execution. Operational versions of vmax that efficiently handle arbitrary dimensional state and action spaces are implemented in the CompEcon Toolbox routine dpsolve, which is discussed in section 9.4.

At the termination of the loops, `f+delta*Ev` is an $n \times m$ matrix whose entries give for each state node (row) and action (column) the current reward `f` plus the expected value next period `Ev` discounted at the rate `delta`. The maximum value in each row of `f+delta*Ev` and the associated column index are the optimal value and action associated with the corresponding state node. In this implementation of `vmax`, the MATLAB vector-maximization routine `max` is used to perform the columnwise maximization in one call, yielding $n \times 1$ vectors `v` and `x` that contain the optimal values and actions associated with the `n` state nodes. Finally, the Jacobian `vjac` of the collocation function is computed by executing a loop over all `K` possible realizations of the discrete shock. For each realization of the shock, the state next period `g` is computed and passed to the CompEcon Toolbox routine `funbas`, which returns the associated basis function values.

Consider now a single state dynamic decision model with a continuous, rather than a discrete, action space. The steps required to solve a continuous choice model using collocation are identical to those required to solve a discrete choice model, with the exception of the optimization routine `vmax`, which must be revised to perform continuous rather than discrete optimization. A routine that performs the optimization for the continuous choice model by iteratively solving the associated Karush-Kuhn-Tucker conditions using Newton's method for complementarity problems is as follows:

```
function [v,x,vjac] = vmax(s,x,c)
[xl,xu] = bfunc(s);
for it=1:maxit
  [f,fx,fxx] = ffunc(s,x);
  Ev=0; Evx=0; Evxx=0;
  for k=1:K
    [g,gx,gxx] = gfunc(s,x,e(k));
    vn      = funeval(c,fspace,g);
    vnder1 = funeval(c,fspace,g,1);
    vnder2 = funeval(c,fspace,g,2);
    Ev   = Ev   + w(k)*vn;
    Evx  = Evx  + w(k)*vnder1.*gx;
    Evxx = Evxx + w(k)*(vnder1.*gxx + vnder2.*gx.^2);
  end
  v    = f + delta*Ev;
  delx = -(fx+delta*Evx)./(fxx+delta*Evxx);
  delx = min(max(delx,xl-x),xu-x);
  x    = x + delx;
  if norm(delx)<tol, break, end;
```

```
end
vjac = 0;
for k=1:K
  g = gfunc(s,x,e(k));
  vjac = vjac + delta*w(k)*funbas(fspace,g);
end
```

This routine assumes that the analyst has coded separate ancillary routines bfunc, ffunc, and gfunc that compute the bounds, rewards, and state transitions specific to the dynamic decision model being solved. The routine bfunc accepts an $n \times 1$ vector of states s and returns $n \times 1$ vectors xl and xu of associated lower and upper bounds on the actions. The routine ffunc accepts $n \times 1$ vectors of states s and actions x and returns $n \times 1$ vectors f, fx, and fxx of associated reward function values, first derivatives, and second derivatives. The routine gfunc accepts $n \times 1$ vectors of states s and actions x and a particular value of the shock e and returns $n \times 1$ vectors g, gx, and gxx of associated state transition function values, first derivatives, and second derivatives.

The continuous action routine vmax begins by computing the lower and upper bounds xl and xu on the actions at the state nodes. The routine then executes a series of Newton iterations that sequentially update the actions x at the state nodes s until the Karush-Kuhn-Tucker conditions of the optimization problem embedded in the Bellman equation are satisfied to a specified tolerance tol. With each iteration, the standard Newton step delx is computed and subsequently shortened, if necessary, to ensure that the updated action x+delx remains within the bounds xl and xu. The standard Newton step delx is the negative of the ratio of the first and second derivatives of the Bellman optimand with respect to the action, fx+delta*Evx and fxx+delta*Evxx. Here, fx and fxx are the first and second derivatives of the reward function, Evx and Evxx are the first and second derivatives of the expected value next period, and delta is the discount rate.

In order to compute the expected value next period and its derivatives, a loop is executed over all K possible realizations of the discrete shock, and probability weighted sums are formed (here, e(k) and w(k) are the kth shock and its probability). For each realization of the shock, the state next period g and its first and second derivatives with respect to the action, gx and gxx, are computed. The state next period is passed to the routine funeval, which computes next period's value and its derivatives using the value function approximant that is identified with the current coefficient vector c. The chain rule is then used to compute the derivatives of the expected value.

Once convergence is achieved and the optimal value and action at the state nodes have been determined, the Jacobian vjac of the collocation function is computed. The Jacobian is an $n \times n$ matrix whose representative ijth entry is the discounted expectation of the jth basis evaluated at the following period's state, given that the current state is the ith state node. To compute the Jacobian, a loop is executed over all $\mathtt{K}$ possible realizations of the discrete shock. For each realization of the shock, the state next period $\mathtt{g}$ is computed and passed to the CompEcon Toolbox routine $\mathtt{funbas}$, which evaluates the basis functions at that state.

Once the collocation equation has apparently been solved, the analyst should perform a diagnostic test to ensure that the computed value function approximant solves the Bellman equation to an acceptable degree of accuracy over the entire approximation interval. In order to perform this test, define the residual function on the domain of the value function as follows:

$$R_c(s) = \max_{x \in X(s)} \left\{ f(s, x) + \delta E_\epsilon \sum_{j=1}^{n} c_j \phi_j \big(g(s, x, \epsilon) \big) \right\} - \sum_{j=1}^{n} c_j \phi_j(s)$$

The residual function measures the difference between the right and left sides of the Bellman equation at arbitrary states s when the value function is replaced with its approximant $\sum_j c_j \phi_j$. The residual would be zero throughout the entire approximation domain for an exact solution. However, in practice, the value function approximant will not generally provide an exact solution, implying that its residual will be nonzero, except at the collocation nodes. Nonetheless, the value function approximant is deemed acceptable if the residual is very nearly zero between the collocation nodes. Otherwise, if large residuals obtain, the model should be solved again with more nodes, different basis functions, or a revised approximation interval, until the residual is reduced to acceptable levels.

In practice, the easiest way to assess the Bellman equation approximation error is to plot the residual function on a fine grid of states spanning the approximation interval. The residual function may be computed at any vector of states using the routines $\mathtt{vmax}$ and $\mathtt{funeval}$. For example, the approximation residual of a discrete action model approximant may be checked as follows:

```
nplot = 500;
splot = nodeunif(nplot,smin,smax);
resid = vmax(splot,c) - funeval(c,fspace,splot);
plot(splot,resid)
```

Here, the CompEcon Toolbox routine $\mathtt{nodeunif}$ is used to generate a vector $\mathtt{splot}$ of 500 equally spaced states spanning the approximation interval. The residual $\mathtt{resid}$ is then computed and plotted at the equally spaced states. Notice that, to compute the residual, $\mathtt{vmax}$ is evaluated at the residual evaluation points, not the collocation nodes. However, careful inspection of the code reveals that `vmax` is designed to solve the optimization problem embedded in the Bellman equation at an arbitrary vector of states, not just the collocation nodes.

There are two common causes of poor approximations. First, the value function may exhibit discontinuous derivatives along a boundary separating regions of the state space where the solution exhibits qualitatively different characteristics. In a discrete-action model, each region may correspond to a set of states at which a given discrete action is optimal. In a continuous action model, the regions may separate states according to whether action constraints are binding or nonbinding. The existence of discontinuous second derivatives in the value function creates difficulties for approximation schemes based on Chebychev polynomials and cubic splines, both of which are twice continuously differentiable. In particular, the residuals will tend to be much larger in magnitude near the kink points. If the kink points are known analytically, which is rarely the case in practice, the residual error can often be reduced by choosing the collocation nodes so as to include the kink points. Another remedy that is often effective is simply to increase the number of basis functions and collocation nodes, though this may not be practical when the state space is higher-dimensional.

Another possible cause of poor residuals is extrapolation beyond the approximation interval. Since interpolants can provide highly inaccurate approximations when evaluated outside the specified approximation interval, one should check whether this difficulty occurs within the routine `vmax` at the final solution. The test can be performed by enumerating all values that can be realized by the state transition function at all possible state collocation nodes, corresponding optimal actions, and shocks, and checking that the value remains between `smin` and `smax`. In MATLAB, this procedure can be executed with the following commands:

```
for k=1:K;
  g = gfunc(s,x,e(k));
  if any(g<smin), disp('Warning: extrapolating beyond smin'), end;
  if any(g>smax), disp('Warning: extrapolating beyond smax'), end;
end
```

If the Bellman residuals are poor and attempts to extrapolate within `vmax` are detected, the minimum or maximum state should be extended, and the model should be solved again. The approximation interval should be repeatedly adjusted in this manner until extrapolation beyond the interval no longer occurs or the residual function becomes acceptably small.

9.4   A Continuous State Dynamic Programming Tool Kit

In order to simplify the process of solving and analyzing continuous-state Markov decision models, the CompEcon Toolbox contains a series of MATLAB routines that efficiently perform many of the necessary operations. The main routine is `dpsolve`, which solves purely continuous state and mixed discrete-continuous state Markov decision models of arbitrary dimensional state and action spaces using the dynamic programming algorithms discussed in the preceding section. The routine, for an infinite horizon model, has a calling sequence of the form:

```
[c,s,v,x,resid] = dpsolve(model,fspace,s,vinit,xinit);
```

Let n denote the number of collocation nodes, let $\hat{n}$ denote the number of residual evaluation points ($\hat{n} \gg n$), and let d_s and d_x denote the dimensions of the state and action spaces, respectively. Then, on input, `model` is a structured variable that contains all necessary information about the model, `fspace` is a structured variable that contains all the necessary information about the basis functions used to construct the value function approximant, `s` is an $n \times d_s$ matrix of collocation nodes, `vinit` is an $n \times 1$ vector of initial guesses for the value function at the collocation nodes, and `xinit` is an $n \times d_x$ vector of initial guesses for the optimal actions at the collocation nodes. On output, `c` is an $n \times 1$ vector of value function approximant basis function coefficients, `s` is an $\hat{n} \times d_s$ matrix of nodes at which the Bellman equation residuals are evaluated (different from the collocation nodes), `v` is an $\hat{n} \times 1$ vector of optimal values at the evaluation nodes, `x` is an $\hat{n} \times d_x$ vector of optimal actions at the evaluation nodes, and `resid` is the $\hat{n} \times 1$ vector of residuals at the evaluation nodes.

The structured variable `model` contains the fields `func`, `discount`, `e`, `w`, `actions`, `discretestates`, and `params`. The required field `func` contains the name of the model function file, which evaluates the bound, reward, and state transition functions as described in the following paragraph. The required field `discount` contains the discount factor, which must be greater than 0 and less than or equal to 1. The fields `e` and `w`, which are specified only when the model is stochastic, contain the discretized random shocks and associated probabilities. The field `action`, which is specified only when the action space is discrete, specifies the action space. The field `discretestates`, which is specified only when the state space contains discrete states variables, specifies the dimension index or indexes of the discrete state variables. And the optional field `params` contains the parameters to be passed to the model function file.

The required, stand-alone model function file has the following calling sequence

```
[out1,out2,out3] = func(flag,s,x,e,additional parameters)
```

On input, s, x, and e are each n-row matrices containing, respectively, state, action, and shock values. The output variables out1, out2, and out3 depend on the value of flag. If flag equals 'b', then out1 and out2 are the lower and upper bounds on the actions associated with the states s; out3 is undefined. If flag equals 'f', then out1 is the value of the reward function, and out2 and out3 are the first and second derivatives of the reward function with respect to the action at the states s and actions x. If flag equals 'g', then out1 is the value of the state transition function, and out2 and out3 are the first and second derivatives of the state transition function with respect to the action at the states s, actions x, and shocks e.

Given the continuous state dynamic programming routines provided in the CompEcon Toolbox, the most significant practical difficulty typically encountered when solving continuous state Markov decision models is writing the model function file and selecting an appropriate set of basis functions and collocation nodes. We demonstrate how to apply dpsolve and related routines in sections 9.6 and 9.7. Section 9.7.8 demonstrates their use in solving a finite horizon problem.

9.5 Postoptimality Analysis

Although the optimal policy and shadow price functions reveal a great deal about the nature of the controlled dynamic process, they give an incomplete picture of the model's implications. Given an economic model, we typically wish to describe the dynamic behavior of the controlled economic process and show how this behavior changes with variations in model parameters or assumptions. Given a dynamic economic model, we typically characterize the model's solution in one of two ways. Steady-state analysis examines the long-run tendencies of the controlled economic process, abstracting from the initial state and the path taken by the process over time. Dynamic path analysis focuses on how the system evolves over time, starting from a given initial condition.

Given a deterministic dynamic model, steady-state and dynamic path analysis are relatively straightforward to perform. As we have seen, the steady state of a controlled deterministic process is typically characterized by a system of nonlinear equations. The system can be solved numerically and totally differentiated to generate explicit expressions describing how the steady state varies with changes in model parameters. Dynamic path analysis can be performed through a simple deterministic simulation of the controlled economic process, which requires repeated evaluations of the optimal policy and state transition functions. In particular, if $x(s)$ is the computed optimal policy and $g(s, x)$ is the transition function, then, given an initial state s_0, the path taken by the state variable may be computed iteratively as follows: $s_{t+1} = g(s_t, x(s_t))$. Given the path of the state variable s_t, it is then usually straightforward to generate the path taken by any other endogenous variable.

The dynamic path analysis of stochastic models is a bit more involved. Stochastic models do not generate a unique, deterministic path from a given initial state. A stochastic process may take any one of many possible paths, depending on the realizations of the random shocks. Often, it is instructive to generate one such possible path to illustrate the volatility that a controlled economic process is capable of exhibiting. This purpose may be accomplished using a simple Monte Carlo simulation in which a sequence of pseudorandom shocks are generated for the controlled process using a random number generator. In particular, given the computed optimal policy $x(s)$, the transition function $g(s, x, \epsilon)$, an initial state s_0, and a pseudorandom sequence of ϵ_t, a representative path may be generated iteratively as follows: $s_{t+1} = g(s_t, x(s_t), \epsilon_{t+1})$.

A more informative analysis of the dynamics generated by a stochastic model is to draw not a single representative path, but rather the expected path of the controlled process. The expected path may be computed by generating a large number of independent representative paths and averaging the results at each point in time. The expected path is typically smooth and converges to a steady-state mean value. The steady state of a controlled stochastic process is a distribution, not a point. Typically, it will suffice to compute the mean and standard deviation of the steady-state distribution for selected endogenous variables. The most common approach to computing steady-state means and variances is through the use of Monte Carlo simulation. Monte Carlo simulation is used to generate a single representative path of long horizon, say 10,000 periods. In the limit, the states thus generated collectively are distributed as per the steady-state distribution of the state variable.

The CompEcon Toolbox provides two utilities for performing dynamic analysis. The first routine, which simulates state paths using Monte Carlo simulation, has the following calling sequence:

```
[spath,xpath] = dpsimul(model,sinit,nper,s,x);
```

Let npath denote the number of simulation paths to be generated. Then here, on input, model is a structured variable that contains all necessary information about the model, sinit is an npath × d_s vector of initial states, nper is the number of periods over which the state process will be simulated, s is the state grid generated by dpsolve, and x is the matrix of corresponding optimal actions generated by dpsolve. On output, spath is an npath × d_s × nper array containing npath paths of the controlled-state process, each nper periods in duration, and xpath is an npath × d_x × nper array containing the corresponding optimal actions.

The utility dpstst computes the steady-state distribution associated with a dynamic programming model by forming and analyzing the h-step ahead transition probability matrix for a finite state approximation. The calling sequence for the procedure is:

```
[ss,pi] = dpstst(model,h,n,s,x);
```

Here, on input, `model` is a structured variable that contains all necessary information about the model, `h` is an integer that influences the degree of smoothing to be performed on the probability distribution histogram, `n` is the number of nodal values used in the finite state approximation (a vector if s is multi-dimensional), `s` is the state grid generated by `dpsolve`, and `x` is the matrix of corresponding optimal actions generated by `dpsolve`. On output, `ss` is a grid of uniformly spaced state values and `pi` is a vector of associated steady-state probabilities (or a cell array of marginal probability distributions if s is multi-dimensional).

The procedure first forms a grid of n values of the state variable. With K possible shocks, there are nK^h possible values of the state h periods ahead. Each of these values is assigned to the nearest grid point and an $n \times n$ transition probability matrix is formed. The transition probability matrix is analyzed using the procedure `markov` discussed in section 7.5.

9.6   Computational Examples: Discrete Choice

9.6.1   Asset Replacement

Consider the asset replacement model of section 8.3.1 assuming that the asset produces $q(a) = 50 - 2.5a - 2.5a^2$ units of output in its ath period of operation. In contrast to the previous model, assume that the asset replacement cost k is an exogenous Markov process $k_{t+1} = g(k_t, \epsilon_{t+1}) = \bar{k} + \gamma(k_t - \bar{k}) + \epsilon_{t+1}$ where ϵ_t is i.i.d. normal$(0, \sigma^2)$, $\bar{k} = 100$, $\gamma = 0.5$, and $\sigma = 15$. Further assume a constant output price $p = 2$ and discount factor $\delta = 0.9$.

The collocation method calls for the analyst to select n basis functions ϕ_j and n collocation nodes (k_i, a_i), and form the value function approximant $V(k, a) \approx \sum_{j=1}^{n} c_j \phi_j(k, a)$ whose coefficients c_j solve the collocation equation

$$\sum_{j=1}^{n} c_j \phi_j(k_i, a_i) = \max \left\{ pq(a_i) + \delta \sum_{k=1}^{K} \sum_{j=1}^{n} w_k c_j \phi_j(\hat{k}_{ik}, a_i + 1), \right.$$

$$\left. pq(0) - k_i + \delta \sum_{k=1}^{K} \sum_{j=1}^{n} w_k c_j \phi_j(\hat{k}_{ik}, 1) \right\}$$

where $\hat{k}_{ik} = g(k_i, \epsilon_k)$ and where ϵ_k and w_k represent quadrature nodes and weights for the normal shock. One may solve the asset replacement model using CompEcon Toolbox routines as follows:

First, one codes a model function file that returns the values of the reward and transition functions at arbitrary vectors of states `s`, actions `x`, and shocks `e`:

```
function out = func(flag,s,x,e,price,kbar,gamma,abar);
k = s(:,1); a = s(:,2);
```

```
switch flag
case 'f';
  out = price*(50-2.5*a-2.5*a.^2).*(1-x)+(price*50-k).*x;
  out(a==abar & x==0) = -inf;
case 'g';
  out(:,1) = kbar + gamma*(k-kbar) + e;
  out(:,2) = (a+1).*(1-x) + x;
end
```

This model function file further requires the model parameters `price`, `kbar`, and `gamma` as input. Passing the flag `'f'` returns the reward function value; passing the flag `'g'` returns the transition function value.

Second, one enters the model parameters. Here, the output price, long-run mean replacement cost, replacement cost mean reversion rate, replacement cost shock standard deviation, and discount factor are specified, respectively:

```
price = 2.0;
kbar  = 100;
gamma = 0.5;
abar  = 6;
sigma = 15;
delta = 0.9;
```

Third, one discretizes the shock. Here, the normally distributed replacement cost shock is discretized using a five-node Gaussian quadrature scheme:

```
nshocks = 5;
[e,w] = qnwnorm(nshocks,0,sigma^2);
```

Fourth, one packs the model structure. Here, `model` is a structured variable whose fields contain the name of the model function file, the discount factor, shock values, shock probabilities, binary action space, index of the discrete state variable (age), and model function parameters, respectively:

```
model.func = 'func';
model.discount = delta;
model.e = e;
model.w = w;
model.actions = [0;1];
```

```
model.discretestates = 2;
model.params = {price kbar gamma abar};
```

Fifth, one specifies the basis functions and collocation nodes. Here, a 100-function cubic spline basis on the interval [30, 190] and the associated standard nodes are used to approximate the value function along its continuous dimension (replacement cost):

```
n      = 100;
kmin   =  30;
kmax   = 190;
fspace = fundefn('spli',n,kmin,kmax,[],[1:10]');
scoord = funnode(fspace);
snodes = gridmake(scoord);
```

Notice how the discrete state is supplied as the last argument to `fundefn`.

Sixth, one solves the decision model:

```
[c,s,v,x,resid] = dpsolve(model,fspace,snodes);
```

Here, the routine `dpsolve` is called to solve the collocation equation using Newton's method, with the value function implicitly initialized to zero. The routine returns the basis coefficients `c`, as well as the optimal values `v`, optimal actions `x`, and Bellman equation residuals `resid` at a refined state grid `s`.

Finally, one performs postoptimality analysis. Figure 9.1a gives the value of the firm as a function of the asset-replacement cost for different asset ages. For any asset age, the value

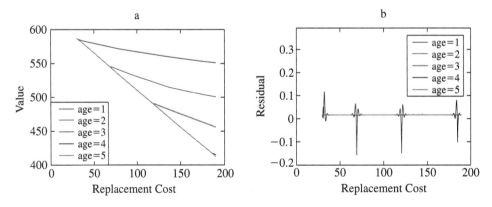

Figure 9.1
Solution to the Asset Replacement Model: (a) Value Function; (b) Approximation Residual

of the firm is a downward-sloping function of the replacement cost, exhibiting a kink at the critical replacement cost below which the asset is replaced. Also, the younger the asset, the greater the value of the firm. Figure 9.1b gives the Bellman equation residual as a function of the asset-replacement cost for different asset ages. The residuals exhibit noticeable spikes at the critical replacement costs, which can be expected as a result of the discontinuous derivatives of the value function at those points. The residuals, however, are very nearly zero elsewhere.

9.6.2 Industry Entry and Exit

Consider the industry entry-exit model of section 8.3.2 assuming that the short-run profit π is an exogenous Markov process $\pi_{t+1} = g(\pi_t, \epsilon_{t+1}) = \bar{\pi} + \gamma(\pi_t - \bar{\pi}) + \epsilon_{t+1}$ where ϵ_t is i.i.d. normal$(0, \sigma^2)$, $\bar{\pi} = 0$, $\gamma = 0.7$, and $\sigma = 1$. Further assume an exit cost $K_0 = 5$, entry cost $K_1 = 10$, and discount factor $\delta = 0.9$.

The collocation method calls for the analyst to select n basis functions ϕ_j and n collocation nodes (π_i, d_i), and form the value function approximant $V(\pi, d) \approx \sum_{j=1}^{n} c_j \phi_j(\pi, d)$ whose coefficients c_j solve the collocation equation

$$\sum_{j=1}^{n} c_j \phi_j(\pi_i, d_i) = \max_{x \in \{0,1\}} \left\{ \pi_i x - K_1(1-d_i)x - K_0 d_i(1-x) + \delta \sum_{k=1}^{K} \sum_{j=1}^{n} w_k c_j \phi_j(\hat{\pi}_{ik}, x) \right\}$$

where $\hat{\pi}_{ik} = g(\pi_i, \epsilon_k)$ and where ϵ_k and w_k represent quadrature nodes and weights for the normal shock. One may solve the industry entry-exit model using CompEcon Toolbox routines as follows:

First, one codes a model function file that returns the values of the reward and transition functions at arbitrary vectors of states s, actions x, and shocks e:

```
function out = func(flag,s,x,e,pibar,gamma,kentry,kexit);
pi = s(:,1); d = s(:,2);
switch flag
case 'f';
   out = (pi-kentry.*(d==0)).*(x==1) - kexit.*(d==1).*(x==0);
case 'g';
   out = [pibar+gamma*(pi-pibar)+e x];
end
```

This model function file further requires the model parameters pibar, gamma, kentry, and kexit as input. Passing the flag 'f' returns the reward function value; passing the flag 'g' returns the transition function value.

Second, one enters the model parameters. Here, the long-run mean profit, rate of mean reversion, entry cost, exit cost, shock standard deviation, and discount factor are specified, respectively:

```
pibar   = 0.0;
gamma   = 0.7;
kentry  =  10;
kexit   =   5;
sigma   = 1.0;
delta   = 0.9;
```

Third, one discretizes the shock. Here, the normally distributed replacement cost shock is discretized using a five-node Gaussian quadrature scheme:

```
nshocks = 5;
[e,w] = qnwnorm(nshocks,0,sigma.^2);
```

Fourth, one packs the model structure. Here, model is a structured variable whose fields contain the name of the model function file, the discount factor, shock values, shock probabilities, binary action space, index of the discrete state variable (profit), and model function parameters, respectively:

```
model.func = 'func';
model.discount = delta;
model.e = e;
model.w = w;
model.actions = [0;1];
model.discretestates = 2;
model.params = {pibar gamma kentry kexit};
```

Fifth, one specifies the basis functions and collocation nodes. Here, a 500-function cubic spline basis on the interval $[-10, 10]$ and the associated standard nodes are used to approximate the value function along its continuous dimension (profit):

```
n       = 500;
pimin   = -10;
pimax   =  10;
fspace = fundefn('spli',n,pimin,pimax,[],[0;1]);
scoord = funnode(fspace);
snodes = gridmake(scoord);
```

Notice how the discrete state is supplied as the last argument to fundefn.

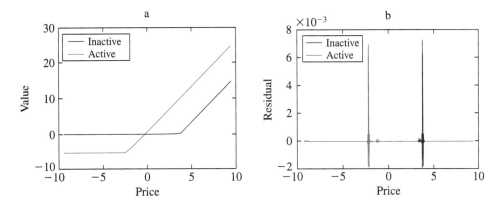

Figure 9.2
Solution to the Industry Entry-Exit Model: (a) Value Function; (b) Approximation Residual

Sixth, one solves the decision model:

```
[c,s,v,x,resid] = dpsolve(model,fspace,snodes);
```

Here, the routine `dpsolve` is called to solve the collocation equation using Newton's method, with the value function implicitly initialized to zero. The routine returns the basis coefficients `c`, as well as the optimal values `v`, optimal actions `x`, and Bellman equation residuals `resid` at a refined state grid `s`.

Finally, one performs postoptimality analysis. Figure 9.2a gives the value of the firm as a function of the short-run profit for both previously active and previously inactive firms. The value of a previously inactive firm is kinked at 3.70, the minimal short-run profit that must be achieved for the firm to enter. The value of a previously active firm is kinked at -2.27, the maximal loss that will be sustained before the firm exits. This result demonstrates the hysteresis phenomenon, where active firms may continue to operate in times of negative profits and inactive firms may decline to enter in times of positive profits. Figure 9.2b gives the Bellman equation residual as a function of the short-run profit for both previously active and previously inactive firms. The residuals exhibit noticeable spikes at the critical short-run profits, which can be expected as a result of the discontinuous derivatives of the value function at those points. The residuals, however, are very nearly zero elsewhere.

9.7   Computational Examples: Continuous Choice

9.7.1   Economic Growth

Consider the optimal economic growth model of section 8.4.1 assuming a social benefit function $u(c) = c^{1-\alpha}/(1 - \alpha)$, an aggregate production function $h(x) = x^\beta$, and an i.i.d. lognormal$(0, \sigma^2)$ production shock ϵ, where $\alpha = 0.2$, $\beta = 0.5$, and $\sigma = 0.1$. Further assume a capital survival rate $\gamma = 0.9$ and discount factor $\delta = 0.9$.

The collocation method calls for the analyst to select n basis functions ϕ_j and n collocation nodes s_i, and form the value function approximant $V(s) \approx \sum_{j=1}^{n} c_j \phi_j(s)$ whose coefficients c_j solve the collocation equation

$$\sum_{j=1}^{n} c_j \phi_j(s_i) = \max_{0 \leq x \leq s_i} \left\{ u(s_i - x) + \delta \sum_{k=1}^{K} \sum_{j=1}^{n} w_k c_j \phi_j \left(\gamma x + \epsilon_k h(x) \right) \right\}$$

where ϵ_k and w_k represent quadrature nodes and weights for the lognormal shock. One may solve the optimal economic growth model using CompEcon Toolbox routines as follows:

First, one codes a model function file that returns the values and derivatives of the reward and transition functions at arbitrary vectors of states s, actions x, and shocks e:

```
function [out1,out2,out3]=func(flag,s,x,e,alpha,beta,gamma);
switch flag
case 'b';
  out1 = zeros(size(s));
  out2 = s;
case 'f';
  out1 = ((s-x).^(1-alpha))/(1-alpha);
  out2 = -(s-x).^(-alpha);
  out3 = -alpha*(s-x).^(-alpha-1);
case 'g';
  out1 = gamma*x + e.*x.^beta;
  out2 = gamma + beta*e.*x.^(beta-1);
  out3 = (beta-1)*beta*e.*x.^(beta-2);
end
```

This model function file further requires the model parameters alpha, beta, and gamma as input. Passing the flag 'b' returns the lower and upper bounds on the action; passing the flag 'f' returns the reward function value and its first and second derivatives with respect to the action; and passing the flag 'g' returns the state transition function value and its first and second derivatives with respect to the action.

Second, one enters the model parameters. Here, the utility function parameter, production elasticity, capital survival rate, production shock standard deviation, and discount factor are specified, respectively:

```
alpha = 0.2;
beta  = 0.5;
gamma = 0.9;
sigma = 0.1;
delta = 0.9;
```

Third, one discretizes the shock. Here, the lognormal production shock is discretized using a three-node Gaussian quadrature scheme:

```
nshocks = 3;
[e,w] = qnwlogn(nshocks,0,sigma^2);
```

Fourth, one packs the model structure. Here, model is a structured variable whose fields contain the name of the model function file, the discount factor, shock values, shock probabilities, and model function parameters, respectively:

```
model.func = 'func';
model.discount = delta;
model.e = e;
model.w = w;
model.params = {alpha beta gamma};
```

Fifth, one specifies the basis functions and collocation nodes. Here, a 10-function Chebychev polynomial basis on the interval [5, 10] and the associated standard nodes are used to approximate the value function:

```
n       = 10;
smin    =  5;
smax    = 10;
fspace = fundefn('cheb',n,smin,smax);
snodes = funnode(fspace);
```

Sixth, one provides judicious guesses for values and actions at the collocation nodes. Here, the certainty-equivalent steady-state shock, action, and state are computed analytically and passed to the CompEcon Toolbox routine `lqapprox`, which returns the linear-quadratic approximation values and actions at the collocation nodes:

```
estar = exp(sigma^2/2);
xstar = ((1-delta*gamma)/(delta*beta))^(1/(beta-1));
sstar = gamma*xstar + xstar^beta;
[vlq,xlq] = lqapprox(model,snodes,sstar,xstar,estar);
```

Seventh, one solves the decision model:

```
[c,s,v,x,resid] = dpsolve(model,fspace,snodes,vlq,xlq);
```

Here, the routine `dpsolve` is called to solve the collocation equation using Newton's method. The routine returns the basis coefficients c, as well as the optimal values v, optimal actions x, and Bellman equation residuals `resid` at a refined state grid s.

Finally, one performs postoptimality analysis. Figure 9.3a gives optimal investment as a percent of wealth computed using both Chebychev collocation and linear-quadratic approximation. The Chebychev collocation approximant is upward sloping and the linear-quadratic approximant is downward sloping, indicating a qualitative difference between the two approximants. Figure 9.3b gives the Bellman equation residual as a function of wealth. The residual possesses zeros at the collocation nodes and exhibits very nearly equal oscillations between the nodes, a property that is typical of Chebychev residuals when the underlying decision model is smooth and effectively unconstrained. In this example, a 10th degree Chebychev approximation was sufficient to solve the Bellman equation to a residual error of order 5×10^{-9}, approximately seven orders of magnitude more accurate than the linear-quadratic approximant over the same domain (residual not drawn). These results suggest that linear-quadratic approximation can yield globally inaccurate solutions even when the underlying model is smooth and the constraints on the actions are not binding.

Figure 9.3c gives the expected path followed by the wealth level over time, beginning from a wealth level of 5. The expected path was computed by performing Monte Carlo simulations involving 2,000 paths of 20 years in duration each, using the CompEcon Toolbox routine `dpsimul`:

```
nyrs  = 20;
npath = 2000;
sinit = 5*ones(npath,1);
[spath,xpath] = dpsimul(model,sinit,nyrs,s,x);
```

As seen in this figure, expected wealth rises at a declining rate, converging asymptotically

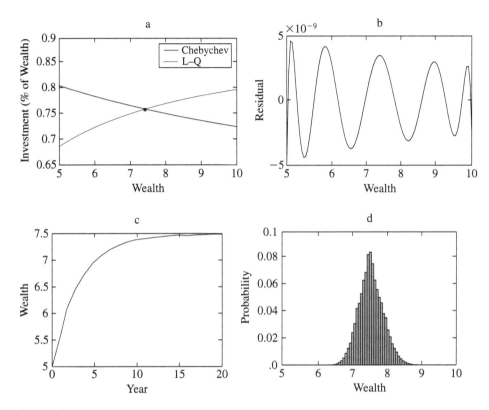

Figure 9.3
Solution to the Optimal Growth Model: (a) Optimal Investment Policy; (b) Approximation Residual; (c) Expected Wealth; (d) Steady-State Distribution

to a steady-state value of approximately 7.5. Figure 9.3d gives the steady-state distribution of the wealth level. The distribution, represented as an 80-bin histogram, was computed using the CompEcon Toolbox routine dpstst with a smoothing parameter of 5:

```
h = 5; nbins = 80;
[ss,pi,xx] = dpstst(model,h,nbins,s,x);
```

As seen in this figure, the steady-state distribution is essentially bell shaped with a mean of approximately 7.5, a result which is consistent with the Monte Carlo state-path simulations.

9.7.2   Renewable Resource Management

Consider the public renewable resource management model of section 8.4.2 assuming an inverse demand function $p(x) = x^{-\gamma}$ and a deterministic reproduction function $g(s, x) = \alpha(s - x) - 0.5\beta(s - x)^2$, where $\gamma = 0.5$, $\alpha = 4.0$, and $\beta = 1.0$. Further assume a unit cost of harvest $\kappa = 0.2$ and discount factor $\delta = 0.9$.

The collocation method calls for the analyst to select n basis functions ϕ_j and n collocation nodes s_i, and form the value function approximant $V(s) \approx \sum_{j=1}^{n} c_j \phi_j(s)$ whose coefficients c_j solve the collocation equation

$$\sum_{j=1}^{n} c_j \phi_j(s_i) = \max_{0 \leq x \leq s_i} \left\{ \frac{x^{1-\gamma}}{1-\gamma} - \kappa x + \delta \sum_{j=1}^{n} c_j \phi_j \big(g(s_i, x) \big) \right\}$$

One may solve the public renewable resource management model using CompEcon Toolbox routines as follows:

First, one codes a model function file that returns the values and derivatives of the reward and transition functions at arbitrary vectors of states s, actions x, and shocks e:

```
function [out1,out2,out3]=func(flag,s,x,e,alpha,beta,gamma,kappa);
switch flag
case 'b';
  out1 = zeros(size(s));
  out2 = s;
case 'f';
  out1 = (x.^(1-gamma))/(1-gamma)-kappa*x;
  out2 = x.^(-gamma)-kappa;
  out3 = -gamma*x.^(-gamma-1);
case 'g';
  out1 = alpha*(s-x) - 0.5*beta*(s-x).^2;
  out2 = -alpha + beta*(s-x);
  out3 = -beta*ones(size(s));
end
```

This model function file further requires the model parameters alpha, beta, gamma, and cost as input. Passing the flag 'b' returns the lower and upper bounds on the action; passing the flag 'f' returns the reward function value and its first and second derivatives with respect to the action; and passing the flag 'g' returns the transition function value and its first and second derivatives with respect to the action.

Second, one enters the model parameters. Here, the growth function parameters, demand function parameter, unit cost of harvest, and discount factor are specified, respectively:

```
alpha = 4.0;
beta  = 1.0;
gamma = 0.5;
kappa = 0.2;
delta = 0.9;
```

Third, one packs the model structure. Here, model is a structured variable whose fields contain the name of the model function file, the discount factor, and model function parameters, respectively:

```
model.func = 'func';
model.discount = delta;
model.params = {alpha beta gamma kappa};
```

Fourth, one specifies the basis functions and collocation nodes. Here, an eight-function Chebychev polynomial basis on the interval [6, 9] and the associated standard nodes are used to approximate the value function:

```
n       = 8;
smin    = 6;
smax    = 9;
fspace  = fundefn('cheb',n,smin,smax);
snodes  = funnode(fspace);
```

Fifth, one provides judicious guesses for values and actions at the collocation nodes. Here, the steady-state state and action are computed analytically and passed to the CompEcon Toolbox routine lqapprox, which returns the linear-quadratic approximation values and actions at the collocation nodes:

```
sstar = (alpha^2-1/delta^2)/(2*beta);
xstar = sstar - (delta*alpha-1)/(delta*beta);
[vlq,xlq] = lqapprox(model,snodes,sstar,xstar);
```

Sixth, one solves the decision model:

```
[c,s,v,x,resid] = dpsolve(model,fspace,snodes,vlq,xlq);
```

Here, the routine dpsolve is called to solve the collocation equation using Newton's method. The routine returns the basis coefficients c, as well as the optimal values v, optimal actions x, and Bellman equation residuals resid at a refined state grid s.

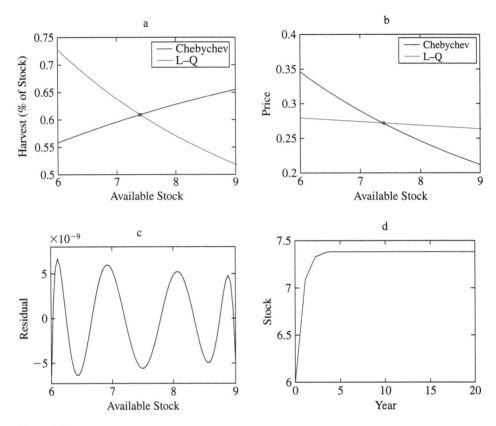

Figure 9.4
Solution to the Renewable Resource Management Model: (a) Optimal Harvest Policy; (b) Shadow Price Function;
(c) Approximation Residual; (d) State Path

Finally, one performs postoptimality analysis. Figure 9.4a gives optimal harvest as a percent of resource stock computed using both Chebychev collocation and linear-quadratic approximation. The Chebychev collocation approximant is upward sloping and the linear-quadratic approximant is downward sloping. Figure 9.4b gives the shadow price of the resource stock computed using both Chebychev collocation and linear-quadratic approximation. Both approximants are downward sloping, but the Chebychev approximant is steeper. Figure 9.4c gives the Bellman equation residual as a function of resource stock. The residual possesses zeros at the collocation nodes and exhibits very nearly equal oscillations between the nodes. In this example, an eight-degree Chebychev approximation was sufficient to solve the Bellman equation to a relative residual error of order 7×10^{-9}.

Figure 9.3d gives the path followed by the resource stock level over a 20-year period, beginning from a level of 6. The path was computed the CompEcon Toolbox routine dpsimul:

```
nyrs  = 20;
sinit = smin;
[spath,xpath] = dpsimul(model,sinit,nyrs,s,x);
```

As seen in this figure, resource stock rises rapidly, effectively converging to its steady-state value of 7.38 within four years.

9.7.3 Nonrenewable Resource Management

Consider the private nonrenewable resource management model of section 8.4.3 assuming an inverse demand function $p(x) = a_1 - a_2 x$ and a cost of extraction function $c(s, x) = b_1 x - 0.5 b_2 x (2s - x)$, where $a_1 = 10$, $a_2 = 0.8$, $b_1 = 12$, and $b_2 = 1$. Further assume a discount factor $\delta = 0.9$.

The collocation method calls for the analyst to select n basis functions ϕ_j and n collocation nodes s_i, and form the value function approximant $V(s) \approx \sum_{j=1}^{n} c_j \phi_j(s)$ whose coefficients c_j solve the collocation equation

$$
\sum_{j=1}^{n} c_j \phi_j(s_i) = \max_{0 \le x \le s_i} \left\{ p(x)\, x - c(s_i, x) + \delta \sum_{j=1}^{n} c_j \phi_j(s_i - x) \right\}
$$

One may solve the private nonrenewable resource management model using CompEcon Toolbox routines as follows:

First, one codes a model function file that returns the values of the reward and transition functions at arbitrary vectors of states s, actions x, and shocks e:

```
function [out1,out2,out3] = func(flag,s,x,e,a,b);
switch flag
case 'b';
  out1 = zeros(size(s));
  out2 = s;
case 'f';
  out1 = (a(1)-a(2)*x/2).*x-b(1)*x+b(2)*x.*(2*s-x)/2;
  out2 = a(1)-b(1)+b(2)*s-(a(2)+b(2))*x;
  out3 = -(a(2)+b(2))*ones(size(s));
case 'g';
  out1 = s-x;
```

```
    out2 = -ones(size(s));
    out3 = zeros(size(s));
end
```

The model function file returns the values and derivatives of the bound, reward, and transition functions at arbitrary vectors of states s and actions x. Passing the flag 'b' returns the lower and upper bounds on the action; passing the flag 'f' returns the reward function value and its first and second derivatives with respect to the action; and passing the flag 'g' returns the transition function value and its first and second derivatives with respect to the action.

Second, one enters the model parameters. Here, the inverse demand function parameters, cost function parameters, and the discount factor are specified, respectively:

```
a = [10 0.8];
b = [12 1.0];
delta = 0.9;
```

Third, one packs the model structure. Here, model is a structured variable whose fields contain the name of the model function file, the discount factor, and model function parameters, respectively:

```
model.func = 'func';
model.discount = delta;
model.params = {a b};
```

Fourth, one specifies the basis functions and collocation nodes. Here, a 101-function cubic spline basis on the interval [0, 10] and the associated standard nodes are used to approximate the value function:

```
n       = 101;
smin    =   0;
smax    =  10;
fspace = fundefn('spli',n,smin,smax);
snodes = funnode(fspace);
```

Fifth, one provides judicious guesses for values and actions at the collocation nodes. Here, since the model has no meaningful steady state, the initial harvest level and value function are both set to zero to initialize the collocation algorithm:

```
xinit = zeros(n,1);
vinit = zeros(n,1);
```

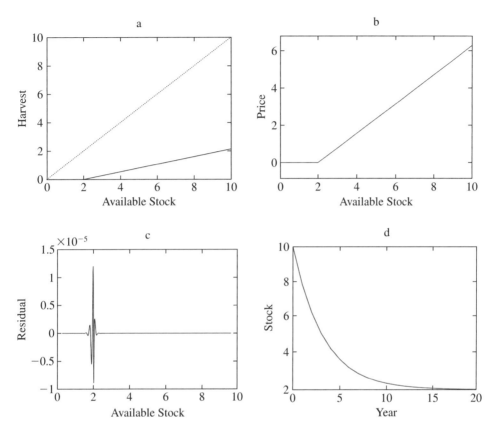

Figure 9.5
Solution to the Nonrenewable Resource Management Model: (a) Optimal Harvest Policy; (b) Shadow Price
Function; (c) Approximation Residual; (d) State Path

Sixth, one solves the decision model:

```
[c,s,v,x,resid] = dpsolve(model,fspace,snodes,vinit,xinit);
```

Here, the routine `dpsolve` is called to solve the collocation equation using Newton's
method. The routine returns the basis coefficients `c`, as well as the optimal values `v`, optimal
actions `x`, and Bellman equation residuals `resid` at a refined state grid `s`.

Finally, one performs postoptimality analysis. Figure 9.5a gives optimal harvest policy
and the 45° line. A salient feature of the optimal policy is that the mine is abandoned
at any stock level below 2. Figure 9.5b gives the shadow price of the resource stock. As
seen in this figure, the shadow price is zero below the critical abandonment level and

exhibits an apparently discontinuous derivative or kink at that point. Figure 9.5c gives the Bellman equation residual as a function of resource stock. The residual exhibits a strong disturbance near the kink point, which is typical of spline approximations in the presence of discontinuities. Still, the residual produced with 101 cubic spline basis functions is small in the vicinity of the kink, on the order of 1.5×10^{-5}, and is several orders of magnitude smaller at stock levels further removed from the kink. As seen in Figure 9.5d, if the initial stock level is 10, extraction levels decline over time, but the content of the mine will be effectively depleted in approximately 20 years.

9.7.4 Water Management

Consider the optimal water management model of section 8.4.4 assuming a farmer benefit function

$$F(x) = \frac{a_1}{1+b_1} x^{1+b_1}$$

a recreational user benefit function

$$U(s - x) = \frac{a_2}{1+b_2} (s - x)^{1+b_2}$$

and an i.i.d. lognormal$(0, \sigma^2)$ rainfall ϵ, where $a_1 = 1$, $b_1 = -2$, $a_2 = 2$, $b_2 = -3$, and $\sigma = 0.2$. Further assume a discount factor $\delta = 0.9$.

The collocation method calls for the analyst to select n basis functions ϕ_j and n collocation nodes s_i, and form the value function approximant $V(s) \approx \sum_{j=1}^{n} c_j \phi_j(s)$ whose coefficients c_j solve the collocation equation

$$\sum_{j=1}^{n} c_j \phi_j(s_i) = \max_{0 \leq x \leq s_i} \left\{ F(x) + U(s_i - x) + \delta \sum_{k=1}^{K} \sum_{j=1}^{n} w_k c_j \phi_j(s - x + \epsilon_k) \right\}$$

where ϵ_k and w_k represent quadrature nodes and weights for the lognormal shock. One may solve the optimal water management model using CompEcon Toolbox routines as follows:

First, one codes a model function file that returns the values of the reward and transition functions at arbitrary vectors of states s, actions x, and shocks e:

```
function [out1,out2,out3]=func(flag,s,x,e,a,b);
switch flag
case 'b';
  out1=zeros(size(s));
  out2=s;
```

```
case 'f';
  out1=(a(1)/(1+b(1)))*x.^(1+b(1))+(a(2)/(1+b(2)))*(s-x).^(1+b(2));
  out2=a(1)*x.^b(1)-a(2)*(s-x).^b(2);
  out3=a(1)*b(1)*x.^(b(1)-1)+a(2)*b(2)*(s-x).^(b(2)-1);
case 'g';
  out1=s-x+e;
  out2=-ones(size(s));
  out3=zeros(size(s));
end
```

The model function file returns the values and derivatives of the bound, reward, and transition functions at arbitrary vectors of states s, actions x, and shocks e. Passing the flag 'b' returns the lower and upper bounds on the action; passing the flag 'f' returns the reward function value and its first and second derivatives with respect to the action; and passing the flag 'g' returns the transition function value and its first and second derivatives with respect to the action.

Second, one enters the model parameters. Here, the farmer benefit function parameters, recreational user benefit function parameters, rainfall standard deviation, and discount factor are specified, respectively:

```
a = [ 1  2];
b = [-2 -3];
sigma = 0.2;
delta = 0.9;
```

Third, one discretizes the shock. Here, the lognormal rainfall shock is discretized using a three-node Gaussian quadrature scheme:

```
nshocks = 3;
[e,w] = qnwlogn(nshocks,0,sigma^2);
```

Fourth, one packs the model structure. Here, model is a structured variable whose fields contain the name of the model function file, the discount factor, shock values, shock probabilities, and model function parameters, respectively:

```
model.func = 'func';
model.discount = delta;
model.e = e;
model.w = w;
model.params = {a b};
```

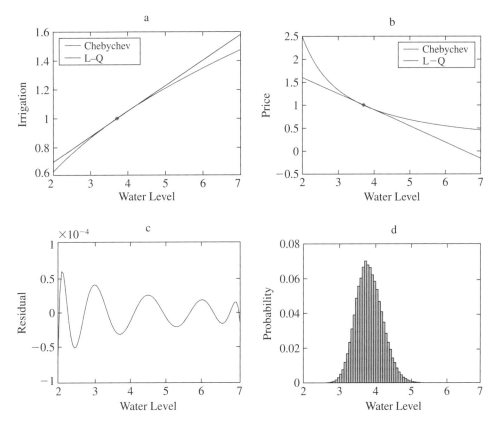

Figure 9.6
Solution to the Water Management Model: (a) Optimal Irrigation Policy; (b) Shadow Price Function; (c) Approximation Residual; (d) Steady-State Distribution

As seen in this figure, the steady-state reservoir level distribution is essentially bell-shaped with a mean of approximately 3.8.

9.7.5 Monetary Policy

Consider the optimal monetary policy model of section 8.4.5 assuming a loss function

$$L(s) = \tfrac{1}{2}(s - s^*)^\top \Omega (s - s^*)$$

a state transition function

$$g(s, x, \epsilon) = \alpha + \beta s + \gamma x + \epsilon$$

and an i.i.d. bivariate normal$(0, \Sigma)$ shock ϵ, where

$$s^* = \begin{bmatrix} 0 \\ 1 \end{bmatrix} \qquad \Omega = \begin{bmatrix} 0.3 & 0.0 \\ 0.0 & 1.0 \end{bmatrix}$$

and

$$\alpha = \begin{bmatrix} 0.9 \\ 0.4 \end{bmatrix} \qquad \beta = \begin{bmatrix} 0.8 & 0.5 \\ 0.2 & 0.6 \end{bmatrix} \qquad \gamma = \begin{bmatrix} -0.8 \\ 0.0 \end{bmatrix} \qquad \Sigma = \begin{bmatrix} 0.4 & 0.0 \\ 0.0 & 0.4 \end{bmatrix}$$

Further assume a discount factor $\delta = 0.9$.

The collocation method calls for the analyst to select n basis functions ϕ_j and n collocation nodes $s_i = (s_{1i}, s_{2i})$, and form the value function approximant $V(s_1, s_2) \approx \sum_{j=1}^{n} c_j \phi_j(s_1, s_2)$ whose coefficients c_j solve the collocation equation

$$\sum_{j=1}^{n} c_j \phi_j(s_i) = \max_{0 \leq x} \left\{ -L(s_i) + \delta \sum_{k=1}^{K} \sum_{j=1}^{n} w_k c_j \phi_j \big(g(s_i, x, \epsilon_k)\big) \right\}$$

where ϵ_k and w_k represent quadrature nodes and weights for the normal shock. This example differs from the preceding continuous choice examples in that the state space is two-dimensional. One may solve the optimal monetary policy model using CompEcon Toolbox routines as follows:

First, one codes a model function file that returns the values of the reward and transition functions at arbitrary vectors of states s, actions x, and shocks e:

```
function [out1,out2,out3]  = ...
func(flag,s,x,e,alpha,beta,gamma,omega,starget);
[n ds]  = size(s);
switch flag
case 'b';
  out1 = zeros(n,1);
  out2 = inf*ones(n,1);
case 'f';
  ss   = s - starget(ones(n,1),:);
  out1 = -0.5*sum((ss*omega).*ss,2);
  out2 = zeros(n,1);
  out3 = zeros(n,1);
case 'g';
  out1 = alpha(ones(n,1),:) + s*beta' + x*gamma + e;
  out2 = gamma(ones(n,1),:);
```

```
  out3 = zeros(n,ds);
end
```

The model function file returns the values and derivatives of the bound, reward, and transition functions at arbitrary vectors of states s, actions x, and shocks e. Passing the flag 'b' returns the lower and upper bounds on the action; passing the flag 'f' returns the reward function value and its first and second derivatives with respect to the action; and passing the flag 'g' returns the transition function value and its first and second derivatives with respect to the action.

Second, one enters the model parameters. Here, the transition function coefficients, banker preference weights, equilibrium targets, shock covariance matrix, and discount factor are specified, respectively:

```
alpha   = [0.9 0.4];
beta    = [0.8 0.5; 0.2 0.6];
gamma   = [-0.8 0.0];
omega   = [0.3 0; 0 1];
starget = [0 1];
sigma   = 0.04*eye(2);
delta   = 0.9;
```

Third, one discretizes the shock. Here, a nine-node discretization of the bivariate normal production shock is constructed by forming the Cartesian product of the three standard univariate nodes in each dimension:

```
nshocks = [3 3];
mu = [0 0];
[e,w] = qnwnorm(nshocks,mu,sigma);
```

Fourth, one packs the model structure. Here, model is a structured variable whose fields contain the name of the model function file, the discount factor, shock values, shock probabilities, and model function parameters, respectively:

```
model.func = 'func';
model.discount = delta;
model.e = e;
model.w = w;
model.params = {alpha beta gamma omega starget};
```

Fourth, one specifies the basis functions and nodes. Here, a 100-function bivariate cubic spline basis on the square $\{(s_1, s_2)| -15 \le s_1 \le 15, -10 \le s_2 \le 10\}$ is constructed by forming the tensor products of 10 univariate cubic B-spline basis functions along each dimension; also, a 100-node collocation grid within the square is constructed by forming the Cartesian product of the 10 standard cubic spline nodes along each dimension:

```
n      = [10 10];
smin   = [-15 -10];
smax   = [ 15  10];
fspace = fundefn('spli',n,smin,smax);
scoord = funnode(fspace);
snodes = gridmake(scoord);
```

Fifth, one provides judicious guesses for values and actions at the collocation nodes. Here, the certainty-equivalent steady-state shock, state, and action are computed analytically and passed to the CompEcon Toolbox routine `lqapprox`, which returns the linear-quadratic approximation values and actions at the collocation nodes:

```
estar = mu;
sstar = starget;
xstar = (sstar(1)-alpha(1)-beta(1,:)*sstar')/gamma(1);
[vlq,xlq] = lqapprox(model,snodes,sstar,xstar,estar);
```

Here, the certainty-equivalent steady-state shock, state, and action are computed analytically and passed to the CompEcon Toolbox routine `lqapprox`, which returns the linear-quadratic approximation values and actions used to initialize the collocation algorithm.

Sixth, one solves the decision model:

```
[c,s,v,x,resid] = dpsolve(model,fspace,snodes,vlq,xlq);
```

Here, the routine `dpsolve` is called to solve the collocation equation using Newton's method. The routine returns the basis coefficients `c`, as well as the optimal values `v`, optimal actions `x`, and Bellman equation residuals `resid` at a refined state grid `s`.

Finally, one performs postoptimality analysis. Figure 9.7a gives optimal nominal interest rate as a function of the underlying inflation rate and GDP gap. A salient feature of the solution is that the nonnegativity constraint on the nominal interest rate is binding for low GDP gaps and inflation rates. Although the model possesses a quadratic objective and a linear state transition function, the exact solution cannot be derived using linear-quadratic methods because of the binding constraint. Figure 9.7b gives the Bellman equation residual as a function of the underlying inflation rate and GDP gap. The residual exhibits discernible turbulence along the boundary at which the nonnegativity constraint becomes binding,

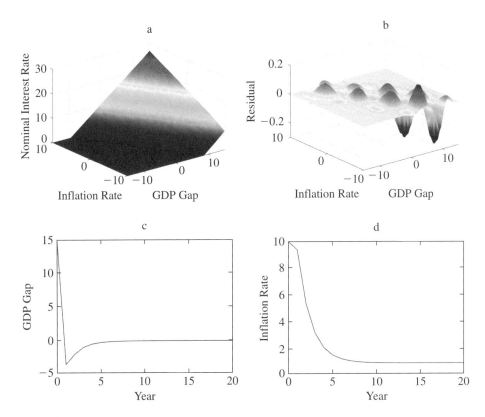

Figure 9.7
Solution to the Monetary Policy Model: (a) Optimal Monetary Policy; (b) Approximation Residual; (c) Expected State Path, GDP Gap; (d) Expected State Path, Inflation Rate

but it is relatively small elsewhere. The residual can be reduced, but only at the expense of additional nodes along each direction. Unfortunately, doubling the basis functions and nodes in each direction quadruples the necessary computational effort because of the product rule construction of the bivariate basis and collocation grid.

The CompEcon Toolbox routine `dpsimul` was used to simulate the model 5,000 times over a 20-year period starting from an initial GDP gap of 15% and inflation rate of 10%. Figure 9.7c indicates that the expected GDP gap will initially drop dramatically, overshooting its target of zero, but over time converges asymptotically to its target. Figure 9.7d, however, indicates that the expected inflation rate will drop monotonically, eventually converging to its target of 1%.

9.7.6 Production-Adjustment Model

Consider the production-adjustment model of section 8.4.6, which has two states, a demand shift variable d and lagged production l, and a single control, current production, q. Assume a linear cost-of-production function $c(q) = \kappa q$, a stochastic constant-elasticity inverse demand curve $dq^{-\beta}$, a quadratic adjustment cost $a(q - l) = 0.5\alpha(q - l)^2$, and an i.i.d. lognormal$(0, \sigma^2)$ demand shock ϵ, where $\alpha = 0.5$, $\beta = 0.5$, $\kappa = 0.5$, and $\sigma = 0.4$. Further assume a discount factor $\delta = 0.9$.

The collocation method calls for the analyst to select n basis functions ϕ_j and n collocation nodes (d_i, l_i), and form the value function approximant $V(d, l) \approx \sum_{j=1}^{n} c_j \phi_j(d, l)$ whose coefficients c_j solve the collocation equation

$$\sum_{j=1}^{n} c_j \phi_j(d_i, l_i) = \max_{0 \leq q} \left\{ d_i q^{1-\beta} - c(q) - a(q - l_i) + \delta \sum_{k=1}^{K} \sum_{j=1}^{n} w_k c_j \phi_j(\epsilon_k, q) \right\}$$

where ϵ_k and w_k represent quadrature nodes and weights for the lognormal shock. One may solve the production-adjustment model using CompEcon Toolbox routines as follows:

First, one codes a model function file that returns the values of the reward and transition functions at arbitrary vectors of states s, actions x, and shocks e:

```
function [out1,out2,out3]=func(flag,s,x,e,alpha,beta,kappa);
n = length(s);
d = s(:,1);
l = s(:,2);
q = x;
switch flag
case 'b';
  out1 = zeros(n,1);
  out2 = inf*ones(n,1);
case 'f';
  out1 = d.*q.^(1-beta) - kappa*q - 0.5*alpha*((q-1).^2);
  out2 = (1-beta)*d.*q.^(-beta) - kappa - alpha*(q-1);
  out3 = -beta*(1-beta)*d.*q.^(-beta-1) - alpha;
case 'g';
  out1 = [e q];
  out2 = [zeros(n,1) ones(n,1)];
  out3 = zeros(n,2);
end
```

The model function file returns the values and derivatives of the bound, reward, and transition functions at arbitrary vectors of states s, actions x, and shocks e. Passing the flag 'b' returns the lower and upper bounds on the action; passing the flag ′f′ returns the reward function value and its first and second derivatives with respect to the action; and passing the flag ′g′ returns the transition function value and its first and second derivatives with respect to the action.

Second, one enters the model parameters. Here, the marginal adjustment cost, demand elasticity, unit cost of production, demand shock standard deviation, and discount factor are specified, respectively:

```
alpha = 0.5;
beta  = 0.5;
kappa = 0.5;
sigma = 0.4;
delta = 0.9;
```

Third, one discretizes the shock. Here, the lognormal demand shock is discretized using a three-node Gaussian quadrature scheme:

```
nshocks = 3;
[e,w] = qnwlogn(nshocks,0,sigma^2);
```

Fourth, one packs the model structure. Here, model is a structured variable whose fields contain the name of the model function file, the discount factor, shock values, shock probabilities, and model function parameters, respectively:

```
model.func = 'func';
model.discount = delta;
model.e = e;
model.w = w;
model.params = {alpha beta kappa};
```

Fifth, one specifies the basis functions and collocation nodes. Here, a 150-function bivariate Chebychev polynomial basis is constructed by forming the tensor products of the first 15 and first 10 univariate Chebychev polynomials along the first and second state dimensions, respectively; also, a 150-node collocation grid is constructed by forming the Cartesian product of the 15 and 10 standard Chebychev nodes along each dimension:

```
n      = [15 10];
smin   = [e(1) xstar-1.0];
smax   = [e(m) xstar+3.0];
fspace = fundefn('cheb',n,smin,smax);
scoord = funnode(fspace);
snodes = gridmake(scoord);
```

Sixth, one provides judicious guesses for values and actions at the collocation nodes. Here, the certainty-equivalent steady-state shock, action, and state are computed analytically and passed to the CompEcon Toolbox routine `lqapprox`, which returns the linear-quadratic approximation values and actions at the collocation nodes:

```
estar = 1;
xstar = ((1-beta)/kappa)^(1/beta);
sstar = [xstar 1];
[vlq,xlq] = lqapprox(model,snodes,sstar,xstar,estar);
```

Sixth, one solves the decision model:

```
[c,s,v,x,resid] = dpsolve(model,fspace,snodes,vlq,xlq);
```

Here, the routine `dpsolve` is called to solve the collocation equation using Newton's method. The routine returns the basis coefficients `c`, and the optimal values `v`, optimal actions `x`, and Bellman equation residuals `resid` at a refined state grid `s`.

Finally, one performs postoptimality analysis. Figure 9.8a shows that optimal production is a monotonically increasing function of the demand shock and the preceding period's production. Figure 9.8b gives the value of the firm as a function of the demand shock and the preceding period's production, which is an increasing function of the demand shock, but a concave function of lagged production. Figure 9.8c gives the Bellman equation residual. The residual exhibits discernible turbulence for low values of the demand shock. However, the maximum residuals are on the order of 1×10^{-6} times the value of the firm. The CompEcon Toolbox routine `dpsimul` was used to simulate the model 5,000 times over a 20-year period starting from a production of 0.3. Figure 9.8d indicates that production can be expected to adjust gradually toward a steady-state mean value of approximately 1.1.

9.7.7 Production-Inventory Model

Consider the production-inventory model of section 8.4.7 assuming a quadratic cost-of-production function $c(q) = c_1 q + 0.5 c_2 q^2$, a quadratic cost-of-storage function $k(x) = k_1 x + 0.5 k_2 x^2$, a market price governed by $p_{t+1} = g(p_t, \epsilon_{t+1}) = \bar{p} + \rho(p_t - \bar{p}) + \epsilon$, and an i.i.d. normal$(0, \sigma^2)$ shock ϵ, where $c_1 = 0.5$, $c_2 = 0.1$, $k_1 = 0.1$, $k_2 = 0.1$, $\bar{p} = 1.0$, $\rho = 0.5$, and $\sigma = 0.2$. Further assume a discount factor $\delta = 0.9$.

The collocation method calls for the analyst to select n basis functions ϕ_j and n collocation nodes (s_i, p_i), and form the value function approximant $V(s, p) \approx \sum_{j=1}^{n} c_j \phi_j(s, p)$ whose coefficients c_j solve the collocation equation

$$\sum_{j=1}^{n} c_j \phi_j(s_i, p_i) = \max_{0 \leq q, 0 \leq x} \left\{ p_i(s_i + q - x) - c(q) - k(x) - \delta \sum_{k=1}^{K} \sum_{j=1}^{n} w_k c_j \phi_j(x, \hat{p}_{ik}) \right\}$$

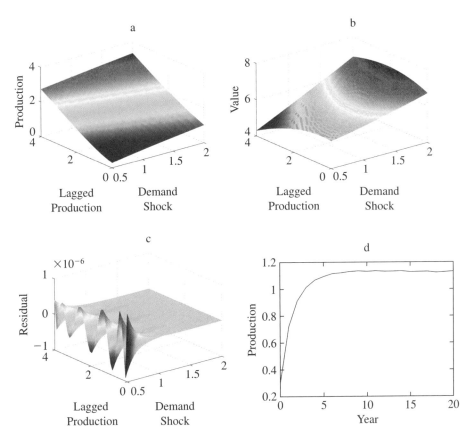

Figure 9.8
Solution to the Production-Adjustment Model: (a) Optimal Production Policy; (b) Value Function; (c) Approximation Residual; (d) Expected Policy Path

where $\hat{p}_{ik} = g(p_i, \epsilon_k)$ and ϵ_k and w_k represent quadrature nodes and weights for the normal shock. One may solve the production-inventory model using CompEcon Toolbox routines as follows:

First, one codes a model function file that returns the values of the reward and transition functions at arbitrary vectors of states s, actions x, and shocks e:

```
function [out1,out2,out3] = func(flag,s,x,e,c,k,pbar,rho);
[n,ds] = size(s);
[n,dx] = size(x);
```

```
switch flag
case 'b'
  out1 = zeros(size(x));
  out2 = inf*ones(size(x));
case 'f'
  out2 = zeros(n,dx);
  out3 = zeros(n,dx,dx);
  out1 = s(:,2).*(s(:,1)+x(:,1)-x(:,2)) ...
          - (c(1)+0.5*c(2)*x(:,1)).*x(:,1) ...
          - (k(1)+0.5*k(2)*x(:,2)).*x(:,2);
  out2(:,1) =  s(:,2) - (c(1)+c(2)*x(:,1));
  out2(:,2) = -s(:,2) - (k(1)+k(2)*x(:,2));
  out3(:,1,1) = -c(2)*ones(n,1);
  out3(:,2,2) = -k(2)*ones(n,1);
case 'g'
  out2 = zeros(n,ds,dx);
  out3 = zeros(n,ds,dx,dx);
  out1 = [x(:,2) pbar+rho*(s(:,2)-pbar)+e];
  out2(:,1,2) = ones(n,1);
end
```

The model function file returns the values and derivatives of the bound, reward, and transition functions at arbitrary vectors of states s, actions x, and shocks e. Passing the flag 'b' returns the lower and upper bounds on the action; passing the flag 'f' returns the reward function value and its first and second derivatives with respect to the action; and passing the flag 'g' returns the transition function value and its first and second derivatives with respect to the action.

Second, one enters the model parameters. Here, the production cost function parameters, storage cost function parameters, long-run mean price, mean reversion rate, price shock standard deviation, and discount factor are specified, respectively:

```
c     = [0.5 0.1];
k     = [0.1 0.1];
pbar  = 1.0;
rho   = 0.5;
sigma = 0.2;
delta = 0.9;
```

Third, one discretizes the shock. Here, the normal demand shock is discretized using a three-node Gaussian quadrature scheme:

```
nshocks = 3;
[e,w] = qnwnorm(nshocks,0,sigma^2);
```

Fourth, one packs the model structure. Here, `model` is a structured variable whose fields contain the name of the model function file, the discount factor, shock values, shock probabilities, and model function parameters, respectively:

```
model.func = 'func';
model.discount = delta;
model.e = e;
model.w = w;
model.params = {c k pbar rho};
```

Fifth, one specifies the basis functions and collocation nodes. Here, an 80-function bivariate cubic spline basis is constructed by forming the tensor products of four and 20 univariate cubic splines along the first and second state dimensions, respectively; also, an 80-node collocation grid is constructed by forming the Cartesian product of the four and 20 standard spline nodes along the two state dimensions:

```
n       = [4 20];
smin    = [0 0.6];
smax    = [2 1.4];
fspace  = fundefn('spli',n,smin,smax);
scoord  = funnode(fspace);
snodes  = gridmake(scoord);
```

Sixth, one provides judicious guesses for values and actions at the collocation nodes. Here, the certainty-equivalent steady-state shock, state, and action are computed analytically and passed to the CompEcon Toolbox routine `lqapprox`, which returns the linear-quadratic approximation values and actions at the collocation nodes:

```
estar = 0;
sstar = [0 pbar];
xstar = [(pbar-c(1))/c(2) 0];
[vlq,xlq] = lqapprox(model,snodes,sstar,xstar,estar);
```

Seventh, one solves the decision model:

```
[c,s,v,x,resid] = dpsolve(model,fspace,snodes,vlq,xlq);
```

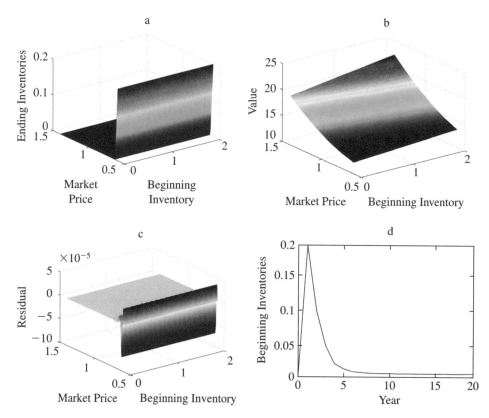

Figure 9.9
Solution to the Production-Inventory Model: (a) Optimal Inventory Policy; (b) Value Function; (c) Approximation
Residual; (d) Expected State Path

Here, the routine `dpsolve` is called to solve the collocation equation using Newton's
method. The routine returns the basis coefficients c, as well as the optimal values v, optimal
actions x, and Bellman equation residuals `resid` at a refined state grid s.

Finally, one performs postoptimality analysis. Figure 9.9a shows that the optimal inventory policy is to store nothing if the price is sufficiently high, given that expected appreciation
of stocks will not be sufficient to cover the cost of storage. However, for sufficiently low
prices, it will be economical to hold inventories; the lower the price, the higher the expected
appreciation, and thus the higher the optimal stock level. Figure 9.9b shows the value of
the firm as an increasing function of both the market price and beginning inventories. The
value is a linear function of beginning inventories with a slope equal to the market price (the
reader is asked to establish this fact theoretically in exercise 8.7 on page 221). Figure 9.9c

gives the Bellman equation residual as a function of beginning inventories and market price. The residual exhibits discernible turbulence for low values of the market price along the boundary at which the stock nonnegativity constraint becomes binding. However, the maximum residuals are on the order of 10^{-5} times the value of the firm, indicating an accurate numerical solution to the Bellman equation.

The CompEcon Toolbox routine `dpsimul` was used to simulate the model 10,000 times over a 20-year period starting from a low price and inventory level. Figure 9.9d indicates that with low prices, the firm acquires substantial stocks at the outset, but can be expected to gradually reduce these stocks over time, eventually reaching a steady-state mean value of approximately 0.0045.

9.7.8   Livestock Feeding

Consider the livestock feeding model of section 8.4.8 assuming a growth function $g(s, x) = \alpha s + x^\beta$ where $\alpha = 0.9$ and $\beta = 0.5$. Further assume that $\kappa = 0.4$, $p = 1$, $T = 6$, and $\delta = 0.9$.

The collocation method calls for the analyst to select n basis functions ϕ_j and n collocation nodes s_i, and form the value function approximants $V_t(s) \approx \sum_{j=1}^{n} c_{tj}\phi_j(s)$ whose coefficients c_{tj} solve the collocation equations

$$\sum_{j=1}^{n} c_{tj}\phi_j(s_i) = \max_{0 \leq x} \left\{ -\kappa x + \delta \sum_{j=1}^{n} c_{t+1,j}\phi_j(\alpha s_i + x^\beta) \right\}$$

One may solve the livestock feeding model using CompEcon Toolbox routines as follows:

First, one codes a model function file that returns the values of the reward and transition functions at arbitrary vectors of states `s`, actions `x`, and shocks `e`:

```
function [out1,out2,out3]=func(flag,s,x,e,alpha,beta,kappa);
switch flag
case 'b';
  n    = length(s);
  out1 = zeros(n,1);
  out2 = inf*ones(n,1);
case 'f';
  n    = length(x);
  out1 = -kappa*x;
  out2 = -kappa*ones(n,1);
  out3 = zeros(n,1);
case 'g';
```

```
    out1 = alpha*s + x.^beta;
    out2 = beta*x.^(beta-1);
    out3 = (beta-1)*beta*x.^(beta-2);
end
```

The model function file returns the values and derivatives of the bound, reward, and transition functions at arbitrary vectors of states s and actions x. Passing the flag 'b' returns the lower and upper bounds on the action; passing the flag 'f' returns the reward function value and its first and second derivatives with respect to the action; and passing the flag 'g' returns the state transition function value and its first and second derivatives with respect to the action.

Second, one enters the model parameters. Here, the growth function parameters, unit cost of feed, unit price of livestock, time horizon, and discount factor are specified, respectively:

```
alpha = 0.9;
beta  = 0.5;
kappa = 0.4;
price = 1.0;
T     = 6;
delta = 0.9;
```

Third, one packs the model structure. Here, model is a structured variable whose fields contain the name of the model function file, time horizon, discount factor, and model function parameters, respectively:

```
model.func = 'func';
model.T = T;
model.discount = delta;
model.params = {alpha beta kappa};
```

Fourth, one specifies the basis functions and collocation nodes. Here, a 50-function cubic spline basis on the interval [0.4, 2.0] and the associated standard nodes are used to approximate the value function:

```
n      = 50;
smin   = 0.4;
smax   = 2.0;
fspace = fundefn('spli',n,smin,smax);
snodes = funnode(fspace);
```

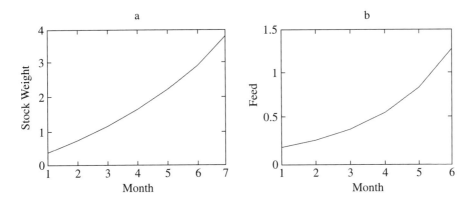

Figure 9.10
Solution to the Livestock Feeding Problem: (a) State Path; (b) Policy Path

Fifth, one specifies the terminal $(T+1)$ values at the collocation nodes and supplies judicious guesses for the actions at the collocation nodes in the terminal decision period (T):

```
xinit = ones(n,1);
vterm = price*snodes;
```

Sixth, one solves the decision model:

```
[c,s,v,x] = dpsolve(model,fspace,snodes,vterm,xinit);
```

Here, the routine `dpsolve` is called to solve the collocation equation using Newton's method. The routine returns the basis coefficients `c`, as well as the optimal values `v`, optimal actions `x`, and Bellman equation residuals `resid` at a refined state grid `s`. Figures 9.10a and 9.10b give the optimal stock weight and feed over time.

9.8 Dynamic Game Methods

Recall from section 8.5 that the Markov perfect equilibrium of an m-agent infinite-horizon dynamic game is characterized by a set of m simultaneous Bellman equations

$$V_p(s) = \max_{x_p \in X_p(s)} \left\{ f_p\left(s, x_p, x^*_{-p}(s)\right) + \delta E_\epsilon V_p\left(g\left(s, x_p, x^*_{-p}(s), \epsilon\right)\right) \right\}$$

$p = 1, 2, \ldots, m$, whose unknowns are the m value functions $V_p(\cdot)$ and the m associated optimal policies $x^*_p(\cdot)$, all of which are defined on the state space S. For the sake of discussion, assume that the state space S is a bounded interval of $\mathbb{R}^m$ and that agent p's actions are constrained to an interval on the real line, $X_p(s) = [a_p(s), b_p(s)]$. Further assume that the reward functions f_p and state transition function g are twice continuously differentiable functions of their arguments.[4]

To compute an approximate solution to the system of Bellman functional equations using collocation, one employs the following strategy: First, write the value function approximants as linear combinations of known basis functions $\phi_1, \phi_2, \ldots, \phi_n$ whose coefficients c_{pj} are to be determined:

$$V_p(s) \approx \sum_{j=1}^{n} c_{pj} \phi_j(s)$$

Second, fix the mn basis function coefficients c_{pj} by requiring the approximants to satisfy their respective m Bellman equations, not at all possible states, but rather at n states $s_1, s_2, \ldots, s_n$, called the collocation nodes.

The collocation strategy replaces the m Bellman functional equations with a system of mn nonlinear equations in mn unknowns. Specifically, to compute the value function approximants, or more precisely, to compute the mn basis coefficients c_{pj} in their basis representations, one solves the equation system

$$\sum_{j=1}^{n} c_{pj} \phi_j(s_i) = \max_{x_p \in X_p(s_i)} \left\{ f_p(s_i, x_p, x_{-pi}) + \delta E_\epsilon \sum_{j=1}^{n} c_{pj} \phi_j \big(g(s_i, x_p, x_{-pi}, \epsilon) \big) \right\}$$

for $p = 1, 2, \ldots, m$ and $i = 1, 2, \ldots, n$, where x_p is the action taken by agent p and x_{-pi} are the actions taken by his competitors when the state is s_i. The nonlinear equation system may be compactly expressed in vector form as a system of simultaneous collocation equations

$$\Phi c_p = v_p(c_p, x_{-p})$$

Here, c_p is the $n \times 1$ vector of basis coefficients of agent p's value function approximant; x_{-p} is the $(m-1)n$ vector of his competitors actions at the state nodes; Φ, the collocation matrix, is the $n \times n$ matrix whose typical ijth element is the jth basis function evaluated at the ith collocation node

$$\Phi_{ij} = \phi_j(s_i)$$

---

4. The presentation generalizes to models with arbitrary-dimensional state and action spaces, but at the expense of cumbersome additional notation that offers little additional insight.

and v_p, agent p's collocation function, is the function from $\mathbb{R}^{mn}$ to $\mathbb{R}^n$ whose typical ith element is

$$v_{pi}(c_p, x_{-p}) = \max_{x_p \in X_p(s_i)} \left\{ f_p(s_i, x_p, x_{-pi}) + \delta E_\epsilon \sum_{j=1}^n c_{pj}\phi_j\big(g(s_i, x_p, x_{-pi}, \epsilon)\big) \right\}$$

Agent p's collocation function evaluated at a particular vector of basis coefficients c_p yields an $n \times 1$ vector v_p whose ith entry is the value obtained by solving the optimization problem embedded in the Bellman equation at the ith collocation node, replacing the value function appearing in the optimand with the approximant $\sum_j c_{pj}\phi_j$ and taking his competitor's vector of current actions x_{-p} at the collocation nodes as given.

Just as in case of a single-agent dynamic optimization model, the simultaneous collocation equations of an m-agent game may be solved using standard nonlinear equation solution methods. However, one cannot solve the individual collocation equations independently because one agent's optimal action depends on the actions taken by others. Still, one can solve collocation equations for the m-agent using iterative strategies that are straightforward generalizations of those used to solve single-agent dynamic optimization models. For example, one may write the collocation equation as a fixed-point problem $c_p = \Phi^{-1}v_p(c_p, x_{-p})$ and use function iteration, which employs the iterative update rule

$$c_p \leftarrow \Phi^{-1}v_p(c_p, x_{-p})$$

In this implementation, the optimal actions of all agents are updated at each iteration with the evaluation of the collocation functions v_p, and passed as arguments to the collocation functions v_p in the subsequent iteration.

Alternatively, one may write the collocation equation as a rootfinding problem $\Phi c_p - v_p(c_p, x_{-p}) = 0$ and solve for c using a pseudo Newton's method, which employs the iterative update rule

$$c_p \leftarrow c_p - [\Phi - v'(x)]^{-1}[\Phi c_p - v_p(c_p, x_{-p})]$$

Here, $v'(x)$ is the common $n \times n$ Jacobian of the collocation functions v_p with respect to the basis coefficient c_p. The typical element of $v'(x)$ may be computed by applying the Envelope Theorem:

$$v'_{ij}(x) = \delta E_\epsilon \phi_j\big(g(s_i, x_i, \epsilon)\big)$$

where x_i is the vector of optimal actions taken by all m agents when the state is s_i.

As with the single-agent model, unless the m-agent game model is deterministic, one must compute expectations in a numerically practical way. Regardless of which quadrature scheme is selected, the continuous random variable ϵ in the state transition function is replaced with a discrete approximant, say, one that assumes values $\epsilon_1, \epsilon_2, \ldots, \epsilon_K$ with probabilities $w_1, w_2, \ldots, w_K$, respectively. In this instance, the collocation functions v_p take the specific form

$$v_{pi}(c_p, x_{-p}) = \max_{x_p \in X_p(s_i)} \left\{ f_p(s_i, x_p, x_{-pi}) + \delta \sum_{k=1}^{K} \sum_{j=1}^{n} w_k c_{pj} \phi_j \left(g(s_i, x_p, x_{-pi}, \epsilon_k) \right) \right\}$$

and their Jacobian takes the form

$$v_{ij}'(x) = \delta \sum_{k=1}^{K} w_k \phi_j \left(g(s_i, x_i, \epsilon_k) \right)$$

The practical steps that must be taken to implement the collocation method for dynamic games in a computer-programming environment are similar to those taken to solve single-agent models. The initial step is to specify the basis functions that will be used to express the value function approximants and the collocation nodes at which the Bellman equations will be required to hold exactly. This step may be executed using the CompEcon Toolbox routines `fundefn`, `funnode`, and `funbas`, which are discussed in Chapter 6:

```
fspace _ fundefn('cheb',n,smin,smax);
s        = funnode(fspace);
Phi      = funbas(fspace);
```

Here, it is presumed that the analyst has previously specified the lower and upper endpoints of the state interval, `smin` and `smax`, and the number of basis functions and collocation nodes n. After execution, `fspace` is a structured variable containing all the information needed to define the approximation space, s is the $n \times 1$ vector of standard collocation nodes for the selected basis, and `Phi` is the associated $n \times n$ collocation matrix. In this specific example, the standard Chebychev polynomial basis functions and collocation nodes are used to form the approximant.

Next, a numerical routine must be coded to evaluate the collocation functions and their common derivative at an arbitrary set of basis coefficient vectors. A version of such a routine in which all basis coefficients and actions are efficiently stored in matrix formats with columns corresponding to different agents would have a calling sequence of the form

```
[v,x,vjac] = vmax(s,x,c) .
```

Here, on input, s is an $n \times 1$ vector of collocation nodes, c is an $n \times m$ matrix of basis coefficients, and x is an $n \times m$ matrix of current optimal actions. On output, v is an $n \times m$ matrix of optimal values at the collocation nodes, x is an $n \times m$ matrix of updated optimal actions at the nodes, and `vjac` is an $n \times n$ Jacobian of the collocation functions. The m columns of `v`, `x`, and `c` correspond to the m agents.

Given a `vmax` function coded as described, the joint collocation equations for the m-agent game can be solved by executing the same steps used to solve the single-agent model. In particular, given the collocation nodes `s`, collocation matrix `Phi`, and collocation function routine `vmax`, and given initial guesses for the basis coefficient matrix `c` and optimal action matrix `x`, the collocation equation may be solved either by function iteration

```
for it=1:maxit
  cold = c;
  [v,x] = vmax(s,x,c);
  c = Phi\v;
  if norm(c-cold,inf)<tol, break, end;
end
```

or by the Newton iteration

```
for it=1:maxit
  cold = c;
  [v,x,vjac] = vmax(s,x,c);
  c = c - [Phi-vjac]\[Phi*c-v];
  if norm(c-cold,inf)<tol, break, end;
end
```

The main challenge in implementing the collocation method for a dynamic game is coding the routine `vmax` that returns the collocation functions and their common derivative, which requires solving the optimization problems embedded in the m Bellman equations at the collocation nodes. A simple routine that performs the optimizations by iteratively solving the associated Karush-Kuhn-Tucker complementarity conditions is as follows:

```
function [v,xnew,vjac] = vmax(s,xold,c)
xnew = xold;
for p=1:m
  x = xold;
  [xl,xu] = bfunc(s,p);
  for it=1:maxit
    [f,fx,fxx] = ffunc(s,x,p);
    Ev=0; Evx=0; Evxx=0;
    for k=1:K
      [g,gx,gxx] = gfunc(s,x,e(k),p);
      vn       = funeval(c(:,p),fspace,g);
```

```
      vnder1 = funeval(c(:,p),fspace,g,1);
      vnder2 = funeval(c(:,p),fspace,g,2);
      Ev   = Ev   + w(k)*vn;
      Evx  = Evx  + w(k)*vnder1.*gx;
      Evxx = Evxx + w(k)*(vnder1.*gxx + vnder2.*gx.^2);
    end
    v    = f + delta*Ev;
    delx = -(fx+delta*Evx)./(fxx+delta*Evxx);
    delx = min(max(delx,xl-x),xu-x);
    x(:,p) = x(:,p) + delx;
    if norm(delx)<tol, break, end;
  end
  xnew(:,p) = x(:,p)
end
vjac = 0;
for k=1:K
  g = gfunc(s,xnew,e(k));
  vjac = vjac + delta*w(k)*funbas(fspace,g);
end
```

The *m*-agent game routine vmax differs from the similarly named routine for single-agent models primarily in that *m* Bellman optimands rather than one must be maximized. In this implementation, an outer loop over the agent index p is executed. For each agent, the collocation function is evaluated using the ancillary routines bfunc, ffunc, and gfunc that compute the bounds, rewards, and state transitions and additionally take the agent's index as an argument. In particular, the routine bfunc accepts the $n \times m$ matrix of states s and the agent's index p and returns $n \times 1$ vectors xl and xu of associated lower and upper bounds on agent p's actions. The routine ffunc accepts the $n \times m$ matrix of states s, the $n \times m$ matrix of actions x, and the agent's index p and returns $n \times 1$ vectors f, fx, and fxx of associated reward function values and derivatives with respect to the agent's actions. The routine gfunc accepts the $n \times m$ matrix of states s, the $n \times m$ matrix of actions x, the agent's index p, and a particular value of the shock e and returns $n \times m$ matrices g, gx, and gxx of associated state transition function values and derivatives with respect to the agent's actions.

Each outer loop in vmax begins by computing the lower and upper bounds xl and xu on agent *p*'s actions at the state nodes. The inner loop executes a series of Newton iterations that sequentially update agent *p*'s actions at the state nodes until the

Karush-Kuhn-Tucker conditions of the optimization problem embedded in the Bellman equation are satisfied to a specified tolerance `tol`. With each iteration, the standard Newton step `delx` is computed and subsequently shortened, if necessary, to ensure that the updated action `x+delx` remains within the bounds `xl` and `xu`. The standard Newton step `delx` is the negative of the ratio of the second and third derivatives of agent p's Bellman optimand with respect to agent p's action, `fx+delta*Evx` and `fxx+delta*Evxx`.

In order to compute the expected value next period and its derivatives, another nested loop is executed over all `K` possible realizations of the discrete shock, and probability-weighted sums are formed (here, `e(k)` and `w(k)` are the kth shock and its probability). For each realization of the shock, the state next period `g` and its first and second derivatives with respect to agent p's action, `gx` and `gxx`, are computed. The state next period is passed to the library routine `funeval`, which computes next period's value and its derivatives using the value function approximant that is identified with agent p's coefficient vector `c(:,p)`. The chain rule is then used to compute the derivatives of the expected value.

Once convergence is achieved and the optimal value and action at the state nodes have been determined, the Jacobian `vjac` of the collocation function is computed. The Jacobian is an $n \times n$ matrix whose representative ijth entry is the discounted expectation of the jth basis evaluated at the following period's state, given that the current state is the ith state node. To compute the Jacobian, a loop is executed over all K possible realizations of the discrete shock. For each realization of the shock, the state next period `g` is computed and passed to the CompEcon Toolbox routine `funbas`, which in turn evaluates the basis functions at that state.

In order to simplify the process of solving and analyzing continuous state Markov dynamic game models, the CompEcon Toolbox contains a routine `gamesolve` that performs the necessary computations that we have described for a two-agent game. The routine has a calling sequence of the form:

```
[c,s,v,x,resid] = gamesolve(model,fspace,vinit,xinit);
```

The input-output conventions for `gamesolve` are similar to those of `dpsolve`, except that the coefficient, value, and policy matrices will contain information about all agents rather than a single agent. The input-output conventions, including the appropriate way to set up the model function file, are presented by example in the following sections.

9.8.1 Capital-Production Game

Consider the capital-production game of section 8.5.1. Assume that the market clearing price is a downward-sloping linear function of the total quantity produced by both firms

$$p(q_1, q_2) = a + b(q_1 + q_2)$$

and that each firm faces a constant unit cost of production that is a declining function of the firm's capital stock:

$$c(k) = \beta_1 + \beta_2/k$$

Also, assume that each firm's cost of investment is a quadratic function of new capital:

$$h(x) = \gamma_1 x + 0.5\gamma_2 x^2$$

Under the assumption that the firms play a Cournot quantity game in the short run, it can be shown that firm p's short-run profit, exclusive of investment costs, will be a function

$$\pi_p(c_1, c_2) = (\alpha_1 - 2c_p + c_{-p})^2/(9\alpha_2)$$

of the firm's unit cost of production c_p and its competitor's unit cost of production c_{-p}.

The collocation method calls for the analyst to select n basis functions ϕ_j and n collocation nodes (k_{1i}, k_{2i}), and form the value function approximants $V_p(k_1, k_2) \approx \sum_{j=1}^{n} c_{pj}\phi_j(k_1, k_2)$ whose coefficients c_{pj} solve the collocation equation

$$\sum_{j=1}^{n} c_{pj}\phi_j(k_{1i}, k_{2i}) = \max_{q_p \geq 0, x_p \geq 0} \left\{ \pi_p\big(c_1(k_{1i}), c_2(k_{2i})\big) - h(x_p) + \delta \sum_{j=1}^{n} c_j\phi_j(\hat{k}_{1i}, \hat{k}_{2i}) \right\}$$

where $\hat{k}_{pi} = (1 - \psi)k_{pi} + x_p$. One may solve the capital-production game using CompEcon Toolbox routines as follows:

First, one codes a model function file that returns the values of the reward and transition functions at arbitrary vectors of states s, actions x, and shocks e:

```
function [out1,out2,out3]=func(flag,s,x,e,alpha,beta,gamma,psi);
[n,m] = size(s);
switch flag
case 'b';
  xl = zeros(n,m);
  xu = inf*ones(n,m);
  out1=xl; out2=xu;
case 'f1';
  c1 = beta(1) + beta(2)./s(:,1);
  c2 = beta(1) + beta(2)./s(:,2);
  pi = ((alpha(1)-2*c1+c2).^2)/(9*alpha(2));
  f  = pi-(gamma(1)*x(:,1)+0.5*gamma(2)*x(:,1).^2);
```

```
   fx = zeros(n,m);
   fx(:,1) = -(gamma(1)+gamma(2)*x(:,1));
   fxx = zeros(n,m,m);
   out1=f; out2=fx; out3=fxx;
case 'f2';
   c1 = beta(1) + beta(2)./s(:,1);
   c2 = beta(1) + beta(2)./s(:,2);
   pi = ((alpha(1)-2*c2+c1).^2)/(9*alpha(2));
   f  = pi-(gamma(1)*x(:,2)+0.5*gamma(2)*x(:,2).^2);
   fx = zeros(n,m);
   fx(:,2) = -(gamma(1)+gamma(2)*x(:,2));
   fxx = zeros(n,m,m);
   out1=f; out2=fx; out3=fxx;
case 'g';
   g = (1-psi)*s + x;
   gx  = zeros(n,m,m);
   gx(:,1,1) = ones(n,1);
   gx(:,2,2) = ones(n,1);
   gxx = zeros(n,m,m,m);
   out1=g; out2=gx; out3=gxx;
end
```

Passing the flag `'b'` returns the lower and upper bounds on the action; passing the flag `'f1'` returns the reward function value and its first two derivatives for agent 1; passing the flag `'f2'` returns the reward function value and its first two derivatives for agent 2; and passing the flag `'g'` returns the transition function value and its first and second derivatives with respect to the action.

Second, one enters the model parameters. Here, the demand function parameters, cost of production parameters, cost of investment parameters, depreciation rate and discount factor are specified, respectively:

```
alpha = [8.0 4.0];
beta  = [1.8 0.2];
gamma = [0.4 3.0];
psi   = 0.1;
delta = 0.9;
```

Third, one packs the model structure. Here, `model` is a structured variable whose fields contain the name of the model function file, the discount factor, and function parameters, respectively:

```
model.func = 'func';
model.discount = delta;
model.params = {alpha beta gamma psi};
```

Fourth, one specifies the basis functions and collocation nodes. Here, a 64-function bivariate Chebychev polynomial basis is constructed by forming the tensor products of eight Chebychev polynomials along both the first and second state dimensions, respectively; also, a 64-node collocation grid is constructed by forming the Cartesian product of the eight standard Chebychev nodes along each of the two state dimensions:

```
n       = [8 8];
smin    = [0.7 0.7];
smax    = [1.3 1.3];
fspace  = fundefn('cheb',n,smin,smax);
scoord  = funnode(fspace);
snodes  = gridmake(scoord);
```

Fifth, one provides judicious guesses for values and actions at the collocation nodes. Here, the investment and the value function are initialized to zero:

```
xinit = zeros(size(snodes));
vinit = zeros(size(snodes));
```

Sixth, one solves the decision model:

```
[c,s,v,x,resid] = gamesolve(model,fspace,vinit,xinit);
```

The CompEcon Toolbox routine `gamesolve` accepts as input the model structure `model`, basis functions `fspace`, and initial guesses for the value function `vinit` and optimal actions `xinit`. It then solves the collocation equation, returning as output the basis coefficients `c` and the optimal values `v`, optimal actions `x`, and Bellman equation residuals `resid` at a refined state grid `s`.

Finally, one performs postoptimality analysis. Figure 9.11a shows agent 1's optimal investment policy as a function of the capital stocks of the two agents. Clearly, optimal investment declines with the level of both capital stocks, though the rate is faster with respect to the agent's own capital stock. Figure 9.11b gives the Bellman equation residual for agent 1's value function approximant. The maximum residuals are on the order of 10^{-9}, indicating that the computed solution offers an acceptably accurate numerical

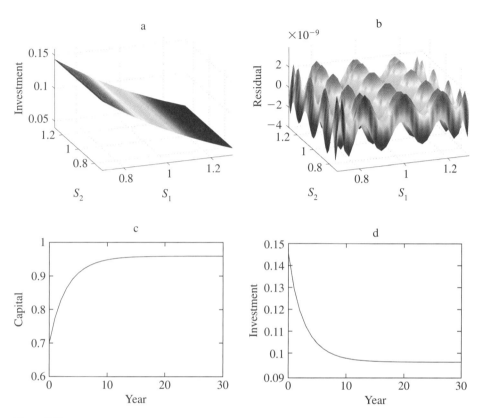

Figure 9.11
Solution to the Capital-Production Game: (a) Investment: Agent 1; (b) Approximation Residual: Agent 1; (c) Expected Capital Stock: Agent 1; (d) Expected Investment: Agent 1

solution to the Bellman equation. The residuals exhibit the equi-oscillation property expected of Chebychev residuals when the underlying model is smooth. The CompEcon Toolbox routine `dpsimul` was used to perform a deterministic simulation of the model over a 20-year period. The capital stock and investment paths are given in Figures 9.12c and 9.12d.

9.8.2   Income Redistribution Game

Consider the income redistribution game of section 8.5.2 assuming that agent p's reward is $u_p(s_p - x_p) = (s_p - x_p)^{1-\alpha_p}/(1 - \alpha_p)$ and his wealth evolves according to $\gamma_p x_p + \epsilon_p x_p^{\beta_p}$, where the production shocks ϵ_p are i.i.d. lognormal$(0, \sigma^2)$. One may solve the income redistribution game using CompEcon Toolbox routines as follows:

First, one codes a model function file that returns the values of the reward and transition functions at arbitrary vectors of states s, actions x, and shocks e:

```
function [out1,out2,out3]=func(flag,s,x,e,alpha,beta,gamma,psi);
[n,m] = size(s);
switch flag
case 'b';
  xl = zeros(n,m);
  xu = 0.99*s;
  out1=xl; out2=xu;
case 'f1'
  fx = zeros(n,m); fxx = zeros(n,m,m);
  f          = ((s(:,1)-x(:,1)).^(1-alpha(1)))/(1-alpha(1));
  fx(:,1)    = -(s(:,1)-x(:,1)).^(-alpha(1));
  fxx(:,1,1) = -alpha(1)*(s(:,1)-x(:,1)).^(-alpha(1)-1);
  out1=f; out2=fx; out3=fxx;
case 'f2'
  fx = zeros(n,m); fxx = zeros(n,m,m);
  f          = ((s(:,2)-x(:,2)).^(1-alpha(2)))/(1-alpha(2));
  fx(:,2)    = -(s(:,2)-x(:,2)).^(-alpha(2));
  fxx(:,2,2) = -alpha(2)*(s(:,2)-x(:,2)).^(-alpha(2)-1);
  out1=f; out2=fx; out3=fxx;
case 'g';
  g = zeros(n,m); gx = zeros(n,m,m); gxx = zeros(n,m,m,m);
  g1   = gamma(1)*x(:,1) + e(:,1).*x(:,1).^beta(1);
  g1x  = gamma(1) + beta(1)*e(:,1).*x(:,1).^(beta(1)-1);
  g1xx = (beta(1)-1)*beta(1)*e(:,1).*x(:,1).^(beta(1)-2);
  g2   = gamma(2)*x(:,2) + e(:,2).*x(:,2).^beta(2);
  g2x  = gamma(2) + beta(2)*e(:,2).*x(:,2).^(beta(2)-1);
  g2xx = (beta(2)-1)*beta(2)*e(:,2).*x(:,2).^(beta(2)-2);
  g(:,1)       = (1-psi)*g1 + share*g2;
  gx(:,1,1)    = (1-psi)*g1x;
  gxx(:,1,1,1) = (1-psi)*g1xx;
  g(:,2)       = (1-psi)*g2 + share*g1;
  gx(:,2,2)    = (1-psi)*g2x;
```

```
    gxx(:,2,2,2) = (1-psi)*g2xx;
    out1=g; out2=gx; out3=gxx;
end
end
```

Passing the flag `'b'` returns the lower and upper bounds on the action; passing the flag `'f1'` returns the reward function value and its first two derivatives for agent 1; passing the flag `'f2'` returns the reward function value and its first two derivatives for agent 2; and passing the flag `'g'` returns the state transition function value and its first and second derivatives with respect to the action.

Second, one enters the model parameters. Here, the utility function parameters, production elasticities, capital survival rates, wealth share rate, production shock volatilities, and discount factor are specified, respectively:

```
alpha = [0.2 0.2];
beta  = [0.5 0.5];
gamma = [0.9 0.9];
psi   = 0.05;
sigma = [0.1 0.1];
delta = 0.9;
```

Third, one discretizes the shock. Here, the lognormal demand shock is discretized using a nine-node Gaussian quadrature scheme:

```
nshocks = [3 3];
[e,w] = qnwlogn(nshocks,[0 0],diag(sigma.^2));
```

Fourth, one packs the model structure. Here, `model` is a structured variable whose fields contain the name of the model function file, the discount factor, shock values, shock probabilities, and model function parameters, respectively:

```
model.func = 'func';
model.discount = delta;
model.e = e;
model.w = w;
model.params = {alpha beta gamma psi};
```

Fifth, one specifies the basis functions and collocation nodes. Here, a 225-function bivariate cubic spline basis is constructed by forming the tensor products of 15 and 15 basis functions along the first and second state dimensions, respectively; also, a 225-node collocation grid is constructed by forming the Cartesian product of the 15 standard cubic spline nodes along each of the two state dimensions:

```
n       = [15 15];
smin    = [ 3  3];
smax    = [11 11];
fspace  = fundefn('spli',n,smin,smax);
scoord  = funnode(fspace);
snodes  = gridmake(scoord);
```

Sixth, one provides judicious guesses for values and actions at the collocation nodes. Here, wealth and investment are initialized by setting them equal to zero:

```
xinit = zeros(size(snodes));
vinit = zeros(size(snodes));
```

Sixth, one solves the decision model:

```
[c,s,v,x,resid] = gamesolve(model,fspace,vinit,xinit);
```

The CompEcon Toolbox routine `gamesolve` accepts as input the model structure `model`, basis functions `fspace`, and initial guesses for the value function `vinit` and optimal actions `xinit`. It then solves the collocation equation, returning as output the basis coefficients `c` and the optimal values `v`, optimal actions `x`, and Bellman equation residuals `resid` at a refined state grid `s`.

Finally, one performs postoptimality analysis. Figure 9.12a shows agent 1's optimal investment policy. Clearly, optimal investment rises with an agent's own wealth but is not significantly affected by the other agent's wealth. Figure 9.12b gives the Bellman equation residual for agent 1's value function approximant. The maximum residuals are on the order of 10^{-6}, indicating that the computed solution offers an acceptably accurate numerical solution to the Bellman equation. The residuals exhibit increased volatility at low own-wealth levels, but relatively little sensitivity with respect to the other agent's wealth. The CompEcon Toolbox routine `dpsimul` was used to simulate the model 2,000 times over a 20-year period starting from the expected steady-state wealth levels in the absence of a redistribution agreement. Figures 9.12c and 9.12d indicate that the introduction of the redistribution agreement lowers investment and ultimately wealth by reducing the incentives for individuals to invest.

9.8.3 Marketing Board Game

Consider the marketing board game of section 8.5.3 assuming a world inverse demand function $P(q_1 + q_2) = (q_1 + q_2)^\gamma$ where $\gamma = -0.5$. Further assume a constant unit cost

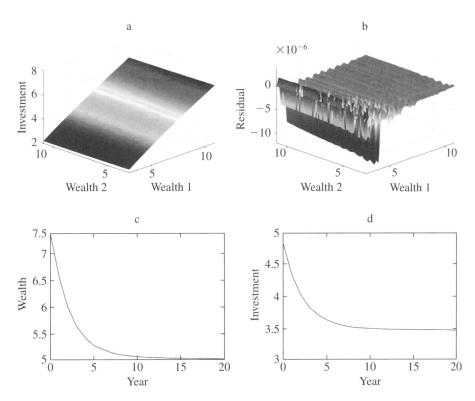

Figure 9.12
Solution to the Income Redistribution Game: (a) Optimal Investment Policy: Agent 1; (b) Approximation Residual: Agent 1; (c) Expected Wealth: Agent 1; (d) Expected Investment: Agent 1

of storage, $c_p(x_p) = \kappa x_p$, with $\kappa = 0.05$, ϵ_p i.i.d. lognormal(μ, σ^2), with $\mu = \ln(0.5)$ and $\sigma = 0.04$, a maximum storage capacity of 0.5, and a discount factor $\delta = 0.95$. One may solve the marketing board game using CompEcon Toolbox routines as follows:

First, one codes a model function file that returns the values of the reward and transition functions at arbitrary vectors of states s, actions x, and shocks e:

```
function [out1,out2,out3]=func(flag,s,x,e,kappa,gamma,xmax);
[n,m] = size(s);
switch flag
case 'b';
  x1 = zeros(n,m);
```

```
   xu = xmax(ones(n,1),:);
   out1=xl; out2=xu;
case 'f1';
   q1  = s(:,1)-x(:,1);
   q2  = s(:,2)-x(:,2);
   p   = (q1+q2).^gamma;
   px  = -gamma*(q1+q2).^(gamma-1);
   pxx = (gamma-1)*gamma*(q1+q2).^(gamma-2);
   f   = p.*q1 - kappa*x(:,1);
   fx  = [-p + px.*q1 - kappa  ones(n,1)];
   fxx = zeros(n,m,m);
   fxx(:,1,1) = -2*px + pxx.*q1;
   out1=f; out2=fx; out3=fxx;
case 'f2';
   q1  = s(:,1)-x(:,1);
   q2  = s(:,2)-x(:,2);
   p   = (q1+q2).^gamma;
   px  = -gamma*(q1+q2).^(gamma-1);
   pxx = (gamma-1)*gamma*(q1+q2).^(gamma-2);
   f   = p.*q2 - kappa*x(:,2);
   fx  = [zeros(n,1) -p + px.*q2 - kappa];
   fxx = zeros(n,m,m);
   fxx(:,2,2) = -2*px + pxx.*q2;
   out1=f; out2=fx; out3=fxx;
case 'g';
   g   = x + e;
   gx  = [ones(n,1) zeros(n,1); zeros(n,1) ones(n,1)];
   gxx = zeros(n,m,m,m);
   out1=g; out2=gx; out3=gxx;
end
```

Passing the flag 'b' returns the lower and upper bounds on the action; passing the flag 'f1' returns the reward function value and its first two derivatives for agent 1; passing the flag 'f2' returns the reward function value and its first two derivatives for agent 2; and passing the flag 'g' returns the transition function value and its first and second derivatives with respect to the action.

Second, one enters the model parameters. Here, the unit storage cost, elasticity of demand, storage capacities, mean log production shock, production shock volatilities, and discount factor are specified, respectively:

```
kappa = 0.05;
gamma = -0.5;
xmax  = 0.4*rho;
mu    = log([0.5 0.5]);
sigma = 0.2;
delta = 0.95;
```

Third, one discretizes the shock. Here, the lognormal production shock is discretized using a nine-node Gaussian quadrature scheme:

```
nshocks = [3 3];
cov     = (sigma^2)*eye(2);
[e,w]   = qnwlogn(nshocks,mu,cov);
```

Fourth, one packs the model structure. Here, `model` is a structured variable whose fields contain the name of the model function file, the discount factor, shock values, shock probabilities, and model function parameters, respectively:

```
model.func = 'func';
model.discount = delta;
model.e = e;
model.w = w;
model.params={kappa gamma xmax};
```

Fifth, one specifies the basis functions and collocation nodes. Here, a 400-function bivariate cubic spline basis is constructed by forming the tensor products of 20 basis functions along each state dimension; also, a 400-node collocation grid is constructed by forming the Cartesian product of the 20 nodes along each state dimension:

```
n       = [20 20];
smin    = min(e);
smax    = max(e)+xmax;
fspace = fundefn('spli',n,smin,smax);
scoord = funnode(fspace);
snodes = gridmake(scoord);
```

Sixth, one provides judicious guesses for values and actions at the collocation nodes.

```
xinit = zeros(size(snodes));
vinit = zeros(size(snodes));
```

Sixth, one solves the decision model:

```
[c,s,v,x,resid] = gamesolve(model,fspace,vinit,xinit);
```

The CompEcon Toolbox routine `gamesolve` accepts as input the model structure `model`, basis functions `fspace`, and initial guesses for the value function `vinit` and optimal actions `xinit`. It then solves the collocation equation, returning as output the basis coefficients `c` and the optimal values `v`, optimal actions `x`, and Bellman equation residuals `resid` at a refined state grid `s`.

Finally, one performs postoptimality analysis. Figure 9.13a shows country 1's optimal storage policy. Clearly, if available supply in country 1 is low, it is optimal not to store. Thus, in this model, the nonnegativity constraint on stockholding is binding. Figure 9.13b gives the Bellman equation residual for country 1's value function approximant. The maximum

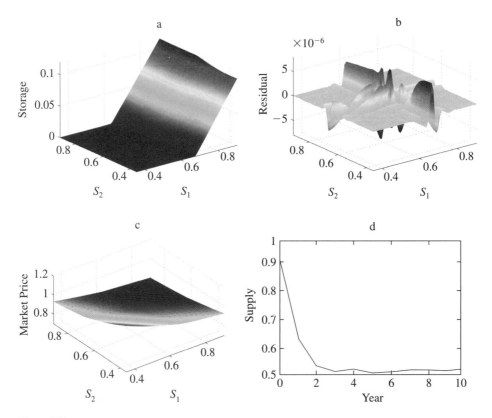

Figure 9.13
Solution to the Marketing Board Game: (a) Storage: Country 1; (b) Approximation Residual: Country 1; (c) Market Price; (d) Expected Supply: Country 1

residuals are on the order of 10^{-5}, indicating that the computed solution offers an acceptably accurate numerical solution to the Bellman equation. The residuals exhibit oscillatory behavior in both dimensions. Figure 9.13c gives the equilibrium market price. Clearly, the market price is a declining function of available supply in each country. The CompEcon Toolbox routine `dpsimul` was used to simulate the model 1,000 times over a 10-year period starting from a relatively high initial supply. Figure 9.13d gives the path followed by the available supply.

9.9 Rational Expectations Methods

Recall the general rational expectations model discussed in section 8.6, which involves solving for the response function $x = x(s)$ when equilibrium is governed by the rootfinding condition

$$f\left(s_t, x_t, E_t h(s_{t+1}, x_{t+1})\right) = 0$$

or, more generally, the complementarity condition

$$CP\left(f\left(s_t, x_t, E_t h(s_{t+1}, x_{t+1})\right), a(s_t), b(s_t)\right)$$

together with the state transition function

$$s_{t+1} = g(s_t, x_t, \epsilon_{t+1})$$

Here, $f : \mathbb{R}^{d_s \times d_x \times d_h} \to \mathbb{R}^{d_x}$, $g : \mathbb{R}^{d_s \times d_x \times d_s} \to \mathbb{R}^{d_s}$, and $h : \mathbb{R}^{d_s \times d_x} \to \mathbb{R}^{d_h}$, where d_s, d_x, and d_h denote the dimensionality of the state space, response space, and expectation space, respectively.

Except in special cases, the rational expectations model poses an infinite dimensional problem that cannot be solved analytically. It may, however, be solved using collocation methods in which the function to be approximated is either the response function $x(s)$ or the expectation function $h(s, x(s))$. The two approaches are equivalent in that $x(s)$ may be recovered from $h(s, x(s))$ and vice versa. In order to describe the collocation method for rational expectations models, we limit our discussion to models with univariate state, response, and expectation variables ($d_s = d_x = d_h = 1$) and in which the responses are unconstrained ($a = -\infty, b = \infty$). The presentation generalizes to models with higher dimensional state, response, and expectation variables and constrained responses, but at the expense of cumbersome additional notation required to track the different dimensions.

Direct response function approximation employs the approximation

$$x(s) \approx \sum_{j=1}^{n} c_j \phi_j(s)$$

Together with a K-valued discretization of the shock process (ϵ_k, w_k), collocation may be used to determine the coefficient vector c by solving the n nonlinear equations

$$f\left(s_i, \sum_{j=1}^{n} c_j \phi_j(s_i), \sum_{k=1}^{K} w_k h(s'_{ik}, x'_{ik})\right) = 0$$

where $s_1, s_2, \ldots, s_n$ are n prescribed collocations nodes and where

$$s'_{ik} = g\left(s_i, \sum_{j=1}^{n} c_j \phi_j(s_i), \epsilon_k\right)$$

and

$$x'_{ik} = \sum_{j=1}^{n} c_j \phi_j(s'_{ik})$$

Although direct response function approximation seems natural, it can lead to difficulties, especially when the response function exhibits kinks resulting from binding constraints. An alternative numerical solution approach is to construct an approximation

$$h\left(s, x(s)\right) \approx \sum_{j=1}^{n} c_j \phi_j(s)$$

for the expectation function. For problems in which the response function is nonsmooth, constructing an approximation for the expectation function will typically encounter fewer practical difficulties because $h(s, x(s))$ will typically be smoother than $x(s)$ itself.[5]

The coefficient vector for the expectation function approximation may be computed using the following iterative scheme. For a given value of the coefficient vector c, determine the equilibrium responses x_i associated with the collocation nodes s_i by solving

$$f\left(s_i, x, \sum_{k=1}^{K} \sum_{j=1}^{n} w_k c_j \phi_j\left(g(s_i, x, \epsilon_k)\right)\right) = 0$$

---

5. This approach breaks down when $f_x = 0$ and $g_x = 0$ because f does not depend on x and hence the equilibrium value of x given c is not defined.

Given the equilibrium responses at the collocation nodes, the coefficient vector c is then updated by solving the n-dimensional linear system

$$\sum_{j=1}^{n} c_j \phi_j(s_i) = h(s_i, x_i)$$

The iterative procedure is repeated until the norm of the difference between successive values of c falls below a prescribed tolerance.

Many of the steps required to implement these two collocation strategies are similar to those taken in solving dynamic programming problems. First, the user must specify the basis used in approximation:

```
fspace = fundefn('cheb',n,smin,smax);
s      = funnode(fspace);
Phi    = funbas(fspace);
```

Here, fspace is a structured variable that contains information that defines the basis functions, s is the vector of associated collocation nodes, and Phi is the associated collocation matrix. It is presumed that the analyst has previously specified the lower and upper endpoints of the state interval, smin and smax, and the number of basis functions and collocation nodes n.

Next, a routine must be coded to solve the equilibrium condition for arbitrary basis coefficients. Such a routine would have a calling sequence of the form

```
[f,x,h] = equisolve(s,x,c)
```

Here, on input, s is an $n \times 1$ vector of collocation nodes, x is an $n \times 1$ vector of responses, and c is an $n \times 1$ vector of basis coefficients for the approximation of the expectation function. On output, f is an $n \times 1$ vector of values of $f(s, x, Eh)$, x is an $n \times 1$ vector of values of x, and h is an $n \times 1$ matrix of values of $h(s, x)$ at the collocation nodes.

Given the collocation nodes s, collocation matrix Phi, and equilibrium solution routine equisolve, and given an initial guess for the basis coefficient vector c, the expectation function approximation may be computed using function iteration:

```
for it=1:maxit
  cold = c;
  [f,x,h] = equisolve(s,x,c);
  c = Phi\h;
  change = norm(c-cold,inf);
  if change<tol, break, end;
end
```

Here, `tol` and `maxit`, which are set by the analyst, specify the convergence tolerance and the maximum number of iterations.

The main challenge in implementing the collocation method is coding the equilibrium routine `equisolve` that solves for the equilibrium response x given c. To accomplish this purpose, `equisolve` must repeatedly evaluate the equilibrium function $f(s, x, Eh)$ and its derivative with respect to x. A routine that computes these values is as follows:[6]

```
function [f,fx] = equifunc(s,x,c)
eh = 0;
ehder = 0;
for k=1:length(w)
  [g,gx] = gfunc(s,x,e(k));
  eh      = eh     + w(k)*funeval(c,fspace,g);
  ehder  = ehder + w(k)*funeval(c,fspace,g,1).*gx;
end
[f,fx,feh] = ffunc(s,x,eh);
fx = fx + feh.*ehder;
```

This routine, in turn, assumes that the user has written separate functions `ffunc` and `gfunc` that evaluate f and g, along with the required derivatives, at arbitrary vectors of states `s`, responses `x`, expectations `eh`, and shocks `e`.

The routine for solving the equilibrium conditions for the equilibrium responses x, given c, can now be described as follows:

```
function [f,x,h] = equisolve(s,x,c)
for it=1:maxit
  xold = x;
  [f,fx] = equifunc(s,x,c);
  deltax = -fx\f;
  x = x + deltax;
  if norm(deltax)< tol, break, end;
end
h = hfunc(s,x);
```

This implementation assumes that the user has coded a routine `hfunc` that accepts an $n \times 1$ vector of state nodes `s` and an $n \times 1$ vector of response variable values `x`, and returns an $n \times 1$ matrix of expectation function values `h`.

---

6. For clarity, the code omits several bookkeeping operations and programming tricks that accelerate execution.

It is important to point out that the solution strategy involves a double iteration. The inner iteration (in `equisolve`) computes the equilibrium response x for a fixed basis coefficient vector c using Newton's method. The outer iteration computes the coefficient vector c using function iteration.

In order to simplify the process of solving and analyzing rational expectations models, the CompEcon Toolbox contains a routine `remsolve` that performs the necessary computations that we have described. The routine has a calling sequence of the form:

```
[c,s,x,h,f,resid] = remsolve(model,fspace,snodes,xinit);
```

The routine accepts as input the model structure `model`, the basis function definition variable `fspace`, the collocation nodes `snodes`, and the initial guess for the response variable `x`. It then solves the collocation equation, returning as output the basis coefficients for the expectation function approximation `c`, states `s`, responses `x`, expectation function values `h`, equilibrium function values `f`, and collocation function residuals `resid`, all evaluated at the refined grid of states `s`. The use of `remsolve` is illustrated in the following sections.

9.9.1 Asset Pricing Model

In some rational expectations models, the collocation equation will be linear in the basis coefficients and can be solved directly without many of the complications described in the preceding section. Consider the asset pricing model of section 8.6.1, which involves an exogenous state process for dividends d

$$d_{t+1} = g(d_t, \epsilon_{t+1})$$

and an endogenous share price p governed by the equilibrium condition

$$u'(d)p(d) - \delta E_\epsilon\left[u'\left(g(d,\epsilon)\right)\left(p\left(g(d,\epsilon)\right) + g(d,\epsilon)\right)\right] = 0$$

In the notation of the general rational expectations model, the expectation function is

$$h(d, p) = u'(d)(p + d)$$

and the equilibrium function is

$$f(d, p, Eh) = u'(d)p - \delta Eh$$

For this model it is relatively easy to compute an approximation of the response function of the form

$$p(d) \approx \sum_{j=1}^{n} c_j \phi_j(d)$$

where the ϕ_j and n basis functions are specified by the analyst. The collocation method requires that the unknown coefficients c_j be fixed by requiring the equilibrium condition to be satisfied exactly at n collocation nodes $d_1, d_2, \ldots, d_n$:

$$u'(d_i) \sum_{j=1}^{n} c_j \phi_j(d_i) - \delta E_\epsilon \left[u'\big(g(d_i, \epsilon)\big) \left(\sum_{j=1}^{n} c_j \phi_j \big(g(d_i, \epsilon)\big) + g(d_i, \epsilon) \right) \right] = 0$$

or, equivalently,

$$Bc = y$$

where c is the $n \times 1$ vector of unknown basis coefficients, B is an $n \times n$ matrix with typical element

$$B_{ij} = u'(d_i)\phi_j(d_i) - \delta E_\epsilon \left[u'\big(g(d_i, \epsilon)\big) \phi_j \big(g(d_i, \epsilon)\big) \right]$$

and y is an $n \times 1$ vector with typical element

$$y_i = \delta E_\epsilon \left[u'\big(g(d_i, \epsilon)\big) g(d_i, \epsilon) \right]$$

In other words, the collocation equation is linear.

To make this example concrete, let $u(c) = (c^{1-\beta} - 1)/(1 - \beta)$, so $u'(c) = c^{-\beta}$. Further, let

$$d_{t+1} = g(d_t, \epsilon_{t+1}) = \bar{d} + \gamma(d_t - \bar{d}) + \epsilon_{t+1}$$

where ϵ is distributed i.i.d. normal$(0, \sigma^2)$. To compute the expectations we can use Gaussian quadrature nodes and weights for the normal shock (ϵ_k and w_k). The model can be solved by the following steps:

First, one enters the model parameters. Here, the long-run mean dividend, dividend mean reversion rate, coefficient of risk aversion, dividend standard deviation, and discount factor are specified, respectively:

```
dbar  = 1.0;
gamma = 0.5;
beta  = 0.4;
sigma = 0.1;
delta = 0.9;
```

Second, one discretizes the shock. Here, the normal dividend shock is discretized using a three-node Gaussian quadrature scheme:

```
nshocks = 3;
[e,w]   = qnwnorm(nshocks,0,sigma^2);
```

Third, one specifies the basis functions and collocation nodes. Here, the first 10 Chebychev polynomials and the corresponding standard Chebychev nodes are selected to serve as basis functions and collocation nodes; also, the minimum and maximum values of d are selected to ensure that d_{t+1} never requires extrapolation:

```
n       = 10;
dmin    = dbar+min(e)/(1-gamma);
dmax    = dbar+max(e)/(1-gamma);
fspace  = fundefn('cheb',n,dmin,dmax);
dnode   = funnode(fspace);
```

Fourth, one solves the decision model:

```
B = diag(dnode.^(-beta))*funbas(fspace,dnode);
y = 0;
for k=1:K
  dnext = dbar + gamma*(dnode-dbar) + e(k);
  B = B - delta*w(k)*diag(dnext.^(-beta))*funbas(fspace,dnext);
  y = y + delta*w(k)*dnext.^(1-beta);
end
c = B\y;
```

The computed value of c provides coefficients for the approximate equilibrium price function, which is plotted along with the solution residuals in Figure 9.14.

Finally, one computes the response function and approximation residuals:

```
d = nodeunif(10*n,dmin,dmax);
p = funeval(c,fspace,d);
Eh=0;
for k=1:m
  dnext = dbar + gamma*(d-dbar) + e(k);
  h     = diag(dnext.^(-beta))*(funeval(c,fspace,dnext)+dnext);
  Eh    = Eh + delta*w(k)*h;
end
resid = d.^(-beta).*p-Eh;
```

Figure 9.14a gives the equilibrium asset price as a function of the exogenous dividend. Figure 9.14b gives the Bellman equation residual, which remains below 10^{-8}.

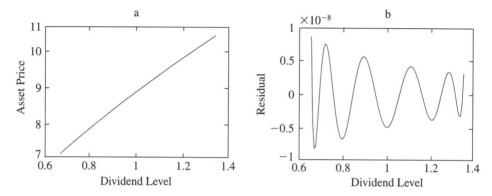

Figure 9.14
Solution to the Asset Pricing Model: (a) Equilibrium Pricing Function; (b) Approximation Residual

9.9.2 Competitive Storage

To solve the competitive storage model of section 8.6.2 we employ the general rational expectations model solver `remsolve`. Recall that the equilibrium storage model with the storage level as the response variable is characterized by the functional complementarity condition

$$\delta E_\epsilon \left[P\left(x(s) + \epsilon - x\left(x(s) + \epsilon \right) \right) \right] - P\left(s - x(s) \right) - c = \mu(s)$$

$$x(s) \geq 0, \qquad \mu(s) \leq 0, \qquad x(s) > 0 \Rightarrow \mu(s) = 0$$

This model can be cast in the generic form with carry-in stocks serving as the state variable and carry-out stocks serving as the response variable. In the notation of the general model

$$h(s, x) = P(s - x)$$

$$g(s, x, \epsilon) = x + \epsilon$$

and

$$f(s, x, Eh) = \delta Eh - P(s - x) - c$$

To make this example concrete, suppose that inverse demand is given by $P(c) = c^{-\gamma}$ and the log of new production ϵ is normally distributed with mean 0 and variance σ^2. The model can be solved with `remsolve` as follows:

First, one codes a model function file that returns the values and (where appropriate) the derivatives of the bound, equilibrium, transition, and expectation functions at arbitrary vectors of states s, actions x, expectations Eh, and shocks e (as well as additional model specific parameters):

```
function[out1,out2,out3]=func(flag,s,x,ep,e,delta,gamma,c,xmax);
n    = length(s);
switch flag
case 'b';
  out1 = zeros(n,1);
  out2 = xmax*ones(n,1);
case 'f';
  out1 = delta*ep-(s-x).^(-gamma)-c;
  out2 = -gamma*(s-x).^(-gamma-1);
  out3 = delta*ones(n,1);
case 'g';
  out1 = x + e;
  out2 = ones(n,1);
case 'h';
  out1 = (s-x).^(-gamma);
  out2 = gamma*(s-x).^(-gamma-1);
  out3 = (-gamma)*(s-x).^(-gamma-1);
end
```

Here, passing the flag 'b' returns the lower and upper bounds on the response variable; passing the flag 'f' returns the equilibrium function value and its first derivatives with respect to the response and the expectation variables, f, fx, and fh; passing the flag 'g' returns the transition function value and its first derivative with respect to the response variable, g and gx; and passing the flag 'h' returns the expectation variable and its first derivative with respect to response variable, h and hx.

Second, one enters the model parameters. Here the discount factor, inverse demand elasticity, storage cost, maximum storage level, and yield volatility are specified, respectively:[7]

```
delta = 0.9;
gamma = 2.0;
c     = 0.1;
xmax  = 0.9;
sigma = 0.2;
```

7. In addition to the model parameters already described, we have added a maximum storage level.

Third, one discretizes the shock. Here, the lognormal production shock is discretized using a five-node Gaussian quadrature scheme:

```
nshocks = 5;
[e,w] = qnwlogn(nshocks,0,sigma^2);
```

Fourth, one packs the model structure. Here, `model` is a structured variable whose fields contain the name of the model function file, shock values, shock probabilities, and model function parameters, respectively:

```
model.func = 'func';
model.e = e;
model.w = w;
model.params = {delta gamma c xmax};
```

Fifth, one specifies the basis functions and collocation nodes. Here, a 50-function cubic spline with evenly spaced breakpoints and standard nodes are selected to serve as basis functions and collocation nodes; also, the domain of the state is taken to be the interval from the minimum production level to the sum of the maximum production level and the maximum storage level, thus ensuring that the next period's carry-in stocks cannot lead to extrapolation beyond the approximation interval:

```
n       = 50;
smin    = min(e);
smax    = max(e)+xmax;
fspace  = fundefn('spli',n,smin,smax);
snodes  = funnode(fspace);
```

Sixth, one provides judicious guesses for values and actions at the collocation nodes:

```
xinit = zeros(n,1);
```

Here, carry-out stocks are initially set to 0.

Seventh, one solves for the rational expectations equilibrium:

```
[c,s,x,h,f,resid] = remsolve(model,fspace,snodes,xinit);
```

The CompEcon Toolbox routine `remsolve` solves the collocation equation, returning, as output, the basis coefficients for the expectation variable `c` and a vector of states `s`, together with the responses `x`, expectation function values `h`, equilibrium function values `f`, and collocation function residuals `resid`, all evaluated at the states in `s`.

Finally, one performs postoptimality analysis. To check on the quality of the solution, both the equilibrium function `f` and the residual function `resid` should be examined. The former is used to demonstrate how well the equilibrium condition is satisfied; the latter is

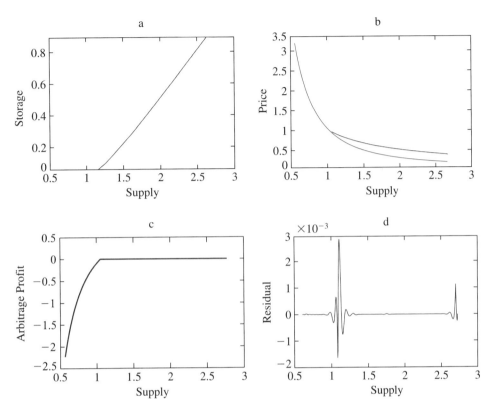

Figure 9.15
Solution to the Commodity Storage Model: (a) Equilibrium Storage Function; (b) Equilibrium Price Function; (c) Arbitrage Profit; (d) Approximation Residual

used to demonstrate how well the approximating function matches the expectation variable. Here, `resid` should be close to 0 for all states, whereas `f` should be close to 0 for all states at which $x(s)$ is positive. Together these functions provide an indication of how accurately the solution has been approximated.

Figure 9.15a gives the equilibrium carry-out stocks as a function of supply (carry-in plus production). Figure 9.15b gives the equilibrium price function with stockholding (above) and without stockholding (below). Figure 9.15c shows that f is essentially zero for supply levels at which the constraints are nonbinding. Notice, however, that for low supply levels the return to storage is negative. The collocation equation, however, shown in Figure 9.15d, indicates that the solution error is small but nontrivial (approximately 1%).

Although using a higher number of basis functions and collocation nodes would provide a more accurate solution, Figures 9.15a and 9.15b exhibit the essential properties of the true rational expectations equilibrium solution for the storage model. Specifically, when supply is low, price is high and storage is zero; as supply rises, however, prices drop and stockholding becomes profitable. Both the response function (carry-out stocks) and the expectation function (price) exhibit kinks at the point at which stockholding becomes profitable.

9.9.3 Government Price Controls

To solve the government price controls model of section 8.6.3 we again use the general rational expectations model solver `remsolve`. Recall that equilibrium in the price controls model is characterized by the functional complementarity condition

$$\delta E_y P\big(x(s) + a(s)y - x\big(x(s) + a(s)y\big)\big)y - c\big(x(s)\big) = 0$$

and

$$x(s) \geq 0, \qquad p^* \leq P\big(s - x(s)\big), \qquad x(s) > 0 \Rightarrow p^* = P\big(s - x(s)\big)$$

In the notation of the general model, the state variable is (s, y), the response variable is (x, a), and the shock is ϵ. The expectation function is

$$h(s, y, x, a) = P(s - x)y$$

$$g(s, y, x, a, \epsilon) = (x + a\epsilon, \epsilon)$$

and the equilibrium function is

$$f(s, y, x, a, Eh) = \big(p^* - P(s - x),\, \delta Eh - c(a)\big)$$

with $a \geq 0$ and $x \geq 0$.

To make this example concrete, suppose that inverse demand is given by $P(q) = q^{-\gamma}$, marginal production cost is given by $c(a) = c_0 + c_1 a$, and the log of yield ϵ is normally distributed with mean 0 and variance σ^2. The model can be solved with `remsolve` as follows:

First, one codes a model function file that returns the values and (where appropriate) the derivatives of the bound, equilibrium, transition, and expectation functions at arbitrary vectors of states s, actions x, expectations Eh, and shocks e (as well as the model-specific additional parameters `delta`, `gamma`, `cost`, and `xmax`).

```
function [out1,out2,out3] = ...
    func(flag,ss,xx,ep,e,delta,xmax,pstar,gamma,c0,c1);
s = ss(:,1);
y = ss(:,2);
x = xx(:,1);
a = xx(:,2);
n = length(s);
```

```
switch flag
case 'b';
  out1 = zeros(n,2);
  out2 = [xmax*ones(n,1) inf*ones(n,1)];
case 'f';
  out1(:,1)   = pstar - (s-x).^(-gamma);
  out1(:,2)   = delta*ep - (c0+c1*a);
  out2(:,1,1) = -gamma*(s-x).^(-gamma-1);
  out2(:,1,2) = zeros(n,1);
  out2(:,2,1) = zeros(n,1);
  out2(:,2,2) = -c1*ones(n,1);
  out3(:,1,1) = zeros(n,1);
  out3(:,2,1) = delta*ones(n,1);
case 'g';
  out1(:,1)   = x + a.*e;
  out1(:,2)   = e;
  out2(:,1,1) = ones(n,1);
  out2(:,1,2) = e;
  out2(:,2,1) = zeros(n,1);
  out2(:,2,2) = zeros(n,1);
case 'h';
  out1 = y.*((s-x).^(-gamma));
  out2(:,1) = y.*(gamma*(s-x).^(-gamma-1));
  out2(:,2) = zeros(n,1);
  out3(:,1) = (-gamma)*y.*(s-x).^(-gamma-1);
  out3(:,2) = (s-x).^(-gamma);
end
```

Here, passing the flag `'b'` returns the lower and upper bounds on the response variable; passing the flag `'f'` returns the equilibrium function value and its first derivatives with respect to the response and the expectation variables, f, fx, and fh; passing the flag `'g'` returns the transition function value and its first derivative with respect to the response variable, g and gx; passing the flag `'h'` returns the expectation variable and its first derivative with respect to the response variable, h and hx.

Second, one enters the model parameters. Here, the discount factor, maximum storage, government support price, inverse demand elasticity, acreage supply parameters, and yield volatility are specified:

```
delta = 0.9;
xmax  = 0.5;
```

```
pstar = 0.9;
gamma = 2.0;
c0    = 0.5;
c1    = 0.5;
sigma = 0.2;
```

Third, one discretizes the shock. Here, the lognormal production shock is discretized using a three-node Gaussian quadrature scheme:

```
nshocks = 3;
[e,w] = qnwlogn(nshocks,0,sigma^2);
```

Fourth, one packs the model structure. Here, `model` is a structured variable whose fields contain the name of the model function file, shock values, shock probabilities, and model function parameters, respectively:

```
model.func = 'func';
model.e = e;
model.w = w;
model.discretestates = 2;
model.params = {delta xmax pstar gamma c0 c1};
```

Fifth, one specifies the basis functions and collocation nodes. Here, a degree 100–function cubic spline basis with its associated standard nodes are selected to serve as basis functions and collocation nodes:

```
n       = 100;
smin    = 0.5;
smax    = 1.5;
fspace = fundefn('spli',n,smin,smax,[],e);
scoord = funnode(fspace);
snodes = gridmake(scoord);
```

Sixth, one provides judicious guesses for values and actions at the collocation nodes.

```
xinit = [zeros(n,1) ones(n,1)];
```

Here, the carry-out stocks are simply set to 0.

Seventh, one solves for the rational expectations equilibrium:

```
[c,s,x,p,f,resid] = remsolve(model,fspace,snodes,xinit);
```

The CompEcon Toolbox routine `remsolve` solves the collocation equation, returning as output the basis coefficients for the expectation variable `c` and a vector of states `s`, together with responses x, expectations variable h, the equilibrium function f, and the collocation residual resid, all evaluated at the values in s.

Finally, one performs postoptimality analysis. To check on the quality of the solution, both the equilibrium function f and the residual function resid should be examined. The former is used to demonstrate how well the equilibrium condition is satisfied; the latter is used to demonstrate how well the approximating function matches the expectation variable. Here, resid should be close to 0 for all states, whereas f should be close to 0 for all states at which $x(s)$ is nonzero. Together these functions provide an indication of how accurately the solution has been approximated.

Figure 9.16a gives the government storage as a function of available supply (carry-in plus production). Figure 9.16b gives the equilibrium acreage planted. Figure 9.16c indicates that the solution error is small but nontrivial (approximately 1%). Figure 9.16d shows the simulated path.

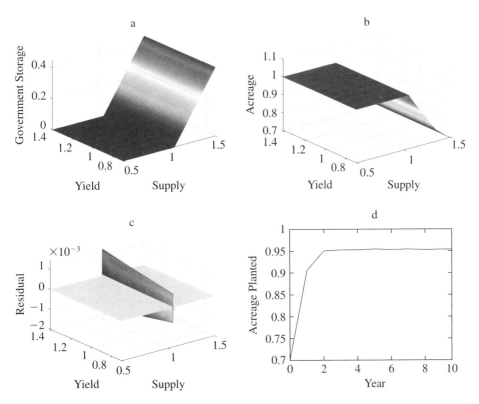

Figure 9.16
Solution to the Government Price Controls Model: (a) Government Policy; (b) Acreage Planted; (c) Approximation Residual; (d) Expected Response Path

Exercises

9.1. Consider an infinitely lived worker searching for a job. At each point in time t, the worker observes a lifetime wage offer w_t. The worker may accept the offer, or he may reject the offer, earning nothing in the current period and waiting for a hopefully better wage offer the following period. The wage offers follow an exogenous Markov process

$$\log(w_{t+1}) = 0.5 \log(w_t) + \epsilon_t$$

where the ϵ_t are i.i.d. normal with mean zero and standard deviation 0.2. The worker's objective is to maximize the present value of wages using a discount factor of 0.9 per period.

a. Solve the model using the collocation method of your choice. Do not use `dpsolve`. Solve the model using only elementary function approximation and discrete maximization routines.

b. What is the minimum wage offer the worker will accept?

c. Plot the shadow price function.

d. Plot the residual function.

9.2. A farmer wishes to maximize the present value of current and future profits over an infinite horizon assuming a constant corn price of \$2.00 per bushel, a constant commercial fertilizer cost of \$0.25 per pound, and an annual discount factor of 0.9. The farmer's corn yield in year t, in bushels per acre, is given by the Mitscherlick-Baule production function

$$y_t = 140[1 - 0.3 \exp(-0.1 s_t)][1 - 0.1 \exp(-1.3 x_t)]$$

where s_t is soil fertilizer carry-in and x_t is fresh fertilizer applied topically at planting time, both measured in pounds per acre. The fertilizer carryover dynamic is

$$s_{t+1} = 9.0 + 0.7 s_t + 0.1 x_t$$

a. Solve the model using linear-quadratic approximation.

b. Solve the model using Chebychev collocation on the interval $[15, 60]$.

c. Plot the optimal fertilizer application policies derived in parts a and b together.

d. Plot the shadow-price functions derived in parts a and b together.

e. Plot the residual function obtained in part b.

f. Plot fertilizer carry-in over a 20-year horizon beginning from a stock level of $s = 15$.

g. Plot fertilizer application over a 20-year horizon beginning from a stock level of $s = 15$.

9.3. As a social planner, you wish to maximize the discounted sum of net social surplus from harvesting a renewable resource over an infinite horizon. Let s_t denote the amount of resource available at the beginning of year t, and let x_t denote the amount harvested. The harvest cost is $c(x_t) = kx_t$, the market-clearing price is $p_t = x_t^{-\gamma}$, and the stock dynamic is $s_{t+1} = \alpha(s_t - x_t) - 0.5\beta(s_t - x_t)^2$. Assume $\gamma = 0.5$, $\alpha = 4$, $\beta = 1.0$, $k = 0.2$, and $\delta = 0.9$.

a. Solve the model using linear-quadratic approximation.

b. Solve the model using Chebychev collocation on the interval $[4, 8]$.

c. Plot the optimal harvest policies derived in parts a and b together.

d. Plot the shadow price functions derived in parts a and b together.

e. Plot the residual function obtained in part b.

f. Plot the resource level over a 20-year horizon beginning from a level of $s = 4$.

9.4. Consider the commodity storage model of section 9.9.2, except now assume that harvest h_{t+1} at the beginning of year $t + 1$ is the product of the acreage a_t planted in year t and a random yield y_{t+1} realized at the beginning of year $t + 1$:

$$h_{t+1} = a_t y_{t+1}$$

Further assume that acreage planted is a function

$$a_t = (E_t p_{t+1})^{0.8}$$

of the price expected to prevail at harvest time conditional on the information known at planting time and that the $\log y_t$ are serially independent and normally distributed with mean 0 and standard deviation 0.2.

a. Write the conditions that characterize the rational expectations equilibrium for this market.

b. Solve the model using Chebychev collocation on the interval $[0.6, 2.0]$.

c. Plot acreage planted in terms of available supply.

d. Plot market price in terms of available supply.

e. Plot storage in terms of available supply.

f. Plot the residual functions.

g. Plot the storage arbitrage profits.

h. Estimate the steady-state mean and variance of price.

9.5. Consider the problem of optimal harvesting of a nonrenewable resource by a competitive price-taking firm:

$$\max E \sum_{t=0}^{\infty} \delta^t \left[p_t x_t - \alpha x_t^\beta \right]$$

s.t. $s_{t+1} = s_t - x_t$

where log price follows a first-order Markov process

$$\log(p_{t+1}) = \gamma \log(p_t) + \epsilon_{t+1}$$

with ϵ distributed i.i.d. normal $(0, \sigma^2)$. Here, x_t denotes harvest and s_t is beginning reserves. Assume that $\delta = 0.9$, $\alpha = 0.2$, $\beta = 1.5$, and $\gamma = 0.5$.

a. Solve the model using cubic spline collocation.

b. Plot the optimal harvest policy.

c. Plot the shadow-price function.

d. Plot the residual function.

e. Plot the resource level over a 20-year horizon beginning from a stock level $s = 10$ and a price level $p = 1$.

f. Plot the harvest level over a 20-year horizon beginning from a stock level $s = 10$ and a price level $p = 1$.

9.6. A social planner wishes to maximize the present value of current and future net social welfare derived from industrial production over an infinite time horizon. Net social welfare in period t is

$$\alpha_0 + \alpha_1 q_t - 0.5 q_t^2 - c s_t$$

where q_t is industrial production in period t and s_t is the pollution level at the beginning of period t. The pollutant stock is related to industrial production as follows:

$$s_{t+1} = s_t^\gamma + q_t$$

Assume $\alpha_0 = 2.0$, $\alpha_1 = 3.0$, $\gamma = 0.6$, $c = 1.0$, and $\delta = 0.9$.

a. Solve the model using linear-quadratic approximation.

b. Solve the model using Chebychev collocation on the interval $[6, 9]$.

c. Plot the optimal production policies derived in parts a and b together.

d. Plot the shadow-price functions derived in parts a and b together.

e. Plot the residual function obtained in part b.

f. Plot the pollution level over a 20-year horizon beginning from a pollution level of $s = 7$.

g. Plot production over a 20-year horizon beginning from a pollution level of $s = 7$.

Bibliographic Notes

The most thorough discussion of collocation and related methods for solving economic models may be found in Judd (1998)and the related articles Judd (1992) and Judd (1994)A thorough treatment of weighted residual methods, of which collocation is a special case, may be found in Fletcher (1984)

Linear quadratic control problems in discrete time are discussed in Kendrick (1981) and RausserHochman 1979). Examples of linear quadratic approximation methods are treated in Christiano (1990). The principle of certainty equivalence was first established in Simon (1956) and Theil (1957). An interesting exposition of alternative methods may be found in TaylorUhlig (1990) and the other articles cited therein and appearing in the same journal volume.

10 Continuous Time Models: Theory and Examples

In this chapter we discuss models that treat time as a continuum. Such models are typically expressed in terms of differential equations, either ordinary or partial. Our discussion proceeds in four sections. First, we discuss models of asset prices that are based on arbitrage considerations alone and that do not depend on solving a decision problem. Many financial assets, including bonds, futures, and some options are in this class. The remaining three sections discuss the topic of stochastic control, that is, of optimal decision making applied to processes that evolve continuously in time. The discussion of control problems is broken into three subtypes. The first, continuous-action problems, have a control that can take any value on a continuum. For the second subtype, discrete-action problems, the control is a choice among a set of discrete states. The third, impulse control, comprises problems for which the optimal control can be exerted at an infinite rate, causing a discrete jump in the value of the state variable.

Continuous time models make extensive use of Ito processes, which are continuous time Markov processes. The ordinary rules of calculus are not applicable to Ito processes, which do not possess well-defined time derivatives. It is therefore necessary to make use of stochastic calculus, especially the extension of the chain rule known as Ito's Lemma and the relationships between expectations and differential equations embodied in so-called forward and backward equations and the Feynman-Kac equation. A review of these topics is provided in Appendix A: Mathematical Background; more details can be found in the references discussed at the end of this chapter.

10.1   Arbitrage-Based Asset Valuation

An important use of continuous time methods results from powerful arbitrage conditions that can be derived in a simple and elegant fashion. Originally developed to solve option pricing problems, arbitrage arguments apply much more broadly. Assets whose values are based on the same underlying stochastic process have values that are related by an arbitrage condition.

Consider two assets whose values V and W both depend on the same random process S. These assets generate income streams (dividends) denoted by δ_V and δ_W. If the assets are time limited (such as bonds or options), their terminal value will also be a function of S. In what follows we show that the lack of arbitrage ensures that the processes V and W are related to each other in a very specific way.

In the following discussion we use the notational conventions that μ, σ, and δ represent drift, diffusion, and payouts associated with random processes; subscripts on these variables identify the process. The symbols V and W represent asset values, which are functions of the underlying state variable S and time; subscripts on these functions refer to partial derivatives.

The underlying stochastic process S is an Ito process, expressed as the stochastic differential equation

$$dS = \mu_S \, dt + \sigma_S \, dz$$

Under suitable regularity conditions, this implies that V and W are also Ito processes, with

$$dV = \mu_V \, dt + \sigma_V \, dz$$

$$dW = \mu_W \, dt + \sigma_W \, dz$$

Suppose one creates a portfolio consisting of one unit of V and h units of W. The value of the portfolio is described by

$$dV + h \, dW = [\mu_V + h\mu_W] \, dt + [\sigma_V + h\sigma_W] \, dz$$

This portfolio can be made risk free by choosing h so as to set the dz term to 0:

$$h = -\sigma_V / \sigma_W$$

Because the portfolio is risk free, it must earn the risk-free rate of return. Therefore, the capital appreciation on the portfolio plus its income stream must equal the risk-free rate times the investment cost:

$$\left[\mu_V - \frac{\sigma_V}{\sigma_W} \mu_W \right] dt + \left[\delta_V - \frac{\sigma_V}{\sigma_W} \delta_W \right] dt = r \left[V - \frac{\sigma_V}{\sigma_W} W \right] dt$$

"Divide" by $\sigma_V \, dt$ and rearrange to conclude that

$$\frac{\mu_V + \delta_V - rV}{\sigma_V} = \frac{\mu_W + \delta_W - rW}{\sigma_W}$$

This expression must hold for any assets that depend on S, and therefore both sides must equal a function $\theta(S, t)$ that does not depend on the specific features of a particular derivative asset. In other words, the function θ is common to all assets whose values depend on S.

To avoid arbitrage opportunities, any asset with value V that depends on S must therefore satisfy

$$\mu_V + \delta_V = rV + \theta\sigma_V$$

This is a fundamental arbitrage condition that is interpreted as saying that the total return on V, $\mu_V + \delta_V$, equals the risk-free return, rV, plus a risk adjustment, $\theta\sigma_V$. This provides a way to interpret θ; it is the additional rate of return required for each unit of volatility and is commonly called the market price of risk.

Ito's Lemma provides a way to evaluate the μ_V and σ_V terms. Specifically,

$$\mu_V = V_t + \mu_S V_S + \tfrac{1}{2}\sigma_S^2 V_{SS}$$

and

$$\sigma_V = \sigma_S V_S$$

Combining with the arbitrage condition and rearranging yields the following linear partial differential equation (PDE):[1]

$$rV = \delta_V + V_t + (\mu_S - \theta\sigma_S)V_S + \tfrac{1}{2}\sigma_S^2 V_{SS} \tag{10.1}$$

This is a remarkable result. It says that to avoid arbitrage opportunities the value of any asset that depends on S must satisfy a linear PDE that is identical except for the income flow term δ_V (assets will also be distinguished by their boundary conditions).

It is important to note that, in general, S may or may not be the price of a traded asset. If it is the price of a traded asset, then the arbitrage condition applies to S itself, so

$$\mu_S - \theta\sigma_S = rS - \delta_S$$

The value of any asset V that depends on the price of a traded S therefore satisfies the partial differential equation

$$rV = \delta_V + V_t + (rS - \delta_S)V_S + \tfrac{1}{2}\sigma_S^2 V_{SS}$$

However, if S is not the price of a traded asset but there is a traded asset or portfolio, W, that depends only on S, then the market price of risk θ can be inferred from the behavior of W:

$$\theta(S, t) = \frac{\mu_W + \delta_W - rW}{\sigma_W}$$

where δ_W is the dividend flow acquired by holding W.

The process

$$dS = [\mu_S - \theta\sigma_S]\,dt + \sigma_S\,d\hat{z} = \hat{\mu}_S\,dt + \sigma_S\,d\hat{z}$$

is sometimes referred to as the risk-neutral or the martingale-equivalent state process. The volatility (diffusion) term is the same as with the original specification of the state process, but the mean (drift) term is adjusted to incorporate the risk premium associated with the

---

1. A linear PDE is one that is linear in the solution function and all its partial derivatives.

asset. Using the risk-neutral process, the no-arbitrage condition (10.1) becomes

$$rV = \delta_V + V_t + \hat{\mu}V_S + \tfrac{1}{2}\sigma_S^2 V_{SS} = \delta_V + d\hat{E}[S]/dt \tag{10.2}$$

Thus the sum of the dividend rate and the expected capital gain is equal to the risk-free return on the value of the asset. The "^" indicates that the expectation is taken with respect to the risk-neutral state process.

The no-arbitrage condition provides a very convenient framework for pricing a wide variety of financial assets. One must specify the nature of the risk-neutral state process ($\hat{\mu}$ and σ) and how the asset and interest rate depend on the state. Any asset that pays a state-dependent return at a fixed terminal date T can then (in principle) be valued. With a little more work one can also value assets that may be terminated early, such as American options and callable bonds (American options are discussed in section 10.4.2).

10.1.1 Bond Pricing

Suppose that the instantaneous rate of interest is described by the (risk-neutral) process

$$dr = \mu(r)\,dt + \sigma(r)\,dz$$

A bond paying 1 unit of account at time T has a current price $B(r, t; T)$ that satisfies the arbitrage condition

$$rB = B_t + \mu(r)B_r + \tfrac{1}{2}\sigma^2(r)B_{rr}$$

subject to the boundary condition at time T that $B(r, T; T) = 1$.

Although this PDE will generally need to be solved numerically, in some special cases an explicit solution can be found. The so-called Vasicek model assumes that the instantaneous interest rate process is

$$dr = \kappa(\alpha - r)\,dt + \sigma\,dz$$

where κ, α, and σ are constants. The bond price can be verified to have the form

$$B(r, t; T) = \theta(t; T)\exp\!\left(-\phi(t; T)r\right)$$

By inserting the form of the answer into the PDE you can show that ϕ and θ must satisfy the following differential equations:

$$\phi_t(t; T) = 1 + \kappa\phi(t; T), \quad \text{s.t. } \phi(T; T) = 0$$

and

$$\theta_t(t; T)/\theta(t; T) = \kappa\alpha\phi(t; T) - \tfrac{1}{2}\sigma^2\phi^2(t; T), \quad \text{s.t. } \theta(T; T) = 1$$

The solutions to these differential equations are

$$\theta(t; T) = \exp\left(\left(\phi - (T - t)\right)\left(\alpha - \frac{\sigma^2}{2\kappa^2}\right) - \frac{\sigma^2\phi^2}{4\kappa}\right)$$

and

$$\phi(t; T) = \frac{1 - e^{-\kappa(T-t)}}{\kappa}$$

For another example with an explicit solution see exercise 10.1 (page 358).

10.1.2 Black-Scholes Option Pricing Formula

Consider a non-dividend-paying (or payout-protected) stock ($\delta_S = 0$), whose price follows

$$dS = \mu S \, dt + \sigma S \, dz$$

where μ and σ are constants. This stochastic differential equation (sometimes denoted $dS/S = \mu \, dt + \sigma \, dz$) describes a so-called geometric Brownian motion process; the log differences, $\ln(S(t + \Delta t)) - \ln(S(t))$, are normally distributed with mean $(\mu - \frac{1}{2}\sigma^2)\Delta t$ and variance $\sigma^2 \Delta t$ (see discussion in section A.5.1, Appendix A, on page 470). The stock is itself an asset with no flow of payments and hence must satisfy the arbitrage condition that

$$\mu(S) - \theta\sigma(S) = rS$$

A derivative asset that depends on S and generates a one-time return at time T therefore has value, $V(S, t)$, that satisfies the arbitrage condition

$$rV = V_t + rSV_S + \tfrac{1}{2}\sigma^2 S^2 V_{SS} \tag{10.3}$$

A European call option on S with a strike price of K has a payout at time T of $S - K$ if $S > K$ and 0 otherwise. The boundary condition for the PDE is, therefore, that

$$V(S, T) = \max(0, S - K) \tag{10.4}$$

The value of such an option is

$$V(S, t) = S\Phi(d) - e^{-r\tau}K\Phi\left(d - \sigma\sqrt{\tau}\right)$$

where $\tau = T - t$,

$$d = \frac{\ln(S/K) + r\tau}{\sigma\sqrt{\tau}} + \tfrac{1}{2}\sigma\sqrt{\tau}$$

and Φ is the standard normal CDF:

$$\Phi(x) = \frac{1}{\sqrt{2\pi}} \int_{-\infty}^{x} e^{-\frac{1}{2}z^2} \, dz$$

Some tedious manipulations will demonstrate that

$$V_S = \Phi(d)$$

$$V_{SS} = \frac{\phi(d)}{\sigma S \sqrt{\tau}}$$

and

$$V_t = -\frac{\sigma S \phi(d)}{2\sqrt{\tau}} - r e^{-r\tau} K \phi \left(d - \frac{\sigma \sqrt{\tau}}{2} \right)$$

where

$$\phi(x) = \Phi'(x) = \frac{e^{-\frac{1}{2}x^2}}{\sqrt{2\pi}}$$

(the partial derivatives are known as the delta, gamma, and theta of the call option and are used in hedging). Using these expressions, it is straightforward to verify that both the arbitrage PDE (10.3) and the boundary condition (10.4) are satisfied.

10.1.3 Stochastic Volatility Model

A model that generalizes the Black-Scholes model to allow for stochastic volatility assumes that there are two risk factors, the price of the underlying asset and a price volatility factor. The (risk-neutral) state process can be written

$$dS = (r - \delta)S \, dt + \sqrt{v} S \, dz_1$$

and

$$dv = \kappa(m - v) \, dt + \sigma \rho \sqrt{v} \, dz_1 + \sigma \sqrt{1 - \rho^2} \sqrt{v} \, dz_2$$

This model assumes that the volatility process is mean reverting at rate κ to a long-run mean of m. Furthermore, the volatility process can be positively or negatively correlated with the price process itself, depending on the sign of ρ. It has been noted that options on securities (and indices of securities) generally exhibit negative correlation between prices and price volatility, whereas the opposite is true for commodities.

The arbitrage equation for $V(S, v, t)$ is

$$rV = V_t + (r - \delta)SV_S + \kappa(m - v)V_v + \tfrac{1}{2}vS^2 V_{SS} + \sigma\rho v S V_{Sv} + \tfrac{1}{2}\sigma^2(1 - \rho^2)v V_{vv}$$

It will prove convenient to convert this model so that the price of the underlying asset is in logs. Let $s = \ln(S)$, and apply Ito's Lemma to see that

$$ds = (r - \delta)\,dt + \sqrt{v}\,dz_1$$

The arbitrage equation for $V(s, v, t)$ is

$$rV = V_t + (r - \delta)V_s + \kappa(m - v)V_v + \tfrac{1}{2}v V_{ss} + \sigma\rho v V_{sv} + \tfrac{1}{2}\sigma^2(1 - \rho^2)v V_{vv}$$

Expressed in terms of s and v, the underlying state process is an example of an affine diffusion, which is discussed further in section 10.1.5. The model does not, however, have an explicit solution.

10.1.4   Exotic Options

The basic no-arbitrage approach can be applied to more complicated derivative assets. We illustrate this approach with several types of so-called exotic options: Asian, lookback, and barrier options.

An Asian option is one for which the payout depends on the average price of the underlying asset over some prespecified period. There are two basic types: the first has a strike price equal to the average, and the second pays the positive difference between the average price and a fixed strike price.

Defining S to be the underlying price and letting the Asian option depend on the average price over the period 0 to T, the relevant average is

$$A = \frac{1}{T}\int_0^T S_t\,dt$$

At time T the average-strike Asian call option pays $\max(S - A, 0)$, and the fixed-strike Asian call option with strike price K pays $\max(A - K, 0)$.

Suppose the dynamics of S are given by

$$dS = \mu(S)\,dt + \sigma(S)\,dz$$

It is not enough, however, to know current S because the average depends on the path S takes; in other words, the option is not Markov in S. We can, however, expand the state space by defining

$$C_t = \int_0^t S_\tau \, d\tau$$

The option's value depends on S, C, and t. Noting that $dC = S \, dt$, the option satisfies the usual no-arbitrage condition

$$rV = V_t + \mu(S)V_S + SV_C + \tfrac{1}{2}\sigma^2(S)V_{SS}$$

with the terminal value equal to

$$V(S, C, T) = \max(S - C/T, 0)$$

or

$$V(S, C, T) = \max(C/T - K, 0)$$

for average- and fixed-strike Asian options, respectively.[2]

A lookback option is one written on the maximum price over the option's life and can be either a lookback strike or a fixed-strike lookback. As with Asian options, one must define an additional state variable to keep track of the maximum price. Let

$$M_t = \max_{\tau \in [0,t]} S_\tau$$

The terminal conditions are $V(S, M, T) = \max(M - K, 0)$ for the fixed-strike lookback call and $V(S, M, T) = M - S$ for the lookback-strike put.

Notice that $dM = 0$ for $S < M$. Hence the no-arbitrage condition for $S < M$ does not involve M:

$$rV = V_t + \mu(S)V_S + \tfrac{1}{2}\sigma^2(S)V_{SS}$$

This does not mean, however, that V doesn't depend on M. At the point $S = M$ the option value must satisfy $V_M(M, M, t) = 0$.

Finally, we consider one of the many types of barrier options, the so-called down-and-out option. This option behaves like a normal put option so long as the underlying price stays above some prespecified barrier B. However, if the price hits B anytime during the life of the option, the option is immediately terminated with some rebate R paid to its holder.

---

2. In some special cases it is possible to simplify the solution for Asian options; exercises 10.4–10.6 provide some examples of this possibility.

Down-and-out options satisfy the usual no-arbitrage condition for $S \in [B, \infty)$. The terminal $(t = T)$ boundary condition is $V(S, T) = \max(K - S, 0)$ for $S > B$ and $V(S, T) = R$ for $S \leq B$. In addition, the following boundary condition at the barrier must be imposed:

$$V(B, t) = R$$

Notice that this implies that $V_t(B, t) = 0$.

Many options and other assets also have compound features; their return is based on the value of another option or other derivative asset. For example, bond options and futures options depend on the value of a specified bond or on a specified futures price at the expiration of the option. To price these, one must first determine the value of the underlying asset and use this value as a terminal condition for the option.

Consider, for example, an option expiring at time T written on a three-month Treasury bond. The value of the Treasury bond satisfies the no-arbitrage condition with $B(S, T + 0.25) = 1$ as a terminal condition. The terminal condition for a call option with a strike price of K is $V(S, T) = \max(B(S, T) - K, 0)$. Using this approach, compound options of considerable complexity can be valued. In general, there will not be closed-form solutions for such assets, but it is relatively easy to price them numerically, as we will see in the next chapter.

10.1.5 Multivariate Affine Asset Pricing Model

As the dimension of the state process increases, the no-arbitrage PDE becomes increasingly difficult to apply in practice. There are some cases, however, for which this so-called curse of dimensionality can be avoided. The most important case is the affine asset pricing model, which has been widely applied, especially in modeling interest rate and futures price term structure and in valuing European options.

Suppose that the d-dimensional risk-neutral state process S can be described by an affine diffusion, which takes the form

$$dS = (a + AS)\, dt + C \, \mathrm{diag}\left(\sqrt{b + BS}\right) dz$$

where a and b are $d \times 1$ and A, B, and C are $d \times d$ (the $\sqrt{}$ operator is applied element by element). Furthermore, the risk-free interest rate is an affine function of the state, $r_0 + rS$, and the log of the terminal value of the asset is an affine function of the state given by $h_0 + hS$ (where r_0 and h_0 are both scalar and where r and h are both $1 \times d$).

Expressing the value of the asset as a function of S and the time to maturity $\tau = T - t$, it can be verified that

$$V(S, \tau) = \exp\left(\beta_0(\tau) + \beta(\tau)S\right)$$

To satisfy the terminal condition, $\beta_0(0) = h_0$ and $\beta(0) = h$. To verify that the proposed value of V satisfies the no-arbitrage condition, substitute it into equation (10.2):

$$(r_0 + rS)V = -[\beta_0'(\tau) + \beta'(\tau)S]V + \beta(\tau)(a + AS)V$$
$$+ \tfrac{1}{2}\mathrm{trace}\big(C\mathrm{diag}(b + BS)C^\top\beta(\tau)^\top\beta(\tau)\big)V \tag{10.5}$$

The variable V is a common term that can be divided out, and the remaining expression is affine in S. Equation (10.5) is therefore satisfied when[3]

$$\beta_0'(\tau) = \beta(\tau)a + \tfrac{1}{2}\beta(\tau)C\mathrm{diag}\big(\beta(\tau)C\big)b - r_0$$

and

$$\beta'(\tau) = \beta(\tau)A + \tfrac{1}{2}\beta(\tau)C\mathrm{diag}\big(\beta(\tau)C\big)B - r$$

The $d + 1$ coefficient functions $\beta_0(\tau)$ and $\beta(\tau)$ are thus solutions to a system of ordinary differential equations, which are easily solved, even when d is quite large. The Vasicek bond pricing model discussed in section 10.1.1 is a one-dimensional example with $b = 1$, $B = 0$, $r_0 = 0$, and $r = 1$. A more interesting example is the Longstaff-Schwartz two-dimensional model, in which A is diagonal, $C = I$, $b = 0$, $B = I$, and $r_0 = 0$. The two factors in this model are independent mean square root processes:

$$dS_i = [a_i + A_{ii}S_i]\,dt + \sqrt{S_i}\,dz_i$$

The instantaneous interest rate is a linear function of these two factors. As a result of its separability, the ODEs to be solved are

$$\beta_i'(\tau) = A_{ii}\beta_i(\tau) + \tfrac{1}{2}\beta_i^2(\tau) - r_i$$

with $\beta_i(0) = 0$, for $i = 1, 2$, and

$$\beta_0'(\tau) = a_1\beta_1(\tau) + a_2\beta_2(\tau)$$

10.2 Continuous Action Control

On an intuitive level, continuous time optimization methods can be viewed as simple extensions of the discrete-time methods discussed in section 8.1. In continuous time one replaces the summation over time in the objective function with an integral evaluated over time and the difference equation defining the state variable transition function with a differential

---

3. We use the facts that $\mathrm{trace}(xyz) = \mathrm{trace}(zxy)$ and, when x and y are vectors, $\mathrm{diag}(x)y = \mathrm{diag}(y)x$.

equation. For nonstochastic models, the optimization problem is

$$\max_{x(\cdot,\cdot)} \left\{ \int_0^T e^{-\rho t} f\left(S_t, x(S_t, t)\right) dt + e^{-\rho T} R(S_T) \right\} \quad \text{with } dS = g(S, x) \, dt$$

where S is the state variable (the state), x is the control variable (the control), f is the reward function, g is the state transition function, and R is a terminal period "salvage" value. The time horizon T can be a fixed constant, but it can also be infinite (in which case R has no meaning) or can even be state dependent (in which case it must be determined endogenously).

For nonstochastic problems, optimal control theory and its antecedent, the calculus of variations, have become standard tools in economists' mathematical toolbox. Unfortunately, neither of these methods lends itself well to extensions involving uncertainty. The other alternative for solving such problems is to use continuous time dynamic programming. Uncertainty can be handled in an elegant way if one restricts oneself to modeling using Ito processes. This is not much of a restriction because the family of Ito processes is rather large and can be used to model a great variety of dynamic behavior (the main restriction is that it does not allow for jumps). Furthermore, for deterministic problems, optimal control theory and dynamic programming are two sides of the same coin and lead to equivalent solutions (see Appendix 10A).

Using dynamic programming, the only change needed to make the problem stochastic is to define the state variable S to be a controllable Ito process, meaning that the control variable, x, influences the value of the state:[4]

$$dS = g(S, x) \, dt + \sigma(S) \, dz$$

To develop the solution approach on an intuitive level, notice that for problems in discrete time, the Bellman equation can be written in the form

$$V(S, t) = \max_x \left\{ f(S, x) \, \Delta t + \frac{1}{1 + \rho \, \Delta t} E_t[V(S_{t+\Delta t}, t + \Delta t)] \right\}$$

Multiplying this by $(1 + \rho \, \Delta t)/\Delta t$ and rearranging:

$$\rho V(S, t) = \max_x \left\{ f(S, x)(1 + \rho \, \Delta t) + \frac{E_t[V(S_{t+\Delta t}, t + \Delta t) - V(S, t)]}{\Delta t} \right\}$$

Taking the limits of this expression at $\Delta t \to 0$ yields the continuous time version of the

---

4. A more general form would allow x to influence the diffusion as well as the drift term; this can be handled in a straightforward fashion but makes exposition somewhat less clear.

Bellman equation:

$$\rho V(S, t) = \max_x \left\{ f(S, x) + \frac{E_t dV(S, t)}{dt} \right\}$$ (10.6)

If we think of V as the value of an asset on a dynamic project, the Bellman equation states that the rate of return on the asset, ρV, must equal the current income flow to the project, f, plus the expected rate of capital gain on the asset, $E[dV]/dt$, both evaluated using the best management strategy (i.e., the optimal control). Thus, the Bellman equation is a kind of intertemporal arbitrage condition.[5]

By Ito's Lemma

$$dV = [V_t + g(S, x)V_S + \tfrac{1}{2}\sigma(S)^2 V_{SS}]\, dt + \sigma(S)V_S\, dz$$

Taking expectations and "dividing" by dt we see that the term $E_t dV(S, t)/dt$ can be replaced, resulting in the following form for the Bellman equation in continuous time:[6]

$$\rho V = \max_x \left\{ f(S, x) + V_t + g(S, x)V_S + \tfrac{1}{2}\sigma^2(S)V_{SS} \right\}$$ (10.7)

The essential task in solving the stochastic control problem is to find a function $V(s, t)$ and a control $x(S, t)$ that jointly satisfy equation (10.7). Furthermore, V should be continuous up to its second derivative in S and its first derivative in t.[7]

The first order condition for the maximization problem is[8]

$$f_x(S, x) + g_x(S, x)V_S = 0$$ (10.8)

leading (in principle) to a solution of the form

$$x = x(S, V_S)$$

The optimal control can be combined with equation (10.7) to form the *concentrated Bellman equation*:

$$\rho V = f\big(S, x(S, V_S)\big) + V_t + g\big(S, x(S, V_S)\big)V_S + \tfrac{1}{2}\sigma^2(S)V_{SS}$$ (10.9)

which must be solved for $V(S)$.

---

5. It is important to note that the arbitrage interpretation requires that the discount rate, ρ, be appropriately chosen (see section 10.2.1 for further discussion).

6. Also known as the Hamilton-Jacobi-Bellman equation.

7. There are a number of regularity conditions and other technical considerations that qualify this brief statement of the problem; see the bibliographical notes for further discussion.

8. If there are additional constraints on the control variables, they typically can be handled in the usual way (using Lagrange multipliers and, for inequality constraints, Karush-Kuhn-Tucker type conditions). Constraints on the state variables are somewhat more problematic (they are discussed in exercise 10.23 on page 365).

Notice that the Bellman equation is not stochastic; the expectation operator and the randomness in the problem have been eliminated by using Ito's Lemma. As with discrete time versions, the state transition equation is incorporated in the Bellman equation.

In finite time horizon problems, the value function is a function of time, and the time derivative V_t appears in the Bellman equation. In infinite time horizon problems with time-autonomous reward and state-transition equations, the value function becomes time invariant, implying that V is a function of S alone and thus $V_t = 0$. In the infinite horizon case the Bellman equation simplifies to

$$\rho V = \max_{x} \left\{ f(S, x) + g(S, x)V_S + \tfrac{1}{2}\sigma^2(S)V_{SS} \right\}$$

We illustrate the dynamic programming approach with a simple example that admits a closed-form solution. Consider

$$V(S_0) = \max_{x(\cdot)} E_0 \left[\int_0^\infty e^{-\rho t} \ln\big(x(S_t)\big) \, dt \right]$$

where

$$dS = (\alpha S - x) \, dt + \sigma S \, dz$$

The Bellman equation is

$$\rho V(S) = \max_{x} \left\{ \ln(x) + (\alpha S - x)V_S(S) + \frac{\sigma^2 S^2}{2} V_{SS}(S) \right\}$$

The associated first-order condition is

$$x = 1/V_S(S)$$

The solution takes the form $V(S) = a + b\ln(S)$. To verify this, we must demonstrate that this function solves the Bellman equation. In the process, we will solve for the undetermined coefficients a and b.

First, note that $V_S(S) = b/S$, so $x = S/b$. Forming the concentrated Bellman equation and making the appropriate substitutions yields

$$\rho[a + b\ln(S)] = \ln(S/b) + (\alpha - 1/b)b - \frac{\sigma^2 b}{2}$$

For this expression to hold for all $S \geq 0$ it must be the case that $b = 1/\rho$. It is then straightforward to show that

$$a = \ln(\rho)/\rho + (\alpha - \rho - \sigma^2/2)/\rho^2$$

Furthermore, notice that the second-order sufficient condition for a maximum is satisfied
for all $S > 0$.

10.2.1 Choice of the Discount Rate

The choice of the appropriate discount rate to use in dynamic-choice problems has been
a topic of considerable discussion in the corporate finance literature. The arbitrage theory
discussed in section 10.1 can be applied fruitfully to this issue. In particular, there is an
equivalence between the choice of a discount rate and the price of risk assigned to the
various sources of risk affecting the problem. In general, if there is a market for assets that
depend on a specific risk, S, then arbitrage constrains the choice of the discount rate that
should be used to value an investment project. If an inappropriate discount rate is used, a
potential arbitrage opportunity is created by either overvaluing or undervaluing the risk of
the project. To see this point, note that the concentrated Bellman equation for a dynamic
project can be written

$$\rho V = \delta_V + V_t + \mu_S V_S + \tfrac{1}{2}\sigma_S V_{SS}$$

where $\delta_V = f(S, x^*, t)$ and $\mu_S = g(S, x^*, t)$, and x^* is the optimal control. To avoid arbitrage, however, equation (10.1) must hold. Together these relationships imply that

$$\rho = r + \theta\sigma_S V_S/V = r + \theta\sigma_V/V \tag{10.10}$$

In practice we can eliminate the need to determine the appropriate discount rate by using
the risk-free rate as the discount rate and acting as if the process S has instantaneous mean
of either

$$\hat{\mu}_S = \mu_S - \theta_S\sigma_S$$

or, if S is the value of a traded asset,

$$\hat{\mu}_S = rS - \delta_S$$

Which form is more useful depends on whether it is easier to obtain empirical estimates
of the market price of risk for S, θ_S, or income stream generated by S, δ_S. Even if the
project involves a nontraded risk, it may be easier to guess the market price of that risk than
to define the appropriate discount rate. For example, if the risk is idiosyncratic and hence
can be diversified away, then a well-diversified agent would set the market price of risk to
zero. An appropriate discount rate is particularly difficult to select when there are multiple
sources of risk (state variables) because the discount rate becomes a complicated function
of the various market prices of risk.

Having said that, there may be cases in which the appropriate discount rate is easier to set. For firm-level capital budgeting, the discount rate is the required rate of return on the project and, in a well-functioning capital market, should equal the firm's cost of capital. Thus the total return on the project must cover the cost of funds:

$$\rho V = \delta_V + \mu_V = rV + \theta_S \sigma_V$$

The cost of funds, ρ, therefore implicitly determines the market price of risk (using equation 10.10).

Summarizing, there are three alternative cases to consider:

1. S is a traded asset for which

$$\mu_S - \theta \sigma_S = rS - \delta_S$$

2. S is not a traded asset, but there is a traded asset whose value W depends on S and the market price of risk can be determined according to

$$\theta = (\mu_W + \delta_W - rW)/\sigma_W$$

3. S represents a nonpriced risk, and either θ or ρ must be determined by other means.

When S is influenced by the control x, the payment stream, $\delta(S, t)$, becomes $f(S, x, t)$, and the drift term, $\mu(S, t)$, becomes $g(S, x, t)$. Thus there are three possible forms of the Bellman equation:

A. $rV = \left\{ \max_x f(S, x, t) + V_t + (rS - \delta_S)V_S + \frac{1}{2}\sigma^2(S, t)V_{SS} \right\}$

B. $rV = \left\{ \max_x f(S, x, t) + V_t + [g(S, x, t) - \theta\sigma(S, t)]V_S + \frac{1}{2}\sigma^2(S, t)V_{SS} \right\}$

C. $\rho V = \left\{ \max_x f(S, x, t) + V_t + g(S, x, t)V_S + \frac{1}{2}\sigma^2(S, t)V_{SS} \right\}$

Any of the three forms can be used when S is a traded asset, although A and B are preferred in that they rely on market information rather than on guesses concerning the appropriate discount rate. When S is not a traded asset but represents a risk priced in the market, B is the preferred form. If S represents a nonpriced asset, then either form B or C may be used, depending on whether it is easier to determine appropriate values for θ or for ρ.

10.2.2 Euler Equation Methods

As in the discrete time case, it may be possible to eliminate the value function (or shadow price function) and express the optimality conditions in terms of the state and control alone (see discussion for discrete time in section 8.2). Such an expression is known as a Euler equation. In the discrete-time case, this approach was most useful in problems for which $g_S(S, x, \epsilon) = 0$. In the continuous time case, however, Euler equation methods are most useful in deterministic problems. As before, we discuss the infinite horizon case and leave the reader to work out the details for the finite horizon case.

Suppose

$$dS = g(S, x)\, dt$$

The Bellman equation is

$$\rho V(S) = \max_x \{ f(S, x) + g(S, x) V'(S) \} \tag{10.11}$$

with first-order condition (FOC)

$$f_x(S, x) + g_x(S, x) V'(S) = 0$$

Let $h(S, x) = -f_x(S, x)/g_x(S, x)$, so the FOC can be written

$$V'(S) = h(S, x) \tag{10.12}$$

Applying the envelope theorem to the Bellman equation (10.11),

$$[\rho - g_S(S, x)]V'(S) - f_S(S, x) = g(S, x)V''(S)$$

and using h and its total derivative with respect to S:

$$V''(S) = h_S(S, x) + h_x(S, x)\frac{dx}{dS}$$

the terms involving V can be eliminated:

$$[\rho - g_S(S, x)]h(S, x) - f_S(S, x) = g(S, x)\left[h_S(S, x) + h_x(S, x)\frac{dx}{dS}\right] \tag{10.13}$$

This is a first-order differential equation that can be solved for the optimal feedback rule, $x(S)$. The "boundary" condition is that the solution passes through the steady state at which $dS/dt = 0$ and $dx/dt = 0$. The first of these conditions is that $g(S, x) = 0$, which in turn implies that the left-hand side of equation (10.13) equals 0:

$$[\rho - g_S(S, x)]h(S, x) - f_S(S, x) = 0$$

These two equations are solved simultaneously (either explicitly or numerically) to yield boundary conditions for the Euler equation.

10.2.3 Bang-Bang Problems

Bang-bang control problems arise when both the reward function and the state-transition dynamics are linear in the control and the control is bounded. In such cases it is optimal to set the control at either its upper or lower bound. The control problem thus becomes one of dividing the state space into a set of points at which the control is at its upper bound and a set at which it is at its lower bound. Equivalently, the problem is to find the boundary between the two sets.

The general bang-bang problem has reward function of the form

$$f_0(S) + f_1(S)x$$

and state dynamics of the form

$$dS = [g_0(S) + g_1(S)x] \, dt + \sigma(S) \, dz$$

Furthermore the control is constrained to lie on a given interval:

$$x_a \le x \le x_b$$

The Bellman equation for this problem is

$$\rho V = \max_{x_a \le x \le x_b} \left\{ f_0(S) + f_1(S)x + [g_0(S) + g_1(S)x]V_S + \tfrac{1}{2}\sigma^2(S)V_{SS} \right\}$$

The Karush-Kuhn-Tucker conditions for this problem indicate that

$$x = \begin{cases} x_a & \text{if } f_1(S) + g_1(S)V_S(S) < 0 \\ x_b & \text{if } f_1(S) + g_1(S)V_S(S) > 0 \end{cases}$$

Let S^a represent the states for which x^a is optimal, and define S^b in a similar way. Furthermore, let S^* be a point at which

$$f_1(S^*) + g_1(S^*)V_S(S^*) = 0 \tag{10.14}$$

This suggests that we must solve for two functions, one that solves

$$\rho V^a = f_0(S) + f_1(S)x_a + [g_0(S) + g_1(S)x_a]V_S^a + \tfrac{1}{2}\sigma^2(S)V_{SS}^a \quad \text{for } S \in S^a \tag{10.15}$$

and the other that solves

$$\rho V^b = f_0(S) + f_1(S)x_b + [g_0(S) + g_1(S)x_b]V_S^b + \tfrac{1}{2}\sigma^2(S)V_{SS}^b \quad \text{for } S \in S^b \tag{10.16}$$

We will need three side conditions at S^* to completely specify the problem and to find the optimal location of S^*, namely that

$$V^a(S^*) = V^b(S^*)$$

$$V_S^a(S^*) = V_S^b(S^*)$$

$$f_1(S^*) + g_1(S^*)V_S(S^*) = 0$$

Combining these conditions with equations (10.15) and (10.16), we see that

$$V_{SS}^a(S^*) = V_{SS}^b(S^*)$$

that is, with the optimal choice of S^*, the value function is continuous up to its second derivative.

10.3   Continuous Action Control Examples

10.3.1   Nonrenewable Resource Management

A firm manages a nonrenewable resource, obtaining a net return flow of $Ax^{1-\alpha}$ per unit of time, where x is the rate at which the resource is extracted. The stock of the resource is governed by

$$dS = -x\,dt$$

The extraction rate is bounded below by 0 ($x \geq 0$) and constrained to equal 0 if the stock is 0 ($S = 0 \Rightarrow x = 0$). The manager seeks to solve

$$V(S_0) = \max_{x(\cdot)} E_0 \left[\int_0^\infty e^{-\rho t} Ax(S_t)^{1-\alpha}\,dt \right]$$

The Bellman equation for the problem is

$$\rho V(S) = \max_x \{Ax^{1-\alpha} - xV_s\}$$

The first-order optimality condition is

$$V_S(S) = (1 - \alpha)Ax^{-\alpha}$$

Using a Euler equation approach, apply the Envelope Theorem to obtain

$$\rho V_S = -xV_{SS}$$

We have an expression for V_S from the optimality condition, and this can be differentiated with respect to S to obtain

$$\rho(1-\alpha)Ax^{-\alpha} = \alpha(1-\alpha)Ax^{-\alpha}\frac{dx}{dS}$$

Simplifying, this equation yields

$$\frac{dx}{dS} = \frac{\rho}{\alpha}$$

which, with the boundary condition that $x = 0$ when $S = 0$, produces the optimal control

$$x(S) = \frac{\rho}{\alpha}S$$

and the value function

$$V(S) = \left(\frac{\alpha}{\rho}\right)^\alpha AS^{1-\alpha}$$

Notice that the time path of the resource satisfies

$$dS = -(\rho/\alpha)S\,dt$$

so the stock

$$S_t = e^{-(\rho/\alpha)t}S_0$$

is exponentially declining.

10.3.2 Neoclassical Growth Model

Production in a single (aggregate) good economy is given by $q(K)$, where K is the level of the capital stock. Output can either be consumed at rate C or invested, thereby increasing the capital stock. A social utility function depends on the rate of consumption, $u(C)$. A social planner attempts to maximize the discounted stream of social utility over an infinite time horizon, using a constant discount factor ρ.

The optimization problem can be expressed in terms of K, the state variable, and C, the control variable, as follows

$$V(K_0) = \max_{C(\cdot)} \int_0^\infty e^{-\rho t} u\big(C(K_t)\big)\, dt$$

subject to the state transition function $dK = [q(K) - C]\, dt$.

This is a deterministic infinite time problem, so V_{KK} and V_t do not enter the Bellman equation:

$$\rho V(K) = \max_C \{u(C) + [q(K) - C]V'(K)\}$$

The maximization problem requires that

$$u'(C) = V'(K) \tag{10.17}$$

A Euler equation for this problem is obtained by eliminating the value function, resulting in a differential equation for consumption in terms of current capital stock. Applying the envelope theorem,

$$\rho V'(K) = q'(K)V'(K) + [q(K) - C]V''(K) \tag{10.18}$$

Combining equations (10.17) and (10.18) with the fact that $V''(K) = U''(C)C'(K)$ yields

$$-\frac{u'(C)}{u''(C)}[q'(K) - \rho] = [q(K) - C]C'(K)$$

Thus the optimal decision rule $C(K)$ solves a first-order differential equation. The boundary condition for this differential equation is that the solution passes through the point (K^*, C^*) which simultaneously solves $dK/dt = 0$ and the Euler condition:

$$q'(K^*) = \rho$$

$$C^* = q(K^*)$$

10.3.3   Optimal Renewable Resource Extraction

The stock of a resource, S, is governed by the controlled stochastic process

$$dS = [B(S) - q]\,dt + \sigma S\,dz$$

where $B(S)$ is a biological growth function and q is the harvest rate of the resource. The marginal cost is constant in the harvest rate but also depends on the stock of the resource. The total cost function thus has the form

$$C(q, S) = c(S)q$$

The total surplus (consumer plus producer) is

$$f(S, q) = \int_0^q D^{-1}(z)\,dz - c(S)q$$

where D is the demand function for the resource.

With a discount rate of ρ, the Bellman equation for this optimization problem is

$$\rho V = \max_q \left\{ \int_0^q D^{-1}(z)\, dz - c(S)q + [B(S) - q]V_S + \tfrac{1}{2}\sigma^2 S^2 V_{SS} \right\}$$

The first-order condition (FOC) for the optimal choice of q is

$$D^{-1}(q) - c(S) - V_S(S) = 0$$

or

$$q = D\big(c(S) + V_S\big)$$

Notice that the FOC implies that the marginal surplus of an additional unit of the harvested resource is equal to the marginal value of an additional unit of the in situ stock:

$$f_q(S, q) \equiv D^{-1}(q) - c(S) = V_S(S)$$

To make the problem more concrete, assume a biological growth function

$$B(S) = \frac{\alpha}{\beta} S[1 - (S/K)^\beta]$$

a demand function

$$D(p) = bp^{-\eta}$$

and a marginal cost function

$$c(S) = cS^{-\gamma}$$

In general this model must be solved numerically, but special cases do exist that admit an explicit solution. Specifically, if $\gamma = 1 + \beta$ and $\eta = 1/(1 + \beta)$, the value function has the form

$$V(S) = -\left(\frac{1}{S^\beta} + \frac{\alpha}{\rho K^\beta} \right) \phi$$

where ϕ solves

$$\theta \phi^{\frac{1+\beta}{\beta}} - \beta\phi - c = 0$$

and

$$\theta = \left(\frac{\alpha + \rho}{b} \frac{\beta}{1 + \beta} - \frac{\beta\sigma^2}{2b} \right)^{\frac{1+\beta}{\beta}}$$

It is straightforward to solve for ϕ using a standard rootfinding routine, and for some values of β a completely explicit solution is possible (see exercise 10.7 on page 360).

10.3.4 Stochastic Growth

An economy is characterized by an exogenous technology shock Y that is governed by

$$dY = \kappa(aY - b)\,dt + \sigma\sqrt{Y}\,dz$$

The capital stock K is influenced by both the technology shock and by current consumption c (the control), according to

$$dK = (\beta KY - c)\,dt + \epsilon K\sqrt{Y}\,dz$$

where the same Brownian motion z that drives the technology shock also causes volatility in the productivity of capital. The social planner's optimization problem is to maximize the present value of the utility of consumption, taken here to be the log utility function, using discount rate ρ.

The Bellman equation for this problem is

$$\rho V = \max_c \left\{ \ln(c) + (\beta KY - c)\,V_K + \kappa(aY - b)V_Y \right.$$
$$\left. + \tfrac{1}{2}\epsilon^2 K^2 Y V_{KK} + \tfrac{1}{2}\sigma^2 Y V_{YY} + \sigma\epsilon KY V_{KY} \right\}$$

The first-order condition associated with the Bellman equation tells us that the optimal c satisfies

$$c = 1/V_K$$

Let us guess that optimal consumption is proportional to the capital stock

$$c = \alpha K$$

If our guess is right, it implies that $V(K, Y) = \ln(K)/\alpha + f(Y)$, where $f(Y)$ is yet to be determined. To verify that this guess is correct, substitute it into the Bellman equation:

$$\rho\left(\frac{\ln(K)}{\alpha} + f(Y)\right) = \ln(\alpha K) + \left(\frac{\beta}{\alpha}Y - 1\right) + \kappa(aY - b)f'(Y) - \frac{\epsilon^2 Y}{2\alpha} + \tfrac{1}{2}\sigma^2 Y f''(Y)$$

Collecting terms and simplifying, we see that $\alpha = \rho$ and that $f(Y)$ solves the following second-order differential equation

$$\rho f(Y) = [\ln(\rho) - 1] + \frac{1}{\rho}\left(\beta - \frac{\epsilon^2}{2}\right)Y + \kappa(aY - b)f'(Y) + \frac{\sigma^2}{2}Y f''(Y)$$

The solution to this differential equation has the form $f(Y) = \theta + \phi Y$, implying that $f'(Y) = \phi$ and $f''(Y) = 0$. This is easily verified:

$$\rho(\theta + \phi Y) = [\ln(\rho) - 1] + \frac{1}{\rho}\left(\beta - \frac{\epsilon^2}{2}\right)Y + \kappa(aY - b)\phi$$

Collecting terms and solving yields

$$\phi = \frac{1}{\rho(\rho - \kappa a)}\left(\beta - \frac{\epsilon^2}{2}\right)$$

and

$$\theta = \frac{1}{\rho}[\ln(\rho) - 1 - \kappa b\phi]$$

10.3.5 Portfolio Choice

The previous examples had a small number of state and control variables. In the example we are about to present, we start with a large number of both state variables and controls; but with a specific assumption about the state dynamics, the dimension of the state is reduced to one. Such a reduction transforms a problem that is essentially impossible to solve in general into one that is relatively straightforward to solve. For some specific classes of reward functions the problem even can be solved explicitly.

Suppose investors can invest in any of a set of n assets, with the per-unit price of these assets generated by an n-dimensional Ito process

$$dP = \mu(P)\,dt + \sigma(P)\,dz$$

where $\sigma(P)$ is an $n \times k$ matrix valued function (i.e., $\sigma : \mathbb{R}^n \mapsto \mathbb{R}^{n \times k}$) and z is a k-dimensional vector of independent Wiener processes. We assume that $\Sigma = \sigma\sigma^{\top}$, the instantaneous covariance matrix for prices, is nonsingular, implying that there are no redundant assets or, equivalently, that there is no riskless asset.[9] A portfolio can be defined by the number of shares, N_i, invested in each asset or as the fraction of wealth held in each asset:

$$w_i = N_i P_i / W$$

Expressed in terms of N_i the wealth process can be described by

$$dW = \sum_{i=1}^{n} N_i\,dP_i$$

---

9. The case in which a riskless asset is available is treated in exercise 10.10.

whereas, in terms of w_i, it is given by

$$dW/W = \sum_{i=1}^{n} w_i\, dP_i/P_i$$

The latter expression is particularly useful if prices are multivariate geometric Brownian motion processes, so $\mu(P) = \mathrm{diag}(P)\mu$ and $\sigma(P) = \mathrm{diag}(P)\sigma$ (where μ and σ are constants), implying that

$$dW/W = w^\top \mu\, dt + w^\top \sigma\, dz$$

that is, W is itself a geometric Brownian motion process. As a result, portfolio decisions can be expressed in terms of wealth alone, without reference to the prices of the underlying assets in the portfolio. Geometric Brownian motion, therefore, allows for a very significant reduction in the dimension of the state (from n to 1). Consider an investor who draws off a flow of consumption expenditures C. The wealth dynamics are then

$$dW = \left[Ww^\top\mu - C\right] dt + Ww^\top\sigma\, dz$$

Suppose the investor seeks to maximize the discounted stream of satisfaction derived from consumption, where utility is given by $u(C)$ and the discount rate is ρ. The Bellman equation for this problem is[10]

$$\rho V = \max_{C,w} \left\{ u(C) + \left[Ww^\top\mu - C\right] V_W + \tfrac{1}{2}W^2 w^\top \Sigma w V_{WW} \right\}$$

s.t. $\sum_i w_i = 1$

The first-order conditions associated with this maximization problem are

$$u'(C) = V_W \tag{10.19a}$$

$$W V_W \mu + W^2 V_{WW} \Sigma w - \lambda \underline{1} = 0 \tag{10.19b}$$

where $\underline{1}$ is a vector of ones and

$$\sum_i w_i = 1 \tag{10.19c}$$

where λ is a Lagrange multiplier introduced to handle the adding-up constraint on the w_i. A bit of linear algebra applied to equations (10.19b) and (10.19c) will demonstrate that the

10. If prices were not geometric Brownian motion, the coefficients μ and σ would be functions of current prices, and the Bellman equation would have additional terms representing derivatives of the value function with respect to prices, which would make the problem considerably harder to solve.

optimal portfolio weight vector, w, can be written as a linear combination of vectors, v and θ, that are independent of the investor's preferences:

$$w = v + \alpha(W)\theta \qquad\qquad (10.20)$$

where

$$v = \frac{\Sigma^{-1}\underline{1}}{\underline{1}^{\top}\Sigma^{-1}\underline{1}}$$

$$\theta = \Sigma^{-1}\left(\mu - \frac{\underline{1}^{\top}\Sigma^{-1}\mu}{\underline{1}^{\top}\Sigma^{-1}\underline{1}}\underline{1}\right)$$

and

$$\alpha(W) = -\frac{V_W}{W V_{WW}}$$

These results have a nice economic interpretation. When asset prices are generated by geometric Brownian motion, a portfolio separation result occurs, much as in the static Capital Asset Pricing Model (CAPM). Only two portfolios are needed to satisfy all investors, regardless of their preferences. One of the portfolios has weights proportional to $\Sigma^{-1}\underline{1}$, the other to $\Sigma^{-1}[\mu - (v^{\top}\mu)\underline{1}]$. The relative amounts held in each portfolio depend on the investor's preferences, with more of the first portfolio being held as the degree of risk aversion rises (as $\alpha(W)$ decreases). This result is understandable when it is noticed that the first portfolio is the minimum risk portfolio; that is, v solves the problem

$$\min_{v} v^{\top}\Sigma v, \quad \text{s.t. } v^{\top}\underline{1} = 1$$

Furthermore, the expected return on the minimum risk portfolio is $v^{\top}\mu$; hence the term $\mu - (v^{\top}\mu)\underline{1}$ can be thought of as an "excess" return vector, that is, the expected returns over the return on the minimum risk portfolio.

The problem is therefore reduced to determining the two decision-rule functions for consumption and investment decisions, $C(W)$ and $\alpha(W)$, that satisfy

$$U'(C(W)) = V_W(W)$$

and

$$\alpha(W) = -\frac{V_W(W)}{W V_{WW}(W)}$$

Notice that the two-fund separation result is due to the assumption that asset prices follow geometric Brownian motions and not the result of any assumption about preferences. Given the enormous simplification that it allows, it is small wonder that financial economists like this assumption.

10.3.6 Production with Adjustment Costs

A competitive firm produces a good that sells for price p, where p is described by the process

$$dp = \mu(p)\,dt + \sigma(p)\,dz$$

The firm produces the good at rate q, incurring a cost of $c(q)$. In addition, it faces an adjustment cost if it changes the production level. Let x be the rate of change in the production rate

$$dq = x\,dt$$

and $a(x)$ the cost of adjustment.

The control for this model is not q but rather the adjustment rate x. The production level q is treated as a controllable state variable along with the stochastic uncontrolled price p. The value function is therefore a function of two variables, $V(p, q)$.

If the firm uses a discount rate of ρ, the Bellman equation is

$$\rho V = \max_x \left\{ pq - c(q) - a(x) + x V_q + \mu(p) V_p + \frac{\sigma^2(p)}{2} V_{pp} \right\}$$

The first-order condition for the maximization problem is

$$a'(x) = V_q(p, q)$$

that is, the marginal adjustment cost must equal the marginal value of a change in the production rate.

To make this model more specific, suppose p is described by the mean-reverting process

$$dp = \kappa(\alpha - p)\,dt + \sigma p\,dz$$

and let two cost functions be given by

$$c(q) = \frac{c}{2} q^2$$

and

$$a(x) = \frac{a}{2} x^2$$

The Bellman equation is

$$\rho V = \max_{x} \left\{ pq - \frac{c}{2}q^2 - \frac{a}{2}x^2 + xV_q + \kappa(\alpha - p)V_p + \frac{\sigma^2 p^2}{2}V_{pp} \right\}$$

The optimal adjustment rate is then

$$x = V_q/a$$

With this parameterization, the production-adjustment model has an explicit solution (see problem 10.14 on page 361).

10.3.7 Harvesting a Renewable Resource

Consider a manager of a renewable biological resource who must determine the optimal harvesting strategy. The state variable, the stock of the resource, is stochastic, fluctuating according to

$$dS = [\alpha S(1 - S) - Sh] dt + \sigma S \, dz$$

where h, the control, is the harvesting effort, which is constrained such that $0 \le h \le H$. The harvesting rate is Sh, and it generates a return of $(p - c/S)Sh$, where p is the sales price on the harvested good and c/S, the marginal harvest cost, is inversely proportional to the total stock. The manager seeks to solve

$$V(S_0) = \max_{0 \le h(\cdot) \le H} E\left[\int_0^\infty e^{-\rho t}(p - c/S_t)S_t h(S_t) \, dt \right]$$

This is a stochastic bang-bang problem. In the notation of general bang-bang problems, $x_a = 0$, $x_b = H$, $f_0(S) = 0$, $f_1(S) = (p - c/S)S$, $g_0(S) = \alpha S(1 - S)$, and $g_1(S) = -S$. The Bellman equation for this problem is

$$\rho V = \max_{0 \le h \le H} \left\{ (p - c/S)Sh + [\alpha S(1 - S) - Sh]V_S + \tfrac{1}{2}\sigma^2 S^2 V_{SS} \right\}$$

The first-order conditions for this problem suggest that it is optimal to set $h = H$ if $V_S < (p - c/S)$ and set $h = 0$ if $V_S > p - c/S$. The interpretation of these conditions is straightforward: only harvest when the value of a harvested unit of the resource is greater than an unharvested one, and then harvest at maximum rate. Thus the problem becomes one of finding the sets

$$S^0 = \{S : V_S > p - c/S\}$$

and

$$S^H = \{S : V_S < p - c/S\}$$

where

$$\rho V - \alpha S(1 - S)V_S - \tfrac{1}{2}\sigma^2 S^2 V_{SS} = 0 \quad \text{on } S^0$$

and

$$\rho V - [\alpha S(1 - S) - SH]V_S - \tfrac{1}{2}\sigma^2 S^2 V_{SS} - (p - c/S)SH = 0 \quad \text{on } S^H$$

The solution must also satisfy continuity conditions at any points S^* such that $V_S(S^*) = p - c/S$. The fact that $\alpha S(1 - S) - Sh$ is concave in S implies that S^* will be a single point, with $S^0 = [0, S^*)$ and $S^H = (S^*, \infty)$. In addition, the assumptions about the stock dynamics imply that $V(0) = 0$ (once the stock reaches zero it never recovers, and hence the resource is worthless). At high levels of the stock, the marginal value of an additional unit to the stock becomes constant, and hence $V_{SS}(\infty) = 0$.

10.3.8 Sequential Learning

More complicated bang-bang problems arise when there are two state variables. The boundary representing the switching points is then a curve, which typically must be approximated. Consider the case of a firm that has developed a new production technique. Initially production costs are relatively high, but they decrease as the firm gains more experience with the process. The firm therefore has an incentive to produce more than it otherwise might because of the future cost reductions it thereby achieves.

To make this model concrete, suppose that marginal and average costs are constant at any point in time but decline at an exponential rate in cumulative production until a minimum marginal cost level is achieved. The problem facing the firm is to determine the output rate x that maximizes the present value of returns (price less cost times output) over an infinite horizon:

$$V(P_0, Q_0) = \max_{0 \le x(\cdot,\cdot) \le x_c} E_0 \left[\int_0^\infty e^{-rt}[P_t - C(Q_t)]x(P_t, Q_t)\, dt \right]$$

where r is the risk-free interest rate; the two state variables are P, the output price, and Q, the cumulative production to date; and x_c is the maximum feasible production rate. The state transition equations are

$$dP = \mu P\, dt + \sigma P\, dz$$

and

$$dQ = x\, dt$$

The price equation should be interpreted as a risk-neutral process. The cost function is given by

$$C(Q) = \begin{cases} ce^{-\gamma Q} & \text{if } Q < Q_m \\ ce^{-\gamma Q_m} = \bar{c} & \text{if } Q \geq Q_m \end{cases}$$

Once $Q \geq Q_m$, the per-unit production cost is a constant, but for $Q < Q_m$ it declines exponentially.

The Bellman equation for this problem is

$$rV = \max_{0 \leq x \leq x_c} \left\{ [P - C(Q)]x + xV_Q + \mu P V_P + \tfrac{1}{2}\sigma^2 P^2 V_{PP} \right\}$$

The problem thus is of the stochastic bang-bang variety with the optimality conditions given by

$$P - C(Q) + V_Q < 0 \Rightarrow x = 0$$

$$P - C(Q) + V_Q > 0 \Rightarrow x = x_c$$

Substituting the optimal production rate into the Bellman equation and rearranging yields the partial differential equation

$$rV(P, Q) = \mu P V_P(P, Q) + \tfrac{1}{2}\sigma^2 P^2 V_{PP} + \max\big(0, P - C(Q) + V_Q(P, Q)\big)x_c$$

The boundary conditions for this problem require that

$$V(0, Q) = 0$$

$$V_P(\infty, Q) = x_c/\delta$$

and that V, V_P, and V_Q be continuous. The first boundary condition reflects the fact that 0 is an absorbing state for P; if P reaches 0, no revenue will ever be generated, and hence the firm has no value. The second condition is derived from computing the expected revenue if the firm always produces at maximum capacity, as it would if the price were to get arbitrarily large (i.e., if the probability that the price falls below marginal cost becomes arbitrarily small). The derivative of the expected revenue is x_c/δ.

The (Q, P) state space for this problem is divided by a curve $P^*(Q)$ that defines a low-price region in which the firm is inactive and a high-price region in which it is active (see

Figure 11.14). Furthermore, for $Q > Q_m$, $P^*(Q)$ is equal to $\bar{c}$ because, once the marginal cost is at its minimum level, there is nothing to be gained from production when the price is less than the marginal production cost.

For $Q > Q_m$ the problem is simplified by the fact that $V_Q = 0$. Thus V is a function of P alone, and the value of the firm satisfies

$$rV(P) = \mu P V_P(P) + \tfrac{1}{2}\sigma^2 P^2 V_{PP} + \max\left(0, P - C(Q)\right)x_c$$

For $Q < Q_m$, however, $V_Q \neq 0$, and the location of the boundary $P^*(Q)$ must be determined simultaneously with the value function.

An additional boundary condition can therefore be specified at $Q = Q_m$:

$$V(P, Q_m) = \bar{V}(P) \quad \text{(defined in the next paragraph)}$$

is a "terminal" condition in Q. Once Q_m units have been produced, the firm has reached its minimum marginal cost. Further production decisions do not depend on Q, nor does the value of the firm, V.

An explicit solution can be derived for $Q > Q_m$:

$$\bar{V}(P) = \begin{cases} A_1 P^{\beta_1} & \text{if } P \leq \bar{c} \\ A_2 P^{\beta_2} + \dfrac{P}{\delta} - \dfrac{\bar{c}}{r} & \text{if } P \geq \bar{c} \end{cases}$$

where the β solve the quadratic equation

$$\tfrac{1}{2}\sigma^2\beta(1-\beta) + (r-\delta)\beta - r = 0$$

and the A_1 and A_2 are computed using the continuity of $\bar{V}$ and $\bar{V}_P$.

The continuity requirements on the value function, even though the control is discontinuous, allow us to determine the free boundary $P^*(Q)$.

Notice that below the free boundary the Bellman equation takes a particularly simple form

$$rV(P, Q) = (r-\delta)P V_P(P, Q) + \tfrac{1}{2}\sigma^2 P^2 V_{PP}$$

which together with the first boundary condition $(V(0, Q) = 0)$, is solved by

$$V(P, Q) = A_1(Q) P^{\beta_1}$$

where $A_1(Q)$ is yet to be determined. Above the boundary, however, there is no closed-form solution. The functions $A_1(Q)$, $P^*(Q)$, and $V(P, Q)$ for $P \geq P^*$ must be approximated numerically.

The solution methods for this problem depend on being able to determine the position of the free boundary. It is therefore worth exploring some of the consequences of the continuity conditions on V. First, consider the known form of the value function below the free boundary and its derivative:

$$V(P, Q) = A_1(Q) P^{\beta_1}$$

$$V_P(P, Q) = \beta_1 A_1(Q) P^{\beta_1 - 1}$$

Eliminating $A_1(Q)$ yields

$$P V_P(P, Q) = \beta_1 V(P, Q)$$

This condition holds at and below the boundary. By the continuity of the V and V_P, it must also hold as the boundary is approached from above. Similarly, the continuity of the second derivative implies that

$$P V_{PP}(P, Q) = (\beta_1 - 1) V_P(P, Q)$$

at the boundary.

10.4   Regime Switching Models

Many problems that arise in economics involve both state variables that are represented as stochastic processes and other states that are discrete in nature, with the control problem consisting of the choice of whether the current discrete state should be maintained or changed. Specifically, there are m discrete states or regimes and there is a controlled process S that, in regime r, is governed by

$$dS = g(S, r) \, dt + \sigma(S, r) \, dz$$

The agent desires a strategy that maximizes the expected flow of returns from the state $f(S, r)$ plus any expected returns generated by switching regimes. The latter is defined by the matrix valued function $R(S)$, where $R_{rq}(S)$ is the reward for switching from regime r to regime q when the stochastic state is S. To avoid the possibility of infinite profits, it must be true that $R_{rq} + R_{qr} \leq 0$. This also ensures that the switches must take place at isolated times or infinite switching costs would be incurred.

   If the agent uses a discount rate of ρ, the solution can be characterized as a set, for each regime, of regions in the continuous state space on which no discrete switch is undertaken. In the interior of the no-switch regions for regime r, the value function satisfies the Feynman-Kac equation

$$\rho V(S, r) = f(S, r) + g(S, r) V_S(S, r) + \tfrac{1}{2}\sigma^2(S, r) V_{SS}(S, r)$$

At the boundary points of the no-switch region, it is optimal to switch to one of the other regimes.

For example, suppose that at S^* it is optimal to switch from discrete state r to discrete state q, i.e., that the optimal control satisfies $x(S^*, r) = q$. The value function must satisfy two conditions at such a point. First, the pre-switch value must equal the post-switch value less the switching costs:

$$V(S^*, r) = V(S^*, q) + R_{rq}(S^*)$$

a condition known as value-matching. This will hold regardless of whether the switching points are chosen optimally and is simply a consequence of the definition of the value function as the sum of discounted net returns from taking a prescribed set of actions.

At the optimal switching points the marginal values before switching must equal the marginal value after switching plus the marginal reward for switching:

$$V_S(S^*, r) = V_S(S^*, q) + R'_{rq}(S^*)$$

a condition known as smooth-pasting.

To understand where this optimality condition comes from, let $U(S, k; S^*)$ be a function that solves the Feynman-Kac equation

$$\rho U = f(S, k) + g(S, k)U_S + \tfrac{1}{2}\sigma^2(S, k)U_{SS}$$

and the value matching condition

$$U(S^*, k, S^*) = U(S^*, k, S^*) + R_{rq}(S^*)$$

for an arbitrary choice of S^*. The value function equals the maximal value of U:

$$V(S, k) = \max_{S^*} U(S, k; S^*)$$

which has the associated first-order condition

$$U_{S^*}(S, k; S^*) = 0$$

The total derivative of the value-matching condition with respect to S^* is

$$U_S(S^*, r; S^*) + U_{S^*}(S^*, r; S^*) - U_S(S^*, q; S^*) - U_{S^*}(S^*, q; S^*) - R'_{rq}(S^*)$$

which is identically equal to zero. Combined with the first-order condition evaluated at $S = S^*$ and at both $k = r$ and $k = q$ yields the smooth-pasting condition.

Characterizing the problem in this way leads to viewing it as a so-called free-boundary problem. We seek a solution to a differential equation, but the location over which that solution must be found is an integral part of the solution itself. In the physical sciences, free-boundary problems are also known as Stefan problems. A commonly used example is the location of the phase change between liquid and ice, where the state space is measured in physical space coordinates. One advantage to viewing the problem in this way is that it allows us to treat the control rule as a problem of finding the boundary values for the no-switch regions. We will exploit this advantage in finding numerical solutions in the next chapter.

The simplest form of discrete action control consists of optimal stopping problems, in which the discrete state represents either continuation or termination. The cost of switching from the terminated state is infinite, thus precluding this possibility. Furthermore, the reward function in the terminated state is zero. Examples of optimal stopping problems include the valuation of American-style options and asset abandonment.

More complicated discrete action problems arise when projects can be activated and deactivated. The problem then becomes one of determining the value of the project if active, given that one can deactivate it, together with the value of the project if inactive, given that it can be activated. The solution involves two boundaries, one that determines when the project should be activated (given that it is currently inactive), the other when it should be deactivated (given that it is currently active). Still more complicated problems may involve more than two discrete states.

It is also possible to view bang-bang problem as discrete state problems. In a bang-bang problem the optimal control is always set to either its lower or its upper bound. The discrete state in this case takes on one of two values depending on which of these two levels is currently operative. As discussed in section 10.2.3, the side conditions for arbitrary values of the switching point consist of continuity of the value function and its first derivative. For the optimal switching point, continuity of the second derivative is also required. This holds true more generally whenever switching costs are zero.

10.4.1 Machine Abandonment

A firm owns a machine that produces an output worth P per unit time, where

$$dP = \mu(P)\,dt + \sigma(P)\,dz$$

The machine has an operating cost of c per unit time. If the machine is shut down, it must be totally abandoned and thus is lost. At issue is the optimal abandonment policy for an agent who maximizes the flow of net returns from the machine discounted at rate ρ.

This is an optimal stopping problem with no reward for termination. The optimal policy can be defined in terms of a switch point P^*. For $P > P^*$ it is optimal to keep the machine running, whereas for $P < P^*$ it is optimal to abandon it.

The current value of the operating machine satisfies the Feynman-Kac equation

$$\rho V = P - c + \mu(P)V_P + \tfrac{1}{2}\sigma^2(P)V_{PP}$$

on $P \in [P^*, \infty)$, where P^* solves

$V(P^*) = 0$ Value-matching condition

$V_P(P^*) = 0$ Smooth-pasting condition

If the drift and diffusion terms describing P are proportional to P (geometric Brownian motion) an explicit solution is possible:

$$V(P) = A_1 P^{\beta_1} + A_2 P^{\beta_2} + P/(\rho - \mu) - c/\rho$$

where the β_i solve

$$\tfrac{1}{2}\sigma^2\beta(\beta - 1) + \mu\beta - \rho = 0$$

and where A_1 and A_2 are constants to be determined by the boundary conditions. For economically meaningful parameter values, one of the β is negative and the other greater than 1. To avoid explosive growth as $P \to \infty$, we set $A_2 = 0$, where β_2 is the positive root.

The value-matching and smooth-pasting conditions are used to determine P^* and A (we drop the subscript on β_1 and A_1):

$$A P^{*^\beta} + P^*/(\rho - \mu) - c/\rho = 0$$

and

$$\beta A P^{*^{\beta-1}} + 1/(\rho - \mu) = 0$$

which are solved by

$$P^* = \frac{(\rho - \mu)\beta}{\rho(\beta - 1)}c \tag{10.21}$$

and

$$A = -\frac{P^{*^{1-\beta}}}{(\rho - \mu)\beta}$$

10.4.2 American Put Option

An American put option, if exercised, pays $K - P$, where K is the exercise or strike price and P is the random price of the underlying asset, which evolves according to

$$dP = \mu(P)\,dt + \sigma(P)\,dz$$

The option pays nothing when it is being held, so $f(P) = 0$. Let T denote the option's expiration date, meaning that it must be exercised on or before $t = T$ (if at all).

Most (though not all) options are written on traded assets, so we may discount at the risk-free rate and replace $\mu(P)$ with $rP - \delta_P$ (see section 10.2.1). The appropriate Feynman-Kac equation is therefore

$$rV = V_t + (rP - \delta_P)\,V_P + \tfrac{1}{2}\sigma^2(P)V_{PP}$$

on the continuation region, where δ represents the income flow (dividend, convenience yield, etc.) from the underlying asset. Notice that the constraint that $t \leq T$ means that the value function is a function of time, and so V_t must be included in the Feynman-Kac equation.

The solution involves determining the optimal exercise boundary, $P^*(t)$. Unlike the previous problem, in which the optimal stopping boundary was a single point, the boundary here is a function of time. For puts, $P^*(t)$ is a lower bound, so the continuation region on which the Feynman-Kac equation is defined is $[P^*, \infty)$. The boundary conditions for the put option are

$V(P, T) = \max(K - P, 0)$ (terminal condition)

$V(P^*, t) = K - P^*$ (value matching)

$V_P(P^*, t) = -1$ (smooth pasting)

and

$V(\infty, t) = 0$

10.4.3 Entry-Exit

A firm can either be producing nothing or be actively producing q units of a good per period at a cost of c per unit. In addition to the binary state δ ($\delta = 0$ for inactive, $\delta = 1$ for active), there is also an exogenous stochastic state representing the return per unit of output, P, which is described by

$$P_t = \mu(P)\,dt + \sigma(P)\,dz$$

The firm faces fixed costs of activating and deactivating of I and E, with $I + E \geq 0$ (to avoid arbitrage opportunities). The value function, for any choice of a switching strategy, is

$$V(P_0, \delta_0) = E_0 \left[\int_0^\infty e^{-\rho t} \delta_t (P_t - c) \, dt - \sum_{i=1}^\infty \left(e^{-\rho t_i^a} I + e^{-\rho t_i^d} E \right) \right]$$

where $\delta = 1$ if active, 0 if inactive, and t_i^a and t_i^d are the times at which activation and deactivation occur.

For positive transition costs, it is reasonable that such switches should be made infrequently. Furthermore it is intuitively reasonable that the optimal strategy is to activate when P is sufficiently high, $P = P_h$, and to deactivate when the price is sufficiently low, $P = P_l$. It should be clear that $P_l < P_h$; otherwise, infinite transactions costs would be incurred. The value function can therefore be thought of as a pair of functions, one for when the firm is active, V^a, and one for when it is inactive, V^i. The former is defined on the interval $[P_l, \infty)$, the latter on the interval $[0, P_h]$. On the interior of these regions the value functions satisfy the Feynman-Kac equations

$$
\begin{aligned}
\rho V^a &= P - c + \mu(P) V_P^a + \sigma^2(P) V_{PP}^a \\
\rho V^i &= \mu(P) V_P^i + \sigma^2(P) V_{PP}^i
\end{aligned}
$$

(10.22)

At the upper boundary point P_h the firm will change from being inactive to active at a cost of I. Value matching requires that the value functions differ by the switching cost: $V^i(P_h) = V^a(P_h) - I$. Similarly at the point P_l the firm changes from an active state to an inactive one; hence $V^a(P_l) = V^i(P_l) - E$.

Value matching holds for arbitrary choices of P_l and P_h. For the optimal choices the smooth-pasting conditions must also be satisfied:

$$V_P^i(P_l) = V_P^a(P_l)$$

and

$$V_P^i(P_h) = V_P^a(P_h)$$

In this problem, the exit is irreversible in the sense that reentry is as expensive as initial investment. A refinement of this approach is to allow for temporary suspension of production, with a per-unit-time maintenance change. Temporary suspension is generally preferable to complete exit (so long as the maintenance charge is not prohibitive). Adding temporary suspension increases the number of values of the discrete state to three; its solution is left as an exercise.

10.5   Impulse Control

In continuous time control problems, the control variable is often the rate of change of one of the state variables. It is conceivable that this rate of change can be made so large (infinite) that the state variable exhibits an instantaneous shift in value. Such problems typically arise when there are transactions costs associated with exerting a control at nonzero levels, in which case it may be optimal to exert the control at an infinite rate at discrete selected times.

The idea of an infinite value for the control may seem puzzling at first, and one may feel that it is unrealistic. In many situations, however, we would like to have the ability to change the state very quickly in relation to the usual time scale of the problem. For example, the time it takes to cut down a timber stand may be very small in relation to the time it takes for the stand to grow to harvestable size. If the control is finite, the state cannot change quickly; essentially the size of the change in the state must be small if the time interval over which the change is measured is small. In such situations, allowing the rate of change in the state to become infinite allows us to change the state very quickly (instantaneously). Although this approach makes the mathematics somewhat more delicate, it also results in simple optimality conditions with intuitive economic interpretations.

We will only consider the single-state case in which the state variable is governed by

$$dS = [\mu(S) + x] \, dt + \sigma(S) \, dz$$

The control x is used to directly change the size of the state. The reward function takes the form $f_0(S) + f_1(S)x$. Thus far this is precisely the form of the bang-bang control discussed in section 10.2.3.[11] In the current context, however, the control is allowed to be unbounded above, below, or both. In addition, if the control is nonzero ($x \neq 0$), a fixed cost of $F \geq 0$ will be assessed.

With continuous time diffusion processes, which are very wiggly, any strategy that involves continuous readjustment of a state variable when there are fixed costs would become infinitely expensive and could not be optimal. Instead, the optimal strategy is to change the state instantly in discrete amounts, thereby incurring the fixed costs only at isolated points in time.

To determine the reward generated by such a strategy, we examine the total reward over time interval Δ using a control that is inversely proportional to Δ ($x = h/\Delta$) and then take limits as $\Delta \to 0$. Ignoring the random component, which is negligible for small Δ, the

---

11. In the general bang-bang problem, the state dynamics are given by

$$dS = [g_0(S) + g_1(S)x] \, dt + \sigma(S) \, dz$$

For g_1 bounded away from 0, however, we can redefine the control as $\tilde{x} = x/g_1(S)$, with the reward given by $f_0(S) + f_1(S)/g_1(S)\tilde{x}$ to put it in the standard format.

change in the state is

$$\Delta S = \int_0^\Delta \mu(S_\tau) + \frac{h}{\Delta} \tau \, d\tau = \int_0^\Delta \mu(S_\tau) \, d\tau + h$$

As $\Delta \to 0$, the first term goes to 0 and so $\Delta S = h$.

The reward over a time interval Δ is

$$\int_0^\Delta f_0 \left(S + \frac{\Delta S}{\Delta} \tau \right) + f_1 \left(S + \frac{\Delta S}{\Delta} \tau \right) \frac{\Delta S}{\Delta} \, d\tau$$

Using the change of variables $x = S + \frac{\Delta S}{\Delta} t$ and letting $S_0 = S$ and $S_1 = S + \Delta S$, this expression is equal to

$$\frac{\Delta}{\Delta S} \int_{S_0}^{S_1} f_0(x) \, dx + \int_{S_0}^{S_1} f_1(x) \, dx$$

which has a limit as $\Delta \to 0$ of[12]

$$R(S_0, S_1) = \int_{S_0}^{S_1} f_1(x) \, dx \tag{10.23}$$

To illustrate with a common example, if the incremental reward function is $f_1(S) = (p - c/S)$, the discrete reward function is $R(S_0, S_1) = p(S_1 - S_0) - c[\ln(S_1) - \ln(S_0)]$.

With impulse control, the state is reset to a new position (a target) whenever a trigger is reached. It may be the case that either or both the trigger and target points are choice variables and hence are endogenous to the problem. For example, in a cash management situation, a bank manager must determine when there is enough cash on hand (the trigger) to warrant investing some of the cash in an interest-bearing account and must also decide how much cash to retain (the target). Alternatively, in an inventory-replacement problem, an inventory is restocked when it drops to zero (the trigger), but the restocking level (the target) must be determined (restocking occurs instantaneously, so there is no reason not to let inventory fall to zero). A third possibility arises in an asset replacement problem, where the age at which an old machine is replaced by a new one must be determined (the trigger), but the target is known (a new asset has age zero).

---

12. Some treatments of impulse control take the reward function $R(S_0, S_1)$ as primitive, often taking the form $R(S_1 - S_0)$. Some of our examples will have this feature. In general we require that $R(S, S) = 0$ and $R_{S_0}(S, S) = -R_{S_1}(S, S)$ for all S. The former says that the reward when $x = 0$ is 0, the latter says that the difference in the reward of going from $S + h$ to S and from S to $S - h$ is negligible as h gets small, as is the difference between the rewards for a movement from S to $S + h$ and from $S - h$ to S.

In any impulse control problem, a Feynman-Kac equation governs the behavior of the value function on the region where control is not being exerted ($x = 0$). In addition, at a trigger, a value-matching condition equates the value function at the trigger point with the value at the target point plus the net reward generated by the jump. Furthermore, if the trigger is subject to choice, an optimality condition is imposed that the marginal value of changing the state is equal to the marginal reward of making the change. A similar optimality condition holds at the target point if it is subject to choice.

In general, the value function satisfies the Feynman-Kac equation

$$\rho V(S) = f_0(S) + \mu(S)V'(S) + \tfrac{1}{2}\sigma^2(S)V''(S)$$

for $S \in [a, b]$. This is a linear-differential equation, which has a solution of the form

$$V(S) = V_0(S) + \alpha_1 V_1(S) + \alpha_2 V_1(S)$$

where α_1 and α_2 are constants to be determined by the choice of targets and triggers.

For any choice of targets and triggers, even if suboptimal, it must be true that the value before an action is taken is equal to the total reward from taking the action plus the value in the state after the action is taken, so $V(S)$ must satisfy the value-matching condition

$$V(S_0) = R(S_0, S_1) - F + V(S_1)$$

To determine the optimal control rule, as we did in section 10.4, define a function $U(S; S_0, S_1)$ that satisfies the Feynman-Kac equations and the value-matching conditions, such that

$$V(S) = \max_{S_0, S_1} U(S; S_0, S_1)$$

The first-order conditions are

$$U_{S_0}(S; S_0, S_1) = 0$$

and

$$U_{S_1}(S; S_0, S_1) = 0$$

These must hold for any S, so they hold specifically for $S = S_0$ and $S = S_1$. Totally differentiating the value-matching condition with respect to S_0 and S_1, we see that, for arbitrary choice of S_0 and S_1,

$$U_S(S_0; S_0, S_1) + U_{S_0}(S_0; S_0, S_1) - R_{S_0}(S_0, S_1) - U_{S_0}(S_1; S_0, S_1) = 0$$

and

$$U_{S_1}(S_0; S_0, S_1) - R_{S_1}(S_0, S_1) - U_S(S_1; S_0, S_1) - U_{S_1}(S_1; S_0, S_1) = 0$$

Combining these with the first-order conditions yields the following necessary conditions for the optimal choice of S_0 and S_1:

$$V'(S_0) = R_{S_0}(S_0, S_1)$$

and

$$V'(S_1) = -R_{S_1}(S_0, S_1)$$

These conditions are often referred to as smooth-pasting conditions, although this is something of a misnomer. In particular, it is not generally true that the marginal values at the trigger and the target are equal, because, in general, $R_{S_0}(S_0, S_1) \neq -R_{S_1}(S_0, S_1)$. A case in point is the example given earlier of $R(S_0, S_1) = p(S_1 - S_0) - c[\ln(S_1) - \ln(S_0)]$. Equality of marginal values will hold, however, in the special case that R has the form $R(S_1 - S_0)$.

In many applications it is useful to distinguish between the rewards and costs associated with positive and negative shifts in the state. We will therefore denote the reward function

$$R(S_0, S_1) = \begin{cases} R^+(S_0, S_1) & \text{for } S_0 < S_1 \\ R^-(S_0, S_1) & \text{for } S_0 > S_1 \end{cases}$$

and

$$F = \begin{cases} F^+ & \text{for } S_0 < S_1 \\ F^- & \text{for } S_0 > S_1 \end{cases}$$

We assume that R has continuous second derivatives except possibly where $S_0 = S_1$, with appropriately defined one-sided derivatives at such points.

We now limit our discussion to situations in which the optimal control keeps the state within some interval $[a, b]$. If a is a trigger, when the state hits a, it is immediately increased to level A. If b is a trigger, when the state hits b, it is immediately decreased to level B. It is also possible that a and/or b are natural boundaries for the problem and that no control is exerted when the state hits these boundaries. In such cases the associated target levels (A and/or B) are undefined.[13]

For the control rule just described, $V(S)$ must satisfy the value-matching conditions

$$V(a) = R^+(a, A) - F^+ + V(A) \quad \text{if } a \text{ is a trigger}$$

---

13. If one of the endpoints is not a trigger, we need an additional boundary condition to uniquely solve the Feynman-Kac equation. In numerical approximations this condition can generally be ignored.

and

$$V(b) = R^-(b, B) - F^- + V(B) \quad \text{if } b \text{ is a trigger}$$

Depending on the nature of the problem, any one of the control parameters (a, A, B or b) can be a choice variable that must satisfy an optimality condition:

$$V'(a) = R^+_{S_0}(a, A) \qquad \text{if } a \text{ is a choice variable}$$

$$V'(A) = -R^+_{S_1}(a, A) \quad \text{if } A \text{ is a choice variable}$$

$$V'(B) = -R^-_{S_1}(b, B) \quad \text{if } B \text{ is a choice variable}$$

and

$$V'(b) = R^-_{S_0}(b, B) \qquad \text{if } b \text{ is a choice variable}$$

It is possible that the state is initially outside of the interval $[a, b]$. In this case, the control should be exerted to bring the state immediately to A, if $S < a$, or to B, if $S > b$. Notice that this control rule implies that

$$V(S) = \begin{cases} R^+(S, A) - F^+ + V(A) & \text{for } S < a \\ R^-(S, B) - F^- + V(B) & \text{for } S > b \end{cases}$$

It is clear from this expression that V is continuous with continuous first derivative at the boundary points a and b. In general, however, the second derivative is not continuous at these points.

If either of the fixed-cost terms F^+ and F^- is equal to zero, the value matching and optimality conditions require modification. It is intuitively reasonable that the size of the shift will decline as the fixed cost approaches 0. In the limit, the control is exerted just enough to keep the state at the trigger, and thus the value-matching condition is tautological and has no meaning. Consider, however, that a trigger at S^* and a target at $S^* + h$ must satisfy

$$V(S^*) = R(S^*, S^* + h) + V(S^* + h)$$

and therefore

$$\frac{V(S^* + h) - V(S^*)}{h} = \frac{-R(S^*, S^* + h)}{h}$$

Taking limits as $h \to 0$ and noting that $R(S, S) \equiv 0$ demonstrates that

$$V'(S^*) = -R_{S_1}(S^*, S^*)$$

Recalling that $R_{S_0}(S, S) = -R_{S_1}(S, S)$, this condition can also be written

$$V'(S^*) = R_{S_0}(S^*, S^*)$$

It is important to note that this condition is not an optimality condition but is a result of maintaining the value-matching condition as the trigger and target approach one another. The relevant optimality condition can be obtained, as before, by defining a function $U(S; S^*)$ that satisfies $U_S(S^*; S^*) = R_{S_0}(S^*, S^*)$ such that

$$V(S) = \max_{S^*} U(S; S^*)$$

The first-order condition is

$$U_{S^*}(S; S^*) = 0$$

The total derivative of $U_S(S^*; S^*) - R_{S_0}(S^*, S^*)$ with respect to S^* is

$$U_S(S^*; S^*) + U_{S^*}(S^*; S^*) - R_{S_0 S_0}(S^*, S^*) - R_{S_0 S_1}(S^*, S^*)$$

and is identically zero when the value-matching condition is met. Combined with the first-order condition for the maximum yields the (necessary) optimality condition

$$V''(S^*) = R_{S_0 S_0}(S^*, S^*) + R_{S_0 S_1}(S^*, S^*)$$

Summarizing, when $F = 0$, the side conditions at a trigger S^* are $V'(S^*) = R_{S_0}(S^*, S^*)$ for any trigger and $V''(S^*) = R_{S_0 S_0}(S^*, S^*) + R_{S_0 S_1}(S^*, S^*)$ for an optimal trigger. Notice that a reward function of the form $R(S_0, S_1) = \int_{S_0}^{S_1} f_1(S) \, dS$ implies that $R_{S_0 S_1} = 0$. However, a reward function of the form $R(S_0, S_1) = R(S_1 - S_0)$ implies that $R_{S_0 S_0} + R_{S_0 S_1} = 0$.

In many cases, the optimal control maintains the state in an interval $[a, b]$. If a is a trigger, when the state hits a, the control is exerted just enough to maintain the state at a. If b is a trigger, when the state hits b, the control is exerted just enough to maintain the state at b. It is also possible that a and/or b are natural boundaries for the problem and that no control is exerted when the state hits these boundaries. For the control rule just described, $V(S)$ must satisfy the value-matching conditions

$$V'(a) = R_{S_0}^+(a, a) \quad \text{if } a \text{ is a trigger}$$

and

$$V'(b) = R_{S_0}^-(b, b) \quad \text{if } b \text{ is a trigger}$$

Depending on the nature of the problem, either or both a and b can be choice variables that must satisfy an optimality condition:

$$V''(a) = R^+_{S_0 S_0}(a, a) + R^+_{S_0 S_1}(a, a) \quad \text{if } a \text{ is a choice variable}$$

and

$$V''(b) = R^-_{S_0 S_0}(b, b) + R^-_{S_0 S_1}(b, b) \quad \text{if } b \text{ is a choice variable}$$

The derivatives of R in these conditions are appropriately defined one-sided derivatives, because of the possible kink in R where $S_0 = S_1$.

It is possible that the state is initially outside the interval $[a, b]$. In this case, the control should be exerted to bring the state immediately to a, if $S < a$, or to b, if $S > b$. Notice that this control rule implies that

$$V(S) = \begin{cases} R^+(S, a) + V(a) & \text{for } S < a \\ R^-(S, b) + V(b) & \text{for } S > b \end{cases}$$

It is clear that this expression implies that V is continuous with continuous first derivative at the boundary points a and b. In general, however, the second derivative is not continuous at these points. For example, for $S > b$, the second derivative is $V''(S) = R^-_{S_0 S_0}(S, b)$, so the right-hand second derivative at b is $R^-_{S_0 S_0}(b, b)$. The left-hand second derivative at b, however, is $R^-_{S_0 S_0}(b, b) + R^-_{S_0 S_1}(b, b)$. Thus the second derivative is continuous at b only if the second cross partial of R is zero.

The limiting case of impulse control as fixed costs go to 0 has been called instantaneous control or barrier control. It can also be viewed as a limiting case of a bang-bang problem as the limits on the control variable become unbounded. To illustrate this point, consider a bang-bang problem with

$$f(S, x) = f_0(S) + f_1(S)x$$

and

$$dS = [\mu(S) + x]\, dt + \sigma(S)\, dW$$

and $x \in [0, \bar{x}]$. The Bellman equation is

$$\rho V(S) = \max_{x \in [0, \bar{x}]} \left\{ f_0(S) + f_1(S)x + [\mu(S) + x]V'(S) + \tfrac{1}{2}\sigma^2(S)V''(S) \right\}$$

The Karush-Kuhn-Tucker condition leads to the decision rule to set $x = \bar{x}$ if $f_1(S) + V'(S) > 0$ and set $x = 0$ if $f_1(S) + V'(S) < 0$. Suppose that there is a unique V and S^* at which $f_1(S^*) + V'(S^*) = 0$ such that

$$\rho V(S) = \begin{cases} f_0(S) + f_1(S)\bar{x} + [\mu(S) + \bar{x}]V'(S) + \frac{1}{2}\sigma^2(S)V''(S) & \text{for } S < S^* \\ f_0(S) + \mu(S)V'(S) + \frac{1}{2}\sigma^2(S)V''(S) & \text{for } S > S^* \end{cases}$$

For both conditions to hold at S^*, it must be true that $V''(S)$ is continuous at S^*. If we let $\bar{x}$ be infinite, it will be optimal to exert the control at an infinite rate whenever $S < S^*$, implying that it is optimal to move the state to S^* whenever $S < S^*$. Notice that this rule implies that, for $S < S^*$, $V(S) = R(S, S^*) + V(S^*)$, and hence that $V'(S) = R_{S_0}(S, S^*) = -f_1(S)$ and $V''(S) = R_{S_0 S_0}(S, S^*) = -f_1'(S)$. The continuity of the first and second derivatives, therefore, leads to the conditions that $V'(S^*) = R_{S_0}(S^*, S^*)$ and $V''(S^*) = R_{S_0 S_0}(S^*, S^*)$ given previously.

10.5.1 Asset Replacement

A firm must decide when to replace an asset that produces a physical output, $y(A)$, where A is the state variable representing the age of the asset. The asset's value depends on its age as well as the net price of the output P and the net cost of replacing the asset c.

This is a deterministic problem for which the state is governed by $dA = dt$. The reward function is $y(A)P$. Thus the Feynman-Kac equation is

$$\rho V(A) = y(A)P + V'(A)$$

This differential equation is solved on the range $A \in [0, A^*]$, where A^* is the optimal replacement age. The value $A = 0$ is a lower boundary point but it is not a trigger. The value A^*, however, is both a trigger and a choice parameter. The target associated with A^* is 0, which is not a choice variable.

There are, therefore, two side conditions on this problem. The value-matching condition is

$$V(A^*) = V(0) - c$$

The optimality (smooth-pasting) condition is

$$V'(A^*) = 0$$

It should be noted that the value function also is well defined for $A > A^*$. An asset older than A^* should always be immediately replaced. Hence, the value function is constant for $A \geq A^*$: $V(A) = V(A^*) = V(0) - c$. Notice that the value-matching and marginality conditions at A^* ensure that the value function is C^1 (a continuous function with continuous first derivative).

Before leaving the example, a potentially misleading interpretation should be discussed. Although it is not unusual to refer to $V(A)$ as the value of an age A asset, this usage is not quite correct. In fact, $V(A)$ represents the value of the current asset, together with the right to earn returns from future replacement assets. The current asset will be replaced at age A^* and has value equal to the discounted stream of returns it generates:

$$\int_0^{A^*-A} e^{-\rho t} P y(A+t) \, dt$$

but the value function is

$$V(A) = \int_0^{A^*-A} e^{-\rho t} P y(A+t) \, dt + e^{-\rho(A^*-A)} V(A^*)$$

Thus the asset at age A has value

$$V(A) - e^{-\rho(A^*-A)} V(A^*)$$

10.5.2   Timber Harvesting

A timber stand will be clear-cut on a date set by the manager. The stand is allowed to grow naturally at a biologically determined rate according to

$$dS = \alpha(m-S) \, dt + \sigma \sqrt{S} \, dz$$

The state variable here represents the biomass of the stand, and the parameter m represents a biological equilibrium point or carrying capacity. When the stand is cut, it is sold for a net return of PS. In addition, the manager incurs a cost of C to replant the stand, which now has size $S = 0$. The decision problem is to determine the optimal cutting and replanting stand size, using a discount rate of ρ.

As in the previous example, 0 is a boundary but not a trigger. The upper bound is both a trigger and a choice variable, and its target is 0. The value function satisfies the Feynman-Kac equation

$$\rho V = \alpha(m-S) V'(S) + \tfrac{1}{2}\sigma^2 S V''(S)$$

for $S \in [0, S^*]$, along with the value-matching condition

$$V(S^*) = V(0) + P S^* - C$$

The optimal choice of S^* additionally satisfies

$$V'(S^*) = P$$

If the stand starts at a size above S^*, it is optimal to cut and replant immediately. Clearly the marginal value of additional timber when $S > S^*$ is the net return from the immediate sale of an additional unit of timber. Hence, for $S > S^*$, $V(S) = V(S^*) + P(S - S^*)$ and $V'(S) = P$.

As in the previous example, the value function refers not to the value of the timber on the stand but rather to the right to cut the timber on the land in perpetuity.

10.5.3 Storage Management

A storage facility has a current stock of S units of a good. As orders are filled (or returns occur) the stock evolves according to

$$dS = \mu\, dt + \sigma\, dz$$

where $\mu < 0$. A flow of payments of kS is required to maintain the stocks. In addition, there is a restocking charge on new supplies of $P \Delta S + F$ (hence $R^+(S_0, S_0) = -(S_1 - S_0)P$ and $F^+ = F$).

The state lies on $[0, \infty)$, with a single nonchoice trigger at 0. The single-choice variable is the target S^* associated with the trigger at 0. For any choice of S^*, the value function satisfies the Feynman-Kac equation

$$\rho V(S) = -kS + \mu V'(K) + \tfrac{1}{2}\sigma^2 V''(S)$$

together with the value-matching condition $V(0) = V(S^*) - PS^* - F$. The optimal choice of S^* satisfies $V'(S^*) = P$.

10.5.4 Capacity Choice

A firm can install capital K to produce an output with a net return P. Capital produces $Q(K)$ units of output per unit of time, but the capital depreciates at rate δ. The firm wants to choose its rate of investment I to solve

$$V(K_t) = \max_{I_\tau} \int_t^\infty e^{-\rho\tau}[Pq(K_\tau) - CI_\tau]\, d\tau$$

subject to the state dynamics

$$dK = (I - \delta K)\, dt$$

and the constraint that $I \geq 0$. This is an infinite-horizon, deterministic control problem. The Bellman equation for this problem is

$$\rho V(K) = \max_I \{Pq(K) - CI + (I - \delta K)V'(K)\}$$

The Karush-Kuhn-Tucker condition associated with optimal I is

$$V'(K) - C \leq 0, \qquad I \geq 0, \qquad \text{and} \qquad [V'(K) - C]I = 0$$

This condition suggests that the rate of investment should be 0 when the marginal value of capital is less than C and that the rate should be sufficiently high (infinite) to ensure that the marginal value of capital never is greater than C.

We assume that capital exhibits positive but declining marginal productivity. The optimal control is specified by a value K^* such that investment is 0 when $K > K^*$ (implying low marginal value of capital) and is sufficiently high to ensure that K does not fall below K^*. If K starts below K^*, the investment policy is to invest at an infinite rate so as to move instantly to K^*, incurring a cost of $(K^* - K)C$ in the process. If K starts at K^*, the investment rate should be just sufficient to counteract the effect of depreciation.

In the impulse control framework we are interested in the value function on $[K^*, \infty)$. The upper bound is obviously not a trigger. The lower bound is both a trigger and a choice variable with associated $R^+ = -C$ and $F^+ = 0$. The value function satisfies the Feynman-Kac equation

$$\rho V(k) = Pq(K) - \delta V'(K)$$

and the marginality condition $V'(K^*) = C$. At the optimal choice of K^*, it also satisfies $V''(K^*) = 0$.

10.5.5 Cash Management

A firm maintains for transactions a cash account subject to random deposits and withdrawals. In the absence of active management the account is described by absolute Brownian motion

$$dS = \mu\, dt + \sigma\, dz$$

The manager must maintain a positive cash balance and can withdraw from or add to an interest-bearing account that pays interest rate r. Adding to the cash account incurs a transactions cost of $c^+ \Delta S + F^+$ as well as an opportunity cost equal to the present value of the forgone interest of $(r/\rho)\Delta S$, where ρ is the manager's discount rate. Withdrawing cash (putting it into the interest-bearing account) incurs a transactions cost of $c^- |\Delta S| + F^-$ as well as an opportunity "reward" of $(r/\rho)|\Delta S|$. In the notation of the general impulse control problem, $f(S) = 0$, $R^+(S_0, S_1) = (-r/\rho - c^+)(S_1 - S_0)$, and $R^- = (r/\rho - c^-)(S_0 - S_1)$. There are two triggers in this problem, 0 and b, and three choice variables, b, A, and B. The value function satisfies the Feynman-Kac equation

$$\rho V(S) = \mu V'(S) + \tfrac{1}{2}\sigma^2(S)V''(S)$$

on $[0, b]$, together with the value-matching conditions

$$V(0) = V(A) - A(c^+ + r/\rho) - F^+$$

and

$$V(b) = V(B) + (B - b)(c^- - r/\rho) - F^-$$

For the optimal choice of A, B, and b, $V'(A) = (r/\rho + c^+)$ and $V'(B) = V'(b) = (r/\rho - c^-)$.

Exercises

10.1. Suppose we take the instantaneous interest-rate process to be

$$dr = \kappa(\alpha - r)\,dt + \sigma\sqrt{r}\,dz$$

where κ, α, and σ are constants. Verify that the bond price takes the form

$$B(r, t, T) = A(t, T)\exp\bigl(-B(t, T)r\bigr)$$

with

$$A(\tau) = \left(\frac{2\gamma e^{(\gamma+\kappa)\tau/2}}{(\gamma + \kappa)(e^{\gamma\tau} - 1) + 2\gamma}\right)^{\psi}$$

and

$$B(\tau) = \frac{2(e^{\gamma\tau} - 1)}{(\gamma + \kappa)(e^{\gamma\tau} - 1) + 2\gamma}$$

In doing so, determine γ and ψ in terms of κ, α, and σ.

10.2. A futures contract maturing in τ periods on a commodity whose price is governed by

$$dS = \mu(S, t)\,dt + \sigma(S, t)\,dz$$

can be shown to satisfy

$$V_\tau(S, \tau) = [rS - \delta(S, t)]V_S(S, \tau) + \tfrac{1}{2}\sigma^2(S, t)V_{SS}(S, \tau)$$

subject to the boundary condition $V(S, 0) = S$. Here δ is interpreted as the convenience yield, that is, the flow of benefits that accrue to the holders of the commodity but not to the holders of a futures contract. Suppose that the volatility term is

$$\sigma(S, t) = \sigma S$$

In a single-factor model one assumes that δ is a function of S and t. Two common assumptions are

$$\delta(S,t) = \delta$$

and

$$\delta(S,t) = \delta S$$

In both cases the resulting V is linear in S. Derive explicit expressions for V given these two assumptions.

10.3. Continuing with the previous question, suppose that the convenience yield is

$$\delta(S,t) = \delta S$$

where δ is a stochastic mean-reverting process governed by

$$d\delta = \alpha(m - \delta)\, dt + \sigma_\delta\, dw$$

with $\mathrm{E}\, dz\, dw = \rho\sigma\sigma_\delta\, dt$. Furthermore, suppose that the market price of the convenience yield risk is a constant θ. Then the futures price solves

$$V_\tau = (r - \delta)SV_S + [\alpha(m - \delta) - \theta\sigma_\delta]\, V_\delta + \tfrac{1}{2}\sigma^2 S^2 V_{SS} + \rho\sigma\sigma_\delta S V_{S\delta} + \tfrac{1}{2}\sigma_\delta^2 V_{\delta\delta}$$

with $V(S, 0) = S$.

Verify that the solution has the form $V = \exp(A(\tau) - B(\tau)\delta)S$ and in doing so derive expressions for $A(\tau)$ and $B(\tau)$.

10.4. Consider the case where S evolves according to a geometric Brownian motion (the assumption made to derive the Black-Scholes formula). Show that an average strike option can be expressed in the form $V(S, C, t) = Cv(y, \tau)$ where $y = S/C$ and $\tau = T - t$. In doing so, provide a PDE for v along with the relevant boundary condition for $\tau = 0$ (assume that the averaging begins at time $t = T - L$).

10.5. The value of the usual fixed-strike Asian option is not proportional to C, and, in fact, no explicit solution exists. An explicit solution does exist, however, for the fixed-strike Asian option when the average is defined as $\exp(\int_0^T \ln S\, dt/T)$ (geometric average). Find this solution.

10.6. Suppose the risk-neutral process associated with a stock price follows

$$dS = (r - \delta)S\, dt + \sigma S\, dW$$

and let

$$M_t = \max_{\tau \in [0,t]} S_\tau$$

Show that a lookback strike put option can be written in the form

$$V(S, M, t) = Sv(y, t)$$

where $y = M/S$. Derive the PDE and boundary conditions satisfied by v.

10.7. For the renewable resource management example of section 10.3.3, determine the explicit solutions when $\gamma = 1 + \beta$ and $\eta = 1/(1 + \beta)$ for $\beta = 1$, $\beta = 0$, and $\beta = -1/2$.

10.8. In the growth model of section 10.3.4, the optimal control is ρK, implying that the value function can be written as

$$V(K, Y) = E_0 \left[\int_0^\infty e^{-\rho t} \ln(\rho K_t) \, dt \right] = \frac{\ln(\rho)}{\rho} + \int_0^\infty e^{-\rho t} E_0 \left[\ln(K_t) \right] \, dt \qquad (10.24)$$

Obtain an expression for the time path of $E[\ln(K)]$, and use it to verify that the value function given in the text equals equation (10.24).

10.9. For the portfolio choice problem of section 10.3.5, show that a utility function of the form $u(C) = (C^{1-\gamma})/(1 - \gamma)$ implies an optimal consumption rule of the form $C(W) = aW$. Determine the constant a, and, in the process, determine the value function and the optimal investment rule $\alpha(W)$.

10.10. Suppose that, in addition to n risky assets, there is also a risk-free asset that earns rate of return r. The controls for the investor's problem are again C, the consumption rate, and the n-vector w, the fractions of wealth held in the risky assets. The fraction of wealth held in the riskless asset is $1 - \sum_i w_i = 1 - w^\top \underline{1}$.

a. Show that the wealth process can be written as follows:

$$\frac{dW}{W} = \{W[r + w^\top(\mu - r\underline{1})] - C\} \, dt + w^\top \sigma \, dz$$

b. Write the Bellman equation for this problem and the associated first-order condition.

c. Show that it is optimal to hold a portfolio consisting of the risk-free asset and a mutual fund with weights proportional to $\Sigma^{-1}(\mu - r\underline{1})$.

d. Derive expressions for $w^\top(\mu - r\underline{1})$ and $w^\top \Sigma w$, and use them to concentrate the Bellman equation with respect to w.

e. Suppose that $u(C) = \frac{C^{1-\gamma}}{1-\gamma}$. Verify that the optimal consumption rate is proportional to the wealth level, and find the constant of proportionality.

10.11. Continuing the previous problem, define $\lambda(W) = -V'(W)/V''(W)$. Show that $C(W)$ and $\lambda(W)$ satisfy a system of first-order differential equations. Use this result to verify that C is affine in W and λ is a constant when $u(C) = -e^{-\gamma C}$.

10.12. Suppose that the resource stock discussed in section 10.3.1 evolves according to

$$dS = -x\,dt + \sigma S\,dz$$

Verify that the optimal control has the form

$$x(S) = \lambda S^{\beta}$$

and, in so doing, determine the values of λ and β. Also obtain an expression for the value function. You should check that your answer in the limiting case that $\sigma = 0$ is the same as that given on page 329.

10.13. As in the example of section 10.3.1, a resource is extracted at rate x, yielding a flow of returns $Ax^{1-\alpha}$. The stock of the resource is governed by $dS = -x\,dt$. Here, however, we treat A as a random shock process because of randomness in the price of the resource governed by

$$dA = \mu(A)\,dt + \sigma(A)\,dz$$

The firm would like to maximize the expected present value of returns to extraction, using a discount rate of ρ.

a. State the firm's optimization problem.

b. State the associated Bellman equation.

c. State the first-order optimality condition, and solve for the optimal extraction rate (as a function of the value function and its derivatives).

10.14. Recall the production with adjustment costs model of section 10.3.6 with the Bellman equation

$$\rho V = \max_{x} \left\{ pq - \frac{c}{2}q^2 - \frac{a}{2}x^2 + xV_q + \kappa(\alpha - p)V_p + \frac{\sigma^2 p^2}{2}V_{pp} \right\}$$

Show that the value function is quadratic in p and q, that is, that it can be written in the form

$$V(p,q) = b_0 + b_1 p + b_2 q + \tfrac{1}{2}C_{11}p^2 + C_{12}pq + \tfrac{1}{2}C_{22}q^2$$

and determine the values of the coefficients b_0, b_1, b_2, C_{11}, C_{12}, and C_{22}.

10.15. A government timber lease allows a timber company to cut timber for T years on a stand with B units of biomass. The price of cut timber is governed by

$$dp = \alpha(\bar{p} - p)\,dt + \sigma\sqrt{p}\,dW$$

If the cutting rate is x and the cutting cost is $Cx^2/2$, discuss how the company can decide what to pay for the lease, given a current price of p and a discount rate of ρ (assume that the company sells timber as it is cut).

Hint: Introduce a remaining stand size, S, with $dS = -x\,dt$ (S is bounded below by 0), and set up the dynamic programming problem.

10.16. Suppose that the timber-harvesting problem discussed in section 10.5.2 is non-stochastic. The Bellman equation can then be rewritten in the form

$$V' = \frac{\rho}{\alpha}\frac{V}{m - S}$$

Verify that the solution is of the form

$$V = k(m - S)^{-\rho/\alpha}$$

where k is a constant of integration to be determined by the boundary conditions. There are two unknowns to be determined, k and S^*. Solve for k in terms of S^*, and derive an optimality condition for S^* as a function of parameters.

10.17. A monopolist manager of a fishery faces a state-transition function

$$dS = [\alpha S(1 - S) - x]\,dt + \sigma S\,dz$$

where S is the stock of fish, x is the harvest rate, and α and σ are constants. The price p is constant, and the cost function has a constant marginal cost that is inversely proportional to the stock level (c/S). In addition, a fixed cost F is incurred if any fishing activity takes place. The reward function can thus be written

$$\left(p - \frac{c}{S}\right)x - F\delta_{x>0}$$

This is an impulse-control problem with two endogenous values of the state, Q and R, with $Q < R$. When $S \geq R$, the stock of fish is harvested down to Q. Express the Feynman-Kac equation for $S \leq R$ and the boundary conditions that determine the location of Q and R (assume a discount rate of ρ).

10.18. Consider an investment situation in which a firm can add to its capital stock K at a cost of C per unit. The capital produces output at rate $q(K)$, and the net return on that output is P. Hence the reward function facing the firm is

$$f(K, P, I) = Pq(K) - CI$$

K is clearly a controllable state, with

$$dK = I\,dt$$

The variable P, however, is stochastic and is assumed to be governed by

$$dP = \mu P\,dt + \sigma P\,dz$$

(geometric Brownian motion). Using a discount rate of ρ, the Bellman equation for this problem is

$$\rho V(K, P) = \max_{I \geq 0} \left\{ Pq(K) - CI + IV_K(K, P) + \mu PV_P(K, P) + \tfrac{1}{2}\sigma^2 P^2 V_{PP}(K, P) \right\}$$

There are, however, no constraints on how fast the firm can add capital, and hence it is reasonable to suppose that, when it invests, it does so at an infinite rate, thereby keeping its investment costs to a minimum.

The optimal policy, therefore, is to add capital whenever the price is high enough and to do so in such a way that the capital stock price remains on or above a curve $K^*(P)$. If $K > K^*(P)$, no investment takes place, and the value function therefore satisfies

$$\rho V(K, P) = Pq(K) + \mu PV_P(K, P) + \tfrac{1}{2}\sigma^2 P^2 V_{PP}(K, P)$$

This is a simpler expression because, for a given K, it can be solved more or less directly. It is easily verified that the solution has the form

$$V(K, P) = A_1(K)P^{\beta_1} + A_2(K)P^{\beta_2} + \frac{Pq(K)}{\rho - \mu}$$

where the β_i solves $\tfrac{1}{2}\sigma^2\beta(\beta - 1) + \mu\beta - \rho = 0$. It can be shown, for $\rho > \mu > 0$, that $\beta_2 < 0$ and $1 < \beta_1$. For the assumed process for P, 0 is an absorbing barrier, so the term associated with the negative root must be forced to equal zero by setting $A_2(K) = 0$ (we can drop the subscripts on $A_1(K)$ and β_1).

At the barrier, the marginal value of capital must just equal the investment cost:

$$V_K(K^*(P), P) = C \tag{10.25}$$

Consider now the situation in which the firm finds itself with $K < K^*(P)$ (for whatever reason). The optimal policy is immediately to invest enough to bring the capital stock to the barrier. The value of the firm for states below the barrier, therefore, is equal to the value at the barrier (for the same P) less the cost of the new capital:

$$V(K, P) = V(K^*(P), P) - [K^*(P) - K]C$$

This expression suggests that the marginal value of capital equals C when $K < K^*(P)$ and hence does not depend on the current price. Thus, in addition to condition (10.25), it must be the case that

$$V_{KP}(K^*(P), P) = 0 \tag{10.26}$$

Use the barrier conditions (10.25) and (10.26) to obtain explicit expressions for the optimal trigger price $P^*(K)$ and the marginal value of capital, $A'(K)$. Notice that to determine $A(K)$ and therefore to completely determine the value function, we must solve a differential equation. The optimal policy, however, does not depend on knowing V, and, furthermore, we have enough information now to determine the marginal value of capital for any value of the state (K, P).

Write a program to compute and plot the optimal trigger price curve using the parameters $\mu = 0, \sigma = 0.2, \rho = 0.05$, and $c = 1$ and the following two alternative specifications for $q(K)$:

$$q(K) = \ln(K + 1)$$

$$q(K) = \sqrt{K}$$

10.19. In the cash management problem (section 10.5.5), the value function can be solved explicitly:

$$V(S) = c_1 \exp(\alpha_1 S) + c_2 \exp(\alpha_2 S)$$

where the α_i are chosen to satisfy the Feynman-Kac equation and the c_i are chosen to satisfy the value-matching conditions.

For a given control rule (i.e., a choice of A, B, and b) and value of the parameters, provide explicit expressions for the α_i and c_i.

10.20. The entry-exit problem discussed in section 10.4.3 can be extended to allow for temporary suspension of production. Suppose that a maintenance fee of m is needed to keep equipment potentially operative. In the simple entry/exit problem there were two switching costs, I and E. Now there are six possible switching costs, which will generically be called F^{ij}. With $\delta = 1$ representing the active production state, $\delta = 2$ the temporarily suspended state, and $\delta = 3$ the exited state, define the Feynman-Kac equations and boundary conditions satisfied by the solution.

10.21. The demand for a nonrenewable resource is given by

$$p = D(q) = q^{-\eta}$$

where q is the extraction rate. For simplicity, assume the resource can be extracted at zero cost. The total stock of the resource is denoted by S (with $S(0) = S_0$) and is governed by the transition function

$$dS = -q\,dt$$

a. For the social planner's problem, with the reward function being the social surplus, state the Bellman equation and the optimality condition, using discount rate ρ. Use the optimality condition to find the concentrated Bellman equation.

b. Guess that $V(S) = \alpha S^{\beta}$. Verify that this guess is correct and, in doing so, determine α and β.

c. Determine the time value T at which the resource is exhausted.

d. Solve the problem using an optimal control (Hamiltonian) approach and verify that the solutions are the same (see Appendix 10A for a discussion of optimal control theory).

10.22. Consider an extension to the renewable resource problem discussed in section 10.3.7. Suppose that the harvest rate is still constrained to lie on $[0, H]$ but that it cannot be adjusted instantaneously. Instead, assume that the rate of adjustment in the harvest rate, x, must lie on $[a, b]$, with $a < 0 < b$, with the proviso that $x \geq 0$ if $h = 0$ and $x \leq 0$ if $h = H$.

This problem can be addressed by defining h to be a second state variable with a deterministic state-transition equation:

$$dh = x\,dt$$

The optimal control for this problem is defined by two regions, one in which $x = a$ and one in which $x = b$. The boundary between these regions is a curve in the space $[0, \infty) \times [0, H]$.

Write the Feynman-Kac equations that must be satisfied by the value functions in each region and the value-matching and smooth-pasting conditions that must hold at the boundaries.

10.23. Consider a situation in which an agent has an inventory of S_0 units of a good in inventory, all of which must be sold within T periods. It costs k dollars per unit of inventory per period to store the good. In this problem there is a single control, the sales rate q, and two state variables, the price P and the inventory level S. The price is an exogenously given Ito process:

$$dP = \mu(P, t)\,dt + \sigma(P, t)\,dz$$

The amount in storage evolves according to

$$dS = -q\,dt$$

Furthermore, it is assumed that both the state and the control must be nonnegative because the agent cannot purchase additional amounts to replenish the inventory. Hence, sales are irreversible.

The problem can be written as

$$V(S_0, P_0, 0) = \max_{q(\cdot,\cdot,\cdot)\geq 0} E_0 \left[\int_0^T e^{-r\tau} \left(q(S_t, P_t, t)P_t - kS_t \right) dt \right].$$

subject to the state transition equations.

What is the Bellman equation for this problem? Treat the problem as an optimal stopping problem so $q = 0$ when the price is low and $q = \infty$ when the price is high. At or above the stopping boundary all inventory is sold instantaneously. State the Feynman-Kac equations for the regions above and below the stopping boundary. State the value-matching and smooth-pasting conditions that hold at the boundary.

10.24. Suppose in the sequential learning problem of section 10.3.8 that the price is deterministic ($\sigma = 0$), that $x_c = 1$ and that $r \geq \delta$. In this case, once production is initiated, it is never stopped. Use this fact to derive an explicit expression for $V(P, Q)$, where $P \geq P^*(Q)$. In this case, because production occurs at all times,

$$V(P, Q) = \int_0^\infty e^{-r\tau}[P_\tau - C(Q_\tau)]\,d\tau$$

where P_t solves the homogeneous first-order differential equation

$$\frac{dP_t}{dt} = (r - \delta)P$$

and

$$\int_0^\infty e^{-r\tau} C(Q_\tau)\,d\tau = \int_0^{Q_m-Q} e^{-r\tau} C(Q_\tau - Q)\,d\tau + \bar{c} \int_{Q_m-Q}^\infty e^{-r\tau}\,d\tau$$

Also show that, for $P < P^*$, the value function can be written in the form

$$V(P, Q) = f\left(P, P^*(Q)\right) V\left(P^*(Q), Q\right)$$

Combining these two results, determine the optimal activation boundary in the deterministic case. Verify that your answer satisfies the Bellman equation.

Appendix 10A: Dynamic Programming and Optimal Control Theory

Many economists are more familiar with optimal control theory than with dynamic programming. This appendix provides a brief discussion of the relationship between the two approaches to solving dynamic optimization problems. As stated previously, optimal-control theory is not naturally applied to stochastic problems, but it is used extensively in deterministic ones.

Consider the Bellman equation in the deterministic case:

$$\rho V = \max_x \{ f(S, x) + V_t + g(S, x) V_S \}$$

Suppose we totally differentiate the marginal value function with respect to time:

$$\frac{dV_S}{dt} = V_{St} + V_{SS} \frac{dS}{dt} = V_{St} + V_{SS} g(S, x)$$

Now apply the envelope theorem to the Bellman equation to determine that

$$\rho V_S = f_S(S, x) + V_{tS} + g(S, x) V_{SS} + V_S g_S(S, x)$$

Combining these expressions and rearranging yields

$$\frac{dV_S}{dt} = \rho V_S - f_S - V_S g_S \qquad (10.27)$$

This expression can be put in a more familiar form by defining $\lambda = V_S$. Then equation (10.27), combined with the first-order conditions for the maximization problem and the state-transition equation, can be written as the following system:

$$0 = f_x(S, x) + \lambda g_x(S, x)$$

$$\frac{d\lambda}{dt} = \rho \lambda - f_S(S, x) - \lambda g_S(S, x)$$

and

$$\frac{dS}{dt} = g(S, x)$$

These relationships are recognizable as the Hamiltonian conditions from optimal control theory, with λ, the costate variable, representing the shadow price of the state variable (expressed in current-value terms).[14]

---

14. See Kamien and Schwartz (1981, pp. 151–152) for further discussion.

The message here is that dynamic programming and optimal control theory are just two approaches to arrive at the same solution. It is important to recognize the distinction between the two approaches, however. Optimal-control theory leads to three equations, two of which are ordinary differential equations in time. Optimal control theory, therefore, leads to expressions for the time paths of the state, control, and costate variables as functions of time: $S(t)$, $x(t)$, and $\lambda(t)$. Dynamic programming leads to expressions for the control and the value function (or its derivative, the costate variable) as functions of time and the state. Thus dynamic programming leads to decision rules rather than time paths. In the stochastic case, it is precisely the decision rules that are of interest, because the future time path, even when the optimal control is used, will always be uncertain. For deterministic problems, however, dynamic programming involves solving partial differential equations, which tend to present more challenges than ordinary differential equations.

Bibliographic Notes

Arbitrage methods for solving financial asset pricing problems originated with Black and Scholes (1973) and Merton (1973). The literature is now vast. A good introductory-level discussion in found in Hull (2000). For a more challenging discussion, see Duffie (1996). The mathematical foundations for modern asset pricing theory are discussed at an introductory level in Hull (2000) and Neftci (1996). See also Shimko (1992). The stochastic volatility model of section 10.1.3 is due to Heston (1993).

Discussions of exotic option pricing models are found in Hull (2000) and Wilmott (1998). Goldman, Sosin, and Gatto (1979) contains the original derivation of the boundary condition for lookback options. Vasicek (1977) and Longstaff and Schwartz (1992) originated the models discussed in section 10.1.5. More general discussions of affine diffusion models are found in Duffie and Kan (1996), Dai and Singleton (2000), and Fackler (2000).

Introductory-level treatments of stochastic control problems are available in Dixit (1993a) and Dixit and Pindyck (1994). These books contain numerous examples as well as links to other references. A more rigorous treatment in found in Fleming and Rishel (1975). Boundary conditions associated with stochastic processes are discussed by Feller (1951), who devised a classification scheme for diffusion processes with singular boundaries (see discussion by Bharucha-Reid, 1960, sec. 3.3, and Karlin and Taylor, 1981, Chap. 15).

Kamien and Schwartz (1981) is a classic text on solving dynamic optimization problems in economics; its primary focus is on deterministic problems solved using calculus of variations and Hamiltonian methods, but it contains a brief treatment of dynamic programming and control of Ito processes (Chapters 20 and 21). Other useful treatments of deterministic problems are found in Dorfman (1969) and Chiang (1999). Malliaris and Brock (1982) contains an overview of Ito processes and stochastic control, with numerous examples in economics and finance. Duffie (1996) contains a brief introductory treatment of stochastic control, with a detailed discussion of the portfolio-choice problem first posed in Merton (1969, 1971).

Free-boundary problems are increasingly common in economics. Dixit (1991, 1993a) and Dixit and Pindyck (1994) contain useful discussions of these problems. Several of the examples are discussed in these sources. Dixit (1993b) provides a good introduction to stochastic control, with an emphasis on free-boundary problems. Our discussion of impulse control draws on Dumas (1991); see also the articles in Lund and Oksendal (1991). Hoffman and Sprekels (1990) and Antonsev, Hoffman, and Khludnev (1992) are proceedings of conferences on free-boundary problems with an emphasis on problems arising in physical sciences.

The renewable resource harvesting problem is from Pindyck (1984), optimal growth with a technology shock from Cox, Ingersoll, and Ross (1985), portfolio choice from Merton (1969, 1971). The original solution to the timber-harvesting problem with replanting is attributed to Martin Faustmann, who discussed it in an article published in 1849. For further discussion see Gaffney (1960) and Hershleifer (1970). Recently, Willassen (1998) discussed the stochastic version of the problem. The entry-exit example originates with Brennan and Schwartz (1985) and McDonald and Siegel (1985). Numerous authors have discussed renewable resource management problems; see especially Mangel (1985). The stochastic bang-bang problem is discussed most fully in Ludwig (1979a) and Ludwig and Varrah (1979), where detailed proofs and a discussion of a multiple-switch-point situation can be found. Exercise 10.22 is due to Ludwig (1979b). The sequential learning example is from Majd and Pindyck (1987) and is also discussed in Dixit and Pindyck (1994).

11 Continuous Time Models: Solution Methods

In the previous chapter we saw how continuous-time economic models, whether deterministic or stochastic, result in economic processes that satisfy differential equations. Ordinary differential equations (ODEs) arise in infinite horizon single-state models or in deterministic problems when the time path of the solution is desired. Partial differential equations (PDEs) arise in models with multiple state variables or in finite horizon problems. From a numerical point of view, the distinction between ODEs and PDEs is less important than the distinction between problems that can be solved in a recursive or evolutionary fashion and those that require the entire solution to be computed simultaneously because the solution at any particular point (in time or space) depends on the solution everywhere else. This is the distinction between initial value problems (IVPs) and boundary value problems (BVPs) discussed in sections 5.7 and 6.9. With an IVP, the solution is known at some point, and the solution near this point can then be (approximately) determined. From this new point the solution at still another point can be approximated and so forth. When possible, it is usually faster to use such recursive solution techniques.

Numerous methods have been developed for solving PDEs. We concentrate on an approach that encompasses a number of the more common methods and that builds nicely on the material already covered in this book. Specifically, the true but unknown solution will be replaced with a convenient approximating function, the parameters of which will be determined using collocation. For initial value problems, this approach will be combined with a recursive algorithm. We will also discuss free-boundary problems that arise in some control problems. The free boundary is an endogenously determined point or set of points at which some discrete action occurs. The basic approach to such problems is to solve the model taking the free boundary as given and then use optimality conditions to identify the location of the boundary.

There are a number of methods for solving PDEs and stochastic control problems that we do not discuss here. These include binary and trinomial tree methods, simulation methods, and methods that discretize control problems and solve the related discrete problem. Although all these methods have their place, we feel that providing a general framework that works to solve a wide variety of problems and builds on general methods developed in previous chapters is of more value than an encyclopedic account of existing approaches. Much of what is discussed here should look and feel familiar to readers who have persevered up to this point.[1] We do, however, include references to other approaches in the bibliographical notes at the end of the chapter.

---

1. It would be useful to at least be familiar with the material in Chapter 6.

11.1   Solving Arbitrage Valuation Problems

In the previous chapter it was shown that financial assets often satisfy an arbitrage condition in the form of second-order partial differential equation (PDE). For expositional simplicity, the single-state variable case with no payment flows (dividends) is discussed here, and the general case is discussed in section 11.1.2. In the simplest case of an asset that pays the state-dependent amount $R(S)$ at time T, the arbitrage PDE is

$$r(S)V = V_t + \mu(S)V_S + \tfrac{1}{2}\sigma^2(S)V_{SS}$$

along with the boundary condition $V(S, T) = R(S)$. For zero-coupon default-free bonds the boundary condition is $R(S) = 1$. For European call options and European put options written on an underlying asset with price $p = P(S)$, the boundary conditions are, respectively, $R(S) = \max(0, P(S) - K)$, and $R(S) = \max(0, K - P(S))$, where K is the option's strike price. For futures prices on an asset with price $p = P(S)$, the boundary condition is $R(S) = P(S)$ with the discount rate $r(S) = 0$.

Asset pricing problems of this kind are more easily expressed in terms of time to maturity rather than calendar time; let $\tau = T - t$. We will work with $V(S, \tau)$ rather than $V(S, t)$, necessitating a change of sign of the time derivative: $V_\tau = -V_t$. This changes the terminal condition at $t = T$ into an initial condition at $\tau = 0$.

The problem, of course, is that the functional form of V is unknown. Suppose, however, that it is approximated with a function of the form $V(S, \tau) \approx \phi(S)c(\tau)$, where ϕ is a suitable basis for an n-dimensional family of approximating functions and $c(\tau)$ is an n-vector of time-varying coefficients. The arbitrage condition can be used to form a differential equation (in c) of the form

$$\phi(S)c'(\tau) \approx \left[\mu(S)\phi'(S) + \tfrac{1}{2}\sigma^2(S)\phi''(S) - r(S)\phi(S)\right]c(\tau) = \psi(S)c(\tau) \qquad (11.1)$$

A collocation approach to determining the $c(\tau)$ is to select a set of n values for S, s_i, and to solve equation (11.1) with equality at these values. The differential equation can then be written in the form

$$\Phi c'(\tau) = \Psi c(\tau) \qquad (11.2)$$

where Φ and Ψ are both $n \times n$ matrices. This is a first-order system of ordinary differential equations in τ, with the known solution expressed in terms of the matrix exponential function:

$$c(\tau) = \exp(\tau B)c_0 \qquad (11.3)$$

where $B = \Phi^{-1}\Psi$ and Φc_0 satisfies the boundary condition $R(S)$ evaluated at the n values of the s_i.[2]

11.1.1   A Simple Bond Pricing Model

The Cox-Ingersoll-Ross (CIR) bond pricing model assumes that the risk-neutral process for the short (instantaneous) interest rate is given by

$$dr = \kappa(\alpha - r)dt + \sigma\sqrt{r}dz$$

Expressing the value of a bond in terms of time to maturity (τ), a bond paying 1 unit of account at maturity, has value $V(r, \tau)$ that solves

$$V_\tau = \kappa(\alpha - r)V_r + \tfrac{1}{2}\sigma^2 r V_{rr} - rV$$

with initial condition $V(r, 0) = 1$.

To solve this model, first choose a family of approximating functions with basis $\phi(r)$ and n collocation nodes, r_i. Letting the basis functions and their first two derivatives at these points be defined as the $n \times n$ matrices Φ_0, Φ_1, and Φ_2, a system of collocation equations is given by

$$\Phi_0 c'(\tau) = \left[\kappa(\alpha - r)\Phi_1 + \tfrac{1}{2}\sigma^2 r \Phi_2 - r\Phi_0\right]c(\tau) = \Psi c(\tau) \tag{11.4}$$

The term $r\Phi_0$ is an abuse of notation; it indicates multiplying the $n \times 1$ vector r by an $n \times n$ matrix Φ_0. Such a term is more properly written as $\mathrm{diag}(r)\Phi_0$; the diag operator applied to a vector forms a diagonal matrix with diagonal elements equal to the elements of the vector. The same comments also apply to the first- and second-order terms.

To illustrate how this approach is implemented we provide a (rather specialized) solver to solve the CIR bond pricing model. The solver uses the syntax

```
function c=cirbond(fspace,tau,kappa,alpha,sigma)
```

The function's input arguments include a function definition structure `fspace` indicating the family of approximating functions desired, as well as the time to maturity τ and the model parameters κ, α, and σ. The procedure returns the coefficient vector c_τ.

---

2. Matrix exponentials satisfy the usual Taylor expansion:

$$\exp(A) = \sum_{i=0}^{\infty} \frac{A^i}{i!}$$

and can be computed using the MATLAB function `expm`.

The solver first gets the standard nodes and basis matrices associated with the `fspace` variable:

```
r = funnode(fspace);
Phi0 = funbas(fspace,r,0);
Phi1 = funbas(fspace,r,1);
Phi2 = funbas(fspace,r,2);
```

It then constructs the B matrix in equation (11.3):

```
n = size(r,1);
m = kappa*(alpha-r);
v = 0.5*sigma.^2*r;
B = spdiags(m,0,n,n)*Phi1+spdiags(v,0,n,n)*Phi2 ...
                       -spdiags(r,0,n,n)*Phi0
B = Phi0\B;
```

The expression diag(r)Φ (with r $n \times 1$ and Φ $n \times m$) can be obtained in MATLAB in several ways. The simplest is `diag(r)*Phi`. Sparse diagonalization can also be used: `spdiags(r,0,n,n)*Phi`. Despite the additional overhead used in indexing sparse matrices, `spdiags` is generally more efficient than `diag`, because less memory is used storing zeros and it avoids arithmetic with the off-diagonal zero values.[3]

The solver routine finishes by computing c_0 and solving for c in equation (11.3):

```
c0 = Phi0\ones(n,1);
c = expm(full(tau*B))*c0;
```

The `full` function is used because MATLAB's matrix exponential function `expm` requires that its argument be a full rather than a sparse matrix. Some basis functions (e.g., spline and piecewise linear) are stored as sparse matrices, so this approach ensures that the code will work regardless of the family of functions used. The solution function for a 30-year bond with parameter values $\kappa = 0.1$, $\alpha = 0.05$, and $\sigma = 0.1$ is plotted in Figure 11.1a, using a Chebychev polynomial approximation of degree $n = 20$ on the interval [0, 2].

---

3. Element-by-element multiplication can also be used:

```
r(:,ones(n,1)).*Phi0
```

This uses more memory than `spdiags` but does not perform the unnecessary arithmetic associated with the use of `diag`.

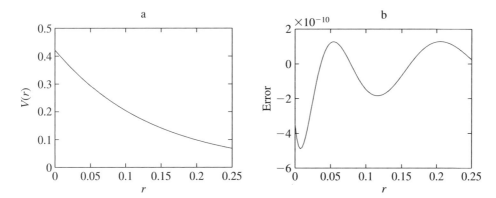

Figure 11.1
Solution of the CIR 30-Year Bond Pricing Model: (a) Bond Price; (b) Approximation Error

Before proceeding, it is important to point out that approximating functions typically require upper and lower bounds to be specified: $S \in [a, b]$. For the process used in the bond pricing example, a natural lower bound of $a = 0$ can be used. The upper bound is trickier, because the natural upper bound is ∞. Knowledge of the underlying nature of the problem, however, should suggest an upper bound for the rate of interest. We have used 2, which should more than suffice for countries that are not experiencing hyperinflation.

More generally, one should use an upper bound that ensures that the result is not sensitive to the choice in regions of the state space that are important. In practice, making this choice may necessitate some experimentation. A useful rule of thumb is that the computed value of $V(S)$ is not sensitive to the choice of b if the probability that $S_T = b$, given $S_t = S$, is negligible. For infinite horizon problems with steady-state probability distributions, one would like the steady-state probability at the boundaries to be negligible.

For this example, a known solution to the bond-pricing problem exists (see exercise 10.1 on page 358). The closed-form solution can be used to compute the approximation error function, which is shown in Figure 11.1b. The example uses a Chebychev polynomial basis of degree $n = 20$; it is evident that this is more than sufficient to obtain a high degree of accuracy.

11.1.2   More General Assets

The approach to solving the asset pricing problems just described replaces the original arbitrage condition with one of the form

$$c'(\tau) = Bc(\tau)$$

and imposes the boundary condition $\Phi c(0) = V_0$. For more general assets the arbitrage PDE takes the form

$$r(S)V = \delta(S) + V_t + V_S\mu(S) + \tfrac{1}{2}\text{trace}\!\left(\sigma(S)\sigma(S)^\top V_{SS}\right)$$

This expression allows for multivariate state processes and for a dividend flow term δ. Using the approximation $V(S, t) = \phi(S)c(t)$, this can be put into the form

$$\phi(S)c'(\tau) = \delta(S) + \psi(S)c(\tau)$$

where

$$\psi(S) = \sum_{i=1}^{d} \mu_i(S)\frac{\partial\phi(S)}{\partial S_i} + \frac{1}{2}\sum_{i=1}^{d}\sum_{j=1}^{d}\Sigma_{ij}(S)\frac{\partial^2\phi(S)}{\partial S_i\partial S_j} - r(S)\phi(S)$$

and

$$\Sigma_{ij}(S) = \sum_{k}\sigma_{ik}(S)\sigma_{jk}(S)$$

Evaluating this expression at n values of S and inverting the resulting $n \times n$ basis matrix Φ, this expression has the form

$$c'(\tau) = b + Bc(\tau) \tag{11.5}$$

which has the known solution

$$c(\tau) = e^{\tau B}\left[\int_0^\tau e^{-tB}dt\right]b + e^{\tau B}\Phi^{-1}V_0$$

If B is nonsingular this is equal to

$$c(\tau) = \left[e^{\tau B} - I\right]B^{-1}b + e^{\tau B}\Phi^{-1}V_0$$

For assets with limiting values as $\tau \to \infty$, the limiting value is given by $-B^{-1}b$.

The solution can be put into a recursive form appropriate for computing the solution at evenly spaced time intervals of size Δ:

$$c\big((i+1)\Delta\big) = e^{\Delta B}\left[\int_0^\Delta e^{-tB}dt\right]b + e^{\Delta B}c(i\Delta)$$

which has the form $c((i + 1)\Delta) = a + Ac(i\Delta)$ (if B is nonsingular, $a = [A - I]B^{-1}b$). The $n \times n$ matrix A and $n \times 1$ vector a need only be computed once, and the recursive relationship may then be used to compute solution values for a whole grid of evenly spaced values of τ.

In the preceding approach, the existence of a known solution to the collocation differential equation is due to the linearity of the arbitrage condition in V and its partial derivatives. If linearity does not hold, we can still express the system in the form $c'(t) = B(c(t))$, which can be solved using any convenient initial value solver such as the Runge-Kutta algorithm described in section 5.7 or any of the suite of MATLAB ODE solvers.

Transforming a PDE into a system of ODEs has been called the extended method of lines. The simple method of lines treats $\Phi = I_n$ and uses finite difference approximations for the first and second derivatives in S. The values contained in the $c(t)$ vector are then simply the n values of $V(s_i, t)$. The extended method of lines simply extends this approach by allowing for arbitrary basis functions. We should point out that the system of ODEs in the extended method of lines is often "stiff." This is a term that is difficult to define precisely, and a full discussion is beyond the scope of this book. Suffice it to say, a stiff ODE is one that operates on very different time scales. The practical import of "stiffness" is that ordinary evolutionary solvers such as Runge-Kutta and its refinements must take very small time steps to solve stiff problems. Fortunately, so-called implicit methods for solving stiff problems do exist.[4]

It is also possible to use finite difference approximations for the derivatives in τ; indeed, this is one of the most common approach to solving PDEs for financial assets. Expressed in terms of time to maturity (τ), a first-order approximation with a forward difference (in τ) leads to a basic valuation condition of the form

$$\phi(S)\frac{c(\tau + \Delta) - c(\tau)}{\Delta} = \delta(S) + \psi(S)c(\tau)$$

or, equivalently,

$$\phi(S)c(\tau + \Delta) = \Delta\delta(S) + [\phi(S) + \Delta\psi(S)]c(\tau)$$

Expressing this in terms of basis matrices evaluated at n values of S leads to

$$c(\tau + \Delta) = \Delta b + [I_n + \Delta B]c(\tau)$$

where b and B are the same as in equation (11.5). This expression provides an evolutionary rule for updating $c(\tau)$, given the initial values $c(0)$. The expression $[I_n + \Delta B]$ is a first-order Taylor approximation (in Δ) of $\exp(\Delta B)$, and ΔI is a first-order approximation to $(e^{\Delta B} - I)B^{-1}$. Hence the first-order differencing approach leads to errors of $O(\Delta^2)$.

---

4. MATLAB's ODE suite provides two stiff solvers, `ode15s` and `ode23s`.

A backward (in τ) differencing scheme can also be used

$$\phi(S)\frac{c(\tau) - c(\tau - \Delta)}{\Delta} = \delta(S) + \psi(S)c(\tau)$$

leading to

$$[I_n - \Delta B]c(\tau) = \Delta b + c(\tau - \Delta)$$

or

$$c(\tau + \Delta) = [I_n - \Delta B]^{-1}[\Delta b + c(\tau)]$$

$I_n - \Delta B$ is a first-order Taylor approximation (in Δ) of $\exp(-\Delta B)$, so this method also has errors of $O(\Delta^2)$.

Although it may seem like the forward and backward approaches are essentially the same, there are two significant differences. First, the backward approach defines $c(\tau)$ implicitly, and the update requires a linear solve using the matrix $[I_n - \Delta B]$. The forward approach is explicit and requires no linear solve.

More important is the fact that the explicit forward approach can be unstable. Both approaches replace the differential system of equations with a system of difference equations of the form

$$x_{\tau+\Delta} = a + Ax_\tau$$

It is well known that such a system is explosive if any of the eigenvalues of A are greater than 1 in absolute value.

In applications of the kind found in financial applications, the matrix $A = [I_n + \Delta B]$ can be assured of having small eigenvalues only by making Δ small enough. However, the implicit method leads to a difference equation for which $A = [I_n - \Delta B]^{-1}$, which can be shown to be stable for any Δ. Practically speaking, this result means that the explicit method may not be faster than the implicit method and may produce garbage if Δ is not chosen properly. If the matrix A is explosive, small errors in the approximation will be magnified as the recursion progresses, causing the computed solution to bear no resemblance to the true solution.

Another popular approach is derived by averaging the explicit and implicit approaches. Note that

$$\frac{c(\tau + \Delta) - c(\tau)}{\Delta} \approx b + \tfrac{1}{2}B[c(\tau + \Delta) + c(\tau)]$$

This expression leads to the recursion

$$c(\tau + \Delta) \approx \left[I - \frac{\Delta}{2}B\right]^{-1} b + \left[I - \frac{\Delta}{2}B\right]^{-1} \left[I + \frac{\Delta}{2}B\right] c(\tau)$$

When the approximating function is piecewise linear with finite-difference derivatives, the result is the so-called Crank-Nicholson method. An interesting fact is that the Crank-Nicholson approach provides a first-order Padé (rational) approximation to $\exp(\Delta B)$.[5]

11.1.3   An Asset Pricing Solver

Due to the common structure of the arbitrage pricing equation across a large class of financial assets, it is possible to write a general procedure for asset pricing. We provide such a procedure called `finsolve`, the input/output syntax for which is

```
function [c,V,A,a]=finsolve(model,fspace,alg,s,N)
```

The first input, `model`, is a structure variable with the following fields:

func	The name of the model function file
T	The time to maturity of the asset
params	A cell array of additional parameters to be passed to `model.func`

The second input is a function definition structure variable that defines the desired family of approximating functions. The remaining arguments are optional. The third argument `alg` defines which algorithm is used and can be one of `lines`, `explicit`, `implicit`, or `CN`. The default is `lines`. The fourth argument `s` is a set of nodal values of the state. If the state is multidimensional, this should be a cell array of vectors. The default is to use the standard nodes associated with `fspace` obtained by the command `s=funnode(fspace)`. The last argument `N` is the number of time steps taken, so the size of the time step is $\Delta = T/N$. The default number of steps is 1, but this is appropriate only if the method of lines is used.

A template for the function definition file is as follows:

```
out=func(flag,s,t,additional parameters);
switch flag
 case 'rho'
   out = instantaneous risk-free interest rate
 case 'mu'
```

---

5. The MATLAB function `expm` uses a sixth-order Padé approximation with rescaling (examine the function `expm1` for details). Typically, Padé approximations are more accurate than are Taylor approximations of the same order.

```
    out = drift on the state process
  case 'sigma'
    out = volatility on the state process
  case 'delta'
    out = the payout flow (dividend) on the derivative asset
  case 'V0'
    out = exercise value of the asset
end
```

The function uses the modified method of lines by default if `alg` is unspecified, but explicit (forward) or implicit (backward) finite differences can also be used to represent the derivative in τ by specifying the `alg` argument to be either `'implicit'` or `'explicit'`. The Crank-Nicholson method can also be obtained by specifying `'CN'`. A simplified version of the procedure, `finsolve1`, that allows one single-dimensional state processes is described in the following paragraphs.[6]

The first task after unpacking the elements of `model` is to compute the basis matrices:

```
n = fspace.n;
Phi0 = funbas(fspace,S,0);
Phi1 = funbas(fspace,S,1);
Phi2 = funbas(fspace,S,2);
```

and then to construct the matrix B

```
mu = feval(probfile,'mu',S,params{:});
sigma = feval(probfile,'sigma',S,params{:});
rho = feval(probfile,'rho',S,params{:});
v = 0.5*sigma.*sigma;
B = spdiags(mu,0,n,n)*Phi1+spdiags(v,0,n,n)*Phi2 ...
      -spdiags(rho,0,n,n)*Phi0;
Phii = inv(Phi0);
B = Phii*B;
```

The constant term b is then computed:

```
delta = feval(probfile,'delta',S,params{:});
hasdiv = ~isempty(delta);
if hasdiv, b = Phii*delta; end
```

---

6. For multidimensional states, the principles are the same, but the implementation is a bit messier. We discuss this topic in Appendix 11A.

If there is no dividend, the model function file can return an empty matrix when passed
the `delta` flag. We define a 0/1 variable `hasdiv`, which is set to 0 in this case. This
step will allow us to avoid unnecessary computations in the no-dividend case. Next the
differencing operator matrices a (if needed) and A are computed according to the requested
algorithm:

```
Delta = T/N;
switch alg
case 'lines'
  A = expm(full(Delta*B));
  if hasdiv, a = (A-speye(n))*(B\a); end
case 'explicit'
  A = speye(n)+Delta*B;
  if hasdiv, a = Delta*a;end
case 'implicit'
  A = full(inv(speye(n)-Delta*B));
  if hasdiv, a = A*(Delta*a);end
case 'CN'
  B = (Delta/2)*B;
  A = speye(n)-B;
  if hasdiv, a = A\(Delta*a); end
  A = full(A\(speye(n)+B));
otherwise
  error('Method option is invalid')
end
```

The code is completed by initializing the coefficient vector and then iterating over all the
time subintervals:

```
V0 = feval(probfile,'V0',S,params{:});
c = Phii*V0;
for i=2:N+1
  if hasdiv, c = a+A*c;
  else, c = A*c;
  end
end
```

This procedure results in an n-vector of coefficients that can be evaluated using `funeval(c,fspace,s)`.[7]

The MATLAB file `demfin01` optionally uses `finsolve` to solve the CIR bond-pricing example. Other examples of the use of this function follow.

11.1.4 Black-Scholes Option Pricing Formula

In section 10.1.2 the Black-Scholes option pricing formula was introduced. The assumption underlying this formula is that the price of a stock that pays dividends at rate $\delta_S S$ has risk-neutral dynamics given by[8]

$$dS = (r - \delta_S)Sdt + \sigma Sdz$$

The arbitrage condition is

$$V_\tau = (r - \delta_S)SV_S + \tfrac{1}{2}\sigma^2 S^2 V_{SS} - rV$$

with the initial condition $V(S, 0) = \max(S - K, 0)$ for a call option or $V(S, 0) = \max(K - S, 0)$ for a put option.

To use `finsolve` one must first create a model function file that specifies ρ, μ, σ, δ_S, and V_0. The model function file for this example follows:

```
function out=func(flag,S,t,r,deltaS,sigma,K,put);
switch flag
case 'rho'
  out = r+zeros(size(S,1),1);
case 'mu'
  out = (r-deltaS)*S;
case 'sigma'
  out = sigma;
case 'delta'
  out = [];
case 'V0'
  if put
    out = max(0,K-S);
```

---

7. The coefficients for every time step can be obtained by using the option `keepall` (`optset('finsolve','keepall',1)`). This returns an $n \times N + 1$ matrix with the first column representing the value of the asset at maturity and the last column representing the value of the asset with T periods until maturity.

8. This expression generalizes the model discussed in section 10.1.2 by allowing the stock to pay a continuous flow of proportional dividends.

```
  else
    out = max(0,S-K);
  end
end
```

Notice that the option pays no dividend, so an empty matrix is returned when the flag `delta` is passed.

The next step is to specify parameter values:

```
r       = 0.05;
deltaS = 0;
sigma  = 0.2;
K       = 1;
put     = 0;
T       = 1;
```

and define the structured variable `model`:

```
model.func = 'func';
model.T = T;
model.params = {r deltaS sigma K put};
```

The family of approximating functions is then defined:

```
n = 51;
fspace = fundefn('lin',n,0,2*K);
s = funnode(fspace);
```

Here we use the family of piecewise linear functions with finite-difference approximations for the derivatives (with prefix `lin`) with 51 evenly spaced nodes on $[0, 2K]$. Notice that this approach ensures that K is a node. Option pricing problems exhibit kinks in their initial (maturity date) conditions, so the family of piecewise linear functions is a good choice, and having K as a node ensures that the initial value can be represented exactly. In general, polynomial approximations perform poorly in option pricing problems. Piecewise linear functions or cubic splines, possibly with extra nodes at $S = K$, are preferable.

Finally, the solver is called:

```
c=finsolve(model,fspace,'lines',s,75);
```

The method of lines with 75 time steps is used. The `finsolve` function returns an n-vector of coefficients. The approximation can be evaluated at arbitrary values of S using `funeval(c,fspace,S)`. The delta and gamma of the option (the first and second derivatives with respect to S) can also be evaluated using `funeval`.

Table 11.1
Option Pricing Approximation Errors

| | Method | | | |
Function Family	Lines	Implicit	Explicit	CN
Piecewise-linear	0.000400	0.000283	0.000540	0.000400
Cubic spline	0.000217	0.000193	0.000335	0.000217

Maximum absolute errors on $[0, 2K]$.
Fifty-one nodes with 75 time steps (explicit cubic spline uses 250 time steps).

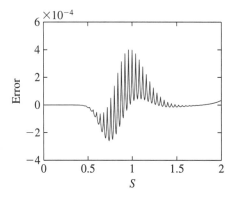

Figure 11.2
Black-Scholes Option Pricing Model: Approximation Error

As an explicit solution exists for this problem, we can plot the approximation errors produced by the method (the procedure bs is available in the CompEcon Toolbox).[9] These are shown in Figure 11.2. The maximum absolute error is 4×10^{-4}. It is simple to experiment with the alternate methods by changing the alg argument to the finsolve function. The family of approximating functions can also be changed easily by changing the input to the fundef function. The approximation errors in Table 11.1 were obtained in this manner.

The approximation errors for all these methods are roughly equivalent, with a slight preference for the cubic spline. Note, however, that the explicit approach using the cubic spline basis is explosive with fewer than 200 time steps, and the table gives approximation errors using 250 time steps. It should also be noted that a polynomial approximation does

9. The explicit solution requires that the Gaussian cumulative probability function be evaluated. Highly reliable code to perform this computation is readily available. The CompEcon Toolbox provides the function cdfn for this purpose.

a very poor job in this problem because of its inability to adequately represent the initial condition, which has a discontinuity at K in its first derivative, and, more generally, because of the high degree of curvature near $S = K$.

The question of which method is best is not a simple one. The accuracy results that we have presented suggest that the Crank-Nicholson method provides a reasonable compromise. However, the method of lines avoids the need for determining the step size required for a given problem and may therefore be preferable for one-time solutions. In higher dimensional problems, memory limitations and the difficulties inherent in the inversion of large matrices become increasingly important (note that the `expm` function used by the method of lines performs matrix inversion). In such cases, it may be necessary to use an explicit method or to modify the implicit methods to avoid forming a matrix inverse.

11.1.5   Stochastic Volatility Model

The stochastic volatility model of section 10.1.3 has a two-dimensional underlying state process. Given the poor experience with polynomials exhibited by the Black-Scholes model, we will use cubic splines to approximate the option value. As the number of dimensions increases, one needs to pay more attention to the details of programming and, in particular, to attempt to exploit sparsity to its greatest extent and to avoid matrix inversion when possible.

In general, the explicit method will become more useful as the number of dimensions grows. We will, of course, need to take small time steps to ensure convergence, but if each time step is executed very quickly, we will come out ahead. In fact, memory limitations may prevent us from using other methods.

We have seen that one can write the basic solution approach in the form

$$\Phi_0 c(t + \Delta) = \Delta \delta + (\Phi_0 + \Delta \Psi) c(t)$$

In general, inverting Φ_0 can be problematic because the sparsity of a matrix is not preserved with inversion. If we are using piecewise linear functions evaluated at the breakpoints, Φ_0 is simply the identity matrix, so sparsity is preserved in this case. It is not preserved, however, for splines, so $B = \Phi_0^{-1}(\Phi_0 + \Delta \Psi)$ will not remain sparse. With the explicit method, however, there is no need to actually form B. Instead, define $a = \Delta \delta$ and $A = \Phi_0 + \Delta \Psi$, and use the following iteration:

$$c \leftarrow \Phi_0^{-1}(a + Ac)$$

With Φ_0 constructed as a tensor product of one-dimensional basis matrices, its inverse is the tensor product of the inverses of the individual one-dimensional basis matrices. These matrices are at most of moderate size and are easily inverted. The CompEcon Toolbox version of `finsolve` is designed to utilize this approach. To solve the stochastic volatility model we first code the model function file.

```
function out=func(flag,S,r,delta,kappa,m,sigma,rho,K,put);
n = size(S,1);
switch flag
case 'rho'
  out = r+zeros(n,1);
case 'mu'
  out = [r-delta-0.5*S(:,2)  kappa*(m-S(:,2))];
case 'sigma'
  out = sqrt(S(:,2));
  out = [out rho*sigma*out zeros(n,1) sqrt(1-rho*rho)*sigma*out];
case 'delta'
  out = [];
case 'V0'
  if put
    out = max(0,K-exp(S(:,1)));
  else
    out = max(0,exp(S(:,1))-K);
  end
end
```

Here the two factors are the log of the price of the underlying asset and the volatility factor v. The mu and sigma flags call for outputs of size $n \times 2$ and $n \times 4$ (or $n \times 2 \times 2$), respectively. For the latter, the columns correspond to σ_{11}, σ_{21}, σ_{12}, and σ_{22}.

Second, we define the model parameters and pack the `model` structure.

```
r     = 0.05;
delta = 0;
kappa = 1;
m     = 0.1;
sigma = 0.2;
rho   = -0.5;
K     = 1;
put   = 1;
T     = 1;
model.func = 'func';
model.T = T;
model.params = {r delta kappa m sigma rho K put};
```

Here we are pricing a European put option with a strike price of $K = 1$. The risk-free interest rate is 5% ($r = 0.05$). The volatility factor has a long-run mean of 0.05. The square root of v can be interpreted as, roughly, the instantaneous coefficient of variation (volatility), which is about 22% here. The value of κ corresponds to a half-life for volatility shocks of $\ln(2)/\kappa = 0.69$, or slightly more than 8 months.

Third, we specify the family of approximating functions.

```
n = [100 10];
smin = [log(0.01*K) 0.1*m]
smax = [log(5*K) 4*m];
fspace = fundefn('spli',n,smin,smax);
s = funnode(fspace);
```

Here we use cubic splines of degree 100 for the price variable and 10 for the volatility variable.

Fourth, we set N to correspond to daily time steps and call the solver.

```
N = fix(T*365+1);
c = finsolve(model,fspace,'explicit',s,N);
```

Figure 11.3a displays the option price for the stochastic volatility model in comparison to the Black-Scholes model. Notice that the option price is greater than the Black-Scholes price at high values of S and is smaller at low values. The differences between the models are highlighted even more in Figure 11.3b, which plots the so-called implied volatility or smile function. This shows the volatility that would produce a Black-Scholes price equal to any given option premium. For options actually priced according to the Black-Scholes formula, the implied volatility is constant in K. We can see, however, that for the parameters chosen, the implied volatility for the stochastic volatility model is downward sloping over the range of K displayed. Other choices of the parameters would lead to other shapes. The correlation between S and v, parameterized by ρ, is particularly influential.

The effect of volatility on the option premium is illustrated in Figure 11.3c. The well-known result that options increase in value as volatility increases is clearly seen in this figure. It is also evident that this effect is most pronounced for prices near the strike price $K = 1$.

11.1.6   American Options

Thus far we have solved problems of valuing European-style options using the extended method of lines, which approximates the value of an option using $V(S, \tau) \approx \phi(S)c(\tau)$. By evaluating $\phi(S)$ at a set of n nodal values, we derived a differential equation of the form

$$c'(\tau) = b + Bc(\tau)$$

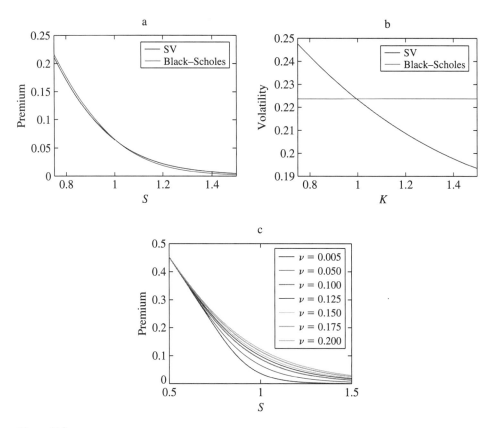

Figure 11.3
Solution of the Stochastic Volatility Option Pricing Model: (a) Option Values; (b) Implied Volatilities; (c) Option Values for Alternative Values of ν

which is solved by

$$c(\tau + \Delta) = a + Ac(\tau)$$

where $A = \exp(\Delta B)$ and $\Phi c(0)$ equals the terminal payout $R(S)$ evaluated at the nodal state values.

American options, which allow early exercise, also satisfy this differential equation but have the additional feature that their value can be no less than $R(S)$. The most commonly used strategy for pricing American-style options solves the closely related problem of determining the value of an option that can be exercised only at a discrete set of dates. Clearly, as the time between dates shrinks, the value of this option converges to the value of one that can be exercised at any time before expiration.

Between exercise dates, the option is effectively European and hence can be approximated using

$$\hat{c}(\tau + \Delta) = a + Ac(\tau)$$

The value of $\phi(S)\hat{c}(\tau + \Delta)$ can then be compared to the value of immediate exercise $R(S)$ and the value function set to the maximum of the two:

$$V(S, \tau + \Delta) \approx \max\left(R(S), \phi(S)\hat{c}(\tau + \Delta)\right)$$

The coefficient vector is updated to approximate this function; that is,

$$c(\tau + \Delta) = \Phi^{-1}\max\left(R, \Phi\hat{c}(\tau + \Delta)\right)$$

The function `finsolve` requires only minor modification to implement this approach to pricing American-style assets. First, add an additional field to the model variable, `model.american`, which takes values of 0 or 1. Then the main iteration loop is changed to the following:

```
for i=2:N+1
   if hasdiv, c = a+A*c;
   else, c = A*c;
   end
   if american
      V = max(V0,Phi*c);
      c = Phii*V;
   end
end
```

This approach was used to produce the plots in Figure 11.4 using the same model function file and parameter values as in section 11.1.4. Unlike the European option case, a closed-form solution does not exist for the American put option, even when the underlying price is geometric Brownian motion. To assess the quality of the approximation, we have computed a different approximation due to Baron-Adesi and Whaley (1987), which is implemented in the CompEcon Toolbox function `baw`. The differences between the approximations are plotted in Figure 11.4b.

With American options it is also useful to approximate the optimal exercise boundary, which is plotted in Figure 11.4c. This is obtained by determining which nodal points that are less than or equal to K are associated with an option that is equal to its intrinsic value of $K - S$. The exercise boundary should lie between the highest such nodal value of S and next nodal value of S. These bounds are shown as dashed lines in Figure 11.4c. A piecewise linear approximation that connects the corners of these bounds (except for endpoint corrections),

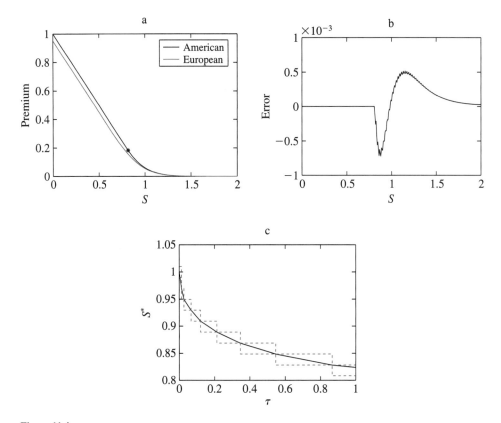

Figure 11.4
Solution of the American Put Option Pricing Model: (a) Option Premium; (b) Approximation Error; (c) Early
Exercise Boundary

represents a reasonable and relatively smooth approximation of the early exercise boundary.
Unfortunately, this approximation can be refined only by increasing the number of nodal
values so they are fairly dense in the region where early exercise may occur (just below the
strike price). Such a dense set of nodal values is rarely needed to improve the accuracy of
the option value, however.

On the positive side, the method of finding an approximation to the value of an option with
a discrete set of exercise dates has two overriding advantages. It is very simple, and it extends
in an obvious way to models with multiple states. On its negative side, the representation
of the optimal exercise boundary is not particularly accurate. If a smoother approximation
of the boundary is needed, the method described in section 11.3.5 can be used.

11.1.7 Exotic Options

The basic solution technique can be applied to solve a variety of other option pricing problems. In this section we discuss barrier, compound, and Asian options. Barrier options are easy to implement but require a modification of `finsolve`. Compound options, at least in their simplest form, can be priced with no modifications to `finsolve`. Asian options typically require an expansion of the state space (as do lookback options). We discuss how to solve Asian options when the underlying asset is described by geometric Brownian motion. In this case a simple variable transformation allows us to avoid expanding the dimensionality of the problem.

To price barrier options, recall that at the barrier, the value of the option is equal to the rebate, and hence the time derivative of the option is 0 (see discussion in section 10.1.4). Therefore, we can substitute

$$\phi(S)c'(\tau) = 0$$

for any value of S that pays the rebate.[10] We must also initialize the option so

$$\phi(S)c(0) = R$$

for any value of S that pays the rebate.

The `finsolve` procedure is designed to handle such cases. Suppose that a rebate of R_a is paid anytime $\beta_a S \leq \alpha_a$ and that a rebate of R_b is paid anytime $\beta_b S \geq \alpha_b$. To specify such a barrier option, an additional field should be added to the `model` variable. For a d-dimensional state process, `model.barrier` is a $2 \times 2 + d$ matrix with the following entries

$$\begin{bmatrix} R_a & \alpha_a & \beta_a \\ R_b & \alpha_b & \beta_b \end{bmatrix}$$

For example, to specify a simple down-and-out call with a single state variable, a knockout barrier at S_b, and no rebate, set `model.barrier` to

$$\begin{bmatrix} 0 & S_b & 1 \\ 0 & \infty & 1 \end{bmatrix}$$

Notice that the second barrier is never crossed because $\alpha_b = \infty$.

---

10. If the rebate is paid at the expiration date, then the time derivative at the barrier is $-r(S)V(S)$.

The `finsolve` procedure is modified in three ways. First, the `barrier` field is read and interpreted.

```
if isfield(model,'barrier')
  barrier = 1;
  temp = model.barrier;
  Ra = temp(1,1); Rb = temp(2,1);
  Binda = S*temp(1,3:end)'< = temp(1,2);
  Bindb = S*temp(2,3:end)'> = temp(2,2);
else
  barrier = 0;
end
```

If a `barrier` field exists, a 0/1 variable `barrier` is set to 1, and two indices are created. `Binda` is a vector of 0/1 variables with a 1 indicating that $\beta_a S \leq \alpha_a$. Similarly, `Bindb` is a vector of 0/1 variables with a 1 indicating that $\beta_b S \leq \alpha_b$. The second modification is to alter the B matrix to impose that the time derivative is equal to 0:[11]

```
if barrier
  B(Binda,:) = 0;
  B(Bindb,:) = 0;
end
```

The third modification is to alter the initial (expiration date) values to incorporate the barriers.

```
if barrier
  V0(Binda) = Ra;
  V0(Bindb) = Rb;
end
```

A few notes of caution: The modifications to B make it singular, meaning that an option that pays dividends cannot be priced as the code is now written (recall that dividends require the computation of $a = (A - I)B^{-1}b$). As dividend-paying barrier options are not typical, it hardly seems worth the bother to modify the code. More importantly, the accuracy of the method depends critically on the placement of the nodes. For a single-dimensional

---

11. This case corresponds to a rebate that is paid when the barrier is hit. For rebates that are paid at the option's expiration date T, the time derivative is $-rV$. For this case, one can set $B(S) = -r\phi(S)$ for each S that triggers the rebate. To price such a barrier using `finsolve`, use `optset` to set the parameter `payatT` to 1.

state process, the accuracy near a lower barrier depends on the size of λ, where $S_b = \lambda s_{i+1} + (1 - \lambda)s_i$ and s_i is the smallest nodal point less than or equal to S_b. The accuracy of the method declines as λ increases from 0 to 1. Thus, to ensure the highest degree of accuracy, the barrier values should equal one of the endpoints of the approximation.

The approach can be illustrated using the same model function file and parameter values as in sections 11.1.4 and 11.1.6. The code to price the option begins with parameter specification.

```
r     = 0.05;
delta = 0;
sigma = 0.2;
K     = 1;
put   = 0;
T     = 1;
Sb    = 0.8;
```

This is a call option with a barrier at $S_b = 0.8$. Then the `model` variable is specified.

```
model.func = 'func';
model.T = T;
model.american = 0;
model.params = {r delta sigma K put};
model.barrier = [0 Sb 1;0 inf 1];
```

We then define a 75-node cubic spline approximation on $[S_b, 2K]$ and call the solver.

```
n = 75;
fspace = fundefn('spli',n,Sb,2*K);
c = finsolve(model,fspace);
```

Figure 11.5a displays the value of the down-and-out call in relationship to the plain vanilla (Black-Scholes) call value. Clearly the barrier option must have value no greater than the vanilla call. For this model, an explicit solution exists and is used to compute the approximation errors shown in Figure 11.5b. The maximum error is roughly 3×10^{-5}, more than accurate enough for practical pricing applications. To emphasize the point about the need to set barrier values equal to nodal points, Figure 11.5c shows the approximation errors when the value of λ is about 0.5. The maximum error here occurs near the barrier and is approximately 100 times larger than for $\lambda = 0$. Experimentation reveals that the maximal error is approximately linear in λ.

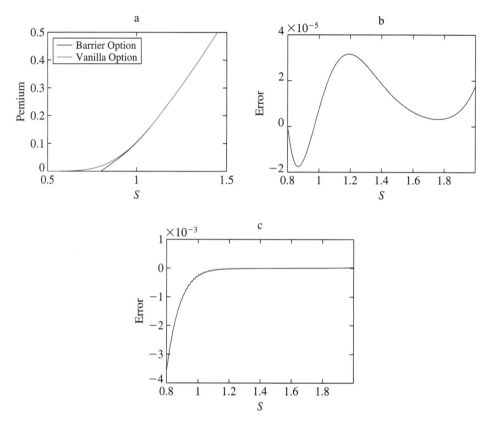

Figure 11.5
Solution of the Barrier Option Pricing Model: (a) Down-and-Out Call Option Premium; (b) Approximation Error; (c) Approximation Error with Barrier Not a Node

Another exotic option that is relatively easy to price is a compound option, which is an option on another derivative. In their simplest form, a European compound option's terminal value depends on the value at maturity of another derivative. Such options are priced by first determining the value of the underlying derivative and using that value to compute the terminal value of the option.

This approach can be illustrated by pricing an option on the same 30-year bond that was priced in section 11.1.1. The model function file must be able to return initial values for both the bond and the option. When `flag` is `V0`, the number of input arguments is checked to determine whether the bond or the option is being priced.

```
function out=func(flag,S,kappa,alpha,sigma,K,put,cB,fspaceB);
n = size(S,1);
switch flag case 'rho'
```

```
  out = S;
case 'mu'
  out = kappa*(alpha-S);;
case 'sigma'
  out = sigma*sqrt(S);
case 'delta'
  out = [];
case 'V0'
  if nargin<6
    out = ones(n,1);
  else
    bondval = funeval(cB,fspaceB,S);
    if put
      out = max(K-bondval,0);
    else
      out = max(bondval-K,0);
    end
  end
end
```

Here we will price a call option with a strike price of $K = 0.2$ and one year to maturity $T_0 = 1$. To solve the model, first specify the parameters:

```
kappa = 0.1;
alpha = 0.05;
sigma = 0.1;
TB    = 30;
K     = 0.2;
put   = 0;
TO    = 1;
```

We have added a "B" to a variable to denote its association with the bond pricing problem and to contrast it with variables having an "O" suffix, which are associated with the option. In the parameter list there are three extra parameters for the option, the strike price K, the 0/1 indicator put and the time to expiration TO.

Next, the value of a 30-year bond is computed.

```
modelB.func = 'func';
modelB.T = TB;
modelB.american = 0;
```

```
modelB.params = {kappa alpha sigma};
n = 20;
fspaceB = fundefn('cheb',n,0,2);
cB = finsolve(modelB,fspaceB);
```

Here, the bond value is approximated with a degree-20 Chebychev polynomial.
   Next, the structured variable model0 for the option is specified:

```
model0.func = 'func';
model0.T = T0;
model0.american = 0;
model0.params = {kappa alpha sigma K put cB fspaceB};
```

A family of approximating functions is then defined and the solver is called:

```
n = 80;
fspace0 = fundefn('spli',n,0,2);
c0 = finsolve(model0,fspace0);
```

Notice that we used a degree-20 polynomial approximation for the bond and a degree-80 cubic spline for the option. As we have seen, low-order polynomials are good for bond pricing but not for option pricing.
   The resulting option price is plotted against r in Figure 11.6a and against the bond price in Figure 11.6b.
   Many types of compound options can be priced in this way, and we leave it to the reader's imagination to explore this approach. There are, however, numerous compound options that

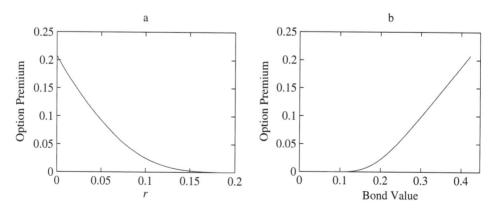

Figure 11.6
Solution of the Compound Option Pricing Model: (a) As a Function of Instantaneous Interest Rate; (b) As a Function of Bond Value

would require modifications to `finsolve` itself. For example, American options cannot be priced simply by setting `model.american` to 1. To see why, notice that as we move through time away from the option's expiration date, the value of the bond as a function of the state also changes. Since the intrinsic value of the option (i.e., its value if exercised) depends on the value of the underlying asset, we would need to simultaneously price the underlying asset to determine the optimal exercise policy. We leave this problem as an exercise.

Asian options have a payoff that depends on the average price over some period $[T - L, T]$. Recall from section 10.1.4 that the pricing of Asians involved the expansion of the state space to include the integral of the price of the underlying asset

$$C_t = \int_{T-L}^{t} S_\tau \, d\tau$$

The option's value satisfies the no-arbitrage condition

$$rV = V_t + \mu(S)V_S + SV_C + \tfrac{1}{2}\sigma^2(S)V_{SS}$$

In the special case in which S evolves according to a geometric Brownian motion (the assumption made to derive the Black-Scholes formula) the problem can be simplified. Suppose that the risk-neutral process for S is

$$dS = (r - \delta)S \, dt + \sigma S \, dz$$

It can be verified that an average strike option can be expressed in the form $V(S, C, t) = Sv(y, \tau)$ where $y = C/S$ and $\tau = T - t$. To verify this assertion, note that the partial derivatives are $V_t = -Cv_\tau$, $V_S = v - yv_y$, $V_{SS} = y^2 v_{yy}/S$, and $V_C = v_y$. These can be substituted into the no-arbitrage condition to derive the expression

$$rSv = -Sv_\tau + (r - \delta)S(v - yv_y) + Sv_y + \tfrac{1}{2}\sigma^2 Sy^2 v_{yy}$$

The variable S is a common term; dividing it out and rearranging results in

$$v_\tau = [1 - (r - \delta)y]v_y + \tfrac{1}{2}\sigma^2 y^2 v_{yy} - \delta v$$

This differential equation is the same that one would get for an asset that evolved according to

$$dy = [1 - (r - \delta)y] \, dt + \sigma y \, dz$$

with an interest rate of δ. Thus, in this special case, the number of state dimensions that require numerical solution is one rather than two and is therefore easier to solve.

We illustrate this approach with an average strike call option with the parameter values $r = 0.1$, $\delta = 0$, and $\sigma = 0.4$, with the averaging occurring over the last six months of the option's life ($L = 0.5$) and three months remaining till maturity ($\tau = 0.25$). The terminal ($\tau = 0$) condition is $v(y, 0) = \max(1 - y/L, 0)$ (the terminal condition for a put is $v(y, 0) = \max(y/L - 1, 0)$).

The model function file for this problem is

```
function out=func(flag,S,r,delta,sigma,L,put);
switch flag
case 'rho'
  n = size(S,1);
  out = delta+zeros(n,1);
case 'mu'
  out = 1-(r-delta)*S;
case 'sigma'
  out = sigma*S;
case 'delta'
  out = [];
case 'V0'
  if put
    out = max(0,S/L-1);
  else
    out = max(0,1-S/L);
  end
end
```

We have an indicator variable `put` that can be set to 1 to solve a put option pricing problem.

The demonstration code begins by defining the parameters and packing the model structure:

```
r              = 0.1;
delta          = 0;
sigma          = 0.4;
L              = 1/2;
put            = 0;
tau            = 1/4;
model.func = 'func';
model.T    = tau;
```

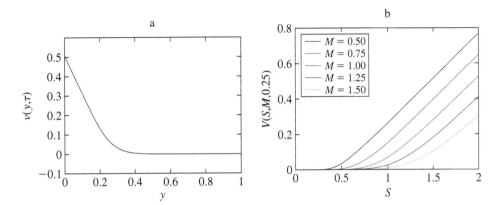

Figure 11.7
Solution of the Asian Option Pricing Model: (a) Approximation Function; (b) Call Option Premium

```
model.american = 0;
model.params = {r delta sigma L put};
```

We then define a piecewise linear function on [0, 1] with 101 nodes to approximate $v(y, \tau)$ and call the solver:

```
n = 101;
fspace = fundefn('lin',n,0,1);
c = finsolve(model,fspace);
```

The resulting approximation of v is displayed in Figure 11.7a. Notice that the function dies out rapidly, suggesting that the interval of approximation is adequate. Although we have defined the option price in terms of C, it is easier to interpret the results in terms of the average to date $M_t = C_t/(L - \tau)$. For given values of S and M, the option premium is computed using

```
y = ((L-tau)*M)./S;
Vhat(:,i) = S.*funeval(c,fspace,y);
Vhat(y>fspace.b,i) = 0;
```

The last line takes account of the fact that for large y (small S), the option premium is 0. Figure 11.7b displays the premium value as a function of S for several values of M.

When the averaging period for the option begins ($\tau = L$), the value of C is identically 0, and so the value of the option is proportional to S_t, with the factor of proportionality equal to $v(0, L)$. Asian options may, however, be traded prior to the beginning of the averaging period. We leave it to the reader to verify that

$$V(S, \tau) = v(0, L)S \exp\big((0.5\sigma^2 - \delta)(\tau - L)\big)$$

for $\tau > L$.

11.1.8 Affine Asset Pricing Models

In section 10.1.5 we discussed a way to partially overcome the curse of dimensionality through the use of affine diffusion processes. When the d-dimensional state process is described by

$$dS = [a + AS]\,dt + C\mathrm{diag}(\sqrt{b + BS})\,dz$$

When the instantaneous interest rate process is $r_0 + rS$, and an asset has terminal value $\exp(h_0 + hS)$, then the asset has value

$$V(S, \tau) = \exp\big(\beta_0(\tau) + \beta(\tau)S\big)$$

where

$$\beta_0'(\tau) = \beta(\tau)a + \tfrac{1}{2}\beta(\tau)C\mathrm{diag}\big(C\beta(\tau)\big)b - r_0$$

and

$$\beta'(\tau) = \beta(\tau)A + \tfrac{1}{2}\beta(\tau)C\mathrm{diag}\big(C\beta(\tau)\big)B - r$$

This approach is easily implemented using ODE solvers such as RK4 provided in the CompEcon Toolbox or the intrinsic solvers provided with MATLAB, such as ODE45.

```
function [beta,beta0]=affasset(tau,a,A,b,B,C,g,g0,h,h0);
AA = [A.';a.'];
BB = [B.';b.']/2;
GG = [g;g0];
[Tau,beta] = ode45('affode',tau,[h.';h0],[],AA,BB,C.',GG);
beta0 = beta(:,end);
beta(:,end) = [];
```

This function takes a vector of time-to-maturity values tau and the problem parameters and returns the values of β and β_0. The functions β and β_0 are solved simultaneously, so some preprocessing of the coefficient matrices is done first. Then the ODE solver is called and the results broken apart and returned. The file affode that is passed to ODE45 computes $[\beta'(\tau)\ \beta_0'(\tau)]^\top$ (the transposition is necessary because ODE solvers work on column vectors rather than row vectors).

```
function dX=AffODE(t,X,flag,AA,BB,Ct,GG)
X = X(1:end-1);
CX = Ct*X;
dX = AA*X+BB*(CX.*CX)-GG;
```

We illustrate the use of `affasset` with a trivial but hopefully illustrative example. The bond pricing model of section 11.1.1 is a simple example of an affine asset pricing model. The state variable S is the instantaneous interest rate itself, so $r = 1$ and $r_0 = 0$. A bond has value 1 at maturity, so $h = h_0 = 0$. The instantaneous interest rate process is described by

$$dS = \kappa(\alpha - S)\,dt + \sigma\sqrt{S}\,dz$$

so $a = \kappa\alpha$, $A = -\kappa$, $C = \sigma$, $b = 0$, and $B = 1$. The following code uses `affasset` to solve this model.

```
T       = 30;
kappa = 0.1;
alpha = 0.05;
sigma = 0.1;
a = kappa*alpha; A = -kappa; C = sigma; b = 0; B = 1;
tau = linspace(0,T,301)';
[beta,beta0] = affasset(tau,a,A,b,B,C,1,0,0,0);
```

This code produces vectors of values of β and β_0 associated with a vector of time-to-maturity values `tau`. To investigate the shape of the term structure of interest rates implied by this model, we compute the yield for several values of the instantaneous interest rate between 3% and 8%.[12]

```
r = (0.03:0.01:0.08);
m = length(r);
R = -(beta0(:,ones(m,1))+beta*r)./tau(:,ones(m,1));
R(1,:) = r;
```

The resulting term structures are plotted in Figure 11.8.

11.1.9   Calibration

The asset pricing models we have discussed define the value of an asset in terms of a set of underlying parameters, which we denote here as θ and a vector of state variables S. We

---

12. The yield on a bond is $-\ln(V(S,\tau))/\tau$, where V is the price of the bond when the instantaneous interest rate is S and there are τ periods until the bond matures. The yield for $\tau = 0$ equals S.

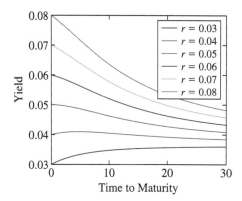

Figure 11.8
Term Structures for Alternative Short Rates

have described how to find the value of an asset as a function of the form $\phi(S)c(t; \theta)$, where the dependence of the coefficients on the parameters is made explicit.

To actually price assets one must provide specific values for both θ and S. The problem of finding reasonable values for θ is well beyond the scope of this book, but we will comment briefly on the problem of obtaining values for S. In some cases S may be directly observed, as is the case for a single-state stock option model, where the state is the price of the stock. Many of the models used in practice, however, involve unobserved state variables. The factors may have some interpretation, such as a stochastic volatility factor, or they may simply be uninterpreted random factors. Unobserved factors can be calibrated to actual market data. Suppose we have observations at a point in time on m different assets. Our model suggests these assets can be priced using $\phi(S)c$, where c is an $n \times m$ matrix with each column associated with one of the assets. Let the $1 \times m$ vector V be the actual (market) prices of these assets.

To determine the value of the d-dimensional state S, we can calibrate the model to the data by solving the least-squares problem

$$\min_S \tfrac{1}{2} \sum_{i=1}^m [\phi(S)c_i - V_i]^2 = \tfrac{1}{2}[\phi(S)c - V][\phi(S)c - V]^\top$$

The Gauss-Newton method uses the iteration

$$S \leftarrow S - [\phi(S)c - V][\phi'(S)^\top cc^\top \phi'(S)]^{-1}$$

(here S is $1 \times d$ and $\phi'(S)$ is treated as a $d \times n$ matrix). In practice, it may be desirable to weight the market data with an m-vector of weights w, so the problem becomes

$$\min_S \tfrac{1}{2}[\phi(S)c - V]\operatorname{diag}(w)[\phi(S)c - V]^\top$$

This approach is implemented in the CompEcon Toolbox function `findstate`, as follows:

```
function s=findstate(c,fspace,s,v,w)
maxit = 100; tol = sqrt(eps);
[n,m] = size(c);
if nargin>4 & ~isempty(w)
  c = (c*spdiags(sqrt(w),0,m,m));
end
s = s(:)';
d = size(s,2);
for i = 1:maxit
  s0 = s;
  X = funeval(c,fspace,s,eye(d));
  y = funeval(c,fspace,s,0)-v;
  s = s-y/X;
  if all(abs(s-s0)<tol), break; end
end
```

We demonstrate this procedure by calibrating the bond pricing model of section 11.1.1 using the parameter values $\kappa = 0.0363$, $\alpha = 0.0692$, and $\sigma = 0.0272$ and Treasury bond yield data for January 7, 1999:

τ	0.25	0.5	1	2	3	5	7	10	30
Yield	4.44	4.49	4.51	4.63	4.63	4.62	4.82	4.77	5.23

The bond price is given by $V = \exp(-\tau y/100)$, where y is the bond yield (in percent).

Using the same model function file as was used for the bond option pricing example in section 11.1.7, we first solve the bond pricing model with 120 time steps over a horizon of 30 years.

```
kappa = 0.0363;
alpha = 0.0692;
sigma = 0.0272;
model.func = 'func';
model.T = 30;
model.american = 0;
model.params = {kappa alpha sigma};
```

```
n = 20;
fspace = fundefn('cheb',n,0,2);
s = funnode(fspace);
optset('finsolve','keepall',1);
c = finsolve(model,fspace,'lines',s,120);
```

This code to price the bond is essentially the same as before except for the parameter values and setting the `keepall` option to ensure that the parameters for all values of τ are available. The data are then entered, and `findstate` is called.

```
t = (0:0.25:30);
tau = [.25 .5 1 2 3 5 7 10 30];
tind = [2 3 5 9 13 21 29 41 121];
y = [4.44 4.49 4.51 4.63 4.63 4.62 4.82 4.77 5.23];
V = exp(-y/100.*tau);
s = findstate(c(:,tind),fspace,alpha,V);
```

The variable `tind` contains the column indices of `c` associated with the observed times-to-maturity in `tau`. Fitted bond prices and yields can then be computed.

```
Vhat = funeval(c,fspace,s);
yhat = -100*log(Vhat)./t;
yhat(1) = 100*s;
```

The actual and fitted yields are plotted in Figure 11.9.

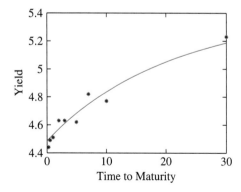

Figure 11.9
Actual and Fitted Bond Yields

11.2   Solving Stochastic Control Problems

In section 10.2 we saw that for problems of the form

$$V(S_0) = \max_{x(\cdot)} E_0 \left[\int_0^\infty e^{-\rho t} f\left(S_t, x(S_t)\right) dt \right]$$

where the state process is described by

$$dS = g(S, x)\, dt + \sigma(S)\, dz$$

the Bellman equation takes the form

$$\rho V(S) = \max_x \left\{ f(S, x) + g(S, x) V'(S) + \tfrac{1}{2}\sigma^2(S) V''(S) \right\}$$

possibly subject to boundary conditions.

When the functional form of the solution is unknown, the basic strategy for solving such problems will be essentially the same as in the discrete time case. The value function will be approximated using $V(S) \approx \phi(S)c$, where c is an n-vector of coefficients.

For infinite horizon problems, the coefficient vector c can be found using policy iteration (Newton's method). Given a guess of the value of c, the optimal value of the control can be solved (in principle) for a set of nodal values s_i for the state variable. The Bellman equation is

$$\rho \phi(s_i)c = \max_x \left\{ f(s_i, x) + g(s_i, x)\phi'(s_i)c + \tfrac{1}{2}\sigma^2(s_i)\phi''(s_i)c \right\}$$

When x can take on a continuum of values, the maximization problem has associated first-order conditions, for each s_i,

$$f_x(s_i, x) + g_x(s_i, x)\phi'(s_i)c = 0$$

which may admit an explicit solution of the form $x_l = x^*(s_i; c)$.

If there are no relevant boundary conditions, n values of s_i are used to form the $n \times n$ basis matrices Φ_0, Φ_1, and Φ_2. The three vectors defined by $f_i = f(s_i, x_i)$, $m_i = g(s_i, x_i)$, and $v_i = 0.5\sigma^2(s_i)$ are also computed. Policy iteration (Newton's method) uses[13]

$$c = [\rho \Phi_0 - m\Phi_1 - v\Phi_2]^{-1} f$$

(as noted earlier, terms like $m\Phi_1$ are an abuse of notation and signify $\mathrm{diag}(m)\Phi_1$).

If there are relevant boundary conditions, the number of nodal values of S can be less than n by the number of additional conditions. Generally, boundary conditions are linear in the value function and its derivatives and hence are linear in the approximation

---

13. A fixed-point iteration method analogous to function iteration can also be defined, but in our experience it is never stable.

coefficients. These conditions can, therefore, be appended to the collocation conditions from the Bellman equation, and c can be updated in essentially the same manner. This approach will be used extensively to solve problems with endogenous switching points (free boundaries) later in this chapter.

A general solver for stochastic control problems with continuous control variables can be developed along the same lines as the solver for the discrete time case (section 9.4). The method starts with an initial guess of the coefficients of an approximation of the value function. It then computes the optimal control given this guess. The value function coefficients are then updated using policy iteration. This iterative process continues until a convergence criterion is met.

There are some distinct computational advantages to using continuous time rather than discrete time models because of three related facts. First, the Bellman equation is not stochastic; there is no need to perform numerical integration to compute an expectation. Second, all the expressions in the Bellman equation need to be evaluated only at nodal values of the state (recall that in discrete-time problems, the next period's value function is evaluated at nonnodal state values). Third, the first-order condition is relatively simple and can often be solved explicitly in the form $x^* = x(S, V_S)$, thereby eliminating entirely the need to use numerical optimization methods to determine the conditional optimal control. Even if no explicit solution is available, numerical optimization requires less computation because the relevant derivatives are evaluated only at nodal points.

11.2.1 A Solver for Stochastic Control Problems

A general solver for continuous time stochastic control problems is provided by `scsolve`. This solver requires that the user specify a model structure and model function file as well as a family of approximating functions, a set of collocation nodes, and initial values for the value function at the collocation nodes. Optionally, an initial value for the optimal control may be passed. The model structure should contain the following fields:

`func`   The name of the model function file

`params`   A cell array of additional parameters to be passed to `model.func`

A template for the model function file named in `model.func` is as follows:

```
function out=func(flag,s,x,Vs,additional parameters)
switch flag
case 'x'
  out = optimal value of the control given S and Vs
case 'f'
  out = reward function given S and x
case 'g'
```

```
  out = drift term in state transition equation given S and x
case 'sigma'
  out = diffusion term in state transition equation given S
        Return [] (empty matrix) for deterministic problems
case 'rho'
  out = discount rate given S
end
```

For many stochastic control problems, an explicit solution giving the optimal control as a function of S and V_S is readily available. The model function file should return these values when a flag value of x is passed.[14]

A simplified (one-dimensional state and action) version of the solver is provided in this subsection. The basic syntax is

```
function cv=scsolve1(model,fspace,snodes,v,x);
```

The collocation problem can be put in the form

$$c = [B - \text{diag}(m)\Phi_1]^{-1} f$$

where m and f depend on x but $B = \rho\Phi_0 - \text{diag}(v)\Phi_2$ does not. We therefore can precompute B:

```
n = size(snodes,1);
rho = feval(func,'rho',snodes,[],[],params{:});
Phi0 = funbas(fspace,snodes,0);
sigma = feval(func,'sigma',snodes,[],[],params{:});
if isempty(sigma)
  B = spdiags(rho,0,n,n)*Phi0;
else
  v = 0.5*sigma.*sigma;
  B = spdiags(rho,0,n,n)*Phi0...
   -spdiags(v,0,n,n)*funbas(fspace,snodes,2);
end
```

Note that for deterministic problems the model function file returns an empty matrix ([ ]) for sigma, so this case needs special handling.

We will need to perform the multiplication $\text{diag}(m)\Phi_1$ at each iteration, so we simply precompute Φ_1 at this point:

```
Phi1 = funbas(fspace,snodes,1);
```

14. If this is not the case, the user must write an auxiliary routine to solve the first-order conditions numerically.

We then initialize the coefficient vector:

```
if nargin>4 & isempty(v)
  f = feval(func,'f',snodes,x,[],params{:});
  g = feval(func,'g',snodes,x,[],params{:});
  cv = (B-spdiags(g,0,n,n)*Phi1)\f;
  v = Phi0*cv;
elseif nargin<4 | isempty(v)
  cv = zeros(n,1);
  v = zeros(n,1);
else
  cv = Phi0\v;
end
```

There are three possibilities here. First, one passes in an initial guess of the optimal control and an empty matrix for the value function. In this case, the optimal coefficient vector is determined, and from it an initial guess of the value function is computed. Second, no initial guesses are passed, in which case a guess of 0 for c is used. Third, an initial guess for the value function is passed, and the initial coefficient vector is found.

The Newton (policy) iteration loop is then performed:

```
for iters=1:maxiters
  Vs = Phi1*cv;
  x = feval(func,'x',snodes,[],Vs,params{:});
  f = feval(func,'f',snodes,x,[],params{:});
  m = feval(func,'g',snodes,x,[],params{:});
  cv = (B-spdiags(m,0,n,n)*Phi1)\f;
  v0 = v;
  v = Phi0*cv;
  e = max(abs(v-v0));
  if e<tol, break; end
end
```

The first part of this code computes the f and g functions at the n state nodes. The collocation equation $[B - \text{diag}(m)\Phi_1]c = f$ can then be solved. Last, the value function is updated and compared to the previous values to determine if the iteration should be terminated.

When the state space is multidimensional, a number of bookkeeping problems arise, and significant computational savings are possible with careful attention to details. Appendix 11A describes some code that handles a number of these details and is used in the multidimensional version of scsolve.

11.2.2 Postoptimality Analysis

Once the solution to the control problem is found, it is often useful to determine how the optimally controlled state process behaves. There are two main ways to accomplish this purpose. First, one can simulate the controlled process and examine the behavior of the simulated time paths and the long-run tendencies of the process. One may also be able to analyze more directly the long-run density function associated with the process.

A simple Euler scheme for simulating Ito processes consists of defining

$$S_{t+\Delta} \approx S_t + \Delta \mu(S_t) + \sqrt{\Delta} \sigma(S_t) e_t$$

where e_t is a standard normal random variate. For controlled problems recall that

$$\mu(S) = g\big(S, x^*\big(S, V_S(S)\big)\big)$$

A MATLAB routine `itosimul` is provided in the CompEcon Toolbox.

```
function s = itosimul(model,s0,T,nstep,cv,fspace)
```

The user must supply a structure variable `model`, an `npath` $\times$ d matrix of starting values `s0`, where `npath` is the number of simulated paths and d is the dimension of the state variable, the time horizon over which the simulation occurs `T`, the number of time steps to use `nstep`, as well as the coefficient vector for the value function approximation `cv` and the function family structure variable `fspace`.[15] The routine returns a `npath` $\times$ d $\times$ `nstep` array.

The structured variable `model` contains four fields

func	the name of the model function file
params	a cell array of additional parameters to be passed to `model.func`
a	a lower bound for the process
b	an upper bound for the process

For unbounded processes set $a = -\infty$ and/or $b = \infty$.

After unpacking the `model` variable, the routine determines the problem size, makes a number of initializations and handles some bookkeeping chores:

```
dt = T/nstep;
sqdt = sqrt(dt);
```

---

15. Uncontrolled models can also be simulated with this routine. One could, therefore, use the routine to do Monte Carlo based asset valuation. Although we do not explicitly discuss this approach, it is further developed in exercise 11.3.

```
[npath,d] = size(s0);
s = zeros(npath,d,nstep);
s(:,:,1) = s0;
st = s0;
a = repmat(reshape(a,1,d),npath,1);
b = repmat(reshape(b,1,d),npath,1);
```

The last two lines expand the bounds a and b into npath × *d* matrices to facilitate comparisons with the simulated values.

The procedure then iterates over the time steps:

```
for i = 2:nstep
  vs = funeval(cv,fspace,st,eye(d));
  x = feval(func,'x',st,[],vs,params{:});
  mu = feval(func,'g',st,x,[],params{:});
  st = st+mu*dt;
  sigma = feval(func,'sigma',st,x,[],params{:});
  if ~isempty(sigma)
    e = randn(npath,d);
    if d==1
      e = sqdt*sigma.*e;
    else
      e = arraymult(sqdt*sigma,e,npath,d,d,1);
    end
    st = st+real(e);
  end
  st = min(max(st,a),b);
  s(:,:,i) = st;
end
```

The main difficulty in this routine occurs in the computation of the shock when $d > 1$. In this case the model function file should return sigma as an npath × *d* × *d* array when passed npath values of the state variable in a npath × *d* matrix. That is, element ijk of sigma represents $\sigma_{jk}(S_i)$. The shock added to element ij of the state process is thus

$$\sqrt{\Delta} \sum_{k=1}^{d} \sigma_{jk}(S_i)e_k$$

where e_k is a $d \times 1$ vector of independent standard normal variates. For $d = 1$ the MATLAB code for this is simply sqdt*sigma.*e but the vectorized version when $d > 1$ uses the

CompEcon Toolbox function `arraymult`, which enables one to perform matrix multiplication on multidimensional arrays.

For one-dimensional state variables it is often possible to determine the long-run probability density function without resorting to simulation. We will not take up the rather complicated issues of whether such a density function exists, except to say that it may not exist because the process is nonstationary or because the process is influenced by the presence of boundaries that result in a mixture of discrete and continuous probability (see the bibliographic notes for references). When the long-run density $\pi(S)$ does exist, however, it will satisfy a forward equation (see Appendix A, section A.5.2) of the form

$$\frac{1}{2} \frac{d^2 \sigma^2(S) \pi(S)}{dS^2} = \frac{d\mu(S)\pi(S)}{dS}$$

Integrating both sides and rearranging terms yields

$$\frac{d\sigma^2(S)\pi(S)}{\sigma^2(S)\pi(S)} = 2\frac{\mu(S)}{\sigma^2(S)}\, dS$$

Integrating both sides again, taking the exponential of both sides, and rearranging terms yields

$$\pi(S) = \frac{c}{\sigma^2(S)} \exp\left(2 \int^S \frac{\mu(s)}{\sigma^2(s)}\, ds\right) \tag{11.6}$$

where c is chosen to ensure that π integrates to 1.

To illustrate, consider the process in which $\mu(S) = \alpha(m - S)$ and $\sigma(S) = \sigma$. The long-run distribution is then equal to

$$\pi(S) \propto \exp\left(2 \int^S \frac{\alpha(m - s)}{\sigma^2}\, ds\right)$$

$$= c \exp\left(\frac{2\alpha m S - \alpha S^2}{\sigma^2}\right)$$

$$\propto \exp\left(-\frac{2\alpha}{2\sigma^2}(S - m)^2\right)$$

which is recognizable as the normal distribution with mean m and variance $\sigma^2/2\alpha$.

When a closed form expression cannot be found, one can approximate the solution. Suppose one has already defined a function definition structure variable `fspace` and computed the values of $m = \mu(S, x^*(S))$ and $v = \sigma^2(S, x^*(S))$ at the n nodal values of the state that compose the vector `s`. First, approximate the integrand in equation (11.6), and integrate the result at each of the nodal state values:

```
c = funfitxy(fspace,s,m./v);
temp = 2*funeval(c,fspace,s,-1);
temp = temp-max(temp);
```

The -1 passed as the last argument to `funeval` requests the integral of the function. The last line is a normalization used to ensure that overflow does not occur.

Next, an approximation is fitted to the integral values divided by the variance term σ^2.

```
p = exp(temp)./v;
c = funfitxy(fspace,s,p);
```

Then the constant of integration is determined and the function normalized to integrate to 1 over the range of approximation:

```
temp = funeval(c,fspace,fspace.b,-1);
c = c./temp;
```

A routine implementing this approach, `itodensity`, is provided. Its syntax is

```
c = itodensity(model,fspace,cv);
```

where the three inputs have the same meaning as for `scsolve`.

11.3   Stochastic Control Examples

11.3.1   Optimal Growth

The neoclassical optimal growth model (section 10.3.2) solves

$$\max_{C(\cdot)} \int_0^\infty e^{-\rho t} u\big(C(K_t)\big)\, dt$$

subject to the state transition function $K' = q(K) - C$. This problem could be solved using a Euler equation approach; we leave this as exercise 11.4 (page 451). Instead, we illustrate how it can be solved using `scsolve`.

To make the problem concrete, suppose that $u(C) = (C^{1-\gamma} - 1)/(1 - \gamma)$ and that $q(K) = \alpha \ln(K+1) - \delta K$. Specific parameter values we use are $\alpha = 0.14, \delta = 0.02, \gamma = 0.5$, and $\rho = 0.05$.

The first step in using `scsolve` is to create the model function file:

```
function out = func(flag,s,x,Vs,alpha,delta,gamma,rho);
n = size(s,1);
switch flag
case 'x';
  out = Vs.^(-1./gamma);
case 'f';
  out = (x.^(1-gamma)-1)./(1-gamma);
case 'g';
  out = alpha*log(s+1)-delta*s-x;
case 'sigma'
  out = [];
case 'rho'
  out = rho+zeros(n,1);
end
```

Next, one defines the parameters and packs the model structure:

```
alpha = 0.14;
delta = 0.02;
gamma = 0.5;
rho   = 0.05;
model.func = 'func';
model.params = {alpha,delta,gamma,rho};
```

The family of functions used to approximate the value function is then defined, along with the nodal state values:

```
n = 20;
smin = 0.2;
smax = 2;
fspace = fundefn('cheb',n,smin,smax);
snodes = funnode(fspace);
```

The state space is defined on $[0, \infty)$, but any interval that contains the steady-state capital stock $K^* = \alpha/(\rho+\delta) - 1$ will provide a good approximation on that interval. In this model the value function becomes problematic as $K \to 0$. Specifically, the value function and its second derivative go to $-\infty$, and its first derivative goes to ∞. We will not be able to capture this kind of behavior with polynomials or splines. For this reason, we have used the interval $[0.2, 2]$ to keep well away from $K = 0$ and to bracket $K^* = 1$.

An initial guess for the value function or the optimal control should then be provided. It is useful for this to look something like what one expects the value function to look like. We use $u(\rho S)/\rho$ as a guess:

```
v0 = ((rho*snodes).^(1-gamma)-1)/(1-gamma)/rho;
```

The solver is then called

```
[cv,s,v,x,resid] = scsolve(model,fspace,snodes,v0);
```

The resulting value, control, and residual functions are plotted in Figure 11.10a–c. The value function plot makes clear that it will be difficult to use polynomial approximations as K gets small.

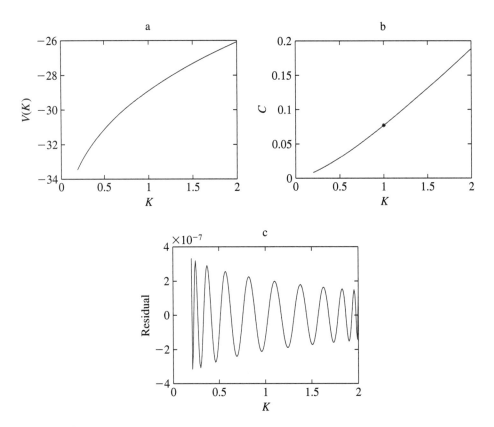

Figure 11.10
Solution to the Optimal Growth Model: (a) Value Function; (b) Optimal Consumption Rule; (c) Approximation Residual

It is often possible to obtain better results through simple variable transformations. For example, the value function seems to behave roughly like a linear function of $\ln(K)$. It may be useful, therefore, to recast the problem in terms of $y = \ln(K)$. Let $v(y) = V(K)$ and thus $v'(y)e^{-y} = V'(K)$. The Bellman equation is

$$\rho v(y) = \max_{C}\{u(C) + [\ln(e^{y} + 1) - \delta e^{y} - C]e^{-y}v'(y)\}$$

with associated first-order condition

$$u'(C) = e^{-y}v'(y)$$

With this modification, one can get more accurate results over a larger interval (e.g., $(0.001, 2)$) with the same degree of approximation. We leave the implementation details as an exercise but note that such variable transformations are often useful in numerical work and that some experimentation is required to find adequate ones.

11.3.2   Renewable Resource Management

In the renewable resource management problem (section 10.3.3) there are a total of nine parameters in the model, α, β, K, b, η, c, γ, σ, and ρ. The model function file for this problem is

```
function out=func(flag,s,x,Vs, ...
    alpha,beta,K,b,eta,c,gamma,sigma,rho)
switch flag
case 'x'
  Cost = c*s.^(-gamma);
  out = b*(Cost+Vs).^(-eta);
case 'f'
  Cost = c*s.^(-gamma);
  if eta~=1
    factor1 = 1-1/eta;
    factor0 = b.^(1/eta)/factor1;
    out = factor0*x.^factor1-Cost.*x;
  else
    out = b*log(x)-Cost.*x;
  end
case 'g'
  if beta~=0
    Growth = alpha/beta*s.*(1-(s/K).^beta);
```

```
   else
     Growth = alpha*s.*log(K./s);
   end
   out = Growth-x;
case 'sigma'
   out = sigma*s;
case 'rho'
   out = rho+zeros(size(s,1),1);
end
```

This code is complicated by the need to handle separately the cases in which $\beta = 0$ or $\eta = 1$ in order to avoid division by 0. For $\beta = 0$, the limiting case is $B(S) = \alpha S \ln(K/S)$. The case of unit-elastic demand ($\eta = 1$) leads to a limiting value for the social surplus function of $b \ln(q) - C(S)q$.

The use of scsolve to obtain a solution is illustrated in this subsection with the parameter values $\alpha = 0.5$, $\beta = 1$, $K = 1$, $b = 1$, $\eta = 0.5$, $c = 0.1$, $\gamma = 2$, $\sigma = 0.1$, and $\rho = 0.05$. One first sets the values of the model parameters, which are stored with the name of the model function file in a structured variable model.

```
alpha = 0.5;
beta  = 1;
K     = 1;
b     = 1;
eta   = 0.5;
c     = 5;
gamma = 2;
sigma = 0.1;
rho   = 0.05;
model.func = 'func';
model.params = {alpha beta K b eta c gamma sigma rho};
```

The family of approximating functions is then defined. The natural state space is $S \in [0, \infty)$. As with all problems involving an unbounded state space, a bounded range of approximation must be selected. For stochastic infinite horizon problems, the general rule of thumb is that the range should include events on which the stationary (long-run) distribution places a nonnegligible probability of occurrence. In this case, there is little probability that the resource stock, if optimally harvested, will ever be close to the biological carrying capacity of K. It is also never optimal to let the stock get too close to zero.

There is another reason why zero is a poor choice for the lower bound of the approximation for this problem. As $S \to 0$, the value function goes to $-\infty$ and the marginal value function goes to ∞. Such behavior is extremely hard to approximate with splines or polynomials. Inclusion of basis functions that exhibit such behavior is possible but requires more work. In this case it is also unnecessary, because the approximation works well with a smaller range of approximation.

Next one defines the space of approximating functions. Here we use a Chebychev polynomial approximation of degree 35 on the interval [0.2, 1.2].

```
n = 35;
smin = 0.2;
smax = 1.2;
fspace = fundefn('cheb',n,smin,smax);
s = funnode(fspace);
```

The solution is obtained with a call to `scsolve`:

```
[cv,S,v,x,resid] = scsolve(model,fspace,s);
```

The long-run density and mean can be obtained with the call

```
[cp,Ex] = itodensity(model,fspace,cv);
```

The marginal value function and the long-run density are shown in Figure 11.11a and 11.11b, respectively. The unboundedness of the marginal value function is suggested as the state goes to 0, but the long-run density also suggests that the probability of this event is vanishingly small (assuming a positive initial stock). Similarly, the probability of achieving the upper bound of the approximation is small, suggesting that the interval of approximation is adequate for numerical computation. The residual function, displayed in Figure 11.11c, confirms the adequacy of the approximation.

An explicit solution exists for the parameter values used here (it is one of the special cases discussed in the previous chapter). Figure 11.11d displays the relative error functions over the range of approximation for the marginal value function and optimal control (i.e., $1 - \hat{V}/V$ and $1 - \hat{x}/x$, where "$\hat{\ }$" indicates the approximation). It can be seen that the relative errors in both functions are quite small, except at the upper end of the range of approximation.

11.3.3   Production with Adjustment Costs

The production-with-adjustment-costs problem of section 10.3.6 presents a somewhat more difficult challenge because there are two state variables. The problem is illustrated here using the parameter values $\kappa = 0.5$, $\alpha = 1$, $\sigma = 0.2$, $a = 4$, $c = 2$, and $\rho = 0.1$.

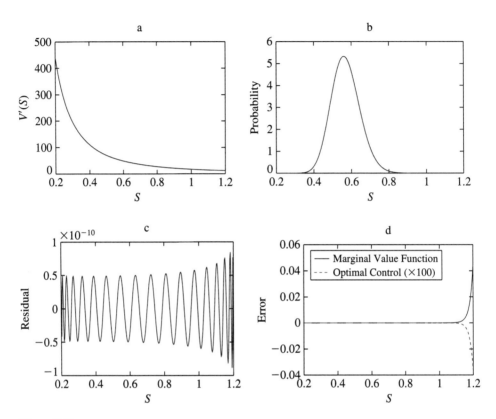

Figure 11.11
Solution to the Renewable Resource Model: (a) Shadow Price; (b) Long-Run State Density; (c) Approximation
Residual; (d) Approximation Error

The first step in solving the problem is to create the model function file:

```
function out=func(flag,s,x,Vs,kappa,alpha,sigma,a,c,rho);
n = size(s,1);
switch flag
case 'x';
  out = Vs(:,2)/a;
case 'f';
  out = s(:,1).*s(:,2) - 0.5*c*s(:,2).^2 - 0.5*a*x.^2;
case 'g';
  out = [kappa*(alpha-s(:,1)) x];
case 'sigma'
  out = [sigma*s(:,1) zeros(n,3)];
```

```
case 'rho'
  out = rho+zeros(n,1);
end
```

The parameter values are specified and are then packed, along with the name of the model function file, into the model structure:

```
kappa = 0.5;
alpha = 1;
sigma = 0.2;
a     = 4;
c     = 2;
rho   = 0.1;
model.func = 'func';
model.params = {kappa alpha sigma a c rho};
```

Then the family of approximating functions is defined, and the nodal values of the states are computed.

```
n = [10 10];
smin = [0.4 0];
smax = [2.5 3];
fspace = fundefn('cheb',n,smin,smax);
scoord = funnode(fspace);
```

Here we use degree-10 Chebychev approximations for both p and q, with the former on the interval [0.4, 2.5] and the latter on the interval [0, 3] (some experimentation is required to determine the appropriate intervals).

We are now ready to call the solver.

```
optset('scsolve','nres',3);
[cv,s,v,x,resid] = scsolve(model,fspace,scoord);
```

The optional parameter `nres` is first set to 3 (rather than its default of 10). This setting instructs the solver to compute the residual function at $(3 \cdot 10)^2 = 900$ points (the default would use $(10 \cdot 10)^2 = 10,000$ points). Nine hundred points should be sufficient to determine if the approximation is adequate. Notice also that no initial guess for the value function is passed to `scsolve` so the default of zero will be used.

Approximation results are displayed in Figure 11.12, including the optimal decision rule (11.12a) and the value function (11.12b). As asserted in exercise 10.14, the value function is quadratic and the decision rule is linear. Not surprisingly, therefore, the residual function is close to machine precision, as demonstrated in Figure 11.12c. Also shown, in Figure 11.12d,

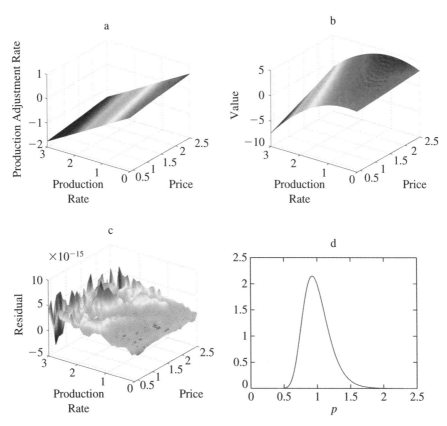

Figure 11.12
Solution to the Production-Adjustment Model: (a) Optimal Production Policy; (b) Value Function; (c) Approximation Residual; (d) Long-Run Price Density

is the long-run density of price, which, in this model, is independent of the agent's actions. The plot makes clear that the range of approximation used for the price ([0.4, 2.5]) captures the range of prices with nontrivial probability of occurrence.

11.3.4 Optimal Fish Harvest

The optimal fish harvesting problem (section 10.3.7) is a bang-bang problem. The first step in using `scsolve` to solve such a problem is to create the model function file:

```
function out=func(flag,s,x,Vs,alpha,sigma,H,P,c,rho)
switch flag
case 'x'
  out = H*(Vs<(P-c./s));
```

```
case 'f'
   out = (P-c./s).*x;
case 'g'
   out = alpha*(1-s).*s-x;
case 'sigma'
   out = sigma*s;
case 'rho'
   out = rho+zeros(size(s,1),1);
end
```

Notice that the optimal control equals H when $V_S(S) < P - c/S$ and equals 0 otherwise.

To solve the problem, first define the parameters and pack the structured variable `model`:

```
alpha = 0.5;
sigma = 0.5;
H     = 1;
P     = 1;
c     = 0.25;
rho   = 0.1;
model.func = 'func';
model.params = {alpha sigma H P c rho};
```

The family of functions used to approximate the value function is then defined, along with the nodal state values:

```
n = 150;
smin = 0.01;
smax = 1.5;
fspace = fundefn('lin',n,smin,smax);
s = funnode(fspace);
```

The state space is defined on $[0, \infty)$, but the probability of a large stock is remote, so we take the upper bound on S to be 1.5. In this model the value function becomes problematic as $S \to 0$. Although the value function is zero at $S = 0$, its first and second derivatives go to ∞ and $-\infty$, respectively. For this reason, we have used the interval $[0.1, 1.5]$ to keep well away from $S = 0$. The second derivative also exhibits a kink at the switching point S^*, so we use a 150-point piecewise linear approximation. As an initial guess for the value function we use $10 \ln(s + 1)$:

```
v0 = 10*log(s+1);
```

The solver is then called

```
[cv,s,v,x,resid] = scsolve(model,fspace,snodes,v0);
```

The routine `itodensity` can be used to compute the long-run state density and its expected value:

```
cp = itodensity(model,fspace,cv);
p = funeval(cp,fspace,s);
```

The value function and its first two derivatives are plotted in Figures 11.13a–c, with the optimal switching point marked as a "*". Notice that the second derivative is kinked at S^*. Figure 11.13b also contains the curve $P - c/S$ as a dashed line. When V' (the value of an unharvested fish) is above $P - c/S$ (the value of a harvested fish), it is optimal not to harvest.

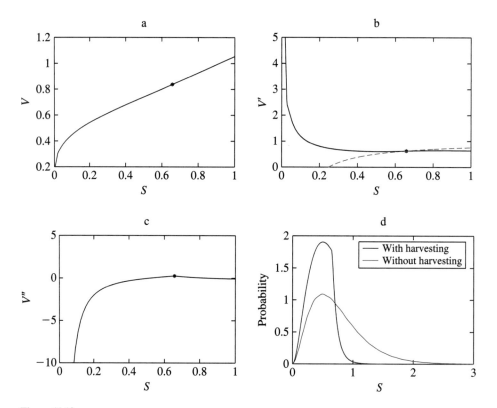

Figure 11.13
Solution to the Fish Harvesting Model (Bounded Harvest Rate): (a) Value Function; (b) Marginal Value Function; (c) Curvature of the Value Function; (d) Long-Run Density of Fish Stocks

The residual function for this problem (not displayed) suggests that the approximation is quite good, with values less than 0.0001 except near 0 and near the switch point.

Figure 11.13d displays the long-run stock density, which is also kinked at S^*. Above S^* the stock is harvested at the maximal rate, but this is not enough to prevent the stock from potentially reaching the carrying capacity ($S = 1$). Also shown in this figure is the long-run density in the absence of any harvesting. The expected value of the stock is 0.46, compared to an expected value of 0.75 in the absence of harvesting. The optimal switching point is 0.67, which is about two-thirds of the carrying capacity.

11.3.5 Sequential Learning

In some problems, one of the state variables may be nonstochastic, meaning that only its first derivative enters the problem. If, in addition, the value function is known at some value of this variable, initial value (evolutionary) type methods can be used to solve the model. We have already seen this type of approach with American options, in which one of the state variables is time to maturity τ, with $d\tau = -dt$. The sequential learning model (section 10.3.8) also has this feature, with the value function being known at $Q = Q_m$ and with $dQ = x\,dt$. In addition, any model with a finite horizon, at which the value function is equal to some known salvage value, is in this class.

The method used for American options, although simple, has the drawback that the free boundary is approximated with a step function. To obtain a smoother approximation of the boundary, without requiring a dense set of state variable nodes, we use an explicit finite difference approximation for the derivative of the first-order variable, while simultaneously solving for the free boundary.

Recall that in the sequential learning problem the cumulative production, Q, acts like a time variable. There is a known terminal condition at $Q = Q_m$, and the solution can be obtained in an evolutionary fashion by working backward in Q from Q_m. Identifying the location of the free boundary, however, is somewhat more involved than with the American option pricing problem.

The Feynman-Kac equation

$$rV = P - c(Q) + V_Q + (r - \delta)PV_P + \tfrac{1}{2}\sigma^2 P^2 V_{PP}$$

holds on $[P^*(Q), \infty) \times [0, Q_m]$, where $P^*(Q)$ is a free boundary to be determined. The boundary conditions are[16]

$$P^*(Q)V_P(P^*(Q), Q) = \beta V(P^*(Q), Q)$$

---

16. Recall that these boundary conditions are due to the fact that, below the free boundary, the solution is of the form $V(P, Q) = A(Q)P^\beta$. We ignore the limiting condition as $P \to \infty$.

and

$$P^*(Q)V_{PP}\big(P^*(Q), Q\big) = (\beta - 1)V_P\big(P^*(Q), Q\big),$$

where β is the positive solution to

$$\tfrac{1}{2}\sigma^2\beta(\beta - 1) + (r - \delta)\beta - r = 0$$

Also a terminal condition at $Q = Q_m$ is essentially known (it will require that we solve, numerically, for the constant $A(Q_m)$).

The difficulty with free boundaries is the unknown shape of the space over which the differential equation must hold. To get around this problem, we use a transformation method that regularizes the boundary; specifically,

$$y = \ln(P) - \ln\big(P^*(Q)\big)$$

with $v(y, Q) = V(P, Q)$. The PDE must be solved for values of P on $[P^*(Q), \infty)$, which translates into values of y on $[0, \infty)$ (in practice we will truncate y). Given this transformation, it is straightforward to verify the following relationships between the original and the transformed problem:

$$v_y(y, Q) = PV_P(P, Q)$$

$$v_{yy} - v_y = P^2 V_{PP}(P, Q)$$

and

$$V_Q = v_Q - \frac{P^{*\prime}(Q)}{P^*(Q)}v_y$$

Substituting these expressions into the Bellman equation and the boundary conditions yields:

$$rv = P^* e^y - C(Q) + v_Q + \big(r - \delta - \tfrac{1}{2}\sigma^2 - P^{*\prime}/P^*\big)v_y + \tfrac{1}{2}\sigma^2 v_{yy}$$

$$v_y(0, Q) - \beta v(0, Q) = 0$$

and

$$v_{yy}(0, Q) - \beta v_y(0, Q) = 0$$

We can approximate $v(y, Q)$ with the function $\phi(y)c(Q)$, where $c(Q) : [0, Q_m] \to \mathbb{R}^n$. The Bellman equation (with suitable rearrangement) can be written as

$$\phi(y)c'(Q) - \frac{\phi'(y)c(Q)}{P^*(Q)}P^{*\prime}(Q) = D(y)c(Q) - e^y P^*(Q) + C(Q)$$

where

$$D(y) = r\phi(y) - \left(r - \delta - \tfrac{1}{2}\sigma^2\right)\phi'(y) - \tfrac{1}{2}\sigma^2\phi''(y)$$

The boundary conditions at $y = 0$ $(P = P^*)$ are

$$[\phi'(0) - \beta\phi(0)]c(Q) = 0$$

and

$$[\phi''(0) - \beta\phi'(0)]c(Q) = 0$$

Treated as system of $n + 1$ unknowns, this is a differential/algebraic equation (DAE) system in Q. It differs from an ordinary system of differential equations because of the boundary conditions, which do not involve the Q derivatives. We will take a simple explicit Euler approach, by replacing the Q derivatives with first-order backward finite differences

$$c'(Q) \approx \frac{c(Q) - c(Q - \Delta)}{\Delta}$$

and

$$P^{*\prime}(Q) \approx \frac{P^*(Q) - P^*(Q - \Delta)}{\Delta}$$

(this approach is explicit because we are working backward in time from a terminal condition). This approach leads to the following system

$$\begin{bmatrix} \Phi_0 & -\dfrac{\Phi_1 c(Q)}{P^*(Q)} \\ \phi'(0) - \beta\phi(0) & 0 \\ \phi''(0) - \beta\phi'(0) & 0 \end{bmatrix} \begin{bmatrix} c(Q - \Delta) \\ P^*(Q - \Delta) \end{bmatrix}$$

$$= \begin{bmatrix} \Phi_0 - \Phi_1 - \Delta D(Y) & \Delta e^Y \\ 0 & 0 \\ 0 & 0 \end{bmatrix} \begin{bmatrix} c(Q) \\ P^*(Q) \end{bmatrix} - \begin{bmatrix} \Delta C(Q)\underline{1} \\ 0 \\ 0 \end{bmatrix}$$

where Φ_0, Φ_1, and D have the usual meaning; that is, they are the functions $\phi(y)$, $\phi'(y)$, and $D(y)$ evaluated at $n - 1$ nodal points. This system has the form

$$Ax_{Q-\Delta} = Bx_Q + C(Q)d \tag{11.7}$$

where A and d are constant matrices and B is a constant matrix except for the first $n - 1$ elements in its last column.

A MATLAB routine `learn` implementing this approach is provided with the following syntax:

```
function [Q,pstar,c,fspace,A1,A2,beta1,beta2] ...
          = learn(r,delta,sigma,Qm,cbar,C,N,n,b)
```

The function takes as inputs the problem parameters r, δ, σ, Q_m, $\bar{c}$, and C, as well as the number of Q steps N and the degree and upper bound of the approximating function n and b. The function returns an $N + 1$ vector of values of Q and an $n \times N + 1$ matrix `c` of coefficients, each column representing one value of Q, with the first column associated with $Q = 0$ and the last with $Q = Q_m$. The output `fspace` is the function definition structure associated with c. The function also returns the parameters associated with the known parts of the solution β_1, β_2, A_1 and A_2.

The routine first computes the solution coefficients β_1, β_2, A_1 and A_2 for $Q \geq Q_m$ (see the discussion on page 340):

```
temp   = 0.5-(r-delta)/sigma.^2;
beta1  = temp+sqrt(temp.^2+2*r/sigma.^2);
beta2  = temp - sqrt(temp.^2+2*r/sigma.^2);
temp   = [cbar.^beta1              -(cbar.^beta2)              ; ...
           beta1*cbar.^(beta1-1)   -beta2*cbar.^(beta2-1)];
temp   = temp\[cbar/delta-cbar/r; 1/delta];
A1     = temp(1);
A2     = temp(2);
```

The approximating functions and nodal values are then defined:

```
Delta  = Qm/N;
Q      = linspace(0,Qm,N+1);
fspace = fundefn('cheb',n-1,0,b);
y      = funnode(fspace);
fspace = fundefn('cheb',n,0,b);
```

Here n Chebychev polynomials are used as a basis. The nodal values are the standard nodes for the degree $n-1$ Chebychev basis because of the need to impose the boundary conditions.

Next, we precompute the collocation matrices A, B and d from equation (11.7):

```
Phi0 = funbas(fspace,y,0);
Phi1 = funbas(fspace,y,1);
Phi2 = funbas(fspace,y,2);
phi0 = funbas(fspace,0,0);
```

```
phi1 = funbas(fspace,0,1);
phi2 = funbas(fspace,0,2);
D    = r*Phi0-(r-delta-0.5*sigma^2)*Phi1-0.5*sigma.^2*Phi2;
A    = [Phi0                    zeros(n-1,1) ;
         phi1-beta1*phi0        0            ;
         phi2-(beta1)*phi1      0            ];
B    = [Phi0-Phi1-Delta*D  Delta*exp(y) ;
               zeros(2,n+1)              ];
d    = [ones(n-1,1);0;0];
```

The cost function values $C(Q)$ are then computed:

```
gamma = log(C/cbar)/Qm;
Cost  = Delta*cbar*exp(gamma*(Qm-Q));
```

and the terminal boundary coefficients $c(Q_m)$ are computed:

```
p           = [cbar;cbar*exp(y)];
c           = zeros(n+1,N+1);
c(1:n,N+1)  = [Phi0;phi1]\(A2*p.^beta2+p/delta-cbar/r);
c(end,N+1)  = cbar;
```

Note that we have appended the switching location P^* to the bottom of the coefficient vector c, resulting in a set of $N+1$ unknowns that are solved at each iteration.

The iteration backward in Q is then performed:

```
for i = N+1:-1:2
  A(1:n-1,end) = Phi1*c(1:n,i)/(-c(end,i));
  c(:,i-1) = A\(B*c(:,i)-Cost(i)*d);
end
```

Finally, we separate c and P^*:

```
pstar = c(end,:)';
c(end,:) = [];
```

Figure 11.14 illustrates the solution to the sequential learning model with parameter values of $r = 0.05$, $\delta = 0.05$, $\sigma = 0.02$, $Q_m = 20$, $\bar{c} = 10$, and $C = 40$. The approximation uses the Chebychev basis of degree $n = 15$ for P and 400 evenly spaced steps for Q.

A few comments are in order. First, this is effectively an explicit method and hence is prone to instability if the number of nodes and Q steps is not picked carefully. Fortunately, it is generally obvious when instability is a problem, as the results will be clearly incorrect.

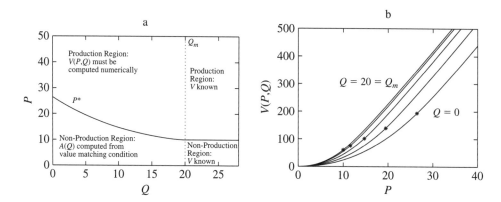

Figure 11.14
Solution to the Sequential Learning Model: (a) Optimal Activation Boundary; (b) Value Function

The other problem concerns the choice of the upper bound, b. This bound represents a value of P equal to $P^*(Q)e^b$. Too small a value leads to distortions in both the value function and the location of the optimal boundary. By experimenting with this value, we found that having an upper limit of $100P^*$ was sufficient to obtain at least three-place accuracy for $P^*(Q)$.

11.4   Regime Switching Models

Suppose that the discrete state variable can take on values in $\{1, \ldots, m\}$.[17] To keep the presentation manageable, we assume that there is only one continuous state variable. We use a degree-n approximating function in the continuous variable with basis functions $\phi_r(S)$ to approximate the value function in the regime r. The solution sought is a collection of m coefficient vectors and m intervals $[a_r, b_r]$.

We assume that enough is known about the problem to be able to identify, for each regime r, which regime will be chosen at the boundaries of its no-switch region. The different possible conditions at each boundary point S_k can be specified with 5 indices r, q, ι_0, ι_1 and ι_2. If S_k is the location of a switching point, then r and q equal the values of the two regimes involved. In general, the conditions that must be satisfied at such a point take the form

$$V^{(p)}(S_k, r) - V^{(p)}(S_k, q) = R_p(S_k, r, q)$$

where $p = 0$, 1 or 2. If such a condition must be met, set $\iota_p = 2$ for an optimality condition

---

17. We can always number discrete states in this manner. For example, a problem with two binary states has a total of four discrete states $(0, 0)$, $(0, 1)$, $(1, 0)$, and $(1, 1)$.

and $\iota_p = 1$ otherwise. If no conditions on the pth derivative are appropriate, then $\iota_p = 0$. If S_k represents a natural boundary, with a condition of the form

$$V^{(p)}(S_k, r) = R(S_k, r)$$

then q is set to 0 and ι_p is set to 1.

For example, suppose that there are two regimes with two unknown switch points S_1 and S_2 and natural boundaries at 0 and 1. Suppose that the no-switch region for regime 1 lies on $[0, S_1]$ and that the no-switch region for regime 2 lies on $[S_2, 1]$. Furthermore, suppose it costs C_{rq} to switch from regime r to regime q and that $V(0, 1) = 0$. The relevant side conditions can be specified by the following table of values:

S	r	q	ι_0	ι_1	ι_2	R_0	R_2	R_2
0	1	0	1	0	0	0	0	0
S_1	1	2	1	2	0	$-C_{12}$	0	0
S_2	2	1	1	2	0	$-C_{21}$	0	0
1	2	0	0	0	0	0	0	0

The last line does not represent a side condition but serves to indicate that 1 is a natural boundary point for the no-switch region of regime 2.

The total number of side conditions imposed on the problem is the sum of the ι values that are greater than 0. The total number of optimality conditions (and therefore of choice variables) is the sum of the ι values that equal 2.

Our solution strategy will be approximate $V(S, r) \approx \phi_r(S)c_r$, where ϕ_r defines a basis for a family of approximating functions on the interval $[a_r, b_r]$. If we take the switching points as given, we can obtain values of the c_r by solving the Feynman-Kac equation

$$[\rho\phi_r(s_i) - \mu(s_i, r)\phi'(s_i, r) + \tfrac{1}{2}\sigma^2(s_i, r)\phi''(s_i, r)]c_r = f(s_i, r)$$

at a set of nodal values s_i, along will the non-optimality side conditions. Given the linearity of the Feynman-Kac equation and the side conditions, a collocation solution involves only a linear solve. The location of the switching points can be determined using a root finding algorithm to solve the optimality conditions.

We have provided a procedure `rssolve` to solve the regime switching problem. The syntax for the procedure is

```
[cv,fspace,x]=rssolve(model,x,n,type)
```

The routine takes as inputs a structured variable model defining the problem, an initial guess of the boundary points x and an m-vector n defining the degree of the approximations to use for each regime. The last input type is optional. It specifies the type of approximating functions, such as 'lin' or 'spli', with the default being 'cheb' (see the discussion in section 6.7).

The procedure returns two cell arrays, each with m elements. The first contains vectors of length n_r representing the approximation coefficients for regime r. The second contains structure variables representing the family of approximations used for regime r. The value function for regime r can then be approximated using funeval(cv{r},fspace{r},s). The third output provides the optimal values of the boundary points.

The model variable has three required fields:

func   the name of the model function file
params   a cell array of additional parameters to be passed to model.func
xindex   a five-column matrix defining the nature of the boundary points

The last field xindex is a matrix with columns corresponding to the indices r, q, ι_0, ι_1, and ι_2 discussed above. Each row of this matrix corresponds to one of the rows of x. A template for the model function file named in model.func is:

```
function out=func(flag,s,r,additional parameters)
switch flag
case 'f'
  out = flow reward function
case 'g'
  out = drift term in state transition equation
case 'sigma'
  out = diffusion term in state transition equation
case 'rho'
  out = discount rate
case 'reward'
  out =  reward at the boundary points
end
```

Except when flag equals reward, this function will be passed a vector of values of the continuous state s and a scalar value r indicating the regime. When flag equals reward, the model function file is passed the current value of the vector x and should return a three column matrix of rewards associated with these values (the R_0, R_1, and R_2 values discussed earlier).

11.4.1   Asset Abandonment

The asset abandonment problem (section 10.4.1) can be solved using `rssolve`. This is an optimal stopping problem. Such problems have two discrete states, but one of the states is trivial. When the asset is abandoned, there are no further rewards, so the value function is identically 0. There is therefore no need to actually represent this regime, so we define the problem as a single-regime model.

Intuitively, the asset is abandoned when the price gets sufficiently low. Thus the active regime lies on $[P^*, \infty)$. It turns out to prove difficult to solve this problem numerically without imposing some condition on the value function at its upper bound. Consider, however, that as the price level gets large, the value function should approach the discounted expected returns that would be forthcoming if the asset was never abandoned, which is equal to $P/(\rho - \mu) - c/\rho$. This observation suggests that the value function is approximately linear in P as P gets large, in turn implying that $V''(P) \to 0$ as $P \to \infty$. The `xindex` variable for this problem can therefore be specified as

$$\begin{bmatrix} 1 & 0 & 1 & 2 & 0 \\ 1 & 0 & 0 & 0 & 1 \end{bmatrix}$$

The first row is associated with the switching point P^* at which both the value function and the first derivative are 0. The second row is used to specify the location of the upper bound for the approximation, which will be set to an appropriately large value. Here the ι_2 value is set to 1 to impose a limiting condition on the second derivative.

We first write the model function file:

```
function out=func(flag,s,x,c,mu,sigma,rho)
switch flag
case 'f'
  out = (s-c);
case 'g'
  out = mu*s;
case 'sigma'
  out = sigma*s;
case 'rho'
  out = rho+zeros(size(s,1),1);
case 'reward'
  out = [0 0 0;s(2)/(rho-mu)-c/rho 1/(rho-mu) 0];
end
```

There are no rewards or costs at abandonment, so the first row of the 2×3 matrix returned when `flag` equals `reward` is set to 0. The second row is set to the limiting values already discussed (this facilitates exploration of the response to alternate specifications of the side condition at the upper bound).

We continue by defining the parameters and packing the model variable:

```
c     = 0.5;
mu    = 0;
sigma = 0.2;
rho   = 0.1;
model.func = 'func';
model.params = {c mu sigma rho};
model.xindex = [1 0 1 2 0;1 0 0 0 1];
```

We will use a degree-50 Chebychev polynomial approximation on the interval $[P^*, 10]$ and set the initial guess for the optimal switching point P^* to 0.

```
n = 50;
x = [0;10];
[cv,fspace,x] = rssolve(model,x,n);
```

Figures 11.15a and 11.15b display the value function and the marginal value (shadow price) functions with the switching point displayed as an asterisk ($P^* = 0.3209$). The residual function for this approximation is displayed in Figure 11.15c. The residuals are relatively small but are increasing in P. As discussed in section 10.4.1, this problem has an explicit solution. The approximation error function is plotted in Figure 11.15d. The accuracy around the switch point is actually quite reasonable. The switch point itself is accurate to about seven significant digits. More troublesome, however, is the loss of accuracy as P increases. This reflects the fact that the price process is nonstationary, leading to a need to use a fairly high upper bound on the approximation of 10 in order to get accurate results near the switching point.

11.4.2   Optimal Fish Harvest

We have already discussed the bang-bang problem of optimal fish harvesting using scsolve (section 11.3.4). It can also be solved using rssolve. The model function file is very similar to the one given in section 11.3.4 and is therefore not displayed here. To solve the problem, first define the parameters:

```
alpha = .5;
sigma = .5;
H     = 1;
P     = 1;
```

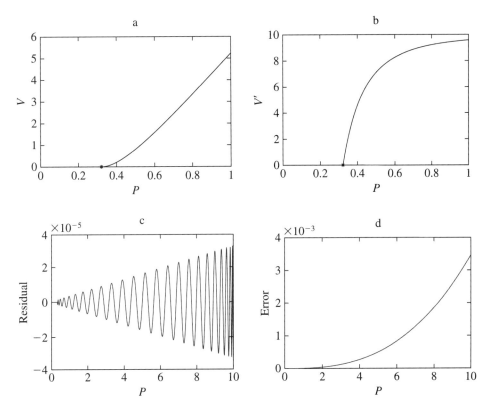

Figure 11.15
Solution to the Asset Abandonment Model: (a) Value Function; (b) Marginal Value Function; (c) Approximation Residual; (d) Approximation Error

```
c     = 0.25;
rho   = 0.1;
```

There are two discrete states, one for zero production, the other for full production. There are no switching costs, so there is a single switch point at which value matching and smooth pasting hold for any arbitrary choice of the switch point and continuity of the second derivative holds for the optimal choice. The structured variable `model` is therefore:

```
model.func = 'func';
model.params = {alpha sigma H P c rho};
```

```
model.xindex=[
   1 0 0 0 0;
   1 2 1 1 2;
   2 0 0 0 0];
```

Here we impose no side conditions at the lower bound for regime 1 or at the upper bound for regime 2.

The approximation for the no-production regime will be located on [0.001, S^*], whereas the full-production regime is located on [S^*, 3]. Of course the natural boundaries for the state are 0 and ∞; we have already discussed the choice of boundaries for this problem in section 11.3.4. We initialize x:

```
x=[0.001;0.5;3];
```

with a guess of $S^* = 0.5$ (half the carrying capacity). We have already seen that the value function is very curved near zero and is nearly linear for high values of S. We will therefore use a degree-75 approximate for the no-production regime and a degree-20 approximate for the full-production regime.

```
n = [75 20];
[cv,fspace,x] = rssolve(model,x,n);
```

Plots of the value function approximation and its derivatives are essentially the same as those of section 11.3.4.

11.4.3 Entry-Exit

In the entry-exit problem discussed in section 10.4.3 there is a fixed cost of I that provided capital to generate a return stream of $P - c$, where we will take the price process to be geometric Brownian motion

$$dP = \mu P \, dt + \sigma P \, dz$$

If capital is in place, it can be abandoned at an exit cost of E. There are two discrete regimes, inactive and active, with four boundary points. It is intuitive that the firm should only abandon if the price is sufficiently low and should only invest if the price is sufficiently high.

The xindex variable for this model is therefore

$$\begin{bmatrix} 1 & 0 & 0 & 0 & 0 \\ 1 & 2 & 1 & 2 & 0 \\ 2 & 1 & 1 & 2 & 0 \\ 2 & 0 & 0 & 0 & 1 \end{bmatrix}$$

with the first regime located on $[x_1, x_2]$ and the second regime located on $[x_3, x_4]$. The natural lower bound for the first regime is 0. The upper bound for regime 2 will be set to a sufficiently high value. As with the asset abandonment problem of section 11.4.1, it proves useful to impose the condition that the value function is linear at the upper bound for regime 2 (the limiting condition is the same here, namely, that $V(S) \rightarrow P/(\rho - \mu) - c/\rho$ as $P \rightarrow \infty$).

We first write the model function file:

```
function out=func(flag,s,x,r,mu,sigma,C,E,I)
switch flag
case 'f'
  out = (s-C).*(x==2);
case 'g'
  out = mu*s;
case 'sigma'
  out = sigma*s;
case 'rho'
  out = r+zeros(size(s,1),1);
case 'reward'
  out = [0 0 0;-I 0 0;-E 0 0;0 0 0];
end
```

The only flow rewards come in the active state ($x = 2$). The rewards at regime switching times are associated with the entry costs in row 2 and the exit costs in row 3 of the matrix that is returned when `flag` is set to `reward`.

One continues by defining the parameters and packing the model variable:

```
r     = 0.05;
mu    = 0;
sigma = 0.2;
C     = 1;
E     = 2;
I     = 5;
model.func = 'mfrs03';
model.params = {r mu sigma C E I};
model.xindex = ...
  [1 0 0 0 0;
   1 2 1 2 0;
   2 1 1 2 0;
   2 0 0 0 1];
```

We will take the upper bound for the active regime to be 50. This may seem large, but we need it to be large because we are working with a nonstationary process (geometric Brownian motion), so we want to minimize any effect the choice of the upper bound has on the calculation of the switch points. We also use a high-degree approximate for the active regime ($n_2 = 85$), but a fairly low degree can be used for the inactive region ($n_1 = 15$). Initial guesses for the switch points are 3 and 1.

```
x = [0;3;1;50];
n = [15 85];
[cv,fspace,x] = rssolve(model,x,n);
```

Figures 11.16a and 11.16b display the value and marginal-value functions with the switching points displayed as asterisks. In the inactive regime, it is optimal to incur the investment cost anytime the price is higher than 2.0827. In the active regime, however, it is optimal

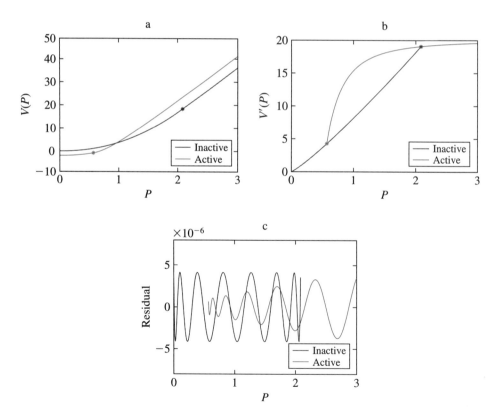

Figure 11.16
Solution to the Entry-Exit Model: (a) Value Functions; (b) Marginal Value Functions; (c) Approximation Residual

to exit the industry anytime the price drops below 0.5687. The residual function for this approximation, which is displayed in Figure 11.16c, suggests that the approximation is a good one.

There is, in fact, a nearly closed form solution to this problem. The switching points computed using polynomial value function approximations provide a solution with the same order of accuracy as the nearly closed form solution (approximately 10^{-8}).

11.5 Impulse Control

Recall that in impulse control problems with a single state variable (section 10.5) the value function satisfies the Feynman-Kac equation

$$\rho V(S) = f(S) + \mu(S)V'(S) + \tfrac{1}{2}\sigma^2(S)V''(S)$$

on some interval $[a, b]$, with boundary conditions at a and/or b if the endpoint is a trigger at which the control is exerted. In addition, for each trigger and target that is subject to choice, there is an additional optimality condition. Suppose that there are m triggers and that there are p triggers and targets to be chosen optimally ($m \in \{1, 2\}$ and $p \in \{1, \ldots, 4\}$).

A collocation approach to finding a solution is to approximate the value function using $V(S) \approx \phi(S)c$, where $\phi(S)$ is an n-vector of basis function values. For a given set of triggers and targets, this function can be uniquely determined by solving

$$\left[\rho\phi(s_i) - \mu(s_i)\phi'(s_i) - \tfrac{1}{2}\sigma^2(s_i)\phi''(s_i)\right]c = f(s_i)$$

at $n - m$ nodal values s_i, plus m boundary conditions. As the boundary conditions are linear in c, the problem of finding the value function for a given control rule involves only a linear solve of size n. The locations of the triggers and targets can then be found by solving the p optimality conditions using a standard rootfinding routine.

In practice, in turns out to make sense to normalize the state variable to lie on the interval $[0, 1]$. Let $u = (S - a)/(b - a)$ and $v(u) = V(S)$. This variable transformation implies that $v'(u)/(b - a) = V'(S)$ and $v''(u)/(b - a)^2 = V''(S)$. The approximation to v solves the Feynman-Kac equation

$$\left[\rho\phi(u_i) - \frac{\mu\big((b-a)u_i+a\big)}{b - a}\phi'(u_i) - \frac{\sigma^2\big((b-a)u_i+a\big)}{2(b - a)^2}\phi''(u_i)\right]c = f\big((b-a)u_i+a\big)$$

This is a system of linear equations of the form $Hc = f$, where H is $n-m \times n$. The $n-m \times n$ matrices Φ_0, Φ_1, and Φ_2 with rows composed of the values of $\phi(u_i)$, $\phi'(u_i)$, and $\phi''(u_i)$ can be precomputed, thereby reducing the cost of computing c for different values of a, b, A, and B.

A solver implementing this approach, provided in the CompEcon Toolbox, uses the syntax

```
function [cv,fspace,x]=icsolve(model,x,n)
```

The routine takes as inputs a structured variable `model` defining the problem, an initial guess `x` of the boundaries, triggers and targets (described in this section), and the degree of approximation `n` desired. The solution will typically be smooth, and hence a polynomial approximation is used by the solver. The outputs are the coefficient vector `cv` and the structured variable `fspace` that define the value function approximation as well as the optimal `x` defining the boundaries, triggers, and targets. The `model` variable has four required fields:

func	The name of the model function file
params	A cell array of additional parameters to be passed to `model.func`
xindex	A 2×2 matrix defining the nature of the triggers and targets
F	A 2×1 vector of fixed costs

A template for the model function file named in `model.func` is as follows:

```
function out=probdef(flag,s,additional parameters)
switch flag
case 'f'
  out = flow reward function
case 'mu'
  out = drift term in state transition equation
case 'sigma'
  out = diffusion term in state transition equation
case 'rho'
  out = discount rate
case 'R+'
  out = discrete reward for S1>S0
case 'R-'
  out = discrete reward for S1<S0
end
```

When `flag` is either `R+` or `R-`, the solver will pass a two-column matrix `s`, with the first column representing the triggers S_0 and the second column representing associated targets S_1. The model function file should return a four-column matrix consisting of

$$[R(S_0, S_1) \quad R_{S_0}(S_0, S_1) \quad R_{S_1}(S_0, S_1) \quad R_{S_0 S_0}(S_0, S_1) + R_{S_0 S_1}(S_0, S_1)]$$

For $S_0 = S_1$ the appropriate one-sided derivatives should be returned.

The state variable takes values in $[a, b]$. If a is a trigger, the control rule specifies that the state is moved to A whenever S hits a. Similarly, if b is a trigger, whenever S hits b the state is moved to B. The 2×2 matrix x contains these values in the following format:

$$x = \begin{bmatrix} a & A \\ b & B \end{bmatrix}$$

Thus the first column of x contains the boundaries/triggers; the second contains the targets. On input to icsolve, x contains initial guesses for any of the choice variables; on output, it contains the optimal values of the choice variables.

To determine the type of problem, the 2×2 variable model.xindex must be specified. The following table can be used to determine the appropriate values, along with the values of the fixed costs in model.F.

a	xindex(1,1)	F(1)
Not a trigger	0	Not used
An unchosen trigger	1	F^+
A chosen trigger	2	F^+
b	xindex(2,1)	F(2)
Not a trigger	0	Not used
An unchosen trigger	1	F^-
A chosen trigger	2	F^-
A	xindex(1,2)	
An unchosen target	0	
A chosen target	1	
B	xindex(2,2)	
An unchosen target	0	
A chosen target	1	

Notice that the sum of all the values in xindex equals $m + p$ and that m equals the number of nonzero elements in the first column of xindex. The routine can handle degenerate cases with zero fixed costs. If $F^+ = 0$, x(1,2) and xindex(1,2) are ignored. Similarly, if $F^- = 0$, x(2,2) and xindex(2,2) are ignored.

11.5.1 Asset Replacement

In the asset replacement problem (section 10.5.1) an asset's productivity depends on its age, A, yielding a net return of $Q(A)P$. The asset can be replaced by paying a fixed cost C. In this subsection the method is demonstrated for the case in which $Q(A) = \beta_0 + \beta_1 A + \beta_2 A^2$ and for specific parameter values $\beta_0 = 1$, $\beta_1 = 0.05$, $\beta_2 = -0.003$, $P = 2$, $C = 3$, and discount rate $\rho = 0.1$.

The model function file is as follows:

```
function out=func(flag,s,beta,P,rho)
switch flag
case 'f'
  Q = (beta(3)*s+beta(2)).*s+beta(1);
  out = P*Q;
case 'mu'
  out = ones(size(s,1),1);
case 'sigma'
  out = [];
case 'rho'
  out = rho+zeros(size(s,1),1);
case 'R+'
  out = zeros(1,4);
case 'R-'
  out = zeros(1,4);
end
```

Notice that there are only fixed costs in this problem, so $R(S_0, S_1) = 0$.

To solve the problem, first define the parameters:

```
beta = [1; 0.05; -0.003];
P    = 2;
C    = 3;
rho  = 0.1;
```

The vector beta is used to hold the parameters of the Q function. The model structure is then packed:

```
model.func = 'func';
model.params = {beta,P,rho};
model.xindex = [0 0;2 0];
model.F = [0;C];
```

There is only one trigger (at b) and its target is 0. Hence the only nonzero element of `xindex` is element $(2, 1)$. An initial guess of the values of the bounds, triggers, and targets is needed:

```
x = [0 0;100 0];
```

We initially set $b = 100$. The target associated with b is 0, which is also the lower bound a. Since a is not a trigger, A is undefined and here is set to equal a. The solver can now be called, here using a degree-15 approximation.

```
n = 15;
[cv,fspace,x] = icsolve(model,x,n);
```

A plot of $V(A)$ is shown in Figure 11.17. The value-matching condition appears in the figure as the difference of $C = 3$ between $V(0)$ and $V(A^*)$ ($A^* \approx 17.64$). The smooth-pasting condition appears as the 0 slope of V at A^*.

11.5.2 Timber Management

In the timber management problem (section 10.5.2) the biomass of a timber stand is governed by

$$dS = \alpha(m - S)\, dt + \sigma\sqrt{S}\, dz$$

When S reaches S^*, the stand is cut, earning a return of PS^* less a replanting cost of C. We solve this equation for parameter values $\alpha = 0.1$, $m = 1$, $\sigma = 0.05$, $P = 3$, $C = 0.15$, and discount rate $\rho = 0.1$.

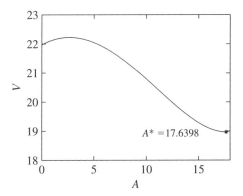

Figure 11.17
Value Function for the Asset Replacement Model

The model function file is as follows:

```
function out=func(flag,s,alpha,m,sigma,P,rho)
switch flag
case 'f'
  out = zeros(size(s,1),1);
case 'mu'
  out = alpha*(m-s);
case 'sigma'
  out = sigma*sqrt(s);
case 'rho'
  out = rho+zeros(size(s,1),1);
case 'R+'
  out = zeros(1,4);
case 'R-'
  out = [P*(s(1)-s(2)) P -P 0];
end
```

To solve the problem, first define the parameters:

```
alpha = 0.1;
m     = 1;
sigma = 0.05;
P     = 3;
C     = 0.15;
rho   = 0.1;
```

The model variable is then defined:

```
model.func = 'func';
model.params = {alpha,m,sigma,P,rho};
model.xindex = [0 0;2 0];
model.F = [0;C];
```

As in the previous example, the upper bound is the only trigger, and it is a choice variable. An initial guess of the values of the bounds, triggers, and targets is needed:

```
x = [0 0;0.5 0];
```

We initially set the upper bound to $b = 0.5$, or one half the carrying capacity m. The target associated with b is 0, which is also the lower bound a. Since a is not a trigger, A is undefined and here is set to equal a.

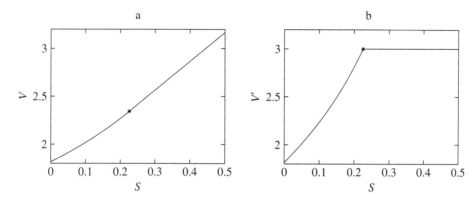

Figure 11.18
Solution to the Timber Harvesting Model: (a) Value Function; (b) Marginal Value

The solver can now be called, here using a degree-15 approximation.

```
n = 15;
[cv,fspace,x] = icsolve(model,x,n);
```

The resulting value and marginal value of the timber stand are shown in Figures 11.18a and 11.18b, with the optimal cutting stock shown as an asterisk. Notice that the marginal value is continuous but kinked at S^*.

11.5.3 Storage Management

In the storage management problem (section 10.5.3) the state is a stock of stored goods S. When the control is not exerted, S evolves according to

$$dS = \mu \, dt + \sigma \, dz$$

The flow reward is $-kS$, the discrete rewards are $R^+(S_0, S_1) = -(S_1 - S_0)P$ and $R^-(S_0, S_1) = 0$, and fixed costs are $F^+ = F$ and $F^- = 0$ (actually R^- and F^- are undefined because the upper bound is not a choice variable). We demonstrate the solution to this problem with $\mu = -0.2$, $\sigma = 0.05$, $k = 0.05$, $P = 2$, $F = 3$, and discount rate $\rho = 0.1$.
    The model function file is as follows:

```
function out=func(flag,s,mu,sigma,k,P,rho)
switch flag
case 'f'
  out = -k*s;
case 'mu'
  out = mu+zeros(size(s,1),1);
```

```
case 'sigma'
  out = sigma+zeros(size(s,1),1);
case 'rho'
  out = rho+zeros(size(s,1),1);
case 'R+'
  out = [P*(s(1)-s(2)) P -P 0];
case 'R-'
  out = zeros(1,4);
end
```

To solve the problem, first define the parameters:

```
mu    = -0.2;
sigma = 0.05;
k     = 0.05;
P     = 2;
F     = 3;
rho   = 0.1;
```

The model structure is then packed:

```
model.func = 'mfic03';
model.params = {mu sigma k P rho};
model.xindex = [1 1;0 0];
model.F = [F;0];
```

In this problem, the lower bound $S = 0$ is a trigger but not a choice variable, and the upper bound is not a trigger. The only choice variable is the target associated with $S = 0$. An initial guess of the values of the bounds, triggers, and targets is needed:

```
smax = 8;
x = [0 smax;smax smax];
```

We set the upper bound and the initial guess of the target to 8, which is larger than we think the trigger should be. Since b is not a trigger, B is undefined and here set to equal b.

The solver can now be called, here using a degree-10 approximation.

```
n = 10;
[cv,fspace,x] = icsolve(model,x,n);
```

The value of storage stocks is shown in Figure 11.19. The optimal restocking level is 1.86 and is shown as an asterisk in Figure 11.19.

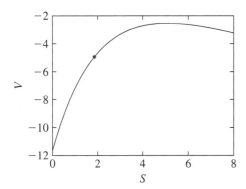

Figure 11.19
Value Function for the Storage Management Model

11.5.4 Cash Management

In the cash management problem (section 10.5.5) the state evolves according to

$$dS = \mu\, dt + \sigma\, dz$$

when the control is not exerted. A reward is generated only when the control is exerted, so $f(S) = 0$. The discrete reward functions are $R^+(S_0, S_1) = (-r/\rho - c^+)(S_1 - S_0)$ and $R^- = (r/\rho - c^-)(S_0 - S_1)$, and there are fixed costs of exerting the control of F^+ and F^-.

The model function file is as follows:

```
function out=func(flag,s,mu,sigma,r,c,C,rho)
switch flag
case 'f'
  out = zeros(size(s,1),1);
case 'mu'
  out = mu+zeros(size(s,1),1);
case 'sigma'
  out = sigma+zeros(size(s,1),1);
case 'rho'
  out = rho+zeros(size(s,1),1);
case 'R+'
  out = [(-c-r/rho)*(s(2)-s(1)) (c+r/rho) (-c-r/rho) 0];
case 'R-'
  out = [(r/rho-C)*(s(1)-s(2)) (r/rho-C) (C-r/rho) 0];
end
```

To solve the problem, first define the parameters:

```
mu      = 0;
sigma   = 0.2;
rho     = 0.04;
r       = 0.05;
c       = 0.75;
C       = 0.25;
f       = 1;
F       = 0.5;
```

The model variable is then defined:

```
model.func = 'func';
model.params = {mu sigma r c C rho};
model.xindex = [1 1;2 1];
model.F = [f;F];
```

In this problem, the lower bound $S = 0$ is a trigger but not a choice variable, whereas the upper bound is both a trigger and a choice variable. Both targets are also choice variables. An initial guess of the values of the bounds, triggers, and targets is needed:

```
x = [0 1;2 1];
```

The broyden algorithm is not guaranteed to converge, so some experimentation may be needed to obtain good starting values.

The solver can now be called, here using a degree-10 approximation.

```
n = 10;
[cv,fspace,x] = icsolve(model,x,n);
```

The value and marginal value functions are shown in Figures 11.20a and 11.20b, with the triggers and targets shown as asterisks. In Figure 11.20b, the horizontal lines at 1 and 2 represent the values of $r/\rho - C$ and $r/\rho + c$. Also, the area above 2 and below $V'(S)$ between a and A equals F^+, and the area above $V'(S)$ and below 1 between B and b equals F^-.

11.5.5   Optimal Fish Harvest

The optimal fish harvesting example (sections 10.3.7, 11.3.4, and 11.4.2) had an upper bound on the rate of harvest. If this bound is removed, so that fish can be harvested at an infinite rate, the problem becomes one of instantaneous or barrier control. We could get a reasonable approximation to a solution by setting the bound to a large number, but we can also use icsolve to get a solution more directly (and more precisely).

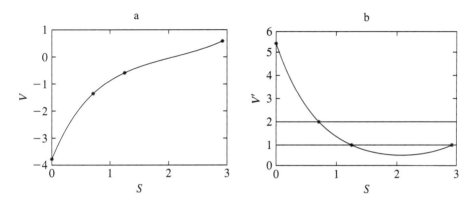

Figure 11.20
Solution to the Cash Management Model: (a) Value Function; (b) Marginal Value Function

The problem as stated, however, does not fit the standard framework required by `icsolve` because the control is the effort rate, not the rate of change in the state. To put it into the standard format, we have the state dynamics given by

$$dS = [\alpha(1 - S)S + x]\,dt + \sigma S\,dz$$

and the flow reward function is

$$f(S, x) = -(P - c/S)x$$

with $x \le 0$, implying that $R^-(S_0, S_1) = P(S_0 - S_1) - c(\ln(S_0) - \ln(S_1))$ (a negative change in the state is a positive amount of fish harvested).

The model function file is as follows:

```
function out=func(flag,s,alpha,sigma,P,c,rho)
switch flag
case 'f'
  out = zeros(size(s,1),1);
case 'mu'
  out = alpha*(1-s).*s;
case 'sigma'
  if sigma==0, out=[];
  else, out = sigma*s;
  end
case 'rho'
  out = rho+zeros(size(s,1),1);
```

```
case 'R+'
   out = zeros(1,4);
case 'R-'
   S0 = s(:,1); S1=s(:,2);
   out = [P*(S0-S1)-c*log(S0./S1) P-c./S0 -P+c./S1 c./S0.^2];
end
```

To solve the problem, first define the parameters and pack the model structure variable:

```
alpha = 0.5;
sigma = 0.5;
P     = 1;
c     = 0.25;
rho   = 0.1;
model.func = 'func';
model.params = {alpha sigma P c rho};
model.xindex = [0 0;2 0];
model.F = [0;0];
```

The upper bound is the only trigger, and it is a choice variable. The trigger is certainly no bigger than the carrying capacity (normalized to equal one). The natural lower bound is 0, but for reasons discussed earlier, it is useful to bound the problem away from 0. We use an initial interval of [0.01, 1].

```
x = [0.01 0;1 0];
```

The values of $x(1,2)$ and $x(2,2)$ are ignored and so are arbitrarily set to zero.

The solver can now be called, here using a degree-50 approximation.

```
n = 50;
[cv,fspace,x] = icsolve(model,x,n);
```

The value function and its first two derivatives are shown in Figures 11.21a–11.21c, with the control barrier shown as an asterisk. Notice that the second derivative is continuous but kinked at S^*. Figure 11.20b also includes the curve $p - c/S$. The marginal-value function lies on this curve for values of S greater than S^* and lies above it for values below S^* when a fish in the sea is worth more than in the market. The control barrier is located at $S^* = 0.76$. This is somewhat higher than the switch point of 0.67 found in section 11.3.4 when the bound on harvest was $H = 1$ (with all other parameters equal).

Figure 11.21d displays the long-run stock density. In this limiting case, the density becomes discontinuous at S^*, with the long-run probability of stocks exceeding the switch

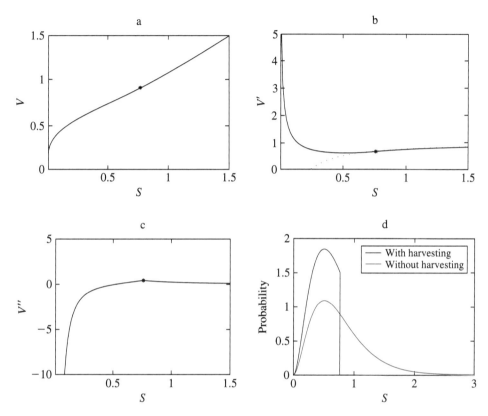

Figure 11.21
Solution to the Fish Harvesting Model (Unbounded Harvest Rate): (a) Value Function; (b) Marginal Value Function; (c) Curvature of Value Function; (d) Long-Run Density of Fish Stocks

point level being identically 0. As in Figure 11.13d, the long-run density with no harvesting is also shown.

As mentioned earlier, the impulse-control approach has the same solution that would be found in the bang-bang formulation of the problem as the upper bound on harvesting effort gets large. The drift rate on the state variable is $\alpha(1 - S)S - HS$, so if $H \gg \alpha(1 - S^*)$, it will be possible, for all practical purposes, to harvest fast enough to keep S at or below S^*. We invite the reader to run the code discussed in section 11.3.4 with the parameter H set to 60. The plots of the value function and its derivatives are essentially the same as those in Figures 11.21a–11.21d.

Exercises

11.1. A one-factor model that encompasses many term-structure models appearing in the literature is based on the process for the instantaneous interest rate (under the risk-neutral measure) given by

$$dr = [\alpha_1 + \alpha_2 r + \alpha_3 r \log(r)]\,dt + [\beta_1 + \beta_2 r]^\nu\,dz$$

State the PDE satisfied by a zero-coupon bond maturing in τ periods, along with the associated boundary condition. Write a function analogous to `cirbond` on page 373 for this case. The function should have the following input/output format:

```
c = bond(fspace,alpha1,alpha2,alpha3,beta1,beta2,nu,tau)
```

Notice that this function returns the coefficients of a function of r defined by the function definition structure variable `fspace`. Verify that your function reproduces correctly the results obtained using `cirbond`, which is a special case of the generalized model. To do so, use the parameters $\tau = 30$, $\kappa = 0.1$, $\alpha = 0.05$, and $\sigma = 0.2$.

11.2. Consider an option that gives its holder the right, in τ^o periods, to buy a bond that pays 1 unit of account τ^b periods after the option expires, at a strike price of K. Using the model for the instantaneous interest rate described in the previous exercise, write a MATLAB function that computes the value of such an option. The function should have the following input/output format:

```
c = bondoption(fspace,alpha1,alpha2,alpha3,beta1,beta2,nu,K,tauo,taub)
```

Determine the value of an option for the CIR model with $K = 1$, $\tau^o = 1$, $\tau^b = 0.25$, $\kappa = 0.1$, $\alpha = 0.05$, and $\sigma = 0.2$.

11.3. The routine `itosimul` can be used to simulate uncontrolled as well as controlled Ito processes. For uncontrolled processes the calling syntax is

```
st=itosimul(model,s0,T,nstep),
```

where `model` has the same form as is used for `finsolve`, `s0` is a npath $\times$ d matrix of starting values, with `npath` the desired number of paths and d the dimension of the state variable, `T` is the time horizon for the simulation, and `nstep` is the number of time steps.

Use `itosimul` to perform a Monte Carlo evaluation of an option on a stock for which the price process has risk-neutral dynamics given by

$$dS = rS\,dt + \sigma S\,dz$$

where r and σ are constants. Use the same parameters as in the example of section 11.1.4: the risk-free interest rate $r = 0.05$, the price volatility $\sigma = 0.2$, the strike price $K = 1$, and the time to maturity $T = 1$. The value of a call option is

$$V(s) = e^{-rT} \hat{E}[\max(K - S_T, 0) \mid S_0 = s]$$

Compare the value obtained by simulation to the values from the explicit Black-Scholes formula and from using `finsolve`.

11.4. Use a Euler equation approach to solve the neoclassical optimal growth model of section 11.3.1:

$$\max_{C(\cdot)} \int_0^\infty e^{-\rho t} u\left(C(K_t)\right) dt$$

subject to the state-transition function $K' = q(K) - C$, where

$$q(K) = \alpha \ln(K + 1) - \delta K$$

and

$$u(C) = (C^{1-\gamma} - 1)/(1 - \gamma)$$

using the parameter values $\rho = 0.05$, $\delta = 0.02$, $\alpha = 2(\rho + \delta) = 0.14$, and $\gamma = 0.5$. Compare your results to those obtained using the `scsolve` equation approach.

11.5. Reformulate and solve the growth model of section 11.3.1 using the variable transformation $y = \ln(K)$, with associated Bellman equation

$$\rho v(y) = \max_C \{ u(C) + [\ln(e^y + 1) - \delta e^y - C] e^{-y} v'(y) \}$$

11.6. In the asset replacement problem discussed in sections 10.5.1 and 11.5.1, the productivity of the asset depended only on its age. Suppose instead that the output of the machine is governed by

$$dQ = -\mu Q \, dt + \sigma \sqrt{Q(\bar{Q} - Q)} \, dz$$

where $\bar{Q}$ is the productivity of a new asset. Notice that the process is singular (the variance is zero) at $Q = 0$ and $Q = \bar{Q}$. At $Q = \bar{Q}$ the drift rate is negative, so productivity is decreasing, whereas $Q = 0$ is an absorbing barrier. The income flow rate from the asset is PQ, for some constant P, the replacement cost of the asset is C, and the discount rate is ρ. Intuitively, there is some value $Q = Q^*$ at which it is optimal to replace the asset.

a. State the Bellman equation and boundary conditions for this problem (be sure to consider what happens if $Q^* = 0$). What is the value function for $Q < Q^*$?

b. Write a MATLAB file that has the following input/output format:

```
[Qstar,c,fspace] = replace(mu,sigma,rho,P,C,Qbar,n)
```

where c and fspace are the coefficients and the function-definition structure defining the value function on the interval $[Q^*, \bar{Q}]$, and n is the degree of the approximation. You may assume an interior solution ($Q^* > 0$).

c. Call the function you wrote with the line

```
[Qstar,c,fspace] = replace(0.02,0.05,0.1,1,2,1,50);
```

Plot the value function on the interval $[0, \bar{Q}]$ (not on $[Q^*, \bar{Q}]$) and mark the point $(Q^*, V(\beta))$ with an asterisk.

11.7. a. Solve the timber-harvesting example from section 10.5.2 with the parameters $\alpha = 0.1$, $m = 1$, $\sigma = 0$, $P = 1$, $C = 0.15$, and $\rho = 0.08$. Plot the value function, indicating the location of the free boundary with an asterisk.

b. Resolve the problem under the assumption that the land will be abandoned and the replanting cost will not be incurred. Add this result to the plot generated for part a.

11.8. Consider the fish-harvesting problem (section 11.3.4) under the assumption that the control is not bounded ($H \to \infty$), making the problem of the barrier control type. Compute and plot the optimal trigger stock level as a function of the maximal harvest rate H, using the example values for other parameters. Demonstrate that the limiting value as $H \to \infty$ computed in section 11.5.5 is correct.

11.9. Consider the problem of determining an investment strategy when a project takes time to complete and completion costs are uncertain. The cost uncertainty takes two forms. The first, technical uncertainty, arises because of unforeseen technical problems that develop as the project progresses. Technical uncertainty is assumed to be diversifiable, and hence the market price of risk is zero. The second type of uncertainty is factor cost uncertainty, which is assumed to have market price of risk θ.

Define K to be the expected remaining cost to complete a project that is worth V upon completion. The dynamics of K are given by

$$dK = -I\,dt + v\sqrt{IK}\,dz + \gamma K\,dw$$

where I, the control, is the current investment rate and dz and dw are independent Weiner processes. The project cannot be completed immediately because I is constrained by $0 \leq I \leq k$. Given the assumptions about the market price of risk, we convert the K process to its risk-neutral form and use the risk-free interest rate, r, to discount the future. Thus we act "as if"

$$dK = -(I + \theta\gamma K)\,dt + v\sqrt{IK}\,dz + \gamma K\,dw$$

and solve

$$F(K_0) = \max_{0 \le I(\cdot) \le k} E_0 \left[e^{-rT} V - \int_0^T e^{-rt} I(K_t) \, dt \right]$$

where T is the (uncertain) completion time given by $K_T = 0$.

The Bellman equation for this problem is

$$rF = \max_{0 \le I \le k} \left\{ -I - (I + \theta \gamma K)F'(K) + \tfrac{1}{2}(v^2 IK + \gamma^2 K^2)F''(K) \right\}$$

with boundary conditions

$$F(0) = V$$

$$F(\infty) = 0$$

The optimal control is of the bang-bang type:

$$I = \begin{cases} 0 & \text{if } K > K^* \\ k & \text{if } K < K^* \end{cases}$$

where K^* solves

$$\tfrac{1}{2}v^2 KF''(K) - F'(K) - 1 = 0$$

Notice that technical uncertainty increases with the level of investment. This is a case in which the variance of the process is influenced by the control. Although we have not dealt with this explicitly, it raises no new problems.

a. Solve F up to an unknown constant for $K > K^*$.

b. Use the result in part a to obtain a boundary condition at $K = K^*$ by utilizing the continuity of F and F'.

c. Solve the deterministic problem ($v = \gamma = 0$), and show that

$$K^* = k \ln(1 + rV/k)/r$$

d. Write the Bellman equation for $K < K^*$, and transform it from the domain $[0, K^*]$ to $[0, 1]$ using $u = K/K^*$. Also transform the boundary conditions.

e. Write a computer program using Chebychev collocation to solve for F and K^* using the following parameters: $V = 10$, $r = 0.05$, $\theta = 0$, $k = 2$, $\gamma = 0.5$, $v = 0.25$.

g. What alterations are needed to handle the case when $\gamma = 0$, and why are they needed?

11.10. Consider an investment project that, upon completion, will have a random value V and will generate a return flow of δV. The value of the completed project evolves, under the risk-neutral measure, according to

$$dV = (r - \delta)V \, dt + \sigma V \, dz$$

where r is the risk-free rate of return. The amount of investment needed to complete the project is K, which is a completely controlled process:

$$dK = -I \, dt$$

where the investment rate is constrained by $0 \leq I \leq k$. In this situation it is optimal to be investing either at the maximum rate or not at all. Let the value of the investment opportunity in these two cases by denoted $F(V, K)$ and $f(V, K)$, respectively. These functions are governed by the following laws of motion:

$$\tfrac{1}{2}\sigma^2 V^2 F_{VV} + (r - \delta)V F_V - rF - kF_K - k = 0$$

and

$$\tfrac{1}{2}\sigma^2 V^2 f_{VV} + (r - \delta)V f_V - rf = 0$$

subject to the boundary conditions

$$F(V, 0) = V$$

$$\lim_{V \to \infty} F_V(V, K) = e^{-\delta K/k}$$

$$f(0, K) = 0$$

$$f(V^*, K) = F(V^*, K)$$

$$f_V(V^*, K) = F_V(V^*, K)$$

The value V^* is the value of the completed project needed to make a positive investment. It can be shown that $f(V) = A(K)V^\beta$, where

$$\beta = \frac{1}{2} - \frac{r - \delta}{\sigma^2} + \sqrt{\left(\frac{1}{2} - \frac{r - \delta}{\sigma^2}\right)^2 + \frac{2r}{\sigma^2}} \tag{11.8}$$

and $A(K)$ is a function that must be determined by the boundary conditions. This may be eliminated by combining the free-boundary conditions to yield

$$\beta F(V^*, K) = V^* F_V(V^*, K)$$

Summarizing, the problem is to solve the following partial differential equation for given values of σ, r, δ, and k:

$$\tfrac{1}{2}\sigma^2 V^2 F_{VV} + (r - \delta) V F_V - r F - k F_K - k = 0$$

subject to

$$F(V, 0) = V$$

$$\lim_{V \to \infty} F_V(V, K) = e^{-\delta K/k}$$

$$\beta F(V^*, K) = V^* F_V(V^*, K)$$

where β is given by equation (11.8). This is a PDE in V and K, with an initial condition for $K = 0$, a limiting boundary condition for large V, and a lower free boundary for V that is a function of K.

The optimal solution must, in addition, satisfy

$$F_K(V^*, K) = 1$$

Write MATLAB code to solve this time-to-build problem for the following parameter values: $\delta = 0, r = 0.02, \sigma = 0.2, k = 1$.

11.11. Review the sequential learning model discussed in sections 10.3.8 and 11.3.5. Note that the Bellman equation provides an expression for V_Q when $P > P^*$. For $P < P^*$, the value function has the form $A(Q)P^{\beta_1}$, and so $V_Q(P, Q) = A'(Q)P^{\beta_1}$.

a. Derive an expression for V_Q for $P > P^*$.

b. Show that V_Q is continuous at $P = P^*$ for $\sigma > 0$.

c. Use this fact to determine $A'(Q)$.

d. Plot V_Q as a function of P for $Q = 0$ using the parameters $r = \delta = 0.05$ and for the values $\sigma = 0.1, 0.2, 0.3, 0.4$, and 0.5.

e. When $\sigma = 0, V_Q$ is discontinuous at $P = P^*$. This case was discussed in exercise 10.24 (page 366). Add this case to the plot from part d.

Appendix 11A: Basis Matrices for Multivariate Models

The basic PDE used in asset-valuation and control problems arising in economics and finance takes the form

$$\rho(S)V = \delta(S) + V_t + V_S\mu(S) + \tfrac{1}{2}\text{trace}\left(\sigma(S)\sigma(S)^\top V_{SS}\right)$$

Generically, S is a d-dimensional vector, V_S is $1 \times d$, $\mu(S)$ is $d \times 1$, V_{SS} is $d \times d$, and $\sigma(S)$ is $d \times d$.

To solve the PDE using collocation one must form appropriate basis matrices for the function and its first two derivatives and must multiply those basis matrices by the appropriate coefficients (ρ, μ, and σ). In a multivariate setting, in particular, this approach requires some bookkeeping tasks that are tedious. To facilitate this process, we provide a function `ctbasemake` to handle these tasks.

For the function itself we require a matrix B_0 such that $B_0 c$ approximates $\rho(S)V(S)$, with each row of B_0 corresponding to one of the N nodal values of S:

$$B_0 = \text{diag}\big(\rho(S)\big)\Phi(S)$$

where ρ is $N \times 1$ and $\Phi(S)$ is $N \times n$.

For the first derivative we seek a matrix B_1 such that $B_1 c$ approximates $V_S(S)\mu(S)$. Hence

$$B_1 = \sum_{j=1}^{d} \text{diag}\big(\mu_j(S)\big)\frac{\partial \Phi(S)}{\partial S_j}$$

For the second derivative we seek a matrix B_2 such that $B_2 c$ approximates

$$\tfrac{1}{2}\text{trace}\big(\sigma(S)\sigma(S)^\top V_{SS}\big)$$

This can be written as

$$B_2 = \frac{1}{2}\sum_{j=1}^{d}\text{diag}\big(\Sigma_{jj}(S)\big)\frac{\partial^2 \Phi(S)}{\partial S_j S_j} + \sum_{j=1}^{d}\sum_{k=j+1}^{d}\text{diag}\big(\Sigma_{jk}(S)\big)\frac{\partial^2 \Phi(S)}{\partial S_j S_k}$$

where

$$\Sigma_{jk}(S) = \sum_{i=1}^{d}\sigma_{ji}(S)\sigma_{ki}(S)$$

Each of the second-partial-derivative matrices is $N \times n$, and each of the Σ_{jk} is $N \times 1$.

One of the most time-consuming parts of these computations lies in obtaining the primitive basis matrices themselves (Φ and its derivatives), which are formed using tensor products of one-dimensional bases (we assume here that the nodal values of S form a regular grid). All the necessary basis matrices can be obtained with a single call to the function `funbasx`:
```
bases = funbasx(fspace,snodes,[0;1;2]).
```
The syntax for our utility function is

```
B = ctbasemake(coeff,bases,order)
```

The last argument `order` should be 0, 1, or 2 and indicates whether B_0, B_1, or B_2 is requested. The first argument `coeff` is an N-row matrix. For $order = 0$ it is the $N \times 1$ vector $\rho(S)$, for $order = 1$ it is the $N \times d$ matrix $\mu(S)$, for $order = 2$ it is the $N \times d \times d$ array (or $N \times d^2$ matrix) $\sigma(S)$.

The function is also structured so the appropriate tensor products can be computed separately from the multiplication of the coefficients. Thus the following syntaxes yield identical results:

```
B1 = ctbasemake(mu,bases,1);
```

and

```
Phi1 = ctbasemake([],bases,1);
B1 = ctbasemake(mu,Phi1,1);
```

The `scsolve` procedure uses this feature to form the B_1 matrix using $\mu(S) = g(S, x)$ evaluated at alternative values of x. The drawback to this method is that it requires additional memory to store `Phi1`, but it results in significant speed improvements if memory is not limited.

Bibliographic Notes

A standard reference on solving PDEs is Ames (1992). It contains a good discussion of stability and convergence analysis; the section on parabolic PDEs is especially relevant for economic applications. Golub and Ortega (1992) contains a useful introductory treatment of the extended method of lines for solving PDEs (sec. 8.4), which they call a semidiscrete method. Most treatments of PDEs begin with a discussion of finite difference methods and may then proceed to finite element and weighted residual methods. The approach we have taken reverses this order by starting with a weighted residual approach (collocation) and demonstrating that finite difference methods can be viewed as a special case with a specific choice of basis functions. We have not discussed finite element methods explicitly, but the same remarks apply to them. Piecewise-linear and cubic-spline bases are common examples of finite element methods.

Numerous references containing discussions of numerical techniques for solving financial-asset models now exist. Hull (2000) contains a good overview of commonly used techniques. See also Duffie (1996) and Wilmott (1998). In addition to finite difference methods, binomial and trinomial trees and Monte Carlo methods are the most commonly used approaches. Heston (1993) suggested an alternative approach to computing the option price for the stochastic volatility model that utilizes Fourier inversion of the characteristic function. The approach has been extended to apply to general affine diffusions by Duffie, Pan, and Singleton (1999).

Tree approaches represent state dynamics using a branching process. Although the conceptual framework seems different from the PDE approach, tree methods are computationally closely related to explicit finite difference methods for solving PDEs. If the solution to an asset pricing model for a given initial value of the state is the only output required from a solution, trees have an advantage over finite difference methods because they require evaluation of far fewer nodal points. If the entire solution function and/or derivatives with respect to the state variable and to time are desired, this advantage disappears. Furthermore, the extended method of lines is quite competitive with tree methods and far more simple to implement.

Monte Carlo techniques are increasingly being used, especially in situations with a high-dimensional state space. The essential approach simulates paths for the state variable using the risk-neutral state process. Many assets can then be priced as the average value of the returns to the asset evaluated along each sample path. This approach is both simple to implement and avoids the need for special treatment of boundary conditions with exotic assets. Numerous refinements exist to increase the efficiency of the approach, including the use of variance-reduction techniques such as antithetic and control variates, as well as the use of quasi-random numbers (low-discrepancy sequences). Monte Carlo approaches have been applied to the calculation of American-style assets with early exercise features, but this approach requires more work.

Merton (1975, Appendix B) contains a useful discussion of long-run densities for Ito processes, including regularity conditions on μ and σ (e.g., they are continuous and $\mu(0) = \sigma(0) = 0$). He points out that there is another solution to the Kolmogorov equation, but that it must be zero when the probability of reaching the boundaries of the state space is zero. This discussion is also related to the Feller classification of boundary conditions in the presence of singularities; see Bharucha-Reid (1960, sec. 3.3) and Karlin and Taylor (1981, Chap. 14). Other approaches to solving stochastic control problems include discretization methods; see, for example, Kushner and Dupuis (1992).

Several of the exercises are based on problems in the literature. The generalized model of the instantaneous interest rate appears in Duffie (1996, pp. 131–133). The fish harvesting problem with adjustment costs was developed by Ludwig (1979a) and Ludwig and Varrah (1979). The cost uncertainty model is discussed in Dixit and Pindyck (1994, pp. 345–351). The time-to-build exercise is from Majd and Pindyck (1987) and is also discussed in Dixit and Pindyck (1994, pp. 328–339).

Appendix A
Mathematical Background

A.1 Normed Linear Spaces

A *linear space* or *vector space* is a nonempty set X endowed with two operations, vector addition ($+$) and scalar multiplication ($\cdot$), that satisfy the following:

- $x + y = y + x$ for all $x, y \in X$.
- $(x + y) + z = x + (y + z)$ for all $x, y, z \in X$.
- There is a $\theta \in X$ such that $x + \theta = x$ for all $x \in X$.
- For each $x \in X$ there is a $y \in X$ such that $x + y = \theta$.
- $(\alpha\beta) \cdot x = \alpha \cdot (\beta \cdot x)$ for all $\alpha, \beta \in \mathbb{R}$ and $x \in X$.
- $\alpha \cdot (x + y) = \alpha \cdot x + \alpha \cdot y$ for all $\alpha \in \mathbb{R}$ and $x, y \in X$.
- $(\alpha + \beta) \cdot x = \alpha \cdot x + \beta \cdot y$ for all $\alpha, \beta \in \mathbb{R}$ and $x \in X$.
- $1 \cdot x = x$ for all $x \in X$.

The elements of X are called vectors.

A normed linear space is a linear space endowed with a real-valued function $|| \cdot ||$ on X, called a norm, that measures the size of vectors. By definition, a norm must satisfy the following:

- $||x|| \geq 0$ for all $x \in X$.
- $||x|| = 0$ if and only if $x = \theta$.
- $||\alpha \cdot x|| = |\alpha| \, ||x||$ for all $\alpha \in \mathbb{R}$ and $x \in X$.
- $||x + y|| \leq ||x|| + ||y||$ for all $x, y \in X$.

Every norm on a linear space induces a metric that measures the distance $d(x, y)$ between arbitrary vectors x and y. The induced metric is defined using the relation $d(x, y) = ||x - y||$. It meets all the conditions we normally expect a distance function to satisfy:

- $d(x, y) = d(y, x) \geq 0$ for all $x, y \in X$.
- $d(x, y) = 0$ if and only if $x = y \in X$.
- $d(x, y) \leq d(x, z) + d(z, y)$ for all $x, y, z \in X$.

Norms and metrics play a critical role in numerical analysis. In many numerical applications, we do not solve a model exactly, but rather compute an approximation using some iterative scheme. The iterative scheme is usually terminated when the change in successive iterates becomes acceptably small, as measured by the norm of the change. The accuracy of the approximation or approximation error is measured by the metric distance between the final approximant and the true solution. Of course, in all meaningful applications, the distance between the approximant and true solution is unknown because the true solution is unknown. However, in many theoretical and practical applications, it is possible to compute upper bounds on the approximation error, thus giving a level of confidence in the approximation. In this book we will work almost exclusively with three classes of normed linear spaces. The first normed linear space is $\mathbb{R}^n$, the space of all real n-vectors. The second normed linear space is $\mathbb{R}^{m \times n}$, the space of all real m-by-n matrices. We will use a variety of norms for real-vector and matrix spaces, all of which are discussed in greater detail in the following section.

The third class of normed linear space is $C(S)$, the space of all bounded continuous real-valued functions defined on $S \subset \mathbb{R}^m$. Addition and scalar multiplication in this space are defined pointwise. Specifically, if $f, g \in C(S)$ and $\alpha \in \mathbb{R}$, then $f + g$ is the function whose value at $x \in S$ is $f(x) + g(x)$, and αf is the function whose value at $x \in S$ is $\alpha f(x)$. We will use only one norm, called the sup or supremum norm, on the function space $C(S)$:

$$||f|| = \sup\{|f(x)| \mid x \in S\}$$

In most applications, S will be a bounded interval of $\mathbb{R}^n$.

A subset Y of a normed linear space X is called a subspace if it is closed under addition and scalar multiplication, and thus is a normed linear space in its own right. More specifically, Y is a subspace of X if $x + y \in Y$ and $\alpha x \in Y$ whenever $x, y \in Y$ and $\alpha \in \mathbb{R}$. A subspace Y is said to be dense in X if for any $x \in X$ and $\epsilon > 0$, we can always find a $y \in Y$ such that $||x - y|| < \epsilon$. Dense linear subspaces play an important role in numerical analysis. When constructing approximants for elements in a normed linear space X, drawing our approximants from a dense linear subspace guarantees that an arbitrarily accurate approximation can always be found, at least in theory.

Given a nonempty subset S of X, span(S) is the set of all finite linear combinations of elements of S:

$$\text{span}(S) = \left\{ \sum_{i=1}^{n} \alpha_i x_i \mid \alpha_i \in \mathbb{R}, x_i \in X, n \text{ an integer} \right\}$$

We say that a subset B is a basis for a subspace Y if $Y = \text{span}(B)$ and if no proper subset of B has this property. A basis has the property that no element of the basis can be written as a linear combination of the other elements in the basis. That is, the elements of the basis are linearly independent.

Except for the trivial subspace $\{\theta\}$, a subspace Y will generally have many distinct bases. However, if Y has a basis with a finite number of elements, then all bases have the same number of nonzero elements, and this number is called the dimension of the subspace. If the subspace has no finite basis, it is said to be infinite dimensional.

Consider some examples. Every normed linear space X has two trivial subspaces: $\{\theta\}$, whose dimension is zero, and X. The sets $\{(0, 1), (1, 0)\}$ and $\{(2, 1), (3, 4)\}$ both are bases for $\mathbb{R}^2$, which is a two-dimensional space; the set $\{(\alpha, 0.5 \cdot \alpha) \mid \alpha \in \mathbb{R}\}$ is a one-dimensional subspace of $\mathbb{R}^2$. In general, $\mathbb{R}^n$ is an n-dimensional space with many possible bases; moreover, the span of any $k < n$ linearly independent n-vectors constitutes a proper k-dimensional subspace of $\mathbb{R}^n$.

The function space $C(S)$ of all real-valued bounded continuous functions on an interval $S \subset \mathbb{R}$ is an infinite-dimensional space. That is, there is no finite number of real-valued bounded continuous functions whose linear combinations span the entire space. This space has a number of subspaces that are important in numerical analysis. The set of all polynomials on S of degree at most n forms an $n + 1$ dimensional subspace of $C(S)$ with one basis being $\{1, x, x^2, \ldots, x^n\}$. The set of all polynomials, regardless of degree, is also a subspace of $C(S)$ and is infinite dimensional. Other subspaces of $C(S)$ of interest include the spaces of piecewise polynomial splines of a given order and breakpoint set. These subspaces are finite dimensional and are discussed further in the text.

A sequence $\{x_k\}$ in a normed linear space X converges to a limit x^* in X if $\lim_{k \longrightarrow \infty} \|x_k - x^*\| = 0$. We write $\lim_{k \longrightarrow \infty} x_k = x^*$ to indicate that the sequence $\{x_k\}$ converges to x^*. If a sequence converges, its limit is necessarily unique. An open ball centered at $x \in X$ is a set of the form $\{y \in X \mid \|x - y\| < \epsilon\}$, where $\epsilon > 0$. A set S in X is open if every element of S is the center of some open ball contained entirely in S. A set S in X is closed if its complement, that is, the set of elements of X not contained in S, is an open set. Equivalently, a set S is closed if it contains the limit of every convergent sequence in S.

The Contraction Mapping Theorem has many uses in computational economics, particularly in existence and convergence theorems. Suppose that X is a complete normed linear space, that T maps a nonempty set $S \subset X$ into itself, and that, for some $\delta < 1$,

$$\|T(x) - T(y)\| \leq \delta \|x - y\|, \quad \text{for all } x, y \in S$$

Then, there is an unique $x^* \in S$ such that $T(x^*) = x^*$. Moreover, if $x_0 \in S$ and $x_{k+1} = T(x_k)$, then $\{x_k\}$ necessarily converges to x^* and

$$\|x_k - x^*\| \leq \frac{\delta}{1 - \delta} \|x_k - x_{k-1}\|$$

If the conditions of the theorem hold, T is said to be a strong contraction on S, and x^* is said to be a fixed point of T in S.

We shall not define what we mean by a complete normed linear space, save to note that $\mathbb{R}^n$, $C(S)$, and all their subspaces are complete.

A.2   Matrix Algebra

We write $x \in \mathbb{R}^n$ to denote that x is an n-vector whose ith entry is x_i. A vector is understood to be in column form unless otherwise noted.

If x and y are n-vectors, then their sum $z = x + y$ is the n-vector whose ith entry is $z_i = x_i + y_i$. Their inner product or dot product, $x \cdot y$, is the real number $\sum_i x_i y_i$ and their array product, $z = x. * y$, is the n-vector whose ith entry is $z_i = x_i y_i$. If α is a scalar, that is, a real number, and x is an n-vector, then their scalar sum $z = \alpha + x = x + \alpha$ is the n-vector whose ith entry is $z_i = \alpha + x_i$. Their scalar product, $z = \alpha x = x \alpha$, is the n-vector whose ith entry is $z_i = \alpha x_i$.

The most useful vector norms are, respectively, the 1-norm or sum norm, the 2-norm or Euclidean norm, and the infinity or sup norm:

$$||x||_1 = \sum_i |x_i|$$

$$||x||_2 = \sqrt{\sum_i |x_i|^2}$$

$$||x||_\infty = \max_i |x_i|$$

In MATLAB, the norms may be computed for any vector x, respectively, by writing `norm(x,1)`, `norm(x,2)`, and `norm(x,inf)`. If we simply write `norm(x)`, the 2-norm or Euclidean norm is computed. All norms on $\mathbb{R}^n$ are equivalent in the sense that a sequence converges in one vector norm if and only if it converges in all other vector norms. This statement is not true generally of all normed linear spaces.

A sequence of vectors $\{x_k\}$ converges to x^* at a rate of order $p \geq 1$ if for some $c \geq 0$ and for sufficiently large n,

$$||x_{k+1} - x^*|| \leq c||x_k - x^*||^p$$

If $p = 1$ and $c < 1$, we say the convergence is linear; if $p > 1$, we say the convergence is superlinear; and if $p = 2$, we say the convergence is quadratic. We write $A \in \mathbb{R}^{m \times n}$ to denote that A is an m-row-by-n-column matrix whose row-i, column-j entry, or, more succinctly, ijth entry, is A_{ij}. If A is an $m \times n$ matrix and B is an $m \times n$ matrix, then their sum $C = A + B$ is the $m \times n$ matrix whose ijth entry is $C_{ij} = A_{ij} + B_{ij}$. If A is an $m \times p$ matrix and B is a $p \times n$ matrix, then their product $C = AB$ is the $m \times n$ matrix whose ijth entry is $C_{ij} = \sum_{k=1}^{p} A_{ik} B_{kj}$. If A and B are both $m \times n$ matrices, then their array product $C = A. * B$ is the $m \times n$ matrix whose ijth entry is $C_{ij} = A_{ij} B_{ij}$.

A matrix A is square if it has an equal number of rows and columns. A square matrix is upper triangular if $A_{ij} = 0$ for $i > j$; it is lower triangular if $A_{ij} = 0$ for $i < j$; it is diagonal if $A_{ij} = 0$ for $i \neq j$; and it is tridiagonal if $A_{ij} = 0$ for $|i - j| > 1$. The identity matrix, denoted I, is a diagonal matrix whose diagonal entries are all 1. In MATLAB, the identity matrix of order n is generated by the statement `eye(n)`.

The transpose of an $m \times n$ matrix A, denoted $A^\top$, is the $n \times m$ matrix whose ijth entry is the jith entry of A. A square matrix is symmetric if $A = A^\top$, that is, if $A_{ij} = A_{ji}$ for all i and j. A square matrix A is orthogonal if $A^\top A = A A^\top$ is diagonal, and orthonormal if $A^\top A = A A^\top = I$. In MATLAB, the transpose of a real matrix `A` is generated by the statement `A'`.

A square matrix A is invertible if there exists a matrix A^{-1}, called the inverse of A, such that $A A^{-1} = A^{-1} A = I$. If the inverse exists, it is unique. In MATLAB, the inverse of a square matrix `A` can be generated by the statement `inv(A)`.

The most useful matrix norms, and the only ones used in this book, are constructed from vector norms. A given n-vector norm $|| \cdot ||$ induces a corresponding matrix norm for $n \times n$ matrices using the relation

$$||A|| = \max_{||x||=1} ||Ax||$$

or, equivalently,

$$||A|| = \max_{||x|| \neq 0} \frac{||Ax||}{||x||}$$

Given corresponding vector and matrix norms,

$$||Ax|| \leq ||A|| \, ||x||$$

Moreover, if A and B are square matrices,

$$||AB|| \leq ||A|| \, ||B||$$

Common matrix norms include the matrix norms induced by the one, two (Euclidean), and infinity norms:

$$||A||_p = \max_{||x||_p = 1} ||Ax||_p$$

for $p = 1, 2, \infty$. In MATLAB, these norms may be computed for any matrix `A`, respectively, by writing `norm(A,1)`, `norm(A,2)`, and `norm(A,inf)`. The two (Euclidean) matrix norm is relatively expensive to compute. The one and infinity norms, however, take a relatively simple form:

$$||A||_1 = \max_{1 \le j \le n} \sum_{i=1}^{n} |A_{ij}|$$

$$||A||_\infty = \max_{\substack{1 \le i \le n \\ 1 \le j \le n}} |A_{ij}|$$

The spectral radius of a square matrix A, denoted $\rho(A)$, is the infimum of all the matrix norms of A. We have $\lim_{k \to \infty} A^k = 0$ if and only if $\rho(A) < 1$, in which case $(I - A)^{-1} = \sum_{k=0}^{\infty} A^k$. Thus, if $||A|| < 1$ in any matrix norm, A^k converges to zero. A square symmetric matrix A is negative semidefinite if $x^\top A x \le 0$ for all x; it is negative definite if $x^\top A x < 0$ for all $x \ne 0$; it is positive semidefinite if $x^\top A x \ge 0$ for all x; and it is positive definite if $x^\top A x > 0$ for all $x \ne 0$.

A.3   Real Analysis

The Jacobian of a vector-valued function $f : \mathbb{R}^n \mapsto \mathbb{R}^m$ is the $m \times n$ matrix-valued function of first partial derivatives of f. More specifically, the Jacobian of f at x, denoted by either $f'(x)$ or $f_x(x)$, is the $m \times n$ matrix whose ijth entry is the partial derivative $\frac{\partial f_i}{\partial x_j}(x)$. More generally, if $f(x_1, x_2)$ is an n-vector-valued function defined for $x_1 \in \mathbb{R}^{n_1}$ and $x_2 \in \mathbb{R}^{n_2}$, then $f_{x_1}(x)$ is the $m \times n_1$ matrix of partial derivatives of f with respect to x_1, and $f_{x_2}(x)$ is the $m \times n_2$ matrix of partial derivatives of f with respect to x_2.

The Hessian of the real-valued function $f : \mathbb{R}^n \mapsto \mathbb{R}$ is the $n \times n$ matrix-valued function of second partial derivatives of f. More specifically, the Hessian of f at x, denoted by either $f''(x)$ or $f_{xx}(x)$, is the symmetric $n \times n$ matrix whose ijth entry is $\frac{\partial^2 f}{\partial x_i \partial x_j}(x)$. More generally, if $f(x_1, x_2)$ is a real-valued function defined for $x_1 \in \mathbb{R}^{n_1}$ and $x_2 \in \mathbb{R}^{n_2}$, then $f_{x_i x_j}(x)$ is the $n_i \times n_j$ submatrix of $f''(x)$ obtained by extracting the rows corresponding to the elements of x_i and the columns corresponding to the columns of x_j.

A real-valued function $f : \mathbb{R}^n \mapsto \mathbb{R}$ is smooth on a convex open set S if its gradient and Hessian are defined and continuous on S. By Taylor's theorem, a smooth function may be approximated locally by either a linear or quadratic function. More specifically, for all x in S,

$$f(x) = f(x_0) + f_x(x_0)(x - x_0) + o(||x - x_0||)$$

and

$$f(x) = f(x_0) + f_x(x_0)(x - x_0) + \tfrac{1}{2}(x - x_0)^\top f_{xx}(x_0)(x - x_0) + o(||x - x_0||^2)$$

where $o(t)$ denotes a term with the property that $\lim_{t \to 0}(o(t)/t) = 0$.

The Intermediate Value Theorem asserts that if a continuous real-valued function attains two values, then it must attain all values in between. More precisely, if f is continuous on a convex set $S \in \mathbb{R}^n$ and $f(x_1) \leq y \leq f(x_2)$ for some $x_1 \in S$, $x_2 \in S$, and $y \in \mathbb{R}$, then $f(x) = y$ for some $x \in S$.

The Implicit Function Theorem gives conditions under which a system of nonlinear equations will have a locally unique solution that will vary continuously with some parameter: Suppose that $F : \mathbb{R}^{m+n} \mapsto \mathbb{R}^n$ is continuously differentiable in a neighborhood of (x_0, y_0), that $x_0 \in \mathbb{R}^m$ and $y_0 \in \mathbb{R}^n$, and that $F(x_0, y_0) = 0$. If $F_y(x_0, y_0)$ is nonsingular, then there is an unique function $f : \mathbb{R}^m \mapsto \mathbb{R}^n$ defined on a neighborhood N of x_0 such that for all $x \in N$, $F(x, f(x)) = 0$. Furthermore, the function f is continuously differentiable on N and $f'(x) = -F_y^{-1}(x, f(x)) F_x(x, f(x))$.

A subset S is bounded if it is contained entirely inside some ball centered at zero. A subset S is compact if it is both closed and bounded. A continuous real-valued function defined on a compact set has well-defined maximum and minimum values; moreover, there will be points in S at which the function attains its maximum and minimum values.

A real-valued function $f : \mathbb{R}^n \mapsto \mathbb{R}$ is concave on a convex set S if $\alpha_1 f(x_1) + \alpha_2 f(x_2) \leq f(\alpha_1 x_1 + \alpha_2 x_2)$ for all distinct $x_1, x_2 \in S$, and $\alpha_1, \alpha_2 > 0$ with $\alpha_1 + \alpha_2 = 1$. It is strictly concave if the inequality is always strict. A smooth function is concave (strictly concave) if and only if $f''(x)$ is negative semidefinite (negative definite) for all $x \in S$. A smooth function f is convex if and only if $-f$ is concave. If a function is concave (convex) on an convex set, then its maximum (minimum), if it exists, is unique.

A.4 Markov Chains

A Markov process is a sequence of random variables $\{X_t \mid t = 0, 1, 2, \ldots\}$ with common state space S whose distributions satisfy

$$\Pr\{X_{t+1} \in A \mid X_t, X_{t-1}, X_{t-2}, \ldots\} = \Pr\{X_{t+1} \in A \mid X_t\} \quad A \subset S$$

A Markov process is often said to be memoryless because the distribution X_{t+1} conditional on the history of the process through time t is completely determined by X_t and, given X_t, is independent of the realizations of the process prior to time t.

A Markov chain is a Markov process with a finite state space $S = \{1, 2, 3, \ldots, n\}$. A Markov chain is completely characterized by its transition probabilities

$$P_{tij} = \Pr\{X_{t+1} = j \mid X_t = i\}, \quad i, j \in S$$

A Markov chain is stationary if its transition probabilities

$$P_{ij} = \Pr\{X_{t+1} = j \mid X_t = i\}, \quad i, j \in S$$

are independent of t. The matrix P is called the transition probability matrix.

The steady-state distribution of a stationary Markov chain is a probability distribution $\{\pi_i \mid i = 1, 2, \ldots, n\}$ on S, such that

$$\pi_j = \lim_{\tau \to \infty} \Pr\{X_\tau = j \mid X_t = i\} \quad i, j \in S$$

The steady-state distribution π, if it exists, completely characterizes the long-run behavior of a stationary Markov chain.

A stationary Markov chain is irreducible if for any i, $j \in S$ there is some $k \geq 1$ such that $\Pr\{X_{t+k} = j \mid X_t = i\} > 0$, that is, if starting from any state there is positive probability of eventually visiting every other state. Given an irreducible Markov chain with transition probability matrix P, if there is an n-vector $\pi \geq 0$ such that

$$P^\top \pi = \pi$$

$$\sum_i \pi_i = 1$$

then the Markov chain has a steady-state distribution π.

In computational economic applications, one often encounters irreducible Markov chains. To compute the steady-state distribution of the Markov chain, one solves the $n + 1$ by n linear equation system

$$\begin{bmatrix} I - P^\top \\ \mathbf{1}^\top \end{bmatrix} \pi = \begin{bmatrix} 0 \\ 1 \end{bmatrix}$$

where P is the probability transition matrix and $\underline{1}$ is the vector consisting of all ones. Due to linear dependency among the probabilities, any one of the first n linear equations is redundant and may be dropped to obtain a uniquely soluble matrix linear equation.

Consider a stationary Markov chain with transition probability matrix

$$P = \begin{bmatrix} 0.5 & 0.2 & 0.3 \\ 0.0 & 0.4 & 0.6 \\ 0.5 & 0.5 & 0.0 \end{bmatrix}$$

Although one cannot reach state 1 from state 2 in one step, one can reach it with positive probability in two steps. Similarly, although one cannot return to state 3 in one step, one can return in two steps. The steady-state distribution π of the Markov chain may be computed by solving the linear equation

$$\begin{bmatrix} 0.5 & 0.0 & -0.5 \\ -0.2 & 0.6 & -0.5 \\ 1.0 & 1.0 & 1.0 \end{bmatrix} \pi = \begin{bmatrix} 0 \\ 0 \\ 1 \end{bmatrix}$$

The solution is

$$\pi = \begin{bmatrix} 0.316 \\ 0.368 \\ 0.316 \end{bmatrix}$$

Thus, over the long run, the Markov process will spend about 31.6 percent of its time in state 1, 36.8 percent of its time in state 2, and 31.6 percent of its time in state 3.

A.5 Continuous Time Mathematics

A.5.1 Ito Processes

The continuous time stochastic processes most commonly used in economic applications are constructed from the so-called standard Wiener process or standard Brownian motion. This process is most intuitively defined as a limit of sums of independent normally distributed random variables:

$$z_{t+\Delta t} - z_t \equiv \int_t^{t+\Delta t} dz = \lim_{n \to \infty} \sqrt{\frac{\Delta t}{n}} \sum_{i=1}^n v_i$$

where the v_i are independently and identically distributed standard normal variates (i.i.d. $N(0, 1)$). The standard Wiener process has the following properties:

1. Time paths are continuous (no jumps).
2. Nonoverlapping increments are independent.
3. Increments are normally distributed with mean zero and variance Δt.

The first property is not obvious, but properties 2 and 3 follow directly from the definition of the process. Each nonoverlapping increment of the process is defined as the sum of independent random variables, and hence the increments are independent. Each of the variables in the sum has expectation zero, and hence so does the sum. The variance is

$$E\Delta z^2 = \Delta t \lim_{n \to \infty} \frac{1}{n} E \left(\sum_{i=1}^n v_i \right)^2 = \Delta t \lim_{n \to \infty} \frac{1}{n} \sum_{i=1}^n E\left[v_i^2\right] = \Delta t$$

Ito diffusion processes are typically represented as stochastic differential equations (SDEs) of the form

$$dS = \mu(S, t) \, dt + \sigma(S, t) \, dz$$

where z is a standard Wiener process.

The Ito process is completely defined in terms of the functions μ and σ, which can be interpreted as the instantaneous mean and standard deviation of the process:

$$E[dS] = \mu(S, t)\, dt$$

and

$$Var[dS] = E[dS^2] - (E[dS])^2 = E[dS^2] - \mu(S, t)^2\, dt^2 = E[dS^2] = \sigma^2(S, t)\, dt$$

μ and σ are also known as the drift and diffusion terms, respectively. This definition is not as limiting as it might appear to be at first, because a wide variety of stochastic behavior can be represented by appropriate definition of the two functions.

The differential representation is a shorthand for the stochastic integral

$$S_{t+\Delta t} = S_t + \int_t^{t+\Delta t} \mu(S_\tau, \tau)\, d\tau + \int_t^{t+\Delta t} \sigma(S_\tau, \tau)\, dz \tag{A.1}$$

The first of the integrals in equation (A.1) is an ordinary (Riemann) integral. The second integral, however, involves the stochastic term dz and requires additional explanation. It is defined in the following way:

$$\int_t^{t+\Delta t} \sigma(S_\tau, \tau)\, dz = \lim_{n\to\infty} \sqrt{\frac{\Delta t}{n}} \sum_{i=0}^{n-1} \sigma(S_{t+ih}, t+ih) v_i \tag{A.2}$$

where $h = \Delta t/n$ and $v_i \sim$ i.i.d. $N(0,1)$. The key feature of this definition is that it is nonanticipating; values of S that are not yet realized are not used to evaluate the σ function. This feature naturally represents the notion that current events cannot be functions of specific realizations of future events.[1] It is useful to note that $E_t\, dS = \mu(S, t)\, dt$; this expression is a direct consequence of the fact that each of the elements of the sum in equation (A.2) has zero expectation. This implies that

$$E_t[S_{t+\Delta t}] = S_t + E_t \int_t^{t+\Delta t} \mu(S_\tau, \tau)\, d\tau$$

1. Standard Riemann integrals of continuous functions are defined as

$$\int_a^b f(x)\, dx = \lim_{n\to\infty} h \sum_{i=0}^{n-1} f(a + (i+\lambda)h)$$

with $h = (b-a)/n$ and λ is any value on $[0, 1]$. With stochastic integrals, alternative values on λ produce different results. Furthermore, any value of λ other than 0 would imply a sort of clairvoyance that makes it unsuitable for applications involving decision making under uncertainty.

From a practical point of view, the definition of an Ito process as the limit of a sum provides a natural method for simulating discrete realizations of the process using

$$S_{t+\Delta t} = S_t + \mu(S_t, t)\Delta t + \sigma(S_t, t)\sqrt{\Delta t}\, v$$

where $v \sim N(0, 1)$. This approximation will be exact when μ and σ are constants.[2] In other cases the approximation will improve as Δt gets small, but it may produce inaccurate results as Δt gets large.

In order to define and work with functions of Ito processes it is necessary to have a calculus that operates consistently with them. Suppose $y = f(t, S)$, with continuous derivatives f_t, f_S, and f_{SS}. In the simplest case S and y are both scalar processes. It is intuitively reasonable to define the differential dy as

$$dy = f_t\, dt + f_S\, dS$$

as would be the case in standard calculus. Unfortunately, this approach will produce incorrect results because it ignores the fact that $(dS)^2 = O(dt)$. To see what this means consider a Taylor expansion of dy at (S, t); that is, totally differentiate the Taylor expansion of $f(S, t)$:

$$dy = f_t\, dt + f_S\, dS + \tfrac{1}{2}f_{tt}(dt)^2 + f_{tS}\, dt\, dS + \tfrac{1}{2}f_{SS}(dS)^2 + \text{ higher order terms}$$

Terms of higher order than dt and dS are then ignored in the differential. In this case, however, the term $(dS)^2$ represents the square of the increments of a random variable that has expectation $\sigma^2\, dt$ and, therefore, cannot be ignored. Including this term results in the differential

$$dy = \left[f_t + \tfrac{1}{2}f_{SS}\sigma^2(S, t)\right]dt + f_S\, dS$$
$$= \left[f_t + f_S\mu(S, t) + \tfrac{1}{2}f_{SS}\sigma^2(S, t)\right]dt + f_S\sigma(S, t)\, dz$$

a result known as Ito's Lemma. An immediate consequence of Ito's Lemma is that functions of Ito processes are also Ito processes (provided the functions have appropriately continuous derivatives).

Multivariate versions of Ito's Lemma are easily defined. Suppose S is an n-vector–valued process and z is a k-vector Wiener process (composed of k independent standard Wiener processes). Then μ is an n-vector–valued function ($\mu : \mathbb{R}^{n+1} \to \mathbb{R}^n$), and σ is an $n \times k$

---

2. When μ and σ are constants, the process is known as absolute Brownian motion. Exact simulation methods also exist for other processes; for example, for geometric Brownian motion process, $dS = \mu S\, dt + \sigma S\, dz$, it will subsequently be shown that $S_{t+\Delta t} = S_t \exp(\mu\Delta t + \sigma\sqrt{\Delta t}v)$, where $v \sim N(0, 1)$.

matrix–valued function ($\sigma : \mathbb{R}^{n+1} \to \mathbb{R}^{n \times k}$). The instantaneous covariance of S is $\sigma \sigma^T$, which may be less than full rank.

For vector-valued S, Ito's Lemma is

$$dy = \left[f_t + f_S \mu(S, t) + \tfrac{1}{2} \text{trace} \left(\sigma^T(S, t) f_{SS} \sigma(S, t) \right) \right] dt + f_S \sigma(S, t)\, dz$$

(the only difference being in the second-order term; derivatives are defined such that f_S is a $(1 \times n)$-vector). The lemma extends in an obvious way if y is vector valued.

Ito's lemma can be used to generate some simple results concerning Ito processes. For example, consider the case of geometric Brownian motion, defined as

$$dS = \mu S\, dt + \sigma S\, dz$$

Define $y = \ln(S)$, implying that $\partial y / \partial t = 0$, $\partial y / \partial S = 1/S$, and $\partial^2 y / \partial S^2 = -1/S^2$. Applying Ito's Lemma yields the result that

$$dy = [\mu - \sigma^2/2]\, dt + \sigma\, dz$$

This is a process with independent increments, $y_{t+\Delta t} - y_t$, that are $N((\mu - \sigma^2/2)\Delta t, \sigma^2 \Delta t)$. Hence a geometric Brownian motion process has conditional probability distributions that are lognormally distributed:

$$\ln(S_{t+\Delta t}) - \ln(S_t) \sim N\left((\mu - \sigma^2/2)\Delta t, \sigma^2 \Delta t\right)$$

A.5.2 Forward and Backward Equations

It is often useful to consider the behavior of a process at some future time, T, from the vantage point of the current time, t. Suppose, for example, we are interested in deriving an expression for $E[S_T \mid S_t = s] = m(s, t, T)$, where $dS_t = \mu\, dt + \sigma\, dz$. Notice that there are two time variables in this function, T and t. It is natural, therefore, that the behavior of the function can be expressed in terms of differential equations in either of these variables. When T is held fixed and t varies, the resulting differential equation is a "backward" equation; when t is held fixed and T varies, it is a "forward" equation.

The forward approach uses the integral representation of the SDE

$$S_T = S_t + \int_t^T \mu(S_\tau, \tau)\, d\tau + \int_t^T \sigma(S_\tau, \tau)\, dz_\tau$$

The diffusion term has expectation 0, so

$$E_t[S_T] = S_t + \int_t^T E_t\left[\mu(S_\tau, \tau)\right] d\tau$$

or, in differential form,

$$\frac{\partial E_t[S_T]}{\partial T} = E_t\left[\mu(S_T, T)\right] \tag{A.3}$$

If μ is affine in S, $\mu(S) = \kappa(\alpha - S)$, this leads to the differential equation $dm/dT = \kappa(\alpha - m)$, with the boundary condition at time t that $m(s, t, t) = s$. Thus

$$E[S_T \mid S_t = s] = \alpha + e^{-\kappa(T-t)}(s - \alpha) \tag{A.4}$$

In contrast, the backward approach holds T fixed. Viewing m as a process that varies in t and using Ito's Lemma

$$dm = \left[m_t + m_S\mu + \tfrac{1}{2}m_{SS}\sigma^2\right]dt + m_S\sigma\,dz \tag{A.5}$$

By the Law of Iterated Expectations, the drift associated with the process m must be 0; hence m solves the partial differential equation (PDE)

$$0 = m_t + m_S\mu + \tfrac{1}{2}m_{SS}\sigma^2$$

subject to the boundary condition that $m(s, T, T) = s$.

For the affine μ, the differential equation is

$$0 = m_t + m_S\kappa(\alpha - S) + \tfrac{1}{2}m_{SS}\sigma^2(S_t, t)$$

Although the σ term appears in this PDE, it actually plays no role. We leave as an exercise the verification that this PDE is solved by the function obtained from the forward equation.

Forward and backward equations can also be derived for expectations of functions of S. Consider the function S_t^2; Ito's Lemma provides an expression for its dynamics:

$$S_T^2 = S_t^2 + \int_t^T S_\tau\mu(S_\tau, \tau) + \sigma^2(S_\tau, \tau)\,d\tau + \int_t^T S_\tau\sigma(S_\tau, \tau)\,dz$$

Taking expectations and subtracting the square of $E_t[S_T]$ provides an expression for the variance of S_T given S_t:

$$Var_t[S_T] = S_t^2 + E_t\left[\int_t^T S_\tau\mu(S_\tau, \tau) + \sigma^2(S_\tau, \tau)\,d\tau\right] - (E_t[S_T])^2$$

Differentiating this with respect to T yields

$$\frac{d\,Var_t[S_T]}{dT} = E_t[\sigma^2(S_T, T)] + 2\big(E_t[S_T\mu(S_T, T)] - E_t[S_T]E_t[\mu(S_T, T)]\big)$$

The boundary condition is that $Var_T[S_T] = 0$; that is, at time T all uncertainty about the value of S_T is resolved. As an exercise, apply this result to the process

$$dS = \kappa(\alpha - S)\,dt + \sigma\,dz$$

(That is, the diffusion term is a constant.)

The backward approach can also be used. Consider again the expression (A.5), noting that the drift equals 0, so

$$dm = m_s(S_t, t, T)\sigma(S_t, t)\,dz$$

Furthermore, $m_T = S_T$, so

$$S_T = m_t + \int_t^T m_s(S_\tau, \tau, T)\sigma(S_\tau, \tau)\,dz_\tau$$

the variance of which is

$$Var_t[S_T] = E_t[(S_T - m_t)^2] = E_t\left[\left(\int_t^T m_s\sigma\,dz_\tau\right)^2\right]$$

Given two functions $f(S_t, t)$ and $g(S_t, t)$, it can be shown that

$$E_t\,[f(S_T, T)g(S_T, T)] = E_t\left[\left[\int_t^T f(S_\tau, \tau)\,dW_\tau\right]\left[\int_t^T g(S_\tau, \tau)\,dW_\tau\right]\right]$$

$$= E_t\left[\int_t^T f(S_\tau, \tau)g(S_\tau, \tau)\,d\tau\right]$$

and therefore

$$Var_t[S_T] = E_t\left[\int_t^T m_s^2(S_\tau, \tau, T)\sigma^2(S_\tau, \tau)\,d\tau\right] \tag{A.6}$$

Another important use of forward and backward equations is in providing expressions for the transition densities associated with stochastic processes. Let $f(S, T; s, t)$ denote the density function defined by

$$Prob[S_T \leq S \mid S_t = s] = \int_{-\infty}^{S} f(S_T, T; s, t) \, dS_T$$

The Kolmogorov forward and backward equations are partial differential equations satisfied by f. The forward equation, which treats S and T as variable, is

$$0 = \frac{\partial f(S, T; s, t)}{\partial T} + \frac{\partial \mu(S, T) f(S, T; s, t)}{\partial S} - \frac{1}{2} \frac{\partial^2 \sigma^2(S, T) f(S, T; s, t)}{\partial S^2}$$

From the definition of the transition density function, f must have a degenerate distribution at $T = t$; that is,

$$f(S, t; s, t) = \delta_s(S)$$

where $\delta_s(S)$ is the Dirac function that concentrates all probability mass at the single point $S = s$.

Similarly, the backward equation, which treats s and t as variable, is

$$0 = \frac{\partial f(S, T; s, t)}{\partial t} + \mu(s, t) \frac{\partial f(S, T; s, t)}{\partial s} + \frac{1}{2} \sigma^2(s, t) \frac{\partial^2 f(S, T; s, t)}{\partial s^2}$$

The boundary condition for the backward equation is the terminal condition

$$f(S, T; s, T) = \delta_S(s)$$

We leave as an exercise the verification that

$$dS = \kappa(\alpha - S) \, dt + \sigma \, dz$$

has Gaussian transition densities, that is

$$f(S, T; s, t) = \frac{1}{\sqrt{2\pi v}} \exp\left(-0.5(S - m)^2 / v\right)$$

where m is given in equation (A.4) and

$$v = \frac{\sigma^2}{2\alpha} \left[1 - e^{-2\kappa(T-t)}\right]$$

A.5.3 The Feynman-Kac Equation

The backward-equation approach to computing moments is a special case of a more general result on the relationship between the solution to certain PDEs and the expectation of functions of diffusion processes. Control theory in continuous time is typically concerned with problems that attempt to choose a control that maximizes an expected discounted return stream over time. It will prove useful, therefore, to have an idea of how to evaluate such a return stream for an arbitrary control. Consider the value

$$V(S_t, t) = E_t \left[\int_t^T e^{-\rho(\tau-t)} f(S_\tau) \, d\tau + e^{-\rho(T-t)} R(S_T) \right]$$

where

$$dS = \mu(S) \, dt + \sigma(S) \, dz$$

An important theorem, generally known in economics as the Feynman-Kac equation, but also known as Dynkin's formula, states that $V(S, t)$ is the solution to the following partial differential equation:

$$\rho V(S, t) = f(S) + V_t(S, t) + \mu(S) V_S(S, t) + \tfrac{1}{2}\sigma^2(S) V_{SS}(S, t)$$

with $V(S, T) = R(S)$. The function R here represents a terminal value of the state, that is, a salvage value.[3]

By applying Ito's Lemma, the Feynman-Kac equation can be expressed as

$$\rho V(S, t) = f(S) + E[dV]/dt \tag{A.7}$$

Equation (A.7) has a natural economic interpretation. Notice that V can be thought of as the value of an asset that generates a stream of payments $f(S)$. The rate of return on the asset, ρV, is composed of two parts, $f(S)$, the current income flow, and $E[dV]/dt$, the expected rate of appreciation of the asset. Alternative names for the components are the dividend flow rate and the expected rate of capital gains. A version of the theorem applicable to infinite-horizon problems states that

$$V(S_t) = E_t \left[\int_t^\infty e^{-\rho(\tau-t)} f(S) \, d\tau \right]$$

is the solution to the differential equation

$$\rho V(S) = f(S) + \mu(S) V_S(S) + \tfrac{1}{2}\sigma^2(S) V_{SS}(S)$$

---

3. The terminal time T need not be fixed but could be a state dependent. Such an interpretation will be used in the discussion of optimal stopping problems (section 10.4).

Although more general versions of the theorem exist (see bibliographic notes), these will suffice for our purposes.

As with any differential equation, boundary conditions are needed to completely specify the solution. In this case, we require that the solution to the differential equation be consistent with the present-value representation as S approaches its boundaries (often 0 and ∞ in economic problems). Generally, economic intuition about the nature of the problem is used to determine the boundary conditions.

A.5.4 Geometric Brownian Motion

Geometric Brownian motion is a particularly convenient stochastic process because it is relatively easy to compute expected values of reward streams. If S is governed by

$$dS = \mu S\, dt + \sigma S\, dz$$

the expected present value of a reward stream $f(S)$ is the solution to

$$\rho V = f(S) + \mu S V_S + \tfrac{1}{2}\sigma^2 S^2 V_{SS}$$

As this is a linear second-order differential equation, the solution can be written as the sum of the solution to the homogeneous problem ($f(S)=0$) and any particular solution that solves the nonhomogeneous problem. The homogeneous problem is solved by

$$V(S) = A_1 S^{\beta_1} + A_2 S^{\beta_2}$$

where the β_i are the roots of the quadratic equation

$$\tfrac{1}{2}\sigma^2 \beta(\beta - 1) + \mu\beta - \rho = 0$$

and the A_i are constants to be determined by boundary conditions. For positive ρ, one of these roots is greater than one, the other is negative: $\beta_1 > 1$, $\beta_2 < 0$.

Consider the problem of finding the expected discounted value of a power of S, ($f(S) = S^\gamma$), assuming, momentarily, that the expectation exists. It is easily verified that a particular solution is

$$V(S) = S^\gamma / \left[\rho - \mu\gamma - \tfrac{1}{2}\sigma^2 \gamma(\gamma - 1)\right] \tag{A.8}$$

All that remains, therefore, is to determine the value of the arbitrary constants A_1 and A_2 that ensure that the solution indeed equals the expected value of the reward stream. This determination is a bit tricky because it need not be the case that the expectation exists (the integral may not converge as its upper limit of integration goes to ∞). It can be shown, however, that the present value is well defined for $\beta_2 < \gamma < \beta_1$, making the numerator in equation (A.8) positive. Furthermore, the boundary conditions require that $A_1 = A_2 = 0$. Thus the particular solution is convenient in that it has a nice economic interpretation as the present value of a stream of returns.

Bibliographic Notes

Many books contain discussions of Ito stochastic calculus with economics and finance orientation, including Neftci (1996) and Hull (2000). At a more advanced level see Duffie (1996); the discussion of the Feynman-Kac equation draws heavily on this source.

A brief but useful discussion of steady-state distributions is found in Appendix B of Merton (1975). For more detail, including discussion of boundary issues, see Karlin and Taylor (1981, Chap. 15) and Bharucha-Reid (1960). Early work in this area is contained in papers by Feller (1950, 1951). A classic text on stochastic processes is Cox and Miller (1965).

Appendix B
A MATLAB Primer

B.1 The Basics

MATLAB® is a programming language and a computing environment that uses matrices as one of its basic data types. It is a commercial product developed and distributed by MathWorks. (MATLAB is a registered trademark of The MathWorks, Inc.) Because it is a high-level language for numerical analysis, numerical code can be written very compactly. For example, suppose you have defined two matrices (more on how to do so presently) that you call A and B and you want to multiply them together to form a new matrix C. This operation is done with the code

```
C=A*B;
```

(note that expressions generally terminate with a semicolon in MATLAB). In addition to multiplication, most standard matrix operations are coded in the natural way for anyone trained in basic matrix algebra. Thus the following can be used:

```
A+B
```

```
A-B
```

`A'` for the transpose of A (for A real)

`inv(A)` for the inverse of A

`det(A)` for determinant of A

`diag(A)` for a vector equal to the diagonal elements of A

With the exception of transposition, all these must be used with appropriate-sized matrices— for example, square matrices for `inv` and `det` and conformable matrices for arithmetic operations.

In addition, standard mathematical operators and functions that operate on each element of a matrix are defined. For example, suppose A is defined as the 2×1 matrix

```
[2 3]
```

then `A.^2` (`.^` is the exponentiation operator) yields

```
[4 9]
```

(not `A*A`, which is not defined for nonsquare matrices anyway). Functions that operate on each element include `exp`, `ln`, `sqrt`, `cos`, `sin`, `tan`, `arccos`, `arcsin`, `arctan`, `abs` Also available are a number of functions useful in statistical work, including `beta`, `betainc`, `erf`, `gamma`, `gammainc gammaln`. The constant π (`pi`) is also available. MATLAB has a large number of built-in functions, far more than can be discussed here.

As you explore the capabilities of MATLAB, a useful tool is MATLAB's help documentation. Try typing `helpwin` at the command prompt; this will open a graphical interface window that will let you explore the various types of functions available. You can also type `help` or `helpwin` followed by a specific command or function name at the command prompt to get help on a specific topic.

Be aware that MATLAB can only find a function if it is either a built-in function or is in a file that is located in a directory specified by the MATLAB path. If you get a "function or variable not found" message, you should check the MATLAB path (using `path`) to see if the function's directory is included or use the command `addpath` to add a directory to the MATLAB path. Also be aware that files with the same name can cause problems. If the MATLAB path has two directories with files called `tiptop.m`, and you try to use the function `tiptop`, you may not get the function you want. You can determine which is being used with the "which" command—for example, `which tiptop`—and the full path to the file where the function is contained will be displayed.

A few other built-in functions or operators are extremely useful, especially

```
index = start:increment:end;
```

creates a row vector of evenly spaced values. For example,

```
i=1:1:10;
```

creates the vector [1 2 3 4 5 6 7 8 9 10]. It is important to keep track of the dimensions of matrices; the `size` function does so. For example, if A is 3×2,

```
size(A,1)
```

returns a 3 and

```
size(A,2)
```

returns a 2. The second argument of the size function is the dimension: the first dimension of a matrix is the rows; the second is the columns. If the dimension is left out, a 1×2 vector is returned:

```
size(A)
```

returns [3 2].

There are a number of ways to create matrices. One is by enumeration

```
X = [1 5;2 1];
```

which defines X to be the 2×2 matrix

$$\begin{bmatrix} 1 & 5 \\ 2 & 1 \end{bmatrix}$$

The semicolon indicates the end of a row (actually it is a concatenation operator that allows you to stack matrices; more on that topic later). Other ways to create matrices include

```
X = ones(m,n);
```

and

```
X = zeros(m,n);
```

which create $m \times n$ matrices with each element equal to 1 or 0, respectively.

MATLAB also has several random-number generators with a similar syntax.

```
X = rand(m,n);
```

creates an $m \times n$ matrix of independent random draws from a uniform distribution (actually they are pseudorandom).

```
X = randn(m,n);
```

draws from the standard normal distribution.

Individual elements of a matrix the size of which has been defined can be accessed using ( ); for example, if you have defined the 3×2 matrix B, you can set element 1,2 equal to $\cos(2.5)$ with the statement

```
B(1,2) = cos(2.5);
```

If you then want to set element 2,1 to the same value, use

```
B[2,1] = B[1,2];
```

A whole column or row of a matrix can be referenced as well in the following way:

```
B(:,1);
```

refers to column 1 of the matrix B and

```
B(3,:);
```

refers to its third row. The colon is an operator that selects all the elements in the row or column. An equivalent expression is

```
B(3,1:end);
```

where "end" indicates the last column in the matrix (it can also be used in refer to the last row of a matrix). You can also pick and choose the elements you want, for example,

```
C = B([1 3],2);
```

results in a new 2×1 matrix equal to

$$\begin{bmatrix} B_{12} \\ B_{32} \end{bmatrix}$$

Also the construction

```
B(1:3,2);
```

is used to refer to rows 1 through 3 and column 2 of the matrix B.

The ability to access parts of a matrix is very useful but also can cause problems. One of the most common programming errors is attempting to access elements of a matrix that don't exist; this will cause an error message. While on the subject of indexing elements of a matrix, you should know that MATLAB actually has two different ways of indexing. One is to use the row and column indices, as before; the other is to use the location in the vectorized matrix. When you vectorize a matrix, you stack its columns on top of each other. So a 3×2 matrix becomes a 6×1 vector composed of a stack of two 3×1 vectors. Element 1,2 of the matrix is element 4 of the vectorized matrix. If you want to create a vectorized matrix the command

```
X(:)
```

will do the trick.

MATLAB has a powerful set of graphics routines that enable you to visualize your data and models. For starters, it will suffice to note the routines `plot`, `mesh`, `surf`, and `contour`. For plotting in two dimensions, use `plot(x,y)`. Passing a string as a third argument gives you control over the color of the plot and the type of line or symbol used. The functions `mesh(x,y,z)` or `surf(x,y,z)` provide plots of a 3-D surface, whereas `contour(x,y,z)` projects a 3-D surface onto two dimensions. It is easy to add titles, labels, and text to the plots using `title`, `xlabel`, `ylabel`, and `text`. Subscripts, superscripts, and Greek letters can be obtained using TEX commands (e.g., `x_t`, `x^2`, and `\alpha\mu` will result in x_t, x^2, and $\alpha\mu$). To gain mastery over graphics takes some time; the documentation *Using MATLAB Graphics* available with MATLAB is as good a place as any to learn more.

You may have noticed that statements sometimes end with a semicolon and sometimes they don't. MATLAB is an interactive environment, meaning it interacts with you as it runs jobs. It communicates things to you by means of your display terminal. Any time MATLAB executes an assignment statement, meaning that it assigns new values to variables, it will display the variable on the screen *unless* the assignment statement ends with a semicolon. It will also tell you the name of the variable, so the command

```
x = 2+4
```

will display

```
x =
    6
```

on your screen, whereas the command

```
x = 2+4;
```

displays nothing. If you ask MATLAB to make some computation but do not assign the result to a variable, MATLAB will assign it to an implicit variable called `ans` (short for "answer"). Thus the command

```
2+4
```

will display

```
ans =
    6
```

B.2   Conditional Statements and Looping

As with any programming language, MATLAB can evaluate boolean expressions such as A>B, A>=B, A<B, A<=B, and A~=B (the last one is "not equal"; ~ is MATLAB's negation operator). Also ~(A>B), ~(A<B), and so on can be used. These need to be used with a bit of care when A and B are not scalars, however. The expression A>B creates a matrix of zeros and ones equal in size to A and B. Determining whether any of the elements of A are bigger than any of the elements of B is the same as checking whether any of the elements of the matrix A>B are nonzero.

MATLAB provides the functions `any` and `all` to evaluate matrices resulting from Boolean expressions. As with many MATLAB functions, `any` and `all` operate on rows and return row vectors with the same number of columns as the original matrix. This applies to the `sum` and `prod` functions as well. The following are equivalent expressions:

```
any(A>B)
```

and

```
sum(A>B)>0
```

The following are also equivalent:

```
all(A>B)
```

and

```
prod(A>B)>0
```

Boolean expressions are mainly used to handle conditional execution of code using one of the following:

```
if expression
...
end
```

```
if expression
...
else
...
end
```

or

```
while expression
...
end
```

The first two of these are single conditionals, for example,

```
if X>0, A = 1/X; else A = 0, end
```

(You should also be aware of the switch command (type `help switch`).) The last is for looping. Usually you use `while` for looping when you don't know how many times the loop is to be executed and use a `for` loop when you know how many times it will be executed. To loop through a procedure n times, for example, one could use the following code:

```
x(1) = 0; for i=2:n, X(i) = 3*X(i-1)+1; end
```

A common use of `while` for our purposes will be to iterate until some convergence criterion is met, such as

```
P = 2.537;
X = 0.5;
DX = 0.5;
while DX<1E-7;
   DX = DX/2;
   if normcdf(X)>P, X = X-DX; else X = X+DX; end
```

```
  disp(X)
end
```

(Can you figure out what this code does?) One thing in this code fragment that has not yet been explained is `disp(X)`. This will write the matrix *X* to the screen.

B.3   Scripts and Functions

When you work in MATLAB, you are working in an interactive environment that stores the variables you have defined and allows you to manipulate them throughout a session. You also have the ability to save groups of commands in files that can be executed many times.

MATLAB has two kinds of command files, called m-files. The first is a script m-file. If you save a bunch of commands in a script file called `MYFILE.m` and then type the word `MYFILE` at the MATLAB command line, the commands in that file will be executed just as if you had run them from the MATLAB command prompt (assuming MATLAB can find where you saved the file). A good way to work with MATLAB is to use it interactively, and then edit your session and save the edited commands to a script file. You can save the session either by cutting and pasting or by turning on the diary feature (use the on-line help to see how this works by typing `help diary`).

The second type of m-file is the function file. One of the most important aspects of MATLAB is the ability to write your own functions, which can then be used and reused just like intrinsic MATLAB functions. A function file is a file with an m extension (e.g., `MYFUNC.m`) that begins with the word `function`.

```
function Z=DiagReplace(X,v)
% DiagReplace Put vector v onto diagonal of matrix X
% SYNTAX:
% Z=DiagReplace(X,v);
n = size(X,1);
Z = X;
ind = (1:n:n*n) + (0:n-1);
Z(ind) = v;
```

You can see how this function works by typing the following code at the MATLAB command line:

```
m = 3; x = randn(m,m); v = rand(m,1); x, v, xv = diagreplace(x,v)
```

Any variables that are defined by the function that are not returned by the function are lost after the function has finished executing (n and `ind` in `DiagReplace`).

Here is another example:

```
function x = randint(k,m,n)
% RANDINT Random integers between 1 and k (inclusive).
% SYNTAX:
%   x = randint(k,m,n);
% Returns an m by n matrix
% Can be used for sampling with replacement.
x = ceil(k*rand(m,n));
```

Documentation of functions (and scripts) is very important. In m-files a % denotes that the rest of the line is a comment. Comments should be used liberally to help you and others who might read your code to understand what the code is intended to do. The top lines of code in a function file are especially important. It is here where you should describe what the function does, what its syntax is, and what each of the input and output variables is. These top lines become an online help feature for your function. For example, typing help randint at the MATLAB command line would display the four commented lines on your screen.

A note of caution on naming files is in order. It is very easy to get unexpected results if you give the same name to different functions, or if you give a name that is already used by MATLAB. Prior to saving a function that you write, it is useful to use the which command to see if the name is already in use.

MATLAB is very flexible about the number of arguments that are passed to and from a function. This flexibility is especially useful if a function has a set of predefined default values that usually provide good results. For example, suppose you write a function that iterates until a convergence criterion is met or a maximum number of iterations has been reached. One way to write such a function is to make the convergence criterion and the maximum number of iterations be optional arguments.

The following function attempts to find the value of x such that $\ln(x)x = a$, where a is a parameter.

```
function x=SolveIt(a,tol,MaxIters)
if nargin<3 | isempty(MaxIters), MaxIters=100; end
if nargin<2 | isempty(tol), tol=sqrt(eps); end
x = a;
for i=1:MaxIters
  lx = log(x);
  fx = x.*lx-a;
  x = x-fx./(lx+1);
```

```
  disp([x fx])
  if abs(fx)<tol, break; end
end
```

In this example, the command `nargin` means "number of input arguments," and the command `isempty` checks to see if a variable is passed but is empty (an empty variable is created by setting it to `[]`). An analogous function for the number of output arguments is `nargout`; many times it is useful to put a statement like

```
if nargout<2, return; end
```

into your function so that the function does not have to do computations that are not requested. It is possible that you may want nothing or more than one thing returned from a procedure, for example,

```
function [m,v]=MeanVar(X)
% MeanVar Computes the mean and variance of a data matrix
% SYNTAX
%      [m,v]=MeanVar(X);
n = size(X,1);
m = mean(X);
if nargout>1
  temp = X-m(ones(n,1),:);
  v = sum(temp.*temp)/(n-1);
end
```

To use this procedure call it with `[mu,sig]=MeanVar(X)`. Notice that it only computes the variance if more than one output is desired. Thus the statement `mu=MeanVar(X)` is correct and returns the mean without computing the variance.

In the following example, the function can accept one or two arguments and checks how many outputs are requested. The function computes the covariance of two or more variables. It can handle both a bivariate case when passed two data vectors and a multivariate case when passed a single data matrix (treating columns as variables and rows as observations). Furthermore, it returns not only the covariance but, if requested, the correlation matrix as well.

```
function [CovMat,CorrMat]=COVARIANCE(X,Y)
% COVARIANCE Computes covariances and correlations
n = size(X,1);
if nargin==2
```

```
   X = [X Y]; % Concatenate X and Y
end
m = mean(X); % Compute the means
X = X-m(ones(n,1),:); % Subtract the means
CovMat = X'*X./n; % Compute the covariance
if nargout==2 % Compute the correlation, if requested
   s = sqrt(diag(CovMat));
   CorrMat = CovMat./(s*s');
end
```

This code executes in different ways depending on the number of input and output arguments used. If two matrices are passed in, they are concatenated before the covariance is computed, thereby allowing the frequently used bivariate case to be handled. The function also checks whether the caller has requested one or two outputs and only computes the correlation if two are requested. Although it would not be a mistake to just go ahead and compute the correlation, there is no point if it is not going to be used. Unless additional output arguments must be computed anyway, it is good practice to compute them only as needed. Some examples of calling this function are

```
c = COVARIANCE(randn(10,3));
[c1,c2] = COVARIANCE((1:10)',(2:2:20)');
```

Good documentation is very important, but it is also useful to include some error checking in your functions. This makes it much easier to track down the nature of problems when they arise. For example, if some arguments are required or their values must satisfy some specific criteria (for example, if they must be in a specified range or be integers), these things are easily checked. For example, consider the function DiagReplace presented earlier. This is intended for a square matrix ($n \times n$) X and an n-vector v. Both inputs are needed, and they must be conformable. The following code puts in error checks:

```
function Z=DiagReplace(X,v)
% DiagReplace Put vector v onto diagonal of matrix X
% SYNTAX:
% Z=DiagReplace(X,v);
if nargin<2, error('2 inputs are required'); end
n = size(X,1);
if size(X,2)~=n, error('X is not square'); end
if prod(size(v))~=n, error('X and v are not conformable'); end
Z = X;
```

```
ind = (1:n:n*n) + (0:n-1);
Z(ind) = v;
```

The command `error` in a function file prints out a specified error message and returns the user to the MATLAB command line.

An important feature of MATLAB is the ability to pass a function to another function. For example, suppose that you want to find the value that maximizes a particular function, say, $f(x) = \exp(-0.5x^2)x$. It would be useful not to have to write the optimization code every time you need to solve a maximization problem. Instead, it would be better to have a solver that handles optimization problems for arbitrary functions and to pass the specific function of interest to the solver. For example, suppose we save the following code as a MATLAB function file called `MYFUNC.m`:

```
function fx=myfunc(x)
fx = exp(-0.5*x.^2).*x;
```

Furthermore, suppose we have another function called `MAXIMIZE.m` that has the following calling syntax:

```
function x=MAXIMIZE(f,x0)
```

The two arguments are the name of the function to be maximized and a starting value where the function will begin its search (this is the way many optimization routines work). One could then call `MAXIMIZE` using

```
x = maximize('myfunc',0)
```

and, if the `MAXIMIZE` function knows what it's doing, it will return the value 1. Notice that the word `myfunc` is enclosed in single quotes. It is the name of the function, passed as a string variable, that is passed to `MAXIMIZE`. The function `MAXIMIZE` can evaluate `MYFUNC` using the `feval` command. For example, the code

```
fx = feval(f,x)
```

is used to evaluate the function. It is important to understand that the first argument to `feval` is a string variable (you may also want to find out about the command `eval`, but this is only a primer, not a manual).

It is often the case that functions have auxiliary parameters. For example, suppose we changed `MYFUNC` to

```
function fx=myfunc(x,mu,sig)
fx = x.*exp(-0.5*((x-mu)./sig).^2);
```

Now two auxiliary parameters are needed, and `MAXIMIZE` needs to be altered to handle this situation. The function `MAXIMIZE` cannot know how many auxiliary parameters are needed, however, so MATLAB provides a special way to handle just this situation. Have the calling sequence be

```
function x=MAXIMIZE(f,x0,varargin)
```

and, to evaluate the function, use

```
fx = feval(f,x,varargin{:})
```

The keyword `varargin` (variable number of input arguments) is a special way that MATLAB has designed to handle variable numbers of input arguments. Although it can be used in a variety of ways, the simplest is shown here, where it simply passes all the input arguments after the second on to `feval`. Don't worry too much if this procedure is confusing at first. Until you start writing code to perform general functions like `MAXIMIZE` you will probably not need to use this feature in your own code, but it is handy to have an idea of what it's for when you are trying to read other people's code.

B.4 Debugging

Bugs in your code are inevitable. Learning how to debug code is very important and will save you lots of time and aggravation. Debugging proceeds in three steps. The first is to ensure that your code is syntactically correct. When you attempt to execute some code, MATLAB first scans the code and reports an error the first time it finds a syntax error. These errors, known as compile errors, are generally quite easy to find and correct (once you know what the right syntax is).

The second step involves finding errors that are generated as the code is executed, known as run-time errors. MATLAB has a built-in editor/debugger, and it is the key to efficient debugging of run-time errors. If your code fails because of run-time errors, MATLAB reports the error and provides a trace of what was being done at the point where the error occurred. Often you will find that an error has occurred in a function that you didn't write but was called by a function that was called by a function that was called by a function (etc.) that you did write. A safe first assumption is that the problem lies in your code and you need to check what your code was doing that led to the eventual error.

The first thing to do with run-time errors is to make sure that you are using the right syntax in calling whatever function you are calling. This means making sure you understand what that syntax is. Most errors of this type occur because you pass the wrong number of arguments, the arguments you pass are not of the proper dimension, or the arguments you pass have inappropriate values.

If the source of the problem is not obvious, it is often useful to use the debugger. To do so, click on "File" and then either "Open" or "New" from within MATLAB. Once in the editor, click on "Debug", then on "Stop if error". Now run your procedure again. When MATLAB encounters an error, it enters a debugging mode that allows you to examine the values of the variables in the various functions that were executing at the time the error occurred. These can be accessed by selecting a function in the stack on the editor's toolbar. Then placing your cursor over the name of a variable in the code will allow you to see what that variable contains. You can also return to the MATLAB command line and type commands. These are executed using the variables in the currently selected workspace (the one selected in the stack). Generally a little investigation will reveal the source of the problem (as in all things, it becomes easier with practice).

There is a third step in debugging. Just because your code runs without generating an error message, it is not necessarily correct. You should check the code to make sure it is doing what you expect. One way to do so is to test it on a problem with a known solution or a solution that can be computed by an alternative method. After you have convinced yourself that it is doing what you want it to, check your documentation and try to think how it might cause errors with other problems, put in error checks as appropriate, and then check it one more time. Then check it one more time.

Here are a few last words of advice on writing code and debugging:

1. Break your problem down into small chunks, and debug each chunk separately. This process usually requires writing lots of small function files (and documenting them).

2. Try to make functions work regardless of the size of the parameters. For example, if you need to evaluate a polynomial function, write a function that accepts a vector of values and a coefficient vector. If you need such a function once, it is likely you will need it again. Also, if you change your problem by using a fifth-order polynomial rather than a fourth-order, you will not need to rewrite your evaluation function.

3. Try to avoid hard-coding parameter values and dimensions into your code. Suppose you have a problem that involves an interest rate of 7%. Don't put a lot of 0.07s into your code. Later on you will want to see what happens when the interest rate is 6%, and you should be able to make this change in a single line with a nice comment attached to it, for example,

```
rho = 0.07;              % the interest rate
```

4. Avoid loops if possible. Loops are slow in MATLAB. It is often possible to do the same thing that a loop does with a *vectorized* command. Learn the available commands and use them.

5. RTFM—internet lingo meaning Read The (F-word of choice) Manual.

6. When you just can't figure it out, check the MATLAB technical support site (MathWorks)

and the MATLAB discussion group (comp.soft-sys.matlab), for postings about your problem (past discussion group postings can be accessed at http://groups.google.com/), if those
efforts turn up nothing, post a question to the discussion group. Don't overdo it, however;
people who abuse these groups are quickly spotted and will have their questions ignored.
(If you are a student, don't ask the group to solve your homework problems. You will get
far more out of attempting them yourself than you'll get out of having someone else tell
you the answer. You are likely to be found out anyway, and it is a form of cheating.)

B.5   Other Data Types

So far we have only used variables that are scalars, vectors, or matrices. MATLAB also
recognizes multidimensional arrays. Element-by-element arithmetic works as usual on these
arrays (including addition and subtraction, as well as Boolean arithmetic). Matrix arithmetic
is not clearly defined for multidimensional arrays, and MATLAB has not attempted to define
a standard. If you try to multiply two multidimensional arrays, you will generate an error
message. Working with multidimensional arrays can get a bit tricky but is often the best
way to handle certain kinds of problems. An alternative to multidimensional arrays is what
MATLAB calls a cell array. A multidimensional array contains numbers for elements. A
cell array is an array (possibly a multidimensional one) that has other data structures as
elements. For example, you can define a 2×1 cell array that contains a 3×1 matrix in it
first cell (i.e., as element $(1, 1)$) and a 4×4 matrix in its second cell. Cell arrays are defined
using braces (curly brackets) rather than square brackets, for example,

```
x = {[1;2],[1 2;3 4]};
```

Other data types that are available in MATLAB include string variables, structure variables, and objects. A string variable is self-explanatory. Structure variables are variables
that have named fields that can be referenced. For example, a structure variable, X, could
have the fields DATE and PRICE. One could then refer to the data contained in these files
using X.DATE and X.PRICE. If the structure variable is itself an array, one could refer to
fields of an element in the structure using X(1).DATE and X(1).PRICE. Object-type
variables are like structures but have methods attached to them. The fields of an object
cannot be directly accessed but must be accessed using the methods associated with the
object. Structures and objects are advanced topics that are not needed to get started using
MATLAB. They are quite useful if you are trying to design user-friendly functions for
other users. It is also useful to understand objects when working with MATLAB's graphical
capabilities, although, again, you can get pretty nice plots without delving into how objects
work.

B.6   Programming Style

In general there are different ways to write a program that produce the same end results. Algorithmic efficiency refers to the execution time and memory used to get the job done. In many cases, especially in a matrix-processing language like MATLAB, there are important trade-offs between execution time and memory use. Often, however, the trade-offs are trivial, and one way of writing the code may be unambiguously better than another.

In MATLAB, the rule of thumb is to avoid loops where possible. MATLAB is a hybrid language that is both interpreted and compiled. A loop executed by the interpreter is generally slower than direct vector operations that are implemented in compiled code. For example, suppose one had a scalar x that one wanted to exponentiate by the integers from 1 to n to create a vector y whose ith entry is $y_i = x^i$. Both of the following code segments produce the desired result:

```
for i=1:n
  y(i) = x^i;
end
```

and

```
y = x.^(1:n);
```

The second way avoids the looping of the first and hence executes substantially faster.

Programmer development effort is another critical resource required in program construction that is sometimes ignored in discussions of efficiency. One reason for using a high-level language such as MATLAB, rather than a low-level language such as Fortran, is that programming time is often greatly reduced. MATLAB carries out many of the housekeeping tasks that the programmer must deal with in lower level languages. Even in MATLAB, however, one should consider carefully how important it is to write very efficient code. If the code will be used infrequently, less effort should be devoted to making the code computationally efficient than if the code will be used often or repeatedly.

Furthermore, computationally efficient code can sometimes be fairly difficult to read. If one plans to revise the code at a later date or if someone else is going to use it, it may be better to approach the problem in a simpler way that is more transparent, though possibly slower. The proper balance of computational efficiency versus clarity and development effort is a judgment call. A good idea, however, is embodied in the saying "Get it to run right, then get it to run fast." In other words, get your code to do what you want it to do first, then look for ways to improve its efficiency.

It is especially important to document one's code. It does not take long for even an experienced programmer to forget what a piece of code does if it is undocumented. We suggest that you get in the habit of writing headers that explain clearly what the code in a file does. If it is a function, the header should contain details on the input and output arguments and on the algorithm used (as appropriate), including references. Within the code it is a good idea to sprinkle reminders about what the code is doing at that point.

Another good programming practice is modularity. Functions that perform simple, well-defined tasks that are to be repeated often should be written separately and called from other functions as needed. The simple functions can be debugged and then depended on to perform their job in a variety of applications. This approach not only saves program development time, but also makes the resulting code far easier to understand. Also, if one decides that there is a better way to write such a function, one need only make the changes in one place. An example of this principle is a function that computes the derivatives of a function numerically. Such a function is used extensively in this book.

References

Ames, William F. 1992. *Numerical Method for Partial Differential Equations,* 3rd ed. San Diego, CA: Academic Press.

Antonsev, S. N., K.-H. Hoffman, and A. M. Khludnev, editors. 1992. *Free Boundary Problems in Continuum Mechanics,* vol. 106 of *International Series of Numerical Mathematics.* Basel: Birkhäuser Verlag, July 15–19.

Atkinson, K. E. 1989. *An Introduction to Numerical Analysis,* 2nd ed. New York: John Wiley and Sons.

Balinski, M. L., and R. W. Cottle, editors. 1978. *Complementarity and Fixed Point Problems,* no. 7 in Mathematical Programming Studies. Amsterdam: North-Holland.

Barone-Adesi, Giovanni, and Robert E. Whaley. 1987. "Efficient Analytic Approximation of American Option Values." *Journal of Finance* 42:301–320.

Bellman, R. E. *Dynamic Programming.* 1957. Princeton, NJ: Princeton University Press.

Bellman, R. E., and S. E. Dreyfus. 1962. *Applied Dynamic Programming.* Princeton, NJ: Princeton University Press.

Bertsekas, D. P. 1976. *Dynamic Programming and Stochastic Control.* New York: Academic Press.

Bertsekas, D. P., and S. E. Shreve. 1978. *Stochastic Optimal Control: The Discrete Time Case.* New York: Academic Press.

Bharucha-Reid, A. T. 1960. *Elements of the Theory of Markov Processes and Their Applications.* New York: McGraw-Hill.

Black, Fischer, and Myron Scholes. 1973. "The Pricing of Options and Corporate Liabilities." *Journal of Political Economy* 81:637–654.

Blackwell, D. "Discrete Dynamic Programming." 1962. *Annals of Mathematical Statistics* 33:719–726.

Blackwell, D. "Discounted Dynamic Programming." 1965. *Annals of Mathematical Statistics* 36:226–235.

Brennan, Michael J., and Eduardo S. Schwartz. 1985. "Evaluating Natural Resource Investments." *Journal of Business* 58:135–157.

Cheney, W., and D. Kincaid. 1985. *Numerical Mathematics and Computers,* 3rd ed. Pacific Grove, CA: Brooks/Cole.

Chiang, Alpha C. 1999. *Elements of Dynamic Optimization.* Prospect Heights, IL: Waveland Press.

Christiano, L. J. 1990. "Solving the Stochastic Growth Model by Linear-Quadratic Approximation and by Value-Function Iteration." *Journal of Business and Economic Statistics* 8:23–26.

Clark, C. W. 1976. *Mathematical Bioeconomics: The Optimal Management of Renewable Resources.* New York: John Wiley and Sons.

Conrad, J. M., and C. W. Clark. 1987. *Natural Resource Economics.* New York: Cambridge University Press.

Cottle, R. W., F. Giannessi, and J-L. Lions, editors. 1980. *Variational Inequalities and Complementarity Problems.* Chichester: John Wiley and Sons.

Cottle, R. W., J.-S. Pang, and R. E. Stone. 1992. *The Linear Complementarity Problem.* San Diego: Academic Press.

Cox, D. R., and H. D. Miller. 1965. *The Theory of Stochastic Processes.* New York: John Wiley and Sons.

Cox, John C., Jonathan E. Ingersoll, and Stephen A. Ross. 1985. "A Theory of the Term Structure of Interest Rates." *Econometrica* 53:385–407.

Dai, Qiang, and Kenneth J. Singleton. 2000. "Specification Analysis for Affine Term Structure Models." *Journal of Finance* 55:1943–1978.

de Boor, Carl. 1978. *A Practical Guide to Splines.* New York: Springer-Verlag.

Denardo, E. V. 1967. "Contraction Mappings in the Theory Underlying Dynamic Programming." *SIAM Review* 9:165–177.

Dennis, Jr., J. E., and R. B. Schnabel. 1983. *Numerical Methods for Unconstrained Optimization and Nonlinear Equations.* Englewood Cliffs, NJ: Prentice-Hall.

Dixit, Avinash. 1989. "Entry and Exit Decisions Under Uncertainty." *Journal of Political Economy* 97:620–638.

Dixit, Avinash. 1991. "A Simplified Treatment of the Theory of Optimal Regulation of Brownian Motion." *Journal of Economic Dynamics and Control* 15:657–673.

Dixit, Avinash. 1993a. *The Art of Smooth Pasting,* vol. 55 of *Fundamentals of Pure and Applied Economics.* Chur, Switzerland: Harwood Academic Publishers.

Dixit, Avinash. 1993b. "Choosing Among Alternative Discrete Investment Projects Under Uncertainty." *Economics Letters* 41:265–268.

Dixit, Avinash K., and Robert S. Pindyck. 1994. *Investment Under Uncertainty.* Princeton, NJ: Princeton University Press.

Dorfman, R. 1969. "An Economic Interpretation of Optimal Control Theory." *American Economic Review* 59: 817–831.

Duffie, Darrell. 1996. *Dynamic Asset Pricing Theory,* 2nd ed. Princeton, NJ: Princeton University Press.

Duffie, Darrell, and Rui Kan. 1996. "A Yield-Factor Model of Interest Rates." *Mathematical Finance* 6:379–406.

Duffie, Darrell, Jun Pan, and Kenneth Singleton. 1999. "Transform Analysis and Asset Pricing for Affine Jump-Diffusions." Graduate School of Business, Stanford University.

Dumas, Bernard. 1991. "Super Contact and Related Optimality Conditions." *Journal of Economic Dynamics and Control* 15:675–685.

Fackler, Paul L. 2000. "Multivariate Option Pricing." North Carolina State University.

Feller, William. 1950. "Diffusion Problems in Genetics." *Proceedings of the Second Symposium on Mathematical Statistics and Probability,* pp. 227–246. Berkeley, July/August.

Feller, William. 1951. "Two Singular Diffusion Problems." *Annals of Mathematics* 54(1): 173–182.

Ferris, Michael C., and Todd S. Munson. 1999. "Interfaces to PATH3.0: Design, Implementation and Usage." *Computational Optimization and Applications* 12:207–227.

Ferris, M. C., and J. S. Pang. 1997. "Engineering and Economic Applications of Complementarity Problems." *SIAM Review* 39:669–713.

Ferris, Michael C., and Christian Kanzow. 1998. "Complementarity and Related Problems: A Survey." University of Wisconsin, Madison.

Ferris, Michael C., Michael Mesnier, and Jorge J. More. 1996. "The NEOS Server for Complementarily Problems: PATH." Computer Sciences Department, University of Wisconsin, Madison, June.

Ferris, Michael C., and Krung Sinapiromsaran. 2000. "Formulating and Solving Nonlinear Programs as Mixed Complementarity Problems," *Optimization,* vol. 481 of *Lecture Notes in Economics and Mathematical Systems,* ed. V. H. Nguyen, J. J. Strodiot, and P. Tossings. New York: Springer-Verlag.

Fleming, Wendell H., and Raymond W. Rishel. 1975. *Deterministic and Stochastic Optimal Control,* no. 1 in Applications of Mathematics. New York: Springer-Verlag.

Fletcher, C.A.J. 1984. *Computational Galerkin Techniques.* New York: Springer-Verlag.

Fletcher, R. 2000. *Practical Methods of Optimization,* 2nd ed. New York: John Wiley and Sons.

Gaffney, M. 1960. "Concepts of Financial Maturity of Timber and Other Assets." Department of Agricultural Economics, North Carolina State College, A.E. Information Series 62.

Gill, P. E., W. Murray, and M. H. Wright. 1981. *Practical Optimization.* New York: Academic Press.

Goldman, M. Barry, Howard B. Sosin, and Mary Ann Gatto. 1979. "Path Dependent Options: 'Buy at the Low, Sell at the High'." *Journal of Finance* 34:1111–1127.

Golub, Gene H., and James M. Ortega. 1992. *Scientific Computing and Differential Equations: An Introduction to Numerical Methods.* San Diego: Academic Press.

Golub, G. H., and C. F. van Loan. 1989. *Matrix Calculations,* 2nd ed. Madison: University of Wisconsin Press.

Hershleifer, J. 1970. *Investment, Interest and Capital.* Englewood Cliffs, NJ: Prentice Hall.

Heston, Steven L. 1993. "A Closed-Form Solution for Options with Stochastic Volatility with Applications to Bond and Currency Options." *Review of Financial Studies* 6:327–343.

Hoffman, K. H., and J. Sprekels, editors. 1990. *Free Boundary Problems: Theory and Applications II,* no. 186 in Pitman Research Notes in Mathematics. Essex, England: Longman Scientific and Technical.

Hotelling, H. 1931. "The Economics of Exhaustible Resources." *Journal of Political Economy* 39:137–175.

Hull, John C. 2000. *Options, Futures and Other Derivative Securities,* 4th ed. Englewood Cliffs, NJ: Prentice Hall.

Judd, Kenneth L. 1992. "Projection Methods for Solving Aggregate Growth Models." *Journal of Economic Theory* 58:410–452.

Judd, Kenneth L. 1994. "Approximation, Perturbation, and Projection Methods in Economic Analysis." *Handbook of Computational Economics,* vol. 1, ed. H. Amman, D. A. Kendrick, and J. Rust, pp. 509–586. New York: North-Holland.

Judd, Kenneth L. 1998. *Numerical Methods in Economics.* Cambridge, MA: MIT Press.

Kamien, M. I., and N. L. Schwartz. 1981. *Dynamic Optimization: The Calculus of Variations and Optimal Control in Economics and Management,* 2nd ed. New York: North-Holland.

Karlin, Samuel, and Howard M. Taylor. 1981. *A Second Course in Stochastic Processes,* 2nd ed. New York: Academic Press.

Kato, Ryo, and Shinichi Nishiyama. 2001. "Optimal Monetary Policy When Interest Rates Are Bounded at Zero." Working Paper, Ohio State University.

Kendrick, D. A. 1981. *Stochastic Control for Economic Models.* New York: McGraw-Hill.

Kennedy, J. O. S. 1986. *Dynamic Programming: Applications to Agriculture and Natural Resources.* New York: Elsevier Publishers.

Kennedy, William J., and James E. Gentle. 1980. *Statistical Computing,* vol. 33 of *Statistics: Textbooks and Monographs.* New York: Marcel Dekker.

Kincaid, D., and W. Cheney. 1991. *Numerical Analysis: Mathematics of Scientific Computing.* Pacific Grove, CA: Brooks/Cole.

Kremers, Hans, and Dolf Talman. 1994. "A New Pivoting Algorithm for the Linear Complementarity Problem Allowing for an Arbitrary Starting Point." *Mathematical Programming* 63:235–252.

Kushner, H. J., and P. G. Dupuis. 1992. *Numerical Methods for Stochastic Control Problems in Continuous Time.* New York: Springer-Verlag.

Leon, Steven J. 1980. *Linear Algebra with Applications.* New York: Macmillan Publishing.

Longstaff, Francis A., and Eduardo S. Schwartz. 1992. "Interest Rate Volatility and the Term Structure: A Two Factor General Equilibrium Model." *Journal of Finance* 47:1259–1282.

Lucas, R. E., Jr. 1978. "Asset Prices in an Exchange Economy." *Econometrica* 46:1429–1445.

Lucas, R. E., Jr., and E. C. Prescott. 1971. "Investment Under Uncertainty." *Econometrica* 39:659–681.

Ludwig, Donald. 1979a. "Optimal Harvesting of a Randomly Fluctuating Resource. I. Application of Perturbation Methods." *SIAM Journal of Applied Mathematics* 37(1): 166–184.

Ludwig, Donald. 1979b. "An Unusual Free Boundary Problem from the Theory of Optimal Harvesting." *Lectures on Mathematics in the Life Sciences* 12:173–209.

Ludwig, Donald, and James M. Varrah. 1979. "Optimal Harvesting of a Randomly Fluctuating Resource. II. Numerical Methods and Results." *SIAM Journal of Applied Mathematics* 37(1): 185–205.

Lund, D., and B. Oksendal, editors. 1991. *Stochastic Models and Option Values.* New York: North-Holland.

Majd, Saman, and Robert S. Pindyck. 1987. "Time to Build, Option Value, and Investment Decisions." *Journal of Financial Economics* 18:7–28.

Majd, Saman, and Robert S. Pindyck. 1989. "The Learning Curve and Optimal Production Under Uncertainty." *Rand Journal of Economics* 20(3): 331–343.

Malliaris, A. G., and W. A. Brock. 1982. *Stochastic Methods in Economics and Finance*, vol. 17 of *Advanced Textbooks in Economics*. Amsterdam: North-Holland.

Mangel, Marc. 1985. *Decision and Control in Uncertain Resource Systems*. Orlando, FL: Academic Press.

McDonald, Robert L., and Daniel R. Siegel. 1985. "Investment and the Valuation of Firms When There Is an Option to Shut Down." *International Economic Review* 26(2): 331–349.

Merton, Robert C. 1969. "Lifetime Portfolio Selection Under Uncertainty: The Continuous-Time Case." *Review of Economics and Statistics* 51:247–257.

Merton, Robert C. 1971. "Optimum Consumption and Portfolio Rules in a Continuous-Time Model." *Journal of Economic Theory* 3:373–413.

Merton, Robert C. 1973. "The Theory of Rational Option Pricing." *Bell Journal of Economics and Management Science* 4:141–183.

Merton, Robert C. 1975. "An Asymptotic Theory of Growth Under Uncertainty." *Review of Economic Studies* 42:375–393.

Miranda, M. J. 1989. "A Computable Rational Expectations Model for Agricultural Price Stabilization Programs." Unpublished paper, Ohio State University.

Miranda, M. J., and J. W. Glauber. 1993. "Estimation of Dynamic Nonlinear Rational Expectations Models of Primary Commodity Markets with Private and Governmental Stockholding." *Review of Economics and Statistics* 75:463–467.

Miranda, M. J., and P. G. Helmberger. 1988. "The Effects of Price Band Buffer Stock Programs." *American Economic Review* 78:46–58.

Miranda, M. J., and X. Rui. 1996. "An Empirical Reassessment of the Nonlinear Rational Expectations Commodity Storage Model." Working Paper, Ohio State University.

Miranda, M. J., and X. Rui. 1997. "Maximum Likelihood Estimation of Nonlinear Rational Expectations Asset Pricing Model." *Journal of Economic Dynamics and Control* 21:1493–1510.

Neftci, Salih N. 1996. *An Introduction to the Mathematics of Financial Derivatives*. San Diego, CA: Academic Press.

Nguyen, Genevieve, and Mario J. Miranda. 1997. "Redistribution of Resources Under Uncertainty and the Dynamics of Indigenous Risk Sharing Institutions." Working Paper, Ohio State University.

Ortega, J. M., and W. C. Rheinboldt. 1970. *Iterative Solution of Nonlinear Equations in Several Variables*. New York: Academic Press.

Pindyck, Robert S. 1978. "Optimal Exploration and Production of a Nonrenewable Resource." *Journal of Political Economy* 86:841–862.

Pindyck, Robert S. 1984. "Uncertainty in the Theory of Renewable Resource Markets." *Review of Economic Studies* 51:289–303.

Press, William H., Saul A. Teukolsky, William T. Vetterling, and Brian P. Flannery. 1992. *Numerical Recipes*, 2nd ed. Cambridge: Cambridge University Press.

Rausser, G. C., and E. Hochman. 1979. *Dynamic Agricultural Systems: Economic Prediction and Control*. New York: North-Holland.

Rivlin, Thoedore J. 1990. *Chebyshev Polynomials: From Approximation Theory to Algebra and Number Theory*, 2nd ed. New York: John Wiley and Sons.

Ross, S. 1983. *Introduction to Stochastic Dynamic Programming*. New York: Academic Press.

Rui, X., and M. J. Miranda. 1996. "Solving Dynamic Games via Orthogal Collocation: An Application to International Commodity Markets." *Annals of Operations Research* 68:87–108.

Sargent, T. J. 1987. *Dynamic Macroeconomic Theory*. Cambridge, MA: Harvard University Press.

Scheinkman, J. A., and J. Schechtman. 1983. "A Simple Competitive Model with Production and Storage." *Review of Economics and Statistics* 50:427–441.

Shimko, David C. 1992. *Finance in Continuous Time: A Primer*. Miami, FL: Kolb Publishing.

Simon, H. A. 1956. "Dynamic Programming Under Uncertainty with a Quadratic Criterion Function." *Econometrica* 24:74–81.

Smith, Vernon L. 1969. "On Models of Commercial Fishing." *Journal of Political Economy* 77(3): 181–198.

Stokey, N. L., and R. E. Lucas. 1989. *Recursive Methods in Economic Dynamics*. Cambridge, MA: Harvard University Press.

Taylor, J. B., and H. Uhlig. 1990. "Solving Nonlinear Stochastic Growth Models: A Comparison of Alternative Solution Methods." *Journal of Business and Economic Statistics* 8:1–18.

Theil, H. 1957. "A Note on Certainty Equivalence in Dynamic Planning." *Econometrica* 25:46–49.

Turnovsky, Stephen J. 2000. *Methods of Macroeconomic Dynamics*, 2nd ed. Cambridge, MA: MIT Press.

Vasicek, Oldrich. 1977. "An Equilibrium Characterization of the Term Structure." *Journal of Financial Economics* 5:177–188.

Vedenov, Dmitry V., and Mario J. Miranda. 2001. "Numerical Solution of Dynamic Oligopoly Games with Capital Investment." *Economic Theory* 18:237–261.

Williams, J. C., and B. D. Wright. 1991. *Storage and Commodity Markets*. New York: Cambridge University Press.

Williassen, Yngve. 1998. "The Stochastic Rotation Problem: A Generalization of Faustmann's Formula to Stochastic Forest Growth." *Journal of Economic Dynamics and Control* 22: 573–596.

Wilmott, Paul. 1998. *Derivatives: The Theory and Practice of Financial Engineering*. Chichester, England: John Wiley and Sons.

Wright, B. D., and J. C. Williams. 1982. "The Economic Role of Commodity Storage." *Economic Journal* 92: 596–614.

Index